BRUCE
SPRINGSTEEN

BOOKS BY DAVE MARSH

Born to Run: The Bruce Springsteen Story Volume 1

The Book of Rock Lists

The Rolling Stone Record Guide

Elvis

Before I Get Old: The Story of the Who

Fortunate Son

The First Rock & Roll Confidential Report

Trapped: Michael Jackson and the Crossover Dream

Glory Days: The Bruce Springsteen Story Volume 2

The Heart of Rock & Soul: The 1001 Best Singles Ever Recorded

Pastures of Plenty: The Uncollected Writings of Woody Guthrie
(edited with Harold Leventhal)

50 Simple Things You Can Do to Fight Censorship

Louie Louie

The New Book of Rock Lists
(with James Bernard)

Dave Marsh

BRUCE SPRINGSTEEN

TWO HEARTS

THE DEFINITIVE BIOGRAPHY,
1972–2003

Routledge
New York and London

Published in 2004 by
Routledge
29 West 35th Street
New York, NY 10001

Published in Great Britain by
Routledge
11 New Fetter Lane
London EC4P 4EE

Bruce Springsteen: Two Hearts combines the complete text of two books previously published by Dave Marsh, *Born to Run* and *Glory Days*, along with new material.

Library of Congress Cataloging-in-Publication Data

Marsh, Dave.
  Bruce Springsteen : two hearts / Dave Marsh.
    p. cm.
  Combines the complete text of two books previously published by Dave Marsh, Born to run and Glory days, along with new material.
  Includes bibliographical references (p.) and index.
  ISBN 0-415-96928-X (pbk. : alk. paper)
    1. Springsteen, Bruce. 2. Rock musicians–United States–Biography. I. Marsh, Dave. Born to run. II. Marsh, Dave. Glory days. III. Title.

ML420.S77M335 2003
782.42166'092–dc21
[B]   2003054801

CONTENTS

II. Glory Days

ACKNOWLEDGMENTS

BORN TO RUN

In 1975, writing a piece about what he called the Rock Critic Establishment, my friend and colleague Robert Christgau was generous enough to remark that my "quickie" paperback on Bruce Springsteen might lend new dignity to that benighted form. But I don't think he thought that my method was going to mean delaying publication for four years. It certainly wasn't what I had in mind.

For me this project has been worth every minute, and I stole lots of them from other things in order to scheme and dream about it. There is a great deal left out, a thousand hilarious stories that just didn't fit. But mostly, I value this book so much because writing it meant making so many friends.

To start with, there was Ron Oberman, who convinced me to listen to Bruce's first album and wooed me to my first Springsteen show. That I didn't adequately appreciate either wasn't his fault.

Jon Landau dragged me away from a TV set in Cambridge one night in 1974 and changed both our lives. I remember his exact words: "If I can't watch Kojak, neither can you. Now get down here." As he tells it, I introduced him to Bruce, but what I remember about the show at Charley's Bar is a blur, with the two of us looking at each other from time to time to make sure what we were seeing was real. I also had the good fortune to edit Jon's *Real Paper* column about Bruce, in which he uttered the sentence heard 'round the world, and to see a lot of Springsteen shows, listen to a lot of records, and talk about the man and the music for hours with Jon. So I know why they call him the King.

Glen Brunman was more than just a Columbia Records publicist to me. He is one of my best friends, and the nights we stayed up till dawn sorting out the past and the future were some of the best of my life. When I did the initial research in 1975, he was indispensable; when I thought I'd never be lucky enough to be typing the final sentences of this manuscript, the Brahma was always there to encourage me. But I remember more than anything our hours on the phone and sitting around the house — there's lots more of that guy in this book than his quotes.

Obie Dziebzic is a miracle worker. She brought me much closer to my own feelings, not just about Bruce but about rock and roll in general. In a funny way, I've always thought that rock 'n' roll is more about the audience than the performer, and Oblie is the best fan any rock 'n' roller could ever hope to have. That such a person could actually become a friend of mine is as much as I have ever hoped for.

There were other fans, too. Hundreds of them wrote me letters asking about Bruce and the book during the period when it lay in limbo; it sustained me to know that so many people were interested in seeing this book come to life. I wish I could thank each of them in person. A few of them, however, I got to know, and they are the faces I saw as ideal readers. Barry Bell and Dick Wingate appear in the text; I thank them again for letting me share their experiences and insights. Dave McGee — who generously shared his file on the lawsuit — Barry Singer, and Wayne King all contributed a great deal to the research. In a different way, so did Lou Cohan, who put it all on the line.

My colleagues Jim Henke, John Milward, Paul Nelson, Jay Cocks, Kit Rachlis, and especially Dave McGee and Greil Marcus also provided invaluable advice, comments, and assistance. My editor at *Rolling Stone*, Barbara Downey, did not work on this book, but she has been the single most important factor in improving my writing in the past few years; for that I thank her.

Miami Steve Van Zandt, Garry Tallent, Max Weinberg, Clarence Clemons, Danny Federici, and Roy Bittan — the E Street Band — gave me companionship and stories as good as their music. There isn't anything better than that. Jim McHale, Bob Chirmside, Mark Brickman, Bruce Jackson, Jim McDuffie, George Travis, Neil Quateman, Harry Sandler, Mike Batlan, and Doug Sutphin of Bruce's road crew all went out of their way to make me comfortable. They ought to be celebrities in their own right.

Rock 'n' roll is supposed to be something closed to all except the youngest. John Hammond helps prove that a lie every day of his life. So do Tex and Marion Vineyard, who showed me a great deal, not just about Bruce, but about courtesy and dignity.

Debts of gratitude are also owed to Stephanie Bennett and all at Delilah; Mike Rock, Ernie Thormahlen, and T.R.A. Studios; Gerry Helferich at Doubleday; and especially Mike Mayer and Ted Nussbaum, who took this book far more seriously than they were obliged to do.

Among the others who contributed to making the book possible are Debbie Gold, Southside Johnny, Kevin Kavanaugh, Ed Sciaky, Kevin Stein, Jimmy Iovine, Mike Pillot, Kathy Heavy, Gary Baker, Marianne Partridge, Susan Ginsberg, Phil Ceccola, Dave Gahr, and the people who first proposed that I write it, Josh Feigenbaum and Bob Zenowich.

And this time around, extra thanks go to Madeline Morel and Steve Leeds, whose promotional efforts helped ensure the success of the first edition; to Debbie Gold and Barbara Downey for their aid with the revisions; to Wayne King, Ellen Shipley, and the guys in Beaver Brown for keeping me honest; and to Sandy Choron at Dell for her faith in me. Not to mention all those fans at the bookstores, faces I'll never forget, and the ones who wrote the letters, which I'll cherish all my days.

Barbara Carr lived though it all without complaining, understanding my obsession even when it got in the way of normal living; for the 3 A.M. noise and for helping me believe, my thanks and my love. And more of the same for Sasha and Kristen, who are still young enough to know what it will mean to look back on the funny side of this someday.

Finally, thanks to Bruce, who contributed much more than the comments on the text. Rock 'n' roll has given me the best moments of my life, and my best moments in rock 'n' roll have come from him. Knowing the guy has been more than I needed; the real inspiration is watching him make dreams come true every night. To Bruce, from all of us, thanks for the lift.

GLORY DAYS

To begin with, there's Sandra Choron. Sandy served this book from the day I thought it up, first as an agent, then as designer and packager. But that's not what she really did; mostly, she did what she has done for the best part of a decade, which is make me believe in myself. Writing is a pretty easy job, compared to some, but when you're in the midst of a difficult and overdue project, it has its own terrors. Because of Sandra Choron, I can tackle those head-on, without looking over my shoulder. In the words of a singer we both love, she "makes my burden a little bit lighter / Makes my life a little bit brighter." If I didn't begin by thanking her, I wouldn't be able to begin at all.

In the spring of 1986, I called Sandy—she was wearing her agent hat—and told her that this book wasn't going to come out that fall. She did not shoot me, for which she deserves undying gratitude. Instead, she listened to what I had to tell her about a still-secret Springsteen project that would alter not only the book's ending but its entire shape. Without knowing exactly what I was talking about, she told me I was right and not to worry. This is not what you pay someone for; this is how you find out that someone is really your friend.

A few days later Sandy and I went to see Wendy Goldwyn, my editor at Pantheon. I told Wendy the same sketchy story. She didn't throw me out of the twenty-eighth-floor window; she listened, said okay, and asked me to step down the hallway to the office of her boss, Andre Schiffrin, who runs the joint.

I had never met Andre Schiffrin, but he didn't run out into the hallway, break open the fire alarm box, and murder me with the axe that he'd have found there. He listened, and then he said Pantheon would get the book out anyway as quickly as it could after the secret project had become a reality.

When I say each of these people is responsible for the existence of *Glory Days*, you see, I'm not kidding.

Bob Oskan deserves some credit, too. His empathetic editing consistently improves hasty writing and half-baked thinking (even if I did crumble some of his grammatical perfection). Thanks, Bob, het's do it again.

I'd also like to thank the following friends, neighbors, colleagues, and general rock 'n' roll riff-raff for various forms of assistance: Lee Ballinger, my indispensable partner in *Rock & Roll Confidential*;

Frank Barsalona; Barry Bell; Bob Benjamin; Bob Brown; Glen Brunman; Harry Choron; George Cole; Greg Drew; Jim "Sneak Preview" Dunning, for many kinds of confidence building; Ben Eicher; Stanley Fischer; Dave Gahr; Barbara Hall; Karen Hall; John Hammond; Frank Joyce; Wayne Kind; Andrew Klein; Barbara Landau; Marilyn Laverty; Greil Marcus; Milo Miles; Bob Muller; Steve Perry; Neal Preston; Neil Quateman; Larry Regan; Maggie Renzi; Marta Renzi; Cynthia Rose; Harry Sandler; John Sayles; Toby Scott; Suzy Shaw, Craig Hankin, and the Springstones; Chris Sprowal; Daniel Wolff. (Apologies to Michael Balhaus for nearly decapitating him with that cue ball.) Also Leslie Nolen, Pantheon's steadiest unrecognized hand.

For putting up with my presence, I'd like to thank the E Street Band, who have given me and several million others a thousand and one unforgettable nights at the opera out on the turnpike. These were their glory days, too. And especially Little Steven at whose feet I have studied soul music of many varieties.

If George Travis didn't exist, somebody would have had to invent a tour director who could work twenty-six-hour days, juggle several dozen egos, face down customs officials without blinking, always make the last flight out, and never complain (although he may sometimes be seen smirking). Travis doesn't do it alone, of course; he heads a crew shaped in the image of that philosophy, and watching them work together throughout the *Born in the U.S.A.* tour was an inspiration. In small ways and large, each of these members of the Springsteen crew went out of their way to help me throughout the tour, and I feel privileged to think of them as friends: Steven DePaul, Bob Thrasher, Lyle Centola, Jim McDuffie, Bruce Jackson, Terry Magovern, Jeff Ravitz, Bob Wein, Max Loubiere, Mike Grizel, Wayne Williams, and Drew Houseworth, with whom I once closed the Philadelphia Spectrum. Without Arthus Rosato, I don't know what I would have done for an ending. Thanks also to Denise Sileci for maintaining her usual air of complete calm, and to Carol Green for making sure everybody was where they were supposed to be.

Personal to Chris Chappel: This was *a lot* more fun than the last trip we went on.

Special thanks to Chuck Plotkin: We ought to do this again sometime in six or seven years.

Jon Landau is a person to whom I owe more things than space

allows me to define or a simple thanks can begin to express. Hopefully, some of the rest is embedded in the story itself.

Extra special thanks to my personal Jersey Girl, Barbara Carr, for keeping me (and everybody else) in line. And to Sasha and Kristen Carr, who for the last three years have functioned well in a house where there was often only one parent. Someday, I hope, you'll look back on this and it will all seem funny.

Finally, I thank Bruce Springsteen—for many things, music and conversation included, but most of all for giving me a chance to tell a true story with a happy ending.

TWO HEARTS

I'd like to thank especially Daniel Wolff and Craig Werner, who affected the new material here. Craig and Daniel also provided edits of the new introduction, "Across the Border," and new chapter, "The Price of the Ticket." My dialogue with each of them over the past few years has been not only instructive but liberating.

Others with whom I've maintained a dialogue about Bruce that colors my sense of what happened include Chris Buhalis, Lou Cohan, Suzy Covey (who was Suzy Shaw the first time around), Mary Feinstein, Stew Francke, John Ingrassia, Sue Martinez, Scott McClatchy, Lauren Onkey, Matt Orel, Chris Papaleonardos, Eric Schumacher-Rasmussen, and the usual suspects. Kevin Kinder, moderator of the much missed Luckytown Digest, did a thankless task brilliantly.

Kevin Gray gave me tremendous perspective on "41 Shots"—the moment when he first heard it will be with me always.

Karen Swymer Shanahan, Laura Swymer Clancy, and Emily Swymer Quinn gave me a glimpse of "faith will be rewarded" that has a value beyond mortal measure. Karen and Laura remain alive in my heart, still dancing with Emily at the edge of the stage that last time in Hartford.

Richard Carlin provided valuable editorial insight and grasped my idea for the new material instantly, offering ideas that much improved it.

Thanking Sandy Choron feels mundane. In my heart, I do it every single day. She remains a lifesaver.

Finally, I want to once again thank Jon Landau, my friend of more than thirty years; Barbara Carr, who has been my wife for a quarter century; and Bruce Springsteen himself, for affirmations of the essentials of the human spirit.

INTRODUCTION

Across the Border

In all the efforts of life, however complicated they may be, if we can isolate the strands in the circumstance, we shall see that each strand in and of itself is consistent. The plaiting of the strands creates patterns that may transcend the logic of any particular strand. Always there is the order; always there is the logic. We are not altogether bound by it because we are living, thinking, deciding, creatures. In this concept there is abiding hope for man.
— Howard Thurman, *Wade in the Water, Children*

I t used to drive me nuts (ok, nuttier) that people swatted me over the head with the term "hagiographer" because of *Born to Run* and *Glory Days*. It doesn't anymore, because I figured out that if you find the most coherent and dramatic rock 'n' roll story of your generation and tell it well enough for people to still be interested after a quarter of a century, you've done the job. If, as a part of the story, you claim that the person you're writing about is not a fraudulent, exploitative scoundrel but in fact honorable, immensely gifted, and inspired, and if, fifteen years later, there is nothing to contradict those claims, then somebody has a problem but it ain't the writer.

These two books brought many gifts into my life, including some of my most cherished friendships. Yet in my mind, the two volumes never quite meshed. As pieces of writing they are quite a bit different—as they ought to be, given that they were separated by six years. Some of *Born to Run* strikes me now as overheated—more the introduction, which is about me, than the rest, which is about Bruce. Maybe that's why, when I wrote *Glory Days*, I couldn't for the life of me see how to begin it without retracing a lot of Bruce's history. I apologize for the repetition.

Both books tell one story, though. Bruce Springsteen has created a career—and, for the most part, a life—with startling continuity. For him the question has never been whether to burn out or fade away but how to keep on keepin' on. That's part of what made him such a perfect biographical subject.

His story also provides a platform for discussing all kinds of ideas, about music and the music business, but also about such issues such as popular art in general, celebrity, and social class. (To make a probably vain attempt to clarify something that seems to confuse many readers: My politics are radical, by which I mean, outside the Democratic/Republican oscillation. Bruce's seem to be on the left edge of liberal.)

The beginning of Bruce's career presents a paradigm of how rock star careers began up to that time. I cannot speak to the end of his career, because I can't find it anywhere in sight; Bruce may now be in the Rock and Roll Hall of Fame, but recently he made a record as good as his best. So let's say I'm impressed by the middle of his career. How many rock 'n' roll (or even popular music) careers have lasted long enough to create a middle?

Keeping on track seems simple enough, a matter of being true to yourself and unwavering in your principles. In fact, it's a tightrope act, with all sorts of forces striving to bring you to earth. Undergoing the process of attaining stardom (and it is a process, no one just "becomes famous") generates a counterforce that drags the performer away from his core; few stars survive with identity, let alone integrity, intact. Maintaining an audience on top of that requires maintaining a public image without allowing that image to set priorities or overwhelm your sense of self. All that struggle means nothing, though, if you can't also come up with work that justifies it. Doubt will drag you down; so will self-assurance.

The worst drag of all comes from preconceptions—the artist's own and those of his audience.

Springsteen serves as an unmistakable American symbol, but since the late 1980s, Europe has been by far the best place to see his shows. The audiences there impose offer Springsteen much more freedom to define himself. Those audiences don't recoil from edgy songs like "41 Shots," since for instance in many ways the song's antipolice surface fulfills *their* preconceptions about the United States. They also gladly take new versions of his all-time concert staples. Their reward—and Bruce's—may be seen in the excerpt from the show in Barcelona that became a 2003 CBS television special. It comes closer than anything I've ever seen—except a Bruce show in the moment of its execution—to demonstrating why he's the greatest live rock performer of his generation. The only problem is that the video offers just a hint of the crowd's response—a cascading cry of love that began the first time he played Barcelona in 1981 and has increased in intensity ever since. They take what he gives them and puzzle it out on their own terms (I guess). You don't feel like he has to fight them to move on.

On the other hand, for many of his fans, especially in the U.S. and more especially in the New Jersey/New York City area, Bruce Springsteen is a known quantity. He does a certain set of things, and those things define him (as he often defines them). There is a whole other set of things he does not do. He's not likely to show up with a sitar or a set of props. He doesn't do commercial endorsements; his tours don't have corporate sponsors or the signage that comes with them. His records and shows emphasize melody and a steady beat, not fractured harmonies and polyrhythms.

The changes in popular music during his career have complicated all this. Hip-hop dominates today's popular music. It functions similarly to rock 'n' roll of the 1950s and 1960s, in part by dividing listeners into camps based, in significant measure, on how open to African-American signifiers they are. Hip-hop tore the cover off the central limitations of Western music, including rock 'n' roll: its refusal or inability to incorporate polyrhythms and its exaltation of melody and harmony over the power of beat.

Bruce never had much of a black audience, although his band has always been integrated. More important, he draws on a musical history developed primarily among African Americans, he sings more often than not in a voice derived from blues, R&B, soul and gospel, and he never backs away from racially charged topics. He lacks that black audience because, as a friend of mine put it, "The bottom of his music is never gonna be as interesting as the top of it," meaning his drum and bass lines stick to one rhythmic pattern per song (or section of a song). Compared to hip-hop, this seems not so much primitive as dull, which is an important part of why Bruce, along with other stars of rock's dominant period, has lost the attention of young Americans.

It's also why he's retained the interest of some pretty conservative people—New York City cops, for instance—long after he made it clear that his politics ran in the other direction. Willful misreadings of Springsteen's lyrics and actions range from Reagan's attempt to expropriate "Born in the U.S.A." to the safe, predictable interpretations (truly, emasculations) that appear in the few surviving publications that identify themselves as "liberal." Springsteen's worked very hard to make his political, as opposed to moral, convictions opaque, and so most of what has been said and written about him and expropriated from him represents less what his work contains than the playing out of a process in which people hear what they want to hear. Springsteen intends to empower his audience, teach them to make up their own minds, not tell them what to think.

But sometimes, when it turns out that Springsteen doesn't share the ever more reactionary white American perspective, big trouble looms. I've never been so frightened at a public event as that night in June 2000 when Bruce and the E Street Band first performed "41 Shots," his song inspired by the police shooting Amadou Diallo, at Madison Square Garden in New York City. In the wake of a single live performance of the song (in Atlanta a week earlier), the police unions and Rudy Giuliani, the city's law'n'order mayor, attacked Springsteen. They declared that, since the cops who shot Diallo had been acquitted—by a jury many miles from where the crime happened—further public comment was out of order. A police union spokesman capped the whole controversy by calling Bruce "a floating fag" (a term that remains undefined, despite diligent research).

The "floating fag" comment showed up the controversy for what it was: an attempt to cut off any dialogue about what had happened since Giuliani had turned the city's dark streets over to cops on "stop and search" missions. The bullying wasn't going to work, since everyone knew he'd sing the song. When your opponents are armed and angry, just singing the song takes some guts. And that night, with Diallo's parents seated just to stage left, the Garden felt close to the edge of real violence.

As I remember it, that night Springsteen opened with a new song, "Code of Silence," whose lyrics—portraying a love relationship where communication had suffered a total breakdown—metaphorically addressed the cops' objections. Then "41 Shots" rang out, a stunning arrangement, particularly if you'd only read the lyrics or heard the bootleg live dubs on the Internet (the song remained not only unreleased but unrecorded). The band sang as if in mourning. This wasn't a flip attack on the police—the lyrics weren't even unsympathetic to the cops, suggesting that they made an honest mistake. "41 Shots" had a subtitle, "American Skin," and that's what it tackled—the reality of race, the truth that all of us fear one another and that it gets some of us killed, and that it's people with the "wrong" skin who do almost all of the dying. Springsteen has walked the edges of despair in a lot of his songs. Here, it was impossible to see how he maintained his equilibrium, for what he skirted was the American abyss. "Is it a gun? Is it a knife?" he asked. "Is it in your heart? Is it in your eyes?"

The Garden didn't get so still you could hear a pin drop. For one thing, the song grew loud. He argued back with just his voice and his band, and this gave him an indomitable dignity.

Still, it felt like someone might try to hurt Springsteen, and I thought I knew who. In front of me sat a cop hurling furious threats and belligerent curses. But as soon as "41 Shots" ended, the cop wound up cheering just as loud as everyone else for the songs that followed. Maybe he'd forgotten his need to ban Springsteen's heretical thoughts; maybe he wasn't even a cop; maybe he just got carried away.

You could understand the guy's sense of betrayal, though. Springsteen turned out not to be the guy in his fantasy. Other Springsteen fans had felt betrayal for lesser reasons: When Bruce fired his drummer and started playing a tighter form of rock 'n' roll; when he made records that attracted people who didn't know Spanish Johnny from Madame Marie, or "Jungleland" from "Hungry Heart." When he married a girl who wasn't from New Jersey; when he wound up in a messy divorce that involved philandering with a Jersey girl. When he broke up the E Street Band and replaced it with a band of mainly black players and singers; when he put the band back together and went on a worldwide reunion tour. When he got rich as a result of satisfying his fans' desires so well; when he refused to stop identifying with the poor. When he stopped writing about the Jersey shore and started writing about the world; when he wrote more about his own life than he did about the world. When he put out records on his dilatory schedule; when he put out two full-priced albums at the same time. When he fired a couple of roadies and only gave them six figure severance pay; when he kept working with managers and producers that some fans didn't care for. Each of these "betrayals" involved the failure to meet a powerful preconception.

Most Springsteen fans didn't share those preconceptions (it's probable, for that matter, that most cops didn't think their representatives — or the mayor — should tell singers what to sing.) Still, you could feel the tension between star and audience in many things Bruce did. He even made fun of it on *The Ghost of Tom Joad*, in a John Prine-ish song called "My Best Was Never Good Enough," each verse a series of bitter clichés capped with the title phrase: "The sun don't shine on a sleepin' dog's ass / But for you my best was never good enough." I took it as a comment on what happened when Springsteen did something his core audience disapproved of — that 1992–1993 tour with a black band and a (slightly) blacker beat. There and then, Bruce found out that the compact of loyalty with his fans ran down a one-way street. All of a sudden he couldn't sell out Cleveland. He didn't sound pissed off, though. Just a little more cynical. Of course, with Bruce Springsteen, a little cynicism goes a long way toward confusing and contradicting any number of issues.

To the cop, it seemed pretty simple, I bet: Springsteen was an American hero, with an American flag on the cover of his biggest selling album. That there might be more than one version of America, that there might even be more than two, was the warp and woof of the issue. It apparently never occurred to that cop that Bruce's sense of what's important in the world might differ from his, just as it seemingly never occurred to the dissident fans that if his manager and producer were in charge, they'd have had to be clinically insane to let his career careen along at such a screwy pace and with so many restraints on making a buck.

All these forces pull at the man on the tightrope, and he's out there by himself. And, as the Band sing, "when he gets to the end, he's got to start all over again." It's a balancing act, and even when Springsteen takes a stand, he fights for equilibrium. In April 2003 radio station chains and politicians campaigned to silence the Dixie Chicks for admitting that being from the same state as George W. Bush embarrassed them. Springsteen responded with a statement on his website:

> The Dixie Chicks have taken a big hit lately for exercising their basic right to express themselves. To me, they're terrific

American artists expressing American values by using their American right to free speech. For them to be banished wholesale from radio stations, and even entire radio networks, for speaking out is un-American.

The pressure coming from the government and big business to enforce conformity of thought concerning the war and politics goes against everything that this country is about—namely freedom. Right now, we are supposedly fighting to create freedom in Iraq, at the same time that some are trying to intimidate and punish people for using that same freedom here at home.

I don't know what happens next, but I do want to add my voice to those who think that the Dixie Chicks are getting a raw deal, and an un-American one to boot. I send them my support.

That's the hardest line Springsteen's ever taken on a public controversy. Unlike the Diallo case, what's happened to the Dixie Chicks can be seen only one way, he insists.

Now try to use that statement to prove that Springsteen opposed the invasion of Iraq. It can't be done. He will tell you that it's important to keep the right to think. But he won't stray into what he thinks about what the Dixie Chicks think. All we know for sure is that in Springsteen's version of America, everybody retains the right to criticize or even mock politicians. That proves only one thing: As much as it goes against convention and public policy, Bruce refuses to surrender his memory.

Without memory, of course, there could be no continuity and the continuity, sustains Springsteen's art and life. But in the every day colored by the spectre of September 11, 2001, acknowledging that there is history and that it has consequences, let alone became a feat. This old trend in America grew like kudzu until it took over almost everything—except those whose sense of survival forced them to resist. Whether Bruce Springsteen wants to be a leader or not, he walks now on a path whose existence most public figures regularly deny.

The continuity here reaches back to the conclusion of his first great song: "Walk tall, or don't walk at all."

This volume represents a chronicle of his journey and my own. There is no one else of my generation I'd rather walk beside.

I | BORN TO RUN

For Barbara
—and all the tramps like us

INTRODUCTION TO THE FIRST EDITION

INDEPENDENCE DAY

"Me and the boys got some work to do. You wanna come along? It ain't like the old days . . . but it'll do."

Edmond O'Brien, *The Wild Bunch*

This book was first written in 1976. Flush with the newness of Springsteen's success, it was shorter, breezier, I guess happier. But that version never appeared, because Mike Appel (who then controlled Bruce Springsteen's song publishing rights) at the last moment withdrew his permission to quote from the lyrics. Perhaps the delay was fortuitous; I now realize that, back then, the story was far too fresh to be fully appreciated.

At any rate, the manuscript moldered in my desk until July 1978, when I finally asked Bruce what he thought about my updating it. I wasn't asking for permission—this isn't an authorized biography— but I felt Bruce was owed a chance to veto. Fortunately for me he accepted the idea.

My reasons for writing this book go beyond its role in rationalizing my Springsteen fanaticism (which justifies itself). When I saw Bruce

Springsteen, the dreams and hopes of what might have been were suddenly restored. For me, this is more than just a story about Bruce Springsteen. It is also a chronicle of rock in the Sixties—and in the Seventies, as its innocence curdled into cynicism.

I believe that rock and roll has saved lives, because I know that it was instrumental in shaping my own. When Bruce speaks of rock reaching down into homes without culture to tell kids that there is another way to live, I understand it personally. That is exactly what happened in my house. If this book succeeds, it's because it takes the measure of the life of a bus driver's son (like Bruce Springsteen)—or a railroad brakeman's son (like myself), or perhaps your own life—and spells out something of what rock and roll has given to them. We had nothing; rock lent us a sense that we could have it all.

But over the past decade, rock has betrayed itself. It gnaws at my marrow to recall a hundred sellouts, from the rock opera movies that were all glamour and no heart, to the photos of rock celebrities with international jet-set fugitives. The inevitable result was records that were made not with feeling but because there was a market demanding a product, and concerts performed with an eye only toward the profit margin. Rock became just another hierarchical system in which consumers took what was offered without question. Asking who was fake and who was for real used to be half the joy of the thing. Losing that option was our own fault, of course, but that doesn't make it hurt less. Rock saved my life. It also broke my heart.

So then the advent of Bruce Springsteen, who made rock and roll a matter of life and death again, seemed nothing short of a miracle to me. Not because it shifted the trend toward sounds I preferred but because it proved that one man could make a difference; because it said that it was every fan's responsibility to root out the corruption that had seeped into rock.

I remember four days in Los Angeles during the summer of 1978. On the first night Bruce climbed atop a six-story building to paint a mustache on the billboard advertising his album on Sunset Strip; "artistic improvement" he called it. The next night he played the Forum, the area's largest arena; it was sold out, but the show was as intimate as any with fifteen thousand participants could be. The night after that, performing with as much intensity as he had at the Forum, Springsteen played with an unknown band from Oklahoma in a roadhouse out in Callabasas that couldn't have held more than fifty people. And on the final evening, Bruce played the Roxy in Los Angeles, before a live audience of five hundred and to thousands of radio listeners. There had been some confusion about tickets, and not everyone who had stood in line all night got them. Springsteen apologized, live on the radio, then played as forcefully as anyone I have ever heard.

Every day now, new rock and rollers appear, fierce with determination not to compromise. "Punks," they often call themselves, and though I'm barely thirty, they make me feel old. For I know that rock can never be for them what it was for me and my friends— itself a means of avoiding compromise. I recognize that some of what I have written here seems overstated. There was no helping it. For Bruce Springsteen is the last of rock's great innocents. There can never be another quite like him.

But as long as weeks like that one in Los Angeles are still possible, even the betrayals seem worth it.

So this book was written to remind myself that these things really happened, as much as to share the story with others. And at the end, what I remember is not one of the happy songs, but one of the saddest. When Bruce sang it that night at the Roxy, he dedicated it to his father. It made me think of mine, and how desperately I've always wanted to communicate to him what's happened in a world he will never know. But tonight, that song also brings back to me the whole story of rock and roll itself. It is called "Independence Day."

> Poppa go to bed now, it's getting late
> Nothing we can say can change anything now
> Because there's different people comin' down here now
> And they see things in different ways
> And soon everything we've known will just be swept away
> So say goodbye, it's Independence Day
> Poppa now I know the things you wanted that you could not
>   say

Say goodbye it's Independence Day
I swear I never meant to take those things away

New York City
April 24, 1979

INTRODUCTION TO THE SECOND EDITION

OUT IN THE STREET

He and his boys up there were keeping it new, at the risk of ruin, destruction, madness, and death, in order to find new ways to make us listen. For, while the tale of how we suffer, and how we are delighted, and how we may triumph is never new, it always must be heard. There isn't any other tale to tell, it's the only light we've got in all this darkness.

James Baldwin, "Sonny's Blues"

Born to Run: The Bruce Springsteen Story set out to be a paradigm, the story of a rock 'n' roll archetype. Don't get me wrong. I thought then, as I think now, that Bruce Springsteen was—is—the brightest rock 'n' roll talent to emerge from the Seventies. But the reason I wanted to write a book about him stemmed only partly from being a fan. It came just as much from journalistic perception of a story taking shape. What happened to Springsteen happened to everyone else, virtually without exception, only it happened to him over and over again in a dramatically charged fashion. This turned out to be true from the way he learned to play guitar to the way in which he finally created a hit record, and it was never more true than in his business affairs. There is a saying in the record industry, "If you're going to have one hit, you'd better have two," meaning that you're certainly going to be ripped off on the first. The post-*Born to Run* lawsuit between Bruce and his former manager Mike Appel played out that axiom as contemporary tragicomedy. (I apologize if the best I could do with it was morality play.)

It had seemed to me, ever since Springsteen first thrust his leg-end-in-the-making into my face upstairs at Max's Kansas City one summer's night in 1973, that some kind of generational gestalt was hard at work within him. Or maybe I was simply cunning enough to recognize a great story when it was taking shape with the boy next door. I could never have written a good story about a musician, however paradigmatic, who didn't move me. And Springsteen's story—more concise and approachable than the Who's, less sprawling and sheltered than Motown's, more conscious and less alien than Elvis's—was the crucial thing that allowed *Born to Run: The Bruce Springsteen Story* to become the first rock 'n' roll best-seller.

Whatever else this book did, it invented that mongrel genre now known as the "rock book." I think it actually contained the proto-types for several styles within that genre, offering a biography, a fan's notes, a photo book (which was the format of the first Doubleday edition), an analysis of the biz and an annotated discography *cum* touring chronology.

I thought all those parts ought to be in there, because, first, they might be useful and one of the things I'd always loved about books was their pure utility, their side-by-side deposits of fact and lore.

Second, I wanted to write a book out of the sensibility that rock 'n' roll had given me. Frankly, none of the earlier books about rock 'n' roll captured its reach; even Nik Cohn's brilliant early encomiums slighted rock's more serious side. Most of the other people who'd tried to capture the experience (as opposed to just lay out the history, à la Charlie Gillett's indispensable *The Sound of the City*) presumed that overwriting to produce a tumult of metaphor, simile and hyperbole could somehow put the auditory experience *on the page*. Nonsense. Nothing puts the auditory experience on the page, which is about the least auditory experience there is. If you can't face that limit, you're not much of a writer, and you're certainly not a music critic.

The job is to lay out what happened, to describe what occurred, and then to embellish it with just the right attitude, an attitude that can't be flip all the time, anymore than Elvis could sing nothing but "Hound Dog" or Dylan nothing but "Rainy Day Women." (Even the Stones do "Dead Flowers" and "Moonlight Mile.") If you happen to be the kind of vernacular poet that James Baldwin was, every once in a while you can say it in a way that gets close to the core of the experience, the way "Sonny's Blues" does. But nobody's prose replaces or replicates the experience itself, and imitating what music's emotional core riles up may be the worst way of trying to emulate it.

The writer's job is to place those riled emotions in some kind of order that might, if you get lucky (and even a poet would need luck for this part), explain what can't be explained to those who previously did not get it. Probably my favorite tribute to this book has been the number of people who've told me that they've given a copy to a parent or teacher or spouse who just couldn't figure out what it was about this rock 'n' roll thing, in the hope that my book would spell it out. I don't know if any of those unrocked readers actually figured out what the book was about (there's a passage in some Joyce Maynard novel that indicates *she* sure didn't), but at least some other obsessives realized that I had cast my bread upon the waters.

In 1979, when *Born to Run: The Bruce Springsteen Story* was first published (the official publication date was September 23, Bruce's thirtieth birthday), the idea that rock listeners would also be interested in reading a story struck publishers as preposterous. The audience presumably consisted of illiterates with short attention spans. (You didn't see a whole lot of editors and publishers at those marathon Springsteen and Dead shows.) Rock books got published only if a star like the Beatles or Elvis grew too big to ignore. Doubleday's big popular culture titles in the autumn of that year were meant to be its books about the Bee Gees (riding high on *Saturday Night Fever*) and the first of *Rolling Stone*'s innumerable tomes on the cast of *Saturday Night Live*. I have never fully understood how Madeline Morel, Stephanie Bennett and the other people at Delilah

Communications convinced Doubleday to take a flyer on a performer who had made only five albums, the first three of which had flopped, and, for that matter, a performer who must have seemed even to the Delilah folks like nothing more than a poorly groomed cult figure. The fact that I had a fairly complete first draft probably helped. Anyway, Doubleday printed 15,000 copies of the first edition, and there weren't meant to be any more, as one could tell from the way the deal was structured—Doubleday had to pay *on delivery* for every copy they distributed, no returns allowed.

We outfoxed their slacker intentions, partly by tapping into the real rock audience, which had always been more devoted to the funky cult hero than to the Next Big Thing. This may or may not still be true, MTV having changed everything, but in trying to figure out the relative importance of rock icons, I try to follow a maxim articulated by John Fogerty, who said that what was really happening wasn't even in the Top 10 but somewhere down around number 16 somewhere.

In 1979, there were no book editors who could have told you who was number 6, let alone number 16. You can only imagine what the sales and marketing people must have thought about this scruffy Springwhozit—*you* can, because thinking it through would be way too depressing for me. So More!, independent promotion man Steve Leeds and myself set out to promote the book as if it were a record, touting it to radio stations, arranging giveaways and personal appearances, traveling from town to town. It was a shoestring version of what's become the "author tour." Nobody in the book business knew quite what to make of what we were up to, but my music industry friends did. "Dave's showing those publishing guys a new idea," Jon Landau said one Sunday afternoon. "He's out there *flogging* the damn things." So *Born to Run: The Bruce Springsteen Story* hit the best-seller lists.

If you're going to pull off something like that, in addition to shameless guts, it helps to have ammunition, and that was just what Bruce Springsteen provided. His fans, though fewer, were even more rabid then. It also helped that, from start to finish, *Born to Run: The Bruce Springsteen Story* spoke with a zealot's conviction that if people simply paid attention to Springsteen's work, they'd come to the same conclusion about its greatness that I had. Most of all, what

I was alleging happened to be pretty much true for a lot of people, and almost all of them wanted tools with which to proselytize. (Also, Springsteen makes albums so slowly that if he owned his own record label he'd have to call it Molasses, and so his cult and its wallets were otherwise unoccupied that fall.)

Somewhere along in there, *Born to Run: The Bruce Springsteen Story* played a role in allowing Bruce Springsteen to fulfill Jon Landau's prophesy that he was "rock 'n' roll future." (The weirdest part is that he actually *was*—even though I thought it was kinda hyperbolic when Landau wrote it. Not that I dislike hyperbole, as this book proves in spades.) As a critic, it's always nice to know when you've gotten one right. As a Bruce Springsteen fan and a rock 'n' roll true-believer—no matter how hard I try to keep some distance—it's damn flattering. But I live as a writer even more than I do as a rock 'n' roll fan, and if the truth be known, I'm proudest of all that *my* version of *Born to Run* succeeded the way Bruce's original did—by breaking a few rules, conjuring a mystery, inspiring some word of mouth, refusing to give up, making people fall in love with it despite its periodic ungainliness. By hacking its own way through the forest and into the sunlight. Sentence for sentence, it's as ramshackle as a Gary Bonds single, but like "Quarter to Three" and all the other midnight classics I listened to while I wrote it, *Born to Run: The Bruce Springsteen Story* gets the job done. This paperback writer never asked for anything more.

September 23, 1995

1 THE E STREET SHUFFLE

August 15, 1975

On this hot night in Greenwich Village, two hundred kids huddle in dank humidity at the corner of Mercer and West Fourth streets. Their faces alternately reflect hope and despair. Some have come from as far away as Philadelphia to see the rock show across the street.

The club is the Bottom Line, the showcase nightclub of the Manhattan music industry. Its fluorescent marquee reads:

Aug. 13-17
Bruce Springsteen
& the E Street Band
Sold Out

Tonight is the middle night of the stand. The crowd is waiting on a chance at the standing-room tickets—fifty per show, all that are left to buy—an opportunity to do nothing but elbow up to the bar or crowd around the coat-check room. They may not see much, but at least they'll be there.

Selling out the Bottom Line for five nights (ten shows) isn't terribly difficult. The club seats only five hundred. But Springsteen's new album, *Born To Run*, his first, is about to be released. In that time his cult has trebled. A tape of the title song is already an underground hit in Boston, Cleveland, Austin and Phoenix. In New York, Springsteen's following is sufficient for WNEW-FM, the city's leading FM rock station, to broadcast tonight's first set live. From the Jersey coast to Connecticut, cassette recorders are hooked to radio receivers.

Springsteen is prepared. Wednesday's opening sets were rocky in all the wrong ways—ragged and nervous. But Thursday's performances turned the corner. Bruce regained his keen edge. Unlike almost every other contemporary rock star, he had earned his following not with records but with stagecraft: charismatic, intense and intimate two-and-one-half-hour shows. By the end, he is drained and so is the crowd. Few leave unconvinced.

Last night's second set ended well after two A.M., with the crowd on its chairs and the band rocking the final encore, "Twist And Shout." Not counting an hour off while the Bottom Line staff cleared the first show customers and let the second group inside, the band had been onstage for more than six hours. And unlike the similar marathons of the Grateful Dead, this was not laid-back hippie music; this was street-level, kick-ass rock and roll and rhythm and blues, music to dance to, conjure with and be overpowered by.

Tonight, passing WNEW's emcee, Dick Neer, Springsteen delivers a spiel patterned after Muhammad Ali's heavyweight title fight boasts. Tonight he's out to prove that he's the champ. He says this into an open mike, and when it reaches the radio listeners milliseconds later, a few are bemused. Of course he's the champ—the only problem is that, at this point, rock has few other contenders for the title.

Still, it requires more than the usual amount of arrogance to make this claim. Since the beginning of the summer, the group has played only in the studio. The four previous Bottom Line sets are the only ones that have included Miami Steve Van Zandt, the new guitarist. But the band lives up to every boast. Van Zandt is ready; he looks like a gunslinger, relaxed but coiled for action. Drummer Max Weinberg is smashing a few practice shots into his kit. Clarence Clemons, the big saxman, thunders scattered notes from his tenor horn; he glowers, white-suited and very black, at the virtually all-white audience, as enticing as he is threatening. Pianist Roy Bittan and organist Danny Federici finger their keyboards, itching to start. Garry Tallent, the implacable bassist, stares past his beard at his shoes, absently plucking his heavy strings.

Suddenly, Bruce hits the stage. A white spot hits him; from the first note, it's clear that Springsteen sees something unusual at stake tonight. Maybe he's thinking of that long line of radio-linked tape recorders rolling from Asbury Park to way up in Westchester, and on out across Long Island. Instead of the solo number he has been opening with, Springsteen grabs the mike and flails his arm like a man falling off a bicycle as the band crashes into "Tenth Avenue Freeze-Out," the story of the band and one of the songs from *Born To Run*.

The band charges into "Spirit In The Night," dedicated "to all the folks down by the Shore, down at Greasy Lake." In the middle, Springsteen crawls onto one of the front tables, prompting squeals of delight from the patrons, to sing a verse up close. He leaps back onstage and finishes the song, then dives into the magic world of the Crystals' "Then She Kissed Me." The beauty of the arrangement has Springsteen almost breathless; he sings as if the song were new to him, as if he really *had* just mustered up the nerve to go up and ask that dream-date if she wanted to dance. His twelve-string guitar notes fall into the night and travel those airwaves like a message home.

Through his comic autobiography, "Growin' Up," its delight balanced between the devilish and the angelic, and into the searing "It's Hard To Be A Saint In The City," which resolves the issue in favor of both sides, the roar of the crowd grows louder. Then the stage goes black. Weinberg begins to snap rimshots like a tired metronome. All at once, a blue spotlight hits Bruce squarely and Bittan strikes some beautiful rolling chords on the piano. The organ slips underneath for a couple of bars, and Miami Steve's wailing guitar cries out. Then Springsteen brings his arm up, and snaps it down.

"Bam!" he cries, leaping into the air. The music rises with him, and as his feet hit the boards, the music falls back.

"It was, uh, about three, four years ago—four years ago, about this time of year, around August," he begins, his voice raspy. "I was working in this bar down on the Shore. I worked there for three, maybe four months, place called the Student Prince." A cheer. Springsteen has made the bars of Asbury Park—his home turf— nearly as famous as he is. And tonight there is a large element in the audience that has been following him long enough to remember those clubs.

"So it was me," he continues, the rhythm ticking away, "and it was Steve here and Garry. Garry was in the band then. And Southside Johnny.

"Do you folks get down to the Shore much?" He's answered with maniacal cheers. The mention is a setup; Bruce has accomplished the virtually impossible feat of making New Jersey fashionable. The shouts of affirmation come even from fans whose summers are spent on the rooftop tar beaches of the city. "Well, you gotta go see Southside Johnny's band, yeah, the Jukes." He croaks this, giggling, half little boy, half adult.

"Anyway, this is about three, four years ago, me and Steve and Garry are working in this bar down there. And we were feelin' like, like real discouraged at the time," he says, as though this is now unbelievable. "Because no one would give us a gig or nothin'. We went into this bar—the only way we got this job was this guy had just bought the bar and we went in there about midnight on a Saturday night. You know, there should be a few folks in there, right? Went into this place, the darkest, dingiest, dampest place you ever seen and there was nobody in there. Right?

"So we walk up to this guy and say we'll play for the door. You know, we'll charge a dollar at the door and we'll play for that. So we had a seven-piece band at the time, a big band. And we brought the band in the first week and we made, hell, we musta made . . .'"

"Thirteen seventy-five," interjects Miami Steve, with a flat air of doom.

"Yeah, we split $13.75 between us," Springsteen goes on, chuckling a bit. "And a few guys quit, you know. The next week I was there with a six-piece band. Threw some cat out—five-piece band.

This went on for a few weeks until we got it down to . . . You get down to your boys when you're starvin'.

"We was playin' this joint and we was always figurin', like, these people was trying to set us up. Like, 'Man, I got the manager from the Byrds comin' down here tonight to check you guys out. So you dudes better be good.' Right? So we would play like mad dogs all night. And about three in the mornin' we'd all be sittin' at this damn little table, sayin', 'Where is the cat? You know? What happened to the joker? Where is the dude?'

"And Steve, Steve was known then for practicin' his guitar, day in and day out, night and day, all the time. Every time I'd see him, he would practice, practice, practice. He always had his guitar with him, everywhere he went, you know. See him on the boardwalk, he's always got his guitar with him. Practice, practice, practice.

"So one night after the gig, we was all feelin' down in the dumps and you know, you're sittin' there sayin' 'Man, we're better than them cats and they got *two* records out. How come we ain't got no record out?' Right? You do all that kind of stuff, you know. Me and Steve was feelin' really, really drug out, and we figured we were gonna walk home. Figured we'd walk north along the boardwalk.

"So we got out there and it was a nasty night. It was rainin' and the club was flooded because some bikers come along and ripped off the front door. Really," he says when the crowd begins to laugh. "They just ripped the sucker off and brought it home with 'em or somethin'. I don't know what they did with it." As though the door, not the flood, were amazing. "They ate that thing. *Right.*

"So we was walkin' down the boardwalk this time of night. It was late—musta been four in the mornin'. Steve had his guitar with him. He was practicin'. And we was just walkin' down the boardwalk, figurin' we wanted to get home." The music continues its slow but inexorable pace, Federici's organ joining the melody every few bars. But Miami Steve has dropped out; he is too engrossed in the story. Springsteen swings over to his side of the stage and they pretend to peer into the distance.

"All of a sudden, we see somethin' comin'. I said, 'Steve, you see somethin' comin' down there?' "

"Umm huh," Van Zandt answers.

"He says yeah. I said, 'I don't know *what* that is.' But we don't want to take no chances, like, we just wanted to get home. We don't wanna fool around. So we ducked in this doorway, you know [they lean back]. And he told me to peek out. And I peek out.

"Whatever it was was comin' in the rain. The wind was blowin', it was in this big mist. And it was dressed all in white."

Clarence Clemons jumps into the spotlight, facing Bruce and Miami Steve. He begins to swing his arms and slowly walk in place, as though approaching them. His size, and their cowering figures, make the saxman seem a true force of nature.

"Dressed all in white with a walkin' stick. Walkin' like there ain't no rain, no wind. I said, 'Steven! Are you . . . am I crazy or is that dude carryin' a *saxophone?*" Now the crowd catches on. It roars with joy.

"So we figured," Bruce, says, as Steven nods in terrified agreement, "any dude walkin' in the rain at four A.M., dressed all in white, walkin' like there's no rain, with a saxophone is not to be messed with! Let the sucker walk on by. Right?

"So we huddled in the doorway, and we were sorta scared. [Steve hides his face, ducks behind Bruce, peers over the singer's shoulder.] We were a little scared. We were thinkin' we didn't want to get messed around or nothin'. I thought, that's all I need—come home with $3.50 and a messed-up face tonight.

"We heard his footsteps comin' closer. [Steve pantomimes the steps, banging on his guitar strings.] And they come closer [banging] and closer. They came even closer than that [final bang]. Now we figured this is no time to look like we were scared. We figured this guy is gonna come along, so we better at least look like we're bad. So here the cat's comin' and we're startin' to get ready." Steve pushes Bruce toward Clarence. Bruce drags his heels, but edges a little nearer. "And this cat comes up and he turned and he faced off right in front of us in the doorway and I just jumped back like this [falls into Steve's arms, as the music continues to swell].

"The first thing we did was, we throw all our money down. Threw *all* the damn money down. Then I still didn't know where the cat was at. He didn't move, he didn't do nothin'. He just stood there. And he held out the saxophone. So I took out my sneakers—I wasn't goin' to take no chances—and I threw them down. I figured he might want me to do that.

"But all he did was . . . put out his hand. [Clarence's hand edges into the spotlight, which is still fixed on Bruce]. So me and Steve leaned back and we got just . . . a little . . . closer. And then when we touched, it was like:

Sparks! fly on E Street
When the boy-prophets walk it handsome and hot
All the little girls' souls grow weak
When the manchild hits 'em with a double shot
The schoolboy pops pull out all the stops
On a Friday night . . .

And suddenly the band and the crowd sing with Bruce, in a moment of unity and passion:

The teenager tramps in skin tight pants do the
E Street dance
And it's all right

In that moment, it is a good deal better than all right.

2 IT'S MY LIFE

B ruce Springsteen has made Asbury Park, New Jersey, famous. But that's not really his hometown. He grew up
fifteen miles inland, in Freehold, a small town of the sort
that has almost disappeared since the freeways re-routed
traffic. It isn't a place of suburban ranch homes and half-
acre lots. It's the kind of community familiar to Americans who grew
up before World War II—more than a bedroom to its residents,
but without the pretensions of a city. There are a couple of factories—the largest makes Nescafe instant coffee—and the seat of
Monmouth County; small shops rather than shopping malls. Towns
like this have been sliding downhill for years; in today's world, the
very concept of such places is outmoded. Still, Freehold has a feeling
of stability that tract housing can never create.

Bruce was born in Freehold on September 23, 1949, the first child
of Adele and Douglas Springsteen. (They would later have two
daughters, Ginny and Pam.) Their surname is Dutch (not Jewish,
as is commonly supposed), but Douglas Springsteen's ancestry is
mostly Irish: his wife is Italian—her maiden name was Zirilli. Bruce

apparently acquired his talent for tale-spinning from his maternal grandfather.

A story Bruce used to tell about his youthful life in Freehold sums up the place, and the time. It is, of course, considerably mythologized, but those who were around in the old days say that almost every word is true.

"I lived eighteen years of my life in a small town in New Jersey, next door to a gas station—Ducky Slattery's Sinclair Station. That was the guy's name, Ducky Slattery. He was an older guy. And I lived next door.

"You know how in a small town, the place where the people hang out these days is down at the gas station. Everybody comes in and sits around at the gas station. Some guy comes in, somebody goes out, pumps the gas, comes back in. Ducky Slattery and this guy Bill who was kinda . . . This cat had a pink Cadillac. It was a sight! Got drunk, smashed it up.

"Ducky Slattery had this one line he ripped off the Marx Brothers. Anybody'd come in, he'd say, 'Wanna buy a duck?' That was his big line—not too original, but it worked. 'Wanna buy a duck?' Whaddya gonna do with a duck?

"I had a duck . . . my father killed a duck for Thanksgiving once. Helped me get out of the draft. Went down to the Army, told 'em ever since I seen my father kill that duck, I go crazy every time I see a duck. Told 'em, if I was out there on the battlefield in Vietnam, and I seen a duck, I might do anything—start killin' generals or something. I could do anything—I don't know what I do when I see a duck."

(Bruce would actually beat the draft in the classic Sixties fashion. "They gave me the forms and I checked everything. Even said I was a homo and all that. Then this guy calls me into his office, talks to me for about three minutes and tells me to go home.")

Douglas Springsteen had a variety of jobs, ranging from factory worker to prison guard. But mostly he drove a bus. "My father was a driver," Bruce recalls. "He liked to get in the car and just drive. He got everybody else in the car, too, and he made *us* drive. He made us all drive." It's a trait Bruce retains to this day; he likes the feeling of being in an automobile, behind the wheel or riding shotgun, cruising slowly or careening recklessly (mostly the latter). His fascination with highway imagery in his songs is not an idle one.

Springsteen attended parochial schools, not the best environment for a headstrong, idealistic kid who refused to learn his place. "I lived half of my first thirteen years in a trance," he has said. "People thought I was weird because I always went around with this look on my face. I was thinking of things, but I was always on the outside looking in."

Bruce was far from the most popular kid in school. Nuns seemed to single him out for harassment. "In the third grade a nun stuffed me in a garbage can under her desk because, she said, that's where I belonged. I also had the distinction of being the only altar boy knocked down by a priest during Mass. The old priest got mad. My mother wanted me to serve Mass, but I didn't know what I was doin' so I was tryin' to fake it."

Some of the trouble may have been self-inflicted. Bruce is by nature reserved; he does not reveal much of himself with any ease. Coupled with an equally strong streak of self-reliance often misinterpreted (even in his adult life) as arrogance, this spelled problems. Once, in fifth or sixth grade, he was sent to a first-grade classroom, as punishment. "I got down there and I was still actin' up. So the nun says to one of the little kids in class, 'Jimmy, I want you to show Bruce how we deal with people who act like that down here.' And this little kid gets up, walks over and slaps me in the face."

He might have hated any school, but parochial school, with its emphasis on discipline and social restraint, was the wrong place for anyone as rebellious as Bruce. "I was there eight years," Bruce says. "That's a long time. I still remember a lot of things about it. But I don't remember anything nice about it, so I guess I didn't enjoy it. It has nothing to do with me. I'm not involved in it. I'm here to play music; I'm in a rock band. Some people pray, some people play music." He attended a public high school.

Conflict was not unknown at home, either. The Springsteens were much less than affluent—from time to time, they lived with Mrs. Springsteen's parents and Douglas was often out of work. Both Bruce and Douglas are headstrong, volatile personalities, without much tolerance for rules. In such circumstances, a son with vision and ambition can seem less than a blessing. Bruce's memories of his early life are a mixture of the hilarious and the bitter. "We had a bathroom with a big gaping hole in it," he told an early interviewer, "and it looked right into this convent. I used to tell the other kids that during the war an airplane crashed into it—to save face, y'know?" (The story has a germ of truth: the bathroom window was broken). The part of Freehold where the Springsteens eventually settled was a weird neighborhood known, for some reason, as "Texas," filled with rundown two-family houses occupied mostly by immigrant Appalachian factory workers.

The family was typical American working class; culture came from television and the daily paper. "I wasn't brought up in a house where there was a lot of reading and stuff. I was brought up on TV," Bruce says. "Who was William Burroughs? They never brought him up in high school in the Sixties—unless you hung around with that kind of crowd. And I didn't hang around with no crowd that was talking about William Burroughs."

The crowd he did hang around with was trouble enough as far as his father was concerned. Although Bruce now speaks of his father with both affectionate humor and a kind of intense identification, there was a time when the mixture of love and hate all adolescents feel for their parents was seriously unbalanced. Introducing an old Animals song, Bruce used to tell this story: "I grew up in this dumpy, two-story, two-family house, next door to this gas station. And my mom, she was a secretary and she worked downtown. She married my pop as soon as he got out of the Army; they got married and she took that job. And my father, he worked a lotta different places, worked in a rug mill for a while, drove a cab for a while, and he was a guard down at the jail for a while. I can remember when he worked down there, he used to always come home real pissed off, drunk, sit in the kitchen.

"At night, about nine o'clock, he used to shut off all the lights, every light in the house. And he used to get real pissed off if me or my sister turned any of 'em on. And he'd sit in the kitchen with a six pack and a cigarette. My mom, she'd set her hair and she would come downstairs and just turn on the TV and sit in the chair and watch TV till she fell asleep. And she'd get up the next morning and go to work again.

"My pop, sometimes he went to bed, sometimes he didn't. Sometimes he got up. Sometimes he didn't get up. And I used to sleep upstairs. In the summertime, when the weather got hot, I used to drag my mattress out the window and sleep on the roof next door to the gas station. And I watched these different guys—the station closed at one and these guys, they'd be pullin' in and pullin' out all night long. They'd be meetin' people there. They'd be rippin' off down the highway.

"As soon as I got sixteen, me and my buddy, we got this car and we started takin' off. We used to take off down to the beach, sleep on top of the beach houses. We used to spin up to the city, just walk around the streets all night long 'til the cops would catch us in the Port Authority and call our pops. My pop, he'd never come and get me. I remember he always sent my mother. Everytime I got in trouble, my mother would always come and she'd always say, 'Your father, he don't even wanna come.'

"I used to always have to go back home. And I'd stand there in that driveway, afraid to go in the house, and I could see the screen door, I could see the light of my pop's cigarette. And I remember I just couldn't wait until I was old enough to take him out once.

"I used to slick my hair back real tight so he couldn't tell how long it was gettin'. And try to sneak through the kitchen. But the old man he'd catch me every night and he'd drag me back into the kitchen. He'd make me sit down at the table in the dark, and he would sit there tellin' me. And in the wintertime, he used to turn on the gas stove and close all the doors so it got real hot in there. And I can remember just sittin' there in the dark, him tellin' me . . . tellin' me, tellin' me, tellin' me. And I could always hear that voice, no matter how long I sat there. But I could never, ever see his face."

Throughout this recitation, the music has kept up an ominous, unresolved figure. The drums rumble, the electric glockenspiel rings remorselessly, bass and guitar mumble the same phrase over and over. But now that phrase resolves itself, swells into something beautiful but aching; the soprano sax squawks in confusion, but through this maze there is a route to freedom. The sound, halfway to cacophony, builds to peak volume. and when Bruce resumes his story, he has to shout to make himself heard.

"We'd start talkin about nothin' much. How I was doin'. Pretty soon he'd ask me what I thought I was doin' with myself, and we'd always end up screamin' at each other. My mother she'd always end up runnin' in from the front room, cryin' and tryin' to pull him off me, try to keep us from fightin' with each other. And I'd always, I'd always end up runnin' out the back door, pullin' away from him, runnin' down the driveway, screamin' at him, tellin' him, tellin' him, tellin' him how it was my life and I was gonna do what I wanted to do."

And the music swells a final time as Bruce sings the famous opening lines:

It's a hard world to get a break in
All the good things have been taken
But I know there's ways
To make certain these days
Though I come dressed in rags
I will wear sable some day
Hear what I say!
[Shouted] Man I'm gonna make for certain . . .
ain't gonna be no more of my time spent . . .
sweatin' rent . . . Hear my command! I'm cuttin'
loose . . . it ain't no use . . . tryin' to hold me
down . . . stickin' 'round
Cause baby [Baby!]
Remember [Remember!]
It's my life and I do what I want
It's my mind and I think what I want
Show me I'm wrong
Hurt me sometimes
But someday I'll treat you real fine

"It's My Life" is a perfect song for Springsteen. The introduction hits so hard because, despite its authentically personal details, it is a universal story of what happened to fathers and sons in the Sixties

. . . perhaps what always happens to parents and children. As a result, watching Bruce go through that epic onstage can be confusing: Should one weep, or dance in joy at his release? Exhilaration is the victor; through music, Springsteen triumphs, leaving the prison of small-time life behind him. It's corny all right—you can see the same sort of scene acted out in the classic John Garfield boxing film, *Body and Soul*—but, like sports and the movies, rock and roll represents for many working-class kids the only prospect of surmounting the despair of their inheritance. As Bruce would later realize, the real miracle was that he and his father had the same goal—both wanted more for Bruce than Douglas had ever been able to have. "What they didn't understand," Bruce would say in 1978, "is that I wanted it *all*." From the beginning, rock and roll was the medium for obtaining it.

It's appropriate that Bruce's first exposure to rock and roll was Elvis Presley on *The Ed Sullivan Show*. Like Bruce, Elvis came from a background that offered neither financial support nor much hope. "Man, when I was nine, I couldn't imagine anyone *not* wanting to be Elvis Presley," Springsteen remembered years later. He was so worked up over the experience that his mother bought him a guitar. "But my hand was too small to get into it. Besides, guitar lessons at the time were like a coma, buzzing on the B-string. I *knew* that wasn't the way Elvis did it." For five years, he put down the guitar. But he still listened, and dreamed.

In 1963, even before the advent of the Beatles, lightning struck. "I was dead until I was thirteen," Bruce says, and he means it. "I didn't have any way of getting my feelings out. Then I found this thing. I was a drummer, but I wasn't working enough to buy a set of drums. So I bought a guitar." With it came an identity: "When I got the guitar, I wasn't getting out of myself. I was already out of myself. I knew myself, and I did not dig me. I was getting into myself."

This guitar came from a pawnshop, for $18. "It was one of the most beautiful sights I'd ever seen in my life. It was a magic scene. There it is: The Guitar. It was real and it stood for something: 'Now *you're* real.' I had found a way to do everything I wanted to do." His cousin Frankie taught him his first few chords. The thrill was immediate. Since the day he began, Springsteen says, "Rock and roll has been everything to me. The first day I can remember looking in a mirror and being able to stand what I was seeing was the day I had a guitar in my hand."

His parents were appalled at this obsession. Springsteen not only believed that rock was all that counted—he acted like it. But no amount of pressure could make him stop. Just playing on his own was enough to lend him a joy he'd never known before.

The radio was an encyclopedia of music. He bought few records except those he wanted to learn to play, but his instincts, while idiosyncratic, were excellent. "I've always listened to what I loved, and watched what I loved. I play the records that I like. But I hate to study anything. The main reason I started doing my own arrangements and writing my own songs was because I hated to pick them up off the records. I didn't have the patience to sit down and listen to them, figure out the notes and stuff. So it's all just assimilation. I've been playing for eleven years and you just assimilate all these things," Bruce said in 1974. "It goes through something in you and it comes out with something of what you've been watching." As Miami Steve says, "Bruce has a real *fast* ear."

He loved the classic artists: Elvis, Chuck Berry, the Beatles, the Rolling Stones. And the second line of the British Invasion: Eric Burdon and the Animals before they went psychedelic, Manfred Mann's early records with Paul Jones as lead vocalist, the Byrds' folk-rock, the Who's power-mad singles. But the radio was full of dense mystery in those years, from the orchestrated paranoia of Phil Spector and Roy Orbison to the odd, crude, supremely energized Gary "U.S." Bonds. Bruce stored away limitless treasures: "Mountain Of Love," by Harold Dorman, Claudine Clark's "Party Lights," soul hits by Sam Cooke, Martha and the Vandellas and the rest of Motown, Sam and Dave, Eddie Floyd and other Stax artists, Mitch Ryder's and the Rascals' white twists on white rhythm and blues. It was perfect music for dance bands; there was no folk music, little Chicago blues (except the numbers the Stones and Animals converted), just rock and soul.

Until early 1965, Bruce simply woodshedded, just another high school kid with a guitar. In another part of Freehold, though, a gang of fifteen-year-olds were carrying the fantasy further, setting up a band of sorts—guitar, bass, drums, voice—in one half of a three-story duplex. In the other half lived a thirty-two-year-old factory worker, "Tex" Vinyard, and his wife, Marion. Tex was, and is, a big, blustering fellow with a booming voice, a salty tongue and a genuine love for kids. But the sound pounded through the walls, driving Marion to distraction. Finally, she convinced Tex to go next door and tell the kids to knock it off.

A few days later, George Theiss, the rhythm guitarist, came by to apologize. Along the way, he suggested that Tex—who was on strike from his factory job—might be interested in managing the Castiles (as the band called themselves, after the soap George used to wash his hair). Marion was not enthusiastic, but where kids are concerned her heart is as soft as her husband's. The dining room furniture was pushed aside, and rehearsals began. When some of the band failed to show up for practice regularly, Tex fired them, and the deposed lead guitarist took with him the band's only microphone and its only amplifier. But Tex soon found a twenty-five-year-old bass player named Frank who owned an amplifier and who was interested in filling in as lead guitarist. Practice resumed. "We were soundin' better," Tex remembers, "but we weren't exactly gettin' anywhere."

Then, on a night when, to use Tex's words, "It was rainin' like a cow pissin' on a flat rock," a kid from a few blocks away knocked on the screen door. "Hi," he said, looking up at the tall, rangy Tex. "My name's Bruce Springsteen. I hear you're lookin' for a guitar player."

"George had told me about this kid in school named Bruce for two or three weeks," Tex says. "And he kept saying, 'I'll ask him.' But really, George kinda had eyes for Bruce's sister, Ginny. So apparently he'd just go over there and get Ginny and forget about Bruce."

Bruce had an old Kent guitar that he'd borrowed. Tex asked if he knew any songs; he didn't really know much, beyond a few chords and snatches of a few guitar parts from songs on the radio. "But I'm quick to learn," he said.

"The kid just had something about him," Tex recalls. "Just like I could see it with George. There was something there. They wanted the band, their heart was set on it. So I said to Frank, 'You teach him.'" Now there were three guitars—Frank switched back to bass, in the end—running through a single amp.

At the end of the rehearsal, Bruce looked up to Tex. "Am I in the band?" he asked. Tex said he wasn't sure. Why didn't Bruce come back when he'd learned say, four or five songs."

"The next night . . ." Tex laughs. "The *next* night, it must have been about eleven o'clock, there was a rap on the door. 'Hi,' he says. 'I'm Bruce Springsteen. Remember me?' I said, 'Yeah. I remember ya.' He says, 'Well I learned a little. You gonna let me play for ya?' I said, 'Yeah.'

"Well, this damn kid sat down and knocked out five songs that would blow your *ears*. Five. Leads. No amplifier but five leads. He said, 'Oh, by the way, I learned a couple more,'" Tex says, rolling his eyes in remembrance.

"Frank teach ya?" Tex asked, playing it cool.

"No," Bruce replied innocently. "I listened on the radio."

"He knocked out a couple more," Tex says, "and I'm sittin' there with my ears goin' WHAT?!? WHAT?!? WHAT?!? I couldn't believe it!"

Tex arranged a special rehearsal two days later for Bruce's audition. The other boys arrived, George feeling especially cocky with a school chum on trial. Tex hadn't let on about the extent of Bruce's newfound repertoire. He still recalls the scene.

"Bruce is standing there with his ass out of his jeans, his damn old boots all run over, always in a T-shirt, pimples all over his face. So George says, 'Bruce, why don't you show us what you learned?'"

Bruce asked Frank to loan him the guitar the older player was using. He then proceeded to tune it, much to Frank's amazement. Then he plugged it in, and knocked out the songs. "Well, Bruce cut loose with those damn things," says Tex, "and you shoulda seen the look on George's face. The drummer dropped his sticks. Bruce is real cool. He says, 'How did I do? All right?' He's serious!

"Well, George just turned around to me and said, 'Hey, Tex, I'm still lead singer, ain't I?'" Vinyard throws back his head and roars. "Bruce says, 'Well, am I gonna make it in the band?' I said, 'Son, as far as I'm concerned, you're in the band.'"

Tex remained on strike, and, with only $21 per week in benefits from the union, he was rapidly falling into debt. But he spent as much time as possible with the boys, and he and Marion soon became deeply attached to them. The boys responded, and so did many of the other kids in the neighborhood. If the other kids weren't allowed inside while the band was rehearsing, they'd pull milk crates up to the window and press their faces against the pane to watch and listen. After forty-five days of rehearsal—steady, two or three times a week, as soon as homework and household chores were done—Tex decided the Castiles were ready for their first gig, a dance at the West Haven Swim Club.

With the big engagement coming up, the Castiles grew nervous, not about their lack of experience but about their impoverished equipment. "The amp was beginning to rattle," Tex remembers. "Now, across the street from us was a music store, next to the pool hall. Here comes the thrill: The boys were all sweet to me and Marion for a week straight. I know they're leadin' up to somethin' but I don't know what.

"All this time, remember, we ain't even got a microphone. We're just singing, without a mike. So they give me this look. 'Tex, have you looked over at Ralph's yet, in the window? Boy, they got a new amp over there. It's the latest and it's a beauty.' Which it was. Detached amp—had a separate head, which in those days was a big deal.

"Well, it was about nine o'clock at night and the store was already closed. 'Tex,' they said, 'let's go take a look at it.' And the owner drove up just then and he says, 'Hey, Texas, what's up?' I said, 'Ah, the boys just want to look at the amp.' He opened the store and let us have a look.

"They went, '*Look!* It's got three inputs!' It was a Danelectro 310, made right over here in Neptune City; biggest amp on the market at the time, except for the Vox Super-Beatle. And it had full reverb—nobody had *reverb*. Bruce coulda played with that thing and got his en-joys.

"I said, 'I'd like to have it. How much is it?' Well, it was a little over $300. Might as well have been three thousand as far as I was concerned. But they had to have it, they just had to have it. Then they had to have two or three microphones, which meant I had to go out and buy a fifty-watt Bogen amp for the PA. The boys got together and found a couple of old amps and glued the speakers together and that was our PA. But the amp was a beautiful thing, and I went into hock for it. I think I gave him $5 down for it and it was $11 bucks a month—for about three years."

The West Haven gig went well; the Castiles closed the show with a favorite of Tex's, Glenn Miller's "In the Mood," rearranged by Bruce. Proudly, they took their $35 and insisted that Vinyard accept his $3.50 commission. "Next day they came over and I bought 'em about $8 worth of picks and about $12 worth of strings."

Tex Vinyard likes to paint himself as crusty and crafty, but the feeling doesn't hold. His delight in dealing with the Castiles remains something special, and one of his fondest memories is the night a couple of years ago that he and Marion were introduced at a local nitery as "the Mom and Pop of rock on the Jersey shore." The appellation was earned. Although the Vinyards have no children of their own, they have helped put about a dozen through college, and not only musicians. In time, Bruce's sister, Ginny, became as frequent a visitor in their home as Bruce himself. Young musicians in the Shore region still often turn to Tex for advice, and he can still tell you what each of them likes to eat for dinner. Marion's private photo albums are filled with smiling teen-age faces eating pizza, listening to records—simpler pleasures out of a time that elsewhere seemed vicious and complicated in unnecessary ways. For the Shore musicians, Tex and Marion's home must have seemed a refuge.

Of all the kids that Tex worked with (he would later manage and book twenty-one bands) the Castiles are still the most special, and Bruce and Ginny (along with George) the most special of the Castiles. "I never loved two kids more in my life," Tex says today. "Many a night they'd sleep over. And many a night Bruce would fall asleep curled up with his guitar." For his part, Bruce played eloquent homage when he delivered a heart-felt dedication to Tex and Marion at his 1978 Madison Square Garden debut.

From the beginning, Marion Vinyard kept scrapbooks, and she has continued them, not only through Bruce's rise to fame, but for the other boys as well. Through these books, one gets a feeling of the time, which was marvelous for rock bands, even young, naive ones. Dances were held at a variety of places: teen clubs, high schools and junior highs, roller rinks, swim and country clubs, Hi Y canteens and CYOs. One Castiles show took place at the grand opening of a Shoprite Supermarket; another time, they played the local drive-in, as openers for *The Russians Are Coming, The Russians Are Coming*. There were charity shows hosted by disc jockeys, with a few top-flight local bands opening for acts like Lenny Welch, Dion and the Belmonts, Anthony and the Imperials. There were battles of the bands, held at Keyport Roller-drome. Tex remembers one where a young girl slipped the results into his pocket a few minutes before the show even began. (The paper is in the scrapbook.) It was a nothing scene. Everywhere, a beginning act like the Castiles was worth $35 per date; top attractions like the Motifs (the biggest local act at the time), $125. Half-hour sets, four or five a night. No original material, just the latest rock hits and perhaps an oldie or two, like "Twist And Shout."

It didn't take long for the Castiles to move up in class. George Theiss was (and is) a first-rate vocalist; Bruce was immediately recognized as an outstanding guitarist. But Springsteen was not allowed to sing; Tex felt his voice wasn't good enough. He took lead vocals on only two songs, Van Morrison's (Them) classic "Mystic Eye" and The Who's anthemic feedback orgy, "My Generation." In the summer of '65 those songs were adventurous stuff, notable mainly for anarchic energy. Tex felt that Springsteen's raw vocal projection fit the bill.

By early 1966, the Castiles were riding a crest. They developed an original song, "Sidewalk," which achieved such popularity that, in the scrapbooks, there is a petition from fans begging for a recording. But the band lacked the resources and the savvy to find a record label, and the boys were far too young anyway. (Frank left the group after a teen club proprietor said that kids didn't want to see a twenty-five-year-old on stage; Bart joined the Army and was killed in Vietnam.)

On May 22, 1966, the Castiles took matters into their own hands. There was a small recording studio in the nearby Brick Mall Shopping Center in Bricktown and on this rainy Sunday, the band piled into Tex's '61 Mercury and went over to cut a couple of sides. Bruce and George wrote the songs in the back of the car on the way over: "That's What You Get" and "Baby I." The record was never released, not even locally, but Tex still has acetate copies. The songs are so crudely recorded that they don't reveal too much, but it is interesting to hear this fresh-faced, effervescent music, with strong melody and propulsive rhythm. On "Baby I," Bruce's guitar cuts through enough to discern a simple but strong style developing. The playing is more remarkable because, during the recording of the first side, Bruce's E-string broke. There was no replacement and no time to go out and buy one. The Castiles had one hour of recording time which cost $50; they settled for what they could get.

At this time, the teenage world was divided into two camps. In the Shore area, they were known as "surfers" and "greasers," which was not quite the same as wimps and hard guys. Surfers were relatively clean cut and listened to white rock; greasers wore leather and denim and preferred soul music—what was sometimes disparagingly referred to as "boogaloo" by the other side. It was a simple and long-standing division among kids; in England it took the form of "rockers" and "mods," while in parts of America farther from the beach, surfers were called "continentals" or "frats," greasers were sometimes known as "hitters." Whatever, the essence of the matter was the same. Surfers had prospects, some hope of a future; greasers often had none. (It was a while yet before the hippie movement then blossoming in cities like New York and San Francisco would penetrate to places like Freehold.)

The Castiles were a hybrid band, and as a result, Bruce remembers that they "took a lot of heat from both sides." Freehold was located equidistant between Route 35, the highway near the Shore which was the main strip for surf clubs, and Route 9, the inland highway where the greaser clubs were located. It was a period of transition for both surfers and greasers—musically, this was reflected in the development of bands that played more than instrumentals. Before the Castiles only about two other Jersey bands had vocalists; everyone else played instrumentals, either the greasers' soul funk, or the surfers' twangy beat ("Night Train" versus "Pipeline," as it were). But at grease clubs, the Castiles had problems because they were too adventurous, splicing songs from the early albums of the Animals and Who into their Motown repertoire. At surf clubs, the British rock was all right—although the smoke bombs the Castiles used were a little *outré*—but the band's looks didn't make it. The Castiles not only wore semi-greaser uniforms (frilly shirts, snakeskin-style vests, black pants and socks, Beatle boots), but they had long hair.

No one had long hair. Greasers still lingered in duck-tail fashion; surfers cropped theirs tight to the skull. At the greaser bars, the Castiles sometimes came close to brawling with the customers. At the surf clubs, particularly the Sea and Surf in Sea Bright (which Bruce remembers as "the surfer stronghold"), the group was spit at, attacked with thrown pennies and generally reviled. "But there was always a minority that dug it," recalls Bruce. That might have had something to do with the Castiles' innovations, which included dragging a lifeguard tower indoors, which Bruce climbed up on to start the set.

Such strokes of innovation were all that separated the Castiles from ten thousand other bands that blossomed in the years following the Beatles. "There were three hundred bands for every job," Tex says, and he's not exaggerating. While it would not be fair to say that all of them sounded the same, it would be accurate to say that almost all of them tried to emulate one of the half-dozen major British bands: Beatles, Stones, The Who, Kinks, Animals, Yardbirds. (Judging from the acetates, the Castiles were very influenced by the Beatles.) This music was unschooled but utterly stylized, ground out in garages and backrooms, occasionally making it to the same kind of tiny two-track studios that the Castiles used. Once in a while, such groups would get lucky and score a hit; the McCoys, from Ohio, with "Hang On, Sloopy"; the Swinging Medallions, from the South, with the soul-influenced "Double Shot"; the Five Americans, from Oklahoma, with "I See the Light"; Count Five, from California, with "Psychotic Reaction," one of many rip-offs of the Yardbirds' "I'm a Man." More often, the records had confined regional success, as was the case with Bob Seger's "Gloria"-like "East Side Story" and Dylan-influenced "Persecution Smith." Sometimes, the musicians would go on to bigger things—John Fogerty's Blue Velvets became Creedence Clearwater—but the music wasn't the sole purpose anyway. As E Street Band drummer Max Weinberg remembers, "When I was fourteen, the band was it. It was your identity."

In later years, such grass-roots music became known as "punk rock," mostly because it was simple, ragged and raw, but emotionally honest, in contrast to the constricted, self-conscious music the bigger names in rock had begun to toy with. Were these musicians punks? Not exactly—they didn't have gangs that swiped cars and hubcaps and they didn't go around looking for fights (although there was sometimes no avoiding them). Punk rock, and its audience, was more concerned with style, a certain posture and attitude that encapsulated a view of life. In a way, this perspective was not dissimilar from hippie ideology: It was equally cynical (if not more so) about jobs, schools, the Army and other institutions.

But the surfers, frats, continentals, greasers and hitters of the mid-Sixties—lump them together as punks, if you will—were different from the hippies in more important ways. For one thing, they did not espouse isolation from the rest of the society the way the hippies did. The punks genuinely regarded the adult world as irrelevant but, in their secret hearts, must have known that this moment was just a teen-age dalliance, part of the natural adolescent transition between childhood and maturity.

Punks did not owe much to the beatnik bohemian tradition. They belonged to an older strain in American culture, one with roots that went back to Billy the Kid. Before Elvis Presley, this outlaw punk tradition was mostly expressed through young male movie stars— James Cagney, John Garfield, Humphrey Bogart, Marlon Brando, and James Dean—who established the punk perspective: bitter, alienated, tough, somewhat sentimental, cynical but also committed to values that seemed forever to be slipping out of reach or fading into oblivion. In *Rebel Without a Cause* and *On the Waterfront*, Dean and Brando established the look for the contemporary rocker version of the punk. The kids in *West Side Story* were a remarkably sweet-tempered version of it, and that film was (despite its inauthentic music) heavily influential, especially on the gang-oriented East Coast.

As Weinberg says, the rock band was another kind of gang, where guitars replaced zip guns. The beatnik/hippie concepts—largely derived from European and Oriental culture—were never terribly accessible to most Americans, except as a fad. Jeans make more sense for people who ride in cars than flowing robes do. Rowdy music has greater resonance for people who spend their life numbed by factory and shopclerk work; and to such people, modal expressions of serenity are meaningless. Drinking overshadowed other drugs for the Sixties punk, and when drugs came onto the scene, they were approached with the same frivolous zest as alcohol, not with the pretensions of enlightenment the hippies claimed for them.

Philosophically, the difference was simple but crucial: For hippies, Western society had disintegrated to the point where it deserved to be mocked and abandoned. For punks, that society's disintegration meant something more various, confused and economically immediate: Rebellion was imperative but so was respect, as if an instinctive, atavistic memory of earlier values remained. Perhaps that is the reason that the hippie ethos was so easily corrupted and merchandised, while in the late Seventies, an attempt to revive and extend the hard-edge spirit of punk was doomed to commercial failure in the United States.

It was Bruce Springsteen's fate to become the key figure in the transition from hippie music back toward a more naturalistic rock style. Springsteen writes of cars and girls, the key icons of this macho movement, the way the hippie writers wrote of drugs and universal peace/love—with commitment and passion. (The downfall of Seventies punk was that too much of it had all the commitment and sneered at the passion.) In Springsteen's songs, a questing, romantic spirit is inevitably scorned and banished; he is torn between his own abandonment of the traditional values and his desire to seek them as a refuge. He is not a dropout; he is an outlaw, in line with what Norman Mailer had written in 1960: "There was a message returned to us by our frontier that the outlaw is worth more than the sheriff." America had eclipsed its frontiers—Vietnam was a disastrous attempt to find a new one, the moonshot was a silly one—but in Springsteen's songs that frontier made a reappearance, both everywhere and nowhere. It was the only thing worth seeking and an impossible goal, simultaneously a chimera and the most potent force in the world. The answer was personal; it had to do with style, give that style whatever name you will. In "Backstreets," Springsteen stated it concisely and perfectly:

Remember all the movies, Terry, we'd go see
Trying to learn to walk like the heroes
We thought we had to be . . .

Musically, this outlaw spirit gave punk music (in its original Sixties incarnation, anyway) a connection with black popular music—soul, not jazz—that the hippies lacked. Hippies attempted to fuse rock with folk, jazz, classical, Indian, Native American, Middle Eastern and twelve-tone elements; punk rock retained the basics, elaborating upon them only slightly, never willing to abandon the basic beat.

But because the punks are rarely articulate, because they more often come from the American underclasses (one reason punks don't drop out is because they can't afford to), mainstream rock went into decline. As the Beatles became baroque and the West Coast bands seemed unable to come up with anything visceral, only a few standard-bearers of the old sound remained: Even the Rolling Stones fiddled with sitars, while The Who toyed with rock opera. John Fogerty of Creedence Clearwater Revival sometimes seemed the last man in the world capable of writing straightforward rock songs—or at least the only one willing to do so. Most of the real heirs of the early rock tradition wound up playing in local bars, struggling to make ends meet—though once Springsteen revived the sensibility, it was surprising how many people seemed to have been waiting to follow suit.

But that was all in the future. For their time, the Castiles were successful. Bruce was developing a style, learning licks (it was said that, hearing a new chord or technique, he could master it in twenty minutes and play it back better than the person who taught it to him), writing songs. He had been writing since he joined the band, even though not much of his material could be included in the stage show. He was in public school now—the switch came in ninth grade—but still on the outside of its social life. "Music became my purpose in life," Bruce told Robert Hilburn of the *Los Angeles Times*. "Before that, I didn't have any purpose. I tried to play football and baseball and all those things. I checked out all the normal alleys and I just didn't fit. I was running through a maze. Music gave me something. It was never just a hobby—it was a reason to live."

Kit Rachlis of *The Boston Phoenix* remembers interviewing Southside Johnny and the Asbury Jukes. Each of the band members told Rachlis the story of how he had come to a crisis point, where a decision finally had to be made whether to pursue music as a career or give it up. "Did everyone you know go through that?" asked Rachlis. "Everyone but Bruce," Southside replied. "Bruce always knew. There was never any question about it as far as he was concerned."

The passion was all-consuming. "One time, George and Skibotts [the drummer who replaced Bart] came to me and said they got a job," Tex remembers. "So I said to Bruce, why don't you go out and get a job and go to work? He went into the living room and jumped into Marion's lap and said, 'Tex is screamin' at me.' She said, 'What's the matter?' He said, 'He told me a dirty word. He told me to *work.*'" Apparently, Bruce viewed outside jobs as a trap, designed to keep him from developing his talent for rock.

He saw sex similarly. There was a time for girls, but they never came first. When one friend got married, Bruce told him flatly, "You ain't never gonna go no further in your music career now." No one was going to trap Bruce Springsteen into a house, kids and a nine-to-five future. In any event, sex would not have been easy for a small-town Catholic boy. "You weren't asking a girl, 'Do you want to dance?'" he remembers. "You were asking her, 'Do you *wanna*? My life is in your hands.' We're not talking about a dance; we're talking about survival." Still, if girls were secondary, they were definitely far ahead of whatever came third.

Drugs weren't even on the list. Although many people thought that Springsteen's twitchy, itchy stage mannerisms meant he must be on *something*, in fact he always abhorred anything stronger than beer. "People take drugs because their friends do it," he said. "At the time, I didn't have many friends. I had a guy I'd see once in a while, and a girl, but outside of that, there was nobody. I wasn't in that circle. Consequently, I was oblivious to a lotta social pressures and stuff within the scene, 'cause I was on the outside, lookin' in— until I started to play. Then people came closer. But by then it was too late. I was totally involved in what I was doing, and I had no need for anything else, or for anybody. I was there, and that was it, for me."

Springsteen is a loner by nature. Even today, he is the sort of person whose favorite moments often involve being alone: speeding down a highway, or just soaking up the atmosphere at four A.M. on a deserted street. This came naturally to him (his father apparently shared it), but in the late Sixties, threatened by the draft on one side and school on the other, Bruce became even more determined to find a way out. And it would be his *own* way—that more than anything was the purpose of his music.

The Castiles were beginning to feel a bit frustrated simply playing the surf bars in New Jersey. They suggested that Tex attempt to find them bookings in New York, in Greenwich Village. Tex, somewhat reluctantly, agreed. "Shit, there were ten thousand bands in New Yawk," Vinyard says. "But the boys said, 'Aw, Tex, you gotta try for us.' Finally, I called the Cafe Wha—that was on the same street with the Night Owl, where the Lovin' Spoonful were getting started, the Mothers of Invention and the Fugs. Anyway, I called for an audition. 'Naw,' they said, 'we ain't auditioning nobody, we got a hunnert bands to audition, and we only got thirty nights open for the rest of the winter.' But finally I convinced them to at least hear us.

"So we got up there, and everybody's real nervous. But Bruce, he says to Curt, the bass player, 'I want some good lead bass. Not plunk, plunk, but lead—with a pick.' He came out with 'My Generation' and I hate to say this, but we got twenty-nine out of the thirty bookings." It was January 1967, a real triumph in a Village scene that was about to explode nationally; with the Spoonful and other groups. But the Castiles, perhaps because their name was not hip, perhaps because their music was a little behind the trend (although in New Jersey, their surf/grease hybrid was called "psychedelic"), were offered no recording contract during their stay in New York.

And by summer, high school would be over for the Castiles. The band had offered an early start, and some madhouse moments. They once played the local asylum. "We were terrified. This guy in a suit got up and introduced us for twenty minutes, saying we were greater than the Beatles," Bruce would remember years later. "Then the doctors came up and took him away." But the innocence was draining out of the rock scene and, with it, the time for high school bands like the Castiles. "Bruce was getting ready and wanted to go on further with music," Tex remembers. "The other boys wanted college or marriage. But we stayed close, and I went with Bruce to gigs many, many times."

3 GREETINGS FROM ASBURY PARK, NEW JERSEY

I t was a summer of massive changes, the year of the hippie and the antiwar movement. The Summer of Love. But in Freehold, it was something different. Bruce took off for New York the night of his high school graduation, which didn't do much for the party his parents had planned. He came back in the middle of the night, but his father made sure he went to the school the next day to get his diploma. Other changes were brewing as well.

The Castiles were over, and Bruce was working with Earth, the first in a series of bands. Influenced by the recent emergence of Cream, with a power trio "heavy metal" sound, Earth played lengthy guitar based songs, heavily influenced by the Doors and Tim Buckley. And Bruce had discovered in nearby Asbury Park a haven for young musicians like himself. Miami Steve remembers Bruce riding into town with a new Les Paul model Gibson guitar, "the fastest guy on the scene." "The concept of taste had not yet entered my thinking," adds Bruce. "I just wanted to play as fast as possible." So he became a sort of Alvin Lee-by-the-sea.

Asbury Park is a small-time beach town, dismal by most standards. Downtown is nearly empty, devastated by municipal default in the Thirties, urban renewal in the Fifties, a race riot in 1970. Cross the railroad tracks driving east toward the beach and life picks up, but only a little. White wooden beach hotels sit next to greasy spoon restaurants. On the boardwalk, there's Madam Marie's, the fortune-telling shack that later turned up in Bruce's "Sandy," and a couple dozen arcades. But the width of the boardwalk nearly exceeds that of the tiny beach which has eroded as much as the man-made landscape around it.

The Ferris wheel is much smaller than those at the resorts farther south. Instead of Atlantic City's Steel Pier, here, at either end of the boardwalk, there are the musty, chipped-paint Casino and the Convention Hall. Even on Fourth of July weekends, the place is only three-quarters occupied. Right next door, only a few feet south of the Casino, begins Ocean Grove, a Methodist camp town where you can't drive on Sunday or drink any day of the week. Farther down the beach, the teen dream lights of Point Pleasant and Seaside, with their more prosperous boardwalks, can be seen on clear nights. This is no idyllic Big Sur landscape, but for anyone with a taste for tackiness, for connoisseurs of junk-food Americana, Asbury still scores points as paradise.

Residential Asbury is tough. The beach homes and some of the old hotels used to be luxurious; the year-round homes were never anything more than humble bungalows. In the winter, people hustle, hoping for a summer drought; rain can spell disaster to the tourist trade.

The real attraction of Asbury had nothing to do with the beach. The draw for musicians was a club called the Upstage, which had two sessions on weekends, one from eight to midnight and another from one to five A.M. Bruce remembered the place in his liner notes for the first Southside Johnny and the Asbury Jukes album, *I Don't Want To Go Home.* "There was a lotta musicians there, 'cause the bands that came down from North Jersey and New York to play in the Top Forty clubs along the shore would usually end up there after their regular gig, along with a lotta different guys from the local areas. Everybody went there 'cause it was open later than the regular clubs and because between one and five in the morning, you could play pretty much whatever you wanted, and if you were good enough, you could choose the guys you wanted to play with.

"The Upstage was run by this beat-type guy named Tom Potter who plastered the walls with black light and pin-ups and showed Fifties smokers to the kids in between the bands . . . It was a great place. He'd slip you five or ten bucks to sit in and you could work it so you'd never have to go home, 'cause by the time you got out of there it was dawn and you could just flop on the beach all day, or you could run home before it got too light, nail the blankets over the windows of your room and just sleep straight through till the night.

"There were these guys . . . Mad Dog Lopez, Big Danny, Fast Eddie Larachi, his brother Little John, Margaret and the Distractions (house band), Black Tiny, White Tiny, Miami Steve and assorted E Streeters plus the heaviest drummer of them all, in terms of both poundage and sheer sonic impact, Biiiiig Baaaaad Bobby Williams, badass king of hearts, so tough he'd go the limit for you every time, all night. You will never see most of these names on another record besides this one, but nonetheless, they're names that should be spoken in reverence at least once, not 'cause they were great musicians (truth is, some of them couldn't play nothin' at all) but because they were each in their own way a living spirit of what, to me, rock and roll is all about. It was music as survival and they lived it down in their souls, night after night. These guys were their own heroes and they never forgot."

Garry Tallent, the E Street Band's bassist, also remembers the Upstage. "I think that club was what was special about Asbury," Garry says. "There weren't many other areas that had places like that. Like I never sat down with a record—I just learned from playing with other people." (Springsteen remembers that he met Tallent because the bassist "used to pull a damn chair out in the middle of the floor and stare at me, until finally we just started talking after a show one night." It would be a couple more years before they were actually in a band together.)

"The whole back wall was speakers," remembers Danny Federici. "Potter had built a crazy system, maybe a hundred 15-inch speakers, 30 twelves, 10 eights, and little Bassman heads in the front of it. You plugged into those amplifiers with the speakers behind you."

Earth was short-lived, because almost as soon as Springsteen became a regular at the club, he had his pick of bandmates. It was

there that Springsteen met Vini Lopez and Danny Federici. Springsteen recalls his first meeting with Vini, being approached by "this
real short-haired guy, real short hair, shorter than Charlie Watts has
now. It was 'Mad Dog' Lopez, just out of jail. He told me about
that, says he's lookin' for a guitarist, because I was the hottest guitarist then. Danny Federici I met in Tom Potter's office; he was
wearing a three-quarter-length black leather jacket, very greaser, and
his wife, Flo, had on a blond wig."

Federici remembers meeting Springsteen just as distinctly. "The
first time I saw Bruce, I knew it right then and there. He was just
a guy who came off the street, but in the musicians' circuit in those
days, it was like, you gotta see this guy Bruce. Bruce from Freehold.
He had a big mane of curly hair, a guinea tee and suspenders, real
tight jeans. He was so fast. He's still fast, but he never plays guitar
like he used to play."

Federici had come down from Flemington, his hometown in
North Jersey. He'd studied classical accordion for several years,
switching to rock and roll on a Cordovox and eventually a full-scale
organ after the Beatles hit. He had, for a time, a band called the
Legends, made up of whichever of his high school friends were available on Friday nights, for which his mother, also his manager, had
four sets of floral print jackets made. (He still wears some of them
onstage.) Federici left high school in his junior year to play with
another musician who would later frequent the Asbury scene, Bill
Chinnock. Chinnock had a singles deal with Artie Ripp, and they
released a record, though on Tristereo, not on Ripp's Kama Sutra
label itself. But Kama Sutra distributed it, and when that label went
bust, Chinnock and Federici were left high and dry.

He'd been playing with Lopez, and when they saw Springsteen,
they immediately suggested he form a band with them and bassist
Vinny Roslyn. They called it Child.

Springsteen soon found out that there was already a rock band
named Child somewhere nearby. So the group's name was changed
to Steel Mill. By most accounts, this was the premiere band of
Springsteen's youth. It would eventually enhance his reputation,
spreading it over the mid-Atlantic coast as far south as Virginia. The
band was enormously popular with beach kids everywhere; there are
still tapes floating around from that era.

What they reveal is illuminating. Steel Mill has always been described as playing heavy metal music, which usually means blues-based, instrumental-oriented rock with a leaden beat. Steel Mill had the blues base—Springsteen's guitar style was obviously patterned after the B. B. King-influenced single-note playing of Eric Clapton, Jeff Beck, Mike Bloomfield and Danny Kalb—but it had a more driving and flexible rhythm foundation. The material was quite remarkable—"Resurrection" was a scathing look at Catholicism, with lines like: "Take me to church on Friday/And we confess our sins/ Special low price on three Hail Marys/My soul is clean again." The mockery, the underlying spirituality and the sound add up to an approach that is pure *Live at Leeds* Who. Steel Mill did other kinds of material—a version of Martha and the Vandellas' "Dancing in the Streets," for instance—but all of it was tough, aggressive and overpowering. It is far from what Bruce would later do, but it is also some of the best heavy-metal music ever played. Steel Mill deserves its legend.

Actually, Steel Mill was formed while Bruce was in Ocean County Community College. College didn't last long (although Bruce did manage to have a couple of poems—not good ones— published in the school literary magazine). Springsteen has a natural instinct for drawing the wrong kinds of attention from authorities. But at college, he was roundly disliked by his fellow students as well as by the faculty. "The times were weird, the students were weird, and the school was weird," he says. The conversation concluding his academic career came after a number of other students had petitioned for his dismissal. He was called in by a counselor.

"Look, you've got problems at home, right?"

"No, things are great. I feel fine."

"Then why do you . . . *look* like that?"

"What are you talking about?"

"There are some students who have . . . complained about you."

"That's their problem."

But Bruce stayed in school a while longer. He finally left after meeting "a record producer in New York," who promised him that he'd have a deal in no time. "Quit school," he said, "you won't have any trouble with the draft." Since Bruce was not exactly in the market for a degree, he left the college—but he never heard from the producer again. Still, he quite easily stayed out of the Army.

In early 1969, Douglas Springsteen decided to seek work in California. Bruce was determined not to go along; he remained in Freehold, living in the family's home until he was finally evicted, after which he moved around, staying with Tex, Miami Steve and other musicians, and for a time in a house with some surfers. ("Surfing was the only thing besides cars and music that I could relate to at that time," he said.) It was a perfect time and place to learn rock and roll, even though New Jersey is a national joke. "When I was eighteen and playing in this bar in California," Bruce recalls, "people would come up to us and say, 'Hey I really dig you guys! Where ya from?' And I'd say New Jersey and they'd just go, 'Yech! Ech!' "

But the isolation of the Jersey Shore, where there was nothing to live up to, was also an advantage. Free to develop a style without pressure of trends and false criteria about what was hip, Springsteen was able to concentrate on music that elsewhere was forgotten: Paul Jones, Manfred Mann's lead singer, became a decisive influence on his vocal style; soul music helped shape his rhythm style. Bruce has most often been compared musically to Bob Dylan and Van Morrison, but the Dylan influence is mostly expressed lyrically, not instrumentally, and what he shares with Morrison, beyond a vague similarity of voice, is mostly a common affection for soul rhythm. As critic-producer Jon Landau has put it, "For twelve years, Bruce had the time to learn to play every kind of rock and roll. He has far more depth than most rock artists because he really had roots in a place—coastal Jersey, where no record company scouts ever went." Absorbing styles and influences that were too quickly forgotten in the music industry centers, Springsteen became not so much a human jukebox as a human synthesizer, with an enormous repertoire of songs, influences, bits and pieces picked up from almost anything on the radio. He built his songs on guitar lines and hit records of vague memory, which gave his most original songs an immediately familiar quality. It's part of the rock dream that even the briefest, most minor hit single might have some eternal quality; Bruce Springsteen distilled the essence of that quality, and shaped it with a genuinely original vision.

That summer, Bruce and Steel Mill headed for California. Tinker

West, the surfboard maker who managed the band, was from California, and he wanted to take them to his old haunts, to "make it." Bruce drove out, but since he didn't know how to shift the car's manual transmission, he had to have a friend change gears for him. In California, Steel Mill's first gig was at Esalen, the original spa of the self-awareness movement. "I'd never been outta Jersey in my life," Bruce said. "Suddenly, I get to Esalen and see all these people walking around in sheets. I see some guys playin' bongos in the woods. One of them turns out to be this guy who grew up around the corner from me." Later, at a date at the Matrix, the Berkeley club founded by the Jefferson Airplane's Marty Balin, Steel Mill drew a rave review from the *San Francisco Examiner*'s Philip Elwood.

Elwood called the band's ninety-minute show "one of the most memorable evenings of rock in a long time," and he added, "I have never been so overwhelmed by an unknown band . . . [Springsteen] is a most impressive composer . . . 'American Song' [has] political-military observations, ranging from Concord Bridge to the present, and there is one called 'Lady Walkin' Down by the River' that is a fascinating juxtaposition of stop-time solos, interesting lyrics and a heavy, heavy ending.

"The band is currently splitting hot dogs four ways to keep things together while delving into the local music scene. They deserve and demand attention." The review drew enough attention to get the band invited to audition night at Bill Graham's Fillmore West, and to be given a chance to cut a three-song demo for Graham's Fillmore Records. Steel Mill was offered a contract but turned it down because the advance money ($1,000) was too small.

Steel Mill returned to New Jersey, a little dejected but certainly just as popular. Miami Steve Van Zandt was soon added as bassist, replacing Vinny Roslyn. Steel Mill became sufficiently popular to earn up to $3,000 a show at local colleges. But Bruce grew tired of Steel Mill's approach, and in early 1971 he let the band fold up, deciding to form a much larger group: ten pieces, with horns and girl singers. While rehearsing that band, Bruce decided to put together a group composed of everyone who wasn't already in another band.

That was Dr. Zoom and the Sonic Boom. It played three dates, one of which was as opening act for the Allman Brothers. The membership changed nightly: "Somebody'd take a solo and we'd all fall down laughing," Springsteen says. The group even featured a Monopoly table set up in the middle of the stage. "That was to give the people who didn't play anything a chance to be in the band," Bruce recalls with a laugh. "You know, so they could say,'Yeah, I'm in Dr. Zoom. I play Monopoly.' " "Everybody made about $5 each," Vini Lopez adds.

Later that summer, Asbury Park went to the ground, in a fire from the race riot. "We went right down with it," Miami Steve says. They lived on a dollar or two a day, developing a series of arcane rituals. Pinball was a passion; Springsteen was the best at that. Monopoly was more complicated. Their version of the game included special cards that assured that the less scrupulous players would win. Springsteen was supposedly Boss here, too, except when Van Zandt showed up. Even then, Bruce had an edge. He'd come well supplied with snacks, and, eventually, he could trade them for property and other considerations.

In this kind of community, the musicians who stuck with it developed special bonds. Insulated from the big time, they knew they were prey for small-time hustlers. As a result, they came to trust no one easily, except one another. Nicknames proliferated ("Southside" for Lyon, the blues fan; "Miami" for Van Zandt, who hated the winter weather; "Big Man" for Clemons, because he was). There was a kind of code, the sort of thing that Western movies propose for outlaws. Loyalty was its first tenet. To this day, the original Asbury Park musicians have bonds unfathomed—and unbreakable—by outsiders.

But Dr. Zoom was meant as nothing more than a stopgap until the ten-piece band was prepared for its debut. Miami Steve, for one, contends that the ten-piece group—the first known as the Bruce Springsteen Band—far outstripped Steel Mill in ability and conception. "Musically, it all kinda ties in with the Jukes and everything, because this was our first experience with horns," said Van Zandt. "We spent six months getting the guys. That was the first time that we ever found out that—forget rock and roll—there's no such thing as rhythm and blues horn players. At least in our area, with white guys; they all wanted to do jazz." But in the process, Springsteen found musicians who would stick with him for years: pianist and guitarist David Sancious, bassist Garry Tallent, Miami Steve (now switched back to guitar), Lopez and Federici were the core of the ten-piece band.

"But after six months, we finally got the band together," Steve continued. "And we played two gigs, and broke up." The ostensible reason was a lack of jobs—promoters simply weren't prepared to deal with such a large band, and it wasn't highly paid enough to be sustaining when there was work. The horns went after the first gig, which was held in Richmond, Virginia, where the band had planned to move. But soon the gang was back in New Jersey, and playing as a five-piece, as described in the E Street Shuffle story in Chapter One. (Indeed, that story is very close to the truth, Clarence Clemons has since revealed. He was playing down the street from the five-piece Bruce Springsteen Band back in Asbury Park, when he encountered Bruce and Steve, standing on the street during a between-sets break.)

The rest of the band still had day jobs. Van Zandt had joined the construction union, using a jackhammer on highway repair. Falling into debt, Steven went out on tour with the Dovells, the Philadelphia act that had hits with "You Can't Sit Down" and "The Bristol Stomp" in the early Sixties. Tallent gave guitar lessons. Clemons did social work with young kids. Only Bruce refused to have any part of a nonmusical job. The problem for everyone else was that there just wasn't enough work—nor enough money. Bruce might occasionally slip off to the Village to play solo dates, but the rest didn't have such options. Under this financial pressure, Bruce eventually had to let the band break up. He would try it as a solo act for a while.

4 THE PUNK MEETS THE GODFATHER

"You see they didn't know what to do with me at first. I was strictly a rock and roller. But they heard these songs and the first record came out sounding like some folk music album."

Bruce Springsteen

Somehow, Tinker West met a pair of songwriters named Mike Appel and Jim Cretecos. Appel and Cretecos had been aspiring performers and producers—actually producing a Mercury Records LP by a heavy metal band called Sir Lord Baltimore—but in order to make a living, the pair had taken jobs as writers in Wes Farrell's songwriting mill, where they had written a hit for the Partridge Family, the era's quintessential teeny-bopper group.

Springsteen's audition was a smash. "He sang as if his life depended on it," Appel remembered years later. "The song was about a deaf, dumb, and blind kid who 'danced to a silent band.'" Appel and Cretecos recognized Bruce's talent immediately. "Look, there was never any doubt in my mind that he was one of the greatest. Onstage in that leather jacket . . . like Elvis. We all want a piece of that leather."

But. Appel and Springsteen lost touch. Bruce went out to California; this time, he said, he wasn't planning to come back. But the experience was horribly frustrating. "I didn't know anybody out there, and I wound up playing with these fourteen-year-old kids in garages," he recalled. And when he got back, Appel had forgotten the name; Bruce had to pressure Mike's secretary to take the call. Finally, it dawned on the songwriters that this was the same kid who'd auditioned for them. They got Bruce to write a batch of songs for them simply by asking him to come by the office. He had the first one finished by the time the bus hit the Lincoln Tunnel.

Prolific Bruce may have been. Shrewd he was not. He signed a long-term management contract only a few days later, on an automobile hood in the unlighted parking lot of a bar.

In early 1972, Springsteen was living in an apartment over a drugstore in Asbury. Although Bruce rarely bothered with books, he did pick up a copy of Tony Scaduto's just-published biography of Bob Dylan. Paging through the book, he came upon the story of Dylan's signing to Columbia Records: Apparently the young folk singer had simply auditioned for a man named John Hammond, who seemed to be some sort of legendary music business figure. In *The Benny Goodman Story*, Bruce remembered, Hammond had been portrayed by Dennis the Menace's father. So when Appel called to tell Springsteen that he had arranged an appointment with Hammond, at least Bruce knew who Mike was talking about. (Actually, Appel had been trying to reach Clive Davis, the president of Columbia Records. But Davis was out of town, so Appel "settled" for the most famous talent scout in recording history.)

In fact, John Hammond had had a hand in some of the greatest events in American musical history. The scion of a branch of the wealthy Vanderbilt family, Hammond developed a passion for jazz and blues while still in his teens. In the early Thirties, he rediscovered Bessie Smith and recorded her best sides. A little later, he was responsible for signing Billie Holiday to Columbia. In 1938, Hammond organized the famous Spirituals To Swing concert, which first brought home-grown American music to Carnegie Hall. In the Fifties, he had recorded the great Aretha Franklin. In the Sixties, he had been among the first to spot Dylan's budding genius. If there is a popular music aristocracy in this country, John Hammond is both its most elegant and most venerated figure. But in 1972, Hammond was some years between major discoveries. His position at Columbia was secure thanks to his past contributions, but many felt that, as a talent scout, he was finished.

Hammond was less than desperate to find a new hit act. That had never been his philosophy in the first place; when he signed Dylan, the cracked-voice singer was known to CBS executives as "Hammond's folly." Unlike most other record company employees, Hammond did his job out of passion, not for personal wealth. After all, he was born with money. But when Appel called, Hammond's secretary, also operating on instinct, made an appointment. Hammond recalls: "She said, 'I think you might do this. He came on very strong.' I said, 'Okay. I have fifteen minutes.'"

Springsteen and Appel entered in a rush of enthusiasm. Appel, who has rarely been described as charming, opened the conversation on the boldest possible note. "You're the guy who discovered Bob Dylan, huh?" Mike snapped. "Well, we want to find out if that was just luck or if you really have ears." To Hammond, whose gentility is almost Old World, this gratuitous abuse came as a shock. "Stop!" he said. "You're making me hate you!"

For his part, Bruce remembers the occasion with comic trepidation. "I went into a state of shock as soon as I walked in. Then Mike starts screamin' and yellin' about me—before I ever played a note, the hype began. I'm shrivelin' up and thinkin', 'Mike, please, give me a break. Let me play a damn song.'"

Hammond scowled as Appel's tirade continued. Finally, he said, "Bruce, why don't you sing something for me." Springsteen got out his guitar and did either "It's Hard To Be A Saint In The City" or "Growing Up," depending on who's telling the tale. Longer and less rocking than his usual style, it was almost a folk song. But its impact, lyrically and musically, was impressive.

"I couldn't believe it," Hammond recalls. "I reacted with a force I've felt maybe three times in my life. I knew at once that he would last a generation." Hammond wondered whether Bruce had ever worked as a single. Springsteen replied that mostly he'd played in bands. Hammond called Sam Hood, who was running the Gaslight, a tiny club in the Village, and quickly arranged an audition performance for that very night. Then he called in a few other CBS colleagues. "The initial reaction was, 'Well, he looks so much like Dylan, he must be a copy of him,'" Hammond says. "But he's not, not even remotely."

At the Gaslight that night, Bruce sang for a crowd of about a dozen people, including Hammond. The talent scout's ears hadn't lied. He arranged an audition recording session for a few days later, to be produced by himself. Appel was requested to make himself scarce.

At the audition, Bruce played piano; while he is not nearly as adept on that instrument as he is on guitar, he is usually not so clumsy as he was that day. The pressure showed as he hammered at the keys, striking them with far more force than was necessary— or effective. But there was a simple strength to the music, and the imagery in many of the songs was prolific and exciting. He did about half the songs from what eventually became his first album, *Greetings from Asbury Park, New Jersey*. But the song that impressed Hammond most was a fluke: He asked Springsteen if there were any song he had written but would never perform live, and Bruce responded by playing "If I Was The Priest." The demo is rough, like all the others, but Hammond was knocked flat by the lyrics:

Well now if Jesus was the sheriff and I was the priest
If my lady was an heiress and my mama was a thief
Oh and papa rode shotgun for the Fargo line
There's still too many outlaws tryin' to work the same line

Anti-Catholic imagery ran rampant: Virgin Mary runs the Holy Grail Saloon; the Holy Ghost runs the burlesque show. It ends with Bruce refusing Sheriff Jesus's request to come up to Dodge City.

The song also cleared up another point for Hammond. "It seemed unlikely that he was Jewish," he laughs today. "But when he sang that song, I knew he could only be Catholic." Indeed.

Hammond took the audition demo tape to Clive Davis. Davis has an autocratic reputation, and Hammond knew an eager reception was far from guaranteed. "You know, I've brought a few stiffs as well as some good people to Columbia," Hammond says. "But Clive loved what he heard on the tape. He said, 'You know, John, he's very amusing, isn't he?' I said, 'He's more than that, Clive. He's fantastic.'"

Hammond asked an attorney—not one who works for CBS—to take a look at Bruce's contract with Appel. "It's a slavery deal," the lawyer reportedly said. Nonetheless, Bruce's faith in Mike was complete. So, on June 9, 1972, Springsteen was signed to CBS Records.

But Springsteen was not signed directly to CBS. In May, he had signed a management agreement—for one year with four one-year options—and another agreement giving Laurel Canyon (the Appel/Cretecos production company) exclusive right to his recordings for the same length of time. The recording agreement provided for a royalty of three percent of the retail selling price, and that Bruce would make five albums for Laurel Canyon.

The Laurel Canyon/CBS agreement, however, provided that Bruce would make a total of *ten* albums, and that Laurel Canyon would receive a royalty of eighteen percent of the wholesale price—about nine percent of the retail price, or approximately three times what Bruce would receive. Naively, Bruce never bothered to have these provisions explained to him by an attorney.

For the moment, it seemed more important that CBS was advancing him $25,000 in a lump sum (to be charged against royalty revenue, of course), and that the contract provided a $40,000 recording budget. Springsteen could finally make an LP. He quickly called together his Asbury Park cronies and began preparations for re-forming the Bruce Springsteen Band with Tallent, Federici, Sancious, Clemons and Lopez.

Federici, for one, hadn't played with Springsteen for more than two years, ever since Steel Mill broke up in the wake of a police raid on a swim club gig in Middletown. "I got a call about a week later," Danny recalls. "Bruce said the band is breaking up. It never occurred to me that I was so involved in the band. Bruce called me at home, and I broke out in tears."

For the next two years, Danny drifted from gig to gig, "playing for the money." He was rehearsing on Long Island when he got word that Bruce had phoned with an offer. "Billy [Chinnock] was standing at this pay phone with me, and he saw the look in my eye. He said, 'You're leaving the band, huh?' I said, 'Yes, I am.' " So Federici went back to Jersey. "I came down and I played and after it was over, I went up to Bruce and said, 'Well, what's the story?' He said, 'It's not an audition.' There was no audition; it was a rehearsal. And we went out on the road seven days later and we've been there ever since."

The record company, Appel and Cretecos were stunned. They saw Springsteen as a solo act in the Bob Dylan/James Taylor bracket, and a rock band was the farthest thing from their minds. At the time, the trend was toward solo writer-performers like Taylor, Carly Simon, Joni Mitchell and Carole King, who recorded with studio musicians and made understated, tasteful pop recordings. Bruce had accurately described his musical history—eight years in rock groups, two months on his own—but, as he would later remark: "They forgot about the eight years and went with the two months."

CBS and the managers gave in only partly. Hammond has steadfastly maintained for years that Bruce is always at his best as a solo writer-performer, and he still seems to cherish the idea that Springsteen will someday make a "pure" album in that style. Appel and Cretecos came around more easily; rock and roll was their past, too, although they still wanted a record that would fit the commercial mainstream.

(Years later, Miami Steve Van Zandt and Jon Landau speculated one evening on why Springsteen had briefly chosen the solo route. "It's the one thing I have never understood." Steve said. "Although he said at the time that he had to be a singer-songwriter, that's all that people were buying at the time." "That's true," Landau said. "But maybe, what he wanted was a record deal for *Bruce Springsteen*.")

In any event, Bruce had no intention of letting down the boys back home now that his chance had finally come. He found the notion of recording with session musicians—who he felt played for the bucks alone—repugnant. The rest of the group was playing a gig down in Richmond when the contract was signed, and they quickly headed back for rehearsals in Jersey. Only Miami Steve was missing, and even he showed up (on a break from the oldies circuit) in time to play a minor role, punching an amplifier head to produce a blast of feedback on "Lost In The Flood."

It was a band of archetypes. Drummer Vini Lopez was a wild man who lived as hard as he played, in the great spirit of Keith Moon. Lopez had a reputation as a barroom brawler—he earned his nickname, "Mad Dog," by giving his own trumpet player a sock in the lip (according to the ever-veracious Miami Steve).

The other half of the rhythm anchor, Garry Tallent, also fit the pattern of rock band personalities. Originally a guitarist, he was intimidated into becoming a bassist by the recorded prowess of master guitar player Jimi Hendrix. Shy and steady, Tallent was like the Rolling Stones' Bill Wyman and The Who's John Entwistle in preferring the back of the stage to the front. Like Entwistle and Wyman, Garry's bass playing is as firm and unobtrusive as his persona; but he has a certain deadpan wit, and he is a passionate rockabilly fan with a record collection—jointly held with Southside Johnny— of immense quantity and quality. Tallent, in fact, claims to have burst into tears after first hearing Roy Orbison's "Running Scared," a song of no little consequence in the Asbury pantheon.

Clarence Clemons is another story. At six foot four, he stands a head taller than anyone else in the band. He is also several years older. Clemons played football at Maryland Eastern Shore University (with Emerson Boozer of the New York Jets), and he had tryouts with the Dallas Cowboys and Cleveland Browns before a knee injury ended his hopes of an NFL career. He is alternately quiet and boisterous (on road trips, his room parties loudest and longest), with a piercing laugh and the sense of humor to go with it. A genuine eccentric known for his generosity, Clarence plays perfectly off Bruce onstage—the relationship has made him a favorite in his own right.

David Sancious is also tall and black, but he is Clemons's opposite in almost every other way. Slender, with the long fingers and huge reach of the keyboard player, he is also a red-hot guitarist, although he rarely had the opportunity to play that instrument with Bruce. (He would later play guitar with Stanley Clarke, the jazz-rock bassist.) Temperamentally, Sancious was unlike the rest. Introspective rather than simply shy like Tallent, Sancious had studied classical music, and jazz as well. His playing added an exotic dimension to the band: He would drop in quotes from Monk during his breaks, or open a set with a selection from a sonata.

The group was completed by Danny Federici, "The Phantom." Federici grew up in Passaic, in North Jersey, far from the rest of the gang, but he fit in neatly. His tough exterior and "dese" and "dose" enunciation hid a softer spirit that came out in the songs; his organ playing, when given free reign, has a warmth and strength that is genuinely soulful, perhaps derived from his classical accordion studies.

With Springsteen as lead guitarist, plus session bassist Richard Davis and pianist Harold Wheeler on a couple of tracks, this was the band with which Springsteen went into the recording studio that June. Appel and Cretecos were the "producers," although they quickly discovered that it was an arduous task to convince Bruce to change any of his musical ideas once his heart was set on them. Of the two, Cretecos seems to have been the more important factor in the studio (until he was cashiered following the second album).

Appel later admitted that he was at first against the band concept. "Perhaps I was too caught up in his lyrics. When Bruce came in and played me 'Spirit In The Night' on guitar, I liked the song, but I didn't extend the tune into the band backing. Bruce said, 'It's just because you listened to it on guitar. You can't tell exactly how it will sound.' "

When the time came to overdub electric guitar on the tracks, Appel was adamant. "Look," he said, "this is supposed to be a folk record and *that* is a rock and roll instrument." Springsteen held out. It was his music, and it would be played his way. ("When I painted houses," as he puts it, "I'd paint any color you wanted. But now I'm playing music, and I do it my way.") But Springsteen's victory was only partial. The production was not sympathetic to rock, and as a consequence Springsteen—already acquiring a reputation as a forceful showman on stage—had a record that made his rock and roll sound tentative, an aberration coming from some sort of "street poet."

Part of the problem with *Greetings from Asbury Park, New Jersey* was that it was finished in only three weeks. "Bruce had a lot of ideas," Appel later said. "But he wasn't knowledgeable about the studio. He had definite ideas, so many that he didn't know which one to pursue. He had so many ways of expressing the same song."

But it was precisely the job of the producer to help Bruce decide on what ideas to use before he entered the studio and began to spend costly studio hours on such decisions. It is a measure of Appel and Cretecos's lack of ability in this area that the album as finally released reveals that those key artistic decisions about arrangements were *still* unresolved.

Not that three weeks is an exceptionally long time in which to make a record, anyway. Had Bruce been recording in an expensive, top-flight Manhattan studio, the excuse offered might have been that time and money simply ran out. But he was working at tiny 914 Studios, in suburban Blauvelt, New York. And the only reason to record there, besides a sympathetic engineer named Louis Lahav, was to save money. (It certainly wasn't convenient, for Bruce and the band, who lived in New Jersey, or for Appel and Cretecos, who lived in Brooklyn.) CBS would advance the full $40,000, regardless of how much was actually spent making the album. By scrimping in the studio, by recording in a cheap but technically inadequate facility and cutting down on mixing and mastering time, Laurel Canyon could save some money to keep the organization going. This practice is not uncommon among undercapitalized rock organizations, but it is, of course, terribly short-sighted. The meals Appel could buy with his savings are long since forgotten, but the album is still around—in that sense, to haunt.

The album might have been completed even more quickly and cheaply, but when Appel first delivered it to CBS, the company sent them back into the studio. "There's no single here," they said. So Bruce recorded "Blinded By The Light" and "Spirit In The Night" for release as the album's potential hits. Some of the band had gone back to Virginia, so the songs were recorded with Bruce playing bass, guitar and piano, and Harold Wheeler adding the other keyboard on those tracks.

Whatever its flaws, *Greetings from Asbury Park, New Jersey* is one of the most ambitious debut albums of the Seventies. The problems are conceptual and technical; Springsteen's writing and performance are outstanding. There is no denying the compelling melodies of

"For You" and "Spirit In The Night," the passion of "Blinded By The Light" and "It's Hard To Be A Saint In The City," or the effervescent good humor of "Growin' Up" and "Does This Bus Stop At 82nd Street?"

It was the lyrics that brought Springsteen the most attention—and no wonder. The opening lines of the album—from "Blinded By The Light"—represent his tumble of images perfectly:

Madman drummer bummers and Indians in the summer with
  a teenage diplomat
In the dumps with the mumps as the adolescent pumps his
  way into his hat

The song continues that way for four verses—pure excess, and pure rock and roll. *Greetings* has ten songs, and, while none of them has the barrage of images of "Blinded By The Light," none of them is streamlined, either. On occasion, such verbose lyrics become cumbersome. "Mary Queen Of Arkansas," with its sexually ambiguous madonna, demands more focused writing than this style can give it, and "The Angel," despite the fact that Springsteen praised it at the time as his most "sophisticated" number, now seems little more than the most pretentious song ever written about an outlaw motorcyclist. More than anything, however, these songs typify the conceptual inadequacy of the singer-songwriter approach: Rather than writing about motorcyclists as observed, Springsteen wandered off into a rather unremarkable fantasy about them. On the other hand, while equally indulging in fantasy, "For You," "Growin' Up" and "It's Hard To Be A Saint In The City," are more tightly focused, minutely observed; onstage, they've become solid rockers.

There were reasons for the excess verbiage. "I let out an incredible number of things at once," Springsteen said of that group of songs. "A million things in each song. They were written in half-hour, fifteen-minute bursts. I don't know *where* they came from. A few of them I worked on for a week or so, but most of them were just jets, a real energy situation." As far as Bruce knew, this might be his only chance to make a record. It is typical of his obsessive drive that he determined to put everything he knew or could imagine on the first album.

At their best, these scattershot lyrics are remarkably effective, flinging epigrams like artillery. The final lines of "Blinded" still stand as the test of Springsteen's ambition and motivation: "Mama always told me not to look into the sights of the sun/Oh, but Mama, that's where the fun is." When such phrases strike home full force, they can freeze a moment or an attitude forever. Like Rod Stewart's "Every Picture Tells a Story," "Growin' Up" offers a marvelous capsule of that moment in adolescence when attitude and style are everything:

> I stood stone-like at midnight, suspended in my masquerade
> I combed my hair 'til it was just right
> And commanded the night brigade

As a whole, the song goes much farther than Stewart's image of hair-combing and mirror-posing, which is soon dropped for a depiction of sexual exploits. "Growin' Up" is the ideal vernacular portrait of the young rebel outsider, lost in the crowd with an improbable vision:

> Well, my feet they finally took root in the earth
> But I got me a nice little place in the stars
> And I swear I found the key to the universe
> In the engine of an old parked car

At that time Springsteen claimed that he had never read many books—Scaduto's *Bob Dylan* and Mario Puzo's *The Godfather* were among the few—but some remarkably sophisticated ideas leap from his songs. Many better educated men have sought futilely to capture the magic of the teen-age dream; Springsteen gets it all in a line. And he refuses to stop there. Most great rock writers are miniaturists, but Bruce reaches for the largest canvas of all—he wants to portray nothing less than existence itself, as seen at a certain time, from a certain perspective. In songs like "Growin' Up," he goes a long way toward achieving that goal, and in the process lends a voice to a group of people that generally goes unheard.

Springsteen's concerns, from the beginning, have been with moral, ethical and spiritual dilemmas. "For You," for instance, is about death—perhaps even suicide. (Oddly, it is also the one song on *Greetings* that heralds the style and concerns of Springsteen's later work.) It is among the best of his love songs, and, as a contemplation of death, Jimi Hendrix's "I Don't Live Today," Jackson Browne's "For a Dancer" and Paul Simon's "Mother and Child Reunion" are the only rock songs that can match it. But Browne, Simon and even Hendrix view death philosophically; Springsteen, while offering some philosophy, concentrates on the very human narrative. By any standards other than rock and roll's, "For You" might be overwrought, but the sheer emotionalism of the performance sweeps such objections aside. (Greg Kihn's later version does not come close to the sweep of Springsteen's, because his much cooler reading is more descriptive than felt.) The story is pure melodrama—the singer is in an ambulance with his girlfriend, who is fading fast—like every corny rock death number since "The Endless Sleep." As life ebbs, we come to know both characters with a startling degree of intimacy, and to grasp the dimensions of their relationship. In the end, "For You" brings those rock death song clichés to life.

As in "For You," the best of Springsteen's imagery is action and character oriented, rather than abstract. We care about the suicide victim not because she is a symbol of death—though we may come to care about the symbol too—but because the singer cares so completely about their lives together. "The point in a lot of my stuff is that they're like scenarios, they're like plays," Bruce has said. "And the power is not so much in the immediate imagery or the immediate physical picture that's presented as it is in a certain battle being waged between just whatever forces are in the songs. So generally, I write things on a bigger-than-life scale in a certain way.

"Plus, I write about moments. I don't write about the everyday . . . I write a lot about action moments, moments when people are pushed to take a certain action, to do something, to do anything to get out of their present situation or circumstances or predicament— to step out, to get out of that boring thing, to break loose. And I think there's a certain romanticism and a certain kind of everyday heroism that is inherent in this. It's something that is very real to me."

The best rock songwriting—songs by people like Chuck Berry, Bob Dylan, John Fogerty, Peter Townshend—has always been heavily populated. In the space of a few lines, subtle characters live full lives. (By this, I don't mean extravaganzas like Dylan's "Sad-Eyed Lady of the Lowlands" or Townshend's *Tommy*. Better examples are found in brief, three-stanza rockers like Berry's "Too Much Monkey Business," Townshend's "I'm a Boy" and "Substitute," and Fogerty's "Fortunate Son.") In that sense, the best rock writing is authentically cinematic, suggestive rather than elaborate. And Springsteen's songs, from the beginning, fit this pattern perfectly. By that measure his writing is a return to the roots of rock. By 1977, Dylan and Townshend, for instance, had begun to write about ideas and abstractions rather than about characters and situations. The best of the singer-songwriters did the same.

Raymond Chandler once wrote that the mystery novelist, Dashiell Hammett, had used his hard-guy realism to "give murder back to the people who commit it for reasons, not just to provide a corpse." Springsteen did something similar for rock, although *Greetings from Asbury Park, New Jersey* only hinted at it. Just as Hammett exposed the empty clichés of the drawing-room detective story, Springsteen's flood of images and characters were an assault upon the dry conventions of contemporary rock songwriting. Like Hammett, a former Pinkerton agent who used his experience among hoodlums and cops to add realism to his stories, Springsteen did not have to invent from scratch the reckless innocents of his songs. Because he lived among ordinary people—rather than in the rock star jet set—such characters were his most natural material.

When Jon Landau speaks of Bruce having "roots in a place— coastal Jersey," he is suggesting that Springsteen's fantasies arise from a natural environment. But since there is little room for physical description in rock songs, Springsteen's eye can't linger on the landscape: The Greasy Lake of "Spirits In The Night" is his equivalent of John Ford's Monument Valley, but he celebrates its inhabitants more than its natural splendor. One understands Greasy Lake as an archetype of similar places the listener has known, just as one understands the characters to be universal versions of figures in real life.

"For You," however, attacks stereotypes with a degree of deliberation. Springsteen has compared his songs to the films of Sergio Leone, the great director of Italian Westerns. That is to say, he is a genre artist, but operating from the *mise en scene* of the hotrod exploitation picture, with its fast cars, easy women and melodramatic tensions. Thus, when critics speak of Springsteen's "overreliance" on such images, they are missing the point (unless one wants to dismiss genre art *per se*—but that means discarding rock and roll, too). As Bruce himself has noted, in genre writing it isn't the situation that makes the difference—that always *seems* to be the same—but the perspective from which that scene is shown. If Springsteen's achievement counts for anything, then, it is for taking the teen milieu of cruising cars and backseat passion out of the hands of outsiders and giving it back to the people who really live it.

So it is not coincidental that "Spirit In The Night," the first complete scenario based on this teenscape, took longer to write than any other song on the first album. No matter how much it is derived from experience, the best fiction is always a work of imagination. It would denigrate Springsteen's work to suggest that it is autobiographical.

"Spirit In The Night" established the genre in which Springsteen would work. Its story, while humorous, achieves some of its emotional resonance from its connections to the teen exploitation pictures of the Fifties and Sixties. But those movies (even the best of them such as *Rebel Without a Cause*) were told from the outside, through adult eyes. Their morality and sensibility are that of filmmakers who belong to another generation; the values of the characters are presented without much sympathy or even much understanding. The point of view is precisely the opposite of rock, which has a value system of its own. (One reason that so many rock songwriters, including Bruce, were stunned by Martin Scorsese's *Mean Streets* is that it was the first film about young adult street life that was not distanced from its protagonists.)

But those early exploitation films did help to create the American rock audience's image of itself. And in the story of a one-night getaway to a lakeside fantasy paradise, Springsteen recalls the motive-less impulse of tales like *The Wild One*—only this time, the adults have been written out of the picture. "Spirit In The Night" is a moment that ought to be forever; the only authority on the scene is the bond of friendship and trust that holds these people together. Not even cops come to bother Wild Billy, Crazy Janey and Hazy Davey. (Not since Chuck Berry's heyday has a rock artist developed so many ludicrously appropriate nicknames.) Unlike Bob Dylan's weirdly named denizens of the night, these kids are close to the sort of people any listener might know—they're dream, not nightmare, creatures. Their achievements are also exaggerated versions of our own. Like Berry, Springsteen creates characters with lives longer than one song. Under various guises, they have followed Springsteen through each of his albums.

The spirit of the night is the spirit of escape—that goes almost without saying. But it is also the spirit of unity, whether sexual or otherwise. When Springsteen sings "Spirit In The Night" in concert, he sings the final verse amidst the crowd. The drunkenness and lovemaking are thus not debauched, as they would be in an exploi-tation story (which flaunts conventional morality to conceal its own cynicism); they are a form of ritual that suggests the richest mo-ments in lives that are otherwise banal. Anyone who has grown up in a small town knows that the goal is to get out, have some fun, seek the Promised Land—just as everyone knows how improbable it is that real fun, genuine escape, true promise, can be found. Of-ten, what seems from a distance to be improvement is, close up, much worse—even a trap. At Greasy Lake, Crazy Janey and her pals gain no permanent freedom; in the end, they must drive off to return to their drudgery. But what matters is the magic unity of this moment: The key word in the final chorus ("Together we moved like spirits in the night") is "together."

"Spirit In The Night" is the heart of *Greetings from Asbury Park, New Jersey,* because it is the album's most fully realized song. But the album is framed by two numbers, "Blinded By The Light" and "It's Hard To Be A Saint In The City," which together create a heroic individual and begin to track his progress from the humdrum existence of the characters in "Spirit" toward a permanent escape.

Although the arrangements work against them, "Blinded" and

"Saint" are both pure products of rock and roll. Their drive is relentless, the action nonstop. But where "Blinded" shows the hero as romantic innocent, "Saint" portrays that man full grown, facing a world that tempts him to abandon his singleminded pursuit of spiritual freedom. Like the protagonist of the Crystals' "Uptown," the hero of "It's Hard To Be A Saint In The City" is nothing except when he's on his own turf:

> I was the king of the alley, mama
> I could talk some trash
> I was the prince of the paupers
> Crowned downtown at the beggars' bash
> I was the pimp's main prophet
> I kept everything cool
> Just a backstreet gambler with the luck to lose

This is pure brag, in the grand tradition of Bo Diddley—simply strutting one's stuff, in the confidence that though the world outside rock and roll can interfere, it can never win. And with this burst of self-assertion, *Greetings from Asbury Park, New Jersey* was delivered into the machinery of the record business.

5 THE SAINT IN THE CITY

From the beginning, rock stood outside the entertainment establishment, not entirely as a matter of choice. When Sam Phillips and Elvis Presley were in Memphis inventing the grandest music of the Fifties, they certainly did not view themselves as outlaws. But to the entertainment establishment—the world of big-dollar television, motion pictures and nightclubs—rock was nothing more than a particularly belligerent and queerly persistent fad.

There was a variety of reasons for the showbiz attitude toward rock, but possibly the two most important were the youth and the working-class background of most of the early rock and roll performers. Rock stars were resented first because they had not traveled through the normal channels. They lacked the grooming of the movie studio and nightclub circuit stars, and they were not only inclined to say and do outrageous things, but often didn't bother to cover them up. Jerry Lee Lewis was banned, remember, not so much for marrying his thirteen-year-old second cousin but for flaunting it. Had he lived, Buddy Holly might have faced similar problems with his marriage to a Latin-American woman.

The early rock stars also came from far less genteel circumstances than most movie or pop music stars of the day would admit to. Elvis Presley was born in a one-room house, and almost until he began recording his family lived on welfare. This was a surmountable problem, but here the lack of grooming (one might almost say, breeding) came into play again: Far from denying his working-class background, the rock star exploited it. Until the end of his life, Elvis remained in some ways a country boy and proud of that, if nothing else. As unruly, unwashed representatives of the class that had traditionally been the audience, not the source, of American popular culture, rock stars were, from the start, entertainment establishment outlaws.

As a result, the major record companies (including RCA, despite its acquisition of Elvis Presley in 1956) virtually ignored early rock. This was a mistake of major proportions, because it gave an edge to smaller, independently distributed record companies like Atlantic in New York, Chess in Chicago, Ace of Jackson, Mississippi, and Specialty of Los Angeles. These companies prospered not by attempting to tailor the images of their performers, but by concentrating on developing distinctive musical styles.

But because the record companies for which they recorded—and often as not the management personnel that handled the performers—were undercapitalized, the success of the early rock stars was often fleeting. Elvis was the great exception, but even when he first played Las Vegas in 1956, he was a bust, not able to make it on supper club terms. He ended up second on the bill to comic Shecky Greene.

When it did decide that rock was something with potential for exploitation, the showbiz establishment had no idea how to sustain such careers. Often, dressing the rock star in a tuxedo and sending him to the nightclubs divorced him from his natural audience—and the white adults there still found rock music too threatening for their own entertainment. The record companies developed a series of teen idols who made exploitation records, crafted with great cynicism to appeal to the teen market, but the careers of Fabian, Frankie Avalon and the rest were even more short-lived.

Part of the problem was a lack of vision among promoters. The powerful booking agents and managers who controlled the talent policies of nightclubs, casinos and resorts—where the big bucks were—had no use for the noise, and it hardly seemed likely that hip-slung jeans and duck-tail haircuts were going to go over big in the Catskills or Vegas, anyway. Most of the rare entrepreneurs with sufficient expertise—Alan Freed, for instance—were ruined in the 1960 payola witch-hunt. With the rise of manufactured rock performers like Fabian and Avalon, the teen market once more became a stepping-stone at the edge of a cliff, as it had almost been for Frank Sinatra. No one entertained the thought that a full-fledged, long-lived career could be built around rock or rhythm and blues.

Meanwhile, however, people were growing up with rock and roll, and not only took its values for granted but regarded the freedom and sense of exhilaration they found in the music as a kind of ideal. It's important that the rebellion of Elvis Presley and his peers (at least as far as conventional entertainment values were concerned) was instinctive, while the outlaw posture of all later rock and roll performers was self-conscious and very deliberate. Much the same can be said of the rock audience. A teen-ager hearing Little Richard's "Tutti Frutti" in 1955 could respond simply to the power of the rhythm. But by the time the Beatles arrived in 1963, it had been drilled into every kid's mind that this was outlaw culture. Mature people—even "mature" teens—frowned upon it.

Having missed Elvis, the major record companies were at least somewhat prepared to cope with the advent of the Beatles, Rolling Stones and the other bands that formed the first wave of the British Invasion of 1963-65. Consequently, the ripples these bands created quadrupled the annual dollar volume of the music industry. Still, the old-line talent packagers were reluctant to become involved with rock. Since, this time, rock didn't go away for even a moment, other talent development mechanisms were created to fill the gap.

Managers were developed from a pool of cronies—the legendary "fifth kid on the block"—Dutch uncles and ex-musicians. A former William Morris mailroom boy, David Geffen, became an agent, left the company with one artist, Laura Nyro, and parlayed her into a combine that eventually included Crosby, Stills, Nash and Young; the founding members of the Eagles; Jackson Browne and Joni Mitchell. In Macon, Georgia, R & B king Otis Redding's manager, Phil Walden, cast about locally for new talent after his star's tragic death in a 1968 plane crash—and found the Allman Brothers Band, Wet Willie, the Marshall Tucker Band and a half-dozen other southern rock groups. They made him a millionaire well before he was thirty and eventually helped elect another Georgian, Jimmy Carter, President of the United States. In New York, Dee Anthony, ex-manager of Tony Bennett, Jerry Vale and Buddy Greco, foresaw the long-term success of British rock and signed up Humble Pie, Emerson Lake and Palmer, Joe Cocker and Ten Years After for American representation. Humble Pie spun off Peter Frampton, who sold ten million albums. In England, Robert Stigwood, an Australian, joined together with Beatles manager Brian Epstein and created a hit act in the Bee Gees, a pop-oriented vocal trio, then cashed in on rock with the first power-trio, Cream. Chas Chandler, the bassist of the Animals, quit playing in order to promote the career of Jimi Hendrix. Epstein's American attorney, Nat Weiss, served as lawyer-manager for James Taylor and Bonnie Raitt. Chris Blackwell, son of a Jamaican planter, began to import reggae, the Caribbean variant of soul music, back to England, then acquired management of Steve Winwood and Traffic. Many of these men also wound up with their own record companies: Geffen with Asylum, Walden's Capricorn, Blackwell's Island and Stigwood's RSO were to become among the most important—and richest—record labels of the next decade.

Concert promotion underwent drastic changes. Before the Beatles, the biggest shows of the year were package tours put together by Dick Clark, in which a dozen acts appeared; even the headliner was fortunate if he had a half-hour onstage. And the places that the Clark Caravans and other, similar tours played were no great improvement over the high school gyms that featured groups like the Castiles—an endless round of roller rinks, decrepit teen clubs and dilapidated auditoriums. The object wasn't a "concert," but a spectacle, a chance to see the hits recreated live.

But led by the imperious Bill Graham, with his Fillmores East and West, a new breed of rock promoter and presentation sprang up: the ballroom circuit with stops in Detroit (the Grande Ballroom), Chicago (the Kinetic Playground), Philadelphia (the Electric Factory) and Boston (the Tea Party) as well as New York (Fillmore East), San Francisco (Fillmore West) and Los Angeles (the one major city without a long-running ballroom). Coupled with a few college gigs to fill in the gaps, a rock circuit developed that was not unlike the storied days of vaudeville—often, the converted theaters where rock groups played *were* old vaudeville stops.

But the most significant entrepreneur of Sixties rock was not a record company president like Atlantic's Ahmet Ertegun or CBS's Clive Davis, or even a sharp promoter like Graham. That title belongs to a balding, rotund booking agent named Frank Barsalona. Barsalona was originally an agent at GAC which was rivaled only by William Morris among the establishment booking agencies. He was one of the few younger agents in the company, and the only one who saw much potential in rock. Barsalona helped Sid Bernstein put together the Beatles tours, including their record-setting engagement at Shea Stadium, but he was unable to convince anyone else that rock was here to stay. "The way the agency treated rock performers was a crime," Barsalona has said. "If you were young and had a hit record, to them you had no talent, you were just lucky and manufactured and they would treat you like that . . . Rock was really the asshole, it really was." Frustrated, Barsalona decided to form his own agency, Premier Talent, and as rock performers and entrepreneurs (particularly British ones) came to understand that he was a man who understood their potential, Premier became the most influential booking agency in the business. Because he is by nature shy, Barsalona himself became a figure of almost mythic proportions. Before him, no one dared to let an act tour the country without a hit—to Barsalona, touring was the essence of hit-making. This, and his instinct for marketing rock at its hardest, were what made him so exceptional.

In the Sixties, Premier was virtually the only rock-based agency in the country. The Who, Joe Cocker and Jimi Hendrix were among the beneficiaries of its expertise; all three made as much or more mileage from live performances as they did from recordings. Premier quickly devised a simple but effective formula for large-scale rock success. It involved frequent national tours, records released at well-spaced intervals (nine months to one year between LPs—anything shorter risked oversaturating the market, anything longer risked being forgotten), and a high degree of coordination between the act's management, record company and the various promoters. It was a familiar process. As Barsalona told Anthony when the latter was considering switching over to rock management, "Dee, it's the same thing you used to do with Bennett, Vale and Greco, but with a different cast of characters."

That should have been all the difference in the world. But theory broke down. The second generation of rock musicians did enter show business as self-conscious rebels. And at first, this attitude armored those stars against selling out. But, when it became clear that enormous sums of money were involved, the rebel attitude became an empty shell that insulated many stars from the realities of their own compromises. By 1973, the political dreams of the Sixties were finished, and whatever allegiance was paid to rock's outlaw spirit was mostly lip service. If the freedom implicit in rock was only personal—not collective—then everyone owed it to himself to make as much money as possible before the bubble burst. So the performers were generally willing, and even eager, to accept the formula rules for success.

The first step in entering what Joni Mitchell has called the "star-making machinery" was obtaining the interest of an individual— usually a record company talent scout (A & R man) or a manager— with access to the apparatus. With recording and booking agency contracts secured, the stipulations for success were simple.

Musically, this didn't seem to involve much compromise. The focus was now on LPs, and many rock acts became successful in those years through albums alone. But the surest way to sell albums was still through radio airplay on a hit single. And radio stations that played "hits"—as opposed to the "freeform" FM stations, which by the early Seventies were on their last legs—required certain kinds of music. Anything too raucous or abrasive, any song with "questionable" lyrics, any performer who dared to flaunt an outlandish lifestyle (and act as though he believed in it) was subject to banishment from the most important radio stations. The pressure to come up with a hit was intense; rhetoric about art was left behind, along with the political jargon.

Without an early hit, there was a natural progression in record sales. The act usually had two or three chances, sometimes a couple more, to make it to the coveted gold-record plateau (five hundred thousand copies sold). If, by the time of the third album, the act had not achieved sales close to that mark, it was in grave danger of being released from its contract. If the act made that goal, then the push to platinum (one million unit sales) began. No one expected to reach that level very often.

There was a similar hierarchy of performances. Young acts began by playing clubs, for little or no money, or—with luck—opening for mid-level stars at the concert halls of the three-thousand to five-thousand-seat variety that had replaced the ballrooms. Middle-level acts starred in such venues, or opened for top-line attractions in sports arenas and outdoor festivals with crowds of ten thousand or more. (On the way back down the ladder, some star acts found themselves opening for people who had begun by opening for them.) The idea was to get exposure, build word-of-mouth and generate sufficient initial sales to encourage radio airplay. As with records, frequency was important. Playing the same town too often risked diminishing returns. Similarly, a brief, well-paced set was in order—forty-five minutes plus an encore was the order of the day. Two-and three-hour marathon performances only risked overtime charges, damaging the profit potential.

Few acts tried to buck the formula. Bands with the communitarian ideals of the Sixties (the Grateful Dead) or strong regional bases (New York Dolls, MC5) found that without well-connected managers or agents, even miles of press clippings and strong record company support were insufficient. Of course, bands like the Dolls and MC5 played harder than most radio programmers preferred, and their behavior and politics were deliberately outrageous. But most groups, especially the big-name British ones, settled easily into the formula. There was no conscious design to destroy rock's early energy and idealism; that wasn't necessary. The net effect of the star-making process was to tame the music, as well as the musicians.

As a result, within the record business, the musician became not much more than an extremely well-paid laborer; having lost whatever pretensions he may have possessed as an artist, he was not quite a businessman since others were calling those shots. And the sounds became as conventional as the promotional mechanics—which from the star-making machine's perspective was ideal, since the closer the sound to some abstract standard, the easier to formalize promotional structures.

Rock stars also suffered a degree of estrangement from their original sources of inspiration, due to over-protectiveness and wealth. This was felt most severely by the Beatles era stars, who for a while literally could not walk down the street without being mobbed. By the time the hysteria quieted, such performers were permanently out of step with their audiences, in ways that had less to do with drug-taking and "hipness" than the natural tendency of all star-making processes to create an aristocracy. (Not to its credit, a good deal of the rock audience played along with this, settling for vicarious experience.)

Rock entrepreneurs had specific tastes. Groups that mumbled about revolution shouldn't speak up. Performers who toyed with ambiguous sexuality or openly used drugs didn't fit into the scheme—although performers who did any of these things at a certain level were admired. Thus, the commentary on decadence represented by Iggy and the Stooges was bastardized into the purely harmless entertainment of Alice Cooper, and the flashy street charisma of the Dolls was repackaged into the costumed theatrics of Aerosmith and Kiss. The development process established by promoters who were, by business standards, visionaries—whether Presley's manager, Colonel Tom Parker, agent Frank Barsalona or promoter Bill Graham—had ossified into a new kind of straitjacket, just as limiting as the system it had replaced.

By 1973, it looked unlikely that anyone could afford even to attempt to break the hegemony of this new rock establishment. Rock had lost its idealism, and even the standard-bearers of the past—the Who and the Rolling Stones, the individual Beatles, Bob Dylan—were sounding tired to a great many ears.

All of this is essential to understanding what happened in January 1973, when *Greetings from Asbury Park, New Jersey* was released by Columbia Records. Without it, Springsteen's task and his impact might have been vastly different.

The label's autocratic president, Clive Davis, made it clear that Springsteen was Columbia's highest priority among new artists. This was a substantial commitment, for CBS was the largest American record company, accounting for nearly one-quarter of the nation's record sales each year. Davis ran a one-man show to a great extent, delegating authority primarily to those who could be trusted to carry out his policies to the letter. If he said that Bruce Springsteen was

Columbia's best shot at a new superstar for '73, no one was about to question it. At least, not within CBS.

Normally, an artist would have been ecstatic about such strong support. But the promotional tactics that Columbia used were a mixed blessing: They offered Springsteen an identity, but not a realistic one. In a way, Columbia's initial approach to Bruce and his music was the single most damaging event of his career; it was an obstacle he fought for years to overcome.

The dominant sound of the year was "soft rock," which was not really rock at all. It was the year of the singer-songwriter. Rock critics had identified the genre, and *Time* and *Newsweek* had certified its importance; the newsweeklies liked soft rock, feeling more comfortable with it than with the belligerent forms of other years. It was an institutional attitude shared by the record business.

Stylistically, the singer-songwriter was never adequately defined. Superficially, it meant any performer who both wrote and performed. But it certainly did not include John Lennon, or even John Fogerty, or a black man such as Sly Stone. In fact, the singer-songwriter archetype was Bob Dylan, but Dylan was such a chameleon that the reference was confusing. The idea seemed to be that there was a group of writer-performers who had emerged in Dylan's wake, with deeply emotional, often confessional lyrics and a light, rock-influenced (but never hard-rocking) sound. Such writers performed their own songs almost exclusively, generally in a style that owed as much to folk music and show tunes as to anything Elvis Presley or James Brown ever sang. The accompaniment was minimal—bass, drums and either guitar or piano. The mood was quiet, tasteful, almost elegant, somewhat in the spirit of Tin Pan Alley show tune composers like Hoagy Carmichael and Cole Porter. What this had to do with any kind of rock is pure guesswork.

But as a pigeonhole, the singer-songwriter tag was a masterstroke. It excused simultaneously writers who could not sing (Kris Kristofferson) and singers who could not write (Carly Simon). But in plain point of fact, the singer-songwriter was antirock—it offered snobs a comfortable place within rock music, and alienated a great many of the most committed listeners. It was yet another attempt to submerge rock within pop music, rather than to distinguish rock as an important pop subgenre in its own right. The success of the singer-songwriter helped diminish the importance of rock and roll, even when the singer-songwriters were as skillful as Randy Newman or John Prine.

The most curious aspect of the singer-songwriter boom was in fact much older: The New Dylan Syndrome. There had been one— or more—of these per year since Eric Andersen was signed by Vanguard in 1964. Phil Ochs, David Blue, Janis Ian, P. F. Sloan, John Prine and a dozen others had been saddled with the designation. In record circles it had come to be regarded as a kiss of death, since none of those performers sold many records while suffering under it. Dylan's achievements were so broad and his stature so great that no one could hope to equal him on his own terms. And it was both arrogant and idiotic for any record company to expect an unknown to do so. But the companies needed some handle with which to distinguish one new act from another.

Both musically and historically, it was incorrect to apply either the "singer-songwriter" or the "New Dylan" labels to Bruce Springsteen. His lyrics were sufficiently intense and personal to work as singer-songwriter material, but they were clearly rooted in the rock tradition, not in the confessional, self-pitying vein of the other genre. Springsteen's music was never sedate and well mannered in the singer-songwriter fashion; none of the performers named above could have written "Blinded By The Light." None of them could have imagined "It's Hard To Be A Saint In The City." Singer-songwriters did not boast; they complained, analyzed and philosophized. Bravado was beneath them—but it was the core of Springsteen's approach. To lump him together with them was as unwieldy as trying to make the singer-songwriters themselves fit the tradition founded by Little Richard, Chuck Berry and Elvis Presley.

The comparisons with Bob Dylan at least had more natural origins. The most obvious and superficial connection, of course, was John Hammond, who had discovered both of them. But there was also a surprising physical resemblance, enhanced by the fact that many thought Springsteen must be a Jewish name. Although Bruce is a bit taller, at five feet nine inches, his piercing eyes, compact, powerful, but slender body and scraggly beard seemed virtually identical to Dylan's. Both men have a mass of curly hair, which under a spotlight acquires the aspect of a halo. On the back cover of *Greet-*

ings, Springsteen looked like Dylan's tough, urban cousin. His blue work shirt might have come from the same Army-Navy store as the one Dylan wears on the cover of his *The Times They Are A-Changin'* LP. So the Columbia ads for *Greetings* featured a quote from Crawdaddy's Peter Knobler equating "Blinded By The Light" with Dylan's "Like a Rolling Stone." It was anything but apt, but it sure was an eye-catcher.

Inevitably, all great rock writing is matched against Dylan's, because Dylan's early work smashed so many boundaries and conventions, in terms of both structure and theme. As Springsteen has acknowledged, it was Bob Dylan "who made it possible for [me] to do the things [I] wanted to do." But Springsteen's similarities to Dylan weren't studied, as were those of many of the solo, acoustic guitar-playing writer-performers on the Greenwich Village scene. In fact, although Dylan's impact on him was immediate and undeniable, Bruce's knowledge of him was centered on Dylan's 1965-66 string of hit singles, not the albums that had influenced most of the singer-songwriters. Arguably, such songs as "I Want You," "Positively 4th Street," "Like a Rolling Stone," "Mr. Tambourine Man" and "It Ain't Me, Babe" are the man's greatest music anyway. All of those—the first three as performed by Dylan himself, "Mr. Tambourine Man" in the Byrds' version and "It Ain't Me, Babe" as performed by the Turtles—had a sound Bruce loved, but not one that he pursued to the exclusion of all else. "Listening to one of his records was always a high point," Bruce said back in 1973—but not *the* high point. As a performer on the radio, Dylan was the equal of, not king amongst, the Stones, Manfred Mann, Mitch Ryder or The Who. None of this diminishes Dylan, but seeing his work out of context can become confusing.

In any event, Columbia's promotion (or hype)of *Greetings* put so much emphasis on the Dylan analogy that it unavoidably alienated consumers, radio people and critics. "The Dylan hype from Columbia was a turn-off," Dave Herman of WNEW-FM in New York has admitted. "I didn't even bother to listen to the album. I didn't want Columbia to think they got me." Similarly, Lester Bangs's *Rolling Stone* review of *Greetings* was so preoccupied with the New Dylan push that it missed much of Bruce's rock appeal.

Greetings almost immediately showed the symptoms of commercial failure—its initial sales could not have been much more than twenty-five thousand copies, a bust by any standard. The Dylan hype wasn't the key factor—the amateurish production and wrong-headed arrangements were the truly insurmountable difficulties—but the hype was the longest-lasting problem that the album created.

Soon after Springsteen was signed to Columbia, Appel also arranged a deal with the William Morris Agency for live bookings. Springsteen was already a seasoned onstage craftsman from his experience working Jersey joints, and agents Sam McKeith and Peter Golden, who made the deal, recognized him as a potential star of major proportions. It would be difficult to book him without a record, but the agency did the best it could.

When the record was released, Springsteen was sent on a comprehensive club tour: The Main Point near Philadelphia, which would become his home turf in years to come; Paul's Mall in Massachusetts; The Quiet Knight and Max's Kansas City in Chicago and New York. There weren't many other clubs to play. A few college bookings, a couple of dates on the West Coast, and, since the album wasn't exactly a smash, that was about it. Only in Boston and Philadelphia was there much success; the strongest place for Springsteen bookings continued to be the bar scene at the Shore.

One person who caught onto Springsteen's appeal immediately was Barry Bell, a secretary at the William Morris Agency (although he was soon to become an agent himself). Springsteen's combination of original songs, tall tales (which might make up as much as half the show) and eccentric musicality—he threw in oldies, he performed with a tuba, a violin, an accordion, you name it—was obviously unique. Slowly, a following did start to build up. Remembers Bell, "You were like the guy who went to a club before it happened. You were there and you knew it was coming." For Bell and certain others—McKeith, Columbia publicity chief Ron Oberman, *Crawdaddy* editor Peter Knobler, free-lance critics Paul Nelson and Karen Berg—Springsteen was already a major star on the horizon.

To spread the word, Columbia arranged for Bruce to appear as the opening act on a tour by the jazz-rock group Chicago. It was a brief tour—only eight or ten dates. But it was a heavy token of support, for Chicago was Columbia's biggest-selling act—each of its nine albums had sold more than a million copies, and several had sold *two* million, which was then unheard of. The concert dates, including one at Madison Square Garden in New York, were certain sellouts.

But the tour was pure disaster for Bruce. It was symptomatic of Columbia's misunderstanding of the nature of Springsteen's talent and ambition. Chicago is a purely commercial proposition; its exploitation of banal rock and jazz riffs in a pop setting qualifies as a kind of cynicism. If nothing else, Chicago is bland, and its appeal is not to people who share Bruce's intense commitment to rock and roll. This slick, adult, middle-class show was the antithesis of Bruce's performance. Naturally, the audiences did not take to this hoody tough, who only delayed the appearance of what they'd paid to see and hear. (Bruce, however, remembers that the members of Chicago were unfailingly courteous, at a time when "most big bands were *not* that nice to opening acts. We got sound checks most nights. I had a lotta fun with those guys.")

In some places, Springsteen remembers, the group had things thrown at them. In Philadelphia, already a good town for Bruce, he was booed. "It was get introduced, walk on stage, blink and that's it. It's hard to show an audience what a band's about in that little time," Bruce said. "I couldn't stand it—everybody was so far away and the band couldn't hear. Maybe if they had come to see me, it would have been different. But I doubt it."

"It left a terrible taste in Bruce's mouth as far as big buildings, as far as opening to anybody. I mean, he got booed in *Philadelphia*," Bell says, with a tone of disbelief. "The Chicago tour was a waste, and it was just sad, almost, after seeing him in the clubs, doing two hours of energy and stories and charisma. Now here he was, just another opening act on stage."

But the worst effect of the Chicago tour was the damage the New York performance at Madison Square Garden did to Springsteen's credibility with the CBS executives who saw it. Without so much as a sound check to help deal with the Garden's voluminous recesses, the group performed horribly. Even the company's biggest Springsteen fans, like Oberman, were shaken. Frustrated, Springsteen vowed he would never find himself treated as just another *anything* ever again.

For Bruce, the music always had a certain existential purity. To play less well, or not to give as much of himself to it as he was capable of doing, was a violation of principle. After the Chicago experience, he decided that the rules of the game would change. He would never again play halls of sports arena size. No more was he to be booked as opening act to anyone, unless he could do his full, two-hour show. He must have his own sound system. Above all, he must be able to perform without any time restrictions.

"That was the most important thing, I think, in Bruce's thinking," Bell says. "You can't take his show out of context. To take a part of it is to ruin it. So from then on, after the Chicago tour, it was An Evening with Bruce Springsteen. He would do the whole show, or there was a nominal opening act, like Jae Mason, the guy who later became the bouncer at the Bottom Line."

But this attitude only increased the disgruntlement at CBS and William Morris. It made both jobs incredibly difficult. "Because you could only book him in places where he could sell tickets—which at that time, was my house and a couple other places in the North-east," said Bell. "So he stayed out of the Midwest for a long, long time." On stops in Phoenix, Houston and eventually Los Angeles, he won sufficient fans to make returning profitable—if enough surrounding dates could be found. As Bell points out, "You can't take a date in St. Louis, even if there's an offer, go all the way out there for $500, if there's no dates around it to support it.

"Some of the other people at the agency were saying, 'He's crazy. He should get on as an opening act, go across the country.' But those are the same people who just don't understand Bruce. There's a lotta things that Bruce does that make people wonder."

Among those wondering was the staff at Columbia Records. And Mike Appel wasn't doing much to cheer people up. When an artist is obstinate the manager takes the blame, and there is no question that Mike Appel was willing to do so for Bruce. But there was more than enough blame to go around, because of Appel's bizarre and abusive style of presenting Springsteen's decisions. John Hammond has said that Appel is "about as offensive as any man I've ever met." Many CBS employees felt even more strongly about him, and this colored their reaction to Springsteen, which was already antagonistic because he had been unable to live up to the initial hype.

It wasn't that Appel was making particularly outrageous demands. Indeed, a good deal of the record company support he was seeking was probably just what any good manager would have requested. But Appel is a former Marine, and when he's in doubt his policy is to attack. He lacks any sense of diplomacy. Given a choice between treating someone rudely and making a conciliatory gesture, Appel never loses a chance to bully and intimidate with the language and demeanor of a drill sergeant. The result, at both Columbia and William Morris, was a good deal of animosity, a fair share of hatred and a general reluctance to cooperate or go out of the way for either Appel or his client. Only those who believed most completely in Bruce—McKeith, Oberman and a few others—continued to work hard on his career.

Appel was also extremely naive. Before the first album was released, he placed a call to the NBC producer in charge of the NFL Super Bowl festivities, suggesting that instead of opening the game with "The Star Spangled Banner," NBC should use Bruce Springsteen singing an original, antiwar song, "Balboa Vs. The Beast Slayer." That anyone who lives in the United States could suggest such a thing is astonishing enough. But when he was immediately and understandably turned down, Appel reportedly became enraged. "Someday I'm gonna give you a call and remind you of this," he told the stunned producer. "Then I'm gonna make another call and you'll be out of a job." (So the story goes. Appel admits making the call and the suggestion but denies the threat: "All I said was, instead of doing something creative, he was gonna do the same old hack thing.")

"Remember," Appel told a new CBS employee, "Bruce Springsteen isn't a rock act. He's a religion." This attitude no one denies. Even Hammond, who clearly finds the man despicable, acknowledged at the time, "Mike is utterly selfless in his devotion to Bruce." Appel has taken the statement about religion further. "I always thought of myself as John the Baptist, heralding Bruce's coming to the world," he says. Since he was operating with little capital and a family to support—he would eventually mortgage his home to keep the organization going—there seems little doubt that such comments were made partly to sustain Appel's own conviction. As Bell says, "I don't think Mike Appel did anything without checking it with Bruce first. I think that was how, to some extent, Mike got into trouble with Bruce. They started having different opinions on things—a lotta things, like where Bruce should go, what he should get paid and all the rest." Left to himself, Appel would never have made the decision to buck the system. But there is no denying that he could have—should have—conducted himself more discreetly and less emotionally.

All of these problems were exacerbated in May 1973, when Clive Davis was mysteriously fired (actually, it seems, in a corporate *putsch*). With the dismal sales record and a poor performance at the CBS Records Convention in San Francisco in July, Springsteen was in big trouble with CBS. And although the live show was coming along, it, too, had problems, mostly stemming from the erratic rhythm section.

The convention appearance was especially damaging to whatever credibility Bruce had left within Columbia Records. "Bruce came on with a chip on his shoulder," Hammond says, "and played way too long. People came to me and said, 'He really can't be that bad, can he, John?' " Many at the record label were prepared to write him off as a particularly embarrassing mistake.

But Bruce remembers differently. "I followed Edgar Winter with his smoke bombs, and the salesmen loved that. You can't compete with that. So Danny and I did 'Sandy,' which I had just written, just accordion and acoustic guitar. Then the band came out to play 'Saint In The City,' 'Thundercrack' and maybe another one. All these ladies in gowns in the front rows had their fingers in their ears, but I thought we played good, and so did [promo man] Mike Pillote, Ron Oberman and [concert producer] Chip Monck. At least, that's what they told me. What can I say?"

As for the rest of the world, it seemed to have forgotten more than it ever wanted to know about Bruce. Disc jockey Dave Herman summarized the attitude: "He was just another media hype that failed. He was already a dead artist who bombed on his first album."

Undaunted, the young corpse prepared to record his second LP.

6 WILD AND INNOCENT

*T*he Wild, The Innocent & The E Street Shuffle was recorded in the summer and fall of 1973 and released that November. At Columbia Records, it was a less-than-ideal moment to be considered a Clive Davis protege, especially if your first album hadn't sold enough copies to justify a heavy promotional budget. *E Street* was released with the absolute minimum of fanfare. The CBS field people who had pushed hard for sales and airplay on *Greetings* now had several projects of much higher priority—not an uncommon circumstance for an artist whose first album has been a widely publicized flop, although it was perhaps taken to extreme lengths by the CBS national promotion man who encouraged a Houston station to cease playing Bruce's record and begin programming Boz Scaggs and Billy Joel instead.

Springsteen did have one small, but vocal, part of the rock establishment on his side: the critics. CBS publicity director Ron Oberman made *The Wild, The Innocent & The E Street Shuffle* his highest personal priority. Oberman was a believer who had attended enough shows to know what Bruce could do onstage. In fact, Oberman was one of very few CBS executives who had seen Springsteen frequently enough to know that the Chicago tour and the convention show were just flukes. In addition, he recognized Springsteen's appeal among the press: Bruce's instinct about what made a great record was completely in line with most rock critics' thinking.

In terms of influence, rock critics have never been as significant in their field as reviewers of drama, film or "serious" music, partly because the audience for rock is often barely literate. Poor reviews will close a Broadway play; good ones in the right places will sometimes make a novel a best seller. But even the top rock critics have exerted little public influence—though their impact on the music industry itself has not always been inconsequential. Oberman didn't need to manipulate the press in this instance—he was too canny to try. Besides, he understood that, from the point of view of critical taste, Bruce's music didn't require hype. Now that the "New Dylan" bullshit had settled down, *The Wild, The Innocent & The E Street Shuffle* was certain to be widely praised. Oberman's publicity job consisted of assuring critics who hadn't seen Bruce that he was everything the others were beginning to say, and encouraging those who had been converted to listen, and to write.

There had been some enthusiasm among critics even for the first album, and the early shows had earned astonishingly good reviews. "Our enthusiasm was sustained because of the press," says Bell. "All you had to do was read the newspaper and you would think that *Greetings* was the Number One album, instead of number one thousand. Every time we booked him anywhere, we got nothing but rave reviews."

This enthusiasm was beginning to trickle down to the promoters, as well. "I *never* have had a phone call when somebody said, 'Boy, Bruce stunk!' or 'What's this guy about?' " Bell said in early 1979. "Which always happens at least once or twice with everybody— including the Rolling Stones. Somebody will call up and say they didn't play good this night. But people were saying, '*This* guy's got potential.' There was always something good coming back."

If Springsteen were still only last year's failed hype to the disc jockeys and the record stores, he was, in the eyes of many writers, a young artist with potential for greatness. Most critics have an his-torical perspective, and one of the startling things about even

Springsteen's early shows was their dramatic sweep of rock history, the way they incorporated songs, styles and fragments from every era. Besides, Springsteen wrote with incisive intelligence of the street life that so many critics idolized (though very few of them had lived any part of the tough-guy image). And his reference points were similar to the kind of half-forgotten, away-from-the-trend nuances critics cherished: early Elvis, Dylan's great Sixties rock, the soul of Motown and Stax (as transmitted through Van Morrison, or so it seemed) and the pop production extravaganzas of Phil Spector and Roy Orbison.

It wasn't surprising, then, that Ken Emerson, writing in *Rolling Stone*, called *E Street* one of the year's best albums, or that Ed Ward, in *Creem*, dubbed it "great." Ward added that he hadn't been "so mystified and entertained by an album since *Astral Weeks*," Van Morrison's most spellbinding record.

For Bruce himself, *The Wild, The Innocent & The E Street Shuffle* was a breakthrough. "On the second album, I started slowly to find out who I am," he said, "and where I wanted to be. It was like coming out of the shadow of various influences and trying to be yourself."

What he found was a sensibility totally shaped by rock and pop culture Americana. The result was not quite pastiche, for Springsteen took the best bits and shaped them into a distinct vision; like many another genre artist, he saw the stock situations from such a personal perspective that they seemed unique. In some senses, *The Wild, The Innocent & The E Street Shuffle* might have been made by a different person than the one who did *Greetings from Asbury Park, New Jersey*. Although the key stylistic elements remained the same, and they were allowed free play, there was no talk about "folk music," this time. The result is a record that is more confident, mature and disciplined—and when the discipline fades, as it sometimes does, one is still left with more than simple sloppiness.

"The new album was a little more what I wanted to do," Springsteen continues. "There was more of the band in there and the songs were written more in the way I wanted to write." And it was at this time that the advantages of New Jersey's isolation from the rock mainstream began to show up. Because Bruce had not been pressured into joining a scene or following a trend, he had never confused the idealism inherent in early rock and roll—the notion that it could set you free—with the mass-marketed bohemianism of the Sixties. So he understood from the start that it was important to retain control of as many aspects of his career as possible. Elvis Presley was the root of his inspiration—Elvis the King, the man who had it all and threw it all away. Springsteen's ambition was just as limitless.

At times, "all" seems the most important word in Bruce's vocabulary. It is the explanation for the sweat-drenched three-hour shows, for the painstaking way he records and for the distance he keeps from rock's cocaine-and-limousine set. Springsteen wants to be the Complete Rock Star: great singer, greater writer, great producer, great arranger, great guitarist, great live performer. Surround himself with the best band, best stage crew, best lighting. To do it *all*, his own way.

Perhaps it is naive, but Bruce's faith in rock and roll and what it can do—not just for him, but for anybody—is complete. Rock and roll is the great spiritual alternative of the age; Bruce understands this as well as anyone, and he articulates it better than any spokesman rock has had since Peter Townshend's heyday.

"Sometimes people ask, who are your favorites?" Bruce told *Creem*'s Robert Duncan in 1978. "My favorites change. Sometimes it's Elvis, sometimes it's Buddy Holly. Different personalities. For me, the *idea* of rock and roll is sort of my favorite. The feeling. Rock and roll came to my house where there seemed to be no way out. It just seemed like a dead-end street, nothing I liked to do, nothing I wanted to do, except roll over and go to sleep or something. And it came into my house—snuck in, ya know, and opened up a whole world of possibilities. Rock and roll. The Beatles opened doors. Ideally, if any stuff I do could ever do that for somebody, that's the best. Can't do anything better than that. Rock and roll motivates. It's the big, gigantic motivator, at least it was for me. There's a whole lot of things involved, but that's what I think you gotta remain true to. That idea, that *feeling*. That's the real spirit of the music."

But at the end of 1973, in pursuit of fame and fortune, the rock machine had forgotten that feeling. When the idealism of the Sixties crashed, more than just political and artistic pretension perished. So did the notion of rock and roll as something bigger than entertainment—the idea that rock was a cause and a salvation, the idea that it offered something greater than fun. That it offered, in Pete Townshend's word, *triumph*.

When rock joined in the typical pop pursuit of big bucks, when the musician ceased to be an outlaw and began to cooperate with the show business establishment, the *idea* of rock was corrupted. It may be true, as British critic Charlie Gillett has said, that any term which can encompass both Elvis Presley and the Velvet Underground is musically meaningless. But it is not *emotionally* meaningless—at least, not until rock becomes a synonym for any pop music, no matter what its inspirational potential. That is the tragedy of the Seventies: Rock became whatever people marketed as rock, rather than something special.

In such a medium, to return to the historical roots and impart new life to them seems more worthwhile than to experiment with such things as "art rock." And in any event, the stars who had made technical breakthroughs in the early Seventies—Pete Townshend himself, Stevie Wonder, Sly Stone—were beginning to run into dead ends, or out of gas. Acting almost as if their experiments had never existed, Springsteen investigated many of the nooks and crannies they and their peers had ignored.

Thus, the methodology by which Springsteen came to his music is perhaps less interesting than the tenacity with which he held to his ideals. Bruce was never caught up with what was fashionable in terms of technique, and because he was a remarkably prolific songwriter, he could discover ruts and dead ends more quickly than those who wrote more slowly. He also had a memory for every honest moment ever put on wax, it sometimes seemed, whether it was Gene Pitney's "Love My Life Away" or Harold Dorman's "Mountain of Love." At a time when the demarcation between black and white popular music was severely drawn, Bruce slipped easily into grooves based on soul rhythm patterns—thus the frequent comparisons to Van Morrison, who, at that time, was almost the only other white performer who consistently used soul music elements in rock. Bruce built a style as deeply imaginative as the Beatles or Bob Dylan had done, because he was one of the few performers who understood that rock did not begin and end with superstars, but with a hundred—or a thousand—half forgotten records whose stars had flick-ered for only an instant. *The Wild, The Innocent & The E Street Shuffle* found an audience without resorting to the usual music busi-ness routine because those who had once been committed to rock couldn't forget it. And because those who were too young to have known it before couldn't help believing it.

The album is certainly flawed, sometimes in fundamental ways. The sound is muddy, and although this time the band arrangements are integral to the sound, the drumming is still erratic, one of the most serious problems from which rock can suffer. The piano parts were recorded on a creaky instrument: the action of the foot pedals can actually be heard during soft passages. The lyrics are still too wordy, but at least they're focused on a single theme per song.

The Wild, The Innocent & The E Street Shuffle is a transitional record, serving for Bruce much the same purpose that albums like *Revolver* and *Bringing It All Back Home* did for the Beatles and Bob Dylan. In essence, the album consolidates Bruce's perspective on the best elements of rock's first twenty years, while making the first step toward a genuinely personal style.

In a way, the album's two sides seem like separate records. The first, "E Street," side is something of a holdover from *Greetings*, full of energetic songs whose potential has not always been fully ex-ploited. But Side Two contains Springsteen's first fully realized the-matic concepts—a three-song suite of tales about wild and innocent kids on the loose.

The themes of Side One deal with escape. "Wild Billy's Circus Story," a mood sketch of an evening at the circus and a young boy's seduction by carnival life, is too mannered in its pursuit of the calliope—it is almost a parody. Similarly, although "The E Street Shuffle," which opens the record, contains wonderful street-life im-agery—"teenage tramps in skintight pants do the E Street dance"—with powerful, soul music horns, the recording lacks the crispness and punch to move it along. This is even more problematical on "Kitty's Back," a classic bar band shouter that is obviously meant as a performance piece, but whose best qualities are swallowed up in the mix. Springsteen's prowess as a guitarist should have been immediately apparent after this song, but because of the fuzzy recording, the playing here reveals itself only with extremely concentrated listening.

In the end, Side One's most fully realized production is "4th of July, Asbury Park (Sandy)," a nearly perfect ballad, the story of the boardwalk kids and their hot rod/pinball environment. The arrangement is built around acoustic guitar and accordion which are haunting in their simplicity. Springsteen's raspy vocals quaver in a way that is reminiscent at times of The Band's Richard Manuel. That's appropriate. The Band sings about an America most of us have felt, but have never seen. Springsteen sings about a version of the nation most of us have seen without feeling.

The story of "Sandy" is a B-movie plot about kids on the loose, running from dream date to low-key rumble. The singer's girl friend (a boardwalk waitress) has left him, and he's looking for new romance and a way out of this ritualized existence. The street is full of "switchblade lovers," "boys . . . with their shirts open," and "greasers in their high heels." A mysterious fortune teller, Madame Marie, is busted by the cops for "telling fortunes better than they do." As the music rises and falls, the singer pleads with Sandy to follow him:

> For me this boardwalk life's through
> You oughta quit this scene, too
> Sandy, the aurora is rising behind us
> The pier lights; our carnival life forever
> Oh love me tonight and I promise I'll love you forever
> Oh I mean it Sandy girl

Here, the boardwalk becomes something more enticing and more ominous than the one pictured on the postcard cover of *Greetings*: a symbol of hope, and an omen of wasted possibilities. In the second verse, the singer wistfully remembers making love to his boss's daughter. (Onstage, Springsteen caps the verse with a simple interjection of delight and pure triumph. "Ain't got no boss, no more," he exults.)

The Wild, The Innocent & The E Street Shuffle's first side is characterized by a remarkable exuberance. Even the slower songs like "Wild Billy" and "Sandy" have a quality of release, a delight in the simple joy of existence. But Side Two is much darker—while it is never defeatist, it is certainly much more raw. All along, Springsteen has had a tale to tell, an epic of life as lived not so much by car-crazy kids or the urban underworld, but on the rough edge, under the thumb of a system that beats back hope for sport. On the first LP, the celebration of the subway rider in "It's Hard To Be A Saint In The City," the shootout in The Bronx that's the peak moment of "Lost In The Flood" and here, Kitty's failed attempt to find a big city romance in "Kitty's Back," are all of a piece. The names change but the characters do not. And all of them point toward the narrative second side of *The Wild, The Innocent & The E Street Shuffle*.

It's a story rich with lust and humor, of victory snatched from the clutches of defeat, of victories lost at the last moment, of life lived for thrills and lives that are barely lived at all. What's most remarkable is that Springsteen's view of this nightworld is, in the end, affectionate. He finds beauty in its empty echoes, in its milieu of dirty sheets and barren cupboards, trashy gutters and broken-down cars. As with any outsider, his belief in the City is stronger than a native could ever afford.

"Rosalita" is Side Two's rocker, sandwiched between the two ballads, "Incident on 57th Street" and "New York City Serenade," the way the weekend is crammed between Friday and Monday. It might have been recorded at a demolition site. And the story is a marvel. Rosalita is locked in her room. Her parents disapprove of her boyfriend—the singer—because he is a rock and roller. The lyric is mostly a plea for her to break past their inane regulations; the singer stands beneath her balcony, shouting like a madman for Rosie to free herself. But she's confused. So he coaxes her, while the wild guitars bump into the horns and finally slams the punch line home:

But now you're sad, your mama's mad
And your papa says he knows that I don't have any money
Well, tell him this is his last chance

To get his daughter in a fine romance
Because the record company, Rosie,
Just gave me a big advance

It's a giddy spoof of a conclusion—for once, the characters really have found a way to beat the trap of their lives. If anybody had doubts that Bruce Springsteen would someday write a classic rock song, "Rosalita" dispelled them. The music is equal to the lyric, literally archetypal rock and roll. For five years, it has been the final number of his show; it may be his final song forever.

"Incident on 57th Street" and "New York City Serenade" begin more quietly, and never gain the raucous heights of "Rosalita." But they lack nothing for energy—long, winding, slower tempo songs they may be, but they both end on emotional peaks. Most writers take years to write songs that meld classical virtues with a unique perspective, but Springsteen did it when he was twenty-three, on his second album. "When I write something and I *know* it's good," Springsteen says, "I get a little spark. It's like a little light that goes off inside me that says, 'Bing! You've just fulfilled your life's purpose.'"

"New York City Serenade" is about exactly such moments of self-discovery. Bruce croons it with all the faith of the truly wild and innocent, describing a fool's paradise and the rules by which one lives within it: "It's midnight in Manhattan/This is no time to get cute. It's a mad dog's promenade. So walk tall ... or, baby, don't walk at all." In the end, the city and the song merge in a single metaphor:

Hey vibes man, hey jazz man, play me your serenade
Any deeper blue and you're playin' in your grave

There's great delicacy in this song, with its acoustic guitar and light piano, rumbling bass and crying strings. But in the guitar, there's an edge like a knife, and Bruce's voice aches with desire. At the very end of the song's ten minutes, the music glides and soars with a singsong celebration of a junkman, whose "singing, singing,

singing" becomes a triumph of life itself. For in this place, beauty is everywhere balanced by something sinister.

It's as though he were whispering secrets and promises in our ear, drawing us just close enough to make us want to hear more. You can imagine Johnny Shines hearing Robert Johnson's blues and finding in them something like this that encouraged him to follow the great country bluesman. The beat is not rock and roll—it is just a rolling heartbeat. But it is something very like Springsteen's own statement of the blues: what it is that matters, how one might gain it, and lose it, and the price paid for the attempt. For if this is not a version of the blues, then it is very like a Pied Piper's tune; one has about as much hope of resisting.

Springsteen does not know the City well. These songs have less sense of place and physical detail than, say, the New York Dolls' demimonde epics. What he does know is the sort of person for whom the place has killer depths, for whom this town chokes off all that's young and beautiful, whom the town uses its own beauty to destroy. It's the same place that the Drifters found, uptown, "On Broadway." That story was too long for one song, or three. It would spill over to the next album, and the next. A simple tale, it's a long way from "Sandy's" Little Eden—a world away, or a lifetime.

In "Incident on 57th Street," Johnny's a flashy dresser, hanging out with hard girls and pimps. Puerto Rican Jane picks him up, but Johnny's torn between his love and his partners in crime. Temptation is the central fact of his existence—temptation and looming failure, demons that only grow larger until he challenges them.

With "Incident on 57th Street," all the funny street names suddenly come to life, leaping from the earlier songs to swagger down boulevards and creep down narrow alleys. The names have changed again, but we recognize the same figures. In the end, these characters bring the teen exploitation era up to date, only this version is truer than ever before. Geographically, Bruce Springsteen is as far from Latin New York as he is from Leonard Bernstein. Spiritually, he has always been there, down with the losers and the hopeless, the not-quick-enough and the dead, where the margin of life is music.

It's the music that makes the difference. In other hands, Spanish Johnny and Puerto Rican Jane's love affair could easily have become maudlin. But Springsteen, marshaling his band like an army, makes the lovers triumphant. Danny Federici's organ is as open and warm as a fresh bullet wound, and Springsteen's own guitar surges at the end like antiaircraft fire. When Johnny says "Good night, Janey," it is not a mournful farewell, but a promise on which he means to deliver; the difference is precisely the intensity of the performance.

The story itself is as old as Romeo and Juliet, but it is told with the passion of someone who must, sometimes in the dark of night, wish that he had lived it—or fear that he still might. This is rock not just on the edge, but over it. The best way—finally the only way—to tell it is to let the boy do it himself.

Incident on 57th Street
By Bruce Springsteen

Spanish Johnny drove in from the underworld last night
With bruised arms and broken rhythm and a beatup old
   Buick
But dressed just like dynamite
He tried sellin' his heart to the hard girls over on Easy Street
But they sighed, "Johnny, it falls apart so easy and you know,
   hearts these days are cheap."
And the pimps swung their axes and said, "Johnny, you're a
   cheater."
Oh the pimps swung their axes and said, "Johnny, you're a
   liar."
And from out of the shadows came a young girl's voice
Sayin' "Johnny, don't cry."
Puerto Rican Jane, oh, won't you tell me, what's your name?
I want to drive you down to the side of the town
Where paradise ain't so crowded and there'll be action goin'
   down on Shanty Lane tonight
All the golden-heeled fairies in a real bitch-fight

Pull .38s
And kiss the girls good night

Good night, it's all right, Jane
Now let them black boys in to light the soul flame
We may find it out on the street tonight, baby
Or we may walk until the daylight, maybe

Well, like a cool Romeo he made his moves
Oh, she looked so fine
Like a late Juliet, she knew he'd never be true
But then she didn't really mind
Upstairs the band was playin'
The singer was singin' something about going home
She whispered, "Spanish Johnny, you can leave me tonight
But just don't leave me alone"
And Johnny cried,
"Puerto Rican Jane! Word is down the cops have found the
    vein."
Them barefoot boys, they left their homes for the woods
Them little barefoot street boys they said their homes ain't
    no good
They left the corners
Threw away all of their switchblade knives
And kissed each other good-bye

Johnny was sittin' on the fire escape
Watchin' the kids playin' down the street
He called down, "Hey little heroes, summer's long
But I guess it ain't very sweet around here any more."
Janey sleeps in sheets damp with sweat
Johnny sits up alone and watches her dream on, dream on
And the sister prays for lost souls

Then breaks down in the chapel after everyone's gone
Jane moves over to share her pillow
But opens her eyes to see Johnny up and putting his clothes
   on
She says, "Those romantic young boys
All they ever wanna do is fight"
Those romantic young boys
They're callin' through the window:
"Hey Spanish Johnny, wanna make a little easy money
   tonight?"

And Johnny whispered
"Good night, it's all right, Jane
I'll meet you tomorrow night on Lover's Lane
We may find it out on the street tonight, baby
Or we may walk until the daylight, maybe

Aw, good night, it's all right, Jane
I'm gonna meet you tomorrow night on Lover's Lane
Now we can find it out on the street tonight, baby
Or we may have to walk until the morning light, maybe."

There are a few precious moments in rock when you can hear a
musician overcoming both his own limits and the restrictions of the
form. At those times, the music flows into something so awesome
that its force is undeniable. Van Morrison's *Astral Weeks*, Eric Clapton's "Layla," Dylan's "Like a Rolling Stone," Phil Spector's "Da
Doo Ron Ron," Roy Orbison's "Running Scared," perhaps Neil
Young on "Helpless" and *Tonight's the Night*, certainly the entire
first Jimi Hendrix Experience LP and The Who's "My Generation"
and "Substitute" are moments such as that. For Springsteen, the
watershed came on his second album. If he has already written
greater music, explored the possibilities of his ideas more completely, made better recordings, none of it can ever sound quite this
fresh. Neither he, nor we, will ever again be quite so astonished by
the dimensions of his talent.

7 FREEZE OUT

"You don't see no music on the records unless you watch the grooves. And that ain't much. That's pretty boring."

Bruce Springsteen

I t may have been clear to rock critics that *The Wild, The Innocent & The E Street Shuffle* was a major piece of rock artistry. But to almost everyone else the album looked like a certified commercial flop. The reasons were more complex than Columbia's lack of promotion, although, as was later demonstrated, the album could have done better if the most elementary promotional efforts had been expended. (For instance, there was not a single trade paper advertisement for *The Wild, The Innocent & The E Street Shuffle*, although at that time record companies routinely took at least one ad for every new release.)

Electronics aside, the differences between AM and FM radio in America are principally matters of demographics. Both sorts of stations have a tendency to seek music that conforms to the bland standards promoted by the rock machine (although that is putting the cart before the horse, since those standards were developed as a response to radio's role as the principal promotional vehicle for American popular music), but rock on AM radio must conform to very different standards than rock on FM—and this difference was much greater in 1974 than it is today.

The most obvious restriction on AM radio concerns time. Such stations are extremely reluctant to play any song more than three minutes, thirty seconds long. Go over four minutes, and you risk kissing the AM Top Forty stations good-bye—not a light matter, since AM is by far the larger marketplace, with audiences measured in potential millions of listeners and with similar benefits in potential sales. Of the seven songs on *The Wild, The Innocent & The E Street Shuffle* not one was less than four and one half minutes long. (At the time, Springsteen claimed that he simply couldn't say or play what he wanted in a briefer format.)

There are also ways to mix the sound of a record to make it sound brighter and more immediately exciting on AM radio, which has very low fidelity and is most often picked up on tinny automobile and table radio speakers. Because *The Wild, The Innocent & The E Street Shuffle* sounded muddy even on expensive stereo equipment, the AM radio market was written off—for all intents and purposes, since no singles were released from it—the moment *E Street* was released. This made it drastically unlikely that the album would achieve sales beyond the quarter-million level.

FM radio is another story. Theoretically, FM—the so-called Album-Oriented Radio of the Seventies (AOR for short)—is much freer than AM, playing hits that are too long or too loud for the broad-based listenership of their brethren. But in 1974 very few stations on even the FM band were willing to take a chance on adventurous sounds. FM programmers liked to blast AM radio for its stale conventions and its preference for bland performers like Kenny Rogers and Elton John. But FM itself was (and is) in something of a rut. What started in the late Sixties as an exciting movement toward radical broadcasting had become merely another trail in the hunt for large listenership; FM rock radio also looked for a least common denominator, although admittedly its ideal sound was a bit more adventuresome.

Only a few loyal disc jockeys, usually at FM stations that allowed the deejays to pick a proportion of their own music, bothered with Springsteen's second album. In New York, WNEW virtually ignored it, at least at the onset, despite the fact that "New York City Serenade"—for one—was a natural for its hometown listeners. KILT in Houston, WBCN in Boston and, above all, Ed Sciaky at WMMR in Philadelphia, Cerph Caldwell at WHFS in Washington D.C., and, later, Kid Leo at WMMS in Cleveland did play Springsteen, partly because they liked the music, partly because the Springsteen cult was growing to substantial proportions—through live shows—in those cities.

This situation is not altogether unusual. There are thousands upon thousands of albums released yearly in the United States, and several hundred others released in the English language abroad. The majority remain unheard on any radio station at all. But the quality of Bruce's songs is so self-evident that it is mystifying that so few FM stations picked up on them. For Mike Appel, who had all of his own and (soon-to-be-departed) Jim Cretecos' savings tied up in Springsteen, the lack of airplay was more than disconcerting. It was infuriating.

Appel began to badger Columbia for more support; again, something many a manager might do, but given Appel's penchant for verbal abuse, the tactic proved self-destructive. The company was unresponsive. Appel hardly cared how he appeared to the record company. His dedication to Springsteen, in whom he had both believed and invested, was complete. But to call his approach to promotion merely counterproductive is to understate the case considerably.

Appel is said to have sent a letter containing torn-up $10 bills (according to another version, photocopied twenties) to stations that he considered the worst offenders; the implications that he thought the programmers took payola could not be more clear. He also phoned and berated them. At Christmas, he sent bags of coal, rather than the usual presents, to everyone he felt was hurting Springsteen's career by not playing his record. (Appel denies that he sent the shredded or photocopied bills. But he admits the rest, contending that the coal was meant as a gag.)

The radio programmers went berserk, but what was worse, Appel's audacity hurt Springsteen with the record company. Columbia, like any other label, cannot afford to offend radio stations; unintentional slights require immediate fence-mending. From the company's point of view, there's always another album to promote, which requires the programmer's continuing cooperation. The coal outraged CBS executives. Appel had left a lot of programmer feathers to smooth—more, many executives felt, than either he or his act were worth. Word came down from near the top: *The Wild, The Innocent & The E Street Shuffle* was a dead issue. What little promotion there was dried up. Rumors began to hit the street that CBS was even thinking of releasing Springsteen from his contract.

Undoubtedly, Springsteen would have been signed by another record company if CBS had dropped him. That was one thing that kept CBS from doing so. But a new label would have meant starting from scratch, and whatever the problems, it was hard to find another label—particularly another New York-based label—that was as effective in selling records as Columbia.

Springsteen found himself blocked at every turn. Radio was not interested. The record company had virtually given up hope. Touring in the usual fashion seemed to violate his artistic conception. Like a one-horse shay, the record machine stopped working all at once.

The point isn't that the machine was attempting to prevent Bruce Springsteen from becoming a success. But confronted with a performer who did not meet specifications, the machinery was simply unable to process him. Unless one believes that rock is purely product, never art, and that therefore the performer is obliged to tailor his work to the standards of the marketplace, the failure was not basically Springsteen's. It was, rather, an indication that the promotional process developed by the rock establishment in the Sixties and early Seventies had lost a great deal of its effectiveness.

Springsteen and Appel fell back on their confidence in themselves. Bruce soon began to think about making another record—although the suggestion from CBS that he try recording with session musicians fell on deaf ears. Springsteen would rather fail than compromise the essence of his sound. As for the live show, they simply slogged it out in the half dozen markets—Philadelphia, New York, Boston, Washington, Phoenix, Austin—where he had caught on. It was mostly club dates and small halls, making just enough money to keep going. The key was Philadelphia, where *E Street* had sold more than half its total copies in the early going.

Of course, this approach contradicted standard music business logic, according to which an artist who made himself available too often in a given market would soon become "overexposed." Why this was supposed to be true of concert attractions and not of records—which are ideally played on radio as often as possible—is mysterious. In any case, it proved untrue: Some of the major success stories of the Seventies (Bob Seger, Ted Nugent, Styx) developed precisely by exploiting this sort of regional popularity.

The judgment was irrelevant in the case of Bruce Springsteen anyway, because anyone who went to see his show more than once did not see the same thing. As agent Bell remembers, "I would go there and I would be surprised every night. With somebody else, after seeing the act two nights in a row, you'd say, 'Okay, let's go home.' But here, you know, I wanted to be there the next night, to see what the new surprise was gonna be, what the new innovation was gonna be, what the new material was gonna be, where would he jump this time, what would he do crazy next time."

In his early dates, Springsteen offered a mix of his own material tied together with a few stories that served as introductions along with the occasional oldie. Although his tales were always more witty than the usual slam-bang introductions, and while the oldies were inevitably performed with zeal, the most unusual fixtures of the early appearances were Danny Federici's accordion and Garry Tallent's tuba. But as Springsteen became more experienced and more confident, he wove the introductory stories into the fabric of the music itself: The material changed endlessly, with old hits recast completely and new material being worked out before the audiences' eyes. And always, the intensity was remarkable, Springsteen was not happy unless he left the stage completely drained. As Bell says, "He would do things that people just weren't used to. They weren't used to commitments like that onstage. His whole concept—he always had the public in mind in his shows. The long sound checks, even in the clubs—everything. There was a reason for his being there. His show was always . . . perfect.

"It was weird. It was spontaneous, yet it was not spontaneous. The spontaneity was so evident, yet you would think that the guy rehearsed for six years before he went on stage. He would always know how to put new material in the show. In the beginning, the pacing of the show wasn't great, but as he performed more and more it got better.

"I think that what most people were just shocked at, when they saw him, was his energy. Everybody else that you would normally see—Chicago, Blood Sweat and Tears—was just *tired* on stage. Everybody was getting used to the forty-five minute set. Bruce was out there for two hours. That was the one complaint we used to get about Bruce: that he was on too long. According to the promoters. You couldn't tell the kids that—the kids would have liked him to play another three hours."

The live show really took off after drummer Ernest "Boom" Carter replaced Vini Lopez. Springsteen agonized over sacking Lopez, with whom he had played since Steel Mill. But the move was necessary. Carter was a last-minute addition when a gig turned up before auditions for a new drummer were completed—he was Sancious's friend, and readily available. Boom's arrival stabilized the rhythm section, letting the natural drive of the songs come through. People began to talk about Springsteen's E Street Band as one of the most powerful club acts in rock. Now Bruce could say truthfully, "I play for two and a half hours every show. I put myself on the line."

The length of his shows was made mandatory by Springsteen's sense of obligation to his audience. "If I leave the stage feeling, well, if I'd played just one more song, maybe somebody out there would have been won over, if I feel I could have given more, it's hard for me to sleep that night," he has said. As a result, despite his fragile looks, Springsteen has the physical condition of an athlete. His biceps ripple, and his agility is notorious; it is not uncommon for him to begin or end a song by leaping headlong from a piano or a speaker column, or to pursue Clarence Clemons around the stage at a furious pace through a one-minute instrumental bridge in "Rosalita." After each show, Springsteen virtually collapses into his dressing room, soaked with sweat. Yet good or bad, his dedication extends into the heart of the night; he leaves the concert hall hours after the show is concluded, but if any fans were still waiting outside, he almost always has time for a few words, an autograph, a joke or two.

The classic rock songs that Springsteen began to drop into his show were more carefully chosen and performed than the oldies used by most singer-songwriters. Whereas someone like Elton John made obvious choices, picking up on ever-present Beatles songs like "I Want To Hold Your Hand" and "Lucy in the Sky with Diamonds," Springsteen picked his older material in a way that integrated it into his own music. Bruce never used more than two or three such songs per show, but when he did Fats Domino's "Let the Four Winds Blow," Chuck Berry's "Little Queenie," or Elvis Presley's "Wear My Ring (Around Your Neck)," he made them his own, without violating the stylistic basis of the original. The archetypal examples of this are Springsteen's version of "Quarter to Three," the half-forgotten Gary "U.S." Bonds hit that became his standard encore, and the Crystals' great Phil Spector production, "Then She Kissed Me." But his version of Bob Dylan's "I Want You," slowed down and intensified, lifted that song from a mixture of lust and disgust to a tune of more aching passion, without sacrificing Dylan's ironic intent.

This was an astute move, because it gave Springsteen access to the entire span of rock and roll at a moment when rock was especially historically self-conscious. If he was more than two steps from the blues, Springsteen was barely one removed from the Sixties' hard rock of the Beatles and the Rolling Stones. Playing for audiences that were not always certain which were his originals and which the "oldies," Bruce simply took everything and stamped it with his own identity. Fans old enough to remember the originals were still jarred by a jolt of reminiscence.

For his part, Springsteen never considered any part of his repertoire "oldies" in the sense of Sha Na Na's bogus nostalgia. "They're just songs that I've always liked. Whenever a song's got that life, that ability to move you and is still very relevant to today, to what's happening, that's important.

"We don't play no oldies. They may be older songs, but they're not nostalgic, really. I was never into that whole nostalgic thing, because it's stupid. But these songs are different. It's obvious by the reaction they get. It's great today, it's great right now, and if somebody plays it and people hear it, they'll still love it tomorrow." In an industry whose sense of history often overwhelmed its sense of tradition, that statement was nearly revolutionary: It drew the line between mechanical masturbation and the genuine ability to perceive and create links between past and present in popular culture.

Springsteen never played other people's songs with reverence, because that would have sapped the life from them. His own material was also not fixed into any single shape or style. On the LP, for example, "The E Street Shuffle" is an approximation of Stax Records' version of soul music, with a jaunty brass section and raspy vocal. Live, it sometimes became a slow ballad or a straightforward rocker. Partly, this was compensation for the E Street Band's lack of a brass section. But it was also a measure of Bruce's relentless searching, his willingness to rethink his material constantly, exploring all of its possibilities. "For You," to take another example, might be performed solo, just Bruce at the piano, on one night, and in a full band version the next, done as a fast-paced rocker or as a slow ballad as the mood struck him. There were a dozen different ways to sing his songs, and Springsteen felt no need to confine himself to the version that was recorded. And this applied not only to whole songs but to details within numbers, as well (although once a song's *lyrics* were recorded they rarely differed onstage.) But rhythm, tempo, instrumentation and phrasing all shifted nightly—that was a major element of the "surprise" that Bell talks about.

But Springsteen's biggest concert risk was playing unrecorded material; most recording artists had long since ceased performing anything but recorded material, for only that material could have a calculated effect. Springsteen used new songs, to let him see whether they fit into the performance and to determine audience reaction: In fact, songs like "Thundercrack" that never made it into any of the albums were audience favorites in Philadelphia. And one could hear Springsteen shifting the good ideas and images from one song to the next: The lines "French cream won't soften those boots, baby/French kisses will not break your heart" originally appeared in a song called "Contessa," but were later incorporated in slightly altered form into "She's the One" from *Born To Run*. The original live performances of "She's the One," in turn, contributed the phrases "hated the truth that ran us down" and "hated you when you went away" to "Backstreets." "Thunder Road" itself had two different verses that changed the narrative line drastically, although certainly the emotional thrust of the song never varied.

Springsteen's show was so far away from the standard rock presentation that it's difficult to compare the two. The live shows of recording artists feature their own material, done in versions as close as possible to the album they're trying to sell; the artists perform songs associated with other performers exceedingly sparingly, for fear of being thought uncreative; new songs aren't performed because they haven't been established as product. In contrast to the others, with their standardized forty-five-minute sets, Springsteen's concerts were epic, not just in length, but in their scope. Yet throughout, they kept the audience on the edge of their seats, with the feeling that anything might happen next.

Oddly, these innovations made Springsteen seem even more the repository of rock and roll tradition: His energy and creativity linked the comparatively primitive experiments of Presley, Little Richard and Chuck Berry to the relative sophistication of the Beatles, Bob Dylan and the Rolling Stones. Yet this is precisely what made his performances so utterly up to date, for Springsteen grafted the enthusiasm and recklessness of the Fifties rockers onto the self-aware innovations of the Sixties.

In addition, Bruce seemed always on the verge of unlocking the last secret cupboard of rock and roll, so that the music would finally stand naked, its essence revealed. Rock history is made up of moments—hit singles that have no follow-up, careers that end in airplane crashes just as they are about to blossom. Because there is not yet an orthodox and complete version of that history, one can never be sure that something hasn't been overlooked. Suppose *the* great rock single had flickered over the airwaves just once, on the night you had passed out in the backseat? Probably not, but still . . . For Bruce, rock and roll has always had this sense of possibility. He brought it back to a great many of his listeners as well.

Ultimately, it was his showmanship—the physical aspect of his presentation—that nailed the point home. Bruce uses his body to dramatize not just the content of his songs, but every moment of his stage life. Faris Bouhafa, who then ran Max's Kansas City, remembers that "Bruce has always done the street rap on stage, and he always had an incredible sense of drama. The first shows were very spontaneous. After a while, every movement looked spontaneous, but he'd been doing it so long, it had to be calculated. He opened the shows acoustically then, and the band was different, but he always captured the audience."

This ability to make the rehearsed appear spontaneous and the spontaneous seem well-crafted is in its way as great a gift as Springsteen's musical instinct. As a result, Springsteen's stories were rarely the random, shaggy dog variety like the one about Ducky Slattery. More often, they are like the introductions to "The E Street Shuffle" and "It's My Life" recounted above. All of them have a point to make about the music—or, rather, the music has a point to make about the stories. "The E Street Shuffle" narrative plays across the notion that blacks are dangerous and innately hip, two ideas central to the broad appeal of Clarence Clemons—a man who probably does know who put the bomp, although he isn't telling.

Eventually, in the introduction to an old Manfred Mann hit, "Pretty Flamingo," Bruce found a way to deal with the one subject that, up to that point, his writing had sometimes shied away from: sex.

"I lived on this street," the story sometimes began. "It was South Street. Highway 9 passed right by my house. But it was real close to town and every day about five o'clock, there was this one girl, she used to work downtown, I guess, and she used to walk past my house, every day. And we'd sit out on the porch and we'd find out what time it is—it's four-thirty, man. And at quarter to five we'd hustle out there and we'd sit down. And I'd say, 'Today, you're gonna go up, Steven, and say, "Hi, my name is Steve. What's your name?"'

" 'Umm humm.'

"See, we'd plan all this stuff out, how we were gonna do this. 'Cause she was one of those girls that you sit there like a fool and you're afraid to go up and say hello to, you know. And we'd try to get everybody, everybody on the street, to go up and try to find out what her *name* was. And the only cat that'd go near her was this one crazy guy. And we'd say, 'Now go on up, go on up to her. You're crazy, see, she won't . . .' "

The laughter drowns him out.

"No, really, if you're crazy, see, you can get away with lots of stuff. People are always afraid of somebody who acts nuts. This guy was a little guy; he was littler than me. I used to hang out with him on weekends. Like, he'd go into pool halls and go up to the table where all the heaviest cats are playin'. You know they got a lot of money on the game. And he'd take the eight ball and throw it across the table, you know, knock it into all the balls. But they never used to beat him up, 'cause they thought he was nuts.

"So I was hangin' out with him, but even he wouldn't go up and say nothin' to her. So this went on for like a few . . . years, I guess. And then, like I moved away. But we never found out what her name was; we used to always call her somethin', we used to have this name—should I tell 'em?

"All the guys on my block called her Flamingo . . ." By the time he finishes the verse, the audience is wild, half in love with its image of the girl, riveted to the song. The guitar line is elegant and the singing impassioned. For a few moments, you're just lost in the magic of a moment, and then Springsteen snaps you out of it. "Gonna find that girl!" he bellows and then:

"Clarence, what can I do? I think I'll hire some private detective. I don't know. I looked in the phone book. I'm gonna hire somebody famous. They found Patty Hearst; it took 'em awhile. Somebody famous—Charlie Chan—somebody with a gun. And when I get 'er, I know what I'm gonna tell her now. I know what I'm gonna tell 'er. I'm gonna tell her, I'm in a *band.*"

"E Street," "It's My Life" and "Pretty Flamingo" are narrative set pieces, but on occasion, Bruce used other songs to the same effect. "Spirit In The Night" can become a full-fledged, detailed narrative, and when Bruce enters the audience to sing the final verse, as he began to do in 1975 and continues doing even in large halls, it is a major thrill. "Kitty's Back" became a tale of terror one night, when Bruce claimed that she had sent a bloodstained knife back-stage. Then he ducked into the audience during the middle of the song, while Clarence Clemons solemnly declaimed: "Ladies and gentlemen, Bruce Springsteen will not be appearing here tonight." Then Bruce raced back to the mike, as if there was a hellhound on his trail, to hit the "Here she comes" chant and explode with "Kitty's back in town!"

At the end of "Incident on 57th Street," Springsteen would describe Spanish Johnny leaving Puerto Rican Jane:

"He pulled on his pants. He pulled on his shirt. He pulled on his *tube socks*. And he went out into the car. [Bluffs turning the ignition several times; the car won't start. Finally he smiles as the engine catches. He begins to sing.] Maybe we can slip away . . . maybe we can steal away." Over and over he repeats those lines, whispering them, seducing everyone. "Just for a minute, just for a second." When the music ends, even a packed room feels drained.

It wasn't just the length of the shows, then, that made them the talk of rock. They built from quiet opening numbers ("New York City Serenade," later "Thunder Road") to the wildest rocking conclusion, "Rosalita," and then into a series of encores: "Quarter to Three," "For You," "Wear My Ring (Around Your Neck)," "Sandy." If it went on long enough. Bruce would call for the Isley Brothers' "Twist and Shout" and finish standing atop the piano.

And this sense of complete exhilaration came along at the perfect moment. Since rock had begun to be taken seriously, an arrogance of musicianship had grown up among the biggest and most popular performers. Aside from a few old timers—The Who, the Stones—showmanship was disdained, particularly by the heavyweight English and Californian groups. The Grateful Dead; Yes; the Eagles; Emerson Lake and Palmer; Led Zeppelin; Crosby, Stills, Nash and Young, regardless of their musical diversity, shared a common refusal to project as entertainers.

A cult of showmanship did appear in the Seventies, partly as a reaction to the standoffish attitude of big-time rock bands. But Elton John and Alice Cooper—later, Kiss as well—put rock in the backseat, playing music that was purely exploitative and derivative. Mick Jagger, Rod Stewart and Roger Daltrey all continued to put on flamboyant shows that complemented their music but they had begun to seem like aging throwbacks. There was not a single American performer who had been able to combine showmanship and creative music. In fact, the very best American rock bands, Creedence Clearwater Revival and The Band, were the most immobile of all. The heyday of Jimi Hendrix and Joe Cocker was barely a memory.

Springsteen, able to see himself as both a fan and a player, was as fed up as some parts of the audience were becoming. "They're just people who wanna crawl back in the womb," he said of such performers, "people who have built their own reality and are afraid of reality itself." It was part of his compact with his fans that he would never isolate himself in that way.

Springsteen felt that his relationship with his audience implied an obligation: "When you're up on that stage, you can't think about you and them. You got to look out there and see yourself as a kid and see how you're reacting to what you're doing. When you lose the kid in you, you can't deal with performing anymore. If you look at things too objectively, you lose that spirit that the audience has come looking for.

"It's just being honest with the audience and yourself," he continues. "You can't conform to the formula of always giving the audience what it wants, or you're killing yourself and you're killing the audience. Because they don't really want it either. Just because they respond to something doesn't mean they want it. I think it has come to the point where they respond automatically to things they think they should respond to. You've got to give them more than that. Someone has to take the initiative and say, 'Let's step out of the mold. Let's try *this*.'"

Bruce Springsteen's combination of showmanship and musicianship, his recklessness, and his dogged commitment to the pursuit of perfection, harked back to the Presley-led Fifties and to the Sixties when Jagger was really sashaying and the Beatles could spin the world with a nod of their heads. Audiences responded immediately because they had missed this combination, or else had never known it. In Springsteen, the Seventies had acquired their first *complete* star, one who did not have to compartmentalize his talents.

Now all that remained was for the rock industry to take notice.

8 THUNDERCRACK

On a chilly Thursday evening in early April 1974, Bruce Springsteen was in the midst of a three-night benefit at Charley's, a small bar near Harvard Square in Cambridge, Massachusetts. The club could not have held more than three hundred people, and it had rarely been so packed. Outside, lines stretched around the corner, despite the weather. Springsteen had been playing in Boston a good deal recently, and word-of-mouth was making him a local cult hero there, as it was all over the Eastern Seaboard.

Springsteen's choice of Charley's for his Boston engagement is indicative of his loyalties. He had originally been slated to play Joe's Place, an even smaller dive that specialized in Chicago blues, because Joe Spadafora (who owned Joe's Place) had booked Springsteen in his scuffling days and they had become friendly. Then, the weekend before, Joe's Place burned to the ground. Springsteen called Mike Appel to tell him he was going to play a benefit for Spadafora, and discovered that William Morris had booked him into the larger more prestigious Performance Center in the heart of Harvard Square for the same nights.

This precipitated a crisis of sorts. The growth of his Boston following would clearly make the April date Springsteen's final club
appearance in the area; next time, the sheer demand for tickets
would make it necessary to move to a concert hall. Bruce felt he
owed Spadafora his final club date.

That upset the booking agency. Once more, Springsteen was refusing to take the course most advantageous to his career (not to
mention reducing their commission). For a time, both the Performance Center and Charley's were advertising the appearance. Eventually, Bruce won—he would play for Spadafora, or not at all.

By Thursday's late show, sweat was pouring off the walls at Charley's, mingling with the stench of spilled beer and stale cigarette
smoke. The crowd was a socially mixed group—a rarity in Cambridge, where audiences tend to be exclusively collegiate or rough-
house townie—and the blend helped make the sense of anticipation
for each set as high as at a concert by the Stones or Led Zeppelin,
while the listeners were as attentive as at shows by Jackson Browne
or Bonnie Raitt.

Reports from the early shows, and repeated listenings to *The Wild,
The Innocent & The E Street Shuffle*, drew the attention of Jon
Landau. Landau, at twenty-six, was probably the most influential
rock critic in the country. From his Concord home, he ran the record review section of *Rolling Stone*, the nation's most prestigious
rock consumer publication. Tall and bespectacled, a former guitarist
himself, Landau was one of the few critics who took the time and
trouble to learn the business side of rock, which further increased
his stature in the record industry. Landau had also produced records—the MC5's second album, *Back in the USA*, plus two by Livingston Taylor, the brother of James—before being forced to return
to journalism because of a chronic intestinal disease. In the Boston-
Cambridge area, Landau's clout was even greater, because of his
regular column in *The Real Paper*, one of the city's two *Village
Voice*-style weeklies. Landau knew how to wield his influence: He
had been instrumental in getting the J. Geils Band signed to Atlantic
Records, and his review of Maria Muldaur's "Midnight At The Oa-
sis" had been a key factor in convincing Warner Bros. Records to
back the song, which eventually became a major hit.

On the Sunday before Springsteen's appearance at Charley's, Landau wrote an anticipatory *Real Paper* column that called *The Wild, The Innocent & The E Street Shuffle* "the most under-rated album so far this year, an impassioned and inspired street fantasy that's as much fun as it is deep."

Landau was ordinarily cautious in his judgments. Because of his position in Boston, and at *Rolling Stone*, such a strong statement would have had some impact on the record company in any event. But unlike other critics, who had celebrated Springsteen's successes without being able to pinpoint the fundamental flaws in his recordings, Landau also spotted the problems. Drummer Lopez, he said, was "the album's consistent weak spot." In addition, he noted, "The album is not as well-produced as it ought to have been . . . The recording is still a mite thin or trebly-sounding, especially when the band moves into the breaks. With Springsteen's voice so rough in the first place, the album occasionally becomes unnecessarily shrill. But these are minor blemishes on a very major work.

"Next time around," he concluded prophetically, "he ought to work a little harder on matching the production to the material, round out a few rough edges and then just throw some more hot ones on the vinyl. The subways he sings so much about keep rolling all night long; and the way this boy rocks, it's just a matter of time before he starts picking up passengers."

Still, at this time, Landau knew virtually nothing about Springsteen. He hadn't listened to the first album, although, after receiving a phone call from Clive Davis, he made certain it was reviewed. And though he had heard from Oberman, *Rolling Stone* reviewer Ken Emerson and others about Bruce's live show, Landau had yet to see it himself.

So it must have been fate that Landau walked up to Charley's that night at just the moment Springsteen had come outside to read the copy of the *Real Paper* column posted in the window. Springsteen was wearing only a light jacket, and to warm himself he was bouncing up and down on his toes as he read. Somehow, the fans standing in line didn't recognize him, but Landau did. Walking over, Jon asked Springsteen if he liked the piece. "It's good," Bruce replied. "I've read better, you know." Then Landau introduced himself. Laughing, they entered the bar.

Inside, Bruce introduced Landau to Mike Appel, who immediately asked, "So you don't like the album's production, huh?" Landau spent the few remaining minutes before the show amplifying and explaining his remarks for Appel, and listening to Bruce and Mike's story of their problems at CBS. Bruce himself said little; he spent most of the time listening to the exchange between the other two.

Despite the rave, Landau's friends were surprised by his appearance at Charley's. He had quit going to concerts, except for performances by real favorites or old friends, yet here was the man who joshingly (but deliberately) styled himself King of Rock and Roll at a concert by a virtual unknown.

That evening's show confirmed Landau's impressions from the album, and raised his hopes. Springsteen opened with "New York City Serenade," accompanied only by David Sancious, who added snatches of Mozart to the song's lush introduction. This could have made for a confusing beginning, but instead it announced that this was one rocker who was bound by no one's preconceptions.

Visually, the band was a hodge-podge. After Bruce, dressed as usual in leather jacket, plain T-shirt, jeans and boots, the focus of attention was Clarence Clemons, whose size dwarfed both his tenor sax and the relatively diminutive Springsteen. Garry Tallent had long hair, and a beard halfway down his chest. Sancious and Boom Carter wore their hair closely cropped, and they dressed neatly, almost as if they were preppies themselves. Danny Federici's long red locks curled down past his shoulders as he swayed at his organ. The music they made was all of a piece—hard, tight, driving. What really impressed Landau, though, was Springsteen's projection of a complete artistic persona. The singing was classically rock and roll, unabashedly passionate and powerful, and Bruce expanded upon it with a series of short introductions, witty stories that served to frame the songs. He also acted out the songs with grand gestures full of the innocence and toughness of the lyrics.

By the time the group came out for their second encore, a raucous version of Fats Domino's "Let the Four Winds Blow," the place was in pandemonium and, surprising even himself, Landau—seated only inches from the stage—led the applause. He left raving, not only to his Boston colleagues but to his fellow editors at *Rolling Stone*, where he made certain that *The Wild, The Innocent & The E Street Shuffle* was named one of the seven best albums of 1973.

A month later, on May 9, Springsteen played Cambridge again. Once more, this ran counter to music-business orthodoxy: Playing the same towns too frequently was "saturating" the market, becoming too available. Still, Springsteen was making it work for him. At the Harvard Square Theatre, he was only the opening act; Bonnie Raitt, the headliner, had agreed to allow him to play his full two-hour show. It was something Raitt may have regretted: Springsteen concluded to a thunderous ovation, and a good portion of the crowd walked out after his set, despite the fact that Cambridge is Raitt's home turf.

It was the night before his twenty-seventh birthday, and Landau drove home in a daze. It was hard for him to believe that he was feeling this way, but by early morning, he had himself so worked up that he sat down and wrote an exceptionally long and intense *Real Paper* column about the experience.

"It's four in the morning and raining," began the "Loose Ends" column that appeared in the May 22, 1974, *Real Paper*. "I'm twenty-seven today, feeling old, listening to my records and remembering that things were different a decade ago." The piece went on to chronicle the richness of Landau's personal history in rock and roll music: the Righteous Brothers, the Four Tops, the Rolling Stones, each initial encounter special and emotionally devastating. Landau told, too, of his disenchantment as the fan became a musician, critic, and producer.

"But tonight," he concluded, "there is someone I can write of the way I used to write, without reservations of any kind. Last Thursday at Harvard Square Theatre, I saw my rock and roll past flash before my eyes. And I saw something else: *I saw rock and roll's future and its name is Bruce Springsteen.* And on a night when I needed to feel young, he made me feel like I was hearing music for the first time."

The piece went on for another column and a half. But that one paragraph, besides containing the most frequently quoted line in the history of rock criticism, sealed Jon Landau's future and, in a way, Bruce Springsteen's. The stage was set. In a few weeks, the "rock and roll future" tag would rocket literally around the world.

9 THE FUTURE DELAYED

olumbia Records seized "I saw rock and roll's future and its name is Bruce Springsteen" and used it as the headline of a full-page ad featuring the last half of Landau's column. The line quickly became one of the most misquoted in rock. Landau's original is almost Dickensian, with its spoofing allusion to the spiritual resurrection of Scrooge, but the other versions made it seem as though Landau were attempting to write advertising copy. Still, if Springsteen's future at Columbia had seemed a bit hazy before, the column went a long way toward clearing it up.

It would be ingenuous to suggest that Landau had not anticipated the effect of his words. There is a certain kind of very partisan criticism that, when written by a highly regarded critic, can raise the level of rhetoric about an artist's work. (Pauline Kael's review of Robert Altman's *Nashville* is an even more celebrated example.) When such reviews appear, they force other critics into a reactive position. Since such an esteemed colleague has called the work a masterpiece, those are the grounds on which it must be judged, rather than the usual terms of good/bad/indifferent/interesting.

Chances are, many lesser critics will follow the lead of the big-time pundit, but even the critic's relative equals must match the stakes laid on the table. Moreover, Landau was not writing about a single work—he was making a claim for the artist *himself*. For the rest of his career, Bruce Springsteen will be judged not on whether he is good, but on whether he is great. The question is no longer whether his style is unique and expressive, but whether it really represents the future direction of rock; not whether his songs are special, but whether they are classics. And because the record business—and in many ways, rock criticism itself—is so short-sighted, Springsteen was immediately faced with the notion that he was the first wave of a trend. Landau had wiped out the middle ground, and although he certainly didn't calculate every effect his article might have, in a general way he understood very well what the column might accomplish. What was more surprising was that so many fans and critics jumped over to his side.

In the next few months, such prestigious critics as Robert Christgau of *The Village Voice* and *Newsday*, John Rockwell of *The New York Times* and Robert Hilburn of the *Los Angeles Times* also wrote enthusiastically of Springsteen. (Hilburn, in fact, had been raving about Springsteen for quite a while.) More importantly, Landau's line struck a responsive chord with Bruce's swelling audience: He had put his finger on just what made people care so passionately about Bruce's music, and about rock in general. If some who saw only the ad were skeptical, those who saw both the ad and Springsteen felt confirmed in their judgments.

CBS reactivated Springsteen's albums, offering a discount to stores that bought them in quantity. Sales (particularly of the second album) picked up fast. By August, *The Wild, The Innocent & The E Street Shuffle* was approaching one hundred thousand sold, a highly respectable figure, particularly considering the company's initial disinterest. (More than half of these initial sales were in Philadelphia, where a pair of WMMR-FM disc jockeys, David Dye and Ed Sciaky, were rabid Springsteen followers.)

Springsteen was of two minds about Landau's quote and the resultant advertisement. He told friends that he resented the ad, because it capitalized on "a very personal thing." But he also appreciated Jon's enthusiasm. "It came at a time when a lot of people—including the record company—were wondering whether I really had it," he says. "It gave me a lot of hope. Landau's quote helped me reaffirm a belief in myself. The band and I were making $50 a week. It helped me go on. I realized I was gettin' through to somebody."

For his part, Jon Landau felt he had found something in the Harvard Square Theatre that he had always been seeking in rock and roll: "When I had my band, my dream was to write a show that would tell the whole history of rock and roll—sort of like Eric Burdon's 'Story of Bo Diddley.' And one night, long after Barry and the Remains [an early Boston band with which Landau was close] had broken up, I saw Barry Tashian actually do it.

"He was playing with this terrible band in some bar in Boston. They began to do Chuck Berry's 'Let It Rock,' which is one of my favorites in the first place. Barry got so deep into it, he just waved off the other guys, one by one, until he was all alone, playing guitar and making up the words. He was telling this incredible story about Elvis, Berry and the rest of it. And that's what I saw in Springsteen: an ability to tell the whole damn story."

Some saw the column as Landau's bid to become Springsteen's record producer. But, the transparent honesty of the piece aside, Landau's Crohn's disease (an intestinal disorder aggravated by stress) made it physically impossible for him to do any producing. That was the reason he had stopped in the first place. However, the column did bring Springsteen and Landau together as friends. Shortly after the article appeared, Springsteen phoned Landau to thank him, and they became embroiled in a lengthy discussion. CBS still felt that Bruce had serious production problems that were preventing him from being successful. What, Springsteen wanted to know, did a producer do, anyway? Landau explained the range of functions a producer might perform: Some are merely engineers, simply responsible for the proper recording of ideas an artist has already worked out thoroughly. Others help arrange songs, or, for artists who do not write, assist in choosing material. At the most extreme, the producer imposes his ideas on the recording to the point where it becomes more his record than the artist's. Springsteen was fascinated; he knew almost nothing about standard record business procedure. (As he once put it, "I never knew anyone who made a record or was involved in the record business. If they'd told me that part of the deal was mopping the floor, I suppose I'd have mopped the floor.") From there, the conversation meandered into more personal matters, winding up with both men promising to stay in touch. They did.

Meanwhile, the pressure was mounting for Bruce to make a record as good as his live show. At the Harvard Square Theatre date, he had played "Born To Run" for the first time live. Shortly afterward, he recorded a four-and-one-half-minute version of "Born To Run," clearly hit-single material although the song was too long in that rendition. Editing it proved almost impossible; Springsteen was stymied. June and July passed with no resolution.

Springsteen had recorded some other material after his second album, including "The Fever," a fine Ray Charles-style R & B number. Bruce decided that he hated it, but not before an enthusiastic Appel had run off a few copies and sent them to disc jockeys who had been supportive. When Bruce arrived in Austin, Texas, and Phoenix, Arizona, for shows that summer, he was barraged with dozens of requests for the song, which had become an underground hit. This displeased CBS, who had hit material, but no product to sell.

"Born To Run" was likewise distributed to a few disc jockeys, with even stronger results. Appel was apparently confident that Springsteen would soon make an album—there was almost enough material for one—so he gave tapes to Sciaky, Kid Leo in Cleveland and a few others. Everybody who heard the tape wanted to buy it, but again, there was no hope of that. It became an even bigger underground hit than "The Fever," Leo playing it every Friday at five fifty-five P.M. on WMMS-FM in Cleveland to "officially launch the weekend."

Columbia was again annoyed; Springsteen's perfectionism stood in the way of obvious sales. "Born To Run" might be too long, but then again, it might be that rare number that becomes a smash despite its length. And according to a hoary record business shibboleth, advance airplay such as this is disastrous to sales. Only certain radio stations had the tape, for one thing, which meant that their competitors would feel slighted and might refuse to play the official release. Perhaps radio stations who had the early tape wouldn't play the record as often when it came out, because their listeners were already too familiar with it. Besides, records are bought on impulse; if a kid goes into a store and asks for a song, it had better be there, because the chance he'll come back—even once—is slim. Yet CBS was stymied. Springsteen was not yet satisfied with "Born To Run," and as far as he was concerned, the song would be perfect before it was released, or it would not be released at all.

A similar perfectionism stalled the recording of the rest of the third album. If things didn't go right during the first couple of sessions in a week, the dates fell apart. And things were not going right. Bruce couldn't put his finger on it, but he felt stalemated in the studio. For one thing, 914 Studios, where the first two LPs had been made, was in Rockland County, New York, more than sixty miles from the Jersey shore where the band members lived. By the time they arrived at the studio, everyone was already tired. Also, 914's tape equipment tended to malfunction and its piano was frequently out of tune.

So Bruce would cancel out, play whatever live dates he could get or just stay at home, writing and arranging material that often never got performed onstage, much less on record. This was nothing new. Those who had known Bruce longest accepted it as his way. Back in the Steel Mill era, Danny Federici remembers, "Bruce was writing about a song per day. It was crazy. It got so I didn't want to go to rehearsal, because every time there'd be this mess of new songs to learn. And they were all gone so soon. Bruce just goes, 'That's yesterday,' and throws 'em away."

Springsteen's attitude in the recording studio itself was similar. Just as his arrangements were becoming increasingly complex, necessitating trying a variety of approaches to each song before laying it down, he wanted to experiment with the recording process. That was one reason for using 914 Studios, where the rates were much lower than in a Manhattan studio. Many of his most unusual effects were created by taking outrageous chances: "Born To Run" itself features strings, more than one dozen guitar tracks, sax, drums, glockenspiel, bass, multiple keyboards and a variety of voices. Because he worked by trial and error, the young wizard proceeded even more slowly.

What sustained the band was its live shows. The band was still being booked by agent Sam McKeith, whose confidence in Springsteen's talent kept enthusiasm alive at William Morris. But McKeith was on vacation that August and so it was Barry Bell who booked Bruce as an opener at an Anne Murray show at the Schaefer Music Festival in Central Park on August 3. "Shep Gordon and Johnny Podell managed and booked Anne Murray [Gordon and Podell were also involved with Alice Cooper.] And [promoter] Ron Delsener wanted to put this package together of Anne Murray, Bruce and an opening act, Brewer and Shipley," says Bell. "So I told Ron, 'That's fine with us. If that's the only date you've got, that's *fine*. We advise you that it would be a good idea if Bruce closes the show.' Ron agreed. However, Shep Gordon did not agree. Shep Gordon wanted Anne Murray to close; he said it was an important New York date for her. Johnny Podell wanted her to close. He said, 'Who's Bruce Springsteen? He has a cult following in New York. "Snowbird" is a big hit. Murray should close.'

"I said, 'Hey, I don't care. I'm just trying to do this for your sake. You're not gonna want to follow Bruce Springsteen in New York City.' But evidently they wanted to follow him in New York City. And they did.

"So Bruce goes out there. There was a buzz in the amplifier, I remember, for which Mike Appel got yelled at after the show. But Bruce goes out there and really kicks ass. It was one of his better shows that I had seen up to that point. Now, he's on for about an hour and twenty minutes. Mike Appel is walking around with his safari hat on; he doesn't even want to talk to Gordon or Podell.

"So they come over to me, like I'm their best friend. 'C'mon, get this guy off the stage.' I said, 'Hey *no*. *You* wanted to follow him. That's just the way it is. You had the choice. We advised you that this was gonna happen. We wanted to close the show. You wouldn't let us. He's got another ten or fifteen minutes to go. He's gonna do it.'

"So then he goes into 'Rosalita' and completely killed the audience. It was about ninety-nine percent Springsteen fans, it seemed. There were about five thousand people there and they went wild.

"Now these people are screaming, 'Get him the fuck outta there!' I said, 'No. He gets his encore.' He does his one encore, I forget what it was. The crowd went wild. Anne Murray went on, and was booed off the stage. 'We want Bruce,' the whole thing. She has never come back to New York since then."

Unfortunately, the Central Park gig was one of the last shows that David Sancious and Boom Carter played with Bruce. Sancious had been offered a recording contract with Epic, Columbia's sister label, and he decided to take it. Carter left with him, as part of a band called Tone, which has since made several electric jazz records. (Sancious has also played with John McLaughlin, Jack Bruce and Stanley Clarke, among others.)

Springsteen respected Sancious's ability enough to appreciate David's need to make his own sound. ("Davey could get off on playing anything," Bruce remembers. "When we first played together, in the ten-piece band, he was a real wild man. He had that rock 'n roll thing in him—it always seemed like he might be the next Jimi Hendrix. He had the potential to be that.") But the absence of a second keyboard player and a drummer made things difficult. For someone else, it might have simplified the recording issue. The obvious move was to hire studio professionals for those instruments. But Springsteen wanted none of that. "I don't hire studio musicians. I don't want guys with big houses playing for me. I just put an ad in the paper and people come out and play. You take a kid off the street and he'll play his heart out for you. If someone's primarily interested in how much money he's going to make, I don't want him playing for me."

Anyway, Springsteen needed replacements who would fit into the live act permanently. And, since Sancious, Tallent, Clemons and Federici worked with Bruce to form one of rock's most distinctive sounds, it would not be easy to find substitutes.

In one way, Springsteen had very little to offer. "I ain't makin' that much money. I've got some great musicians in my band, and I'm payin' 'em terrible money," he said around this time. "I pay myself the same, but it's terrible for me, too. I mean, we're barely makin' a livin' scrapin' by." But there was no lack of candidates for the new post. Springsteen and Appel placed an ad in *The Village Voice*: "Drummer and keyboard player wanted for Bruce Springsteen and the E Street Band. Must sing."

Calls flooded Appel's office. With characteristic serendipity, after auditioning about thirty other performers, Springsteen found a pair of musicians who not only matched Carter and Sancious, but who brought whole new dimensions to the band.

The drummer, saturnine "Mighty" Max Weinberg, was another Jersey boy, who had come to New York to study with Bernard "Pretty" Purdie, the great soul drummer. Max had played in rock bands since he was thirteen, and later in pit bands with Broadway shows like *The Magic Show* and *Godspell*. But rock and roll was closest to Weinberg's heart; he played with something of the power of Keith Moon, though with a good deal more restraint. And the pit band experience made him a grand onstage foil for Bruce—Weinberg keyed the rhythm to Springsteen's physical and vocal movements, no matter how unpredictable. Max added drama to the band, and enhanced its rhythmic power. He was a real find.

Pianist Roy Bittan was, if anything, even more of a discovery; he quickly became known as technically the best player in the group. He so impressed Bruce that the diminutive, balding keyboard wiz (who looks a bit like film director Martin Scorsese) was dubbed "The Professor." He ate up all the Sancious parts and reached for more. Having grown up in Far Rockaway, near Coney Island, Bittan was the only non-New Jersey kid in the band. Roy was also the only member who had recorded with anyone but Bruce. And, in addition to an array of rock bands, he'd toured with *Jesus Christ, Superstar*; he'd served as musical director of a Broadway flop, and he'd even played with the Pittsburgh Symphony.

The addition of Weinberg and Bittan was crucial to Springsteen's sound, because they professionalized it without losing its essential spirit. Tallent was steady as a rock, while Clemons and Federici were highly stylized players—neither Clarence nor Danny could be described as master technicians, but they had heart. Max and Roy were pros with the sense not to let what was "correct" get in the way of what felt right. They let Bruce range as far as his imagination.

The band at this time also had a sort of floating seventh member—the willowy blond violinist Suki Lahav, wife of engineer Louis Lahav, who worked on the first two LP's and the early stages of *Born To Run*. Onstage, Suki's ghostly pale figure was a fine contrast to Bruce's darkness and toughness, and, musically, the addition of a violin was a luxury that quickly became a necessity in songs like

"Incident on 57th Street," "New York City Serenade," Dylan's "I Want You" and a new song called "Jungleland."

Now all that was left was for Bittan and Weinberg to learn the material, and for Bruce to adapt it to their style. Then the record could be completed. But November 1974—the first anniversary of the release of *The Wild, The Innocent & The E Street Shuffle*—came and went with no progress. Sales of the second album had passed one hundred fifty thousand, but a new record was needed to spread Bruce's name beyond the East Coast. Things still weren't right in the studio; no one seemed to understand why not.

Outwardly, Bruce was as phlegmatic as ever, although he, too, must have been disheartened by the lack of progress. "When it's ready, it'll be there. I can't be pressured," he said. "I decided a long time ago, I know who I am and where I come from. And I know what it is to be caught up in the pressure. You start thinking that you're something else. You start becoming a product of the entertainment business. I try to keep my perspective on the thing. It's even for the good of the record company that I do that, because I'll give 'em my best and it'll work out for the best in the end."

However, Bruce wasn't nearly so decisive in the studio, agonizing for hours and sometimes days over details some thought irrelevant. He was essentially marking time. CBS was unimpressed by his rationale—like any corporation, it cared more about his biggest-selling than his best work. Yet, although he hadn't seemed very important when the year began, Columbia Records entered 1975 with Bruce Springsteen once more near the top of its priorities. All he had to do was get a record out.

10 PRISONER OF ROCK AND ROLL

"The record company was confused. The kids in the audience were going nuts, but the record wasn't selling. It got obvious that we needed a rock and roll album."

Bruce Springsteen, September 1975

What Springsteen needed more than anything, some thought, was a relatively objective third party to assist him and Mike Appel in the studio. (Perhaps this was a function Jim Cretecos had performed on the first two records, which at least were completed in short order.) Because Springsteen thought of a "producer" as someone who would separate him from control of his own music, he was hostile to the idea. But CBS never quite gave up on it. As a record company spokesman put it early in 1975: "It's true that his recordings have been rather poor. But I have yet to meet anyone who knows more about what he's after than Springsteen does. He's really fascinated by the studio, and he has a great ear. The problem is that he's not interested in documenting what he's learned. He does not cater to marketing."

In June 1974, Jon Landau entered the hospital for an operation that would cure his stomach trouble; he spent four weeks flat on his back in a hospital bed, and could barely get around for another month or two. When Bruce and Mike saw him at Springsteen's October 29 show at the Boston Music Hall, Landau had lost so much weight they hardly recognized him. Bruce again let Jon know how much he appreciated the *Real Paper* column, and reiterated his difficulties with CBS about record production.

They didn't see one another again until late November. By then, Landau was fully recovered from the operation and in the midst of a divorce. As a result, Jon was moving to New York, where he and Bruce spent an afternoon going through records and evaluating their production, talking generally, and ending up at the movies, where they ran into Jim Cretecos. A couple of weeks later, Bruce phoned Jon, and they met again. This time, Bruce played him a demo of "Jungleland" and asked what Landau thought of the production. Jon suggested they compare it to the second album. When they did, it was clear that little, if any, progress had been made.

For Landau, this was a time of decision. He was sufficiently re-covered to think about record production again, but he was leaning toward working in a record company for a while to get some more experience. Producing Springsteen was at the back of his mind, per-haps, but Landau considered that possibility only with caution. Be-sides, he still had some obligations to *Rolling Stone*, which had kept him on salary during his convalesence.

There were other considerations, too. Landau's last rock band pro-duction, of the MC5, had been controversial; a later attempt at producing his friends, the J. Geils Band, had not worked out. While the more folk-oriented Livingston Taylor productions had both sold better and sounded more professional, Springsteen would mean tak-ing a third shot at rock and roll. If the record was bad, Landau's reputation would suffer—though after the *Real Paper* column, that was true no matter who produced. As Landau moved back to the city where he'd grown up, his mind seemed settled. He would work in the record business and he would someday produce more records, but at the moment, Bruce Springsteen was too hot to handle.

Still, Jon and Bruce formed a natural friendship. If Bruce found himself stranded in Manhattan, after the last bus back to New Jersey, he would call Landau and stay at his Eighty-fourth Street apartment, where they would stay up all night, talking about a hundred things, but most of all about the difficulty of getting a record out. During this period, Landau heard demo versions of "Backstreets," "Born To Run" and "Jungleland." Later, Paul Nelson, writing in *The Village Voice*, caught the essence of their relationship: "If Landau was somewhat in awe of the kind of instinctual genius who could resolve esthetic problems by compounding them, Bruce had no less respect for someone who invariably got to ten by counting out nine individual numbers, one at a time. It was the ideal artistic marriage of creative madness and controlling method."

In February, Springsteen invited Landau to visit one of the sessions at 914 Studios. It was a frustrating night. Playing the same song over and over again is part of the studio process, but Bruce didn't seem to be making any progress. Drawing Jon aside, Springsteen asked him what he thought. Landau suggested that the essential problem was in the rhythm section, which fit with Springsteen's own thinking.

A month or so later, Springsteen and Appel invited Landau to stop by a late-night mixing session at the CBS Studios on Fifty-second Street. By the time Landau arrived at two A.M. there was no hope left of accomplishing much that night. The aim had been to put together a version of "Born To Run" suitable for single release, but the chemistry just wasn't right. After the session broke up, Bruce asked Jon if he could stay at the Eighty-fourth Street apartment. They stopped off for a bite to eat, and it was then that Bruce first suggested that he would like Landau to work on the album. Despite his qualms, Jon was interested. A meeting with Appel to work out the business details was arranged. But Jon and Mike couldn't come to terms.

A few weeks later, Bruce invited Landau to come down to New Jersey for a band rehearsal. Landau agreed, spending the night on a ratty old couch which, Springsteen told him the next day, had been rescued from a neighbor's trash. It was indicative of the group's $100-a-week living conditions.

When they arrived at the rehearsal hall, Landau was surprised to find that Springsteen expected him to participate as more than a friend. Bruce expected Jon to give suggestions, and even some orders. The song was "Thunder Road," and the problem was a sax break in the middle of the song that disrupted the flow of the tune. Jon suggested moving the solo to the end, which worked beautifully. He also tinkered a bit with the rest of the arrangement, cutting the rendition from more than seven minutes to about four. Both Bruce and the group were impressed; the next day, at Springsteen's insistence, Landau was hired as the album's co-producer with Bruce and Mike.

Mike Appel must have been perplexed that Bruce had chosen this upstart rock critic to assist them—after all, Landau's other rock records had been flops—but he went along. Not that anyone has much choice when Springsteen sets his mind to something. Still, the album was not yet set, primarily because the songs were not yet written. Also, 914 Studios was technically not as good for the kind of record Springsteen wanted to make as some Manhattan facilities. After only one session with Landau at the Westchester studio, the project was moved to the Record Plant, near Times Square, a studio favored by hard rockers like Aerosmith and John Lennon. They also signed on a young engineer named Jimmy Iovine, from Red Hook, Brooklyn, whose previous work had been done principally with Lennon, on the Harry Nilsson *Pussycats* album and with Lennon and Phil Spector, on John's *Rock and Roll* oldies set.

Publicly Springsteen was still confident. "I just don't work on a schedule," he would say. "If I'm gonna do this, it's gonna be fun." But the strain did begin to show; Paul Williams recounted one instance in his 1975 *Gallery* piece on Springsteen.

"At a recent concert, he mentioned between songs that his former piano player, David Sancious, would have an album coming out soon. A voice from the audience shouted: 'What about you?' Bruce paused for just a moment. 'Me? I'm not putting out records any more. I'm just . . . ' He paused again, aware that his joke could turn into a putdown. 'No, y'know, pretty soon. . . . I don't know, it sorta tells me. It's like . . . ' And the band began the next song."

"The album became a monster," Springsteen remembered later. "It wanted everything. It just ate up everyone's life."

Of the songs Springsteen had written—"Born To Run," "She's

the One," "Thunder Road" and "Jungleland"—none were short enough to qualify as hit singles. Both "Born To Run" and "Thunder Road" were immediately memorable, but neither was less than four minutes long. "Jungleland" was a ten minute narrative, and it was impossible to shorten it. "She's the One" could have been adapted but Bruce wasn't even sure he wanted to include the song on the album. If one of those songs had been a possible single, it could have been released immediately to slake the appetites of fans and the record machinery. But Springsteen just didn't feel that he had a single to give them.

Various attempts were made to edit "Born To Run," which had not been recorded terribly well—the tempo falls apart near the end—but which had the inexpressible quality of magic that is the hallmark of great rock. The record company had a staff engineer make a few passes at an edit; Springsteen literally laughed at the results. "Born To Run" is a pure creation of the studio, an incredible hodge-podge of effects. If any part is eliminated, the rest of the song becomes a jumble.

The addition of Landau to the production team was the first encouraging sign in weeks. Bruce would finish a few live dates booked for April, then do nothing but work on the record. Certainly, there was no reason it couldn't be finished in a month or two. The album would surely be out by July.

It was going to be an educational summer.

Landau's greatest contributions to the project were, first, a firm commitment to the concept of a hard rock LP, and second, professionalizing the recording process. The symbol of the latter was the Record Plant. There were no long delays for mechanical failure here, and Iovine, trained by Record Plant boss Roy Cicala and further educated by Lennon and Spector, knew exactly how to get the block sound—without needless instrumental separation—they needed. Iovine's engineering and the more up-to-date standards of the studio contributed to the closest approximation yet of Bruce's live sound on vinyl.

Landau also encouraged Springsteen to go for a focused rock sound, which would concentrate on just those elements the first two albums had underplayed. The original idea, spawned by the track of "Born To Run," was to do a group of guitar-based songs. But for some reason, Springsteen wasn't comfortable playing guitar in the studio, or with experimenting with the instrument as he had done in Steel Mill. He found the requirement of playing the same figure identically on each take too restrictive. In the end, the mass of guitars on "Born To Run" made the album *seem* guitar dominated, although in fact the most important instruments are Roy Bittan's piano and Clarence Clemon's saxophone. As Bruce puts it: "We decided to make a guitar album, but then I wrote all the songs on piano."

In any event, people expected a rock album. But the decision to do one also gave the record a cohesive organizing principle. And someone had finally made decisions in an organization riddled with an inability to decide anything. "The indecision came from fear," Landau later said. "If you do one thing, that means you can't do another. Bruce wants it all; he always wants it all."

By his own admission, Springsteen was simply trapped in the forest of his own ambition. "It was the weirdest thing I have ever seen. We did attempt to work on it earlier. We did 'Born To Run' a year ago. And over that period, we did attempt to start the record many times. But we'd always get bogged down. Things broke. Sessions didn't work.

"The main factor that changed things around, I guess, was Jon Landau. He was an interested party. He said, 'Listen, man, you gotta make an album.' Like he said, I wasn't doing right by myself putting the album off as long as I did. He sorta impressed on me this fact. Whenever we talked, he'd have something important to tell me. It became obvious that I needed somebody with an outside perspective.

"But it wasn't like he came in and said, 'Don't do it your way; do it my way.' When Jon came in, he just said, 'Do it your way. But *do it!*' " The problem was that Bruce wasn't certain what his way was.

There was another psychological advantage to stalling. The third album was make-it-or-break-it time; the world was waiting. The longer Springsteen could delay, the longer he could put off his day of reckoning. As he said at the time, "Here comes the third album, and I guess everybody's excited about it. My time has come, but I'm not going to count on it. I don't count on nothing. I stopped doing that a long time ago. Anything that happens now is icing on the cake."

There was no problem recording basic tracks for the songs already written—"Jungleland," "She's the One" and "Thunder Road" were swiftly laid out. It was decided that "Born To Run" was not to be tampered with, since fiddling with the song only confused it. The remaining difficulties were twofold: finishing the writing and adding overdubs that would flesh out the songs. The vocals weren't difficult to get down—that was mostly a matter of concentration. But, for the first time, the other songs only trickled from Bruce's pen. And it took the band some time to learn them, which could only be done after Springsteen was sure he knew what arrangement he wanted to use, which often took days.

Prodded by Landau, Springsteen agonized over the arrangements. It was mostly a choice of what to leave out. Unlike Phil Spector, Springsteen could not use all the instruments of his dreams in his songs. Sometimes, there were minor battles, but everyone worked with the knowledge that, in Landau's words, "Bruce works instinctively. He is incredibly intense and concentrates deeply. Underneath his shyness is the strongest will I've ever encountered. If there's something he doesn't want to do, he won't." And he took his time making up his mind, too. The work was intensive, from three P.M. to six A.M., and often longer, every day. Pressure couldn't speed things up; only constant, gentle prodding spurred Springsteen on. At anything else, he balked.

Almost any other artist would have tried to rush. Bruce would not. As he brought in new songs, he would sit and rework the lyrics with assiduous attention to detail, sometimes calling on Landau's editorial experience. The wordiness of the previous record was curbed; every image was streamlined, and as a result, each one packed more punch.

But whatever advice he may have taken from his co-producers, as Landau says, "Bruce made every important artistic decision on the LP. The biggest thing I learned from him was the ability to concentrate on the big picture. 'Hey, wait a minute,' he'd say, 'the release date is just one day. The record is forever.' "

Occasionally, they all must have felt condemned to a lifetime in the Record Plant, endlessly waiting to complete just a little bit more.

Unlike most delayed sessions, the production problems with *Born To Run* weren't a matter of trying to get things musically correct or of searching for the right song. The task was lengthy and arduous because Springsteen had unleashed his drive for perfection; every note and nuance had to be perfect, exactly what he intended, with no possibilities overlooked.

Occasionally, all that kept voices down and fists unclenched were long walks around the seedy block in the middle of the night. By August, neither Bruce nor Landau nor Appel had any vestige of a tan; their skins were ivory white, like rock and roll ghosts. Outsiders didn't notice that. Around the Record Plant, the word from the start was that an extraordinary album was being created. Everybody who dropped by the studio inquired about its progress or tried (usually with no luck) to hear some of it.

Robert Duncan published Bruce's ghoulish version of the experience in *Creem* magazine that winter:

"Let me tell ya, I had this *horrible* pressure in the studio, and for the whole last part of the record, I was livin' in this certain inn in New York over on the West Side. And the room there had this crooked mirror . . . and every night when I'd come home, that mirror was *crooked* again. Every time. That crooked mirror . . . it just couldn't stay straight.

"So I'm in there with this crooked mirror, and after about a week, the room started to look like Nagasaki. . . ." He pauses suspended in a gesture that indicates the room, and begins again. "Junk all over the place. So every day I'd go in the studio and that was *that*— every day was *supposed* to be the last, it stretched out for weeks— and then I'd come home and there'd be this crooked mirror.

"One night," he says, getting serious once more, "toward the end of the record, I was sittin' there at the piano tryin' to get down the last cut, 'She's the One,' and Landau's in the booth, and we've been at it for hours and hours. I just lean my head down on the piano. It just won't come. And everybody's tryin' to tell me how to do it— they were all there to help me and they were really tryin'—and Landau's sayin' this and that and freakin' out . . . and, all of a sudden, everybody looks around and Landau has just disappeared, just walked off into the night—night, it was like *six* A.M.—couldn't take it.

"He was smart to go home and get some sleep. The whole thing was like that. And when I got home around ten in the morning, to the room with the crooked mirror, my girl friend, she says to me— she says it every night when I come home—'Is it finished?'

"And I say, 'No.' I could've cried. I almost cried. Well, maybe I did cry a little." (Springsteen himself became so exhausted that he dozed off during the mix of "Thunder Road," with the result that the sax part which he intended to use only on the final chorus was left in the entire song.)

When the horn parts for "Tenth Avenue Freeze-Out" had to be added, Bruce realized that he wanted some saxes and trumpets to accompany Clarence Clemons's sax. But nobody seemed able to articulate what was needed. Bruce and Roy Bittan wrote some charts that sounded like Chicago, which was far from what they had in mind. "There was no direction. Everybody was waiting for Bruce. The date's falling apart and all these expensive guys [the Brecker Brothers] are out there," Landau remembers. "Then I notice this guy, Miami Steve, standing around."

Landau had met Van Zandt in Asbury Park the previous winter, when Steve was playing guitar in the Asbury Jukes with Southside Johnny Lyon—a group that featured precisely the Stax soul music that the "Tenth Avenue" horn part was supposed to evoke. Springsteen pointed to Van Zandt, and Steve moved to the door separating the control room from the musicians. "Okay, Steve, this is the big time," said Landau.

Van Zandt looked about nervously. Like many another natural-born rock and roller, he does not cut a commanding figure—sort of a cross between the anarchic Keith Moon and the irrepressible Keith Richard. But when he entered the studio and confronted the superstar sessionmen, he became cocky. Putting his straw hat firmly on his head, he marched up to the Brecker Brothers and said to the most experienced studio horn players in Manhattan, "Okay, boys, put those charts away." In the control room, eyes were popping. Everyone knew Steve, but no one knew whether he could pull this off. That is, not until he *sang* each horn player his part, with the lines, the timing and the inflection all perfect. The sessionmen obediently played their parts, and the horns were recorded. When they'd finished, Springsteen turned to Mike Appel, "Okay," he said.

"It's time to put the boy on the payroll. I've been meaning to tell you—he's the new guitar player." From that night, Miami Steve has been a fixture in the E Street Band.

Bruce made precisely one commercial concession. "Every letter I got about the second album—and I got a bunch—asked why the lyrics weren't printed on the sleeve. I'll be glad to give 'em that," he said.

Fittingly, the recording itself went right down to the wire. As Springsteen finished the final vocals, he, Landau and Iovine mixed them in another room, supervised band rehearsals for the forthcoming tour in a third room, and made certain that the lyrics were accurately transcribed. In fact, Bruce did a few shows during the mastering period, afterward flying or driving back to Manhattan to work on the album. Finally, just before a gig at the Carter Baron Theatre in Washington, D.C., that would take Bruce out of town for the best part of a week, every detail was complete. Sort of.

Mixing is a major part of record-making that involves placing all the sonic elements in their proper relationship, since too much of this guitar or that backing vocal and the record doesn't sound as good. But even the best mix can be spoiled by an inferior master. Mastering involves translating the tape mix accurately to the metal parts from which the records are actually pressed. It is precision work that only a few people do well. Bruce rejected almost a dozen *Born To Run* masters. "Once, down in Virginia," he remembered, "Jimmy sent down a master and I had to go to a local hi-fi store and ask the guy to let me play it. It was defective and the guy musta thought we were nuts." Another master was so bad that Bruce flung it out of his hotel room window and into a river.

Iovine now acknowledges that Bruce was right about the first few masters, but, he claims, Springsteen was "nuts" about the last one. In Washington, where Bruce got the master, the only available record player was an $89.95 cheapie portable, and that's what he and the band heard it on. Low fidelity was the word, and Bruce decided he hated the whole damn thing. He was going to scrap half of it, he told Appel, and substitute live recordings from upcoming dates at the Bottom Line in New York.

Landau got the word in San Francisco, where he had gone on vacation. Landau is usually reserved, but this time he lost his cool.

No one knows exactly what he said, but he has reported the gist of what he told Bruce on the phone that night. "Look," he told him, *"you're* not supposed to like it. You think Chuck Berry sits around listening to 'Maybellene'? And when he does hear it, don't you think that he wishes a few things could be changed? Now c'mon, it's time to put the record out." It was an argument Springsteen could understand, and he accepted it. So it was over. The "monster" was tamed at last. Springsteen could now answer the question, "Where's the album?" with, "It'll be out in two weeks."

11 THUNDER ROAD

*B*orn To Run was an instant classic. Anyone who loves rock and roll must respond to its catalogue of styles, the rough and tough music, the lyrics that sum up the brightest hopes—and some of the darkest aspects—of the rock and roll dream. The album may have been a monster in the making, but it was also, as Greil Marcus has said, "like a '57 Chevy running on melted-down Crystals records. And it shuts down every claim that has been made for him."

Born To Run makes no stylistic breakthroughs, as the fundamental Elvis Presley and Beatles recordings had done. But it does represent the culmination of twenty years of rock and roll, and when it was released in October 1975 it was the strongest possible testimony to the continued vitality of that tradition. Springsteen had synthesized his music largely from secondary sources. Rather than delving directly into blues or gospel or even early rock, he went for what he recalled of the forgotten, sometimes junky hit singles he and his friends had loved when they were kids.

There is something about a one-shot hitmaker, like Little Eva, or an underrated one, like Roy Orbison, that is more fascinating than the big league musicians who have been prominent for years. Springsteen's record recalled, and in a sense redeemed, this important part of rock and roll. Part of the appeal of these brief successes is what they tell the fans about themselves, people who love the music as a secret world not easily discovered, and whose place in the music is confirmed through a memory that is more than nostalgic.

Another part of the magic of one-shot hits lies in what they tell about the transience of success and failure. Rock and roll, in this sense, typifies the American dream: The star on the wane, like the one-shot hit, reminds us that everyone has a shot at the top. And *Born To Run* takes us out there among those whose shot has arced off into the distance, beyond the possibility of recovery. It is a record that explores the horizon and examines people whose horizons are closing in. "My early albums were about being someplace and what it was like there," says Bruce. "*Born To Run* is about being nowhere at all."

But Nowhere is not Anywhere. *Born To Run* is as locked into an America of screen doors, fast cars and casual violence as the Beatles' "Penny Lane" is locked into the English everyday. To miss the point is to miss the reason why Bruce Springsteen is such a powerful influence on his fans. As the American Incarnate, he has become the first American hard rock hero since . . . well, I'll argue, since Elvis himself.

With one exception, the figures who unified the Sixties rock scene were British. And that exception, Bob Dylan, lacked a commitment to rock as music; his rock period was, in fact, brief—lasting only from *Bringing It All Back Home* (1965) through *Blonde On Blonde* (1966) and *The Basement Tapes* (recorded 1967, released 1977). Before and after, Dylan played music that could be identified as rock only through its association with a similar audience.

In fact, none of the American groups of the Sixties had the sort of commitment to rock and roll as a form that The Who, the Rolling Stones and (at their best) the Beatles brought to it. The Beach Boys diddled with dandified, if complex, pop forms after 1966. The folk rock bands—the Lovin' Spoonful, the Byrds, Buffalo Springfield— were too concerned with their own cool. So were the acid rock bands of the San Francisco sound; their LSD experimentalism may have been chic, but that sort of music never had much connection with rhythm and blues or the Elvis Presley/Buddy Holly rockabilly school. It was, instead, a melange of effects pilfered from West Coast jazz, from the cool school, from campus folk music, from country and western—from almost anything but rock and soul themselves.

In any event, none of these groups had a figure of sufficient charisma to challenge British rockers like Keith Richard, John Lennon or Pete Townshend. Only three American stars of the Sixties had the commitment and personal magnetism to challenge the English rock hegemony. Of them, the Berkeley-bred John Fogerty was dishonored in his own backyard, as a result of which he denied his natural instinct in vain attempts to make Creedence Clearwater Revival conform to the artificial aesthetic of the "album rock" groups across San Francisco Bay. Nevertheless, Fogerty's great series of CCR hits is the closest thing to rockabilly since the Fifties.

Sly Stone was an inspirational figure in his own right, but he rarely turned his considerable imagination to rock itself, preferring instead to demolish the conventions of soul music and afterward to march to his own distinctive beat. (In the Seventies, Sly's rhythm inventions would be codified and repackaged as disco music—a form which has more merit than the white rock audience is willing to grant it, but which only recently has moved beyond Sly's original concepts.)

After Presley's decline in Hollywood, the closest we came to an American rock hero was Jimi Hendrix. Not only was Hendrix black, which presented problems of perception (rock racism did not *start* with the antidisco movement) but he had to escape to England to live out his fantasy that a black man could do what Dylan and Presley had done. Hendrix was great at everything he set his hand to, but even today his immeasurable influence is underacknowledged. And in the Sixties the rock audience in America was already too far gone on its pretentious path to see Jimi for what he was: The One.

Everybody else was either a hippie or an entertainer. Left without an American rock star, the underclass rebels who formed rock and roll's natural constituency drifted away from music, toward motorcycles and petty crime. The few who stuck with the music listened more often to black music than to white sounds, which left an enormous vacuum. Bruce Springsteen was the first American rock performer in nearly a decade—since Jimi's death—to attempt to fill that space. And his emergence would create, in surprising ways, a flood of followers and would reopen issues many had thought closed. If the meaning of "punk" has changed drastically since 1975, *Born To Run* must be counted as the record that set the stage for its re-emergence at all. It was a record that took the music's possibilities from the hands of craftsmen and profiteers and gave them back to the sort of people who loved rock because they lived it.

But *Born To Run* is much more than a resurrection of the proto-punk esthetic. It is also the story of where such people had been since the rocker became an *artiste*: truly Nowhere. *Born To Run* is a record for everyone who grew up during the heyday of Woodstock and peace and love and couldn't embrace such foppish trappings. Everyone in America with a chip on his shoulder can accept these stories. In fact, the little stories add up to one big story, one that simply follows a boy and his girl friend through a long, tragicomic day, a bit like *American Graffiti* without the saccharine. In some ways, though, it is more like *Mean Street*: There is a sense that every life we encounter has a half-realized potential not just for violence but for catastrophe.

This time, Springsteen's concept was deliberate. At one point, it was jokingly suggested that the album's opening song, "Thunder Road," might begin with a clock radio clicking on and blaring Orbison's "Only the Lonely." In fact, Bruce wrote the song in a morning mood, adding a reference to the Orbison song in the fifth line.

The record moves through a series of encounters, some of which are flashbacks—"Tenth Avenue Freeze-Out," "Night," "She's the One"—but all of which are harrowingly current in their emotions. "Backstreets" ends Side One evoking the heat of the afternoon; "Born To Run" begins the second side with the early evening mist. By the time "Jungleland" is over, we have reached dawn of the next day. Much has happened, here in Nowhere, but nothing is finished. There is the feeling that these characters may be condemned to repeat such days forever.

"Thunder Road" is a statement of purpose; in its way, it encapsulates the whole story of the album. It celebrates the virtues of day-to-day living and loving, while articulating the hero's deepest fears:

So you're scared and you're thinkin'
That maybe we ain't that young anymore
Show a little faith! There's magic in the night
You ain't a beauty but hey, you're all right
And that's all right with me

This is not a story of salvation or heroism (searching for such imponderables is declared a "waste"), yet there's always a chance if the girl (here Mary, though she has other names) will only believe as deeply as the singer: "Roll down your window and let the wind blow back your hair/The night's bustin' open/These two lanes will take us anywhere."

Cars and guitars are not a panacea, of course—but they may be a way of escaping these cruel streets, of leaving the poverty and desperation of the empty lives around them. The singer has both car and guitar, and he's splitting; it's up to Mary (and to every listener) to take a chance with him, or to risk being trapped. To call this temptation isn't fair—anyone half-alive has to take the chance; this romantic ambition is too seductive to ignore. Plus, we know these characters—from time to time, we may have been them—and we have to find out what's coming next. The past is a gang of departed lovers:

They haunt this dusty beach road
In the skeleton frames of burned-out Chevrolets
They scream your name at night in the street
Your graduation gown lies in rags at their feet
And in the lonely cool before dawn,
You hear their engines roaring on
But when you get to the porch, they're gone
On the wind—so, Mary, climb in
It's a town fulla losers
And I'm pullin' outta here to win!

It is such a brave boast that the fact that they're going to drive in circles doesn't really matter—at the moment. Later, it might be the only thing that counts.

"Backstreets" and "Born To Run" are alternate consequences of running away. (Perhaps "running away" is a bit extreme; as Pete Townshend has said, rock will not let you run away from your problems—but it will let you dance all over them.) Neither of the songs' locations is geographically far removed from the other, but physically the distance is extreme. Taken separately, they are impressive. Taken together, these two numbers alone would be enough to make Springsteen's reputation as one of the great rock writers, singers and musicians.

Musically, the songs are opposites. Both are bursting with ideas, riffs, images, throwaway lines that burn into the memory. But "Born To Run" is driven, possessed (the man with the hellhound on his trail once again), propelled by the mighty roar of God-knows-how-many Fender guitars slamming into the same riff, racing to a climax on a dead-end street. "Backstreets," on the other hand, owes more to the stately, fuguelike music of the electric Dylan. It is led along by organ and piano interplay, the guitar understated and used to punctuate the phrases mathematically (as Dylan described Robbie Robertson's playing). Both songs are reaching for an orchestral effect, and largely achieve it, though there's nothing remotely European about them. Springsteen sings "Born To Run" flat out, as though his life depends on getting through a tight corner at maximum speed. He sings "Backstreets" with true grief, so mournful that he seems ready to swallow the whole world for solace.

In "Born To Run," Wendy and the singer are racing down a cruising strip right out of real life, the endless highway, lined on either side by drive-in restaurants, movie theaters and amusement arcades, the kind of street that seems to run through every town with more than a handful of teen-agers. Springsteen has temporarily slipped away from Jersey—there are a minimum of references to the Shore, nothing so explicit as in "Sandy," which is really the same story at a more conservative speed. This place may be Nowhere but it is now a Universal Nowhere.

There's something furious about the song's celebration of life; there's a sense of what price a man must pay to attain such peak experiences in this world. Even here Springsteen hasn't completely escaped the world of small town New Jersey—in fact, he doesn't seem to want to. Perhaps it's symbolic that Springsteen the man still chooses to reside there. As Jay Gatsby discovered (and as Magic Rat will learn in a few moments) there is no way out:

In the day we sweat it out on the streets of a runaway
    American dream
At night we ride through mansions of glory in suicide
    machines . . .
Baby this town rips the bones from your back
It's a death trap, a suicide rap
We gotta get out while we're young
'Cause tramps like us, baby, we were born to run

"Born To Run" is a snapshot of this endlessly circled paradise, girls primping their hair, boys trying on hard faces. It is impossible to hear it without some apprehension—what might happen is anyone's guess: The place can explode at any second. In its way, "Born To Run," as lively a piece of music as anyone has ever made, is a song about death; consider the title's allusion to the old punk tattoo, "Born To Lose." It is a message of hope, but also a message of doom. Like the ghost-lovers of "Thunder Road," the heroes of "Born To Run" are condemned to roam the strip forever, seeking what cannot be found.

In "Backstreets," Springsteen's roving punk loses everything to love. In the midst of all this fantasy, the song serves as a blast of icy reality—a paranoid's reality, maybe, but real enough. "Backstreets" is a song in which innocence is not so much lost as discarded. But it is also a song about how even rebels try to hold onto their illusions. Its opening lines are ominous:

One soft, infested summer
Me and Terry became friends
Tryin' in vain to breathe the fire
We was born in

Those words come as close to poetry as any lyrics in rock but they have much more to offer than verbal felicity. "Backstreets" establishes a situation in which a man and a woman are not just lovers, but best friends; in which the lover's loss is not mourned because she is an idealized angel, but because it robs the singer of a special companion who shares what seemingly cannot be shared. In a medium that has been noted for its unyielding dominance by males, and for its callous attitude toward women, "Backstreets" is a landmark. Terry is neither Bob Dylan's goddess/angel "Isis," nor the "Stupid Girl" of Mick Jagger's and Neil Young's fantasies. If she seems a dream, that's only because she is an equal—something people rarely are in life.

But Terry leaves the singer, and he is crushed, bellowing his hurt and disbelief throughout the song. Without her, he may have to grow up—in the worst sense of that term—exchanging his dreams and hopes for "maturity," or whatever it is that society calls a life without prospects.

It would be a mistake to consider Springsteen the protagonist of these songs. The emotions are real, but the actions aren't his. The characters are idealized and universalized, and their function is to symbolize and develop the themes of the songs. In a sense, Springsteen is all of the men and most of the women on this album; but in that same sense, so is any listener.

This is never more clear than in "Jungleland," the mini-opera that ends *Born To Run*. Springsteen is no more Magic Rat in this song than director Martin Scorsese is one of the crazy aspiring hoods in *Mean Streets*. But, like Scorsese's, Springsteen's remove is not the detachment of the exploiter; rather, he keeps his distance in order to maintain artistic perspective. And his ability to create dramatic situations and arresting characters is unparalleled in contemporary popular music. The links between his characters are by now patent—Magic Rat *is* Spanish Johnny, and Bruce has suggested that "Jungleland" might be what happened to Johnny after he left Puerto Rican Jane's bed and went into the night at the conclusion of "Incident on 57th Street."

In the two most menacing songs on the album, Springsteen's characters find their fate. The stranger of the two—and the shorter—is "Meeting Across the River," a terse, moody vignette that parallels the small-town hustlers of "Born To Run" to the big city hoods of the second album. "Meeting Across the River" is unlike anything Springsteen had previously done—brief, spare, nonrock: The arrangement features Bruce's voice set against piano and trumpets, only. Originally called "The Heist," it depicts two small-time hoods getting ready for the big score, preparing to meet the kind of guys who "don't dance." Although "Meeting" is striking on its own terms, on the album it serves primarily as an introduction to "Jungleland" shifting the mood of the record from exuberance to exhaustion.

"Jungleland" opens with a sweet violin passage that gives way to a tinkling piano. As Magic Rat pulls into town and picks up his girl, there's no sense that anything but another romantic interlude is taking place. But that mood is suddenly shattered as the Rat and the girl move across a twisted landscape, pursued for unknown reasons by Maximum Lawmen. Although their crime is unstated, the fact that, this time, the escapees are pursued for real casts a new light on the hope that was held out in the early songs. In the second verse, the guitars explode and the drums crash in:

From the churches to the jails
Tonight all is silence in the world
As we take our stand
Down . . . in . . . Jungleland.

From this point, the song takes on a furious pace and tone. Even the rock and roll bands, which represent the route out of the town full of losers, are transformed into street-fighting gangs. An Exxon sign looms on the horizon like Moby Dick. The faces have hardened: The characters have become a battalion rather than a bunch of hot-rod innocents. This moment is Springsteen's way of saying, "You can be my partner in crime."

The scene moves to a wild dance party, then changes again, via a smoky sax solo, to a funky bedroom where lovers wrestle but love can't win. Outside the window, Rat, the potential hero, is smashed to the pavement. Uncaring, the girl inside reaches for the light. As it goes out, Springsteen sings, "Outside the street's on fire/In a real death waltz," and the music smashes in for the kill, threatening, lethal, expressive of all the destructive potential of these mean streets.

And the poets down here
Don't write nothin' at all
They just stand back and let it all be
And in the quick of the night
They reach for their moment
And try to make an honest stand
But they wind up wounded,
Not even dead
Tonight in Jungleland

Springsteen's voice takes over, soaring above strings and sax, flat-out wailing. Anyone who ever says he isn't a great vocalist—this isn't exactly singing—is going to have to reckon with this moment, when Bruce simply lets the pure anger, frustration, pain and glory of rock and roll ooze out of him.

Magic Rat isn't dead, though. There's hope. It is not clear how much more Rat (or we) could stand—but the idea remains that we have seen only the beginning of his story, even now.

Next time, the world will wait to hear it.

12 "HYPE"

I n Philadelphia, Washington, D.C., and Boston, *Born To Run* sold more in advance than any other album in history. In D.C., orders tripled those for Elton John's current record. *Born To Run* made *Record World*'s Top Ten its first week out (something only Led Zeppelin and Elton John had done previously), selling well even in a few areas where Springsteen had not often performed. The demand was so heavy, in fact, that FM airplay was saturated with Springsteen for more than two weeks, with nearly every station in the country reporting that they had programmed it.

In Philly, the Top Forty AM station, WFIL, was so impressed by phone requests and retail sales that it began playing "Born To Run" without waiting for Columbia officially to release a single. For its part, the record company wasted no time in naming "Born To Run" as the single from the album, and, despite its four-and-one-half-minute length, the song began a steady march up the charts. The album lingered in the national Top Ten.

Springsteen began his first national tour ever, playing forty dates from coast to coast. Reaction to the shows everywhere was incredible; the Bottom Line dates had especially helped to spread the word, because CBS had specially flown in a number of non-New York press and radio figures. And where Springsteen played, he sold records. *Born To Run* quickly went gold, and it was clear that the album would reach the platinum level in a matter of a few months.

Born To Run also received an extraordinary display of press attention. *Rolling Stone* ran a feature, a long record review and a review of the live show. John Rockwell, pop critic for *The New York Times*, wrote a lengthy piece on the Bottom Line gig. Nearly every daily, college newspaper and life-style weekly in the country devoted some space to the Springsteen album, tour, phenomenon.

Moreover, nearly every album review was an outburst of praise, and, if anything, the live reviews were even more glowing. The demand for interview time became so great that Mike Appel granted access only to those publications that agreed to feature Springsteen on their front cover. An exception was made for *Playboy*, but Appel counseled the sex magazine that if it was serious, as it claimed, about changing its image, putting rock's "next big sex symbol" on the cover would be to its advantage.

It's important to understand, though, that the press could not have made Springsteen's record a hit. In the end, reviews have little to do with record sales, except that they encourage people to check out the show. It was the live appearances, in conjunction with radio play, that accounted for the tremendous sales of *Born To Run*.

Still, the press had played a very important role for Springsteen, nurturing his talent when everyone else seemed to have given up. And even more importantly, it provided a more sympathetic (if not necessarily more accurate) image for Bruce than the one that the record company was able to give him. After all, it is Springsteen's identity that assures him, not of hits, but of a career. "Born To Run" might have established him in any case, or it might have simply become a lost one-shot for the next inspired outsider to draw upon. But Springsteen created a remarkably strong image on stage, and it was the press—more than, and long before, radio—that exposed that image to the rock audience. Bruce's mug, staring out from all those review illustrations, was easily the most distinctive that rock had produced in years; Springsteen with one Top Thirty hit became more indentifiable than faceless groups like Chicago, the Doobie Brothers and the Guess Who, who had had whole strings of Top Ten songs.

The press explosion was in fact a groundswell. Nonetheless, the massive press coverage Springsteen received, and its overwhelmingly favorable tone, led those who knew little or nothing about rock (which includes most of the straight media, and even a great many on the staff of such "rock journals" as *Rolling Stone*) to conclude that it was all a gigantic hype. *Rolling Stone*, although it had an inside story, did not put Springsteen on its cover in 1975, because of its San Francisco bias and oversensitivity to Jon Landau's involvement. Instead, it ran a twenty-five hundred word profile by John Rockwell.

Admittedly, CBS spent a great deal of money promoting *Born To Run*: Initial expenditures probably totalled around $250,000 for advertising, concert tickets and related expenses. But CBS spent more time merely trying to keep pace with the press demand for interviews and concert seats than it did trying to engineer favorable comments. Indeed, since the departure of Ron Oberman to the West Coast marketing department, the New York publicity staff—with the notable exception of Glen Brunman, who was theoretically responsible only for liaison with "out-of-town" papers—had not been exceptionally enthusiastic in its support of Springsteen. Brunman became known as the key man in getting access to Bruce, but he was hardly well enough known among most writers to have pulled off the supposed publicity coup single-handed. Glen wound up with two grocery boxes full of *Born To Run* clippings, but it was all he could do to gather them in and make certain that those who were supposed to see the show did.

As Brunman points out, the regional reviews—outside the East Coast media centers—were at least as important to Springsteen's 1975 success as were the big city reviews. In fact, the sheer quantity of clippings was a factor in *Newsweek*'s final decision to run their "Making of a Rock Star" cover story. But Brunman acknowledges that he talked Bruce up from a "go-see-for-yourself" angle, which is a long way from a hard sell. "Everything I said was designed to push people to see him," says Brunman. "But only because I knew he could back it up. Which he did."

The fact is that the press was presold on Springsteen. Jon Landau's influence had something to do with this, as did that of several other prestigious New York writers, including John Rockwell, Paul Nelson, Robert Christgau, and myself, a group that Christgau later dubbed the Rock Critic Establishment. And, as Christgau has recognized, Springsteen was made to order for that Establishment, who believed, in Christgau's words, that "the early 60's were a rich if somewhat silly period that nurtured both the soul style . . . and a wealth of not-so-ephemeral pop rock and roll, consummated in the enlightened hedonism of the Beach Boys and the great production machines of Motown and Phil Spector. This is Springsteen's era—he may talk Berry and Presley, but his encore is Gary 'U.S.' Bonds. I sometimes wonder whether half of Springsteen's [critical] fans aren't delighted by his music because they weren't lucky enough to have been glued to their radios in 1963; clearly, the other half are delighted to experience the most unequivocal pleasure of their adolescence all over again . . . The stock explanation of why successful media professionals identify so intensely with an idealized youth rebel like Springsteen is that they want to preserve their own youth, but this is stupid. Say rather that they want to preserve their rebellion."

The most significant articles about Springsteen were written by just such professional fans. Robert Hilburn in the *Los Angeles Times*, Peter Knobler at *Crawdaddy*, Paul Nelson in the *Voice* itself—not to mention Landau—wrote pieces closer to critical essays than objective reportage. In terms of the media brouhaha to follow, this was not terribly significant. As Christgau pointed out, "The first tenet of newsroom cynicism . . . is that hard news 'digging' is a more blessed endeavor than feature writing, of which reviewing is the lowliest example." It was not the reviews in the rock papers, or even the daily paper critiques, that landed Springsteen on the covers of *Time* and *Newsweek* simultaneously.

Rockwell's piece in the daily *Times* on the phenomenon of *Born To Run* piqued the interest of Henry Edwards, rock critic without portfolio (or interest, or much expertise) for the Sunday *New York Times* Arts & Leisure section. He wrote a piece called "If There Hadn't Been a Bruce Springsteen, Then the Critics Would Have Made Him Up," which ran in the *Times* on October 5. Written with

The Castiles. George Theiss is in the center. Bruce appears at the far right, in fashionable boots. Photo: Tex Vinyard collection

The Castiles. George Theiss stands in the center. Bruce is second from the right. Photo: Tex Vinyard

Photo: Phil A. Ceccola

The E Street Band in 1973. Left to right: Garry Tallent, David Sancious, Vini Lopez, Bruce, Danny Federici, Clarence Clemons. Photo: David Gahr

Photo: Phil A. Ceccola

In Long Branch, New Jersey. Photo: David Gahr

At the piano. Photo: Phil A. Ceccola

Bruce meets the press: Lester Bangs gives his sign of approval. Photo: Chuck Pulin

At his first-ever show in Memphis, in 1976, Bruce visits backstage with Eddie Floyd, the soul singer who sang "Knock on Wood" with him that night. Photo: Belinda Taylor

Clarence, Bruce, and Miami Steve on stage. Photo: Richard Aaron

So I said, "A SAXophone!?!?" Photo: Phil A. Ceccola

At the Asbury Park Casino, 1974. Photo: Peter Jay Philbin

Born to Run. Photo: CBS/Eric Meola

Photo: David Gahr

Photo: Chuck Pulin

Producer Miami Steve shows his approval of Ronnie Spector (sitting on case in rear), whose single "Say Goodbye to Hollywood" he produced, while the rest of the band enjoys the scene, backstage in Cleveland, 1976. Photo: David Gahr

Photo: Frank Stefanko

Photo: Michael Putland

The audience goes wild. Photo: New Haven *Journal Courier*

Bruce gets a few pointers from his mother, onstage at Madison Square Garden, 1978. (She wanted another encore.) Photo: Bob Gruen

Clarence and Bruce rock on. Photo: David Gahr

The band in a serious moment. Left to right: Clarence, Roy, Max, Miami Steve, Bruce, Danny, and Garry. Photo: Frank Stefanko

Photo: New Haven *Journal Courier*

all the felicity of phrasing embodied in its title, the piece's highlight was an attack on Springsteen for repeating the phrase "hiding on the backstreets" twenty-five times (which count, incidentally, is incorrect).

Edwards's central points were that Springsteen appealed to rock critics purely out of nostalgia and that the critics alone had made him a phenomenon. Nevertheless, the two contradictory articles in *The New York Times* were just the sort of controversy needed to generate interest among the other Establishment press organs. *Newsweek* senior editor Lynn Young had been contemplating doing a piece on the "making of a rock star," and she decided that the Springsteen "hype" was worth a cover story.

It is clear that *Newsweek* approached the story with the premise that no rock star could make it big on merit alone. Newsweeklies— not to mention the majority of American publications—are run by the sort of people who can't understand why rock continued to exist after the "scandal" of payola was exposed in 1960. The magazine had already done a brief Springsteen piece in its September 8 issue, which concluded on this ironic note: "Still the star's manager, Mike Appel, was reluctant to spring Springsteen into the full spotlight, banning interviews 'except for a cover story.' "

There was also a note of sour grapes: When *Time*'s Joan Downs had done a Springsteen piece the year before, he had talked with her.

Young determined that the magazine would do an "inside story on how the music industry creates a star." Unfortunately, she had chosen the one star that the music industry had *not* created—the one performer of the past five years who had not allowed himself to be packaged. But *Newsweek*'s real intent was to discredit Springsteen, and hopefully the rock business, for which the publication does not conceal its disdain. Maureen Orth, a glamour sniper recently returned from a European vacation, was assigned to research and write the story. Orth had occasionally written about rock performers before, although her style is about as compatible with rock as cannibalism is with missionary work.

One way or another, Jay Cocks of *Time* got wind of *Newsweek*'s plans and convinced his editors that they should not be scooped. Cocks was the magazine's film critic, but he was also a rock fan (in

1978, he would become *Time's* rock critic). He had the support of staffers Downs, James Willwerth (who had coauthored Clive Davis's book, *Clive: Inside the Music Business*) and researcher Jean Vallely. *Time,* too, decided to do the Springsteen story as a cover: Willwerth interviewed the principals, Vallely talked with some others, and Cocks did the writing.

Columbia's public relations people could hardly believe what seemed to be their good fortune. It was all they could do to keep the two ferociously competitive reporting teams separate. (According to some versions of this story, it was also all Columbia could do to get Bruce to agree to interviews for either piece.)

Time and *Newsweek* used almost identical material to write diametric stories. Orth's thesis was that Springsteen was the creation of CBS—although she never got around to explaining just how CBS had done the job, despite the "Making of a Rock Star" cover headline. According to *Newsweek,* Springsteen was an unlettered dummy, and Landau and Appel were shadowy, subcriminal figures manipulating gullible press people who in turn twisted a captious public around their typing fingers.

In *Time,* Cocks championed Springsteen, while acknowledging that the press reception might have gone a trifle overboard. His piece, which, like Orth's, appeared in the issue dated October 27, 1975, accepted the "hype" as a natural consequence of exposure to Bruce's talent. The resulting furor over the simultaneous covers was not dignified with comment by Walter Cronkite on the CBS evening news—but Cronkite seemed to be the only pundit in the country who didn't claim that the two newsweeklies were only expanding the "hype."

In its next issue, *Newsweek* felt compelled to run an "explanation" of the double-cover barrage, assuring its readers that there had been no collusion between the two magazines. To its credit, *Time* refrained from bitching about the situation in print. But some time later, editor-in-chief Henry Gruenwald was allegedly heard at a party to say that he considered the Springsteen cover the greatest embarrassment of his career.

Glenn Brunman put the newsweeklies' impact in perspective: "Before the *Time* and *Newsweek* covers, Bruce Springsteen was being compared to Dylan, to Van Morrison, to a whole bunch of people.

After the cover stories, he became someone to whom others were compared."

The rest of the print media had a field day with the double-cover sweep. Snide remarks and intimations of idiocy were the rule of the day, reflecting the national news media's antagonism toward rock and roll, or toward any other expression of non-Milquetoast culture. In truth, the *Time* and *Newsweek* stories reflected the bankruptcy of American cultural coverage more than anything else. Lacking any grasp of artistic phenomena not certified by Europeans and/or academics, such publications almost invariably play follow the leader, the leaders in this case being John Rockwell of the *Times* and Jay Cocks at *Time*, who were the only critics at any of the Establishment bastions who had any feeling for what was going on at street level.

"The covers and all the press on Bruce," said Brunman, "completed the change in the definition of hype. It used to be that hype meant exaggeration, creative lying and stretching the truth. Hype now came to mean any highly enthusiastic statement, regardless of how true it was."

The pity was that somewhere in the midst of this the music was forgotten. *Born To Run* might never have been reviewed with much real insight anyway, because Landau's quote had blown it out of proportion. But with the *Time* and *Newsweek* autohype, the fact that this record was one of the finest and most startling of the decade was lost in the ensuing controversy. Springsteen's success, and the album itself, had raised many questions about the state of rock and roll, but with the exception of Christgau's *Voice* piece and one by Langdon Winner in the *Real Paper*, almost nothing written about the man or his album touched on those issues. The editors of *Time* and *Newsweek* may have felt that they were just running a story on another popular entertainer, like the bland Elton John or the elegant, empty vocalizer and political groupie Linda Ronstadt. But Bruce Springsteen was something else: An authentic American street kid, who wasn't particularly interested in the insular concerns of media management, and whose music was so unpalatable to the pop tastes of nonrockers that it inevitably spawned a backlash.

The real irony was the amount of space the press spent pondering its own actions. The obvious parallel is the Evel Knievel story. After Knievel's abortive Snake River Canyon jump, nearly every editor that had sent along a reporter to cover the story then assigned long articles questioning whether such events were in fact newsworthy, or simply exploitative—"hype" again. It is a pathetic commentary on American journalism that such issues are not considered in advance. But, in the Springsteen case, none of the commentators (except rock critic Christgau) were able to see past their own biases clearly enough to resolve such issues.

"Ironically," adds Brunman, "a good deal of the backlash consisted of writers who initially had been outlandish in their praise of Bruce turning around several months later and attacking that praise, without admitting that they had been party to it. If anyone over-hyped Bruce Springsteen—and I don't think anyone did—it was the press." Notable among the backlash were critics Ken Emerson and Ed Ward, although Brunman says that about twenty or thirty such articles were written by the next spring in papers around the country.

Of course, the stories and recriminations took their toll on Springsteen himself. Three years later, during his summer 1978 tour, he could look back with some humor on those days. "It's later been written that it was all hype," he said. "And that's silly. 'Cause it wasn't. There wasn't a lotta hype. There were a lotta good stories and positive things written about the band, but there was no bullshit involved.

"Like the *Time* and *Newsweek* thing, which for a long time I had funny feelings about. Now I look back and think that it was good, because we got the record out to maybe more people than might have otherwise heard it. And that was the important thing for me. . : . My pop said the best thing about it. 'Why not you on the cover of *Time?*' he says. 'Better you than another picture of the president.' "

But in October 1975, the hype charges were not a matter for joking. It was almost as if the specter of the promotional debacle on the first album had returned to haunt Springsteen. Certainly, everything written about him for the next few years—maybe forever—would be colored by this incident. Bruce retreated, tried to readjust to both notoriety and success. For a few weeks, it was hard for him to believe that he was the same person.

"One night in Detroit," Springsteen told Robert Hilburn years later, "I didn't want to go on stage. That was the only time in my life—that period—that happened. At that moment, I could see how people get into drinking or into drugs, because the one thing you want at a time like that is to be distracted—in a big way. I was lucky. I had my band, which was people I had grown up with. No matter where we went they were always there for support."

For Springsteen's early fans and most ardent supporters, it was difficult to believe that, despite the fact that he had become a star of major importance, rock had not immediately turned back toward its earlier values. But Springsteen's success was not the sort that creates a watershed, as Elvis Presley and the Beatles had done; the rock audience was by now too fragmented for any single figure to unite it. Presley and the Beatles were able to catch their fans (and their detractors) unawares, but these days both the rock crowd and the media are too self-conscious for anything like that.

But *Born To Run* did set the stage for fundamental challenges to big-time rock and roll. Springsteen clearly was the key influence on struggling Midwestern rocker Bob Seger and his "Night Moves," which was the best hit single since "Born To Run," until Bruce's own "Hungry Heart." It is also hard to believe that an impassioned British rebel like Graham Parker would have gotten much of a hearing without *Born To Run* and its emphasis on root values. Springsteen set people thinking about fundamental issues again, so that when a new generation of punk rockers did emerge in the next two years—beginning with Patti Smith and the Ramones and winding up with a bagful of English antistars such as the Sex Pistols and the Clash—the established interests had to reckon with it.

As for Bruce himself, he soon recovered from the flap. By the time the tour hit L.A., he could laugh about it a little. When the cheers died down at his second show at the Roxy, he was exuberant. "There ain't nobody here from *Billboard* tonight!" he exulted, glad to feel at home with ordinary fans. And by the final show of the *Born To Run* tour, in Philadelphia on New Year's Eve, he seemed fully in command again, even changing the key verse of "Rosalita" to:

Tell your daddy I ain't no freak
'Cause I got my picture on the cover of *Time* and *Newsweek*!

In 1976, there would rarely be cause for such joy.

13 KILLERS IN THE SUN

The *Born To Run* tour was a triumph not just for Bruce Springsteen, but also for the E Street Band, to which people were beginning to pay special attention. Playing across the country, solidly booked for two months at three-thousand-seat theaters and concert halls, improved everything—the sound was fine, and Marc Brickman's lights were beginning to reach for unparalleled effects, working on tighter cues than anyone else in rock, bathing the songs in sheets of color that perfectly complemented the music. Most important, the band was growing together musically, knitting into a genuinely individual sound. Springsteen himself had that much more flexibility, able now simply to sing on some songs where previously he had also had to play guitar, able also to accentuate his moves through Max Weinberg's precision percussion, with Clemons and Van Zandt standing by to lend dramatic support. The net effect was of a group of professionals who played for much more than money.

The key factor in this transformation was Miami Steve Van Zandt, not because he led the band, but because he balanced its diverse tendencies. The professionalism would have come eventually in any case; although Weinberg and Bittan had originally signed on for salaries of only $75 weekly, their seasoning in studios and pit bands guaranteed a new technical polish. Federici, Clemons and Tallent, on the other hand, were notable for a close-knit feeling, stylized but not studied. It was these two diverse approaches that Miami Steve was able to blend. As a charter member of the Asbury Park Upstage crowd—while still in high school—he was part of the casualness and intimacy of the older members. But after his period on the road with Dion, the Dovells and other oldies acts, Van Zandt also understood the rules of the game for hired guns. Van Zandt was capable of saying that "If I had it my way, we'd do the records in mono," but he also recognized the value of professional technique.

Van Zandt's presence was also personally important for Springsteen. Federici, Clemons and Tallent had played with Bruce for years—Danny had been with him even longer than Steve—but, except for Clarence, they were as reclusive as Bruce himself. Like him, other Asbury Park players believed that, in Bruce's words, "What you dig is the respect for doing what you do, not the attention." "Attention without respect is jive. Plus, I was always the kind of guy who liked to walk around and slip back into the shadows."

But Van Zandt is as voluble as Springsteen is taciturn. Steve makes friends quickly and easily, regaling them with quick wisecracks, self-deprecating shaggy dog stories and the rocker's perspective that necessitates dancing on every grave, including (especially) your own. Steve found it simple to take people at their word, socially, and hope for the best. He did not hang back, although while Bruce could forgive almost anything in a friend—once you're in, you're in—Steve believed that friendship was proved by adhering to certain rules of behavior, and those who broke them ought to get themselves lost. It is no coincidence that Van Zandt's favorite is Sixties soul music, loose and convivial, while Springsteen's tastes lean toward the more insular white rock and roll of the Sixties.

But when the chips were down, there was no doubt that the two stood together. Both were driven by a sense of rock and roll as the Way Out of the Trap, into which almost everyone with whom they'd grown up had fallen. And Van Zandt was intensely loyal to Springsteen, seeing in Bruce the one-of-a-kind friend and band leader most musicians must dream about. "Bruce is the best possible boss," he has said. "He's hip enough to let everybody do other things, to express themselves in other ways. All that does is make your gig better. When you go back to playing in the band, it's like coming home to foundation and security."

As an emotional liaison between Bruce and the band, Steve's role was crucial. Although things were terrific onstage, behind the scenes, as far as the group was concerned, the joint was a mess. Springsteen cared nothing about money or business, but the band watched such things closely, and what they saw made them wary. Equipment that should have been purchased was rented. Laurel Canyon didn't always make Clarence Clemon's child support payments on time, once forcing Clarence to spend a night in jail until Appel showed up to bail him out. Steve's guitar was stolen from a rehearsal studio, forcing him to play an important Boston gig with an unfamiliar instrument; he was so depressed that Springsteen played off him for the whole show, just to try and cheer his friend up.

Mike Appel managed Bruce Springsteen, but not the E Street Band. It was a situation Appel wanted to change; he offered contracts to all the members, and Danny Federici and Clarence Clemons actually signed them. When the rest of the band convinced Danny and Clarence that they had made a foolish move, Springsteen asked Appel to tear the documents up. To his credit, Appel did so. But the band was left with the impression that Danny and Clarence, the band's great innocents, had been tricked.

As far as Springsteen was concerned, such problems were of little consequence. But the band never hid its dislike of Appel, nor its distrust of him. Neither did the road crew, which is the backbone of any rock touring organization. When Appel showed up at the E Street Christmas party that year, the celebration was in full swing. Within minutes after his arrival, the room was empty. Bruce viewed such incidents with chagrin. He well understood that Appel was abrasive and rude; during the *Born To Run* sessions, he had asked Mike to stay away from the studio for a month because of the counterproductive tensions he created. (It was Jon Landau, ironically, who engineered Mike's return.) Yet Bruce also saw the other side of the man. "I can't help it—I like the guy," he told friends.

It was hard not to think that "like" was stretching it. Like Pike

Bishop in Sam Peckinpah's *The Wild Bunch*, Bruce believes that "When you side with a man, you stay with him. And if you don't do that, you're like some animal." Mike Appel was the first music business pro to believe in Springsteen's talent—or anyway, the first one who had any notion of what to do with his skill—which made up for a great deal. Certainly, any intelligent person must have seen that Appel created a problem for every one that he solved. Yet Springsteen's loyalty ran deep; it was predicated on trust. Once you're in, you're in.

Born To Run was a success on every level—with the fans, with the press, in radio airplay, and among other musicians. "After the Bottom Line," remembers Barry Bell, "Bruce went from a Northeastern cult figure to a nationwide figure—by playing ten shows. When I look back on that I can't understand how he did it. He would start at eight o'clock at night and end up at five o'clock in the morning. It was like he was punching a clock, he did so many hours—he'd be like a wet rag when it was all over."

From Bell's point of view, the hype issue was also an advantage. "Look," he says, "if a guy writes in Beaumont, Illinois, that Bruce Springsteen is all hype and he can't be as good as he is, then the people are gonna come out and judge for themselves. I can remember that in Seattle or Portland, one of those, he sold out a two thousand seater going in for the first time, just based on all the word going around. And after the show, the kids were screaming for more while they were tearing the set down. I always knew that once Bruce got his audience there, they'd never lose him."

Yet even Bell is willing to admit that "it was not a tremendously successful tour as far as business. We did what we wanted to do as far as exposure in certain markets. It was a process of building him up."

In Los Angeles, the show drew all sorts of scenemakers: Carole King, Jackie DeShannon, Joni Mitchell, Nils Lofgren, Jackson Browne, Tom Waits and actors Robert De Niro and Jack Nicholson. The latter, in fact, another boy from the Jersey coast, led the cheering from atop his table. That same week, Springsteen encountered his penultimate idol, Phil Spector. (He would never meet the ultimate idol, Elvis, although as we shall see, he tried.) Spector was typically cool. "I'm hip to what the kid is doing. I'm mildly interested," said the man to whom *Born To Run*'s wall of sound paid homage.

Spector invited Bruce to visit a session he was producing for Dion. It was a more relaxed encounter, although describing anything about Spector as relaxed risks overstatement. Iovine, who had worked with Spector on Lennon's records, was in town, and Miami Steve knew Dion well from the oldies circuit. The session lasted five hours, peppered with wisecracks from the maestro: "Okay, fellas. Bruce Spring*street* is here. He's on the cover of *Time* and he's born to run. So let's show him how to make a record." But during the evening, the former boy genius drew the new one aside. "If I were with you, your records would be clearer and better," said the man who had produced *Let It Be*, the muddiest of all Beatles LPs, "and you'd sell five times as many." Bruce reportedly thought the offer attractive, though others were amused: Spector, too, has a reputation for taking a long time to finish records.

Spector was reserved about Springsteen, but only up to a point. When one of the producer's friends suggested that the meeting was like introducing the great Sixties pitcher Sandy Koufax to the new Dodger star Don Sutton, Spector corrected him, "No, it's more like Babe Ruth and Hank Aaron." Home-run kings.

Musically, the show was constantly growing. Playing in Detroit for the first time, the group worked up a medley of Mitch Ryder hits, a perfect opportunity for Weinberg—by now, known as Mighty Max—to shine. The so-called "Detroit Medley" worked so well that it remained as a semipermanent encore. In Oakland, California, the crowd was so wild by the end of the set that the balcony nearly collapsed.

Somehow, though, Springsteen was uneasy with success. It was true that he'd come all the way, from virtual rags to potential riches. Life should have been a dream come true. But it wasn't. Things just weren't going right, though knowing Bruce's penchant for perfectionism this might only have meant that they were not going perfectly. And the things that went right were a bit too smooth to be trusted. "You ride in a limousine the first time, it's a thrill," said Bruce. "But after that, it's just a stupid car." The items that got messed up, on the other hand, were just those that mattered most—ones involving Bruce's ideas of integrity and independence.

In Washington, D.C., for instance, Appel and William Morris booked Springsteen into a ten-thousand-seat hall. No one had bothered to consult Bruce, and cancellations, explanations, apologies, rebookings and recriminations ensued—with predictable fallout in the press.

Then disaster set in on a brief European jaunt in November featuring two dates in London and one-nighters in Amsterdam and Stockholm. The mini-tour was booked by William Morris, but its promotion was largely in the hands of CBS International, which didn't quite get the picture. London was chosen for the most excessive hype, partly because of a series of enthusiastic articles written over the past year by Mick Watts and other American correspondents for *Melody Maker*, the largest of the English pop weeklies. The city was plastered with stickers bearing the "I saw rock and roll future and its name is Bruce Springsteen" quote; Hammersmith Odeon, the theater where the shows were held, was festooned with "At Last London Is Ready For Bruce Springsteen!" posters and flyers (which, before the show, Bruce went around tearing off the walls and ripping to shreds). The tour went by in a daze—the All-American eating habits of the band were confounded by European cuisine, the brevity of the tour left little time to recover from jet lag, and on the final night, in his London hotel, Clarence Clemons was denied permission to bring his—black—friends up to his room. (Clarence, never at a loss, changed into his most outrageous clothing and returning to the lobby, glowered at the white businessmen, arriving with their hookers, challenging all who entered as to whether all of *their* party was registered.)

When the band returned to the States, Springsteen withdrew, hardly seeing anyone—not the band, not Appel, not Landau. He spent most of his time with his girl friend, an odd circumstance for a man who had often stated, "I can't have any women. I gotta give everything to my music. And I'm not ready to write married music yet." At that moment, Springsteen felt the need for a truly private life. He had felt the pressure earlier, asking Jack Nicholson in Los Angeles how the movie star had dealt with fame. But Nicholson's reply—that he had waited a long, long time for stardom and so welcomed it with little reservation—was no help.

Springsteen's somber mood affected the show. Bruce changed

from the black leather jacket, jeans and T-shirts he had previously worn to a pair of baggy pants and a long-billed cap that made him look more like one of Ducky Slattery's gas-pump jockeys than the hard-edged punk of the past. The effect was comic but soothing, removing some of the bluster from the shows.

Mike Appel was determined that the fourth Bruce Springsteen album should be recorded live, preferably as a double or triple set. To this end, he recorded a few shows at the end of the year, using the Record Plant's mobile unit with Jimmy Iovine at the controls. (The live broadcasts from the Bottom Line in New York and the Roxy in Los Angeles were among those put on tape, as were the shows at C. W. Post College on Long Island, at the Tower Theatre in Philadelphia, and at Ryerson Theatre in Toronto.) Bruce, however, was convinced that the live album—for which fans had been clamoring since *The Wild, The Innocent & The E Street Shuffle*— was still premature. His attitude wasn't simply obstinate, although one factor was certainly his suspicion that making records by just going out and playing was too easy. He felt that the band's onstage excitement wasn't ready to be captured yet; when he heard the shows on tape, Bruce thought that the playing lacked consistency, particularly in terms of tempo. Also, he was confident that his fourth album should be a set of completely new songs.

Once more, Springsteen was flying in the face of the rock formula. It is instructive to compare his career with that of Peter Frampton, the young English rocker whose solo career (after leaving Humble Pie) had started about the same time as Springsteen's. Frampton released three studio albums with increasing success (although none went gold) and followed with a live set that was the blockbuster of 1976. *Frampton Comes Alive* sold between five and ten million copies (depending on whose figures one believes), an absolutely unheard-of sum that kicked off the record industry's multiplatinum binge of the late Seventies.

Frampton was managed by Dee Anthony and booked by Frank Barsalona's Premier Talent Agency, and he had followed their rock packaging ideas to the letter, touring as many as two hundred nights a year, more for exposure than for profit, interspersed with albums released at clockwork intervals. As it happened, *Comes Alive* wasn't a bad record, given Frampton's limited talents. But the volume of sales it generated disoriented Frampton, and his follow-up record, *I'm In You*, was burdened with syrupy pop arrangements that overlooked his most distinctive ability (as a guitarist) in favor of teen-idol singing. Although the singer has remained a formidable concert attraction, *I'm In You* sold less than half as many copies as the live set, and Frampton did not release another LP until May 1979. His career seems as damaged as that of any teen idol before him, particularly given his catastrophic "acting" debut with the Bee Gees in Robert Stigwood's horrid film version of *Sgt. Pepper's Lonely Hearts Club Band*.

Peter Frampton is perhaps the classic example of the limitations of rock's starmaking machinery. It is doubtful whether Frampton will ever be a creative—or even commercial—force in rock music again. His credibility is simply exhausted, for although he had worked hard to gain it, his gigantic victory was premature and based on a forced image. The formula could turn drastically counterproductive. Only his instinctive mistrust of the easy ways had saved Springsteen.

In the end, the only product of Appel's 1975 live recordings was a tape of the holiday chestnut "Santa Claus Is Coming to Town," based on Phil Spector's arrangement for the Crystals, which was sent out to a few radio stations during the Christmas season. The song has been given considerable airplay every year since then, some of it on major Top Forty stations such as WRKO-AM in Boston, but "Santa Claus" has never been officially released to the public.

Perhaps the final measure of the toll that fame was taking on Springsteen was that the ordinarily prolific songwriter performed no new material on the *Born To Run* tour. His set instead consisted of the complete new album, minus only "Meeting Across the River," plus highlights from the first two LPs and a few older songs; toward the end of the year, "Santa Claus" and "It's My Life," complete with the story about his adolescence, were added. But Bruce wrote no new songs, or at least none that he was ready to sing in public.

The *Born To Run* tour ended with four sold-out shows at the three-thousand-seat Tower Theatre in Philadelphia. Ticket requests numbered ninety thousand; it was clear that Springsteen would either have to play someplace larger next time or simply work full-time in Philly, if he wanted to reach all of his fans in the area.

When the last set was over, long after midnight on New Year's Eve, no one was terribly surprised when Bruce expressed more relief than exhilaration. Now he could relax, grow into his new situation. His life would never be so simple again.

14 EAST OF EDEN

"Lee said uneasily, 'I told you when you asked me that it was all in yourself. I told you you could control it if you wanted to. . . . He couldn't help it, Cal. That's his nature. It was the only way he knew. He didn't have a choice. But you have. Don't you hear me? You have a choice.'"

John Steinbeck, *East of Eden*

The early days of 1976 were filled with promise. Jon Landau flew to Los Angeles to begin recording a new Jackson Browne album, *The Pretender*. Pianist Roy Bittan was in Philadelphia, working with David Bowie on *Station to Station*, an album for which Bowie recorded two Springsteen songs, "Saint in the City" and "Growin' Up" (they never appeared). Miami Steve got back to Asbury Park and decided that his old band—retitled Southside Johnny and the Asbury Jukes—was ready to record. With Van Zandt producing and Jimmy Iovine engineering, the Jukes cut a debut album called *I Don't Want To Go Home* for the CBS Epic label; its highlights were the title track, written by Steve, and Bruce's "The Fever." Pure mainline soul in the old style, with guest appearances by Lee ("Ya Ya") Dorsey and ex-Ronette Ronnie Spector, *I Don't Want To Go Home* sold acceptably for a debut record—more than one hundred thousand—and the Jukes began a national tour.

Toward the end of 1975, Barry Bell and Mike Appel began discussions about creating a new booking agency with Bell running the business and Appel providing the office space—a small enterprise with only Bruce and a couple of others as clients. Barry was eager to leave William Morris, and there was a feeling among the E Streeters that the big agency wasn't right for them.

If anyone was unhappy, it was Mike Appel. He had, perhaps, supposed that success would make Bruce see the light about large concert halls and other methods of maximizing profits. But it soon became clear that, left to himself, Springsteen had no intentions of making such concessions to stardom. Appel had big ideas—he wanted to set up a cross-country tour in a circus tent, establish the booking agency, release a live album as quickly as possible to cash in on the *Born To Run* success. At the very least, Appel felt, he needed additional protection as Springsteen's manager. While Bruce was still contracted to Laurel Canyon for two more albums (and to CBS for seven), the management contract had only one year to run.

The *Born To Run* tour hadn't been profitable; it had not lost much money, but playing in small theaters, traveling with more than twenty people in the crew, keeping the band on salary year-round, the debts had increased. The obvious solution was to play some big gigs and cash in—Larry Magid offered Bruce $500,000 for playing the one-hundred-thousand-seat JFK Stadium in Philadelphia on the Bicentennial Independence Day. But Springsteen rejected anything so gross and obvious—which had Appel worried.

Mike arranged for CBS to advance Laurel Canyon $500,000 against future Springsteen earnings. The company was happy to do so, the success of *Born To Run* (nine-hundred-thousand units sold and counting) having proved that if Springsteen were not *the* future, at least he had one.

What happened next is unclear. According to Appel's attorney,

Leonard Marks (as reported in *Rolling Stone*), "When things started looking up, Appel offered to renegotiate the contracts with Springsteen—including giving him half the stock of all Laurel Canyon companies. Springsteen said he didn't want to deal with a written contract but wanted to work it out with Appel on a day-to-day basis with a verbal agreement based on trust. Appel had an audit done by Mason and Company and then sent Springsteen a letter saying that 'the books are open' and invited another outside audit by Springsteen."

That is certainly accurate. But Appel's tactics while renegotiating proved rather heavy-handed. He told Springsteen of the half-million-dollar CBS advance, saying that half of it could be his—if Bruce agreed to re-sign with Laurel Canyon Management for an extended period of time. Otherwise, Appel assured him, he would have to hold Springsteen to the letter of their agreement—and Appel made it clear, for the first time, the disadvantages of the contracts Springsteen had originally signed. For instance, Bruce was entitled to a three and one-half percent (about ten cents) record royalty (based on wholesale price), while Laurel Canyon's agreement with CBS gave Appel's company at least forty cents per LP. The manager/producer kept the difference. Similarly, the management contract did not specify the standard fifteen or twenty percent commission to Laurel Canyon/Appel; in high-earnings situations, it provided for a *fifty percent* commission. Springsteen did not control his own song publishing rights either; Laurel Canyon held them, and could grant or refuse right to use the material to whomever it chose, whatever Springsteen's wishes.

Springsteen found this shocking, since he had never bothered to read the contracts when he signed them. "It was my own fault," he would later say. "I knew what a lawyer was." If he didn't, he was soon to find out. Still, in January and February 1976, Springsteen wasn't taking Appel's assertions too seriously; mostly, they were about money, and cash had never been at the top of Bruce's priorities. He retained his confidence that matters could be worked out.

On the other hand, he had to be sure. Heading to California to visit his parents, Springsteen stopped off to visit Landau in Los Angeles. He had the contracts with him, and asked Jon to read them. Asked what he thought, Landau replied that Springsteen clearly needed the advice of an attorney. A few weeks later, when both men were back in New York, they visited the offices of Mike Mayer, of Mayer, Nussbaum and Katz, a respected music business law firm that represented—in addition to Landau himself—Atlantic Records, Phil Walden of Capricorn Records, the Otis Redding estate and Rod Stewart.

Mayer immediately saw the unfairness of the contracts, and the conflicts inherent in Appel representing Bruce's overall career on one hand and acting as his record production company on the other. Bruce retained Mayer, Nussbaum and Katz to represent him in renegotiating the deals. He also had accountant Stephen Tenenbaum audit his dealings with Appel, from early 1972 through February 1976. Springsteen regarded these maneuvers as overdue but simply matters of form—he was preparing to work out some sort of agreement with Appel—not for a lawsuit. Despite Appel's admissions about the nature of the contracts, there were still bonds between them.

Meanwhile, Appel continued to plan a booking agency with Barry Bell. "We were all ready for the next tour," Bell recalls. "But a lotta things started to happen. It began slowly. I was at Bruce's house and Mike still hadn't made an arrangement with me yet, so he and Cheauteau Merrill, his assistant, had started to book a small tour out of Mike's office. Bruce says to me, 'What do you think about Cheauteau booking my tour?' I said, 'You're asking the wrong guy, 'cause I want to do it.'

"Mike was telling me that what was holding the deal up was that Bruce wasn't sure he wanted to do it. I said, 'You can't just hire anybody to do the booking. We're [agents are] professionals. You want the best of everything else. You should also have the best agent.'

"Bruce said, 'Oh I didn't realize that was it; I thought it was something else.' By the time the conversation ended, what it came down to was him saying, 'Look, Mike Appel's my manager, he's my producer; I don't want him to be my agent, too.' So I assured him that every dollar he paid to an agent was going to go to me. All Mike was doing was giving me an office and a telephone; if I signed any other acts, I'd give him some of what I got in order to pay the expenses. But Bruce was my thing. I told him, 'You will not sign any contract with Mike Appel as far as an agency.' He said, 'Fine, let's do it.' And we went off to the Carole King show at the Palladium, had a great time; Bruce jammed with Carole. It was a great night in my life."

The next day, Bell called Appel to tell him that everything was resolved. Appel said they should have lunch, and over the meal explained that Bruce's deal was running out and that Springsteen was reluctant to sign a new one. "I don't know why I should have to give him a new deal," Appel said. "I've already got him on paper." Bell could see that the sides were being drawn, which worried him, especially because the rumors that he was starting his own agency were starting to filter through the music business grapevine. If the gossip ever got back to the bosses at the agency, Bell knew, he wouldn't be able to quit—he would be summarily dismissed for his contemplation of competition.

"Now what happens is they really start to spread apart," Bell says. "Then they get back together. And Bruce calls me up one night, I think it was in February. He says, 'Okay, quit your job tomorrow and let's roll.' That was exactly what I wanted to hear. I said, 'Wow, you worked it out.' Bruce says, 'Yeah, Mike agreed to my deal.'

"The next day, I go into the office with a big grin on my face, ready to say, 'See ya.' But a sixth sense says I should call Mike Appel and congratulate him on making the deal. And Mike didn't pick up my call. Now I'm starting to sweat bullets.

"Around five thirty I finally reached him—I'd spent the day in the office without quitting. I said, 'Mike, what's going on?' And in the most hyper, nervous voice I have ever heard on the telephone, he says, 'The whole thing's off, the deal's off, I changed my mind, I talked to my father and it was not a good deal; I can't do it!'"

So they went to the mats.

Appel started out with crucial leverage: the half-million dollars from CBS. Except for whatever publishing royalties trickled in, that was all the income he had, since he represented no other clients. But it was enough.

Springsteen, on the other hand, was jammed for cash. He needed money to mount the tour that Appel had booked for him, and since CBS had courteously paid off Mike, the record company wasn't the place to get it. William Morris agreed to lend him the money, provided he would re-sign with the agency for another year. This Bruce agreed to do, and Bell and Sam McKeith, his co-agents at the time, arranged for the cash to be advanced.

The tour was meant to cover secondary markets, but it had not been properly structured. William Morris did its best to straighten the gigs out, but Springsteen was still left with a long jaunt through the South, the area of the country where he had the least appeal. The tour featured, for instance, five dates in Tennessee, where Bruce had never before appeared, and where he eventually would not draw terribly well. The band called it the "Chicken Scratch Tour" because the routing seemed to have been arranged by inking the legs of a fowl and sending it on a walk across the map.

Still, Bruce kept his spirits up. After his show in Memphis on April 29, mid-way through the tour, he and Miami Steve, along with publicist Glen Brunman, got into a taxi to look for a bite to eat. "We told the cab driver, take us someplace quiet," Bruce later recalled. "He said, 'Are you guys celebrities?' 'Yeah.' So he said he'd take us out along the highway, by Elvis's house. I said, 'You *gotta* take me to Elvis's house.' He says, 'Okay. Do you mind if I call the dispatcher and tell him where we're going?' So he calls the guy, says, 'We got some celebrities here. We got . . . ' and he shoves the mike in my face, so I say, 'Bruce Springsteen.' They didn't know who I was, but they were *pretendin'* to, y'know? He told the dispatcher we were going to Elvis's house; he was crackin' up because the dispatcher thought we were gonna drink coffee with Elvis.

"When we got to the gate, I looked through. It was three A.M., but all the lights in the house were on. I said, 'I gotta go see if he's home.' So I climbed over and started up the driveway; it's a long walk 'cause the house is set way back. And I was almost at the front door, just getting ready to knock, when I see this guy looking at me from the trees. He says, 'Hey, come here a minute.' I said, 'Is Elvis here?' He said, no, he was in Lake Tahoe or something.

"Well, now I'm pullin' out all the cheap shots I can think of— you know, I was on *Time*, I play guitar, Elvis is my hero, all the things I never say to anybody. Because I figure I've gotta get a message through. But he just said, 'Yeah, sure. Why don't you let me walk you down to the gate. You gotta get out of here.' He thought I was just another crazy fan—which I was."

Springsteen was also writing songs again—notably a new rocker,

"Frankie"—in preparation for his fourth album, which he and Jon Landau hoped to begin recording as soon as this tour was completed, in late May or early June—provided that Jon could finish the Jackson Browne LP, which was also dragging on.

Mike Appel, meanwhile, was making plans of his own. He requested in several places that concert receipts be held in escrow so that he could be sure of obtaining his management commissions; in the few places where the courts granted his plea, however, Appel found that the money had been paid in advance—there was no box office money to attach. This was crucial for the coming struggle, for Springsteen's only hope of generating income was through live performances.

On May 14, Laurel Canyon sent Springsteen a check for $67,368.78 "which represent[ed] the balance of all monies due [him] from the inception of our relationship through March 31, 1976." But it is interesting to note that this was the first accounting Springsteen had ever received from Laurel Canyon, although the relationship began in March 1972, more than four years previously; under the contract, he was owed accountings every three months. The audit also disclosed some interesting facts: Although Laurel Canyon's Springsteen-derived income over the four-year period totaled between one and two million dollars, Springsteen's total income for the period was less than $100,000 through March 31, 1976. Only one tax payment, from 1975, was recorded. Although some of this was explained by the fact that most money was turned over to the organization for salaries and expenses, accountant Tenenbaum's report said that Appel's records showed that Laurel Canyon had "conducted Springsteen's business in a slipshod, wasteful and neglectful manner; that he failed to maintain adequate and complete books and records relating to Springsteen's activities; and that enormous amounts of expenses and disbursements are charged to Springsteen which are in large measure unsubstantiated. . . . My audit reveals a classic case of the unconscionable exploitation of an unsophisticated and unrepresented performer by his manager for the manager's primary economic benefit."

Certainly, Mike Appel hadn't gotten rich off Bruce Springsteen, but just as certainly, Springsteen was entitled to more than ten percent of the money he had generated. Bruce clearly had a right to expect that his management organization would make sure that his taxes were paid; not to do so is the kind of fiscal irresponsibility that has so often resulted in catastrophe for entertainment and sports figures (the fighter Joe Louis is only the most obvious example).

Meanwhile, it was clear that the Jackson Browne sessions were not going to be completed by June 1. That was no real problem, since, despite Springsteen's many ideas for new songs, he'd actually completed only a few. But on July 2, Appel sent Springsteen a letter stating in no uncertain terms that he would not allow Jon Landau to produce the fourth LP, citing paragraph 2 (b) of their contract as his authority. Three weeks later, on July 27, 1976, Springsteen filed suit in federal court in Manhattan, alleging fraud (in that Appel had represented himself as a knowledgeable and experienced businessman), undue influence and breach of trust. In the legal parlance, Appel had allegedly breached his "fiduciary" trust as manager— which trust obliged him to act first and honorably in the best interests of his client.

According to Springsteen's lawsuit, the Laurel Canyon management was a massive conflict of interest, in that Appel's managerial responsibility was suspended in any of Springsteen's dealings with Laurel Canyon companies and in that it attempted to deny Springsteen the right to any advisers other than Mike Appel. In dealing with any of Appel's companies, in other words, Springsteen stood naked.

The CBS contract boondoggle, in which the number of albums Laurel Canyon contracted for was twice as many as Bruce was obliged to give the production company, was also revealed in the suit. Springsteen said that far from being advised of his rights in these matters, he had seen only one page of the CBS agreement— the one which he signed, ironically enough, on the hood of a car in a dark New Jersey parking lot.

Two days later, on July 29, Appel filed suit in New York State Supreme Court, asking the court to bar Bruce and Landau from entering a recording studio together. In an affidavit, Appel claimed that only Laurel Canyon had the right to appoint a producer, and, he said, he preferred the "winning combination" of himself and Springsteen, conveniently ignoring the fact that only one track, "Born To Run," had been produced by that pair without assistance of a third party.

Springsteen's legal team had apparently underestimated the persuasiveness of Appel's argument. Judge Arnold Fein, who has a reputation for taking the phrase "unique and exclusive services" in a contract very seriously, saw only that Appel's rights were being infringed, and granted the injunction, effectively barring Bruce and Jon Landau from recording together. Appel had gained the upper hand, dividing the opposition.

Springsteen was not barred from recording; he was only barred from recording with *Jon Landau*. (Appel would later attempt to appoint as producer Brooks Arthur, owner of 914 Sound Studios and producer of previous hits by Janis Ian—a move that Bruce would greet derisively in a later affidavit.)

CBS was involved in the lawsuit, against its corporate instinct. Indeed, company attorney Walter Dean would later characterize CBS as "an innocent third party," which was hardly the case. The truth was that CBS could hardly afford to have the case go to trial, for if it were determined that Appel's contracts were invalid, the CBS deal might be voided along with them. And, as a free agent, Springsteen would clearly be worth millions. The company was pushed into a position of false neutrality very much to Appel's advantage.

Landau was effectively isolated by Appel's strategy and by Fein's strongly worded opinion, which said that Jon had "no rights under these agreements." Since part of Appel's suit alleged that Landau had engaged in a "campaign to sabotage the relations between Springsteen and [him]self," Landau—the figure with whom Bruce was most comfortable—had to tread carefully.

In Fein's formal opinion he stated: "The real issue appears to be whether Landau may act as the producer over the plaintiff's objection." But this was true only so long as Springsteen was viewed as merely a "capital generator"—as he would later refer to himself— the maker of a unique product. If Bruce were seen as an artist who was "fighting for [his] life," as he told the judge, the picture would change. In human terms, it was unconscionable to deny Springsteen the opportunity to work with Landau, who was a key influence on his work and who was the only person he knew who could help him shape it properly. Obviously, this argument is extralegal; but any assessment of the lawsuit without considering these factors is blinder than justice was ever meant to be.

There was a further factor in Springsteen's motivation in the case, and it is a key to why he was passive for so long (his early depositions were so disastrous that *Appel* released excerpts from them to the press). Bruce was willing to forgive whatever financial wrongdoing might have been done, but the moment he realized that he did not own his own songs, he realized that he was fighting for his creative life. The notion that he could be denied rights to *his* work incensed Bruce, and he fought ferociously to regain control of his career, which he saw slipping away. Everything he had done in contravention of record business formula had been designed to insure the integrity of his songs and his music, and when he saw that the litigation threatened that integrity, he hit back, hard. Although they have never been publicly released, Springsteen's later depositions are said to be as dramatic and pointed as any of his shows. Asked why he refused to go on tour in the circus tent, for instance, Bruce reportedly snapped, "Why don't you try practicing law in a tent for a while? Then I'll think about playing my guitar in one."

Still, Appel was winning the case. He had enough money to wait the situation out, for months or even years if necessary. And even if the issues at hand in the state court were settled, the validity of the contracts could not be tested there—those were tied up in federal court, where it could take more than a year just to get on the docket.

In October, Springsteen switched attorneys, retaining Michael Tannen, who represented the business interests of Paul Simon, John Lennon and the Rolling Stones, among others, and Peter Parcher, a skilled litigation specialist. The new lawyers turned the case around. "The day we hired Michael Tannen was the day we won the case," Bruce says now. Together with Parcher, Springsteen began to roll the record back and rumors of a settlement began to circulate.

In August, to earn some money, Bruce had played a week-long engagement in Red Bank, New Jersey, where he debuted a remarkable new song, "The Promise," as well as a new lighting design by Brickman that was nothing short of breathtaking. And in late September, he headed out on a longer tour, opening in Phoenix, Arizona, where he performed in the Coliseum, a 7,500-seat leviathan of the variety he had always refused to play; the show was instrumental in convincing Springsteen that he could go over well in a larger arena. Two dates in Santa Monica made him a major draw in Los Angeles.

But the most important gigs once again came at the end of the tour. In Philadelphia, Bruce was finally convinced to appear in a full-size sports arena, the Spectrum, where the Philadelphia Flyers and 76ers played. "I brought it up to him," says Bell. "I said, 'Bruce, you're gonna have to—for the first time in your own mind—*think* about playing the big halls in Philadelphia.' The way I put it to him was: 'You're worried about the kids, how they're gonna be affected. But if you were a kid, would you rather sit in the last row of the Spectrum or ask your friend how good he was at the Tower? If I was a kid, I'd rather get in there somehow.' "

Springsteen reached a rapprochement with the huge hall by screening off the back of the stage with a large curtain, and, for insurance, hiring Clare Brothers, the best rock concert sound specialists, to run the P.A. As a triple precaution, he played a four-hour sound check that nearly exhausted the band before there was a patron in the house. But as Bell said, "What he found out was that you could get good sound in a big hall—if you were willing to make the effort."

Even without a new record, the '76 tour was a triumph. "He was becoming a major star even with a legal problem," says Bell. And as if to confirm it, the tour ended with six sold-out shows at the Palladium Theatre, a 2,800-seat opera house in Manhattan.

Springsteen's prolific writing was also beginning to slip back into gear. The sets opened with "Rendezvous," a new rocker that evoked the spirit of the Manfred Mann and Searchers Sixties hits that Springsteen loved to sing. And the shows featured two new ballads, "Something in the Night," a tale of pure desolation, and "The Promise," a ballad written very much in the romantic spirit epitomized by the Beach Boys' "Don't Worry Baby."

"The Promise" represented a crucial turning point in Bruce's career, and a new kind of maturity in his lyrical perspective. When he heard the song for the first time at a concert in South Bend, Indiana, the *Chicago Reader* critic John Milward was moved to write: "The song's metaphor is 'The Challenger,' a race car that the singer has built by hand 'to carry the broken dreams of all those who have lost.' But the real twist comes during the song's bridge, when he sings the words 'thunder road' and immediately transforms his car into his rock and roll dreams. In 'The Promise,' Springsteen mythologizes himself and compares his struggle to be true to his art to the desperate struggle of the young racer. He sings in 'Thunder Road' that 'tonight's the night all the promises will be broken,' but the dream etched in 'The Promise' and put into perspective by Springsteen's own experience is clearly a romantic notion that is not easily shattered. Despite a landscape filled with losers—the singer eventually sells his car when he needs money—it's clear that in Springsteen's heart the Challenger's potential will never die."

When Milward refers to "Springsteen's own experience," he is clearly alluding to the lawsuit, but Milward is canny enough to know that the lawsuit itself is only a symbol of what Bruce had undergone since *Born To Run* catapulted him to fame. ("I don't write songs about lawsuits," Bruce says tersely, and the fact that people might think that "The Promise" was concerned only with legalities kept it off his fourth album.) "The Promise" is rather about the price everyone pays for success—and the dangers of settling for anything less.

The weirdest anomaly of success is that it requires compromises never demanded of failure. It isn't just the minor infringements on one's humanity—such as signing autographs at meals, which reduces the very act of eating to a promotional event. It's also the expectation, and the possibility, that one will do *anything* to keep from losing what's been gained. And this, of course, is antithetical to the rock and roll dream, which says that the only way to possess anything of true importance is to risk losing all. "We were gonna take it all . . . and throw it all away," says Springsteen at the end of "The Promise"— which puts a fine point on rock's version of succeeding.

Rock and roll is about promises—covenants between the audience and the star (and vice versa, since the latter is only an idealized version of the former). This is a central tenet of *Mystery Train*, Greil Marcus's great critical study of the music, which in fact may have served as the inspiration for "The Promise." For Marcus, such promises are an inherent part of America itself; they are at least as old as the Mayflower Compact, and their centrality to the Declaration of Independence and the Constitution is likewise clear. For Bruce, these promises are simply the foundation of the world he knows. He believed in the ideals he'd been raised up on; compromise such things and you *are* "like an animal." And so when he sings, "When the promise is·broken/You go right on living/But it takes something from down in your soul/Like when the truth is spoken/And it don't make no difference/And something in your heart grows cold," he has assessed the price of every syllable.

These are emotions far outside the scope of the punks on *Born To Run*—the feeling is definitely adult, although it certainly does not lack anything in the way of rock spirit. (Which recalls Christgau's line that grown-up rockers wish not to preserve their youth but only their rebellion.) Still, Springsteen was not quite ready to adopt this dour perspective completely. On the 1976 tour, introducing "Growin' Up," Bruce made light of the pressure: "I went in and did my audition with this song. I remember I went up to the record building, you know . . . All these lawyers. Everybody had one but me." Then he broke up in a fit of giggles, as Roy Bittan began to play the tinkling introduction. "Awwww, so *what!*" Springsteen shouted as he began to sing the verses.

But in the middle of the song, the music fell away again, and Bruce stepped forward to tell a fairy tale about fame. Only a pinging electronic sound came from the guitar, while the piano and Danny Federici's glockenspiel tinkled away in the background.

"There we was," Bruce said, punctuating the drama with giggles. "It was me, and the Big Man, and Miami. We were drivin' down this old dark road. All of a sudden (bang!) we got a flat. We were in a '63 Impala, absolutely nothing done to it; a real piece o' shit my old man gave me. It was the only thing we had to get around with, screamin' down the back road, doin' alla fifty-five. Boom! Flat tire.

"We pull over. Course, we ain't got no spare; this is a budget operation. So we try to convince Miami to run with it, while we got to a gas station. But we didn't know where we was. It was dark; it was so dark; there was no moon out. Everybody was hidin' that night. There was trees, a deep dark forest, we couldn't see nothin'.

"And we looked, looked way off, and deep in the forest we saw this light just sorta shinin' there. And we said, somebody must live there, we oughta go find out, get some help, y'know. So we stomped back through the woods—got mud all over us, right? And there in the middle of the forest was this old gypsy lady, sittin' around this fire.

"So we walked up to her and she looked at us and said, 'Got a flat tire, huh?' We felt a little nervous there, you know, how'd she know we have a flat tire, you know? It's like, we were waaay out there on the road. We said, 'Yeah.' She said, 'What'd they send you suckers back here for? Whaddya want? You just tell the gypsy lady—she'll straighten you out right now.'

" 'First of all,' she sez, 'you look like a buncha bums.' This is about six years ago, right? 'First, you cats are not presentable, you know, to do *anything*.' So like, she waved this stick and . . . BAM! Miami's standin' there in a red suit in the middle of the woods. She waved it again . . . BOOM! The Big Man's standin' there in a white suit, right in the middle of the woods. She waved it again, in front of me. Boom! Nothin' happened.

"She says, 'Don't work alla time. Some people gotta work at bein' bums. Others are born that way.' So I say, 'Hey, gypsy lady, you owe me one—you owe me one now.' She said, 'All right, all right. What can I do for ya?' So I thought real hard, said, 'Well . . . ' Thought about a new transmission. Naw, ain't nothin' gonna help that old car—the thing's a goner. I thought about uh . . .

"She said, 'Well you gotta just tell me, man. You wanna be a king? You wanna be an emperor? You wanna own your own Pizza Hut? Just tell me, tell the gypsy lady, I'm right here.'

"I said, 'Well. Well, to be honest with ya . . . not to pull any punches . . . what I really had in mind . . . I think I could dig . . . I think I wanna be, I think I wanna be, I think I wanna be . . . A Rock and Roll Star!" Max's drums exploded like tympani, as the band rushed back into the song, playing hard and fast. As Bruce hit the last lines, he looked out at the crowd. For a moment, only a moment, he seemed caught up, really that cosmic kid he sang about. "Then I hit 'em with my guitar," he exulted.

The legal maneuvering proceeded throughout the winter months. Bruce's depositions had helped, although at one point, he became so bellicose, peppering his aggressive statements with obscenities, that Appel's lawyers had him hauled before Judge Arnold Fein, who asked him to cool it. But even that worked out for the best—Bruce was able to clarify his personal position to Judge Fein (whose children were reportedly mighty impressed at whose trial he was overseeing), and the incident conveyed to Appel's attorneys the impression that a man so carried away was not about to give in easily. For his part, Mike Appel was anything but a quitter; he, too, was willing to carry the fight to the bitter end.

But the true test of the case was in the legal trenchwork of motions and countermotions. In his initial decision, Fein hadn't flatly refused to hear a case that would resolve the "underlying issue"—which was nothing less than the validity of the contracts, the grounds on which Springsteen initiated his complaint. Therefore, on November 18, Peter Parcher submitted an affidavit asking that the federal and state cases be joined. Parcher's affidavit was bolstered by supporting ones from Jim Cretecos, Appel's former partner, and Robert Spitz, a former Appel employee, both of whom claimed that Appel had reneged on verbal promises made to Springsteen at the beginning of their relationship. "On numerous occasions," said Spitz, "Appel stated to me that he hoped Springsteen never became aware of those agreements. Appel also expressed to me on a number of occasions that he was aware that a court of law would find them unconscionable." Why, then, had Appel instigated an action that would encourage Bruce to investigate the nature of his contracts? Maybe he just couldn't believe Bruce would really get mad.

On December 8, Springsteen submitted a key document, in which he requested permission to record an album with Landau producing and CBS advancing the recording costs, the tapes from which would be kept by the court until the suit was resolved. Fein denied this request. But in making his plea, Springsteen also outlined the potential damage that the delay was causing.

In closing, Springsteen pointed out that, while Appel's interest in the case was strictly financial, his own was his career, which until then had held the promise of making a significant contribution to "an entire generation of music. No amount of money could compensate me if I were to lose this opportunity," Springsteen concluded. This was lawyer talk—but highly persuasive and emotional stuff of its kind. This affidavit was the turning point in making Fein see that the issue of record production was unavoidably linked to the other issues in the case.

On March 22, 1977, Springsteen won a motion to submit an amended answer to Appel's state court complaint. That opened the door for resolution of almost all the federal issues in one trial. It also allowed him to assert as a defense Appel's breach of fiduciary obligation—his conflicts of interest, failure to provide proper accountings and the like. Once more, Springsteen was on the offensive. Bruce was clearly in a position to win if the case came to trial, and since Judge Fein had issued a "speedy trial" order, it was possible to push ahead toward one. It was at this point that a settlement became a genuine possibility, since Appel could not afford a trial he was likely to lose anyway, and since Springsteen, Landau and CBS, for their part, were more interested in getting back to making records.

A final settlement was reached at three A.M. on May 28, 1977. The details of the settlement were never officially released—the final document in the case file simply says that an amicable settlement had been reached and that the parties could not sue one another again. Both sides claimed victory, of course. Appel said he won because he had gotten some cash (reportedly as much as $1 million), retained some share of the profits from the first three albums and obtained a five-year production deal for Laurel Canyon with CBS. On the other hand, Appel had lost a better artist than he was likely to find again, and the production deal may not have been terribly significant: Appel's first post-Springsteen production client, Arlyn Gale (who looks, but doesn't sound like Bruce), was released through United Artists not CBS.

Springsteen felt he had won because he'd gained his freedom. He controlled his music again, in terms of both production and publishing, and he was able to work with Jon Landau. In fact, the pair entered Atlantic Studios in New York with the E Street Band only five days after the settlement, on June 1. The recording contract with Columbia had been renegotiated, with the rate adjusted upward, if not to superstar terms, at least to ones reasonable for a successful performer.

Confident that Landau and Springsteen could record together quickly, CBS laid plans for a Christmastime release of Springsteen's fourth LP.

15 RAISING CAIN

ntering the studio that June, Springsteen felt prepared. The sessions were being held in Atlantic Records' new studio in Manhattan, running from early evening to about midnight, after which the Rolling Stones came to mix *Love You Live*. (Typically, it was not Bruce but Miami Steve who struck up a quick friendship with Keith Richards; Keith admired Steve's soul-style songwriting, which he'd heard on the Jukes albums.)

The first evening was spent laying down demos of about twenty songs Bruce had written and more or less completed during the lawsuit. They included "Rendezvous," "The Promise," "Frankie" and "Something in the Night" from the live shows of the previous year, and several of the numbers that eventually wound up on *Darkness on the Edge of Town*, including the title song, plus some still-unreleased numbers such as the screaming rocker, "Don't Look Back."

At first things seemed to be progressing smoothly. Landau had gained a great deal of confidence while working with Los Angeles studio professionals on the Jackson Browne album; Jimmy Iovine had engineered and produced a number of acts since *Born To Run*. The E Street Band surprised both of them, however. "The amazing thing about those guys is how much energy they have," Landau told a friend. "With sessionmen, you almost always get the song done in two or three takes, and after that, it's time to move on to something different; the enthusiasm doesn't last. But with this band, the more takes you do, the better they get." Of course, the difference is that the E Street Band knows it is not playing a song for the final time when it is recorded; they still have a few hundred performances onstage left in them.

After a few weeks at Atlantic, though, it became obvious that something was wrong. No one was happy with the drum sound, and the studio wasn't terribly liveable, the latter an important consideration since the recording would inevitably drag on for several months. So the sessions were moved back to the Record Plant, where *Born To Run* was made.

Had Bruce been satisfied with the material he'd written before the recording started, the sessions might have progressed as quickly as planned. But Bruce wanted more than a set of listenable, craftsmanlike songs. One of his goals was to create a set of songs consciously linked, perhaps as a continuation of the story begun with *Born To Run*. Aided by Landau's insight, he now saw threads of continuity in all of his work. "There's a progression that goes through the records," Springsteen later told Walter Dawson of the *Memphis Commercial Appeal*. "The first album, that was sort of out of my control, except for the material. . . . And on *The Wild, The Innocent & The E Street Shuffle*, I brought my band in and that had real warm songs and a lot of characters, and there was more of an in-society type feeling. Even if it was low rent, it was more involvement in groups of people.

"And then on *Born To Run*, it sort of gets cut down to usually a guy and a girl. And for me, *Born To Run* maintains some warmth, but there was a certain element, a certain fear that starts to come in. I don't know why.

"And on this record, I think it's less romantic—it's got more, a little more, isolation. It's sort of like I said, 'Well, listen, I'm twenty-eight years old and the people in the album are around my age.' I perceive 'em to be that old. And they don't know what to do. . . .

There's less of a sense of a free ride than there is on *Born To Run*. There's more of a sense of: If you wanna ride, you're gonna pay. And you'd better keep riding."

It was more difficult for Springsteen to conceptualize his fourth album because it really should have been his fifth; the lawsuit had kept him from making an album the year before, and in the early days of recording *Darkness on the Edge of Town*, he must have been torn between making the record he would have made in the previous year, and the one he was ready to do now. Eventually, he opted to discard the past and push forward. It was the only sane choice, but it slowed things considerably.

Among the influences that helped shape Springsteen's ideas during this time were the kind of movies Landau had loved as a film critic—the Italian Westerns of Sergio Leone (*A Fistful of Dollars*, *Once Upon a Time in the West*), and John Ford classics like *The Searchers*. *East of Eden*, with James Dean, inspired "Adam Raised a Cain." Bruce came to understand himself and his songs better by viewing the work of filmmakers who could depict almost identical situations a dozen times and yet make each of them different.

Intrigued by the hero others saw in him, Bruce also took a closer look at his own role models. In July, soon after moving to the Record Plant, Bruce and the band found some advance copies of *Elvis: What Happened?*, Steve Dunleavy's muckraking book about Presley, in a bookshop around the corner. The influence of the King clicked back in, and for several weeks, the studio took on the look of an Elvis shrine. Bruce identified with Elvis's career, the way it seemed totally in the artist's control at one moment, and careening without guidance the next. "He was an artist, and he wanted to be an artist," Bruce said soon after Presley died, which also summed up Bruce's feelings about himself. But he wasn't about to allow himself to be caught up in anyone's expectations, as Elvis had done. "Mike Appel thought he would be Colonel Parker and I'd be Elvis," Springsteen would later say. "Only he wasn't the Colonel, and I wasn't Elvis."

The lessons of hype, the lawsuit, the failures of his idol, Elvis, and the natural maturity that came with simply being twenty-eight worked a transformation in Springsteen and his music. If he had sometimes been passive about the way others were exploiting his work, he now saw such apathy as the gravest irresponsibility. In "The

Promised Land," Springsteen says proudly: "Mister I ain't a boy/No I'm a man." So *Darkness on the Edge of Town* evolved into a statement of what had transpired, not in the courtroom or the recording studio, but in Springsteen's life, and the lives of the sort of people he knew.

Eventually, the album sifted down into thirteen songs—the ten that finally appeared on *Darkness on the Edge of Town* plus "The Promise," "Independence Day," and "Don't Look Back." "The trouble was that any way you sequenced them, it came out being a different record," Landau remembered. Not willing to overlook any possibility, Bruce shuffled the songs back and forth for weeks. Eventually, "The Promise" was eliminated, because too many reviewers of the live show had construed it as being "about" the lawsuit and because Springsteen saw it as too desolate for the message he meant to convey. "Don't Look Back" was not selected because it made Side Two sound too harsh. "Independence Day," Bruce thought, really belonged in the next chapter of the story—what happened to the character after he had survived being cut off from society.

Springsteen threw away songs around which others would build albums. He gave "Fire" (a Presley-style love song written in the manner of Doc Pomus and Mort Shuman's early Sixties Elvis hits such as "Marie's Her Name," "Little Sister," and "Viva Las Vegas!") to Robert Gordon, a young New York rockabilly singer he'd met through Garry Tallent. After Jimmy Iovine took a demo for "Because the Night" to the studio next door, where he was producing a record for Patti Smith, Springsteen let Smith finish the lyric (although he does not sing her version onstage) and the song gave Smith a Top Twenty hit in 1978.

Mixing began in early 1978, with Landau, Springsteen, Iovine and Miami Steve acting as collective midwife. But Landau soon placed a call to Charles Plotkin, who was head of Elektra/Asylum's A & R and with whom Jon had become friendly while Landau was making *The Pretender* in Los Angeles. They respected one another's ideas about production, and Landau asked Plotkin to visit the mix sessions when Plotkin came to New York to produce a Harry Chapin record soon afterward. Plotkin immediately grasped the mixture of West Coast clarity and hard rock density Springsteen was after, and his intense, joking personality proved a catalyst that pushed Bruce toward making decisions about the mix much more quickly than he would have otherwise.

The mixing was complete by early spring; this time, the mastering was done in Los Angeles, and it went much more smoothly. But there were other difficulties. Perhaps the most important was the album cover art. Bruce had selected a photograph by a virtually unknown New Jersey photographer, Frank Stefanko, that he felt reflected the starkness and energy of the record. But Stefanko's picture was not easy to reproduce; Columbia's art director John Berg insisted he could do the job, but after several cover proofs were submitted from Berg, it became clear to Springsteen that there had been a breakdown in communication. He turned to his product manager, Dick Wingate, for help.

About the same age as Bruce, Wingate had been a Springsteen fan since his days as an FM disc jockey in Rhode Island in the early Seventies. He was one of the few people at the record company Bruce felt he could trust. As product manager, Wingate was principally responsible for marketing the album, but in this situation he became involved as *de facto* art director as well.

Dick was in Minneapolis, where he had just seen the opening date of an Elvis Costello tour, when he received a one-thirty A.M. call from Landau and Springsteen, who were then in Los Angeles. Jon and Bruce had just received another cover proof, with no improvement. In fact, it was so far from what they wanted that Springsteen was on the verge of chucking the whole concept and going to a simpler black-and-white picture. The record release date of mid-May was imperative, because the national tour was set to start then. The album delays had forced the tour to be pushed back several times already, and it was felt that postponing it further would cost too much credibility with local promoters. The next morning, Wingate was on a plane to Los Angeles.

"I went out for the specific purpose of taking Bruce to the engraver, L.A. Color Service, which he had heard was the best. So we went to the place, and spent a couple of hours with these people, going through every fine step of how a cover is made. We wound up going out there two or three times. So the cover proof was finally done to his satisfaction.

"Then the whole scene shifts to New York. And we're down to a matter of days, if we want to get this album out in advance of the tour. After a lot of hassles and delays, it is finally decided that the cover will be printed at Ivy Hill lithographers, because they can do it fastest and supposedly they'll do it as well as anybody. So the day comes for Bruce to do something that no artist in the history of Columbia Records has ever done. Usually, you know, artists approve proofs of their cover, and then it's printed. But Bruce actually wants to go to the place where they print the cover.

"So the morning arrives, around the middle of May—the tour starts the twenty-third of May. We jump into a limo with the Ivy Hill people and head out to their printing plant. Bruce is jovial. And we get to Ivy Hill, spend quite a bit of time on the printing press, adjusting the color to exactly how Bruce wants it. It's the kind of art that's very sensitive to the slightest color changes. And you could see it right on the printing press. But Bruce finally says, 'This is it. Let's go.' We're all very happy; for me a six week trauma had come to an end.

"On the way back in the car, Bruce is telling stories, really opening up in front of a lot of people. I drop him off at the hotel. An hour later, I'm on the phone with Landau, saying, 'Jon, Bruce just approved the cover. We're smokin'; it looks like the album's gonna be out before the tour.' And Jon says, 'Dick, I couldn't tell you this this morning, but I got some bad news for ya. Bruce and I are going back to L.A. at six o'clock tonight to remix "The Promised Land." ' They were going to put the guitar solo back in. I couldn't believe it.

"But what really killed me was Bruce. He'd been obsessed with making this record for eleven months; it must have been gnawing at him all day, that he had to go back to L.A. and remix this song. Because that meant that the whole side would have to be remastered, and there was no way the album would be out for the first week of the tour. But he never rushed us; we took our time to get back to New York; he was in a joking mood, as if he had no place to go. And he had to make that plane. It was unbelievable."

Wingate had one final problem to solve. "Bruce didn't want any advertising for the album at first. What he conceived of, if he could have had it his way, was that the record would just appear one day in the stores, as if by magic."

Springsteen had had enough of hype; as far as he was concerned,

Darkness on the Edge of Town would rise and fall completely on its own merits. But he was ultimately concerned with something else. The key factor was that each of his other records had slipped from his personal control. *Darkness* would be different; this album would be his responsibility, start to finish. That way, if anything went wrong, he'd know why. Wingate finally prevailed about advertising by using exactly that rationale; there would be local advertising for the record in every town where Springsteen appeared in concert. If Bruce didn't design an ad, he was going to be seeing a lot of ads he hated. It was the kind of thinking Springsteen appreciated.

"He wanted to come back in total control of his career," Wingate says. "He became totally involved in his career as it related to the record company."

16 DARKNESS

arkness on the Edge of Town is a cycle of songs that
continually turns back upon itself in obsessive pursuit of
Big Secrets. But the record's themes might be understood even without lyrics. The sound is pounding and
relentless; the guitar screams, the organ howls, the vocals
roar, the drums crash. The music lets up only grudgingly, and then
not for long. All of it points toward something—not the darkness
per se, but what might be concealed there, discoverable only by
those with immense vision and will.

You could say that this music is about survival, but not the easy
kind that pop musicians and consciousness cults like to talk about.
This sort of survival isn't about being "happy" or having "fun," or
resolving the dilemmas of being sensually satiated. In this context,
that kind of "survival"—in which demons are neither conquered
nor conquering, but simply ignored—is far more meaningless than
death itself could ever be. For Springsteen, survival is a matter of
facing up to everything that saps psychic and physical strength; it
means taking life on its own terms, and never giving in. "When

Bruce Springsteen sings on his new album, that's not about 'fun,' "
said Pete Townshend, "that's fucking *triumph*, man."

The price for living to the hilt is paid in the currency of eternal
vigilance. It costs something to beat back the slack moments and
refuse the petty terrors of the everyday. "I wanna go out tonight,"
Springsteen sings on "Badlands," the song that opens the record. "I
want to find out what I got."

At the end of the album, a man stands alone at the bottom of a
hill. He has never had much in a material way; by now, he has been
stripped of what little he once possessed. Around him is little but
wreckage and the temptation to join it. And in the face of this, this
man raises his chin and sings:

> Tonight I'll be on that hill, cause I can't stop
> I'll be on that hill with everything I got
> I'll be there on time and I'll pay the cost
> Of wanting things that can only be found
> In the darkness on the edge of town

The singing now becomes a wordless moan, symbolic not of pain
but of effort, the labor of a man trying to raise himself above his
circumstances. There is not a hint of defeat. And the music continues, as we watch this man climb his hill, until he simply fades away,
leaving us to wonder what's at the top, desperate to know, convinced
that it's all been worth it.

But the violence of "Darkness" is far different from the stylized
fighting of "Incident on 57th Street" or the ritualized battles of
"Jungleland." This time, the grappling is clumsy, brutal, ugly—not
the romantic violence Springsteen imagined when roaming city
streets, but the real-life variety he saw in small towns back home.
"You can just tell some of these guys are looking for trouble,"
Springsteen said, recalling the faces in working-class bars in New
Jersey. "But they're not looking to punch anybody out. They want
to *be* punched."

For Springsteen, the most striking part of *The Grapes of Wrath*
is the early scene where the Dust Bowl farmer is trying to find out

who has evicted him from his land and is confronted with only images of faceless corporations. Similarly, a vague, disembodied "they" creeps into songs like "Something in the Night," "Prove It All Night" and "Streets of Fire" to deny people their most full-blooded possibilities.

Yet, for all the cars, the violence and the searching, the dominant image of *Darkness on the Edge of Town* is labor. There are lines about working in "Badlands," "Adam Raised a Cain," "Racing in the Streets," "The Promised Land," "Factory," and "Prove It All Night" and in three of the other four songs, there are references to wealth or the lack of it. But Springsteen's art is not socialist realism; he speaks so much of working because jobs are the overwhelming concern of the lives he writes about.

"I know what it's like not to be able to do what you want to do, because when I go home, that's what I see. It's not fun, it's no joke," Bruce told Robert Duncan. "I see some of my best friends. They're living the lives of my parents in a certain kind of way. They got kids; they're working hard. These are people, you can see something in their eyes. . . . I asked my friend, 'What do you do for fun?' 'I don't have any fun,' she says. She wasn't kidding."

So when Springsteen wants to compare those who are still alive to those who are just waiting to die, he expresses it in terms of what people do when work is done:

Some guys they just give up living
And start dying little by little, piece by piece
Some guys come home from work and wash up
And go racing in the streets

To me, those lines explain everything about *Darkness on the Edge of Town*, including its seeming obsession with auto imagery. But in the verse that follows, Springsteen makes a fine distinction that would probably occur only to someone who had lived among such people. The singer finds a girl, and loves her, but she can't share his dream. At the end of the song, she is staring off "into the night

with the eyes of one who hates for just being born." Springsteen
does not desert her, though he sings lines of utter compassion, lines
that reveal his knowledge of just how hard it is to keep from being
swallowed up by such niggardly existence:

> For all the shutdown strangers and hot rod angels
> Rumblin' through this promised land
> Tonight my baby and me are gonna drive to the sea
> And wash these sins off our hands

There's love in those words, and understanding, for precisely
those people who are ordinarily shut out of American life: commonplace, anonymous Americans, undistinguished by ethnicity or
other cultural memory. These are the sort of people who are ro-
manticized, depicted as the backbone of democracy, but almost
never allowed to speak for themselves. *Darkness on the Edge of Town*
is an album about such people. It's not an accident that the end of
"Racing in the Streets," where Danny Federici's organ blends with
Roy Bittan's piano in a fuguelike cry, is the warmest, most affectionate moment on this stark album.

Springsteen had spent most of his young lifetime trying to escape
working-class America, only to discover that he remained a product
of that society. As Thomas Massey wrote in a *Washington Monthly*
article published around the time that *Darkness on the Edge of Town*
was being completed, the differences in class life in this country
"can be defined in terms of income . . . culture . . . education and
occupation and prestige. But the single clearest class difference, the
sum of all the other parts, is the feeling of *control.*" It was precisely
this feeling that he did not run his own life that had spurred Springsteen toward rock and roll.

Darkness on the Edge of Town is the fruit of Springsteen's growing
awareness of these facts. And in a way, its most remarkable accomplishment is its spirit of compassion and reconciliation for everyone
and everything that had ever been falsely blamed. The apex of that
spirit is "Adam Raised a Cain," in which Springsteen sees himself
not only as a product of a specific social situation, but literally as
his father's heir:

In the Bible Cain slew Abel and East of Eden he was cast
You're born into this life payin' for the sins of somebody
    else's past
Well Daddy worked his whole life for nothin' but the pain
Now he walks these empty rooms lookin' for somethin' to
    blame
You inherit the sins, you inherit the flames
Adam raised a Cain

Like "It's My Life," this is the story of all sons, all fathers. And by telling it in terms of murder—the first murder, a fratricide—Springsteen makes all generations brothers, understanding once and for all that if there is an enemy, its face is not necessarily human. The fractured chords that lead into the song render the guitar a torture device and establish the motivation of the entire album: determination to break out of the vicious circle of pain and futility that robs people of the best parts of their lives.

The fact that music released him from this environment is why Bruce holds onto rock and roll so religiously. "If you grow up in a home where the concept of art is like twenty minutes in school everyday that you *hate*, the lift of rock is just incredible," he once told Paul Nelson. "There's a little barrier that gets broken down, a consciousness barrier. Rock and roll reached down into all those homes where there was no music or books or anything. And it infiltrated that whole thing. That's what happened in my house."

Perhaps, then, it is not surprising that rock critics (who for the most part have lived middle-class lives where such cultural poverty is unknown) found *Darkness on the Edge of Town* depressing. On the contrary, Springsteen isn't only describing working-class lives at their bleakest, he is writing about people who are breaking through these barriers. "The characters ain't kids," Bruce once told Tony Parsons of *New Musical Express*, "they're older—you been beat, you been hurt. But there's still hope, there's always hope. They throw dirt on you all your life, and some people get buried so deep in the dirt that they'll never get out. The album's about people who will never admit that they're buried that deep."

And so the final verse of the record's first song, "Badlands," is both an invocation and a benediction, Bruce Springsteen attempting to do for every listener what rock and roll had done for him:

For the ones who had a notion
A notion deep inside
That it ain't no sin to be glad you're alive.

17 THE PROMISE

Bruce Springsteen returned to the stage—and a life sealed off by neither lawsuits nor recording hassles—on May 23, 1978, at Shea's Buffalo Theatre. It was the first stop on a tour that would last until January 1, 1979—with only one lengthy break, from October 1 to November 1—and that would see Springsteen and the E Street Band play one hundred and nine shows in eighty-six cities, more than twice as many as they had ever done on a single tour. It was a triumphal tour, selling out even in some places where Bruce had never played before; the best shows came in the biggest halls, too, proving that Springsteen had broken through that final barrier, on his own terms.

But the world in which *Darkness on the Edge of Town* appeared in 1978 was drastically different than the one that *Born To Run* had conquered. The earlier album had signified the reemergence of rock's underclass, dividing rock and roll between those who were perpetuating an entertainment aristocracy and those who still believed in the fundamental ideals of the music's early days. By 1978, that challenge to the hegemony of rock's show business interests had been picked up by a self-conscious third wave of performers called "punks," who made the threat much more explicit, literally spitting on the conventional values of big-time rock.

The punk movement began in New York, with performers like the poet and sometime rock critic Patti Smith and a strange band called the Ramones. Both Smith and the Ramones developed a sound based on inspired amateurism. Their music had a sameness that bordered on monotony, but the energy of the revved-up guitars and unsyncopated drumming could not be denied. When the Ramones toured England in 1976, they left in their wake dozens of kids determined to emulate their raw, crude sound. In fact, the punks' strongest impact was felt in Britain; in America, they remained a cult of fringe eccentrics.

American punk was never a unified movement. The Ramones were deliberate satirists of pop-song conventions; songs like "I Wanna Sniff Some Glue" and "I Don't Wanna Walk Around with You" ridiculed the druggy romanticism of rock's previous generation. Smith was herself a product of that generation, and while her music blasted with less delicacy and craftsmanship than American rock of the Sixties and early Seventies, her mystical lyrics had specific roots in the work of the Doors, the Velvet Underground and Jimi Hendrix. The other American punks believed with Richard Hell of the group Television that they were part of a "blank generation," and they cultivated an apolitical, amoral apathy that flattered itself with pretensions to nihilism. Their attitude reflected their roots in bohemian dilettantism; most of the so-called "new wave" in New York—and later, Boston, San Francisco and Los Angeles—was in fact much closer spiritually to the pretensions of Seventies British art-rock performers like Brian Eno and Robert Fripp than to the basic rock and roll of Smith and the Ramones—much less the Sixties punks.

However, in Britain (where rock has the status of a major industry), the reaction to the punk possibility was decidedly political; if not always committed to leftist idealism, the punks certainly rejected the Rock Establishment's aristocratic pretensions. As the most revolutionary band since the MC5, the Clash took this to the furthest extreme. In general, English punk was not a matter of groups—in rejecting the rock aristocrats, the punks denied careerism most explicitly. Punk made rock once more a music of one-shot hits. The perfect example of this is the Sex Pistols, who were to the English outlaw rockers what the New York Dolls had been to Americans in the early Seventies. Threading a fine line between populist outrage and cult decadence, the Sex Pistols mocked such British institutions as the Queen's Silver Jubilee and threatened not apathy but "Anarchy in the U.K.," all with a wink and a grin that did nothing to belie the seriousness of their intent. Living up to their own beliefs, after recording a half dozen singles and one album, the Pistols broke up.

British punk also produced its fair share of exploiters, frauds and morons: Sham 69, who did for the revolutionary Clash what Alice Cooper did for Iggy Pop's sexual ambiguity; the Stranglers, whose sexism was perhaps more offensive than any of the traditional macho men of rock; the Damned, who had all the crudeness and none of the imagination of original punk greats like Count Five. But punk's best moments came on the kind of one-shots (Chelsea's "Right to Work," Magazine's "Shot by Both Sides") that the Rock Establishment could never have created. British punk also inspired a host of small record companies to challenge the marketing strategies of the major corporations—these labels were mostly short-lived or soon bought off in distribution pacts with the majors, but they contributed to an atmosphere of freedom and experimentation. So did the so-called new wave—artists whose philosophy was somehow linked with the punks but whose music was more carefully crafted or less outrageous: Elvis Costello, Graham Parker and Ian Dury, all affiliated with the Stiff Records' combine, were perhaps the most significant.

Parker and Costello had ties to a new group of American and British artists who had emerged in the wake of *Born To Run*; these included Bob Seger, Thin Lizzy (an Irish band featuring Phil Lynott), the Boomtown Rats (another Irish group, led by Bob Geldoff), Joe Jackson and, on the West Coast, Warren Zevon. It would be a mistake to say that all of these performers were inspired by the success of *Born To Run*, although Seger's hit, "Night Moves," and Thin Lizzy's "The Boys Are Back in Town" certainly were—but it is clear that without Springsteen's breakthrough, record companies would have been considerably less eager to sign up this kind of tough-but-tender, relatively nonconformist performer. There were also a variety of attempts to create synthetic Springsteens during Bruce's long absence from the studio: Appel's Arlyn Gale, for instance, Johnny Cougar and Billy Falcon. The most commercially successful of the lot was Meatloaf, a three-hundred-pound actor/ singer whose *Showboat* vocal style and cynically teen-tailored lyrics were redeemed only slightly by the appearance of Roy Bittan and Max Weinberg on his debut album.

If rock had changed enormously in three years, the pop industry had changed even more. Part of the reason was the emergence of a new form of black dance music, disco, as a potent commercial force. Some lamented the virtual disappearance of the old soul crooning style, regarding disco as a mechanical dance machine that stripped singers of their personality. While this is clearly true in some cases, it is also true that some of the best pop records of the late Seventies were done in that format.

More important, from a business perspective, the punk and disco movements loosened the power structure's stranglehold on popular music. Punk and disco records could be made quickly and cheaply, meaning that it was now once again feasible to make music that did not conform to the narrow requirements of the Establishment's tastes. The major record companies were easily able to attach themselves to the most profitable performers in both idioms, but at least they had to recognize the blacks and gays who originated disco, the uncouth youths who spawned punk.

Sadly, the older rock performers seemed more bankrupt than ever. When Linda Ronstadt recorded Elvis Costello's "Alison" and the Rolling Stones scored a disco hit with "Miss You," the results seemed less acts of rapprochement than products of a desperate cynicism. Ronstadt and the Stones were at a loss for a formula to replace their old one, which had begun to fall apart in the face of the new divisions among the audience.

Meanwhile, Springsteen decided to change booking agencies, moving from William Morris to Frank Barsalona's Premier Talent in early 1977. In 1976, Barsalona had signed the Asbury Jukes, and Springsteen first met him through Miami Steve, but their alliance seemed natural. More than any other Rock Establishment figure, Barsalona had greeted the changes of the preceding years with open arms, signing Patti Smith, the Ramones, the Sex Pistols and Graham

Parker. Barsalona was canny enough to understand Springsteen's need to determine his own style as a performer. (He was also shrewd enough to hire Barry Bell away from William Morris late in 1977, in time for Bell to work on the *Darkness* tour.)

Of course, attaching himself to Columbia Records and Premier Talent was not a particularly radical position for Bruce to assume. But he had resolved his conflicts about the business world; as he explained to interviewers, after having worked so hard to make the best record possible, he would have been stupid not to attempt to reach as many listeners as possible. Besides, with the aid of Jon Landau (who became Springsteen's manager officially in July 1978), he was confident he could effectively manipulate the system. That's always a dangerous presumption, of course, but Springsteen is so single-minded that it seemed likely that he could make it work without any undue compromises. Certainly, by playing sports arenas so successfully Springsteen proved that he could have both quality and quantity; in fact, he got a clearer, more powerful sound in Madison Square Garden than many acts have at the Palladium or the Bottom Line.

To both old wave and new, Springsteen remained an outsider. Rock aristocrats mistrusted his high level of commitment to his fans, which sharply contrast with the way the others kept their distance from their own fans. When Mick Jagger wished to get close to his audience at Madison Square Garden, he teased them by swinging overhead on a rope, just out of reach. When Bruce Springsteen wanted to be with his fans, he climbed offstage and sang from their midst, confident that he would not be ripped to shreds. Such things did nothing to endear him to the more insecure stars of old-line rock.

Oddly, Springsteen was threatening to the punks in much the same way. Because punk ideology was absolutely antisentimental, the humanism of *Darkness on the Edge of Town* seemed old-fashioned to many new wave ideologues. And Springsteen's devotion to the needs of his audience, and his willingness to go much farther than halfway to meet those stood in stark contrast to the icy isolation of Elvis Costello, the Sex Pistols and the Clash, all of whom viewed their listeners with at least as much suspicion as they regarded their corporate sponsors. Actually, the comparison is unfair—

with the exception of the Pistols' Johnny Rotten, punk has not produced a figure with a fraction of Bruce's charisma. Despite the legitimate claims of others to be taken seriously, Bruce Springsteen often seems like the last rock star, or at least the last one innocent of cynicism.

To anyone witnessing a single show, Springsteen's 1978 tour was reassuring; there was still plenty of vitality in rock and roll. For those lucky enough to follow the progress of the tour, though, it was epochal. Dick Wingate remembers trying to schedule filming a concert for a TV commercial. Someone suggested that Bruce could pick a town where the camera crew's interference onstage really wouldn't matter. "There's no such place," Springsteen immediately replied. And that was the way the tour went, night after night, three-and four-hour shows back to back, then a couple of hours of interviews backstage. After singing all of *Darkness*, all of *Born To Run*, selections from the first two albums, and a few oldies, Bruce was almost always the very last person to leave the auditorium. But if there were any kids still hanging around the backstage door, he'd remain there until every last one of them had a fragment of what he wanted—a couple of moments of conversation, an autograph, just recognition.

The *Darkness* songs went over well, but that didn't prevent Bruce from introducing new material into the show. He did "The Promise" once in a while and "Independence Day" about as often; by early July, he already was performing a newly written song called "Point Blank," a ballad that extended the *Darkness* story into its next phase.

The rockabilly listening of the past year paid off, too, with versions of Buddy Holly's "Not Fade Away," Eddie Cochran's "Summertime Blues," Jerry Lee Lewis's "High School Confidential" and Elvis's "Heartbreak Hotel." But the greatest rockabilly moment came one night at Madison Square Garden: "I hear you got a newspaper strike in town," Bruce said as he stepped to the mike for the first song. "Well, have you heard the news?" The band roared into a version of Elvis's milestone "Good Rockin' Tonight" that could have lifted the roof.

There was much more; too much to absorb. For every moment

cited, another begs for inclusion. That's the way it's supposed to be. The very best moments of the tour were the ones when you could see how far Springsteen had come—they were the times when he'd simply lean forward and smile, laugh, shake his head at a band member as if to say that it was all too good to be true. "You know," said Max Weinberg, "when I was twelve years old, this is *exactly* what I wanted to be doing." Trying to explain that would really be like trying to tell a stranger about rock and roll.

If Bruce Springsteen's story has a central issue, it's whether dawning maturity is compatible with the rock and roll spirit. During the 1978 tour Bruce told a story similar to the one he'd told in 1976 about the gypsy lady. It has the ring of truth, though just how much only Bruce himself can say. In the middle of "Growin' Up," Bruce would step forward with a smile:

"When I was growing up, there were two things that were unpopular in my house. One was me and the other was my guitar. We had this grate, like the heat was supposed to come through, except it wasn't hooked up to any heating ducts; it was just open straight down to the kitchen, and there was a gas stove right underneath it. When I used to start playing, my pop used to turn on the gas jets and try to smoke me outta my room. And I had to go hide out on the roof or something.

"He always used to call the guitar, never Fender guitar or Gibson guitar, it was always the *God-damned* guitar. Every time he'd knock on my door, that was all I'd hear: 'Turn down that God-*damn* guitar.' He musta thought everything in my room was the same brand: God-damn guitar, God-damn stereo, God-damn radio.

"Anyway, one day my mom and pop, they come to me and say, 'Bruce, it's time to get serious with your life. This guitar thing . . . it's okay as a hobby but you need something to fall back on.' My father, he said, 'You should be a lawyer'—which I coulda used later on in my career. He says, 'Lawyers, they run the world.' But I didn't think that they did—and I still don't.

"But my mother used to say, 'No, no, no, he should be an author, he should write books; that's a good life. You can get a little something for yourself.' But me, I wanted to play the guitar.

"Now my mother, she's real Italian, and my father, he's Irish. So they say, 'This is a big thing. You should go see the priest. Tell him we want you to be a lawyer or an author. But don't say *nothin'* about that God-damn guitar.'

"So I went to the rectory and knocked on the door. 'Hi, Father Ray, I'm Mr. Springsteen's son.' I tell him, 'I got this problem. My father, he thinks I should be a lawyer, and my mother wants me to be an author. But me, I got this guitar.'

"Father Ray says, 'This is too big a deal for me. You got to talk to God,' who I didn't know too well at the time. 'Tell him about the lawyer and the author,' Father Ray says, 'but don't say *nothin'* about that guitar.'

"Now I was worried. Where was I gonna find God, right? So I go find Clarence—he knows everybody. Clarence says, 'No sweat. I know right where he is.' So I show up at Clarence's house in my mother's car—an old Nash Rambler. Clarence looks at me. He says, 'You gonna go visit God in that? Man, he's got like, people in Cadillacs, you know. He ain't gonna pay attention to anybody shows up in a Nash Rambler.' But it's all I got.

"So we drive way out of town, along this old dark road. We drive a long ways, and I say to Clarence, 'Man, you sure you know where we're goin'?' Clarence says, 'Sure, I just took a guy out here the other day.' So we finally come to this little house, way out in the woods, nothing around, but all the lights are on inside. There's music blasting out and a little hole in the door.

"I knock and this eye peeps out. I say, 'Uh, Clarence sent me.' So they let me in. And there's God, behind the drums. On the bass drum it says: 'G-O-D.' So I said, 'God, I got this problem. My father, he wants me to be a lawyer, 'cause he says lawyers rule the world. And my mother, she wants me to be an author, get a little something for myself. But they just don't understand—I got this guitar.'

"God looks at me. He says, 'I know, I know. See, what they don't understand is, Moses screwed up. There was supposed to be an Eleventh Commandment. Actually, Moses was so scared after ten—it was a great show, the burning bush, the thunder, lightning, you shoulda seen it—he went back down the mountain. You see, what those guys don't understand is that there was *supposed* to be an Eleventh Commandment. And all it said was:

"LET IT ROCK!"

18 THE PRICE YOU PAY

Now some say forget the past
And some say don't look back
But for every breath you take, you leave a track
And though it don't seem fair, for every smiling place,
The tears fall somewhere
Oh the price you pay

Bruce Springsteen

The 1978 tour ended with concerts in Cleveland on New Year's Eve and New Year's Day. It had been a triumphal tour, the band's longest and the first one ever to show much profit. Over its 150 nights, Bruce Springsteen and the E Street Band played to more than a million fans, and almost every one of them had come away marveling at the sweetness and innocence, the ecstasy and the intensity.

But at the stroke of midnight on New Year's Eve, a fan, over-zealous or just plain dumb, hurled a fire cracker at the stage. It exploded just beneath Bruce's right eye. Hardly missing a beat, Springsteen snapped, "I'm gonna have a good new year anyway," then pushed the band into "Good Rockin' Tonight."

When the song was finished, he left the stage without a word. The band was left to mill around, the crowd to grow restive. Bruce appeared a few moments later wearing a clean shirt. He stepped up to the mike and turned the air blue with his anger. And though Springsteen got back into a groove after a few more numbers and played his show the next night without incident, the firecracker soured what should have been the tour's celebratory conclusion.

Afterward, Springsteen took a break to the California sun, then went home to write songs for his fifth album. Only two new numbers had been worked out on the road, "The Ties that Bind" and "Point Blank." Yet he could approach this album with uncommon confidence, for his affairs had never been so well ordered. The tour had confirmed his stature as the premier American rock act on stage, and if *Darkness on the Edge of Town* hadn't expanded his audience as much, it had at least successfully presented another aspect of his talent to more than a million listeners. Business was less of a problem than ever. And the band had grown in skill and dexterity, capable of transforming "Prove It All Night," so slight on record that it is almost a throwaway, into an eight-minute explosion on stage.

By the end of March, Bruce had written enough material to start rehearsing the band. A few days later, the band was in the recording studio, this time the Power Station on West Fifty-third Street in Manhattan. The studio, housed in an old church, had a huge cathedral-style main room perfect for getting the big sound that the production team—Bruce, Jon and, for the first time officially, Steve Van Zandt—wanted.

The band's early progress was so swift and efficient that CBS flatly predicted that the record would be in the stores by mid-September. While most people understood this to mean sometime around Christmas, or right after the first of the new year, for Springsteen even those release dates would have meant lightninglike speed.

But in mid-April, Robin Williams, then storming the country as Mork from Ork, hit town for some live shows. An old friend of Barry Bell, Williams had met Springsteen at an earlier session, and now he and Bell decided to drive out to Springsteen's house in New

Jersey on a Saturday afternoon. When they arrived, Bruce and his girl friend, actress Joyce Heiser, were cavorting on a three-wheeled off-the-road motorbike. As Williams and Bell came up the drive, Springsteen let his concentration on the terrain lapse, and the bike crashed, jamming Bruce's leg between the machine and a tree, damaging a muscle in his leg. Visibly in pain, Springsteen resisted going to the hospital until much later that evening; by then the leg was badly swollen, and the doctors quickly diagnosed severe muscle damage and ordered him completely off his feet for the next three weeks.

If it had only broken the momentum of the recording sessions, the injury would have been frustrating. But the inactivity drove Springsteen to grouchy distraction. His energy seethed and he raged and grew depressed. It was a bad time, and the rumors made it worse.

As utterly accessible as Springsteen can be when he's touring, he's equally isolated during recording sessions. Since it would have been pretentious for Bruce to issue progress reports on the albums, the more active imaginations among his fans and the media were given free play.

During his months in the studio, there were at least a dozen wild tales told about Springsteen's activities. He was said to be making screen tests for at least three movies and to have approved a script based on "Racing in the Street." He was recording at home, with a mobile studio, or making a live album, or turning to disco music. He was producing Stevie Nicks, making a duet album with Rickie Lee Jones, writing songs with Bob Seger, and going out with sixteen-year-old Rachel Sweet. The E Street Band was breaking up. Each of these rumors appeared in several publications ranging from *Rolling Stone* to *Carcraft*, *Playboy* to the *New Musical Express*.

The news of Springsteen's injury broke on WNEW-FM, the New York rock station, and quickly spread to Liz Smith's daily gossip column, where it was syndicated around the country. According to these reports, Springsteen was in a hospital with an injury to his back that had caused him to be placed in traction.

As rumors go, this one was minor and it was quickly dispelled, but its inaccuracy was symptomatic. It was only that Springsteen had hurt his leg not his back, and was recuperating at home not in the hospital, and he was never in traction. These were the only facts the media got wrong.

By the first of May, when Bruce got back to recording, the pace quickly picked up. And the material was once more spurting forth: about twenty songs altogether, not all of them finished, but rough melodies and arrangements, fragmentary lyrics, the typical state of a Springsteen composition when the band begins to record it. In addition to the "Needles and Pins"-style "The Ties that Bind" and the doomy "Point Blank," there was "Hungry Heart," which sounded as much like a hit as anything he had done; "Roulette," a paranoid rocker that was written just after the near-meltdown at Three Mile Island; "Cindy," the sweetest love song he'd ever written; and the brutal, thunderous "Jackson Cage." There were also a couple of numbers left over from the *Darkness* sessions: "Sherry Darling" (considered as a possible single that summer) and "Ramrod." The E Street Band played these songs brilliantly; Landau suggested that if the album was delayed, the only reason he could see might be that everyone was enjoying the sessions so much.

In late May a problem arose, and although it was fairly minor at the time, it symptomized what was becoming an important issue. Through lax studio security, someone got hold of a cassette of some practice and rehearsal tapes. Fortunately, he was a novice, and not knowing what to do with the tape, played it for a Manhattan record shop owner, over his store's sound system, during business hours. Naturally, word immediately got back to the studio, and within a few days the situation was corrected—dramatically. Bruce's tapes were henceforward placed in an anvil case, fitted with enough locks to foil Houdini, and stored in a locked room to which only engineer Neil Dorfsman, roadie Doug Sutphin and Landau's assistant, Debbie Gold, had keys.

In general, however, bootlegging was getting out of hand. Down near the Shore, record stores were bold enough to display whole stacks of illicit LPs, and Landau and Springsteen, with the involvement of CBS, moved to halt the trade in Springsteen bootlegs, through the courts.

In some ways, Springsteen had cooperated all along with efforts to quash the bootlegging. But onstage, at one of the many 1978 shows that were broadcast live, he had often said things that tended to give tacit approval to such records. Stepping to the mike to begin his second set at the Roxy in Los Angeles, for instance, Springsteen had shouted: "Bootleggers! Roll your tapes." And he didn't sound like he was speaking in a spirit of resignation.

Rehearsal and studio tapes were also bootlegged, which was a different matter. At least the concerts were meant to be heard publicly. But taken together, the rash of Springsteen bootlegs that popped up during the later months of 1978 and the first half of 1979 presented a set of financial, artistic and ethical problems.

Financially, the problem wasn't that serious, since anyone devoted enough to shell out the often exorbitant prices the bootleggers charged would surely spend the much more reasonable price CBS charged for official recordings. Anyway, such albums were rarely pressed in quantities of more than ten thousand. Legally, however, Springsteen had to stop the bootlegs or jeopardize his copyright control of the music.

Worse, the bootlegs were obviously exploitative of the audience Springsteen otherwise worked so hard to protect. The pressings were of inferior vinyl, the sound quality was inevitably lousy and they were often outrageously priced, sometimes costing as much as $15 to $20 per disc.

Artistically, Springsteen felt strongly that only he had the right to determine which of his songs should be issued, and in what form. If he rejected a song because it didn't fit an album conceptually, or because of the performance quality, or just because he developed an irrational hatred of the thing, that choice belonged to him, no one else.

The fans who bought bootlegs felt otherwise. In their view, they had a right to Springsteen's work, and since he "refused" to satisfy their demand, they also had a right to go out and find more of it as best they could. When one heard songs as striking as the acoustic version of "Thunder Road" on the *E Ticket* bootleg, or music as historically important to Springsteen's artistic development as that on *Fire on the Fingertips* (another bootleg LP), it was hard to disagree.

But as Jon Landau would later tell *Rolling Stone*, "Bruce spends a year of his life conceiving and executing an album so that it will perfectly reflect the musical statement he wants to make. Then these people come along and confiscate material that was never intended for release on an album, sell it and make a profit on it without ever paying anyone that's involved. It's just out-and-out theft; somebody has stolen something and we want it back."

Music is recorded and performed in the studio for two reasons: to help the artist grow and to communicate what he's learned. If anyone but the artist determines the shape of that communication, then the historical record is distorted. It is no more fair or just to release the scraps and fragments of a performer's work without his consent than it would be to publish the crumpled first draft of a book, or the cutting room floor out-takes of a movie.

In August, CBS Records and Springsteen filed suit in federal district court in Los Angeles against five defendants, asking $1.75 million damages on charges ranging from copyright infringement and unfair competition to unauthoritzed use of name and likeness and unjust enrichment. In November, a similar suit was filed against a New Jersey man in federal district court in Newark. "You've got to understand something about Bruce," Peter Parcher, who was handling this litigation also, told reporters. "He works forever to get a record out. He has very strong feelings about what kinds of records he wants out." Although these suits were not always pursued to their conclusion, they served their purposes: getting the bootlegged records off the streets and scaring off new ones. Parcher adds that Springsteen's assertion of his rights has again established an important precedent for other performers.

The bootlegging and tape theft problems were part of a more fundamental difficulty in Springsteen's approach to his work. "We're slow—I'm slow in the studio. I take a long time," he said in 1980. For fans, this was enormously frustrating, and after a point, it became just as frustrating for the band and the others Springsteen worked with. There was no telling how long finishing this record might really take; though CBS was sticking to an optimistic autumn estimate of the album's release, the kids were stuck with their memories of the three-year wait for *Darkness*.

Springsteen denies that he is frustrated by the slowness. "I'm lucky," he says. "I'm in there, I'm seeing it every step of the way. I would assume that if you didn't know what was going on, and you cared about it, it would be frustrating. With me, it was not frustrating."

No fan could say as much, and some fairly bizarre activity took place as a result. Perhaps the strangest was the campaign, led by Carol Miller, the WPIJ New York disc jockey, to have "Born To Run" made New Jersey's state song. In early 1979, she'd read an article that said that the state was looking for an official song, and she began to encourage her listeners to write letters to the state assembly saying that "Born To Run" should be the one chosen.

As a shrewd media professional with a law degree (and with the aid a salesman at the station who was the son of an important assemblyman) Miller had an instinct for the way such things are accomplished. In March, a resolution was introduced to the Assembly, calling for "Born To Run" to be selected as the State of New Jersey's "Unofficial Youth Rock Anthem" and for Bruce Springsteen to be appointed the state's "Youth Ambassador" to the world, touching off a furor.

Given its mordant view of the state, "Born To Run" was an unlikely choice. But Springsteen was now so popular in New Jersey that, as one state legislator said, he could have swung almost any election with his endorsement. (Significantly, U.S. senator Bill Bradley visited the band in the studio that spring.) So, despite objections, and without any comment by Springsteen, the Assembly passed the resolution on June 12. (The section designating Bruce as Youth Ambassador had been mercifully deleted.)

Springsteen must have found such attention both embarrassing and flattering. But he also must have known that it was indicative of the new responsibilities his stature gave him.

In May, Springsteen was in Los Angeles for light man Marc Brickman's wedding. While there, he met with Tom Campbell, a veteran antinuclear energy activist. Springsteen had met Campbell while in California the previous winter, at an antinuclear energy benefit at which Graham Nash and Jackson Browne appeared. Since then, of course, the near-meltdown at the Three Mile Island nuclear reactor had occurred.

Three Mile Island affected Springsteen deeply, both because it was such a nearly cataclysmic public event, and because the area of Pennsylvania where it occurred was less than a hundred miles from central New Jersey, where Bruce lived.

A number of West Coast musicians, not only Browne and Nash but also Bonnie Raitt, John Hall and others, had a long history of antinuclear activity. Three Mile Island had finally made the issue a matter of prominent national interest, and in its wake, Raitt, Hall, Nash, Browne and some others got together with some full-time political activists, including Campbell, to form MUSE (Musicians United for Safe Energy). Their first order of business was to set up a full-scale benefit concert in New York, at Madison Square Garden, to raise funds and further interest in the issue.

Now Campbell was asking if Springsteen would consider performing at the shows, tentatively scheduled for September. Surprisingly, Springsteen was immediately enthusiastic.

Springsteen had always kept himself aloof from any specific political involvements. Obviously, MUSE was not the first to ask for his involvement, but Springsteen had always shied away from any specific political statements (even though there were strong political threads in his work from the beginning). Secondly, Springsteen was a perpetual outsider and resisted aligning himself with other musicians (an alliance with such musicians as these—the very American Rock Establishment itself—must have been the most shocking factor of all). Finally, the antinuclear movement was associated with the rural, post-hippie ecology movement, the very back-to-the-land types who stood diametrically opposite the urban and small-town working people Springsteen sang for and about.

But even though Bruce didn't give MUSE a firm commitment for several weeks, it wasn't because he was weighing such considerations. It was simply his natural talent for procrastination, which lets him delay making any decision until it absolutely must be made. If there were questions in his mind about MUSE, they had little to do with political considerations, but with the logistics of the event itself.

Springsteen was getting close to completing his album, which meant the work intensified. In the meantime, Landau had several meetings with various MUSE representatives, at which it was agreed that Springsteen would play only a one-hour edition of his show, that the ticket price of $18.50 was acceptable, and that Springsteen would allow the shows to be recorded and lend one of his tracks to the projected concert LP. MUSE also planned to film the shows, but Springsteen and Landau hedged on that proposition, agreeing to let their show be filmed but not committing themselves to allow the footage to be used.

The only additional request Springsteen made was that the concert's official photographer, Lynn Goldsmith, not shoot his shows. Lynn and Bruce had had a romance during the 1978 tour during which time Goldsmith took a great many photos of the performer. Then they broke up. So before the shows, Bruce called Lynn and said that while he understood her desire to be involved with MUSE, he hoped that she'd understand that he didn't want her shooting his sets. Goldsmith agreed.

When Springsteen's shows were announced, they quickly sold out, something that the other nights, with the Doobie Brothers as headliners, had not done. Springsteen's involvement had turned the economic prospects of the shows from iffy to solid. And, of course, his involvement doubled media interest.

Why had Springsteen decided to play the shows? Both politicians and musicians wondered, and Springsteen wasn't answering. Besides the obvious answers suggested above, Springsteen has never said. And this made many people suspicious.

The politicians felt that Bruce's involvement, particularly as the headliner of the shows, was especially suspect since he'd never been associated with politics before, and had declined to issue an antinuclear statement of principle in the program for the shows, as all the other performers had done.

In fact, Springsteen's refusal to make any comments about the politics of antinuclear energy confused just about everybody, especially the part of his audience who were already suspicious of MUSE because of its soft rock, hippie ethic background, and probably the other performers at the shows themselves. Springsteen said that his music was his statement, the fact of his appearance spoke for itself, but that didn't really answer any of several interesting questions: Why MUSE? Why align himself with that Rock Establishment?

The latter question probably didn't bother Springsteen much at all, even if he was aware that people might be intrigued by it. As a musician, he had an intrinsic respect for other musicians; if he sometimes spoke with the voice of a rock critic, that did not make him one. For Springsteen, his appearance was statement enough for him, and the same was true for the other performers there.

Springsteen probably didn't make a political statement because nuclear energy was not an issue with whose details he was especially familiar. As reflected in "Roulette," the song he wrote soon after Three Mile Island, his concerns were primarily with the human dimensions of the problem. In that song, Springsteen portrays a man evacuated from his hometown after just such a disaster; he reflects on that home and how desolate it *always* has been. But this man also knows that he is not being told the full story, and so he attempts to return, is trapped at a police road-block, but escapes, and finally does get back home, only to find greater devastation than he had been able to imagine.

The music is scarifying, blasting in like Del Shannon's "Stranger in Town," which is to say, with a full gust of paranoia. Max Weinberg plays the same pattern he used for "Candy's Room," only moved to the toms and made more ominous; the guitar part is all power chords, wrenched from the gut, and the singing moves from a virtual whisper to a sustained scream. The music is as riveting as anything Springsteen's ever done, and it rides right over a good many of the words, so that only fragments are understandable. In the end, what you hear are lines like these:

Roulette! Bullet in the chamber
Roulette! Gun to your head
Roulette! Finger to the trigger
Roulette! No more danger

You could say that Springsteen had managed to take the most dramatic public event in recent history and render it melodramatic. But you can't say that this melodrama cheapens the event, because he has also taken a great impersonal force that affects everyone's life and given it human scale. "Roulette" performs the prime function of political art, taking a series of lies (that Three Mile Island was an "isolated accident"; that because the place didn't blow up or melt down it was "safe"; that no one got hurt) and stands it on its head. Hearing that song is like experiencing those days in the spring of 1979 all over again, and that is its value. This is a piece of music that tries to make sure that you *never* forget.

And if that wasn't why Bruce Springsteen played MUSE, it should have been.

But "Roulette" has never been released. (It was not even included in the final batch of songs mixed for the album.) Nor has it ever been performed live. So the closest that Springsteen has ever come to an explicit statement about why he played those shows is a more general comment. "It's the *whole* thing," he said. "It's terrible, it's horrible. Somewhere along the way, the idea, which I think initially was to get some fair transaction between people, went out the window. And what came in was: the most you can get, the most you can get, and the least you can give." Springsteen was speaking a couple of nights after Ronald Reagan had been elected President, and here, he laughed one of his quizzical laughs. "That's why cars are the way they are today. It's just an erosion of all the things that were true and right about the original idea."

So maybe what it boiled down to was that Bruce Springsteen played MUSE as a simple act of good citizenship. Having chosen to lead a public life, and reap the rewards, he was now living up to the duties incurred. It probably helped that such a dramatic event— MUSE would be a four-night event at the Garden, with enough stars to insure its stature as a major media event—appealed to his innate sense of showmanship. And that having been cooped up in the studio since spring, he was itching to get back onstage.

This does not answer all the political questions about MUSE— its politics remained smug and terribly narrow, and its proposal for "decentralized" solar power as a nuclear alternative was clearly un- workable in an urban environment. But given that Springsteen was going to act out his social obligation as a star, he had to align him- self with someone, and the rock and roll left, at least in America, was hardly organized enough to pull off anything on the scale of MUSE—and besides, the politics of the rock and roll left were no less blinkered and elitist.

The concerts themselves were remarkable, despite being over- booked in a vain attempt to satisfy various artistic and political constituencies. The shows the Doobies headlined were acceptable entertainment, at least, and the week as a whole was an event of sufficient importance to generate a lot of media attention.

But more than anything, Springsteen was the story of those five nights. He was one of the few stars who was appearing at the height of fame, and the only one who was appearing in his own backyard. So the thunder began before he ever reached the stage: long swelling moans—"Broooooce!"—that were a constant background to all the other acts. It sounded enough like "Boo!" to make Chaka Khan and Bonnie Raitt inquire nervously. (The next Monday, when the performers assembled at *Rolling Stone* for a cover photograph session, Bruce was (naturally) the last to arrive, and as he came through the door, the others took up the chant. "Brooce!" they clamored. Were they converted?)

"The response Springsteen received as he walked onstage Friday night . . . was the most frenzied I've ever heard," wrote Kit Rachlis in the *Boston Phoenix*. "He was frightened, I suspect, but he never let it overwhelm him. Nor did he cut back; he simply made sure that it took him where he wanted to go. It was that acknowledgment of his own fear and his recognition that he was invoking something larger than himself that made his appearance, in MUSE terms, the most mythic and political gesture of all." Not everyone might agree, but it was certainly true that the response Springsteen received was the only gesture of total unity about anything on that night. And he played over his head, despite the fact that both the band and himself were out of condition. His set featured "Promised Land," "Prove It All Night," "Thunder Road," "Rosalita," one new ballad, "The River," and a duet with Jackson Browne on "Stay," leading up to the climactic encore, "Quarter to Three." When it was over, the house came down.

The next night was far less joyous. It began in much the same spirit, and with perhaps even higher expectations, because the act leading to Springsteen was Tom Petty, a young Floridian who played in a similar style, though a good deal more laconically. And as Springsteen took the stage, and the chanting and roaring of "Broooooce" once more filled the room, it seemed like an instant replay.

But it was Springsteen's thirtieth birthday, a milestone in the life of any rock star, and one that he seemed to take especially hard. "Well, I'm over thirty now," he said, after enough cries of Happy Birthday had reached the stage. "I guess I can't trust myself anymore." The irony was well intentioned. Yet a few moments later, when someone in the crowd passed up a birthday cake, Springsteen impulsively threw it out into the crowd. As he watched it spatter the clothing of the crowd in that section of the floor, Bruce snarled, "Send me the cleaning bill." It was an uncharacteristically ugly scene.

And the night got worse. Although Springsteen managed to keep the music going at an acceptable level, he was agitated. During "Rosalita," he began gesturing to the road crew, pointing out some disturbance in the front rows. But when the security force investigated, they saw nothing, not so much as an argument, much less a fight, which is what they were looking for. Yet Springsteen called them back again, and they still found nothing.

Finally, Springsteen took matters into his own hands. He leaped from the stage and went down into the front rows. When he reappeared, he had Lynn Goldsmith by the arm, pulling her with him up onto the stage. "This is my ex-girl friend," Springsteen shouted into the mike, and then he picked Lynn up and carried her to the rear of the stage, where she was quickly hustled from the hall.

Backstage, no one was quite sure how to react. Was this moving, or funny, or what? It was, in the end, the most stupid public act of Springsteen's career, and one which, for that instant, at least, made his rock and roll idealism hypocritical. Goldsmith *had* been snapping away, in violation of their agreement. (She later claimed that Springsteen had asked only that she not take pictures of him from the photographer's pit immediately in front of the stage, but that's not believable.) But Goldsmith's offense was hardly so major that it required such drastic action on Bruce's part.

Although Goldsmith might have expected the treatment she got—if there is anything Springsteen hates, it's deceit—this incident isn't forgivable. Maybe it could be written off as an overreaction on a night when the stress level was running pretty high, but it was still a major embarrassment. And Springsteen seemed to know it. Right afterward, he stood in front of the mike, trembling, shaking his head. Clarence Clemons looked at him, questioningly. "I don't know," Bruce said. "Some nights, I just don't know. . . ." Then he spun back into the song.

Surprisingly, not very much was made of this incident in the reports following the shows. Not until the following Monday, at least, when a report appeared in the *New York Post*, quoting Goldsmith as saying that she was considering suing Springsteen for $3 million for public humiliation and for being "manhandled" backstage. It didn't seem likely that she had much of a case; a good part of the crowd that night thought she was being honored, for one thing, and for another, it was clear in the film of the show that Springsteen had handled her pretty gently, and that Goldsmith was laughing in his face. In any case, no lawsuit was ever filed.

MUSE ended in triumph anyway, with a version of "Quarter to Three" packed with spoofing James Brown drama—a nurse (Heiser) and two attendants in white coats lugging Bruce offstage on a stretcher, and then Springsteen bounding back onstage, as if revived by the band's continued playing. It took the taste of that nasty moment out of one's mouth, if not one's memory.

MUSE was only a marginal success on other levels—instead of $750,000, the originally projected profit, it made only about $300,000, because of overtime charges and some extravagant expenses (parties at the superstar nitery, Trax), and because of a hastily assembled fifth concert, starring Crosby, Stills and Nash, which was played with the Garden only a bit more than half full and therefore lost money.

But for Springsteen, the two nights were a success on every level. Although he had already sold out three nights at the Garden on his own, although he had often played better, MUSE placed Springsteen firmly and permanently in the pantheon of American superstars.

Springsteen went back to the studio with his head buzzing. He was now thirty, an age at which almost all of his role models had begun to deteriorate, and that was worth worrying about. He would later tell *Los Angeles Times* critic Robert Hilburn that he decided that it didn't have to be that way—he wouldn't let it be. But in the meantime, he was feeling uneasy about his new album. CBS had revised their prediction; now they felt that the record would be out by Christmas, or the first of the year at the latest. Mixing was almost ready to begin, and the songs had been chosen. Indeed, even the sequence had been established: Side One was to include "The Ties that Bind," "Cindy," "Hungry Heart," "Stolen Car" and "Be True." Side Two was to include "The River," "You Can Look (But You Better Not Touch)," "The Price You Pay," "I Wanna Marry You," and the album's closer, "Loose Ends." But somehow, Bruce was getting cold feet; he later explained that the exuberance of the audience at MUSE had just made the album seem inadequate.

So they scrapped it and went back into the studio to record more songs. Springsteen continued to write material, but more than anything he was trying to discover a way to balance the two sides of his music: the joyousness expressed on *Born To Run*, and the tragic vision captured on *Darkness*.

"I just said, 'I don't understand all these things. I don't see where all these things fit. I don't see how all these things can work together,'" he remembered when the ordeal was over. "It was because I was always focusing in on some small thing; when I stepped back, they made a sense of their own. It was just a situation of living with all those contradictions. And that's what happens. There's never any resolution. You have moments of clarity, things become clear to you that you didn't understand before. But there's never any making ends meet or finding any type of long-standing peace of mind about something." But in October 1979, Springsteen was still some months away from that realization.

Later in the month, a more pressing circumstance came up. The MUSE concerts were being released, as a double disc live album; pressured by Jackson Browne, Bruce mixed the song they had sung together, a version of the Maurice Williams and the Zodiacs' hit "Stay," in only a few days. Then it was decided that in order to better represent all of the artists who had appeared, it was necessary to make the album a three-record set. But if there was more than enough obvious material for two records, it was harder to fill up a third.

Browne, Springsteen, Landau and Van Zandt spent hours in the studio, trying to find the right additional song. At first, they thought they wanted "Thunder Road." But, playing "Stay" over and over again, they heard and liked the transition, a particularly seamless one, from "Stay" into the band's medley of Mitch Ryder hits "Jenny

Take a Ride" and "Devil with a Blue Dress/Good Golly Miss Molly." Finally, Landau suggested that the Detroit Medley was probably what should go on the record with "Stay." The others agreed.

"The Devil with a Blue Dress Medley," as it's listed on the LP, presented a problem. In the midst of the song, Springsteen paused to urgently warn of the health hazards the high-voltage excitement about to come would present. He suggested that the faint of heart leave the building, or at least go out in the hall. It was a very funny, very long story, and it made the track too long for the album's purposes. Landau, Browne and Van Zandt each made his respective attempt to edit the story, and each version seemed more ridiculous than the last; it was like trying to cut down "Born To Run."

So Springsteen solved the problem. In a gesture that probably stands as one definition of his artistic approach, he simply ordered the story cut out altogether, and joined the musical sections together. It worked, too; unless you know what you're looking for, the splice is barely evident.

And when the *No Nukes* album was released just before Christmas, it was "The Devil with a Blue Dress Medley" that had the overwhelming airplay and was the critical favorite. If the music was not quite as magical as one would have expected Springsteen's first officially released live music to be, that was, as anyone who had seen him knew, because what he did live could not be expressed in only one medium—nor could it be captured in five or ten minutes. But "The Devil with the Blue Dress Medley," despite that minor shortcoming, was as good a live track as anyone had put out in recent years. And that was more than enough to sustain a fan's hopes against the coming of a full LP in the new year.

But 1980 dawned with no resolution to Springsteen's artistic quandary in sight. Often, Bruce would cancel studio time at the last minute, frustrating even those he worked with and squandering a good deal of money. (The album budget soared past $500,000.) Yet sometimes, when Springsteen did come in with a new song, the pieces looked ready to fall together.

In the meantime, the band was keeping itself occupied with its own changes. There was a heavy load of session work for all but Miami Steve, who saw the production through minute by minute. Roy Bittan helped arrange David Bowie's *Scary Monsters*, on which he also played, and in addition produced a fine album for Jimmie Mack, the gravel-voiced hard rocker. He also played on records by Dire Straits, Graham Parker (to which Danny Federici and even Springsteen himself also contributed), Jim Steinman, Ellen Foley, Ian Hunter and Garland Jeffreys. Max Weinberg played with Steinman, Foley, Hunter and Jeffreys. Clarence Clemons and Garry Tallent dabbled with record production and appeared on some other albums. Clemons played with Janis Ian and Michael Stanley. Danny Federici played on Joan Armatrading's album with Clarence and Jeffreys; he also appeared as an accordion player in a movie called *You Better Watch Out*. The band was coming into its own and going through its own growing pains. Garry got divorced; Roy, Danny and Max got engaged.

When Springsteen scrapped the first version of the album, the sessions stopped being fun. Now everyone was on edge: The recording became grueling, and the waiting interminably boring. Yet progress was made, and in the spring the end was in sight. Springsteen had now recorded, in one form or another, about forty songs. The last few weeks were spent on fine-polishing details of the twenty-five of them that he wanted to mix. "Drive All Night" was given a drastically different arrangement and vocal, with Roy on organ and Springsteen himself at the piano. "You Can Look (But You Better Not Touch)," which had been a rockabilly trio number—just Bruce, Max and Garry—became a fleshed-out rocker, with the rockabilly left in at the edges. In the end, it wasn't until the mixing sessions some months later that Springsteen added a chilling monologue to the center of "Point Blank," and the final "Drive All Night" vocal only a week before the recording was completed. In the meantime, Landau, Springsteen and Van Zandt flew to Los Angeles to mix the record with Chuck Plotkin at his Clover Studio.

It was early May by now, and though no one was saying that the record would be completed any minute, there was high hope for a late summer release. But it couldn't be that simple. The twenty-five songs that went with them not only needed to be mixed and sequenced, Bruce also had to choose which ones to leave out.

Already the idea of a two-disc set had been suggested. Landau finalized some business arrangements with CBS, and the project moved in that direction. This meant Springsteen could use twenty songs, with five left over for potential B sides. (Actually, twenty-one were included on the first master, but "Held Up Without a Gun" was held over to be the first B side.)

There were a number of good reasons for releasing a two-record set. It would help amortize the costs of spending all that time in the studio. The material was certainly sufficient in quantity and quality to carry the project through. And it would give Bruce the scope to tell the full story that he felt blossoming inside him. "I could let all those people out that usually I'd put aside," is the way he put it.

In the end, the record wasn't done until a few days before rehearsals for the group's first worldwide tour (not only America but England and the Continent, Australia and Japan) began. This time, it was a production problem with the album cover that held up the release, nothing to do with Springsteen's decision-making delays. But as he stepped onstage in Ann Arbor, Michigan, on October 3, 1980, to begin his first tour in two years, Bruce knew his audience still hadn't heard the new music on which he'd worked so hard.

He opened with "Born To Run." But as he stepped to the mike, he forgot the words. "I knew it was gonna happen, 'cause I'd just listened to the song about ten times backstage, tryin' to remember 'em," he said later, laughing. "But my mind just went blank. All of a sudden, though, I heard the words in the back of my head, and I realized, holy smokes, the kids are singing them to me. It was a real nice gift." And he cruised through a four-hour show, doing more than thirty songs, more than half of them from the new album. It was an auspicious beginning for a tour that established Springsteen as one of the top draws in the world.

Sometimes the tickets went in minutes, sometimes in hours, but everywhere, even in towns where he'd barely been able to fill half a house two years before, the tickets were quickly gobbled up. The tour sold out everywhere. No one seemed certain why.

Barry Bell said, in essence, that this is how the rock business works. You've got to pay your dues, but once you do, the proceeds roll in like profits on the world's most successful chain letter. Bruce himself said that he figured, since the band had played "real hard, every night" in 1978, "people just remembered," although in this case, people who hadn't even seen those shows were remembering.

Some thought it was MUSE, but the album had not been an over-whelming success, and though Springsteen's reviews for the film were great, the movie (released in New York in late summer) had not even been distributed in most areas of the country.

Maybe Greil Marcus came closest to the truth: "Rock and roll today is too big for any center," he wrote. "It is so big in fact that no single event . . . can be much more than peripheral." Marcus went on to a detailed description of the advantages and disadvantages of that situation. The lack of a center broke down conventional ideas of what rock "had" to be, but it also meant that rock and roll was no longer such an aggressive part of popular culture, and that circumstances robbed it of its ability to challenge some other barriers. The importance of Springsteen's tour, Marcus wrote, is that "he performs as if none of the above were true. The implicit promise of a Bruce Springsteen concert is that This Is What It's All About— This Is The Rock."

In seven years, Bruce Springsteen had progressed from being an artist at the fringe of American pop music to one who embodied the center of that music, as a series of musical traditions and as a compact between performer and audience. And he'd done it the hard way: by remaining himself. He had changed a great deal, but not in terms of the essentials, which is to say, he minimized the irony and contradictions of fame by containing them, insisting not on the "correctness" of what he did, but on its sheer necessity. And if this made him a symbol of Rock and Roll itself at this moment, well then, that had its share of necessity too. He wasn't about to squander the opportunity to make such stature count. So *The River* flowed.

19 BRINGING IT ALL BACK HOME

"To lose the earth you know, for great knowing; to lose the life you have, for greater life; to leave the friends you loved, for greater loving; to find a land more kind than home, more larger than earth—

" '—Whereon the pillars of the earth are founded, toward which the conscience of the world is tending—a wind is rising and the rivers flow.' "

Thomas Wolfe, *You Can't Go Home Again*

With a snare shot as loud and deadly as small arms fire, *The River* announces itself, as boldly as "Like a Rolling Stone" did, and for the same purpose. With this album, Bruce Springsteen is not out to summarize his past achievements, but to surpass them, to integrate what they have taught him into a larger vision of the world.

Particularly in the images of its final song, *Darkness on the Edge of Town* emerges as an heroic parable—a rock and roll translation of the Quest for the Holy Grail, told not through devices of chivalry and romance but ones of pain and psychic devastation. The ending is a glorious symbol of transcendence; the hero reaches his mountaintop. But for a popular artist like Springsteen, the problem immediately presents itself: How do you top that act?

"That guy at the end of *Darkness* has reached a point where you just have to strip yourself of everything to get yourself together," Springsteen said. "For a minute sometimes you just have to get rid of everything, just to get yourself together inside, be able to push everything away. I think that's what happens at the end of the record. . . . And then there's the thing where the guy comes back."

So this Hero goes home again, bringing with him a new perspective. He's felt smothered by this place, and he's tried to escape it; he's vowed to transform it, and he's tried to live without it. Now he slips into the mainstream of its life so completely that he almost disappears. Only a few of these songs ("Independence Day," "I'm a Rocker," "The Ties that Bind," "Point Blank" and "Drive All Night") are really about that character. But he's a presence in the rest; the lost souls of "Jackson Cage" and "Two Hearts" are seen through his eyes, and because we know what this hero has experienced, the wild-ass rebel rockers of "Ramrod," "Out in the Streets" and "Cadillac Ranch" don't seem innocent, young and bold anymore, but naive and crazy and terribly vulnerable.

On the surface, the stories aren't that different from those Springsteen has told before. It's only when you slice beneath the surface of the songs themselves that the sadness in a song like "Cadillac Ranch" or the joy in one like "Drive All Night" becomes apparent. And it is only when the songs are heard in terms of their interrelationships that *The River* begins to make sense as the successor to *Born To Run* and *Darkness*, if not their summation, and ultimately, their culmination. "Rock and roll has always been this joy, this certain happiness that is in its way the most beautiful thing in life," Springsteen told Robert Hilburn. "But rock also is about hardness and coldness and being alone. With *Darkness* it was hard for me to make those things coexist. How could a happy song like 'Sherry

Darling' coexist with 'Point Blank' or 'Darkness on the Edge of Town'? I couldn't face that.

"I wasn't ready for some reason within myself to feel those things. It was too confusing, too paradoxical. But I finally got to the place where I realized life had paradoxes, a lot of them, and you've got to live with them."

The River is a record about inescapable realities, including the reality of always trying to escape and always falling back. That is why Springsteen can describe "Ramrod," which is in many ways an even more joyous counterpart to "Born To Run," as "one of the saddest songs I've ever written." Time is running out on some of these characters. While this album was being made, the very gas pumps that fueled the fantasies of *Born To Run* nearly ran dry. And in that sort of world, how does one hold on to faith in hemi-powered drones?

On *The River*, no one is transcending anything; everybody's too busy just trying to get on with their lives. Or they are busy dying or burying the dead or just trying to avoid the stink. These songs are filled with corpses and ghosts. The people we encounter are older, tied down to jobs or looking for work, and it is the jobs—and the joblessness—that dominate, not the odd, reflective or ribald moments in which they're sometimes seen.

Thus, it is Springsteen's first album without anthems. Every song that might be one is undercut. Faith, Springsteen seems to be saying, will get you so far, and not a step more. The rest is down to work and struggle, and you'd better not stop, except maybe to dance, and then you'd better make sure you're dancing as well as a man with a pistol pointed at his toes.

The music is remarkable; the E Street Band brought to the studio the cohesion and intensity developed on the 1978 tour. Each player has his featured moments and each rises to the occasion; more important, no one lets down in between. The constants in the sound are Garry Tallent's bass, resonant with rhythm and melody; and Max Weinberg's drums, which crash and splash as though recorded live. The other elements constantly float in and out of perspective. For once, it's easy to see why Springsteen spent so much time in the mixing room. Sometimes the highlights pass by so fleetingly you miss them—like Roy Bittan's marvelous, country-tinged piano play-ing—or are so firmly grounded in the bedrock of the arrangement that you take them for granted, as with Miami Steve's grand twelve-string guitar playing. The relentless elements are here, too, of course, in Clarence Clemons's ripped-from-the-heart sax solos and Danny Federici's obsessively pumping organ chords. But it is the delicate touches that make the epic sprawl of *The River* worthwhile. It's Springsteen's most subtle record; it gives nothing away.

The River courses through a dozen styles: the rockabilly nuances of "Cadillac Ranch," the Stones-like raunch of "Crush on You," the British Invasion beat of "The Ties that Bind," the folk rock of "The River," the white soul of "I Wanna Marry You," the Duane Eddy twang of "Ramrod," the frat-party noise of "Sherry Darling," the plainspoken country-western voice of "Wreck on the Highway" and the ballads that are a mutant form, derived from Dylan and Van Morrison, but now recognizably Springsteen's: "Stolen Car," "Point Blank," "The Price You Pay," "Independence Day." These are part of a genre all their own. Some of this music is offhandedly casual, more so than any Springsteen has ever recorded, as though he'd assembled the hot rod of his hopes from junk he'd discovered lying around the neighborhood. It's tempting to catalogue all of it: to add up the references to cars and highways, to enumerate the allusions to rock history and to earlier Springsteen songs, to follow the images from song to song, to number the ghosts and corpses and count the tears. It is also beside the point.

What is important is the assurance Springsteen brings to this vast work. The landmark double-disc rock albums are Bob Dylan's *Blonde on Blonde* and the Rolling Stones' *Exile on Main Street*, the former recorded by an artist just reaching maturity, the latter made by artists trying to figure out what to do with theirs. Springsteen's exists between these two archetypes. Its first two sides are a chronicle of people awakening to the fact that they aren't young anymore, that their futures are no longer limitless. In the words of "Jackson Cage," these people confront one hard question:

Are you tough enough to play the game they play
Or will you just do your time and fade away?

Or, to put it in the words of the title song, "Is a dream a lie if it don't come true, or is it something worse?"

The last two sides, on the other hand, describe one version of how someone bred on rock and roll dreams comes to terms with the knowledge that he has aged. These sides are heavy with mortality; their most cheering moments are cut with the poisons of rage and futility, and the happiest song of all, "I'm a Rocker," is just a comic book fantasy (although part of the point might be that Springsteen is able to bring this fantasy to life, so much so that one wants to walk up and ask to see his 007 watch and his I-Spy beeper). It's no coincidence that this is the record Springsteen made when he was thirty, that mythical breaking point for rock and roll stars.

But even those first sides are firmly grounded in the reality set forth in the first song: "No man can break the ties that bind." In a time of solipsism, you could call ,this a bold assertion. But Springsteen explains it further in "Two Hearts":

Once I spent my time playing tough guy scenes
But I was living in a world of childish dreams
Someday these childish dreams must end
To become a man and grow up to dream again
Now I believe in the end
Two hearts are better than one
Two hearts, girl, get the job done

But quoting those lines that way cheats Springsteen of half his meaning. On the lyric sheet, and for a brief second as he sings them, there's a break after "I believe in the end." For someone who believes so strongly in rock and in the way that it seems to hold out promises of eternal youth, the awareness that there *is* an end must be the greatest shock of all. Earlier in this book, Springsteen's "For You" is praised as one of the greatest rock songs ever to tackle the topic of death. *The River* has half a dozen better ones.

If *The River* is cut in half by its self-awareness, it is given the greatest continuity of any of Springsteen's albums by the music. By now, Springsteen has come full circle in his use of the rock band:

Born To Run featured the saxophone and piano, *Darkness on the Edge of Town* organ, bass drum and snarling electric guitar. Here, the music is built around the upper half of the drum kit, the electric bass, and guitar lines that are more light and spindly. More than anything, *The River* finally sounds like Springsteen has figured out how to record a *rock band*. So the unity of the songs is only an analogue for the unity of the playing.

But most of all, *The River* is dominated by voices. Springsteen's own voice has a new assurance, symbolized by his willingness to push it forward in the mixes, for the first time, placing it on top of the instrumental bed. But there are also the crooning *aah's* of Flo and Eddie on "Hungry Heart," and the choral backgrounds of "Stolen Car," "The Ties that Bind" and some of the others. More than anything, there is the constant support of Steve Van Zandt, Springsteen's perfect foil. Some of these songs—"Marry You," and "Fade Away," especially—amount to duets. If Springsteen's voice is strength and power, Van Zandt's is pure vulnerability, a heart about to break.

At the end of "Out in the Street," Springsteen and Van Zandt play their voices against each other in the final chorus, shouting "Meet me out in the street" over and over. Then, for one line, Bruce drops out, and Steve is left alone. "Meet me out in the street," he sings, and it is not an assertion of his right to prowl Broadway but a plea to *be* met.

You can hear a dozen things in that line. It's a voice that thinks hope is a rumor and can't surpass its own worst fears about the cruising idyll it's been describing. It is a voice that has only a little faith in its own best intentions. It's a soul man at the end of his rope. And it's why "Two Hearts" is true.

In the next line, Springsteen's voice joins Van Zandt's on the same words, and the picture shifts focus. What you hear now is conviction, two men bound together, quite simply beyond embarrassment. In that moment, Bruce and Steve meet each other, heart to heart, and you understand why *The River* does not entirely let go of its rock and roll fantasies. It is because the dream is remembered and relived that the cruelty can be endured—and maybe conquered.

But that's an old story, old as "Thunder Road" and "Backstreets" and "Born To Run" itself. It takes the final side of *The River*, just four songs, to write an end to this saga.

"Ramrod," "The Price You Pay," "Drive All Night" and "Wreck on the Highway" have virtually nothing in common musically. "Ramrod" is a rocker built around Duane Eddy guitar and Dave "Baby" Cortez organ. "The Price You Pay" is stock Springsteen, cut from the mold of "The Promised Land" and "Thunder Road." "Drive All Night" is something else—a rock and roll blues number or a beleaguered philosophical ballad, a song that doesn't really belong to a genre, unless that genre is confession. And "Wreck on the Highway" is a country song, taking its title and its melodrama from Roy Acuff, its melody and sense of doom from Hank Williams himself.

Any of these songs could have ended the album, "Ramrod" on a note of false ecstasy, "The Price You Pay" with unconvincing optimism, "Drive All Night" with overblown yet poignant romanticism. Yet it's "Wreck on the Highway" which does end it, and in doing so redeems them all—the finest example of the way these songs work together to make their points. These songs close the album one after another, like a series of shades being drawn, doors being pulled shut, lights being snapped out. Each of them is a farewell: "Ramrod" to the petroleum squandering days of rumbles and cruising, "The Price You Pay" to the innocent optimism that has almost (but not quite) become a cliché in Springsteen's work, "Drive All Night" to the illusions of melodrama that are the backbone of that work.

Yet if Springsteen is now putting these sentiments and styles away, it is not because he loves them less. You can hear this especially in the closing moments of "The Price You Pay," which might have been an anthem on any other album. It's the sort of song that has most influenced his imitators, brimming with innocence, wearing its heart on the very edge of its sleeve. But now he's ready to smash the mold from which it came. Through the stock guitar and harp and sax breaks, Springsteen virtually embraces this music before releasing it. But when he reaches the end of the song, Springsteen takes a knife to the cliché:

But just across a county line [he sings, the E Street chorale
　　swelling behind him] a stranger passing through puts up a
　　sign
That counts the men fallen away to the price you pay

Then the chorus drops out, and Springsteen's voice stands alone, like
a man about to shoot a favored pet to put it out of its misery:

But girl before the end of the day
I'm gonna tear it down and throw it away

The River exploits Springsteen's self-consciousness constantly.
"I'm just a thinkin' fool," he said soon after it came out. "Nothin'
I can do about it." And accepting that some of what he did, so
transparently calculated, was going to strike some as pretentious no
matter what he did, he was able to relax to a much greater degree
and produce music that was more spontaneous and had a much
greater sense of groove—and was, incredibly, even more self-
referential than his other albums.

"Drive All Night," though, takes this self-awareness to an edge.
As the singer rejoins his lover and tries to focus her attention on
their love rather than on the distractions outside the walls they're
huddled within, he's also saying good-bye to the people on his earlier
records:

Tonight there's fallen angels and they're waitin' for us down
　　in the street
Tonight there's calling strangers, hear them crying, in defeat
Let them go, let them go, let them go
Do their dances of the dead

"Drive All Night" strips the situation back down again: the hero
and his girl again, like a reprise of the "Born To Run" experience.
But this time, they're not bursting free, but cuddling, looking for
some warmth in the face of the chill outside.

At the end of "Jungleland," as that girl switches off her bedroom
light, she is totally unknowing about the world beyond her walls.

Her lover lies bleeding in the street, but she remains innocent. The image recurs at the end of "Drive All Night," but this time, the couple together know everything that's out there, and they're quite deliberately protecting each other from it—for a time. Springsteen wanted to operate in the manner of John Ford: images that were dropped casually into a frame years before suddenly appear again, seen in a different light. "Drive All Night" is the song in which he reaches that goal.

But "Wreck on the Highway" pares it down even further, to one man facing the world again. He might be, as Springsteen himself suggests, the guy in "Cadillac Ranch" or the one in "Ramrod," the man in "Stolen Car" or the one in "The River," the boy in "Born To Run" or the hero of "Darkness on the Edge of Town." Whoever he is, he sees and speaks and sings for all of them.

The singer is driving down a bleak highway, long after dark, when he comes upon a wreck. He gets out, and though it's raining, goes over to see if he can help. But he's too late. And as he stands looking down, pelted by the rain, he gazes at this broken body and sees— himself. And he imagines a life, and what's left of those who shared it. It flashes before his eyes, and there's no helping what he feels, and no getting rid of it either. For the rest of his days, he will be haunted by this knowledge.

This is a scene not from John Ford but from Frank Capra's *It's a Wonderful Life*. But Springsteen offers nothing so romantic as a suicide, or an angel to explain. He just tells us what he knows, and what he can imagine. And when he returns home, he says, these images will not leave him:

Sometimes I sit up in the darkness
And watch my baby as she sleeps
Then I climb in bed and I hold her tight
I just lay there awake in the middle of the night
Thinking 'bout the wreck on the highway

At least the hero has what he has always wanted: a knowledge of life from start to finish, and someone with whom to share it. And at the end of an album strewn with images of death and marriage, he concludes by holding both in his arms at once. The song fades out, the bass and piano and guitar ticking the beats away, like time—too precious to squander—ticking off a clock, without hope of ever being returned. The beat does not weaken; it does not quiver in the face of what he's found out. And so this man discovers for sure that one last rock and roll cliché is a lie: It is never better to burn out than to fade away.

The River flows two ways. Some of it is locked into a land that is imbedded with its memories of the past; it was a home once, but it can never be rebuilt. And it holds up a light to a future that might be another kind of home, if only one could reach it. These twin visions are as far apart as separate lifetimes, and as close as the next breath you take. Neither is imaginable without the other.

In that remarkable Thomas Wolfe novel, *You Can't Go Home Again*, this story's epitaph is written. Like *The River*, these lines might be history or a prayer for the future. Chances are, they are both:

"For he had learned some of the things that every man must find out for himself, and he had found out about them as one has to find out—through error and through trial, through fantasy and illusion, through falsehood and his own damn foolishness, through being mistaken and wrong and an idiot and egotistical and aspiring and hopeful and believing and confused. . . . Each thing he learned was so simple and obvious, once he grasped it, that he wondered why he had not always known it. All together, they wove into a kind of leading thread, trailing backward through his past and out into the future. And he thought that now, perhaps, he could begin to shape his life to mastery, for he felt a new sense of direction deep within him."

The tour that Bruce Springsteen and the E Street Band began in the fall of 1980 took them across America more than once, east to west and, in midwinter, north to south. Later, it would take them to Europe and Japan and Australia, and back home to New Jersey. Almost everywhere, Springsteen was greeted with mad glee and fierce devotion, crowds that sang the songs for him and picked up on his every cue. The stars in the audience, when he came to the metropolises, went away impressed and convinced.

It should have been a time to let up a bit, to relax and explore. Instead, Springsteen only worked harder. The show grew from three hours to four, and on special nights, which were many, it went on longer. The band had perhaps forty songs in its repertoire, and that number grew all the time, as Springsteen dragged his old material forth and put some standards away. One night, early on, he called for "In the Midnight Hour," and though the band had never played it together before, they cut through it fine. And it stayed in the show, reappearing from time to time.

Springsteen had it made, yet he wouldn't let himself rest, and the strangest thing of all was that what exhausted everyone else, even the band, seemed to rejuvenate him. He would show up at the concert hall in late afternoon, looking like hell. But when he hit the stage his eyes were bright, and after the show he would stay, talking into the night to all comers, until nearly dawn. Was he a man possessed? Anyone who's read this far has his own answer.

But each night, at the end of the show, Springsteen gave his own reply. In the midst of the Detroit Medley, he would pause and pull Garry, Clarence and Steve to the center of the stage with him. Pointing to the farthest reaches of whatever arena they happened to be playing, he would gaze out and say, "I have a vision. I see . . . a train." Then he'd begin to sing: "I see a train, coming down the line, train train train, coming down the line."

This song did not have a name. It didn't need one. But it contained echoes of a dozen songs, some older than Springsteen himself. There was Roy Acuff and "The Wabash Cannonball." The Impressions and "People Get Ready." James Brown aboard the "Night Train." Elvis Presley and Little Junior Parker on that "Mystery Train"—that one most of all. And also Johnny Cash's "Hey Porter," the blue yodels of singing brakeman Jimmy Rodgers, and the lonesome wail of the original Sonny Boy Williamson.

It was a song you had been hearing, if you had been raised on American music, all your life. It was rhythm and blues and rock and roll and country-western, and inevitably, it was the blues. It was indivisible, a nondescript fragment and everything that he needed to say.

After a few bars, Springsteen would begin to pump his arm, and as the audience began to catch on, they would chant *"woo-woo"* in rhythm. "All aboard," Springsteen would shout. "*Woo-woo*," they would reply. Over and over they sang this together and then Bruce began to yell: "Ann Arbor, Michigan. All abooard!" "Chicago, Illinois. All abooard!" "Oakland, California. All abooard!" And it would go on, through the tour itinerary, until he reached that night's stop.

As a gesture, this song needed no explanation. As a statement of faith, it was perfect. It included everyone: "You don't need no ticket/ You just get on board." In this vision, there was no "on the bus and off the bus," no tickets to ride, and if anyone left, they were always welcomed back, their seats clearly marked.

Springsteen made this song an invitation and a command. It was hard to imagine anyone resisting. It was a promise of adventure, and each night as I heard him sing it, the same thought came into my head. "Where are we headed?" I wondered. "Where are we bound?"

Then I'd shake my head and smile and hop aboard myself. The answer was clear: together, we would try to make it home again.

II GLORY DAYS

For Sasha and Kristen

Take a good look around . . .

Once I spent my time playing tough guy scenes
But I was living in a world of childish dreams
Someday these childish dreams must end
To become a man and grow up to dream again
Now I believe in the end
Two hearts are better than one
— *"Two Hearts"*

INTRODUCTION TO THE FIRST EDITION

"**W**hen the legend becomes fact, print the legend, not the fact," says the newspaper editor in John Ford's *The Man Who Shot Liberty Valance*, an aphorism as useful as it is dangerous. But neither Ford nor anyone else tells you what to do when the facts and legend converge.

This book is a sequel to *Born to Run: The Bruce Springsteen Story*, which I wrote in 1979. That was my first book, and I wrote it partly as an attempt to convince people who didn't like rock and roll and/or Bruce Springsteen that both were great and worthy subjects. *Glory Days* is something like the eleventh book that I've written or edited, and though I'm still capable of the occasional harangue, I now understand that they're for the benefit of my own soul as much, or more than, anyone else's. If you find these arguments convincing, thanks; if not, well . . . I do.

I don't mean to imply that *Glory Days* is any more "objective" than *Born to Run*. Even if I believed that objectivity existed, that's a quality this book couldn't possess. Bruce Springsteen is my friend, as is Jon Landau, as are most of the other characters in the tale. Barbara Carr, who plays a role or two herein, is my wife and, now that this book is finally written, we're feeling a hell of a lot friendlier, too.

Having all these relationships didn't make writing this book easier (although I suppose it made it possible). It's much more difficult to sit and think and pry and analyze when you're likely to be sitting next to one of the principals at dinner tomorrow night. *Glory Days* isn't authorized—in fact, I'm sure all the principals disagree with some things in it—but everybody concerned, especially Bruce and Jon, cut me miles of slack. I hope I've done the story and them some justice.

The personal backdrop for everything here is this: In 1974 Jon Landau and I went to see Bruce Springsteen and the E Street Band in a Boston bar. Both of us have seen a lot of music performed in a lot of bars but never with an effect like that. I can remember it now as clearly as I did the next morning—as a complete blur but the most glorious blur I'd ever run into.

What began that night is essentially the subject of *Born to Run: The Bruce Springsteen Story*. That book bottled enough lightning to make the best-seller lists. At the time, nobody had ever done this by writing a book about a rock musician of lesser celebrity than Elvis Presley or the Beatles. I was never under the illusion that the book sold for any reason other than its topic, which left me less surprised than most when the story continued to develop. *Born to Run* was updated in 1981, in the midst of the tour following *The River*, and the story by then had an air of completion, if not finality. But the protagonists continued to stir.

In 1984, a few weeks before *Born in the U.S.A.* was released, I proposed writing a sequel, on the grounds that the new album would create a new story, too different and complex to simply be tacked onto *Born to Run*. What did that mean? Something different then than now. Everybody who heard *Born in the U.S.A.* knew that there were hit singles on it, and that having hits would not only expand Bruce's audience but change it. It seemed to me that how he dealt with those changes and how he'd already dealt with the changes behind *Nebraska* would constitute a story.

But who would have dared to dream that the story would be this good? Certainly, nobody could have expected that Bruce would become quite this famous or that he would more than maintain his equilibrium, continuing to grow in the face of celebrity pressure. After all, hardly anybody else ever has. As for the rest, I didn't even know he was going to get married (which is okay, because neither did he). I'll take credit for being right about one thing, though, because it's the one that matters: This is a great story.

It's been about fifteen years since I first heard a test pressing of *Greetings from Asbury Park, New Jersey*. In that time, rock and roll dreams and dreamers have come and gone, but the music and the story behind it have remained a fascination every single day. As a writer rather than a rock star, I don't have to apologize for sittin' around thinking about it, which is a good thing, since, as numerous great men have said over the years, it's too late to stop now. But then, why would anybody want to?

INTRODUCTION TO THE FIRST PAPERBACK EDITION (1990)

I was the pimp's main prophet, I kept everything cool
Just a back-street gambler with the luck to lose
And when the heat came down it was left on the ground
— It's Hard to Be a Saint in the City

There is not yet an unambiguous ending to the post-*Glory Days* events in Bruce Springsteen's life and career. Since the Amnesty tour, he has been subject to a lawsuit filed by a pair of former roadies, a drama right out of Abbott and Costello; disbanded the E Street Band; bought a $14 million spread in Beverly Hills; licensed his most famous song to Luther Campbell of 2 Live Crew for an anticensorship parody called "Banned in the U.S.A."; and, with Patti Scialfa, become the parent of a son, Evan. He even spent a whole summer—Memorial Day to Labor Day—without once snagging the stage away from a bar band at the Jersey shore.

These events belong to the same life that's described in this book, but to a different story. Bruce Springsteen in the Nineties is about a guy who's come to terms with his stardom, at least to the extent that he now lives where stars live, records with seasoned professionals rather than old cronies, and does business like a professional, rather than a guardian of cultural mysteries. How he makes music is the most interesting and relevant question, and one which only time will answer, though given his recent pace, it would be extremely unsurprising to have one about the time this edition hits the street.

But whatever happens to Bruce Springsteen, we'll all move on. I spent a little more than a decade covering Bruce Springsteen's career from as close up as I could get, had a lot of fun, learned a lot, and wound up with a couple of books of which I'm still proud, though they're far from flawless. That's one reason why my friend and colleague Steve Perry combed through the original edition of *Glory Days* and made a number of cuts. In this way we've attempted to meet the universal criticism that the book was too long.

There was another strain of criticism, however, which can be met only by me, and only head on. Such reviewers began with the premise that my friendship with Bruce Springsteen and my marriage to one of his managers ought to have disqualified me from writing this book, and that these relationships constituted a great hidden conspiracy, a story beneath the story.

The dishonesty of that allegation must be immediately apparent to anyone who reaches the third paragraph of the introduction. But the idea that I've tried to conceal these facts remains infuriating, so I bring it up here.

The reasons why it persists are interesting, however. Bruce Springsteen himself is beyond attack in today's celebrity-driven magazines, while a biography that contends that he is a decent, complex human being is not. Additionally, at the very moment that *Glory Days* reached the shelves, two disgruntled former roadies were attempting to sell a story based on the "scandal" of their employment—during which they were paid fifty thousand dollars a year, and upon their departures received bonuses of more than a hundred thousand dollars each. Thus, in two of the most prominent music publications, *Rolling Stone* and England's *New Musical Express*, I found myself accused of suppressing evidence of Springsteen's misbehavior, because these comic-opera supplicants hadn't been interviewed. Neither reviewer noted that I also hadn't interviewed the E Street Band. (The last thing *Glory Days* needs is another half-dozen speakers.) In any event, I didn't know that these hearty crewmen felt that they had a story to tell, since they made no effort to tell it to me—although if they had, what they claim in their lawsuit is so patently blown out of proportion that it would have been left on the cutting room floor anyway.

Similarly, this version of the legend of *Glory Days* contends that I omitted mention of Springsteen's public humiliation of his former girlfriend, photographer Lynn Goldsmith, at the 1979 M.U.S.E. concerts. The date of that event and the subtitle of this book ought to give you one clue about why that is, but if you need another, pick up a copy of the paperback of *Born to Run*, and there you'll find it fully reported, with the lack of sympathy Bruce's behavior deserved.

The fundamental idea behind such criticisms is that nobody could have attained Bruce Springsteen's level of fame, success, artistic recognition, and human connection without being a fundamentally corrupt person. This is a basic tenet of ideologies both left and right; from Theodor Adorno and Herbert Marcuse to William Bennett and Alan Bloom, even those who take pleasure in popular culture see its human effects as inherently trivializing and fundamentally dangerous.

Glory Days based itself on the opposite premise: Pop stardom could be used to make art of real substance and the pop star himself could be a responsible citizen. Without presenting Bruce Springsteen as a civics class caricature, it takes stock of a person struggling to maintain humanity against all the temptations and challenges offered by stardom's massive machinery. In my view, he did this successfully—more successfully, certainly, than any other popular-music star ever had.

Is this interpretation of the events recounted in *Glory Days* "hype" of the sort that could only be created by a writer on the take? It's an accusation worth taking seriously, because the people making it are employed by publications whose stock in trade is hype in its grossest dimension.

The consequences aren't trivial either. If the expert assessment of these full-time hypesters is accurate, we're all immobilized. Anyone who can be heard—even if what they're saying is "No"—must be hopelessly corrupt. There is no hope of telling the truth, spelling out the facts, reinterpreting the lies of the phony patriots, undoing the false promises. And the public is too sated and stupid to know the difference anyway.

Glory Days was written against those implications, not only because of my own emotional and ideological sympathies, but because the facts of Bruce Springsteen's career refute them. I once called this a true story with a happy ending. It seems to me now that what's really important is that it's a true story that draws hopeful conclusions.

That's why I'm proud of it, and it's why I don't need to write any more books about Bruce Springsteen. Unfashionable as it may be to admit it, I did find what I was looking for. *Glory Days* is the journal of that search.

July 31, 1990

INTRODUCTION TO THE 1995 EDITION

SOULS OF THE DEPARTED

Shams and delusions are esteemed for soundest truths, while reality is fabulous. If men would steadily observe realities only, and not allow themselves to be deluded, life, to compare it with such things as we know, would be like a fairy tale and the Arabian Nights' Entertainments.

—*Henry David Thoreau*

The new material I wrote for the Dell paperback edition of this book, took Bruce Springsteen's story through *Tunnel of Love*, a radically new chapter in his work. Its discussion of the professional and artistic issues that confronted Springsteen and his admirers then remains relevant, even though in the period since it was written, Bruce has recorded and released two albums of new material, scored one of the biggest hit singles of his career, prepared his first *Greatest Hits* anthology, won his first big-league Grammys and an Oscar, broke up and reunited the E Street Band, toured with another group for the first time in a quarter-century, fathered two more children, moved back and forth between New Jersey and California enough times that only his accountants know for sure where he actually resides, and suffered the worst reviews and first commercial stumbling blocks of his post-*Born in the U.S.A.* career.

By some standards, the pot's already boiling for Volume Three. But now, I really *am* disqualified from commenting too much upon what has happened to Bruce—not for professional reasons, but for personal ones.

When you write a book about someone, even if that book is as concerned with the shape of a career as it is with the psychology of the subject, you think you know something about the person, and perhaps you do. But you don't really know anyone until you've faced an ultimate stress together.

In 1992, my relationship with Bruce Springsteen, and everyone else I know, was put to the ultimate test. My daughter, Kristen Ann Carr, the product of Barbara Carr's first marriage but raised by me since she was three years old, had developed liposcarcoma, a very rare cancer. Kristen loved Bruce the way you love a person you've known from infancy and have watched grow into a virtually mythic figure while remaining someone sitting next to you on the couch. That summer, she worked for him on his European tour with the "new band"—Roy Bittan, drummer Zach Alford, bassist Tommy Sims, guitarist Shayne Fontayne, multi-instrumentalist Crystal Taliaferro, and singers Bobby King, Carol Dennis, Cleo Kennedy, Gia Ciambotti and Angel Rogers. In Europe, Kristen and her boyfriend, Michael Solomon, became unofficial social directors for the band (who were, save for Roy and the singers, closer to their age than Bruce's), leading them through clubs, sightseeing and other exploits from Sweden to Spain, and on to Germany, France and Italy.

It was the best possible summer to spend with Bruce in Europe. In America and England, his dismissal of the E Street ensemble and his hiring of session professionals in Los Angeles was taken as a betrayal, so much so that the records he made with them—which I think are good, though I prefer the polished neosoul of *Human Touch* to the raw folk-rock of *Lucky Town*—went for the most part unheard. Maybe what Springsteen tried to sing about, particularly in such *Human Touch* songs as "Real World," "Man's Job" and "Soul Driver," reflected a view of love and relationships so adult that it outstripped the rock audience's ability to deal with them, or maybe it was just too hubristic (or flat-out confusing) to release the two albums on the same day at full list price. Or maybe Springsteen's portrayal of a man content with his fate— though not everyone else's fate—simply contradicted most people's experience of this life. Speaking for myself, I probably wouldn't have sent off an album that opened with a song called "Better Days" into the teeth of a Presidential election being contested amidst a national economic crisis, and might even have been daunted by putting out two discs simultaneously in the midst of a recession, but maybe that's where my mentality becomes analytic rather than artistic.

Anyway, none of those circumstances obtained in Europe. There, Bruce was more popular than ever, and his tour traveled from high note to high note, climaxed by an amazing show in a Barcelona bull-ring. Backstage that night just before he went on, Bruce ran across Kristen perched on an equipment case. As he related, she gave him a smile that said," 'Hello Mr. Rock Star.' It made me feel a little foolish, in a good way. It reminded me who I am. It was her gift to me." As always, the delivery of the challenge sparked Bruce to meet it. (I'm not saying that Barcelona, the most beautiful city in Europe, with the most rabid Springsteen fans, wouldn't have sparked something special anyway. I'm just telling the story as it was told to me.)

After Kristen came home, her cancer progressed far more rapidly than anyone anticipated. Bruce, Patti and Jon Landau joined a large group of friends who saw her through those grave days. They went to the hospital, they came to the apartment, they called, they sent food, they gave us hugs. One night, Patti brought Evan and Jessica over to the hospital so I could go out to dinner with the tots, a potent symbol of life. I remember only glimpses of those days and nights, even though the whole crisis lasted nine weeks. What stayed with me was a feeling of security. Just before Christmas, I told Barbara that I felt like a man trying to stop a runaway train with his bare hands, but because our friends rallied to us our family maintained that sense of hope which all cancer patients and their loved ones hang onto.

Christmas was a trial. New Year's, always the Springsteen calendar's most important revel, was a nightmare. Just after 9 A. M. on Sunday, January 3, 1993, with Sasha, Barbara, Michael and me holding her hands, Kristen died.

Two days later, Bruce and Patti sang "If I Should Fall Behind"—which Kristen and Michael had planned as their wedding song—at her funeral. Our friends continued to surround us for weeks, then months. Bruce had to go back to Europe; Barbara went along, this time with Sasha in tow. In May, Barbara flew back to New York and announced in a meeting at the office of Arthur Indursky, Bruce's attorney and our close friend, that Bruce would play a benefit to help us endow a Kristen Ann Carr Fund for Sarcoma Research. The show would be on June 26, 1993; top ticket price would be $1,000. (Try scalping *that.*) It would be the final show of his 1992-1993 tour.

Our music industry friends rallied once again. Sony Music bought 250 top-price tickets, and dozens of other record executives, artists and others made contributions. Madison Square Garden gave us a break on the rent, and then made a donation equal to what they charged us.

Bruce invited Terence Trent D'Arby—one of Kristen's prime heroes-to sing, and he flew in from London to be with us. Dozens of other people worked for free. With a beautiful vase of Kristen's beloved pink roses placed downstage left, as if she herself were present, Bruce opened with a spectral version of Woody Guthrie's "You've Got to Walk That Lonesome Valley," sharing lines with Terence, Joe Ely, Cleo, Carol and Tommy. Four hours later, the show ended with Bruce singing "Follow That Dream." I sat in the loge, the kind of seat where I first saw Bruce with Chicago in 1973, and sobbed. Mainly, I cried for my kid, but partly I cried for the kind of friendship and love that had been poured over us.

The concert raised more than $1.5 million, more than twice what was needed to hire our sarcoma researcher. Today, in addition to the fellowship, the Kristen Ann Carr Fund sponsors support services for teenagers, young adults, and sarcoma patients. Each year, our friends at the Hard Rock Cafe in New York work with the Fund to sponsor a Christmas party for all the pediatric patients at Memorial Sloan Kettering Cancer Center.

None of that would be possible without Bruce. We have simply done what any parents with our resources would do in loving memory of their child. He did his part out of the greatness of spirit that I talk about throughout this book, made more personal by our long friendship.

Later in 1993, director Jonathan Demme asked Bruce to write a song for his upcoming movie about a Philadelphia lawyer fighting AIDS and the law firm that fired him because of antihomosexual bigotry. Bruce responded by writing a beautiful, somber song called "Streets of Philadelphia." Whether it's a great song about AIDS, I don't know; but having studied the subject more than a little (see my *Born to Run: The Bruce Springsteen Story* and *The New Book of Rock Lists*), I know it's one of the greatest rock songs about death and dying. The first time I heard Bruce sing one of its most poignant lines—". . . my clothes don't fit me no more"—I knew that Kristen had left her mark on the song. When Bruce accepted his Grammy for Song of the Year in 1994, he thanked Kristen, "whose spirit is in this song."

I love my kids and my wife, and I do my best to love myself. All that comes with the territory. For two books—call them histories, biographies, hagiographies, whatever—I did my best to explain why I loved Bruce Springsteen's music while avoiding talking about why I love *him*. At the time, that seemed to come with that territory. But now that

Bruce has demonstrated his love for my family in such tangible and intangible fashion, I'm in a place beyond words. So I will not speak further but leave you as is only appropriate with lines from Bruce Springsteen:

> *But the stars are burnin' bright like some mystery uncovered*
> *I'll keep movin' through the dark with you in my heart*
> *My blood brother.*

September 27, 1995

PART 1

ONLY THE LONELY

Only the lonely

Know the way I feel tonight

Only the lonely

Know this feeling ain't right

—Roy Orbison

1 DANCING IN THE DARK

His mother told him someday you will be a man,

And you will be a leader of a big ol' band

Many people comin' from miles around

To hear you play your music when the sun goes down.

—Chuck Berry

In the heart of a city, darkness gathers and a crowd accumulates—fifty, sixty, eighty thousand and more, pulling up in sports cars and jalopies, wearing custom-cut slacks and Levis on their last legs. They file into the stadium, a cross section of white America, as much like football fans (only younger, more often female) as rock and rollers (but older, better mannered).

This could be any of half-a-hundred American towns in the summers of 1984 and 1985, but as it happens, the place is the Los Angeles Coliseum and the biggest tour in rock and roll history is just a night or two from its end. In the full moon's light, the Coliseum is beautiful, looking as ancient and hallowed as its name. The air is clear and crisp, as befits the end of September anywhere, and it cools sharply as the night seeps in, so that the fans must huddle while milling for seats, snacks, and souvenirs.

The atmosphere crackles. The crowd knows what it's in for: a four-hour spectacle that is both sheer intoxication and a ritual invocation of the human spirit in the most peculiarly American way. For the first time since Elvis Presley, the king of rock and roll is native-born and, maybe for the first time ever, that crown is worn not lightly but with the full weight of adult awareness. In the crowd almost everybody bounces with anticipation, but there are fewer drunken bleats than you'd expect. Beneath the taped music blaring from the huge stacks of speakers surrounding the stage, a hungry murmur builds.

Backstage, the singer has a few last-minute words with his aides, sneaks a final glance in the mirror, gives his wife a farewell kiss and, for the one-hundred-sixty-second time in the past eighteen months, steps through the dressing room door ready to rock. In the hallway, his bandmates already await him.

Together they set out for the stage, the singer's motorcycle boots clumping on the concrete. As they move, a few quips and good-luck grins are exchanged with stagehands and buddies, forced jokes working off last-minute nerves. But the band passes only a few individuals on the way, most of whom are hard at work. With each step, the group begins to zero in on each other, converging in a mutual tunnel of concentration.

The sun has dimmed now, sunk beneath the stadium's rim, eclipsing the crowd, which looked so colorful—all reds, whites, and blues—just half an hour before. From above, the audience seems a single primitive organism.

The three-story stage has been set up beneath the Coliseum's giant arch, which looms above the stage in the twilight. When they reach it, the band members look at one another, draw a collective deep breath, and descend, their way lit by flashlights held by the crew. They clamber quickly down the concrete stairs, past broad sections of empty seats. They're led blind into the hungry murmur, which builds a bit as those on the fringes of the crowd spot their movement. The house lights go black and the murmur raises its pitch and volume, becomes a scream.

The musicians stride to their places. Behind them hangs a fifty-foot flag, flat without a flutter, at once an icon of the most deeply fixed symbolism and a blank slate on which the evening's meaning will be inscribed. You could write almost anything here, and for the past eighteen months, everybody from the President of the United States on down has tried. But right now, all that's clear is the ambiguity of the image and the intensity of the figures it dwarfs.

The singer glances left, right, and behind, nods his head. Mumbling a greeting into the howling face of the mob, he signals his readiness and raises his guitar before him like a sword. An instant later, white hot light smacks him in the face as he snaps off the cadence—"One-two, one-two-three-four." Synthesizers and drums rumble to life.

For a moment he stands, legs splayed, swinging his guitar like a weapon. Then, taking a stride to the microphone and gripping it with his right fist, he begins his tale at the beginning. It starts with a sound sharp and cruel as the first slap on a baby's fanny. The noise that explodes from his mouth could be called a scream or a bellow, but it's really just a bawl:

> *Born down in a dead man's town*
>
> *First kick I took was when I hit the ground*
>
> *You end up like a dog that's been beat too much*
>
> *Till you spend half your life just coverin' up*

In a sense, Bruce Springsteen has spent half *his* lifetime uncovering those lines, cutting to the core of himself, and in the process unleashing the mighty energy that unites his audience. The power he has focused stems straight from the intensity of his conviction that such a feat is possible, and from the incredible assertion of will required to bring it about. It's exactly what has made him the first white American to approach the mystique and popularity of Elvis Presley. It's what presidents and paupers fight over. It's the essence of this story. And it didn't happen as suddenly as it might seem.

◆

Who was Bruce Springsteen in the months and years before he became such a visibly fortunate son? Even though it must seem so to noninitiates, he didn't just vanish into a woodshed in the time between his near-disastrous simultaneous appearance on the covers of *Time* and *Newsweek* on October 27, 1975, and the release of *Born in the U.S.A.* on June 4, 1984. Unlike Peter Frampton, the other great rock phenomenon of 1975, Bruce Springsteen was never a burnt-out rock star. To have fallen into that valley and reclimbed the heights of megastardom Springsteen reached in the mid-Eighties would have surpassed the recuperative powers of Lazarus. No. Between *Born to Run* and *Born in the U.S.A.*, Bruce Springsteen occupied himself as one of the biggest stars in the world—or at least in the world of rock and roll.

Springsteen survived the hype surrounding *Born to Run* because the hype was of two distinct kinds. Most obviously, there was the enthusiastic hyperbole poured out by rock critics, disc jockeys, and fans with the zeal of fundamentalist converts. This hype was lubricated—but not fueled—by a $250,000 Columbia Records promotion campaign. The fuel was provided by Springsteen himself, partly through the excellence of the *Born to Run* album, but primarily through his three- and four-hour stage shows—rock and roll marathons that combined the bluesy bite and drive of rock at its best with a theatrical production that packed in more tragicomedy than anything since the heyday of James Brown. No performer has ever extended himself further than Springsteen did onstage in those years, risking everything in headlong dives into the audience, revealing himself with stories of growin' up young and poor in central New Jersey, continually concocting a series of minor events and holidays to celebrate as the show concluded in an apex of mugging and riot. Imagine *The Honeymooners* with amplifiers, an all-male cast, and a live audience, and you'll know what it was like at the end of those nights. Imagine reinventing "art rock" as something that ignored Beethoven's Ninth in favor of Del Shannon's "Runaway" and the Ronettes' "Walking in the Rain." All CBS really had to do was spread the word.

There was also a negative hype at work, driven by naysayers who saw the very innocence that allowed Springsteen to balance so precariously between artfulness and slapstick as a kind of cultivated naïveté, who heard his theatricality as closer to Howard Keel than to Jackie Wilson, who saw his all-American-loser-made-good persona as a backdoor mechanism for returning rock and roll to the greaseball dummies from which it (presumably) sprang. At the time, there seemed nearly as many critics, deejays, and rock fans devoted to denying Springsteen's greatness as to celebrating it. "Springsteen needs to learn that operettic pomposity insults the Ronettes and that pseudotragic beautiful-loser fatalism insults us all," wrote critic Robert Christgau, who admired *Born to Run* but despised the mythology on which it was founded.

Corny as it may have seemed to modernist intellectuals, Springsteen's mythos was the very thing that enabled him to recast the rock and roll version of the old American dreams—right down to waving the flag in mourning rather than in joy. Within rock's narrow world, this made Springsteen an eccentric icon and provided the leverage for altering the terms on which at least one section of rock and roll was made and understood. But to those for whom Liverpool, London, and San Francisco had completely overshadowed Memphis, Detroit, and Muscle Shoals, the entire exercise must have seemed preposterous. With punk in the process of being born and the British rock bands of the late Sixties and their American imitators stumbling to dinosaur deaths, what Springsteen was about just didn't seem feasible, much less desirable. In fact, Springsteen's effort to tap the abandoned American folk mythology at the core of Elvis Presley and Chuck Berry's version of rock and roll may have seemed like just what Christgau implied it was: a task for the half-bright in alliance with the cynical.

But Springsteen is neither dim nor a hypocrite. "I was a big daydreamer when I was in grammar school. Kids used to tease me, call me dreamer. It's something that got worse as I got older, I think," Springsteen told Kurt Loder in 1984. But in 1975, he didn't feel that way at all. "I looked at *Born to Run* and the things people were saying about it, that it was just a romantic fantasy and all that, and I thought, 'No, this is me. This is my story.' And I really felt good about it," Springsteen said in early 1986. "But later, as time went on, I started to look around and see what other stories there were to tell. And that was really when I started to see the lives of my friends and the people I knew, and they weren't that way at all."

A big part of Springsteen's own story wasn't that way, either. Born on September 23, 1949, at the height of the postwar baby boom, he grew up in the richest country in the world during the greatest period of material prosperity in human history. Yet the Springsteen family was never economically prosperous; they continually struggled to make ends meet. The Springsteens certainly never knew the depths of poverty so many black musicians experienced as a matter of course, but they were clearly—and through no fault of their own—at the poorer end of the American working class.

After *Born to Run*—and an ensuing lawsuit with his former manager, Mike Appel—Bruce began to work intensively on a follow-up album. It was 1977, and as one result of the lawsuit, his closest adviser was now his manager/producer, Jon Landau. A former rock and film critic, Landau is a deeply introspective and relentlessly analytical person, and he brought out many of the same qualities in Bruce. Springsteen had always shared those characteristics, but they'd been dormant for lack of stimulation and guidance—or worse, had to be hidden because psychological insight and intense analysis were scorned in the working-class culture in which Bruce grew up.

The legacy of such passivity is more of the same, generation upon generation. For a long time Springsteen believed he'd succeeded where so many, including his own father, had failed because of his almost superstitious belief in hard work and personal conviction. "I believe in the love and the hope and the faith," he sang at the beginning of 1978's *Darkness on the Edge of Town*, the sequel to *Born to Run* and the first album in which he began to portray and assess the living shambles around him. But as the Seventies wore on and more and more men of bright hopes and good intentions were discarded or destroyed, it became obvious that the tragedy of lives such as Doug Springsteen's weren't the result of individual failure at all.

Springsteen's performance legend grew. *Darkness on the Edge of Town*, like *Born to Run*, sold something more than a million copies, but Springsteen concert tickets sold out of all proportion to his popularity in the record stores or on Top Forty radio. He could sell out 20,000-seat sports arenas faster and more often than artists who sold four or five times as many records. By 1980, when he completed his fifth album, the double-disc *The River*, he was acclaimed as the greatest performer in rock. The stage show had changed somewhat since *Born to Run*, adding scads of new material, but its essential framework remained the same, as did the essential message: Believe in yourself and the world will work better.

With the assistance of his first Top Ten single, "Hungry Heart," *The River* expanded his album audience to 2 million. Yet, at a time when the Bee Gees, the Eagles, and Fleetwood Mac were selling more than 5 million consistently and more than 10 million copies of their biggest hits, Springsteen was basically still reaching only a cult of initiates, and the initiates were largely those who had seen their dreams pay off as well—nonconforming yuppies. To the vast majority of pop music listeners, whose lives were often as bleak as the vistas of his darkest ballads, Springsteen had barely begun to speak [at all].

"Springsteen's wholeness—the fact that he embodies rock and roll as no one person ever has, except Elvis—springs from his noble-savage persona. Such shocking innocence can't be faked, but it also suggests that Springsteen scarcely exists outside the rock and roll world that created him," wrote critic Stephen Holden in his review of *The River*.

"Fifteen years ago, rock and roll music stormed the frontier of contemporary culture, and the major albums of the day addressed the moment. *The River* doesn't—it addresses rock and roll. The product of one thirty-year-old man's incredible exertion and faith, it conjures an American-provincial world of a guy, a girl, and a car hurtling into the night, fleeing time itself."

In one sense, this scenario reflected a brilliant and complete expression of Springsteen's artistic vision. But it also represented the frustration of his talents. Though he had grown immensely as a songwriter and recordmaker, his themes refused to expand. Pump them up as he might, they continued to revolve around the same small center. What Springsteen really hoped to do was call a halt to the flights of which Holden spoke. To do so would require a confrontation with his most cherished beliefs about himself, his music, and the world. Yet it was only after he had faced down his own ruptured dreams that Springsteen could step forth and speak not just to the world of rock and roll, but to everyone willing to listen.

When he did, the results were tangible in the most extreme sense: 10 million albums sold in the United States; 18 million worldwide; seven Top Ten singles; the highest-grossing, longest-running concert tour in rock history; a quartet of successful videos and the increased visual identification that went with them; community support and political clout; status as a legend not only of rock and roll but of popular culture. But in order to attain that status, Springsteen first had to cross more fields of fire than latecomers or casual observers could have imagined.

2 IN ANOTHER LAND

For the ex-colonials, the declaration of an American identity meant the assumption of a mask, and it imposed not only the discipline of national self-consciousness, it gave Americans an ironic awareness of the joke that always lies between appearance and reality, between the discontinuity of social tradition and that sense of the past which clings to the mind.

—Ralph Ellison, Change the Joke and Slip the Yoke

Bruce Springsteen and the E Street Band landed at Frankfurt, West Germany, on April 5, 1981. It was two days before the first show of their first full-scale European tour, but they were already way off schedule.

The tour was originally set to start two weeks earlier, in England. Tickets for shows in Newcastle, Manchester, Brighton, Stafford, and Birmingham, as well as six nights at London's Wembley Arena, the Madison Square Garden of the U.K., sold out in hours. Tickets for April dates on the Continent went equally quickly. Even though Springsteen's only previous European concerts had been a pair of London dates at 3,000-seat Hammersmith Odeon and single shows at theaters in Amsterdam and Stockholm six years previously, the legend of his concert marathons preceded him.

Then on March 12, only days before the first gig, manager Jon Landau got a late-night call from Springsteen. Bruce was sick; he needed rest. Landau immediately rang U.K. promoter Harvey Goldsmith to tell him that the English dates were postponed.

Awakened before the British dawn, Goldsmith first thought Landau must be kidding; finally convinced that the decision was for real, he spent the better part of an hour trying to talk the manager out of it. The next morning, he issued the statement Landau gave him: "Bruce is simply exhausted and suffering from the assorted ailments that can crop up during a grueling tour. While his health is not in serious danger, doing his first full tour of the U.K. without adequate rest would run the risk of later cancellations. Bruce regrets any inconvenience to his U.K. fans." The shows were rescheduled for the last three weeks of May and the first week in June. Rather than beginning in England, Bruce's first full-scale European tour would end there.

"The risk of later cancellations" was no bluff. A few weeks before, on the final leg of his U.S. tour, a cold in Bruce's throat caused the postponement of early February shows in Indianapolis and Lexington, Kentucky. The physical breakdown wasn't surprising: The band had been on the road for five months, since the week before his fifth album, *The River*, was released, with only one two-week break, at New Year's. And once the European tour started, missed shows would have to be cancelled, not just pushed back. Bruce wasn't willing to risk such a calamity. The memory of his first trip abroad, during the *Born to Run* tour, and of the hype surrounding it, lingered.

The hoopla had peaked in London when Bruce arrived for his debut appearance outside North America on November 18, 1975. Playing by the rules of the more gimmicky, sensationalized British pop star game, CBS had planned to launch a Springsteen frenzy. So they plastered the city with round blue stickers bearing Landau's quote, "I saw rock and roll future and its name is Bruce Springsteen." Landau had written this in 1974, when he was a music critic; his production and management role with Springsteen evolved later. Bruce needed the push then, but by the time of his London appearance, the statement had been so robbed of context (it was originally part of a highly personal 2,000-word article) that its only meaning was an obnoxious assertion of superiority. No one in the Springsteen camp could look upon it any longer without annoyance.

When Bruce arrived at Hammersmith Odeon several hours before showtime, the theater was festooned with posters and flyers reading, "At Last London Is Ready for Bruce Springsteen!" Suddenly he snapped, roaring through the hall, tearing the offending posters down. He performed in a sullen rage that evening, spending a large portion of the night with his back to the crowd.

Springsteen had never before seemed especially disturbed by his record label's blowout promotions, but his seeming passivity obscured the intense purpose with which he pursued his rock and roll dream.

Springsteen believed deeply in the inherent worth and dignity of popular music and in his own responsibility to its traditions, which he was convinced had saved him from a life of frustration and fury. "A businesslike attitude toward that sort of thing is not appropriate," he once said. "I want our band to deliver something that you can't buy. That's the idea behind it."

To those, including many in the media and show business, who believed that cooperation with modern merchandising machinery was inherently corrupting, those sentiments couldn't just be idealistic; they were either hopelessly naïve or rankly opportunistic. In 1975, Springsteen had barely had time to demonstrate that they were neither, just a statement of convictions that he meant to uphold. That he'd been able to maintain such an attitude through the process of making and selling three albums and being acclaimed both "the new Dylan" and "rock and roll future" spoke to his ferocity of will and his ability to reconcile opposites simply by letting things be.

In America, Springsteen was sheltered from some of the contradictions of his career—particularly the tension between his desire for stardom and the anxious populist sentiments of his work—by a devoted following of writers and disc jockeys who had seen his shows and come away gasping. But even in the States in 1975, that network of professional supporters existed only in pockets—the Northeast, Cleveland, Austin, and Phoenix, most notably—and the hype spawned a counterreaction that focused on the naked mechanics of CBS salesmanship and proclaimed him a fraud. In Britain, only a few writers had seen Springsteen, and with the notable exception of *Melody Maker's* Michael Watts, the idea of an American appearing to reclaim the title of champion rock and roller after fifteen years of British dominance of the white pop music scene struck many as beyond the realm of possibility, especially since Bruce's music and image were throwbacks to pre-Beatles American rock and soul music and late Lennonism respectively. Concurrent with the idea that Bruce Springsteen could single-handedly save rock from its mid-Seventies doldrums, there sprang up the notion that he was the biggest con job of the decade, a pure creation of the CBS Records publicity machinery.

"That bothered me a lot, being perceived as an invention, a ship passing by," he told journalist Kit Rachlis in 1980. "I'd been playing for ten years. I knew where I came from, every inch of the way. I knew what I believed and what I wanted." And at the same time, "there was all the publicity and all the backlash. I felt the thing I wanted most in life—my music—being swept away, and I didn't know if I could do anything about it."

During the U.S. dates of the *Born to Run* tour, Bruce kept calm, rarely asserting his doubts, preferring to withdraw. "I felt I was in my *I Walked with a Zombie* routine," he told Rachlis. Maybe, working on home turf, he was just more certain that the show would get over on its merits. Outside the States, robbed of context and without any clues about what to expect, he couldn't be so sure. The London shows brought him out of a defensive shell and forced him to confront his own doubts about the way his music was being presented and sold.

To Mike Appel, then his manager, Hammersmith felt like the beginning of the end. "Bruce was so mad that night in London. He went really nuts. And I guess I looked just as guilty to him as CBS . . . He wanted that fame and glory, but I guess he wanted it on his own terms," Appel told Robert Hilburn many years later. What Hammersmith really began was Springsteen's insistence on defining those terms—and *that* is the point at which Mike Appel, whose method was the hype, found himself gone despite his complete emotional commitment to Springsteen and his music.

Bruce knew exactly where to lay the blame. "It was nothin' to do with the place. It was me. It was the inside world. It's a hard thing to explain, but I learned a lot about my strengths and weaknesses in those days, especially on that particular night," he said to Rachlis on a night when the 1981 European dates might have been very much on his mind.

Bruce took the European tour, particularly the 1981 British shows, too seriously to play at less than top condition. Back in the States, Springsteen had effectively rubbed out the repercussions of the *Born to Run* hype during the 1978 tour that followed *Darkness on the Edge of Town*, his bitterest, most resolute album. The screaming intensity of those '78 shows are part of rock and roll legend in the same way as Dylan's 1966 shows with the Band, the Rolling Stones' tours of 1969 and 1972, and the *Who's Tommy* tour of 1969: benchmarks of an era.

The legend traveled but it created strange resonances in foreign ears. Almost no one in Europe had ever seen him play. In most countries his records sold respectably, but no better. Furthermore, the entire basis of European—particularly British—pop music had changed after the twin revolutions of disco and punk, while Bruce stuck to rock and roll basics as established by Elvis and Chuck Berry, Dylan, the Stones, and the Beatles. Finally, Springsteen was a quintessentially American artist appearing in Europe at a time of enormous anti-American sentiment created by the U.S. government's recent foreign policy, particularly the insistence on foisting upon such NATO allies as West Germany and Britain missile systems that made those countries the likely frontlines of a so-called "limited nuclear war." Springsteen would also be playing in halls ranging in size from 3,000 to 10,000 seats—a radical change from the 10,000-to 20,000-seat sports arenas of North America, which just didn't exist in Europe.

No one could be sure that this very American show would translate well in foreign settings. For one thing, Bruce's concerts generally involved a fair amount of storytelling and dialogue with the audience. How would he speak to an audience that for the most part didn't understand English, much less the highly vernacular American he spoke? Yet that aspect of the show was crucial to creating a sense of shared revelation between the musicians and the crowd.

By reputation the Springsteen show was a bigger-than-life extravaganza recapturing that Nirvana Under the Boardwalk created for Bruce (among others) by early Sixties rock and soul songs, in which beauty and dignity, self-respect and love, were the basis of all relationships. It was the ideal behind that music, his own wonder at it, and his frustration that so little of it had been realized that made Bruce Springsteen exert himself so strenuously onstage; it was what kept him on the road. The show's nightly ritual arose from the belief that by completely absorbing self and audience, player and spectator, in a prolonged ritual, some great, transcendent community would be formed.

How did he do it? Partly, by working harder than anybody in the house did at his or her day job. After a sound check that lasted anywhere from thirty minutes to a couple of hours, during which Bruce was liable to run through any new song he'd lately written or some obscure oldie that had just caught his fancy, the arena doors were opened and the crowd filed in. Then the E Streeters played for about two hours, the length of a normal headline set. After a twenty-minute break, they came back to do another ninety minutes or so, followed by encores—in effect, a *third* set—that lasted anywhere from thirty to sixty minutes. The show hadn't finished in under three hours in years; many nights, the band was up there for more than four.

They played so long because Bruce still thought of himself as a bar band musician. As he once pointed out, "In the bars, you do five sets and they're like, you know, forty-five minutes. And then as you go along, usually when you first make records, you'll play two or sometimes three shows a night that are maybe an hour long. So [our show is] actually about the same amount of time." He laughed and continued less glibly:

"Mainly I did it because there was a point where just playing the one set didn't seem enough. People came wanting to hear certain favorite songs of theirs which I still liked playing. . . . It was just really to allow for more expression. It wasn't a plan to play for a real long time, or it wasn't even a plan to give people their money's worth or whatever. It was just expression. You know, if a fan goes out, it's a whole night out. It's three hours, and he should be much more tired than me when he walks out. 'Cause I do it all the time." He finished, laughing again.

Half hidden between his jokes is the greatest distinction of Springsteen's show: its purpose and the fact that it has one. Springsteen wants to entertain—he can be rock's greatest ham—but he can't quit until he has also inspired.

In the Pentecostal churches whose gospel music spawned so much of rock and roll, the purpose of music is to enhance interaction between congregation and performers. What Springsteen idealized in early rock and roll music were attempts to achieve something similar. (Listen to Sam Cooke's *Live at the Harlem Square Club*, for instance.) But by the late Sixties, the rock ritual had become so empty that the performers' exhortations actually confirmed their distance from the crowd. (Listen to *Woodstock*.) Springsteen seemed a throwback because it was his intention to regain that dialogue with the audience. It was as if he couldn't rest until the distance between artist and onlooker was obliterated.

Six months earlier, dining on fried chicken and grilled cheese in an Arizona hotel room while recuperating after yet another of these marathons, Springsteen spoke of what touring gave *him*. He remembered feeling itchy by the end of the prolonged sessions for *The River*, anxious to get back onstage.

"When I was in the studio and wanted to play, it wasn't the way I felt in a physical kind of way, it was what I felt mentally," he said. "I was excited about the record and I wanted to play those songs live. I wanted to get out there and travel around the world with people who were my friends. And see every place and play just as hard as we could play, every place in the world. Just get into things, see things, see what happens. . . . All I knew when I was in the studio, sometimes, was that I felt great that day. And I was wishing I was somewhere strange, playing. I guess that's the thing I love doing the most. And it's the thing that makes me feel most alert and alive."

But hadn't stardom been isolating? The question pushed at Springsteen's entire purpose.

"Usually . . . you can do anything you want to do," he said, speaking hesitantly at first, as if testing to see if the idea would play, then with increasingly passionate conviction. "The idea that you can't walk down the street is in people's minds. You can walk down any street, any time. What you gonna be afraid of, someone coming up to you? In general, it's not that different than it ever was, except you meet people you ordinarily might not meet—you meet some strangers and you talk to 'em for a little while.

"The other night I went out, I went driving—we were in Denver. Got a car and went out, drove all around. Went to the movies by myself, walked in, got my popcorn. This guy comes up to me, real nice guy. He says, 'Listen, you want to sit with me and my sister?' I said, 'All right.' So we watch the movie. It was great, too, because it was that Woody Allen movie [*Stardust Memories*]—the guy's slammin' it to his fans. And I'm sittin' there and this poor kid says, 'Jesus, I don't know what to say to ya. Is this the way it is? Is this how you feel?' I said, 'No. I don't feel like that so much.' And he had the amazing courage to come up to me at the end of the movie and ask if I'd go home and meet his mother and his father. I said, 'What time is it?' It was eleven o'clock, so I said, 'Well, okay.'

"So I go home with him; he lives out in some suburb. So we get over to the house and here's his mother and father, laying out on the couch, watching TV and reading the paper. He brings me in and he says, 'Hey, I got Bruce Springsteen here.' And they don't believe him. So he pulls me over and he says, 'This is Bruce Springsteen.' 'Aw, g'wan,' they say. So he runs in his room and brings out an album and he holds it up to my face. And his mother says [breathlessly], 'Ohhh *yeah!*' She starts yelling, 'Yeah,' she starts screaming.

"And for two hours I was in this kid's house, talking with these people; they were really nice, they cooked me up all this food, watermelon, and the guy gave me a ride home a few hours later.

"I felt so good that night. Because here are these strange people I didn't know; they take you in their house, treat you fantastic—and this kid was real nice, they were real nice. That is something that can happen to me that can't happen to most people. And when it does happen, it's fantastic. You get somebody's whole life in three hours. You get their parents, you get their sister, you get their family life, in three hours. And I went back to that hotel and felt really good because I thought, 'Wow [now he was almost whispering], what a thing to be able to do. What an experience to be able to have, to be able to step into some stranger's life.' "

In 1981 his munitions were mostly drawn from *Born to Run, Darkness on the Edge of Town,* and *The River.* Some of his audience missed the more eclectic early material, of which only "Rosalita," which had closed every Springsteen performance since he wrote it in 1973, regularly survived. But the saga of American innocence found and lost contained in his last three records gave Springsteen a musical center in rock and roll and a ready-made dramatic structure. He also drew on a repertoire of rock, folk, and soul classics: Woody Guthrie's "This Land Is Your Land," the Beatles' "Twist and Shout," Arthur Conley's "Sweet Soul Music," John Fogerty's "Who'll Stop the Rain." Together they added up to a sweeping story that felt as if it had a new chapter written every night.

◆

Bruce hadn't returned to Europe only to work. He wanted to learn about that part of the world, gain some feeling for its famous cities, internationalize his horizons. Neither he nor the band, personally or professionally, had ever spent any significant amount of time outside the United States. So the tour was arranged with a leisurely schedule, with days off in each town. That was a luxury—every idle date on tour costs thousands of dollars in hotel and meal fees—but even professionally, the purpose of this junket wasn't just to cash in: It was to build a base in the same way they'd done in the States.

So the tour began with free-lance visits to Hamburg's notorious Reeperbahn, a squalid district of whorehouses and dives storied now in rock and roll lore (as it has been among sailors for decades) because the Beatles got their start there—carrying especially poignant memories, because it was only weeks after the murder of John Lennon.

For the most part, the band and crew hung together, as travelers will. They were entertained and shown the sights by the local promoters or by the local CBS Records staff, to whom extending such courtesies was the customary way of coping with the arrival of an offshore rock group.

In a way, after so many months of touring the U.S., another round of hotels and airplanes and concert halls must have felt more normal than being home. After a while, as a veteran tour manager once said, you get so you have to look out the window and check the language of the street signs to know which country you're in. The shows themselves become a sort of maze, the band winding from one to another until they finally work their way out and return to homes they barely recall. It's no life for someone who doesn't love it. And it's no life for anyone who isn't traveling with friends. Most rock bands are not, their internal grappling for position reflected even among the road crew.

The E Street Band was a little different for two reasons: First, everyone knew that Bruce alone occupied the tour's top slot, and second, Bruce insisted that the band and crew stay in the same hotels wherever possible and that all parties be held for everyone or no one. Both stipulations reflected wisdom accumulated over a decade of playing clubs for small wages and no glory. One result was that Springsteen had been working with an identical band and much of the same crew since those scuffling days. To call them a family would have been to succumb to an illusion, but there was an aspect of camaraderie and cooperation among the crew that was rare, and it added to the Springsteen legend in professional circles.

"It's funny, I go back a certain amount of time with the same guys. We can think of nights when we were sixteen, playing in this teen club, and we get into all the stuff that's come down in between," Bruce once commented. "It doesn't feel that much different. What happens inside you is very much the same."

In fact, the E Street Band had held together under his leadership much longer than anyone could have expected. The newest member, guitarist Miami Steve Van Zandt, officially joined in 1975, but he and Bruce had been playing together since those teen club days back at the Jersey Shore. So had organist Danny Federici and bassist Garry

Tallent. Saxophonist Clarence (Big Man) Clemons had appeared one night out of the mist, entering a Jersey boardwalk club as a gust of wind ripped the door off in his hand. He stuck around to play the King Curtis riffs that were one of the signatures of Bruce's early sound and to serve as Springsteen's most important stage foil. Drummer Max Weinberg and pianist Roy Bittan signed up in 1974. If they couldn't remember clear back to the days of Bruce's search for a record deal, seven years is still a very long time in show business, much less rock and roll.

Nevertheless, it would be hard to think of a more personally diverse group of musicians. They were all the same age, in their early thirties, except for Clarence, who was nearing forty, and they all came from the East Coast. But personal resemblances stopped there. Their dress ranged from Bittan's elegant *couture* to Van Zandt's piratical pop star gear. Their musical tastes spanned the gamut, from Tallent's rockabilly record collecting to the boogie-all-night hard partying of Clemons. Their offstage personalities went every which way. Weinberg's hotel room had to meet precise standards, and he padded his drums with only a specific brand of paper towels; Federici tended to disappear into his own world between shows. Perhaps they came together with such force onstage because they were pulled in so many directions off it. What they had in common was a belief in Bruce Springsteen's music that led to an unwavering willingness to follow his direction.

◆

The previous November, German promoter Fritz Rau had flown to New York to see Bruce's Madison Square Garden shows. Rau, a concert promoter for thirty years, was astonished by what he saw, but the frenzied response of the audience worried him. "Now, don't be upset when everybody just sits there and applauds politely," he continually warned Bruce and the band after their arrival in Europe. "That's what happens here. European audiences are much more reserved than those you're used to. They will be very appreciative but don't expect them to rise up out of their seats cheering."

Bruce hadn't known what to expect in 1975, and like any newcomer to a foreign land, he needed orientation. But there's such a thing as overcompensation. "Bruce must have heard this a hundred times in the three days between when he got to Germany and when he did the first show," Landau remembered. "It got to the level of 'Listen, if they stone you, don't worry about it, that's just the audience, they really love it.'"

Rau's worries were reasonable but ultimately unnecessary. Part of what Bruce had learned from the *Born to Run* tour was the need to distinguish between the audience interaction that he wished to create and his own need for a specific reaction. "The moment you begin to depend on audience reaction, you're doing the wrong thing. You're doin' it wrong, it's a mistake, it's not right. You can't allow yourself, no matter what, to depend on them," he said a few months before leaving for Europe. "You gotta have your thing completely together— boom!—right there with you. When I put that mike out to the crowd, you have a certain faith that somebody's gonna yell somethin' back. Some nights it's louder than other nights, and some nights they do and on some songs they don't. But that's the idea. That's what makes nights special and what makes nights different from other nights."

Nevertheless, the E Street Band entered Hamburg's beautiful Congress Center, a modern 4,000-seat concert hall, with the sense that after five years of knowing just what to expect, they were lighting out into unknown territory. And if all this should have been irrelevant in theory, all the players felt a twinge of contradiction in the quivers of their nerves.

They took the stage just after eight, starting out, as always, with some of Bruce's strongest songs: "Thunder Road," "The Ties That Bind," "Out in the Streets," anthemic rockers that would have brought an American audience to its feet from the first familiar chord. But though the applause after each song was enthusiastic, there was no leaping from the chairs, no rush to the stage or dancing in the aisles. This crowd sat down.

Bruce hadn't changed his set at all. As he would during any show in the States, after twenty minutes of sizing up the audience, Springsteen called for "Tenth Avenue Freeze-out." In America he sang that song (or its alter ego, "Spirit in the Night,") leaning far forward over the crowd until he came to the next-to-last verse. Then he'd slip to his knees and slither over the lip of the stage into the front row, where he'd be eagerly engulfed by the crowd, and sing the rest of his song surrounded by them. It was a terrifying act of complete confidence in his audience, a physical expression of the show's central idea—one-to-one interplay between performer and listeners.

Back home, this had always meant leaping into a crowd already clamoring for contact. In Hamburg, however, the audience still sat in perfect decorum. And when Bruce called for "Tenth Avenue" on this night, nobody in the band or crew really thought he'd make the leap.

"I was watching and wondering to myself," remembered Landau. "The whole move of going out into the crowd seems predicated on the fact that the audience is physically involved, and there's that sharing and that physical interaction and, you know, all the weird things that used to happen: People'd pick him up and put him on their shoulders, people'd give him their seats and he'd stand on somebody's seat and sing that stretch in 'Spirit in the Night.' There's all the interplay and what're you going to do if everybody's just sitting there?

"Of course, he went out in the crowd. And people didn't really get up, but it was great anyway. It was like it was important for him to do it. He was havin' a great time, it seemed to me. He had this look of, 'It's fine. It's just fine. People want to sit down, that's fine. People want to stand up, that's fine. But I'm out here doing my thing.'

"He has that lack of fear about maybe making a fool of yourself. You've got a bunch of people who are all sitting down and you know that they're friendly, but they don't know how to respond to the situation, and you say, 'I'm gonna do it anyway; maybe it'll look silly.' And I'm sure that the idea that it might look silly didn't cross his mind at that moment . . . but to any of us, looking at him, you'd say, 'Jeez, wouldn't I be worried about makin' a fool of myself if I were the person up there at that point?' "

The payoff was bigger and better than the risk. The rest of the set roared by. Roy Bittan began the final number with a quietly beautiful piano introduction based on Ennio Morricone's score for *Once Upon a Time in the West*, the greatest European Western ever made. From within this delicate music, Max Weinberg's drums suddenly erupted in march time and the guitars shot off like cannons and Springsteen leaned into the mike, bearing down hard, shouting the opening lines of "Badlands":

> *Lights out tonight, trouble in the heartland*
> *Got a head-on collision, smashin' in my guts, man*

As if on cue, half the crowd exploded from its seats. Onstage, the band looked out at the crowd in amazement, watching as first one person, then another, finally decided to dare it all and rose, until everyone in the house was standing, fists upraised, shouting and dancing. When the song ended and they'd taken their bows and vowed to return for more, the band stepped backstage with tears in every eye.

At the very beginning of the tour, the band had begun playing the first verse and chorus of "Hungry Heart" as an instrumental, then starting over with Bruce's vocal. Then in Chicago, their first stop after "Hungry Heart" hit the Top Ten, the crowd sang the lyrics back to them. Bruce stuck out his mike to encourage them and a ritual was born. It became one of the show's telltale moments. Some audiences sang strongly, some faltered; some were off-pitch, some sounded sweet. The point was the adventure itself.

"Hungry Heart" wasn't a hit single in Germany, but half an hour into the second set the crowd was still wild and willing for whatever was to come. When the band hit that rolling riff and Bruce stuck out his mike, the Hamburg fans took the cue and began to sing. But they didn't really know the words. "The verse in that song and the chorus have the same music," said Landau. "So some people were singing the verse, some people were singing the chorus, some people were singing in English, and some people were singing in German. But everybody was singing something, in the spot where you're supposed to sing.

"As I watched him, Bruce seemed to be quite overwhelmed with the moment. I think it was just experiencing the most basic thing of music being something that communicates across borders—and Bruce experiencing the fact that he had the capacity to create work whose ability to communicate was not limited. It was not limited to New Jersey, it was not limited to the East Coast, it wasn't limited to the United States, it was not limited to any country. He was just making music for people. And all different kinds of people are able to understand what he's doing. I think that was the night we all got it. There it was, you could see it. It was just . . . international."

After that, the show ascended into what Landau termed "a phenomenal level of amiable disorder." And as if to seal his victory, Springsteen closed the show by debuting a brand-new number, John Fogerty's "Rockin' All Over the World," as the Hamburgers stood and stomped and roared their approval.

Soaked in sweat, Springsteen came bubbling off the stage. Before he reached his dressing room, Fritz Rau, a dignified gentleman thirty years his senior, came up to him once more, this time wearing a huge smile.

"*What* have you done to my Germans?" he asked.

"Well," said Bruce, "I guess they know how to stand up."

◆

The unquestionable triumph of the German shows set the tone of the European tour. Bruce and the band played some of the finest music of their career, and the audiences proved amazingly responsive. Whatever might have been lost in the translation was instead transformed into a series of unspoken understandings. Bruce never told as many stories as he did to those half-comprehending crowds, and few performers have ever been met with such a fervent combination of respect and delight. The shows in Berlin, Frankfurt, and Zurich were the equal of Hamburg, and the German swing closed with a date in Munich that was almost *too* good-naturedly rowdy.

To Miami Steve, at least, this was no surprise. "Just before we went to Europe, as the American part of the tour ended, we started to focus in on musical things," he said. "A lot of conversation was going on. We just started re-examining. We tended to play for each other for the first time, I think, in many years. We just tended to pull in a little bit, and consequently we were just . . . great."

Then the band played Paris on Easter weekend, where Bruce began to tinker with the show the same way he would have back in the States, adding new songs, repositioning others, adapting to circumstances and new experiences. He made one significant modification from the start of the tour: Just before singing the evening's first slow song, he requested the audience's quiet attention, a subtle way of acknowledging that many in the crowd would have trouble keeping up with his highly vernacular English and, equally important, of asserting his control over the proceedings, making sure he could do a concert and not just a flat-out rock and roll show. And from the start, he was rewarded with rapt silence, a stillness so deep in its attention that you could actually hear people listening. European crowds may not have known how to rock out as automatically as Americans, but they listened up far more smartly.

In Paris he appeared unaccompanied for the first encore, holding an acoustic guitar. He thanked the audience, then serenaded them with a number he'd never before sung publicly, "my favorite Elvis song," the *Blue Hawaii* ballad "Can't Help Falling in Love." As corny as it was haunting, the song was written way out of Bruce's range. His voice cracked and faltered as he sang it, but that only made the moment more poignant, taking what had been an ironic undercurrent in Elvis's version—the song as the ultimate tease of his devotees—and turning it into a bittersweet tribute to the faceless fan.

The next night, he stepped on stage and without preamble debuted his version of another Elvis hit, "Follow That Dream." Springsteen reinvented the song, one of Presley's bits of movie-era jive, keeping just the basic melody and the chorus: "You gotta follow that dream, wherever that dream may lead/You gotta follow that dream, to find the love you need." Springsteen's version was slow, echoing like a haunt until he reached the new verse he'd written for himself.

Now every man has the right to live

The right to the chance

To give what he has to give

The right to fight

For the things he believes

For the things that come to him in dreams

Baby in dreams, baby in dreams

◆

In one sense, the recast "Follow That Dream" was simply Bruce's most eloquent tribute to the one artist he idolized. Seeing Elvis first made thirteen-year-old Springsteen want a guitar, and he reveled in the King of Rock and Roll's commanding power, his sexiness, the pure freedom his presence suggested. But more importantly, it was Elvis who first gave Bruce a glimpse of rock and roll as a means of expressing a vision: "*It was like he came along and whispered a dream in everybody's ear and then we dreamed it,*" Bruce once said from the stage.

"Follow That Dream" was also a reflection of Bruce's changing concept of his role as a rock star, of the secret dream *he* wished to breathe into the public ear. As early as his first album, Springsteen had expressed complicated social ideas—listen to "Lost in the Flood," as good a song as was written about Vietnam during the war—and both *Darkness on the Edge of Town* and *The River* are steeped in class-consciousness. But it wasn't until the *No Nukes* concerts in 1979 that Bruce began to connect his (and his characters') class origins to a more specifically political outlook. Springsteen's tendency was to look at his life and those of his friends and the characters he invented as roles played in an ongoing drama, caught up in processes great and small. It was only after *The River* that he began to understand those processes as the product of something larger than the circumstances of individual lives. Springsteen had to escape the relatively narrow idea that "politics" is something that only happens when you vote or attend a protest rally, in order to reveal the powerful political undercurrents that surged in his songs from the very beginning.

Springsteen is an extremely cautious man, and he'd always been extra careful not to speak out about issues he didn't fully understand. This was an admirable way to avoid becoming "the new Jane Fonda," but it sometimes meant he sold himself short. At *No Nukes*, for example, he was the only artist who didn't make a statement on the issue in the concert program. Rhetorically, this was supposed to mean that he preferred to let his music speak for him, but an unavoidable implication was that he didn't really feel that he knew what he was talking about (and as the unreleased song "Roulette" proved, that just wasn't true).

So a radical alteration in attitude was apparent when he played Arizona State University on November 5, 1980, the night after Ronald Reagan's wipeout of Jimmy Carter. "I don't know what you thought about what happened last night," Bruce told the crowd. "But I thought it was pretty terrifying." Then he smashed into "Badlands." That was all he said, but it was far more than he'd ever risked before. And while some of the change was just due to current events, Bruce's ability to see Reagan as a bogeyman wasn't all there was to it. Bruce Springsteen himself was changing.

That same Arizona evening, Bruce was given a copy of Joe Klein's *Woody Guthrie: A Life*, the biography of America's best-known folk singer. Reading the book over the next few weeks, Bruce became fascinated by Guthrie, an eccentric character whose mingling of personal and political topics had a lot in common with Springsteen's own songwriting, and whose ambiguous relationship to celebrity was not unlike a rock star's.

For Springsteen, Guthrie had been little more than a name. Despite the Dylan comparisons made early in his career, rock and soul were pretty much the only kinds of music Bruce was aware of back then. He knew more about *West Side Story* than folk music; he could tell you succinctly and persuasively why the Dave Clark Five's hits were critically underrated, but he'd never heard the great bluesman Robert Johnson. Folk and country blues were campus music, and Springsteen had spent only about a hot minute at the local community college before dropping out.

Working with Jon Landau began to change his awareness of where his music came from. Landau grew up around the Boston folk music scene. He'd played bluegrass and rock and roll. He had both a passionate and scholarly knowledge of blues, gospel, country, bluegrass, and R&B, the bedrock on which rock and soul were built. Bruce and Jon's relationship was based on personal as much as professional considerations, even at the outset, and one of the ways in which they'd gotten to know each other was by talking about music—the latest pop hits, old rock and roll they both knew, personal favorites of Jon's, or records Bruce might have read about but never had the chance to hear.

Bruce reacted to such musical encounters as though given a key with which to tap the memories of his ancestors. His songs drew more and more on what he heard there, though not in the sometimes shamelessly overt way he recast old rock songs. For instance, he based "The River" on lines from Hank Williams's "Long Gone Lonesome Blues," although no one had ever guessed it until he mentioned the fact in an interview.

Springsteen was no folkie; his instincts were those of an inheritor, not a preservationist. "My music utilizes things from the past, because that's what the past is for. It's to learn from. It's not to limit you, you shouldn't be limited by it," he said in 1980. "I don't want to make a record like they made in the Fifties or Sixties or Seventies. I want to make a record like today, one that's right now.

"To do that, I go back, back further all the time. Back into Hank Williams, back into Jimmie Rodgers. Because the human thing in those records is just beautiful and awesome. Wow! What inspiration! It's got that beauty and the purity. The same thing with a lot of the great Fifties records, and the early rockabilly . . . Those records are filled with mystery; they're shrouded with mystery. Like these wild men came out from somewhere, and man, they were so *alive*."

Obviously, Bruce Springsteen saw himself as another wild man come out from somewhere that might as well have been nowhere. The myth said that he'd grown up on the New Jersey seashore, in rundown but romantic Asbury Park. The fact was he'd spent the first eighteen years of his life in Freehold, New Jersey (where his first band rehearsed), in a neighborhood called Texas because it was so dominated by immigrants from the southern United States, the kind of people who looked and spoke a little like the singers from the mountains and cottonfields. Texas was on the wrong side of the railroad tracks; it bordered the town's black ghetto. Springsteen's background was East Coast working-class prosaic: Irish and Italian, with a smattering of Dutch (whence the surname). But he could identify with the rockabillies because he'd known people like them in his youth: crackers, white trash, folks who hadn't gotten their cut of postwar prosperity.

This background primed Bruce to hear Woody Guthrie, who marched out of the Dust Bowl to take Manhattan by storm, then turned his back and walked away whistling, as a kindred spirit. Bruce was particularly taken by Joe Klein's story of how Guthrie's American anthem, "This Land Is Your Land," was written. Guthrie wrote the song as a furious response to "God Bless America," written by that other great people's balladeer, Irving Berlin. Guthrie made a song of many verses, and he went to his grave immensely troubled that the most radical of his lyrics were forgotten as his finest song was adopted by the very jingoists and false patriots the song meant to attack.

The irony, perhaps, is that Springsteen's interpretation of what the song was about was smack dab in the middle between Woody Guthrie, who wrote as a Marxist disillusioned with the America of fable, and Irving Berlin, who wrote as a man who had seen his every dream fulfilled and in one lifetime moved from the hellish pits of New York's Lower East Side to Beekman Place, the shortest, most exclusive street uptown. What "God Bless America" and "This Land Is Your Land" have in common is that both were written out of certainty. Springsteen didn't see things that clearly. You could almost think he sang "This Land" instead of "God Bless" simply because he preferred the ambiguity of Guthrie's words. He performed the song at the shows he did at Nassau Coliseum at New Year's; more surprisingly, he kept doing the song when he got to Europe.

It's hard to think of a song more indivisibly American than "This Land Is Your Land." Singing it in Europe, given America's role there as a cultural usurper, added a rich additional layer of ambiguity. Better yet, singing the song in places where "this land is your land" is still a principle to fight over, not simply a slogan, wrenched it out of its context as a great folk cliché. "This is an old song about an old dream," Springsteen told his Paris audience. "It's hard to think what to say about this song, because it's sung a whole lot in the States and it's been misinterpreted a whole lot. It was written as a fighting song and it was written, I feel, as a question everybody has to ask themselves about the land they live in, every day."

◆

In a sense, asking questions was exactly what the European tour was about for Bruce—exploring a new environment, amazed at the perspectives it opened for him , including the light it shed upon life back home. A simple example suffices: In Gothenburg, Sweden, Roy Bittan's wife, Amy, was forced to undergo an emergency appendectomy. Beyond the worry caused by illness 3,000 miles from home, the surgery was simple and everyone was impressed with what they saw of Sweden's socialized medicine. Although private rooms and telephones weren't available, it was taken for granted that any person's health needs were an immediate priority, regardless of that person's nationality or income. The comparison with America was unavoidable and, in this case, unflattering.

The tour moved on from Paris to Barcelona, in Spain's Catalonia; doubled back to France for shows in Lyons; then went on to Brussels, Rotterdam, Copenhagen, Gothenburg, Oslo, and Stockholm. From Paris to Brussels, Bruce was accompanied by his girlfriend, actress Joyce Hyser, but most of the time, he was on his own, often able to simply get out and wander the streets of towns he'd never imagined seeing.

There were sights to see—from the surrealistic Gaudi architecture of Barcelona to the opening-day fireworks of Copenhagen's Tivoli Gardens, which was a long way from the boardwalk in every way—and museums to visit, restaurants that had to be fitted in. But more than anything, the tour gave Bruce exactly the opportunity he wanted: "Going to France and Germany and Japan and meeting Japanese people and French people and German people. Meeting them and seeing what they think, and being able to go over there with something. To go over there with a pocketful of ideas or to go over there with just something, to be able to take something over. And boom! To do it!" He didn't get to Japan on this go-'round but, offstage and on, he otherwise fulfilled that program exactly.

Great stories could be told about almost every show on the tour. In Lyons the show was delayed for a night because of the national elections; President Giscard d'Estaing had preempted the local Palais des Sports to hold his party's election-eve rally. The result was that the show was played the next night in a room whose ceiling was filled with red, white, and blue tricolor balloons. But the finest moment of that evening came when Roy Bittan hit the Morricone-based introduction to "Badlands." The crowd *sang along* to that spectral melody, making a beautiful, haunting sound that no one could have predicted, upsetting and enriching the spectacle of the show. (It turned out that the *Once Upon a Time in the West* theme had been a jukebox hit in northern Italy, where about a third of the crowd came from.) In Paris the band played the Palais des Sports, where the audience didn't expect chairs. The audience simply folded them up and stacked them aside, leaving Bruce to play a festival-seating show whether he wanted one or not. In Brussels, which is NATO headquarters, a sizable percentage of the audience was American military personnel, but in the evening's still moments you could hear whispered translations going on in several languages simultaneously.

Rock and roll represents one basic thing around the world—a dream of freedom. In part, the dream is false. By itself, music is not a liberating force and, anyway, the particular kind of freedom of which rock fans often dream is really a kind of license to do what they will, damn the consequences, or worse, the freedom to sit back as fat and sassy consumers who never move a muscle.

But another part of that dream is true—or can be, under the right circumstances. The dream that Elvis Presley whispered into the ear of the world had such long-lasting echoes and repercussions because it was a peculiarly American expression of the fantasies of mobility, liberation, rebellion, and success that are dreamed the world over. Yet Elvis had never played a single show in Europe, and after him the States produced hardly any figures capable of carrying the myth and only one—Bob Dylan—who did. With Dylan in an artistic decline, Bruce's reception picked up a lot of the slack. You could be sure that when he said the words *United States* the cheers would be as loud as when he mentioned whatever town he happened to be playing. So he toured as a symbol of what people loved about America, leaving him immune, at least for the hours onstage, to all the caveats and criticisms.

Back in the States, looking for something to read while on the road, Bruce had picked up a copy of Henry Steele Commager and Allen Nevins' *History of the United States*, a textbook-length paperback that describes U.S. history in pluralist terms. Far from radical, the book nevertheless opened his eyes time and again, reinforcing an interest in the iconography of America that had been quickened by earlier encounters with such novels and films as *The Grapes of Wrath* and *The Searchers*.

One of the more fascinating bits of byplay on the European tour took place late one night on a bus ride from Copenhagen to Gothenburg. Bruce and Clarence sat in a dimly lit seat with an atlas spread across their laps, Clemons listening attentively while Springsteen explained the German army's pincer movement in World War II. However unlettered his roots, Bruce responded to art—or even just plain old information skillfully presented—with the enthusiasm of an intellectual, and despite his shyness at moments like *No Nukes*, in private he was becoming more and more confident that he knew a little bit. Simply by exposing him to so much more, Europe was accelerating the reformation of Springsteen from an attitude-is-everything street punk to a mature adult; a transformation that was vital if he was to remain a productive, functioning artist.

"I started reading this book, *The History of the United States*, and it seemed that things weren't the way they were meant to be—like the way my old man was living, and his old man, and the life that was waiting for me—that wasn't the original idea," he said one night in England. "But even if you find those things out, it's so hard to change those things. And it wasn't until I started listening to the radio, and I heard something in those singers' voices that said there was more to life than what my old man was doing and the life that I was living. And they held out a promise, and it was a promise that every man has a right to live his life with some decency and some dignity. And it's a promise that gets broken every day, in the most violent way. But it's a promise that never, ever dies, and it's always inside of you."

That was what Bruce brought to his exchanges with the European audiences. What did they give him? He summed it up on the band's last night on the Continent, in Stockholm, before an audience that was just on the friendly side of riotous. (Sweden was probably the country in Europe where Bruce's popularity was greatest.)

"There's a Marvin Gaye and Tammi Terrell song; it's called 'It Takes Two,' " Bruce began, speaking with unusual nervousness. "In the song, Marvin Gaye sings, 'It takes one to dream but it takes two to make a dream come true.' And I guess that's why we're here tonight talking to you and you guys are talking to us.

"Because it's funny, you know, on this tour, since we've been over here, I've learned, I've learned . . . I've learned a lot over here. I've learned the importance of the audience, the importance of you in the show.

"Because we come out and we play, and we play hard and try to tell you about the things that mean a lot to us, and when you respond the way that you have tonight and last night, it's like . . . it's a big, like '*me too*,' you know." Here he paused to laugh one of his short, nervous giggles, and the applause, which had periodically interrupted him, swelled to its fullest.

"It's in a buncha little things. I want you to know that it means a lot to us just how quiet you've been on the slow songs since we've been here. I want to thank you a lot for doing that . . ." He did not continue. Maybe the emotion was too great; perhaps whatever came next just didn't require words. After a moment, he picked up again.

"This song is about two people that once had that kinda connection and for some reason it got broken apart. And it's like a song ain't no good until somebody hears it. By yourself, you can't have an effect. You have to reach out. This is a song about someone who loses that power, which is the most powerful thing in the world—your ability to affect your friends' lives . . ." He hesitated, and then spoke very quickly: "and my life . . . and maybe I can do somethin' for you. So . . . this is called 'Point Blank.' "

◆

They moved on to England, where the language barrier dissolved and others replaced it. And the pressure lurked again, as Bruce and the band headed for London, the one capital of rock and roll they hadn't yet conquered. Despite all the Continental triumphs, until the Wembley shows, their task wasn't complete.

They started out at Newcastle City Hall on May 11, the smallest venue on the tour with the wildest crowd, 2,000 ale-swigging Geordies. Then on to Manchester and Edinburgh, Scotland, for two shows apiece, before moving to a London hotel headquarters and driving out for one night at Stafford's Bingley Hall—which still smelled of livestock exhibitions—and a pair at Brighton's Congress Center, which, in late May, seemed still prepared for the Mods and Rockers riots of twenty years before.

The provincial English shows were mostly uneventful, although in Manchester Bruce debuted a new song, "Bye Bye Johnny" (later retitled "Johnny Bye Bye"), about the death of Elvis Presley. He sang it for the first time, ironically, in a show in which he dedicated "This Land Is Your Land" to reggae king Bob Marley, who had just died in New York City of cancer. (Springsteen had been the opening act for Marley and the Wailers when they made their U.S. debut at Max's Kansas City in 1973.)

"Bye Bye Johnny" wasn't just the product of an obsession with rock stars who died too young, though. It was the result of four years of brooding about the useless way that Elvis Presley allowed his life to decompose. "I think everybody remembers where they were when Elvis died," Bruce said. The memory seemed to exhaust him, an emotion reflected in the music, clocklike block beats setting up a thin wash of synthesizer and guitar.

The story begins with lines from Chuck Berry's "Bye Bye Johnny" that capture the romantic promise of rock and roll stardom, twisted now into a portent of death: "Leaving Memphis with a guitar in his hand/With a one-way ticket to the promised land." In the ensuing verses, the whole mythic romance of the Elvis legend is replayed, right down to a beautiful vision of the funeral procession itself. But at the end, the song turns its gaze unflinchingly upon the ugly fact:

> *They found him slumped up against the drain*
> *With a whole lotta nothin' runnin' through his veins*
> *Now bye bye Johnny, oh, Johnny bye bye*
> *You didn't have to die, you didn't have to die*

In the studio the song would pick up a quicker tempo and a neater arrangement; the released version could almost be an Elvis song. Bruce never let go of the first verse or that last one, but he changed a lot of the other lyrics. The result was a better, more professional song, but it also distanced him from the original's emotion. Not everyone *does* recall where they were when Elvis died, nor did they spend years trying to figure out how the King's death could have happened. It didn't even bother most people in rock and roll, much less the rest of show business, that much. An early, gruesome demise is built into the legend of pop stardom as most of us understand it.

Speaking of Elvis in such universal terms, Bruce Springsteen was revealing both a compulsive fascination with rock's king and his own ambitions and fears. The fascination went back to his childhood. To this child of poverty, Elvis Presley, so obviously the transcendent product of similar everyday misery, loomed like an interstate highway, eight lanes screaming full tilt in both directions *somewhere*. "I remember when I was nine years old and I was sittin' in front of the TV set and my mother had Ed Sullivan on and on came Elvis," Bruce told another audience later that summer. "I remember right from that time, I looked at her and I said, 'I wanna be *just . . . like . . . that.'*

"But I grew up and I didn't want to be just like that no more. Because he was like the biggest dreamer. He was like a big liberator. I remember I was sittin' at home when a friend of mine called and told me that he died, which wasn't that big a surprise at the time because I'd seen him a few months earlier in Philadelphia. I thought a lot about it—how somebody who could've had so much could in the end lose so bad and how dreams don't mean nothin' unless you're strong enough to fight for 'em and make 'em come true. You gotta hold onto yourself."

Never has a performer given advice more clearly meant for himself. In those lines Springsteen effectively summarized his lust for stardom and his terrible desire to have the world know him, and his equally terrible fear of what the consequences of such fame and such knowledge might be. It would be glib and unfair to describe him as the world's greatest Elvis imitator—unless you were willing to include in that category, at one time or another, everyone from James Brown to Bob Dylan, Jackie Wilson to John Lennon. Then you'd have a clearer picture of where Springsteen fit in.

More important, however, is his flat statement about where his path and Elvis's diverged: *"But I grew up and I didn't want to be just like that no more."*

In the time of punk and disco, however, Bruce's music not only seemed to be a throwback; in some important ways it really was one. It could be argued, on the evidence of his rockabilly rhythms and persistent optimism, that he hadn't a radical bone in his body and perhaps far too many conservative ones. Yet in another way, he represented the most radical of all threats to the juvenile hegemony within rock and roll. He represented the idea that performers and audiences *could* grow up, assume adult responsibility, and tackle serious themes, without abandoning rock and roll's kernel of joy.

As a prototypical all-American boy, Bruce Springsteen had learned that might and main and sparks of invention could carry you much farther than rationalists and cynics ever dreamed. His show was the most outstanding example of the efficacy of sheer will in modern popular culture, yet it was the product of more than hard work and raw talent, too. His entire career was a triumph of conviction over trendiness and, more important, of content over form, reversing the typical priorities of contemporary artists. His songs lacked disco's total devotion to groove and the impudent purity of punk, not because he rejected either form of music (he wrote a song for Donna Summer, loved the Clash) but because Bruce Springsteen, all but alone among post-Beatles pop singers, seemed immune to nihilism. Despair was a familiar companion in his recent songs, but dark portents were always overwhelmed, if not dispelled, by cascading affirmations of the tenet succinctly summarized in "Badlands": "It ain't no sin to be glad you're alive." What he learned from Elvis was the importance of that principle and the potential price of ignoring it.

◆

The London of 1981 was transformed from the city Bruce had visited six years before. The British national economy had disintegrated along with the last vestiges of empire; unemployment rose toward fifteen percent, and many kids left school knowing they'd never in their lifetimes have a steady job. Government policy was to ignore such wasted lives. (In this respect, the political economy of Great Britain was a couple of years ahead of America's.)

Pop music was both an important component of England's foreign trade and one of the few available vehicles for the working class to make any headway in a brutally class-stratified system. In this respect, rock stardom, for all its rebellious and outrageous poses, provided an essential safety valve by creating a veneer of mobility. Having made it, on the other hand, pop stars were absorbed into a sort of aristocracy, an acceptable development during the expansionist Sixties but a traitorous move when the roof fell in.

Thousands of England's disenfranchised young people turned against the star-making machinery. Rock had become flatulent and arty; many of the stars were now pompous, self-impressed buffoons. The spirit of engagement and vitality had disappeared. Punk rock arose as the antidote. From 1976 to 1978, a horde of nasty-tempered tatterdemalion bands spat and shouted their way through brief, ultra-fast, musically primitive records, thrilling declarations of disgust and determination to overturn the rotted corpse of pop and the social structure that created it: The Sex Pistols' "Anarchy in the U.K.," "God Save the Queen," and "Holiday in the Sun"; and the Clash's "I'm So Bored with the U.S.A.," "Complete Control," and "White Man in Hammersmith Palais" were only the best of it.

As music, punk was as exhilarating as anything since Little Richard first hollered "Awopbopaloobop, awopbamboom." As political insurrection, it was doomed. As a means of disrupting the British pop industry and replacing one star system with another, it was brilliantly if accidentally effective.

Punk ideology proclaimed that anyone could become a star; it was replaced by the idea that anything was permissible in pursuit of stardom. Since this was Britain, where every new pop moment must have a name and be accompanied by a fashion fad, those who crawled out from under the rock punk had tipped over became "the new romantics." In the spring of 1981, new romanticism was the current fad in trendy London quarters, where the current fad is everything. No one could define exactly what new romanticism *was*, of course, but in a way, that just made it better, in the grand tradition of "The men don't know but the little girls understand."

As Dave Rimmer wrote in *Like Punk Never Happened*, his excellent study of British pop in punk's wake, "In refusing to be pinned down to any one particular style or sound, new romantic successfully avoided being marketable and thus also avoided becoming The Next Big Thing. It didn't turn into a new center, but it eroded enough of the old one—

challenging traditional rock patterns of consumption at least to the extent of shifting attention from live concerts to club life, from weighty LPs to dance-mix 12-inch singles—to leave everyone wondering just what was going on. Once it was clear that the toy-soldier look—the frilly shirts and velvet breeches usually associated with the term *new romantic*—was definitely not hip, nor even saleable in the high street, it was suddenly very hard to work out what was.

"Into the uncertain vacuum roared a confusion of sounds and styles. There was a new fad or revival every week. Rockabilly, most notably in the shape of the Stray Cats, enjoyed a brief renaissance. . . . Brief revisits of psychedelia, be-bop and beatnik all failed to stick. As people cast around for the right new sound, anything became grist to the pop mill. Jazz, Latin, northern soul, funk, Euro-disco, African, Indian and Chinese musics were all variously used as ethnic spice to enliven the staples of mainstream pop. In the case of African music, for example, this boiled down to little more than Adam [Ant] and Bow Wow Wow basing their sound round the drums of Burundi. But it all added to the confusion of a restless, rowdy, eclectic and ultimately brilliant year for white pop music. In 1981 there seemed to be only one rule: don't stand still.

"What was happening was a complete dissolution of the traditional British relationship between music, style and subculture. . . . style was now no longer a badge of allegiance. It was simply this week's outfit. Something to wear for a night but hardly something worth getting into a fight over. Fashion, and pop music along with it, seemed suddenly to have lost its old importance."

From the perspective of an insider like Rimmer, the waning of new romanticism and the dawn of eclecticism took place after Steve Strange and Rusty Egan's Valentine's Day 1981 People's Palace event, in which the decadent, androgynous Soho underground centered around clubs like Blitz moved up to the working class residential neighborhoods in North London. Nevertheless, when the E Street Band landed in London near the end of May, there was still sufficient polyphony of weirdness accumulated in the chic shopping streets to make a Saturday tour of King's Road a block-by-block adventure.

To trendy London, Bruce's roots rock and soul approach, his lack of pomp and splendor, his eschewing of trappings and fashion, must have looked suspicious or too corny for words. Punk hadn't discernibly affected his music—in America it was a fringe movement that had little popular effect—but Bruce was well aware of it. Perhaps he seemed anachronistic to London's trendies. If so, he wasn't concerned about it. But all this made the shows he was about to do at crumbling Wembley Arena that much more difficult and that much more crucial. Bruce was glad to be there. He'd learned a tremendous amount just by soaking up the atmosphere walking down King's Road on a Saturday afternoon, where every block brought another jolt of outrageousness and unconventional finery. But his job was still to transmit a much more homespun and unadorned idea of popular music to the 10,000 per night who'd be there to meet him.

◆

That first show would finally happen, after the months of delay, on Friday, May 29. Before showtime the band and crew rehearsed, dressed, and ate with no histrionics, but you could feel the nervous tension. Springsteen's principle was that every show counted equally, but there were nights when more chips were on the table than usual, and there was no denying that this was one of them.

In the end, it was still up to him to go out and do the show that needed to be done, the one that made *him* feel right at the end of the night. He'd done it that way in Los Angeles, at the Forum, and he'd gone the same route, after years of resistance, at Madison Square Garden. London was the last crucial capital of rock and roll, and in a way it counted more than everything from Hamburg to Manchester rolled into one. People's choice he may have been—he'd sold out six shows in England's largest and most prestigious arena without having had a hit record there—but in these citadels of the fickle, you never knew.

They reached the stage a half hour late and opened with "Thunder Road." The crowd roared its approval and before the end of the third song, almost everyone was on their feet. But the band didn't know that. Onstage, with the glare of spotlights in their eyes, it's impossible for performers to see more than a couple dozen rows into the crowd. And the band couldn't count on hearing the response accurately, either, since the sound is amplified in strictly one direction.

For just this reason, Springsteen's contract provided that no tickets were to be taken for use by the band, the crew, the promoter, or the record company in the first twenty rows. But somehow, promoter Harvey Goldsmith had missed that stipulation, and the first few rows were packed with music business insiders.

As usual, Bruce dove into the audience during "Tenth Avenue Freeze-out," although this time with more risk than usual—the London town council had threatened to revoke permits for the final three shows if he dared to do anything as dangerous as entering the crowd. What he read there was hard to say—probably not the reticence of Hamburg. This crowd knew just what he was up to, and there was no social sanction preventing them from joining in. But first-night crowds in London are a show-me bunch; to get over with this gang, the band really would have to prove it all night.

Thirty minutes into the show, ninety percent of the hall was roaring on its feet, all but saluting. But the band saw only the complacent sitters in front of them. And the band, if not Bruce, seemed taken aback, maybe a little dejected, by that response. They hadn't seen this much resistance since the first set in Germany.

Bruce spoke very little, as if on this night it was especially crucial that his songs speak for him by themselves. He said nothing even when, near the end of the first set, he began a new song. Anyone who didn't know better would have sworn it was an original, and he provided no additional information.

The music surged around a skeletal structure, much like the revamped "Run Through the Jungle," but the lyrics were even more amazing, a cruel and vivid crescendo that built to the point of snapping and ended each verse and chorus with an expostulated "Trapped!" As it turned out, the song had been found on an old Jimmy Cliff cassette that Bruce had purchased in the Amsterdam airport, and about all the E Street arrangement altered was the rhythm, which was flat rock without a hint of reggae.

The idea of debuting a song, much less such a daring one, in the midst of one of the most crucial sets of his career, got even the deadheads down front into it. As the band segued into the powerhouse chords of "Badlands," the whole room once again exploded. Suddenly, there wasn't a sitter in the house. The sight incited the band; you could see them *lift*, kicking up their heels as they rocked to the set's conclusion. They'd cracked London, once and for all.

Before the end, Bruce still found it necessary to apologize, not only for the postponement of the March tour dates but for the 1975 gig at

Hammersmith. But the gesture was needless. Tough as the Wembley crowd may have been, it went home convinced.

The tour ended in euphoria, with the final five shows at Wembley and the last two at Birmingham serving as the coming-out party of a band that had no more worlds within rock and roll to conquer. In Birmingham, as if to pass the torch, the Who's great guitarist, Pete Townshend, showed up to play along on "Born to Run."

"That tour was tremendously exciting," Bruce remembered five years later. "We really reached out around the world, and it gave the band tremendous confidence. I can remember coming home in the end and everyone feeling it was one of the best experiences of our whole lives."

3 OPEN ALL NIGHT

The story that follows was told to a New Jersey audience in 1984. It is almost certainly true. In any event, it summarizes quite tidily the relationship between our hero and his native province, then, now, and forever.

"Now this, this is a song about the Golden Roadway of the East, the New Jersey Turnpike. I used to work up in New York City, so I'd always have to drive home late at night—and my girlfriend lived down farther in southern Jersey.

"I used to kinda like to ride. I'd get out there around three-thirty . . . Just start drivin', put the window down a little bit. I never had too much trouble on the Turnpike, but if you get off at Exit Eight, that's the Freehold exit, you gotta ride through Hightstown down Thirty-three to the shore. Out in Hightstown, these guys don't have nothin' to do but sit around and wait for ya all night long.

"So I's drivin' home one night and I was thinkin' about seein' my girlfriend and thinkin' about raidin' the refrigerator, seein' my girl, makin' a peanut butter and jelly sandwich, and seein' my girl and makin' a ham and cheese sandwich and raidin' the refrigerator and goin' back to the refrigerator—no." He laughs. "And I know I wasn't speedin', but I musta been goin' suspiciously slow. Because all of a sudden I see them red lights, I get pulled over and . . . 'License, registration, please.'

"Now, I didn't have any. See, I always forget my wallet—one of them people always leaves their wallet home. So I give 'im my name and he goes back and sits in the patrol car and he calls me back in about five minutes and kinda looks at me and he says, 'Hey are you . . . are you that rock and roll singer?' So I say, 'Yeah! Yeah, that's me.'

" 'You the guy that wrote that "Born to Run" song?'

"I say, 'Yeah! Yeah, I wrote that one. That's me.'

"He says, 'Yeah, well, you know, I got some of your albums at home. And, son, you're in a lotta trouble.'

"So they took me in, impounded my truck. But the weirdest thing about it was I had to go to traffic court. And when you go to traffic court there are generally three pleas that you can plead. One is innocent, which hardly nobody pleads that. The other one is guilty, which not many people plead *that*. But the one that almost everybody pleads is guilty with an explanation. If you sit in traffic court all night, you figure out that the whole world is guilty with an explanation.

"And what that means is that you really did what they said you did but now you got about five minutes to bullshit your way out of it.

"So like, I'm sittin' in there and some guy recognizes me and comes over, and he's one of the people when they sit down they sit so close to you that you gotta like lean away. And he was drunk. He gets up before me, and he was caught doin' sixty on a residential side street. And his explanation was that he was drunk and thought he was on the main highway.

"So anyway, my turn came and I got up and they got a little microphone. You gotta stand there and everybody's lookin' at you and you feel like a complete jerk. I said, 'Well, judge, now let me start at the beginning' . . ." Against a rockabilly beat, he sings long crazy, unpunctuated lines:

> *Your eyes get itchy in the wee wee hours sun's just a*
>
> *red ball risin' over them refinery towers*
>
> *Radio's jammed up with gospel stations lost souls callin'*
>
> *long distance salvation*

Hey Mr. Deejay woncha hear my last prayer hey ho

rock 'n roll deliver me from nowhere

◆

When I was a kid, I really understood failure. In my family, you lived deep in its shadow.

During the midwinter break before leaving for that European tour, Steve Van Zandt produced an album for Gary "U.S." Bonds, one of his and Bruce's heroes of the soul era. (For years, Bonds's greatest hit, "Quarter to Three," served as their final encore.) The album, *Dedication*, featured four songs written and co-produced by Bruce, including a revamped version of the Cajun classic "Jole Blon," which Springsteen and Bonds sang as a duet. When *Dedication* was released, just about the time that the E Street contingent landed in Paris, its first single, the Springsteen-penned "This Little Girl" became a hit, Bonds's first chart record in nineteen years.

Steve Van Zandt had met Bonds in the mid-Seventies, while both were touring on the oldies circuit (where Van Zandt was the Dovells' band leader for a time). When Bonds first met Springsteen the summer before *The River* was released, he had no idea who Bruce was: "You know, Springsteen, I thought it could have been an old car . . . or a sandwich or something."

Van Zandt wrote the album's finest number, "Daddy's Come Home," selected such bold songs as Bob Dylan's "From a Buick Six" and Jackson Browne's "The Pretender" for Bonds to sing, arranged and produced everything. Bruce was also involved in a limited way. Steve and Bruce had worked this way before, notably on the three albums that Miami produced for Southside Johnny and the Asbury Jukes, but the Jukes albums never had more than moderate commercial success. "This Little Girl" reached thousands who had no idea of that history, and Bruce got a lot of credit for the Bonds comeback. (No artist had ever spent so many years off the charts and returned to the Top Twenty.)

Gary Bonds's hit, the triumph in Europe (sparsely covered as it was in the States), and the lingering memory of the 1980 tour contributed to an upsurge in Brucemania that reached the band the moment they returned to the States. The key was the U.S. tour, which grew in stature as fans and critics looked back. In a sense, Bruce's show was taken for granted while he was doing it; only after he'd been gone awhile and there were other tours to compare it with did it become clear how remarkable it really was.

The tour forged its own context. "Rock and roll is, today, too big for any center. It is so big, in fact, that no single event . . . can be much more than peripheral," critic Greil Marcus wrote around this time. "In one sense, this is salutary and inevitable. The lack of a center means the lack of a conventional definition of what rock and roll is, and that fosters novelty. . . . But this state of affairs is also debilitating and dispiriting. The fact that the most adventurous music of the day seems to have taken up residence in the darker corners of the marketplace contradicts the idea of rock and roll as an aggressively popular culture that tears up boundaries of race, class, geography and (oh yes) music. The belief that the mass audience can be reached and changed has—until now—been the deepest source of the music's magic and power.

"The music does not now provide much evidence that this belief is based on anything like reality. . . . Bands with very broad—or at least very big—audiences continue to exist, of course, but they don't destroy boundaries; they disguise them, purveying music characterized principally by emotional vapidity and social vagueness.

"A concert by Bruce Springsteen offers many thrills, and one is that he performs as if none of the above is true. . . . His show is, among other things, an argument about the nature of rock and roll after twenty-five years. The argument is that rock and roll is a means to fun that can acknowledge the most bitter defeats, that it has a coherent tradition which, when performed, will reveal possibilities of rock and roll the tradition did not previously contain."

Springsteen's confidence in this tradition—not just in its existence, but in the idea that the general principle Marcus describes still worked—was singular at this time. Others operating inside the tradition used it as a crutch, so that it became a substitute for the transaction between artist and audience. Because Springsteen was so internally centered, that problem never arose for him. He poured all his energy and imagination into *what* he wanted and needed to say, not worrying about how. He could do this in part because he was such a naturally gifted rock and roll musician: Songs sprang out of him by the dozen, where they trickled from others, and his music was focused in styles that endured, which allowed him to be oblivious to fashion in ways that almost no other rock performer could afford.

One result was that he made solving the most difficult problem pop performers face look ridiculously easy. But it was never easy for Springsteen, only simple. He was not afraid to show the strain of getting it right when that struck him as appropriate. But it's also true that talking about his faith in tradition misses the mark. ("Having posited a tradition," Marcus commented, "Springsteen acts as if every bit of it is backing him up—rooting for him.") What really distinguished Springsteen was that he wanted desperately to communicate—something he believed counted, that would make a difference in the lives of those who experienced it, including himself. Invest yourself in that way and the world will beat a path to your door.

Yet the contradiction between Springsteen's live appeal and his record sales and radio airplay persisted. "Fade Away," the follow up to "Hungry Heart," had stalled at Number Twenty, and there was no third single. *The River* spent four weeks at Number One. It sold about 2 million copies, substantially more than any of Bruce's other albums but not equal to the day's biggest record acts, who sold 5 million or more copies of their biggest hits. While Springsteen was king of the hill at album-oriented radio (AOR), he remained a marginal figure at more-influential Top Forty stations, and it was Top Forty exposure that sold records in multiplatinum quantities.

All of this indicated the ultimate irony of Springsteen's situation: Though he was celebrated and loved as the last true believer in the possibility of speaking meaningfully to a mass audience, he spoke essentially only to a very large cult.

Bruce shunned talk of marketing. His discoverer, the venerable producer and talent scout John Hammond, once commented that Springsteen was the only performer he'd met in forty years in the business who cared nothing about money, which happens to be true, however unbelievable. And his lack of interest in commerce went way beyond money. For most performers, the claim that their work comes first is merely serviceable rhetoric. To Bruce the work was literally the only thing that mattered. When he entertained any discussion of how to sell himself, it was solely as a means of getting people to hear his work.

So other acts selling more records never fazed Springsteen. He was not competing with what anybody else had to say. His concern was always what happened to the people who *did* hear him, not those who didn't, a reflection of the inverted optimism built into the bedrock of his personality at an early age.

"I never got into being discouraged, because I never got into hoping," Bruce once told Robert Hilburn. "When I was a kid, I never got used to expecting success. I got used to failing. Once you do that, the rest is real easy. It took a lot of the pressure off. I just said, 'Hell, I'm a loser. I don't have to worry about anything.' I assumed immediately that nothing was happening.

"But that's not the same as giving up. You keep trying, but you don't count on things. It can be a strength. Because I know some people who sweat out winning so much it kills them. So, in the end, they lose anyway."

Again, Springsteen makes his outlook seem too simple: just a matter of common sense. And in this particular case, he was being disingenuous, since fame and success gave him more than his share of problems. That was obvious even when it came to simple matters. For years he refused to play sports arenas for fear that it would disrupt his rapport with his audience, as though that intimacy were created by physical proximity, not his own passion. The latest wrinkle in concert promotion was "tour merchandise," the selling of T-shirts, programs, buttons, and other souvenirs. For most of the 1980 tour, he held out against providing a significant array of such trinkets, even though his fans were clearly eager for them, and the graphics and programs he did allow were understated and unpretentious to a fault.

For that matter, his lack of hit singles boiled down to a kind of avoidance. "If success was what it was like with *Born to Run*," Landau remarked, "Bruce didn't want that. He didn't want to have one song that could be taken out of context and interfere with what he wanted the album to represent."

His records may not have been played on Top Forty radio much, but his songs were staples there. Others picked up on his material and had half a dozen Top Ten hits in the late Seventies and early Eighties. The biggest hits came with songs that could just as easily have fitted into his own albums—the Pointer Sisters' "Fire" and Patti Smith's "Because the Night."

Nevertheless, when he returned from Europe, Springsteen had to change, and not only as a result of what he'd seen and learned there. Whether or not he had any use for celebrity, he'd become a huge star. And the U.S. tour planned for that summer, playing multiple arena dates in the dozen cities where he was already biggest, amounted to a victory lap.

4 WAY BACK HOME

I never will forget those nights
I wonder if it was a dream
Remember how you made me crazy?
Remember how I made you scream

—*Don Henley, "The Boys of Summer"*

Bruce Springsteen's six-night run at the Brendan Byrne Arena in New Jersey's Meadowlands Sports complex played to more than 120,000 people, two or three times the capacity of Giants Stadium next door. But even that number was dwarfed by the demand. Tickets for the Jersey shows were sold by mail, and when the first day's orders arrived, Meadowlands general manager Loris Smith reported, there were enough requests for twenty-two shows. And because the shows would also mark the new arena's inauguration, there was a full complement of political brass squabbling for seats; Springsteen's associates prevailed over the promoters, and the public won that round.

Mostly, the huge attendance reflected a massive outpouring of love by the area's rock and roll fans, teenagers to middle-agers. When Bruce came onstage for the first show on July 2, the greeting was so huge— a long screech and stomp rising and swelling to all but overwhelm the first song, which was, inevitably, "Born to Run," Bruce's first anthem— it almost seemed the new building might not survive.

Not a bad welcome for a kid who had grown up on the wrong side of Freehold, one of the seedier towns in the seediest state in the union. Pretty impressive for a boy who had seemed so weird twelve years before that he was requested to leave Ocean County Community College by his fellow students, all of whom now remembered him fondly. A bitter man would have savored the irony. Bruce Springsteen just played his heart out.

If anything, the second night's crowd and show were even wilder. The dignitaries had split, making more room for hard-core Springsteen fanatics. These were fans to whom Bruce Springsteen spoke forcefully and almost across the board. His songs illuminated the glory and the tragedy of dead-end lives played out in dead towns; they also seemed to celebrate the ability to rise in the world, to make it. Yuppies in their cups, teenagers with their hopes up, workers down on their luck in an economy gone sour, could all listen to the words of *"The River"*—"Is a dream a lie if it don't come true/Or is it something worse?"—and hear a fragment of their own stories. It may have been that the Yuppies heard what they feared, a story about what they believed had been left behind, and that others heard a tale much more realistic. But everybody heard a story no one else was telling, and they loved the teller as much as the tale.

Bruce's shows opened with a series of cornerstone rockers, but the middle of the first set was somber, as if he were setting the crowd up for the good times ahead by reminding them of the price that had to be paid, not only that night but every day. He opened the third show, on July 5, with "Thunder Road" and a smoking "Prove It All Night," rollicked through "The Ties That Bind," then pulled the mood back down for "Darkness on the Edge of Town" and "Factory." During the latter, the night's first fireworks went off.

"I'd like to just make one announcement," Bruce said as soon as the song was done. His tone was quiet but stern. "If by any chance you brought any fireworks with you, please don't set 'em off in the hall. Keep 'em in your pocket or throw 'em away. If you see somebody settin' 'em off, tell the usher or tell the security guard because I want 'em thrown out. 'Cause you're gonna hurt yourself or hurt somebody that's around ya.

"That's not what 'Independence Day' is about anyway." On cue, music began, the organ and piano chords that led into the song.

"I remember when I was a little kid, every Fourth of July my mother and father used to take me out to the racetrack in Freehold," Bruce said. "I guess they don't have fireworks no more down there, but they used to have 'em every Fourth of July. And there used to be this cemetery that was right on the outside of the track, and there was this hill called Cemetery Hill, and everybody used to go up there and park and sit up on the hill and watch the skyrockets.

"When I was little I didn't know what it was about. I just knew that on Fourth of July we'd go out there and there were all these fireworks and stuff.

"We just spent a couple of months over in Europe. And I found myself thinkin' of home a lot more than usual, from being away. I'd never been away from the States for so long. And I started to read this book called *History of the United States*. And in it, I found a lot of things that were important to know, because they helped me understand the way that my life was and the way that my life developed. They helped me understand how when I was a kid all I remember was my father worked in a factory, his father worked in a factory . . ." His voice just faded out, as if speaking of a chain too endless to recount.

"And the main reason was that they didn't know enough," he said, echoing his Stockholm rap. "They didn't know enough about themselves, and they didn't know enough about the forces that controlled their lives.

"I started to read this book and the thing that most impressed me was the idealism. It was like when you were a kid and you leave home. You leave home because you believe in yourself or you think you're gonna do somethin'. And because you wanna be different—you wanna be different than your old man was. . . ." He stopped, drowned out by cheers, then began again as they died down.

"And that's what happened here. The idea was that there'd be a place for everybody, no matter where you came from, no matter what religion you were or what color you were, you could help make a life that had some decency and some dignity to it.

"But like all ideals, that idea got real corrupted. And as I read through the book and I got up into the Sixties and the Seventies . . . in the Seventies I was in my twenties and I was in my teens in the Sixties, but I felt like I'd been sleepin' all the time through all those years. 'Cause I didn't know what was goin' on; I didn't know what the government that I live under was doing.

"It's important to know about yourself, that's all, and know about the things around you. So, you get a chance, read that book, *History of the United States*. It's good!"

He launched into a memorably tender version of the song, one of his finest and most important, in which a father is laid to rest by a son still struggling to resolve the hopelessness of their lives together. He had performed the song in moods ranging from rage to anguish, he'd recorded it as what sounded like the recessional from a folk mass funeral, but tonight he simply sang it as a gentle confession of incomprehension—two people so close that they were blinded to one another: "There was just no way this house could hold the two of us/I guess that we were just too much of the same kind." After that introduction, the song became, at least for this night, an act of absolution.

In a way, this was the closest Bruce came during the Meadowlands shows to explaining to his audience what had happened in Europe. His efforts at a direct explanation petered out. The difference seemed to express itself most often when he was unable to control the behavior of his expanded audience, when it lacked the respect and empathy that he had found in the overseas crowds. On July fifth, during "Racing in the Street," another firecracker exploded. When the song ended, Bruce spoke in a tone he virtually never used from the stage: cold fury.

"When I was over in Europe"—he broke off, fighting to command himself—"one of the things that I hadn't thought about that much before, that I started to think about, was the importance of the audience at the show." Cheers forced him to pause again; when he began speaking it was in the tone of a parent who had just been given the perfect setup for the lesson to come.

"And I just want to say that I'm proud that everybody's come down to see us. And whoever it is—and there's only one person or two out of, I guess, twenty thousand people here tonight—that has to set off a firework in the middle of a song, the only thing I can . . ."—he paused to rein himself in again—". . . I can say is, you can do me a favor and never come back to one of my shows ever again. Because if you don't . . . if you don't have the respect for yourself, you should at least have respect for the people that are around you. And if you don't have that, you should at least have the guts to do it where I can see you."

For the most part, Bruce's shows were not confrontational occasions. He ripped into the firecracker crowd all through the Meadowlands series because such activities spoiled the creative atmosphere he wanted. Springsteen's concerts were a refutation of the idea that rock was anarchic rebellion. If anything, his shows were a masterwork of crowd control, an adventure in pure cooperation, a challenge to chaos.

After angrily cursing the final firecracker thrower of the Meadowlands series, on the last night of the stand, Bruce snarled, "Whoever you are, you're no friend of mine." It was the worst epithet he could conceive.

By the same token, politics weren't really the focus of Springsteen's essays in public speaking. His introductions were an art in themselves, a crucial and revealing segment of his performances, but their focus was always on personal revelations of various kinds. His references to Europe, to studying United States history, to the hidden American class system, were profoundly *prepolitical.* He had no ideology to sell; in that sense, he was continually groping to coalesce these interests and incidents into a coherent shape that would do nothing so much as explain himself to himself. He was never so naïve as to believe that the good fortune that rained upon him could happen to just anyone. "I wrote this song because I've been lucky—I've got about as much freedom as money can buy in this country," he remarked later that summer. "And it seems like you're never really free until everybody else is." The song that followed was "Jackson Cage," perhaps the most overtly *psychological* number from *The River*, the story of a woman trapped in her own house by an existence too trivialized to make sense.

It was just such moments of revelation that kept the Springsteen cult returning to his shows, night after night, with a thirst that approached greed. One of the few problems associated with the Springsteen tour was ticket-scalping, not because scalping was particularly worse around his shows than at those of other superstars, but because his fans were convinced that scalping violated the principles those shows epitomized (without considering that those principles were in direct conflict with a market economy) and because every Springsteen fan was sure that an equitable distribution would never leave him or her out. The fact that concerts are inherently inequitable—that there are only a finite number of seats in the front rows, only a finite number of seats in "good" locations, that playing any sort of facility imposes a limit on the number of people who can enter it—was deemed irrelevant. And the reason for it all was that if you missed one of Bruce's shows, you might really be missing something. It didn't have to be a new song or a new story; it could just be a juxtaposition of images or songs, a matter of tone or inflection.

On this final leg of *The River* tour, though, Bruce's onstage musing acquired an almost compulsive character. You could hear in his anxious breathing that he was probing at parts of himself that were extremely discomfiting, dredging up aspects of his life that perhaps did not really want to emerge—certainly, aspects that almost no other performer would have found it necessary or desirable to expose.

A classic example, and one that also shows the process by which the same song and story could have their meanings transformed from night to night, lay in the comments he made before the final "Independence Day" of the Meadowlands shows. Like all such stories, it began in childhood.

"I grew up in this house where nobody ever talked to each other," he began, sounding miserable. "We used to live on the left side of this little three-room house. There was a front room and then the kitchen and two bedrooms and a bathroom upstairs. With everybody livin' that close, it seemed that nobody ever sat down without being angry, tellin' each other what was on their mind. I could never talk to my old man, he could never talk to me, my mother couldn't talk to him . . .

"So I was glad when I finally got old enough and I started to live alone. Then, for about ten years I never saw my folks that much. And just recently, we came back from Europe . . . If you get a chance, you gotta go there because you can't imagine it—it's not what you think it is or what you read in the papers. But we got back and I got a phone call a night or two later that my father had gotten sick. And I went out to California where he was in the hospital there.

"I started thinkin' on the way out about all the things that I always wanted to say to him that I never said and I always figured, well, someday we'll sit down and we'll talk about all this stuff—talk about why it was the way it was when I was young, talk about why he felt the way he did.

"But the years go by and it never comes up. I guess it feels like a dangerous subject or something. But he got sick and I realized that he was gettin' old and that . . . and that if I had somethin' to say to him, I should say it now . . . 'cause family is forever and it's somethin' that . . ." Here he was drowned out by cheers but continued anyway, the audience all but irrelevant. "It's somethin' that don't ever go away, no matter how far you move away from each other or no matter what your feelin's are towards each other. It's just there in your blood all the time, in your blood.

"So if you got folks at home and have been waitin', waitin' to say stuff to 'em, don't waste too much time. 'Cause you'll always regret it." He said the last line in a mumble, so low and muttered that it was doubtful anybody ten feet from the mike heard him, although the listener who mattered most at that moment surely did. The song that night was nothing less than an act of contrition.

◆

When the band returned from Europe, they took the rest of June off. While in California with his parents after his father's stroke, Bruce wound up playing two shows, the Survival Sunday antinuclear benefit with Jackson Browne and a number of others, and a Gary Bonds gig at San Francisco's Old Waldorf nightclub. Clarence Clemons busied himself—against Bruce's advice, it later developed—preparing to launch a Red Bank rock club, Big Man's West. The others relaxed, but not too much. They'd been on the road for six of the past eight months, but the tour still had a long way to go.

Even before going to Europe, Jon Landau and Springsteen had planned another swing around the States. They'd be playing many of the same towns as in the fall, but with a difference. "The concept was to go back to cities that had been very special in Bruce's career," Landau later explained. "Basically, come in and stay for a while and play a little bit in depth. You know, when you're in the city for more than a day, when you're not just on the bus coming in that day and driving out after the show, you go out, you get a feeling for the place, maybe you drop in on a club. You have a chance to personalize your visit to that particular town."

The result encompassed thirty-five shows in only ten cities. In every city except San Diego, Springsteen played for at least two nights in the city's largest arena. In addition to the six nights at the Meadowlands, he played five shows in Philadelphia and five in Los Angeles. In every town, the issue was not whether he sold out, but how quickly the tickets went. In most places there were enough requests to have played two or three times more shows, even considering that, in a mail-order ticket lottery, many customers apply several times, and in Springsteen's case, just as many were bent on seeing *all* of his performances in their town.

This level of fanaticism was not unprecedented. The Who, the Grateful Dead, the Rolling Stones, Led Zeppelin, and a few other top rock acts had acquired equally devoted followings. What made Springsteen's massive cult surprising was that he did not have the Sixties cachet of those other groups. He was the one concert superstar whose career was entirely post-Woodstock.

More significantly, what each of these groups had in common was that they represented an idea. Superficially, that idea could be almost anything, from the macho 'n' mysticism of Zeppelin to the spaced-out good vibes of the Dead. But underneath it all, each of these bands acted out a form of community, whether with the aristocratic-bohemian arrogance of the Rolling Stones or the familial squabbling of the Who. Each of the central figures of rock history had this in common; even those seemingly monolithic individuals, Elvis Presley and Bob Dylan, acquired much of their force from this idea. In their cases, though, the community was not something they acted out so much as a phenomenon that gathered around them.

In a sense, Bruce Springsteen and the E Street Band had it both ways. In reaching out so intimately to his audience, Bruce conveyed an especially lucid idea of community; by making demands on that audience—demands of stamina, attention, and increasingly after the European tour, responsibility—he became continuously more articulate about the community that he was trying to shape. Bruce played several roles in this sense, alternately acting as goodnatured older brother, the most incorrigible and charming juvenile in town, stern parent, generous uncle.

On the other hand, the internal dynamics of the E Street Band represented another form of community, as rock bands always have. In this respect, the polyglot look of the group was even an advantage, for looking from Bittan to Clemons to Van Zandt, one was given the firm impression that no one—at least, no one male—was excluded.

Bruce's relation to all of this was especially fascinating because he was privately such a loner. He always had been. "In the beginning, my goals were pretty modest," he said. "I wanted to learn to play rhythm guitar, just so I could get in a band—just to be in a band; I didn't want to be the lead singer or I didn't want to be the lead guitarist. I didn't become a lead guitarist until I got thrown out of the first band I was in. I just wanted to play rhythm guitar, just find my spot, kinda stand there in the background, just, you know, just be in the band." Even though being in a band was of such tremendous importance to him, he kept to himself offstage, communicating with the band (except Steve) and crew mostly at the hall. Back at the hotel, he was no party animal. Bruce never took drugs—and that means he never took a single pill for pleasure (he was reluctant to swallow medication) or smoked a single joint of grass. He never smoked cigarettes, for that matter. He drank rarely, and when he did, he got wasted (and silly) fast.

"He's so unlike everything you think a real successful rock star would be," exclaimed pianist Bittan. But Bruce's abstemiousness made him mysterious and that made him more attractive. As the audience weaned on rock grew up, it became ready for a more wholesome and constant kind of rock star, someone who would both act out fantasies and provide a model of values. Maybe for the first time in the history of pop stardom, someone like Bruce could become an idol.

Compared to Mick Jagger, much less Johnny Rotten, Springsteen was conservative. The term seems a bit misleading—despite rock's anarchist propaganda, restraint and caution aren't reactionary tendencies—but it was one Bruce himself accepted, at least when it came to creativity. "Generally, I'm pretty conservative in some ways," he said. "I don't really have a desire to experiment for the sake of experimentation, because mainly what I'm tryin' to do is get an idea across. I'm not really that concerned with style. I wanted our thing to be basically real content-oriented. It's what you're sayin'. So I kinda go from there. I go from like, Is this a good song? Is there a human being in this song? If I sing this song, do you hear a real person's voice? And then, what's their story, what are they sayin'? Is it something that's worth takin' up people's time with?"

One part of punk's legacy was the introduction of modernist (and academic "postmodernist") ideas into pop discourse. "Rock was, after all, a modern form—the expression of dislocated, rootless youth," wrote critic Tom Carson. "Its public images and media masks were of a piece with the technological leaps-into-the-void that made it feasible. We didn't respond to Jagger because he was being himself; we responded because he was acting out ploys and stratagems open to us. We expected the truth from our avatars, but not candor." For Carson, Springsteen (until *Born in the U.S.A.*) "was never an entirely satisfying rock star," and the reason was quite basic: "He thought rock and roll was basically wholesome. It was an alternative, an escape—but not a rebellion, either as a route to forbidden sexual or social fruit, or, by extension, as a rejection of conventional society. To him, rock *redeemed* conventional society." Carson pointed to Springsteen's use of rock to work through his relationship to his parents, and to the friendly but generally unsexual way that women were portrayed in Bruce's songs as examples. Critic Milo Miles neatly summed up the problem Springsteen presented for postpunk partisans: "Granted, *Born to Run* sent a tremor through West Coast soft-rockies and warned that several hundred thousand pop fans were spoiling for an old-fashioned rumble, but at bottom the record proved that the avant-garde of rock and roll was out of the hands of extremists."

In this respect, Springsteen's subordination of form to content is not so much reactionary as anachronistic. Even his repetition of themes and images—his fixation on automobiles and driving metaphors, for instance—was a pragmatic rather than theoretical device. This approach may not have been critically fashionable, but it played perfectly in a pop climate in which a substantial portion of the audience had been deadened by the dictum of change for its own sake.

The summer tour confirmed Bruce's stature—and it did something more. "As a band, I think we were different, and not only just musically," Van Zandt said. "Once you communicate internationally, you feel that, even if it's subconscious. You're never the same." Bruce simply said that when he got back home, "I wasn't really sure what was going on, I just knew something had changed."

However great the changes in his audience and in his band, the greatest changes of all were taking place within Bruce Springsteen. He'd entered the record business as a twenty-one-year-old who had barely earned his high school diploma. It wasn't really until 1974, when he and Jon Landau became friendly, that Springsteen began to develop intellectually. Landau's relationship to Bruce was significant not only because he encouraged the singer to believe that he really was as good as his dreams, but also because in the course of spending time together—at first on the phone, then socially, and finally in the recording studio—Jon exposed his new friend to the very idea of art. Bruce became extremely attentive to classic Hollywood films and began to read classic American literature. By 1981, a rather arty film like John Huston's adaptation of Flannery O'Connor's *Wise Blood* had become as inspiring to Springsteen as the Ronettes and Rolling Stones.

Landau didn't deliberately set out to educate Bruce, but his enthusiasms were infectious. When Bruce complained that he couldn't stand to watch John Ford's *The Grapes of Wrath* on television, Landau simply sat down with him the next time it was on and showed him what he was missing. Landau played an extremely useful role in the process by which Springsteen made records; as manager, Jon translated Bruce's ideas into businesslike terms as no less empathetic figure could have done. But if there was a bottom line to their relationship, it was simpler and stranger: Jon Landau was the first person who had ever realized that Bruce Springsteen had not only an amazing talent but was also extremely intelligent. Explaining himself to a Paris audience, Bruce paid tribute to what that meant to him: "I was lucky, too, because I met this guy when I was in my middle twenties who said you should watch this or you should read this. And most people, where I come from, never have someone try and help them in that way."

As he gained a better grasp of himself and his world, Springsteen was able to channel this understanding more and more clearly into his work. When he returned to America, seeing his own country with fresh eyes and confronting an audience that was increasingly huge and anonymous, Bruce began to think about a way of returning some of what he'd been given. In part, this meant money, but just as much, it meant opportunity—the opportunity to have one's story heard and case presented.

Of all the shut-out groups of Americans he knew, Bruce was most moved and intrigued by the plight of the Vietnam veterans. He was no Rambo, and he frankly admitted doing everything he could to avoid being drafted. "I had no real political standpoint whatsoever when I was eighteen. And neither did any of my friends," he said. "The whole draft thing, it was just a pure street thing. You didn't want to go. You didn't want to go because you'd seen other people go and not come back. The first drummer in my first band, the Castiles, enlisted and he came back in his uniform and he was 'Oh here I go, I'm goin' to Vietnam.' Kinda laughin' and joking about it and that was it. He went and he was killed. There were a lotta guys from my neighborhood, guys in bands . . . One of the best singers in the neighborhood, he was drafted and he went and he was missing in action.

"And so it got to be a thing. We didn't even know where Vietnam was when I was eighteen, seventeen. We just knew we didn't want to go and die. It wasn't until probably later in the Seventies that the awareness of the type of war it was, what it meant, the way it felt to be a subversion of all the true American ideals, twisted the country inside out—it wasn't until then that we had any what you would call political awareness about it."

Springsteen was 4-F because of a brain concussion received in a 1968 motorcycle accident in which he also badly injured his leg. Getting out of the draft wasn't that simple though. Springsteen filled out forms crazily, didn't take tests, did his best to get out of serving. But he never forgot how near he'd come.

"When I got on the bus to go take my physical, I thought one thing: *I ain't goin'.* I had tried to go to college, and I didn't really fit in. I went to a real narrow-minded school where people gave me a lot of trouble and I was hounded off the campus—I just looked different and acted different, so I left school. And I remember bein' on that bus, me and a couple of guys in my band, and the rest of the bus was probably sixty, seventy percent black guys from Asbury Park. And I remember thinkin', like, what makes my life, or my friends' lives, more expendable than that of somebody who's goin' to school? It didn't seem right."

By 1981 Springsteen's position on the war hadn't changed and neither had his feelings for those who couldn't escape fighting it. The war had been wrong and worse, and the men and women who fought it had been badly betrayed—not by "lack of national will," but by a government that was eager to use them to carry out pernicious foreign policy objectives and then discarded them without thanks when they returned defeated.

Bruce read *Born on the Fourth of July,* the memoir of Ron Kovic, a paraplegic vet who had joined the antiwar movement, and was deeply moved, both by Kovic's personal story and by the tragedy that had befallen all the Vietnam veterans.

Largely conscripts, the vets had nonetheless volunteered for combat duty, believing they were fighting for civics class ideals. But when they arrived in the jungle, they found themselves shooting and being shot at only to maintain corrupt regimes both in Saigon and Washington. Returning to national scorn, they found no G.I. Bill. The Veterans Administration, set up to cope with the aging veterans of Korea and World War II, wanted as little as possible to do with these vets who were young, often black or Latin, almost always working-class, and justifiably furious. And if the government's treatment was inept, the public was simply callous. Americans didn't want to know about the vets at all. The war had revealed a massive split in American society, and acknowledging the vets' existence could tear it open again.

Meantime the veterans, who had come from the poorest sections of society in the first place, were visited with all sorts of plagues, from mental exhaustion to drug addiction to the aftereffects of Agent Orange, a defoliant that caused various cancers in affected soldiers and produced genetic defects in their children. Americans sufficiently well-to-do to afford higher education had been spared military service; in the face of the double digit unemployment of the early Eighties, the poor and poorly trained Vietnam vet was one of the citizens most likely to be found destitute.

Having thought about the veterans, having read about them, and with the memory of his friend, drummer Bart Hanes, still in his mind, Bruce decided that he wanted to help. He asked Jon Landau to locate a Vietnam veterans' organization and find out what kind of help might be provided. Landau, who had also been against the war, asked Joe Klein, his former *Rolling Stone* colleague who had written the Woody Guthrie biography. Klein was just beginning research on a book about Vietnam veterans that was eventually published under the title *Payback* in 1985. He told Landau that the organization most worthy of aid was Vietnam Veterans of America.

Landau got in touch with VVA president Bob Muller, a thirty-six-year-old former Marine Corps first lieutenant who was left paraplegic after being shot in the spine in 1969 at Con Tien, just outside the demilitarized zone.

When he returned to the States and was finally released from a VA hospital (an experience he said was even more depressing than what he underwent in 'Nam), Muller joined Vietnam Veterans Against the War, the most militant of the veterans groups within the antiwar movement. After the war ended, VVAW died out. By 1978 Muller determined to form a more broadly based group to fight for the rights of Vietnam-era soldiers, which the American Legion and Veterans of Foreign Wars basically refused to do. This was the Vietnam Veterans of America.

By 1981, Muller and VVA had gotten precisely nowhere. The government continued its policy of benign neglect toward the Vietnam vets, refusing to acknowledge their special problems. Muller worked unceasingly, and he was effective in getting some media attention for the veterans. *The Washington Post* wrote thirty-five editorials in favor of Vietnam vets' rights. Muller was named one of the fifty "future leaders of America" by *The New York Times Magazine*. Such establishment credentials gave him access to every key figure associated with the war, including all the major policy-makers, and he arranged meetings with everyone from former Secretary of Defense Melvin Laird to former *Time* editor Henry Gruenwald. "They all told me to go away," he said. Although VVA chapters were proliferating, because it was the *only* game in town for Vietnam vets, Muller couldn't raise enough money to create a functioning home office or even put out a regular newsletter.

Rock and roll was probably the last place Muller would have thought to turn for support. The music's historic association with the antiwar movement suggested hostility toward the vets. But when Landau called and invited him to come to the Meadowlands shows and meet afterward with Bruce, Muller went eagerly. No matter what rock musicians thought of Vietnam veterans, most of the vets were rock fans.

After Jersey shows, Bruce was inevitably tied up for a couple of hours, first recovering from the rigors of the show, then greeting family and friends. Because Bruce didn't want to place a time limit on his meeting with Muller, Bobby came in last. The wait was worth it for everyone concerned. The two men hit it off immediately, forming a friendship that extended beyond the bounds of politics. They talked for forty-five minutes. "I think Bruce decided right then, five minutes into the conversation, that he was going to hook something up with him," Landau said.

Muller may not have been looking for a main chance, but he was smart enough to grab one when it presented itself. Soon after meeting Bruce, he began pursuing other rock stars. After some discussion, Bruce agreed to do his first show in Los Angeles, on September 20, as a benefit, with all proceeds donated to VVA and several Southern California veterans' aid facilities. Meantime, Muller lined up similar commitments from singer Pat Benatar and country-rocker Charlie Daniels (who was not a vet but had a road crew of veterans). Bruce's show was a guaranteed sell-out, and the others did about as well. In all, nearly a quarter of a million dollars was raised. "Without Bruce and that evening, we would not have made it," Muller has said repeatedly since then. "We would have had to close down." Today VVA operates with a multimillion-dollar annual budget and has a Congressional charter. It is the only recognized, effective national organization for Vietnam veterans. Muller has also become one of the key figures in attempting to rebuild diplomatic relations between the United States and Vietnam.

After the Jersey shows, Bruce and the entire band spent a stifling

Saturday night closing out the grand opening of Big Man's West. A couple of days later, the tour proceeded to Philadelphia and ground to a temporary halt. On the first night at the Spectrum, the air-conditioning failed; when the cooling system came back to life for the second show, it was overpowering. By the time the run ended, Bruce's throat was too sore for singing. Shows scheduled for Chicago and Cincinnati's Riverfront Coliseum had to be postponed, flipped to the end of the tour.

After a ten-day layoff, Bruce got back on track with his three-gig stint in Largo, Maryland (between Washington and Baltimore), and the tour charged through Detroit and Denver on its way to the West Coast. The band had never played better. Even a downpour that drenched the crowd and had Bruce playing "Who'll Stop the Rain" to open the show at Denver's outdoor Red Rocks amphitheater couldn't dampen spirits. (Bruce came out and offered either to postpone the show or play on through the rain; he clearly thought it would be a good idea to start all over another night. The crowd voted him down.)

Arriving in Los Angeles, Bruce and Landau's associate, Barbara Carr, spent an entire day at the local veterans' center, meeting with several dozen men and women, a great many of them still suffering from war wounds. Those confined to wheelchairs were the least of it. There were vets who would never leave their hospital gurney tables, and there were men whose bodies were intact but whose minds were in pieces. All of them were coming to the show—so many wanted to attend that tickets were ultimately provided for all the L.A. shows.

Visiting the vets center left a deep impression on Bruce. He told Muller that he'd barely slept the night before the benefit, just thinking about what he was going to have to do. "He said he was petrified, that when he walked onstage without the guitar, he felt naked." Muller had his own worries. He'd made speeches for years, but how was he going to get across to 20,000 rock fans screaming for their hero?

At the Los Angeles Sports Arena, tour manager George Travis built a kind of gallery along the side of the stage for the disabled. On the night of the benefit, dozens of paraplegic and quadriplegic vets were ushered into the special section, honored onlookers who served—that night and on those that followed—as a visible reminder of what the occasion was all about.

At showtime, Bruce walked out, picked up the mike, and began to speak in an unusually nervous tone. At the same time, what he had to say was forceful and considered. He wasn't telling a story or introducing a song; he was making a speech, but he did it with the same combination of straight-from-the shoulder plainspokenness and artful metaphor he always used.

"Listen. Listen for a second," he said. "Tonight we're here for the men and the women that fought in the Vietnam war. Yesterday I was lucky enough and I met some of these guys. And it was funny, because I'm used to comin' out in front of a lot of people and I realized that I was nervous and I was a little embarrassed about not knowin' what to say to 'em.

"And it's like when you feel like you're walkin' down a dark street at night and out of the corner of your eye you see somebody gettin' hurt or somebody gettin' hit in the dark alley but you keep walkin' on because you think it don't have nothin' to do with you and you just wanna get home.

"Well, Vietnam turned this whole country into that dark street. And unless we're able to walk down those dark alleys and look into the eyes of the men and the women that are down there and the things that happened, we're never gonna be able to get home . . . and then it's only a chance."

He looked out to the restless crowd, over at the vets, and began speaking more loudly, his tone sharpened. "You guys! You guys out there that are eighteen and nineteen years old—it happened once and it can happen again." He broke off momentarily to let the cheers subside.

"So," he sighed, "I guess all I'm sayin' is, You gotta go down there and you gotta look. And we got the easy part, because there's a lotta guys here tonight who had to live it and live it every day. And there's a lotta guys who made it home to America but died and didn't make it here tonight. So what I want to ask you to do is, I wanna ask you to give a few minutes of your attention and listen to a friend of mine, a Vietnam veteran named Bob Muller."

Muller wheeled forward into the spotlight. The crowd may have been eager for the show to start, but he was greeted warmly. "It's very exciting to be here tonight," he said eagerly. "It's a great night for Vietnam veterans. You may have been hearin' about Vietnam veterans and not really understanding what it's all about. Very simply, there was a lotta controversy and there was a lotta pain surrounding the tragedy of Vietnam. Because of that, a lotta people have tried to forget it and pretend that it never happened. That doesn't do much for the families of the fifty-five thousand Americans that were killed in Vietnam. It doesn't do much for the three hundred thousand that were wounded fighting that war.

"But tonight is the first step in ending the silence that has surrounded Vietnam." Cheers stopped him. "It is the beginning of taking all the people that have worked so hard for these years all over the country—people like in L.A., the Shad Meshads, the team leaders from the vet centers, the Center for Veterans Rights, *all* the Vietnam veterans—and it's bringin' us together. And by that, it'll make sure that the programs are enacted, it'll make sure that the lessons are learned and that the Vietnams aren't allowed to happen again." Cheers interrupted.

When Muller spoke again, his voice had risen with excitement. He'd been waiting for this part of what he had to say for weeks; it still seemed too good to be true. He wasn't making a speech anymore. He was celebrating an alliance that could not only help keep his organization alive but would push it much closer to victory.

"The last thing I gotta say: It's a little bit ironic that for the years that we've been tryin', when the businesses haven't come behind us and the political leaders have failed to rally behind us that, when you remember the divisions within our own generation about the war, it ultimately turns out to be the very symbol of our generation—rock and roll!—that brings us together. And it is rock and roll that is going to provide the healing process that everybody needs."

Now Muller was shouting like a Top Forty deejay: "So let's not talk about it, let's get down to it, let's rock and roll it!"

Quickly, the E Street Band took its place and Bruce strode to the mike. Counting it off quickly, they hit John Fogerty's "Who'll Stop the Rain," a song probably written about Woodstock but adopted by Vietnam veterans as their anthem. At least two members of the group played the song that night with tears in their eyes. Bruce told Muller afterward that when he counted off the song, his emotions were at such a pitch that he felt as if he'd already played an entire show.

The music simply exploded off the stage, a contained but frenzied pounding that surged with all the complicated emotions the war still evoked. And out front, Bruce Springsteen's voice crackled with mourning and fury against the almost elegant chords. They sailed out of it with Bruce shouting with all his might, demanding, "I wanna know!

Well, I wanna know!" Over and over, pounding it in, as if by the act of singing this song and *getting it right* he could revive all the lost hopes and wasted lives.

They played the whole show that way, pounding through remarkable versions of "Prove It All Night," "Darkness on the Edge of Town," "Trapped," "Badlands," "This Land Is Your Land," and "Hungry Heart." This was the band that played every note, every night, as if it counted. Still, it must have been news even to them that they could play a whole set at such a peak. Given an occasion, even something so slight as a birthday, Bruce always rose to the moment. Given lives at stake, he could take those lines from "The Promised Land"—"Take a knife and rip this pain from my heart"—and make them bleed.

When they came out for the first encore, he spoke again through the music of another. The song was the Byrds' "Ballad of Easy Rider," another song written for a contradictory purpose but adopted by vets who had no songs of their own. Roger McGuinn and Bob Dylan's plain lyrics said next to nothing, but the song told everything there was to know.

What was amazing was the gentleness with which Bruce sang. After four hours of frenzy and fifteen years of madness, it came down to this almost still moment in which the wound began to heal through nothing more and nothing less than the beauty of the music. Five years later, talking with Muller about old times, Springsteen explained that he had always wanted his music "to be useful," to help people who needed it. "When I did that benefit for you guys was the first time I got to do that," he said. If there's an explanation of why the night rose so high, maybe that's it. Bruce Springsteen wasn't doing the Vietnam veterans a favor; they were working *together*. And so when he sang those lines from "Easy Rider"—"Well, all he wanted was to be free/ And in the end, that's how it turned out to be"—he was saying something for himself as well as for them.

It would still be years before Vietnam veterans began to get the respect they deserved, and when they did, it was often for all the wrong reasons: as an attempt to deny that the war had been lost for good reason, as a setup for the nation to wage similar battles once again. But in the music made that night, you could hear a different process beginning—the wounds starting to heal. So believe Bobby Muller when he says, "Without Bruce Springsteen, there would be no Vietnam veterans movement."

Bruce also turned a corner that night. Not so much because he'd come out and made a political statement, or even because he'd spoken his mind so clearly about a complex issue and been understood. It was because he'd made his dream tangible.

"I know this is idealistic," he once said, "but part of the idea our band had from the beginning was that you did not have to lose your connection to the people you write for. I don't believe that fame or success means that you lose that connection, and I don't believe that makin' more money means you lose it. Because that's not where the essence of what you are lies. That's not what separates people. What separates people are things that are in their heart. So I just can never surrender to that idea. Because I know that before I started playing, I was alone. And one of the reasons I picked up the guitar was that I wanted to be part of something. And I practiced and I studied and I worked real hard to do that, and I ain't about to give it up now."

More than that, maintaining his connections was a form of self-protection. "One of the things that was always on my mind to do was to maintain connections with the people I'd grown up with, and the sense of the community where I came from," Bruce remarked a couple of years later. "That's why I stayed in New Jersey. The danger of fame is in *forgetting*, or being distracted. You see it happen to so many people . . . The type of fame that Elvis had, and that I think Michael Jackson has, the pressure of it, and the isolation that it seems to require, has gotta be really painful. I wasn't gonna let that happen to me. I wasn't gonna get to a place where I said, 'I can't go in here. I can't go to this bar. I can't go outside.' "

The only sure way—the only way at all—to keep things in perspective was to keep a visceral connection with everyone else.

Yet Bruce faced an even more difficult obstacle to keeping life "normal": his wealth. "Most rich men will tell you that money don't mean a thing," he said. "But that's not true. It's freedom. But you also got to keep that up-from-under thing that rock and roll has always been about. That's the constant vigilance . . . When Steve and I were young, we said we wanted to be as big as the Rolling Stones, that we'd have all the girls we wanted, fancy clothes. That's all we wanted. Well, when you get there, sometimes the pants don't fit. Or maybe we've grown up too much to enjoy it or want it."

It was this resistance to decadence that earned Springsteen the respect of even doubters like critic Carson. "The limitation of rock-as-rebellion, and even of rock-as-fun, was that both equated rebellion and fun with youth, or at least youthfulness," wrote Carson. "But to Springsteen, with his belief in rock-as-*life*—not to mention a capacity for one-plus-one thinking—a far from negligible asset—it seemed purely natural and obvious that if people grew up, rock should encompass that, too. And once he saw that, he had to open himself up to lives where rock might tell the tale but couldn't provide the salvation."

Springsteen had begun to imagine such lives in the songs of *Darkness* and *The River*. "I wanted to make the characters grow up," he said. "You got to. Everybody has to." There is no more concrete refutation of the premise of bohemianism. But to Bruce, no theoretical question was involved; for better or worse, he lacked much interest in that kind of abstraction. After *Born to Run*, he remembered, "I said, 'Well, how old am I? I'm this old, so I wanna address that in some fashion—address it as it is in some fashion,' and I didn't see that that was done a whole lot."

It didn't occur to him to ask why—or at least, asking why and getting back answers like Carson's didn't deter him. "To me it seemed like, hey, it's just life, you know. It's nothin' but life. Let's get it in there."

His involvement with VVA was a significant extension of the same idea. By striking the first public blow for a group of Americans robbed of their health, their identity, their right to stand free, Bruce had done more than live up to his own ideals. He had begun to live them out. So when the tour finally ended three weeks later in Cincinnati's hockey rink, it was the most joyous conclusion anyone could have wished to see, a funny extravaganza.

But the tour didn't really finish until dawn the next day. Bruce kept the entire touring party and a couple of dozen visitors up all night, drinking and dancing to Dave Clark Five hits. In the end, he laid 'em all to waste and retired, having boogied two consecutive crowds straight into the ground. He made his plane back to Newark the next morning with a smile on his face. After it landed, he had time on his hands for the first time in three years.

5 ON FIRE

idway through the show now, and Bruce stands soaked in sweat. He wears nothing more than T-shirt, jeans, and boots. All are sopping. From the floor, he looks so wet you want to check for rain.

Out in the seats, a night breeze fades the day's heat. Onstage, hot white spots and barely cooler red, blue, and yellow gels lock the band in an inferno. But even the musicians escape for a moment or two between songs or during the solo numbers. Not Bruce. He does his three-hour show without ever leaving that spotlight glow—and pays the price.

Heading into some slow numbers, the fatigue—not just tonight's, but the accumulated weariness of nineteen months of campaigning—begins to tell. Bruce stumps to the microphone, his right leg dragging a little from his old motorcycle wound, and you can see him catch his breath, reach out to adjust the pace, gather his thoughts. He's visibly incorporating that weariness into his demeanor, making it part of the show, as if to say, "Okay, that was the *tough* part. Everybody's a little winded now."

Bruce dedicates his song to Little Steven "and my band, because—" Cheers stop him before he can continue. He laughs right along, the show out of his hands for a second. "We're gonna get kinda senti-mental tonight, now—it's the last night." Then regaining command: "There's no way I can ever measure what their friendship has meant to me over the years. So here's to my band . . . and here's to friend-ship." Gently, carefully, he sings "No Surrender," his song about what it meant to be a desolate kid in the Sixties and join a band—teaming up not just with fellow musicians, but entering into the kind of com-munity from which he'd always feared himself excluded.

Sung with no accompaniment save his own guitar and harmonica, the song's most outrageous pronouncements are presented as flat fact—"We learned more from a three-minute record than we ever learned in school"—and its boldest hopes glimmer brightly before be-ginning to fade toward today: "Out on the street tonight, the lights are growin' dim/The walls of my room are closin' in/But it's good to see your smilin' face and to hear your laughter again/Now we can sleep in the twilight, by the river bed/With a wide open country in our hearts and these romantic dreams in our head." On record, backed by the band at full throttle, these words have an edge of desperation; the song's a reluctant farewell. Sung without the rock backing, the lines are weary and lonesome; if anybody's sleeping under the stars, it's not because they're running away but because they've earned a rest.

Quietly, the band files back into position. Bruce turns alongside the mike in its stand and faces the crowd, still drenched, hair limp, his arms hung down from shoulders squared but sagging. Turns and looks at the crowd, piercing them with a gaze that would be fierce were it not simply pained. Behind him begins the music, a guitar strangling in its own electronic echoes, followed by synthesizer moans.

He picks up the microphone and speaks in a hush. "I remember growin' up, my folks always havin' to work so hard all the time. I remember my dad in the morning, goin' out in the backyard, under the hood of one of the old cars he bought, tryin' to get it started to go to work." He pauses, stares out, says nothing but looks as if he wonders how to get through. The music continues. "And my mom goin' down to the finance company, borrowin' money for Christmas, and gettin' it paid back in time to borrow money for Easter, gettin' it paid back in time to borrow money to get us clothes to go to school in."

He stops again and looks bleakly out into the crowd, as much as to say that probably no one believes him. After a moment, despairing of explanation, he continues anyway.

"When I was really young, I don't remember thinkin' about it much." A brief pause. A sigh. "But as I got a little older, I watched my father . . . how he would come home from work and just sit in the kitchen all night. Like there was somethin' dyin' inside of him, or like he'd never had a chance to live." He emphasizes this last word ever so slightly, in such a way that you can't tell whether he is puzzled or bitter or both. "Until I started to feel there was somethin' dyin' inside of me. And I'd lay up in bed at night and feel like, if somethin' didn't happen . . . I was just gonna . . ." He takes a breath, squeezes it out; his voice is beginning to crack. "That someday I'd just . . ." Breathing harder now as if struggling with some massive weight that continues to press him down, he pushes on: "I felt like I was just gonna . . . If somethin' didn't happen, I was just . . . I felt like I was just . . ." Now he pants, pushing out his breath, gasping, gulping, forcing the words. "Like I was just gonna . . . just gonna . . ."

One last push and the song is born from his breath, the guitar melting into melody, the synth figure losing its sinister cast and becoming a beckoning horn. Now only the words are nasty:

> At night, I wake up with the sheets soakin' wet
>
> And a freight train runnin' in the middle of my head

Toward the end, he abandons the lyric for a kind of mumbled prayer: "Won't you shut out the lights . . . Yeah, won't you shut out the lights now . . . Won't somebody shut out the lights . . . Someone shut out the lights now . . ." Then he simply walks away from the mike and leaves it to the band, ticking the song away, beat by beat, like a transfusion.

MIDNIGHT SPECIAL

I never knew anybody who was unhappy with their job and was happy with their life. It's your sense of purpose. Now, some people can find it elsewhere. Some people can work a job and find it someplace else . . . But I don't know if that's lasting. But people do, they find ways.

Or else . . . ?

[Long pause] Or else they join the Ku Klux Klan or something. That's where it can take you, you know. It can take you a lot of strange places.

—from an interview, 1980

Only a few days after the tour ended, Clarence Clemons flew to Maui to be married. Bruce flew out a little later; he'd be the best man. Many of the other band and crew members also attended. Conspicuously absent was Steve Van Zandt, already back in the recording studio, preparing a second album for Gary "U.S." Bonds and quietly working on a project of his own.

Clarence's decision to remarry was a shock. He was married and the father of two when he joined the E Street Band in 1971, employed as a youth counselor and playing sax only on weekends. Bruce and the band members were making fifty bucks a week—when times were good. Amidst the scuffling, Clarence's marriage soon disintegrated, and for ten years Clemons was the epitome of the party-hearty rock musician. ("I'd just lie back and watch the house jump up and down the block," he later said of those days.)

But in Stockholm during the European tour, Clarence again met Christina Sandgren, a Swede ten years his junior whom he'd first encountered while in Stockholm in 1975. Clarence and Christina (called Tina) hadn't seen one another in the intervening six years. During that time only one brief letter had passed between them. Yet Clemons later said that he had returned to Stockholm determined to find her, and while in Sweden he asked her to marry him. She immediately came to the States and traveled with Clarence through the summer tour of America. Their wedding was held in Hawaii partly because Clarence had been there previously and loved it and also because the Big Man's brother was a minister in the islands.

"You got to be ready to want to do it," said Clarence of his reasons for changing his attitude. "I think that those six years that we didn't see each other were perfect. She lived her life, I lived mine. We needed this time to grow up. I hadn't grown up at the time of my first marriage. People have to experience life before they do something. You'll always wonder what's out there if you don't." Clarence was not inexperienced.

Shortly after the wedding, Bruce flew back to New Jersey. He didn't "go home," because he didn't really have a home to go to. Although now a multimillionaire, he didn't own a house. Well, he'd purchased a place in Los Angeles, but that was easy. He still lacked a home at home, though. The lease had run out on the farmhouse on Telegraph Avenue in Holmdel—just behind the Garden State Arts Center, "the opera out on the turnpike" of "Jungleland"—where he'd lived while working on *Darkness* and *The River*. Since then Bruce had bounced around quite a bit whenever he wasn't holed up in a Manhattan or Hollywood studio or out on the road.

This lack of a house wasn't entirely a matter of being unable to find a suitable place. It was just about a point of principle. "I always want to have a feeling of leanness, of not dragging too much stuff around," Bruce told his friend British journalist Michael Watts in 1981. "I guess that's one of the reasons why I've avoided buying a house—things just clutter up your life."

That attitude hadn't altered over the years. "I throw out almost everything I ever own," he'd told *Melody Maker's* Ray Coleman during his first visit to England. "I don't believe in collecting anything. The less you have to lose, the better you are, because the more chances you'll take. The more you've got, the worse off you get." And Bruce's philosophy applied to a lot more than houses. When his friend George Theiss, the lead vocalist of their first band, the Castiles, got married in 1969, Bruce told him flat out, "Man, you'll never make it now."

It was an icy comment, but in those days Bruce could be equally cold about himself. "You know, you have to be self-contained," he proclaimed in the mid-Seventies. "That way you don't get pushed around. It depends on what you need. I eat loneliness, man. I feed off it. I live on a lotta different levels, y'know, because I've learned to cope with people, which is—be cool all the time . . . I can roll with the punches. It's a way of getting along."

That idea helped make Bruce self-sufficient in his twenties. But he was entering his thirties now, and some of his dogmatism seemed dubious, even to himself. Unlike Clarence, his shyness of marriage applied exclusively to himself. But there were still blocks and barricades about the possibility of domesticity in his life, and he'd put them there himself.

The contrast with the ideals of his concerts and songs was unmissable. Even Bruce knew that. "All my houses seem to have been way stations," he said many months later. "Which is funny, because the things that I admire and the things that mean a lot to me all have to do with roots and home, and myself, personally, I'm the opposite. I'm very rootless in that sense. I never attach myself to any place that I am.

"I always felt most at home when I was like in the car or on the road, which is, I guess, why I always wrote about it. I was very distant from my family for quite a while in my early twenties. Not with any animosity; I just had to feel loose. Independence always meant a lot to me. I had to feel I could go anywhere, anytime, in order to get my particular job done. And that's basically the way I've always lived.

"I think when I was young I did it intentionally, because I knew I only had sixty dollars that month, and I had to live on sixty dollars, and I couldn't get married or I couldn't get involved at the time. And then it just became my way of life."

The professional requirement to travel was also a convenient excuse, one for which Bruce had developed the perfect rationale—big-hearted, idealistic, functional, and abstractly accurate: "Part of the idea of rock and roll is to go on the road. There's a very different feeling that happens when you get out there in the Midwest, really out there where there's nothing for miles and miles around. The thing we got the most from was touring, getting people to come out, to leave their houses and come down to the show."

But whatever the justification, Bruce was coming off the road, where he'd been happily surrounded by band, crew, and crowds for over a year, and returning to a house he'd rarely slept in. It was a nice place overlooking a reservoir in Colt's Neck, the heart of Monmouth County's horse country. But it wasn't a home.

Mythologically, home was Asbury Park, over on the shore, a beat-up beach town with mystique, where Bruce had made his bones as a bar-band rocker and where he'd found almost all of his bandmates. In truth, home was Freehold, fifteen miles inland, a pre-Revolutionary War tank town of 10,000 souls divided—black from white, rich from poor—by railroad tracks. The town of Freehold is in turn surrounded by Freehold Township, which has a wealthier landscape of large suburban homes and horse and truck farms. Freehold is the kind of place where the inferiority complex is built in, rubbed in the face of residents every time they hit Route 33 and head on past the city limits. It has none of Asbury Park's faded charm.

"It's just a small town—it's just a small, narrowminded town," Bruce remembered later. "No different than probably any other provincial town. It was just the kind of area where it was real conservative. There was a time in the late Sixties when I couldn't walk down the streets, you know,'cause of the way you looked. It was very stagnating, there were some factories and some farms and stuff that, if you didn't go to college, you ended up in. There really wasn't that much, you know; there wasn't that much."

Bruce grew up in a working-class neighborhood of Freehold, where families who'd been in Jersey for generations lived alongside transplanted Southerners and recently arrived blacks, all working at the A and M Karagheushian rug mill, a Nestlé's chocolate plant, a 3M factory, or various smaller factories and businesses. All were located within a mile or so of the Springsteens' various homes, not far from the center of town. When the *Asbury Park Evening Press* for Saturday, September 24, 1949, wrote, "Mr. and Mrs. Douglas Springstein [sic], 87 Randolph Street, Freehold, are parents of a boy born yesterday at Monmouth Memorial hospital," any local would have known by the address that they lived in a working-class neighborhood of neatly kept but poorly appointed houses. In fact, the house had been in the family of Bruce's paternal grandmother for a couple of generations, and Doug and Adele Springsteen were living there in part to take care of his parents.

When Bruce was six years old, the younger Springsteens moved nearby to Institute Street, where they lived in a two-bedroom cold-water duplex. Later, when Doug's parents again needed to live with them, they moved to a house on South Street, where Bruce spent his high school years.

In the 1950s and 1960s, when Bruce Springsteen was growing up, working men and women in industrial towns all across North America took for granted the ability to purchase a second car—perhaps a boat, or even a second home—to make enough between wages and overtime to set up some kind of side business (and to work in conditions that left them in some kind of shape for leisure or personal investment). Workers came to welcome short, seasonal layoffs or brief strikes as opportunities. Wages rose; hours shrank. For almost twenty years, even with periodic "adjustments" for recession, American industry provided a majority of workers a standard of living beyond anything previously known.

As long as it's recited in extremely precise terms, this conventional picture of U.S. life in those decades is accurate. But prosperity didn't reach everyone. Few black and Latin workers found things so fat. And even among white workers, there were those who slipped through the boomtime cracks and never found work steady or life satisfying.

Doug and Adele Springsteen both worked, Adele in the same job as a legal secretary throughout Bruce's childhood, Doug at a variety of jobs: taxi driver, rug mill worker, bus driver, guard at the county jail. But they were supporting not only themselves, Bruce, his younger sister, Virginia, and later, when Bruce was in junior high, his sister Pam, but also Doug's parents. The Springsteen kids always had the necessities, but there was little room for luxury, especially since Doug's work was often unsteady.

The key to the family's stability was Adele. "My mother is the great energy—she's the energy of the show," Bruce said. "The consistency, the steadiness, day after day—that's her. And the refusal to be disheartened, even though she was really up against it a lot of the time.

"My mother lived with an immense amount of stress and pressure all her life and she was a person of immense control. It was she who created the sense of stability in the family, so that we never felt threatened through all the hard times." Onstage, Bruce has often told stories of his conflicts with his father, but it was his mother's love of radio music, especially Elvis Presley's, that shaped the joyous side of his sound.

To describe Springsteen's childhood as ordinary, which in the case of male adolescents usually means feeling like a misfit, misses the mark. Compared to most people in America (especially those who grow up to report and interpret events), Bruce's early life was abject but, equally importantly, eccentric: "The loner thing started from the very beginning," he said. "My father's entire family were outsiders." His grandfather, the radio man, restored secondhand appliances and sold them to the laborers in the work camps outside of town. Bruce's night-owl hours began before he started school, and he was imbued by his grandparents with an extreme sense of independence. "They didn't give a damn what anybody thought," he said. On the other hand, he was imbued with a sense of hard work by his parents, especially Adele, who was working a steady job and also having to maintain a household for six people.

Doug and Adele Springsteen didn't miss out on the luxuries of post-war America because they were lazy. They missed out because there was only a limited amount of room in that abundant society. Bruce, whose public recollections of his childhood have sometimes been bitter, also knew the other side: the frustrating battle just to make little things work. "My father worked a lot of jobs that take everything from you and give you barely nothing back," he said in 1980. "Some people get a chance to change the world, and other people, they get the chance to make sure the world don't fall apart." That was even more the case with Adele Springsteen, whom Bruce describes as "real smart, real strong, real creative—what I am doing today is directly connected to my mother." So Bruce was taught the inadequacy of the best intentions from the very beginning.

It was only at the beginning of the Eighties—just a few months before Doug's stroke—that Bruce was able to begin sorting out bad from good in his upbringing and to laugh about it some. Before *The River*, his stories of adolescence had been all hurt and anger. He couldn't really explain the change, except to say, "I sort of have a perspective on those times, right now, maybe more than I did then." He didn't seem to understand why he felt so obsessed by his past, why he kept mulling over old times, why so many of his onstage raps began, "When I was growin' up . . ."

He'd turned thirty but he was no nostalgist. America was entering a political and economic phase in which a lot more lives were being wasted as the Springsteens' had been and a lot more intelligent, talented kids like Bruce were being manhandled by a system completely insensitive to their needs. The real horror, as Bruce later realized, was that the lives didn't die, even though expectations might strangle. "My father sat there every night for, I guess, about eighteen years, and I never once asked him what he was thinking about, what was on his mind. I always felt he was cutting me short, and I guess in a lot of ways I was cutting him short. 'Cause I thought he didn't dream no more, and I was real wrong about that."

He dreamed better lives for his kids, for one thing. One way or another Doug and Adele found the money to send their kids to the nearby parochial school, St. Rose of Lima. Unfortunately, it was an extravagance neither Bruce nor the nuns appreciated, and one that turned grade school into a battleground of further humiliations. And not only because of the nuns. "I was a big daydreamer when I was in grammar school. Kids used to tease me, call me dreamer. It's something that got worse as I got older, I think—until I realized that I felt like I was dying, for some reason, and I really didn't know why." In ninth grade Bruce transferred to the public Freehold Regional High School.

Bruce didn't fit in there either. "I didn't even make it to class clown," he claimed. "I had nowhere near that amount of notoriety." Nevertheless, in the end he had to skip his own graduation, according to Robert Hilburn, because "one of the school's teachers thought Springsteen's long hair was disrespectful, so she appealed to his classmates. If they let him go through the graduation lines with hair that long, she said, they would be telling the whole community that a high school degree wasn't worth respect. No one came to Bruce's aid."

Bruce's teenage social problems are rather difficult to understand at this distance. In a sense, it was all mystifying even to him. "I was the kind of kid that never got into trouble, but trouble would gravitate around me—not even serious stuff, ridiculous kinds of things. I didn't have anything to hold on to, or any connections whatsoever—I was just reeling through space and bouncing off the walls and bouncing off people." He was drug-free and neither boisterous nor troublesome. True, his hair fell frizzily past his shoulders, and in those days that could be enough for ostracism—by adults. Maybe the trouble was just that he didn't make—or even know how to make—any special effort to socialize and that the students at Freehold Regional were just like kids everywhere else: brutal conformists whose instincts were to stamp out whatever failed to fit in. Bruce later dropped out of Ocean County Community College (which, like all such two-year institutions, had a high school atmosphere), but only after his fellow students petitioned for his dismissal on grounds of unacceptable weirdness.

One result was that Bruce remained in some ways innocent of his own times. Explaining the complete lack of appeal drugs had for him, Bruce said, "When I was at that age when it was popular, I wasn't really in a social scene a whole lot. I was practicing in my room with my guitar. So I didn't have the type of pressure that kids might have today. Plus, I was very concerned with being in control at the time."

He found more than solace in his solitude; he found advantage. As he said in 1978, "It was like I didn't exist. It was the wall, then me. But I was working on the inside all the time. A lot of rock and roll people went through this solitary existence. If you're gonna be good at something, you've gotta be alone a lot to practice. There has to be a certain involuntariness to it. Like my youngest sister, she could play if she wanted to. But she's too pretty. She's popular, you know what I mean? She ain't gonna sit in the house in her room no eight hours a day and play the piano. No way."

The few friends he made were among fellow rock and roll musicians who hung out at a late-night teen club called the Upstage, in Asbury Park. The kids Bruce met there had to reckon with him because he was the best musician they'd ever seen, a great guitarist who could figure out how to play the latest licks in an instant. Musically, he was, of all things, a *leader*—though, of course, the rock and roll he perfected was as socially disreputable as he was. In the loving liner notes he wrote for Southside Johnny's first album, *I Don't Want to Go Home*, Bruce speaks of the Upstage as his greatest teenage refuge: ". . . you could work it so you'd never have to go home,'cause by the time you got out of there it was dawn and you could just flop on the beach all day, or you could run home before it got too light, nail the blankets over the windows of your room, and just sleep straight through till the night."

To top his misery off, he was receiving an education guaranteed to murder any desire to learn. Bruce was a poor student—he got Bs and Cs when things were going well, but could do worse—and the school gave him no incentive to do better. Like a lot of kids back then, he probably finished high school at least partly because it kept him out of the Army. Years later, when he wrote in "No Surrender," "We learned more from a three-minute record than we ever learned in school," the line was publicly chastised by voices as various as Elvis Costello and John Fogerty. "It must have been a pretty good record," remarked a rock critic. Anyone who attended a working-class high school knew the punchline: ". . . or a pretty bad school."

Bruce's own perspective is less jaundiced. He focused, as he preferred to do with most things, on the positive side of the question. "There's a lot of people who just fall through the bottom of the educational system. Not because they're stupid but because people don't know how to reach them, number one; and number two, the kids themselves don't know how to open up their own consciousness. Which is what rock and roll did for me. It was like it just opened up my consciousness. It gave me a much wider sense of awareness."

This sense of rock and roll as revelation is an important part of what set Springsteen apart from the beginning of his career. Even as late as 1984 he told *People's* Chet Flippo, "I know that rock and roll changed my life. It was something for me to hold on to. I had nothing. Before then the whole thing was a washout for me. It really gave me a sense of myself, and it allowed me to become useful, which I think most people want to be."

To Bruce, the music was an answer to anonymity, not only in his own life but potentially in everyone's. "I never look out at my crowd and see a bunch of faces. It's never happened. Any night I've ever been onstage, I see people—individual people in individual seats out there. That's why, before the show, we go out and we check the sound in every section of the room. Because there's some guy sittin' back here, and he's got a girl with him, and, you know, it's like this is their seat. And what you hope for is that the same thing goes the other way— that when they look up at you, they don't just see some person with a guitar." Always, he has delivered his music and his ideas with the sense that there could be someone just like himself out there, lacking only one small inspiration to begin the process of self-transformation. Always, he has played with the sense that he needs them at least as much.

Many other arts could have reached Bruce, but it makes a big difference that the one that did was rock and roll. First of all, rock was *there*—in the air, on the radio, in the car—available, inescapable, everywhere one went. Then, too, rock spoke in ways with which Bruce was familiar: In those late Fifties, early Sixties Top Forty hits, you could hear not only the voices of teenagers but the accents of the blacks and white Southerners who had migrated to places like Freehold. So while it could have been any other art, it isn't surprising that rock and roll is what reached Bruce. Nowhere else in the arts and media (much less the educational system) did such people speak, much less talk on their own terms. That's one reason Bruce latched on to American singers like Gary Bonds and the Ronettes at least as enthusiastically as the English rock bands on which his kind of rock band music is more often modeled. And it was partly by using American girl group and soul models that he set his own style apart. There was vision in all of the rock and roll of his youth; he related more closely than most to that which derived from lives close to home.

Rock and roll has so often been described as a music of youthful rebellion that it's easy to miss a contradictory fact: namely, that for many of its greatest practitioners—think only of Elvis Presley or any black man or woman who's ever stepped to the mike—it was a way of finding a place to stand in the everyday world. In the spring of 1986, Bruce put it more bluntly: "I started playing music because I wanted to *fit in*." The fact that white rock was taken over by bohemians in the mid-to late Sixties couldn't change the fact that for many working-class kids it remained a vehicle to forms of success, and possibly even respectability, they otherwise could only dream about. One reason Bruce found being the best rock musician in his area so fulfilling was that when others had to come to him to learn things, he could keep up his loner's facade but still have some sense of connection—a setup a live audience only intensified. On his own, everything told him he was nothing and nobody; in these situations, he was somebody.

Finally, there was what rock and roll did not ask him to do. It didn't require any betrayal of his working-class roots or even of that environment's deepseated anti-intellectualism, which infected Bruce as much as the next kid. Playing music was a *job*. You sweated while you did it; it was (or at least, Bruce made it) an extremely physical form of labor. He could avoid the fact that the foundation of all the stress and strain was—maybe before anything else—his songwriting and his conceptualizing of the show, which are sweatless and extremely mental forms of work.

Most of the time, playing rock and roll didn't pay very well, which meant that the most extreme contradiction of all—the contradiction of the working man grown wealthy—could be safely ducked for a very long time, although after the multi-platinum sales of *The River* and the highly profitable tour, that was no longer true. But that didn't mean Bruce was ready to reckon with such consequences. That was another reason he didn't own a home.

Bruce's fear of becoming just another rich guy only led back to the most deeply seated contradiction of all. As hard as he'd worked to become a rock star, he mistrusted his own fame and fortune as badly as he wanted them. "During the lawsuit [with Appel], I understood that it's the music that keeps me alive. That and my relationship with my friends, and my attachment to the people and the places I've known. That's my lifeblood. And to give that up for, like, the TV, the cars, the houses—that's not the American dream. Those are the booby prizes. And if you fall for them—if, when you achieve them, you believe that this is the end in and of itself—then you've been suckered in. Because those are the consolation prizes, if you're not careful, for selling yourself out or lettin' the best of yourself slip away. So you gotta be vigilant. You gotta carry the idea you began with further. And you gotta hope that you're headed for higher ground."

On the other hand, Bruce was not prepared to follow the punks in abandoning attempts to relate and communicate. That was not what the guy who wanted to become one of the guys did. "I always felt that *Born to Run* was my birthday album. All of a sudden, *bang!* Something happened, something crystallized, and you don't even know what. And now what are you gonna do? That's the big question. You have an audience; you have a relationship with that audience; it's just as real as any relationship you have with your friends."

If there was nothing wrong with harboring a lust for recognition, there was nothing irrational about being afraid of what fame could do. After all, every role model anyone could point out had too quickly washed up on the shores of indulgence and confusion. In the end, the one thing Bruce Springsteen was most determined to do was avoid ending up like his inspiration. "I think about Elvis a lot and what happened to him. The demands that this profession make on you are unreasonable. It's very strange to go out and have people look at you like you're Santa Claus or the Easter Bunny.

"It's a confusing experience for them, too. Who are they meeting? They're not quite sure. If you don't respond exactly as they imagined or something, which you're not gonna . . . it can be a strange experience. If you expect it to be a reasonable thing, it can drive you crazy. The answer is trying to stay healthy—mentally, physically, spiritually—all under a lot of pressure."

In the autumn of 1981, thrust once more into isolation, it seemed that it was time to stand back and confront many things. It was time to write some songs and figure out a way to make a record of them.

◆

You know the old saying: Trust the art, not the artist. I think that's true. I think somebody can do real good work and be a fool in a variety of ways. I think my music is probably better than I am. I mean, like, your music is your ideals a lot of times, and you don't live up to those ideals all the time. You try, but you fall short and you disappoint your-self.

For Bruce Springsteen, record making is a way to illuminate the dark corners of highly personal issues and situations. He does this in a highly metaphorical way that emphasizes the universality of such problems, but the records are inextricably connected to the things he has felt and experienced and is trying to figure out. As producer Chuck Plotkin said, "With Bruce, the album actually is about something. It may not be about something that you can reduce to some paragraph of exposition, but it's about something."

For Plotkin that was the central advantage of working with Bruce. "There was nothing too serious or too strange or too remote or too apparently disconnected from record making that couldn't be talked about with a sense of its relevance to the record-making process. The records were *about something,* and anything that you knew about any-thing relevant was fodder for the record-making mill with Bruce. Something that happened on the street on the way to the studio that sensitized you to some issue that you felt deeply about and that was related to some thing that one of the songs was dealing with. Nothing was irrelevant."

On the other hand, all this information was digested and distilled into songs that were utterly personal. This was true even though Springsteen could be the most derivative of rock artists (and rock is an enormously derivative medium). His songs bristle with quotations and allusions, musical and lyrical.

Bruce's first two albums spoke in such a clash and babble of meta-phor that it was easy to miss the true topics of their songs, not to mention their revealing aspects. Beginning with *Born to Run,* however,

Springsteen made a leap. By his own account, *Born to Run* "really dealt with faith and a searching for answers. . . . I laid out a set of values. A set of ideas . . . intangibles like faith and hope, belief in friendship and in a better way." That was his story, he later said. So it ended triumphantly—*he* had pulled out of his "town full of losers" and won.

But Bruce added a note of warning. "You don't really know what those values are worth until you test them," he said.

It's tempting to conclude that this test began with the lawsuit between Springsteen and former manager Mike Appel, that the stresses it applied caused Bruce to question the emotional laissez-faire articulated in *Born to Run*. In fact, Bruce said, the summer of the lawsuit was one of the best of his life. "I had a truck and a motorcycle; I was living out there in the farmhouse; we had a pond and a pool. Every once in a while, I'd have to go up to the city and talk with the lawyers, but that wasn't so bad—it was just a different thing to do, you know." The legal complications—Appel, as well as obtaining an injunction forbidding Bruce to record, had the CBS royalties for Bruce's first million-selling album tied up—kept money tight, but being broke was nothing new.

For Bruce, the test took the shape of an internal struggle. "I guess in a funny way I began to do that test after *Born to Run* and through *Nebraska*. Those records were kind of my reaction, not necessarily to my success, but to what I was singing and writing about and what I was feeling—what I felt the role of the musician should be, what an artist should be. The one thing I did feel after *Born to Run* was a real sense of responsibility to what I was singing and to the audience. I didn't have an audience before that, not much of one. I was concerned with living up to that responsibility.

"So I just dove into it. I decided to look around. I decided to move into the darkness and look around and write about what I knew and what I saw and what I was feeling. I was trying to find something to hold on to that doesn't disappear out from under you."

Maybe Bruce believed he was just poking at the tattered edges of other lives, but he was really toying with more explosive forces. Each of his albums asked more probing questions, not only about the state of America but about the meaning of life. Whether he knew it or not, he was trying to rationally resolve questions that don't have rational answers. When anyone does that, one consequence can be that what you've taken for common sense stops shaping the world into a believable picture.

"Stolen Car" and "Wreck on the Highway," two of the key songs on the second disc of *The River*, seem central to this probing process because they represent a break in mood from Springsteen's earlier work. Previously Bruce was as unfailingly optimistic in his songs as he was in his everyday interpretations of events. Not only was he the sort of person who could see opportunity in a lawsuit that prevented him from recording and hampered his touring for more than a year, he was the sort of artist who could describe life's most brutal moments of defeat and frustration—as he did over and over on *Darkness on the Edge of Town* and *The River*—and still find a way to turn those songs into affirmations. "What happens to most people is when their first dreams get killed off nothing ever takes its place," he said. "The important thing is to keep holding out for possibilities, even if no one ever really makes it."

The protagonists of "Stolen Car" and "Wreck on the Highway" are past the point of holding out. It's not just that their stories are so grim, though they are that: In "Stolen Car" the singer's loneliness has driven him to compulsive car theft (a kind of joyless-riding), while the protagonist of "Wreck" is kept awake at night by the memory of finding a hit-and-run victim on a rainy, lonesome highway. What really makes these songs spooky, though, is their haunted music. "Wreck" aspires to country (it's modeled after Roy Acuff's song of the same name, though without recourse to Jesus or Mothers Against Drunk Driving moralism), but it never makes it. Its very cadences reject the sentimentality a country song could never abandon. In "Stolen Car" Bruce sings against piano, synthesizer, a few muted voices—all of it ectoplasmic, except the drums, which thump like tympani or a shattered heartbeat. When Bruce sings, "I ride by night and I travel in fear/That in this darkness I will disappear," there is nothing left for the music to do but fade away, which it does without a nuance of reluctance. There is nothing more here—just a waste of life and a man brave or stupid enough to watch it trickle away.

Those stories are true to life, and yet not much else in rock and roll (let alone the rest of popular culture) was willing to face up to them. Bruce said he heard such tales sometimes in the music of punk groups, particularly the Clash, but in general, as he noted in the midst of the *River* tour, "there wasn't too much stuff in America happening. It just seemed to me that's the story. But there was a crucial level of things missing, and it is today still. Maybe it's just me getting older and seeing things more as they are."

It was more than that. The artistic success of *The River* as a whole lay largely in Springsteen's finally achieving some kind of balance between songs and topics he considered trivial and those obviously heavier. Songs like "Cadillac Ranch" and "Ramrod" made dinosaurs dance, and more portentous songs like "Point Blank" were offset by escapades like "I'm a Rocker." Springsteen was finally letting some of the songs he'd suppressed see the light of day, relinquishing a smidgen of control in order to build a broader and thus truer picture of the world he wanted his records to represent.

"When I did *The River*, I tried to accept the fact that the world is a paradox, and that's the way it is. And the only thing you can do with a paradox is live with it. On the album, I just said, 'I don't understand all these things. I don't see where all these things fit. I don't see how all these things can work together,' " he said when the eighteen-month agony of assembling it was finished. "It was because I was always focusing in on some small thing; when I stepped back, they made a sense of their own. It was just a situation of living with all those contradictions. And that's what happens. There's never any resolution. You have moments of clarity, things become clear to you that you didn't understand before. But there's never any making ends meet or finding any kind of long-standing peace of mind."

When Bruce began writing songs for his next album, just after he returned from Hawaii, these were the things he felt compelled to explore, the mysteries he wanted his music to help him reconcile. Already, during the later part of the tour, he'd written one new tune, "Mansion on the Hill," which had some of the dreamlike quality of "Stolen Car" but was written much more concretely. This was what Bruce was shooting for in his new lyrics. After seeing Huston's *Wise Blood*, he'd begun reading Flannery O'Connor's stories, and he was especially impressed by their minute precision, the way O'Connor could enliven a character by sketching in just a few details. And the way she used those details to create a world of claustrophobic lower-class Catholic guilt must have seemed especially familiar to the reprobate of St. Rose of Lima.

Bruce also saw (on television) Terrence Malick's 1974 film *Badlands*, a barely fictionalized account of the 1958 spree during which Charles

Starkweather and Caril Fugate killed ten people in eight days across the barren landscape stretching from Lincoln, Nebraska, to eastern Wyoming. The movie led him to Ninette Beaver's book, *Caril*, the definitive Starkweather account. Impressed, Bruce called Beaver, now a fifty-year-old assignment editor at KMTV in Omaha.

"Honest to God, I know I should know who you are, but I'm just drawing a blank," Beaver told him. They talked for a half hour about Starkweather (executed in 1959) and Fugate (who served eighteen years in prison and was paroled in 1976). Playing Lincoln in 1984, Bruce dedicated the song to Beaver, who attended as his guest.

Punk bands and their New Wave successors had been writing songs about characters like Starkweather for years. The obvious examples are the Adverts' "Gary Gilmore's Eyes," about the Utah prisoner who demanded a public execution, and the Boomtown Rats' "I Don't Like Mondays," about a California teenager who shot up her high school's faculty and some of her classmates, then offered that line as her explanation. In a way, though, "Nebraska" was closer to the Sex Pistols' "Holiday in the Sun":

> *I don't want a holiday in the sun*
>
> *I wanna go to the new Belsen*
>
> *I wanna see some history . . .*

Even if Bruce had regularly trafficked in shock and outrage, "Nebraska" wouldn't quite have fit the stereotype. His song spoke in a horrifyingly blank first-person voice, and it went on to meet questions head-on that the others merely skirted or tackled at an angle. Bruce's Starkweather recites the facts of what he has done without much emotion; he's more excited by the memory of first seeing his girlfriend and by the anticipation of his own execution, which he greets as a chance to realize some wishes, including the hope that Fugate will find herself "sittin' right there on my lap."

But in the final verse, the song shifts gears. Starkweather speaks of the greatest consequences of all, with no more sorrow than a man remembering a pet lost in childhood:

> *They declared me unfit to live, said into that great void*
>
> *my soul'd be hurled*

They wanted to know why I did what I did

Well, sir, I guess there's just a meanness in this world

Charlie Starkweather never said or thought any such thing. He was all but illiterate, and he killed as he did in part because he was superstitious as only a half-wit can be. Starkweather certainly never harbored hope of any judgment anywhere so neutral or mystical as the "great void." Nor was he that matter-of-fact about the murders. He claimed that he killed in self-defense, and he made sure he dragged his girlfriend down with him. Starkweather, said one of the psychiatrists who testified at his trial, "tends to perceive things in a somewhat distorted way. He will pick out things which are not important because of his particular way of looking at things. The act of killing meant to him no more than stepping on a bug." Starkweather later told another psychiatrist that he wished he had a bomb so he could kill the first shrink.

That isn't the man who sings that last verse, and Bruce had done enough research to know it. The man who'd weighed those final lines and found they fit was Bruce Springsteen. It was as if Bruce had recast himself mentally, portraying what could have happened if he had not imagined his way out of the dead ends of Freehold, what the consequences would have been of hearing only static on his latenight radio. In 1975 critic Greil Marcus suggested that the source of "Born to Run" was the old juvenile delinquent tattoo "Born to Lose." "Nebraska" brought to life that tattoo and all it implied, and the person who had to live with its excruciatingly specific detail was the songwriter himself.

Bruce wrote a whole series of such songs: "Atlantic City," "Reason to Believe," "Johnny 99," "Highway Patrolman," "State Trooper," and "Open All Night" were all songs of complete despair. All of them imagined the worst things happening, often to characters very like the most lovingly familiar people in his earlier songs. The guy begging the state cops not to bust him on the Jersey Turnpike could have been the lonesome joyrider from "Stolen Car," the man roaring to meet his baby in the middle of the night on the same highway was "Ramrod" revisited, the loser daring the big score in "Atlantic City" was a near relation to the one in "Meeting Across the River," the brothers in "Highway Patrolman" were a doomed version of the dragstrip partners in "Racing in the Street." These new folks were all locked into situations in which there was no hope, no moment of relief or respite, from which there was no escape. There was nothing good in their lives and whatever had once been good had rotted.

Bruce wasn't sure exactly where the songs came from. "I wrote 'em real fast. Two months, the whole record, and for me that's real quick. I just sat at my desk, and it was something that was really fascinating for me. It was one of those times when you're not really thinking about it. You're working on it, but you're doing something that you didn't think you would be doing."

But certainly, rapidity and lack of self-consciousness weren't the major mysteries about these songs. They represented a rupture with Bruce's previous perspective. "It just seemed to be a mood that I was in at the time," he told interviewers in 1984. "I was living in a house on this reservoir, and I didn't go out much, and for some reason I just started to write. I wrote 'Nebraska,' all those songs, in a couple of months. I was interested in writing kind of *smaller* than I had been, writing with just detail."

He acknowledged that he was "going through some things" at the time, but declined to discuss them other than to say, "It was just kinda growin' up, growin' into the particular shoes I was wearing."

In fact, what was troubling Bruce personally was not far removed from what he'd already conceived as the central problem *The River* had tried to tackle: "People want to be part of a group yet they also want to disassociate themselves. People go through those conflicts every day in little ways: Do you wanna go to the movies tonight with your friends, or stay home? I wanted to get part of that on the record— the need for community, which is what 'Out in the Street' is about. Songs like 'The Ties That Bind' and 'Two Hearts' deal with that, too. But there's also the other side, the need to be alone."

Bruce was beginning to feel the downside of his loner's life—his need to be alone was becoming something tougher, more pernicious: loneliness. He later compared his emotions to the scene in *The Grapes of Wrath* in which an Okie farmer tries to hold off eviction with a shotgun, only to be told that the men he wants to shoot are faceless, hidden away in boardrooms hundreds of miles away. "I felt the same way he did: Where do I point the gun?" Bruce said. "In the Seventies and Eighties, especially compared to the Sixties, it became awfully hard to identify an enemy." Right now, though, Springsteen was fighting the enemy within.

There was more to it than that, though. Bruce was also responding to many things that were happening in America at this time. Maybe playing in Europe had helped him see the stark contrast between the land of his ideals and what the country had become. This was a response to the Age of Reagan, but it wasn't only Reaganomics to which he was responding. It was something more basic.

"In America there's a promise that gets made, and over there it gets called the American Dream, which is just the right to be able to live your life with some decency and dignity," he'd told the crowd that final night in Stockholm. "But over there, and a lot of places in the world now, that dream is only true for a very, very few people. It seems if you weren't born in the right place or if you didn't come from the right town, or if you believed in something that was different from the next person, y'know . . .

"Right now in the States, there's a lot of hard times, and when that happens there's always a resurgence of groups like the Ku Klux Klan and the National Socialists, and it seems like hard times turn people against each other, people that have common interests, people that don't understand that the enemy is not the guy down the street who looks different than you. But it's hard in the States, because the enemy is something that when you're brought up as a kid you're taught to respect. And it's something that you can't see; it's something that works on you and eats its way inside every day of your life and twists the good things that you have in you into nothing." And he sang "This Land Is Your Land," which he called "a song about living free, about the land that you live in, that should belong to each and every one of you, and that you have a right and a promise to life, to fulfill yourself inside."

In the songs of *Nebraska*, Bruce found himself exploring what happened to those basic values in such a society, looking for hard answers and recoiling from what he learned. "I think you can get to a point where nihilism, if that's the right word, is overwhelming, and the basic laws that society has set up—either religious or social laws—become meaningless," Bruce said of his fascination with Starkweather. "Things just get really dark. You lose those constraints, and then anything goes. The forces that set in motion, I don't know exactly what they'd be— I think, just a lot of frustration, lack of findin' somethin' that you can hold on to, lack of contact with *people*, you know? That's one of the most dangerous things, I think—isolation. *Nebraska* was about that American isolation: what happens to people when they're alienated from their friends and their community and their government and their job. Because those are the things that keep you sane, that give meaning to life in some fashion. And if they slip away, and you start to exist in some void where the basic constraints of society are a joke, then life becomes kind of a joke. And anything can happen."

It would be misguided to suggest that Bruce understood all this in late 1981 (the quote is from 1984), and it would be even more misleading to suggest that the songs of *Nebraska* were primarily a political response. Undoubtedly, what Bruce was doing, as he wrote and then taped, was responding to the changing context of his own life. In 1982 it meant something very different to be a loner in America—it meant facing up to a society in which the isolation was built in, perhaps even promulgated. As he later put it, "In a way, I felt like the album had the tone of what it felt like when I was a kid, growin' up. At the same time, it felt like the tone of what the country felt like to me at that moment. That was kinda the heart that I was drawing from." The two factors are inextricable.

And though Bruce has described himself as "a thinkin' fool," a person who analyzes almost everything, his concept of where such ideas came from was probably no more concrete than the songs that expressed them. It may even have seemed that his loneliness would end as soon as he got into the studio with his bandmates and other collaborators. His response to the mysteries of this music was to throw himself deeper into his work. By Christmastime of 1981 Bruce had completed writing a cycle of songs that he felt would form the body of his next record, and he set to work getting them in shape for the studio.

One of the things that concerned Bruce was the length of time it took to make his records. *Born to Run* had been a year-long struggle; even subtracting time off for the lawsuit, *Darkness on the Edge of Town* had taken about fifteen months; *The River* had been more like two years. The first Springsteen album came out in 1973; so did the second. The third arrived in 1975, followed by records in 1978 and 1980. Even though Bruce claimed that he was reconciled to these intervals, he hoped to move faster now.

"I told Mike [Batlan], the guy that does my guitars, 'Mike, go get a tape player so I can record these songs.' I figured what takes me so long in the studio is not having the songs written. So I said, I'm gonna write 'em and I'm gonna tape 'em. If I can make them sound good with just me, then I know they'll be fine. Then I can play 'em with the band. 'Cause if you rehearse with the band, the band can trick you. The band can play so good you think you've got something going. Then you go in and record it, and you realize the band's playing really good, but there's no song there. So I'd record for a month, get a couple of things, go home, write some more, record for another month—it wasn't very efficient.

"So this time, I got a little Teac four-track cassette machine, and I said, 'I'm gonna record these songs, and if they sound good with just me doin' 'em, then I'll teach 'em to the band.' I could sing and play the guitar, and then I had two tracks to do somethin' else, like overdub a guitar or add a harmony. It was just gonna be a demo. Then I had an old beat-up Echoplex that I mixed through, and that was it. It was real old, which is why the sound was kinda deep.

"And so, that was the idea. I got this little cassette recorder, plugged it in, turned it on, and the first song I did was 'Nebraska.' I just kinda sat there; you can hear the chair creaking on 'Highway Patrolman' in particular. I recorded them in a couple of days. Some songs I only did once, like 'Highway Patrolman.' The other songs I did maybe two times, three times at the most.

"I put the tape in my pocket, carried it around a couple of weeks, 'cause I was gonna teach the songs to the band. After a couple of days, I looked at the thing and said, 'Uh-oh, I'd better stop carrying this around like this. Can somebody make a copy of this?'"

Bruce made the tape on January 3, 1982, and mixed it over the next few days. First to hear it was Jon Landau. "He came up to the office one day—he'd let me know he was gonna have something—and he gave me a notebook and a cassette," Landau remembers. "And it was all the *Nebraska* songs, except for 'My Father's House.' And the tape had many other *Nebraska*-style songs, performed in the *Nebraska* style. There were versions of 'Downbound Train,' 'Born in the U.S.A.,' and, I think, 'Working on the Highway.' But basically it was the *Nebraska* album and other *Nebraska*-style songs. That's what he presented to me at that time, with this notebook, saying, in effect, 'Here it is; here's where I'm going with the next album.'"

Landau was tremendously moved by the tape, finding both songs and performances "surprising and very beautiful." However, he was somewhat taken aback at the dark tenor of so much of the material. "On *The River* tour Bruce was able to enjoy what he'd accomplished, more than at any other time I'd known him—to enjoy, for example, opening the Meadowlands. And in a funny way, these songs were so dark that it concerned me on a friendship level."

A few days later Landau drove down to New Jersey to confer with Bruce about the songs and how to prepare to record them. He already had some specific ideas.

Landau had been involved with the folk music revival in Boston, his hometown, and, as he put it, "I had some fairly developed ideas, when you get into that folk music area—not that I would strictly speaking call *Nebraska* folk music, but let's call it a folk-related style—about when the application of things like drums and a full rhythm section and so forth is suitable: When is it likely to sort of desensitize the material as opposed to when is it likely to add something? And I was somewhat skeptical right from the beginning that some of this material was gonna function better with a full rhythm-type thing. The immediate thing that came to mind, going on the assumption—as we were—that most of this stuff was gonna take the . . . well, gee, the band is gonna have to play very differently than they've ever played before for this to work."

Landau felt that certain songs could easily be given arrangements that would enhance them; he suggests that "Nebraska" itself could have worked with the kind of somber arrangement used on James Taylor's "Fire and Rain": string bass, piano, brushed drums. But he also understood that the way the material was voiced and sung on the tape, which was clearly a substantial part of its power, argued against a full rock group.

"On the tape that became the album, Bruce basically sings unusually softly. As soon as you're talking about having drums, you're talking about having to sing out—not necessarily singing loud or harshly, but you must sing with a certain amount of force. If there's no drums, it's easier to sing in a purely conversational fashion. And when you hear the *Nebraska* songs done even with a modest arrangement, in the show and on the live album, Bruce has to push harder. It's just a natural thing to do. But on *Nebraska*, he's almost singing to himself."

But even with that in mind, it was still terribly unclear how the majority of the songs would function as Bruce Springsteen music. Landau certainly didn't have any idea yet how to make the music add up as an album. But then, he probably didn't expect to. Even if Bruce felt that cutting demos would expedite the recording process, Jon had been through three previous albums with him and wasn't expecting a rapid resolution of anything.

Landau and Springsteen spent some time talking about arrangement ideas, which songs seemed most likely to work out, which were probably not destined for the record—like any demo, this one had its false starts and dead spots.

"I remember one thing we talked about," Landau said. "This *Nebraska* version of 'Born in the U.S.A.' seemed to stand out as the one song that just didn't seem to be working in this context. And in fact, to me, when you heard just the acoustic guitar version, it didn't even seem like a particularly good song. It was a real odd thing, and it was not like anything else on the *Nebraska* album. And it was not like any other thing I've ever heard from Bruce—it sounded alien. It just didn't sound like it fit. I knew it was a great idea for a song and there were great things about it, but basically we had so many other good things goin' on the *Nebraska* tape that the song disappeared from consideration fairly quickly."

In the *Nebraska* demo version, "Born in the U.S.A." (the title inspired by an unproduced filmscript by Paul Schrader and by Ron Kovic's *Born on the Fourth of July*) was much faster than it finally turned out to be, and it had a different melody, although the lyrics were the same. Speeded up and played on an acoustic guitar, it was just a protest song, and that was the opposite of what Bruce wanted or needed.

There was no immediate progress toward making a record out of the demo in the first few months of 1982, anyway, because Bruce got caught up in recording the second Gary Bonds album, *On the Line*. Bruce wrote seven out of the record's eleven tracks, notably "Rendezvous," a perennial near-hit that had been kicking around since before *Darkness*; "Angelyne," a reprise of the "Jole Blon" theme; "Out of Work," a mock-topical single; and a scathing soul ballad, "Club Soul City," which Bonds sang as a duet with fellow soul veteran Chuck Jackson. Bruce played a greater role than he had on *Dedication*, and his presence added a much darker cast to the music.

When it came time to mix the album, neither Bruce nor Steve Van Zandt could get a proper handle on it. So they called Chuck Plotkin in Los Angeles. Plotkin had served as mixer of Bruce's last two albums, and he was slated to be part of the next album's production team as well. Plotkin had some time on his hands, and he agreed to take on mixing the Bonds album.

Meantime, Van Zandt was nearing completion of his solo project. The idea for a Miami Steve solo album had been brewing for years. Steve was a talented songwriter in his own right; he could sing and he'd functioned as producer and even manager of Southside Johnny and the Asbury Jukes. When Gary Gersh, who was in charge of the Bonds albums at EMI-America Records, indicated the label would be interested in a Van Zandt solo effort, Steve was intrigued and, as soon as the 1981 tour ended, began to pursue that possibility.

Steve was Bruce's oldest friend, but he was every bit as brash as his buddy was cautious. Burning up with the idea of an album of his own, he set to work on it without waiting for a contract to be signed, which meant without a company to foot the bills for studio time. In the meantime, Steve decided he didn't want to embark on a solo career under the name Miami Steve, which is how he was known to E Street Band fans. To him that smacked too much of piggybacking on the Springsteen reputation. So he became Little Steven.

Then he decided that he ought to have a fulltime band, replete with horn section. (Among Steve's salient virtues was an ability to organize proper Stax-style horn charts.) That meant a big band, and *that* meant heavy expenses; it also meant that the group would have to go out and work if Steve wanted to hold it together. Steve found some excellent players, centered around himself and the Miami Horns—an ad hoc aggregation he'd put together for Bruce to use on the occasions when Springsteen wanted to add horns to his show—plus Dino Danelli, the rhythm sparkplug of the Young Rascals, on drums. The group was filled out by a cast of talented unknowns, including bassist Jean Beauvoir, who later went on to a solo career of his own.

Steve finished the tapes for his album around the same time as the Bonds record. But he had even more trouble mixing them. He, too, called Chuck Plotkin, and Chuck agreed to take a crack at them. Steve sent out some material and Plotkin came up with ideas that resolved some of the mixing difficulties. They agreed to do more when Steve reached L.A.

Meantime, a friend of Landau's, record executive David Geffen, asked if Bruce would be interested in writing a song for Donna Summer, who had just been signed to Geffen's label. Summer was recording her first album with producer Quincy Jones, who was hot off making Michael Jackson's *Off the Wall*. There was even some talk of Bruce and Donna performing a duet. It was an intriguing idea: the

King of Rock and Roll recording with the Queen of Disco. Bruce wasn't entirely certain how he wanted to proceed, but he did write a song. While in the studio with Bonds, he gathered the E Street Band for a demo session.

When Jon Landau heard the result, a song called "Cover Me," combining Springsteen's rock combustion with a sledgehammer version of the typical Summer dance beat, he smelled a hit. Bruce had played a tremendous guitar solo, and though the band had hurried through the song (this was just a demo, a guide for somebody else), the track was a keeper. "You aren't giving this one away," he told Bruce. Bruce didn't think much of the song, but he took Landau's idea seriously enough to write another number around a similar idea. "Protection" was sent to Summer and Jones, and while the idea for a vocal duet was discarded, it was arranged that Bruce would play guitar on the track while he was in Hollywood. (The Summer record didn't come to much, although Bruce played another hot solo, and he and Jones struck up a friendly acquaintance. Jones called Bruce "one of the nicest people I have ever worked with. He had an open mind. No preconceived notions. The man has more musical knowledge than a lot of people think and has a deep sense of commitment to music. You could feel his spirit in the sessions. He did every take like it was the last show at Madison Square Garden. He really gave it up. Instead of fading the song, he gave every song an in-concert ending. Fantastic.")

So in February, Steve and Bruce flew to California to work with Plotkin for a few weeks. Bruce's album project stayed on the back burner until late April.

◆

Back in New Jersey that spring, Bruce slated band rehearsals to prepare for recording. In late April Chuck Plotkin flew in from Los Angeles, where he'd finally finished his other assignments.

"This was the first album that I came out to work on from the beginning," Plotkin said. "I lived in Los Angeles at the time, and I wasn't generally available to work in New York." He'd begun his association with Landau when Jon was producing Jackson Browne's *The Pretender* for Asylum Records, where Plotkin was then head of A&R. When *Darkness* was entering the mixing phase, Plotkin was spending considerable time in New York making a Harry Chapin record, *Living*

Room Suite. Jon had then suggested Chuck to Bruce as somebody who could be of help mixing *Darkness.*

Plotkin never quite saw it that way. "I wasn't really a mixer, and I always felt somewhat miscast as a mixer. My background had been record production; I didn't even mix my own albums. *Darkness on the Edge of Town* was the first album I ever mixed, because they needed a mixer. It's just that what was left to be done when I joined them on *Darkness on the Edge of Town* was to mix the record."

Within the tight-knit world of the Springsteen camp, especially in the first months after Bruce's liberation from Mike Appel, the introduction of any new face was a major and potentially traumatic event, to be approached with great caution. What must have recommended Plotkin to Landau for this task was Chuck's ferocious attention to detail and his interest in the process of record making itself. For Bruce, part of the task of making records—especially around the time of *Darkness*—was learning the process, getting an education.

"Essentially when you work with Bruce, that's basically what you do: You're available to communicate with him on various different levels about whatever it is that's going on," Plotkin said. "I think Jon perceived that, given the way Bruce worked, hiring some fancy mixer to come in and mix the record was not really what they needed. They needed to have somebody who was essentially sympathetic to the artist's role in even something like mixing—and someone who understood that, among other things, the process, for Bruce, was learning about how all this stuff worked. I mean Bruce, as accomplished an artist as he was even at that time, had only made four records."

In the process of mixing *Darkness* and then *The River*, which took six months and involved some rerecording and restructuring of songs, Bruce and Plotkin found a friendship that their work only deepened. "Both of us seemed to be able to and interested in staying in the saddle until the thing was right," Plotkin said. "Neither one of us was afraid to work and neither one of us was the least bit disinterested in the subtle refinement of all kinds of details. I mean, after twelve hours we were both still there working and not becoming disinterested in the things we were learning about a particular piece of music while we were putting the mix together."

In some ways, Plotkin's background was even more different from Bruce's than Landau's. He'd lived in California all his life, he'd attended prep schools, he was married and the father of a then three-year-old son. Gray-haired and gravel-voiced, Chuck provided a sharp contrast with Bruce, who seemed in some ways younger in the early Eighties than he had been five years before. Plotkin had worked for a record company, and he'd made a couple dozen records, working almost always with new artists; he was a part of the record industry in a way that Springsteen and Landau were not. What he shared with them, in addition to a cutting sense of humor and a trencherman's appetite, was a ferocious commitment to the idea that what they were doing was not merely entertainment and an equally strong resolve to get the details right.

"Bruce was the first artist I had ever met or worked with who took this art form as seriously as I did," said Plotkin. "I've thought to myself many times that if I hadn't met Bruce when I did, I might very well have stopped making records at some point soon after that. The guy was able to bite off some amazingly thick, complex things and work at them in this medium. It just revitalized my sense of what could be done with popular music and encouraged me to believe that there was at least somebody out there working with whom I could actually bring everything that I knew about everything into the process of making records.

"It's like for years I remember having said to various different people—about theater, about motion pictures, about records—people who talked about, 'Well, you've got to be entertaining.' Well, what entertains me is a beautiful, deep, rich, difficult exposition in some form or another of some deep and important human question or human experience. The other stuff just doesn't hold my attention. And it didn't hold his, either."

However, the Springsteen production team was crowded and it was unlikely that there would be any dropouts. *The River* was credited to Springsteen, Landau, and Van Zandt—that is, the artist and his two best friends. Plotkin was recognized as mixer, together with engineer Toby Scott, even though that wasn't a fully accurate description of his contribution. But credit wasn't really the issue.

"At the end of *The River*, when Jon and Bruce were taking off, I said, 'Hey look, you guys, next time I'd like to show up for appetizers and the main course as well'—just because there were certain things we were dealing with in the mixing that if I'd been there from step one, the presumption was that we might avoid some of the technical problems. And also just . . . you know, being involved from early on and helping to conceptualize the piece and set a kind of sound picture for it. As much for the pleasure of the experience as anything else—just being able to be involved from the beginning."

The *Nebraska* sessions promised to be different. In late January 1982 Plotkin was called and asked to come to New York in May to begin working on the new album. He was a welcome addition for several reasons: First, given that the essence of producing a Springsteen record is "staying in the saddle," he'd proven that he was as well suited to it as either Landau, with his management duties, or Van Zandt, whose idea of production was to keep things swift and simple in the first place and, anyway, who was increasingly wrapped up in his own solo career.

When he first heard Bruce's demos, Plotkin was taken aback by the emotional atmosphere of the songs. "It was frontier material for all of us—it was on the front edge of what Bruce had been doing for the six months before we started. And he had fetched something that was at the time mysterious to him. I think in some way it remained mysterious for a long period of time," Plotkin said. "It came from a place that was so deep inside himself and had been so unexplored prior to the exploration that flowered into those songs that he really just didn't know where it came from. The sound of his voice—he found a new voice!"

It was true. What was startling about the demo cassette was not just the unrelenting bleakness of the songs themselves. It was also the performances. Bruce had been signed to Columbia Records by John Hammond (discoverer of Aretha Franklin, Billie Holiday, Count Basie, Benny Goodman, and most relevant, Bob Dylan) at the height of the singer-songwriter era; and Hammond heard him as a solo artist. But aside from a few gigs around that time, Bruce had never been a "folk" singer. His background was entirely in rock and roll and rhythm and blues: band music. Bruce insisted on making his first album with what became the E Street Band and never looked back.

But around the time of *The River* and all through the tour that followed, Bruce had listened to music he'd never heard before: Jimmie Rodgers, Hank Williams, Woody Guthrie, the obscure singers on the Folkways *American Folk Music Anthology*, stuff he dug up for himself and on tapes given to him by friends. As a result, the *Nebraska* demos had the quality of stillness associated with the great Library of Congress folk recordings of the 1930s and 1940s, by performers artfully described by critic Paul Nelson as "traditional (and nonprofessional) singers and musicians you've probably never heard of: poor folks, mostly from the rural South, just sitting at home in front of that inexpensive tape or disc machine and telling their stories, sometimes artfully and sometimes artlessly, undoubtedly amazed that anyone from the urban world would place any value on what they were saying or how they were saying it . . . You did the song once, the way you'd been doing it your whole life, and that was it. That was it, all right: the song, your whole life, and every so often, a considerable piece of Americana. Like an aural FSA photo."

The *Nebraska* demos turned the idea of urban folk music on its head. Rather than appropriating the folk songs themselves, Springsteen worked with his own characteristic melodic ideas and lyrics that were utterly contemporary. The touches that felt like folk music came from the doing: the guitar trills that rang like mandolins, the strange diction of lyrics in which the listener was so often addressed as "sir," the blank directness of that intimate singing voice, which sounded more relaxed and easy—if not confident—than any rock and roll vocals Bruce had ever sung.

Everyone heard the new material as a departure. Steve Van Zandt remembered Bruce giving him the tape and saying, "I don't know what this is. It's just what's on my mind. I did this in the house. Whaddaya think?" What Van Zandt thought—everyone recalls his reaction—was, "I love this. This is an album."

As Steve points out, "There was no basis for anyone to think about it that way. [But] it was a special moment. An artist could never get closer to his audience than this. Not because it was done with an acoustic guitar, but because he was literally singing for himself. It's like the most direct, personal, accomplished artistic statement that you can make." And like Landau and Plotkin, Steve had his doubts about how much the demo tape could be improved. But they were going to try. "At that point, I felt, we were just going in, it would probably be another year before something came out—realistically, at least that long. Looking at the pattern of recording, you could safely say two or even three."

The rehearsals ended almost as swiftly as they began. "We became aware after the second day of rehearsals that we were gonna start squeezing some of the vitality out of this stuff if we continued this process," said Plotkin. "The first time something came out great in a rehearsal, which was either the first afternoon or early the second afternoon, we all went, 'We should have had the tape running. This is crazy. Let's not waste ourselves here.' "

So the sessions moved to the Power Station recording studio on New York City's West Side. Bruce's ways in the studio are peculiar, an uneasy amalgam of what's instinctive and the height of calculation. A session might be devoted to a number from the demo tape, but there was an equal chance that it would be given over to something that Bruce showed up with that night. Or songs could simply pop up as Bruce stood in the studio fiddling with guitar, piano, or microphone. Such a song might disappear after the first take, or it might be worked on intensely for several days, after which it might become lost in a black hole or even resurface many months later. A song might be *finished* after the first take, and that was increasingly the case.

For all these reasons, Toby Scott kept a two-track tape machine running at all times, and when the action heated up even slightly, the twenty-four-track master tape began to roll.

This practice paid off one May night during a dinner break. Whenever Bruce had a few extra minutes during such quiet times he'd often stand at his vocal mike, leafing through the pages of the spiralbound notebook containing his lyrics. On this particular evening, he started a somber riff and then stopped just as Roy Bittan and Max Weinberg came back into the studio. "Let's do something with this right now!" Landau said excitedly from the control room. Max and Roy quickly fit themselves into the song, which they had never heard before, and several takes were cut on the spot, without any bass or the rest of the band. The result was "I'm on Fire."

Bruce could come up with such material almost effortlessly, it seemed, and by now the band was able to keep up in the same spirit. Every song they cut showed it. Max Weinberg, in particular, had spent months practicing drum rudiments, regaining a sense of nuanced time that tended to get buried in the excited rush of stage shows but was crucial to record making. Bruce was belatedly becoming interested in synthesizers; Roy Bittan, by several miles the most technically accomplished player in the band (Landau said he remembers Roy making two mistakes in ten years of recording), was already proficient with them. "I'm on Fire" is a good example of the highly atmospheric use Bittan made of the new machines. Garry Tallent's bass-playing had begun to come into its own on *The River*, and it stayed at a very high level. With the addition of Bruce's guitar, this four-piece ensemble was the core of the new music they were making. Steve, Danny, and Clarence added their distinctive touches as coloration, but it was the basic four-piece rock band setup of guitar, bass, drums, and keyboards that drove the sound.

As Bruce was reaching for a greater sense of detail in his lyrics, the band's arrangements were taking on a similar cast. His earlier wall-of-sound approach, in which all parts coalesced into one gigantic Spectorian noise, was replaced by one in which every sound stood out sharply and the whole built from the integrity of these parts.

Be that as it may, the fact was that the material on Bruce's demo cassette wasn't going anywhere. For two weeks, they slugged it out with the same tunes. "I remember the main one we kept whackin' away at was 'Atlantic City,' which was a song that sounded like it was gonna really lend itself to the band," said Landau. "That was one song that seemed like it wasn't gonna be any problem. And *that* was goin' nowhere. No way was it as good as what he had goin' on that demo tape. Then we tried 'Nebraska' for a while, and Bruce had a whole little arrangement for it that had been rehearsed." Again, no success.

They tried other songs, notably "Mansion on the Hill," with an equal lack of results. "The stuff on the demo tape was astounding. It was an incredibly evocative piece of work. And we were losing more than we were picking up," said Plotkin. "I wouldn't even say that the stuff didn't come out beautifully. But the big thing was gone. The stillness was gone, the intimacy was gone. It was being scaled incorrectly."

After two weeks of frustration, Bruce agreed to put aside the material on the demo cassette and work on the songs he'd written since then. The earlier material wasn't being abandoned, however. As far as Bruce was concerned, it was still what his next record was about. It was just being put aside for a time, while other strategies for arranging and recording it were devised. It was senseless to waste studio time getting nowhere, and since the studio time was already booked, it was time to try some different material. (Unlike most other performers, Bruce never suffered any shortage of songs—it's hard to think of a more prolific writer.) So they went back in the next Monday evening to try to salvage something from the remaining sessions.

The first thing Bruce called for was "Born in the U.S.A.," which shocked everyone. Landau had forgotten about the song, since it had been cut from consideration so long before. Plotkin hadn't paid it any special mind on the demo; Steve didn't even remember it being on his cassette. The band hadn't rehearsed.

"To me, it was a dead song. It was one of the lesser songs on the *Nebraska* tape. Clearly the words and the music didn't go together," said Landau.

"What turned out to be the case was that Bruce, who had not forgotten about it, had discovered the key, which is that the words were right but they had to be in the right setting. It needed the turbulence and that scale—*there's* the song! He needed music that could evoke the emotional center of the character; he needed evocative music. In other words, an acoustic guitar wasn't gonna get you there on this song. He needed a band that could feel the way this song was supposed to feel.

"Well, we go through this thing, it was just a quick run-through. And even that is just basically 'Get your parts,' so you're not really getting a feeling for the thing. They started to play this thing and for everybody there, I know to this day, it was the most exciting thing that ever happened in a recording studio."

"We just kinda did it off the cuff," Bruce remembered. "I went in and said, 'Roy, get this riff.' And he just pulled out that sound, played the riff on the synthesizer. We played it two times and our second take is the record. That's why the guys are really on the edge. You can hear Max—to me, he was right up there with the best of them on that song. There was no arrangement. I said, 'When I stop, keep the drums going.' That thing in the end with all the drums, that just kinda happened."

"We did about five takes of it," recalled Landau. "I think the tape that we used was actually the second complete take. The first take could have been used—I mean, they were all incredible. It was just one of those things where it happened real fast, and it was one of those deals where nobody had anything to say. I mean, it was like your producers and engineer just sitting there and it's unfolding . . . I was in complete shock.

"To me, it was one of the most ultimate things of Bruce's gift, the way he had not let go of this song—he had so fully seen its potential and he had just somewhere on his own, instinctively, found his way to the solution. Because it was the same words, the music was different."

Different, certainly, from anything Bruce had ever done before. In some strange way, the song echoed the Rolling Stones' "Jumpin' Jack Flash" and "Street Fighting Man," but then again, Bittan's hastily conceived synthesizer part evoked a martial fife and drum right out of a corny Revolutionary War engraving, played at intervals that suggested Asian music. And in another way, the song just took in everything spread out between those landmarks and slammed it home into something new, something different, with all the high-impact force of Max Weinberg's drums. The song began with a resonant bass chord, which thrummed through the bottom of the first verse as the snare drum beat mercilessly against that fifelike synthesizer figure and Bruce chanted out the words at the top of his lungs.

At the top of the second verse, the rest of the band thundered into life and the turbulent story that the lyrics told—a kid who gets into trouble is sent to the Army and then to Vietnam, where he survives to return home and face facts—is matched by the metallic clash of drum against synthesizer. All through the middle of the song, this struggle for control continues and no one's winning the battle. The words are brittle images torn from the pages of a life gone to seed, and they tell the truth that America was still afraid to admit about the war, the truth that's just about all this vet has left to his name:

> Had a brother at Khe Sanh, fightin' off the Viet Cong
> They're still there; he's all gone . . .

The music rises to a flourish; the singer just stops—there is no finish to this thought. The next image follows immediately:

> He had a woman he loved in Saigon
> I got a picture of him in her arms now

Then the music breaks down again—just that drumbeat and the synthesizer like a call to arms and the voice bawling out its hopes and fears, shattering against its own best intentions: "Bawwwwn inna Yewww Esss Ayyy/Bawwwwn inna Yewww Esss Ayyy/Bawwwwn inna Yewww Esss Ayyy," until the singer makes his final, impenetrable declaration, biting down hard on each word:

> I'm a cool rockin' daddy in the U.S.A. now.

Who knows what this means? And yet, it seems the truest residue not only of this war but of many, including the war between Bruce Springsteen, Rock and Roll Natural, and Bruce Springsteen, Thinkin' Fool. The music slashes and burns on for another ninety seconds of rock and roll pyrotechnics—guitar feedback, drum breakdowns, bass swoops, whooping vocalizations and imprecations—but it is never resolved, it just fades away as old, discarded soldiers do.

That night they knew they'd really begun making an album. And over the next three weeks, one song after another fell into place, usually in just a few takes: "Glory Days," "Downbound Train," "Darlington County" (a song they'd originally done during the *Darkness on the Edge of Town* sessions in 1978!), "Working on the Highway" (recast from its *Nebraska* arrangement), "I'm on Fire," "I'm Goin' Down." A little more than half of what became the *Born in the U.S.A.* album, released in 1984, was recorded in those few nights in May 1982. All cut live, in the studio, and eventually released with few, if any, overdubs. Plus a hilarious "Working on the Highway" companion piece; the brutal "Murder, Inc"; "Frankie," another *Darkness* leftover; and several others that were of release quality but never got out.

Things were going great, everyone was ecstatic—except Bruce. He was still fixing his attention on the first batch of songs, the material from the demo cassette. Landau remembered thinking, "He's sending me a signal saying, 'Hey, I know everybody's excited about how great this rock and roll stuff is, but this stuff over here is what's really important to me right now. And I'm not dealin' with this stuff until I figure out what I'm doin' with that stuff.' "

The initial, obvious idea was to mix the two batches of material together, which wouldn't be easy, since some of the moods contrasted so sharply. But even that prospect was stymied by the incontrovertible fact that the band versions of the *Nebraska* material lacked the intrinsic atmosphere that made the demos great.

If it had been up to anyone else, they could have progressed with the material that had burbled up during the second set of sessions and made the rock and roll record everyone had shown up to record. "If at the end of the evening, your night's work is you cut 'Born in the U.S.A.' or 'Glory Days,' you feel pretty good. We knew what we had at the time. You go in and you spend six hours cutting 'Atlantic City' and at the end of the night you play the demo against what you did for the last six hours and you're nowhere, you feel pretty bad," said

Landau. But Bruce remained adamant about wanting to make the core of his next album from the demo material.

No one had much idea what to do. So the era of uneasy feelings went on. "I was troubled by what was happening," said Plotkin. "The problem was that the demo tape was great and our treatments of the *Nebraska* stuff in the studio were adequate and they were less meaningful. They were less emotionally compelling, they were less honest; we were reducing the stuff, we were making less of it. We ran into a brick wall. Two thirds of the stuff isn't working. We're screwing it up. What do we do here?

"There was a meeting one night that I remember, in the studio. And I think Jon had pretty much made up his mind—Jon had pretty much decided himself or thought his way through the issues and had pretty much decided himself that he thought we could and ought to treat this thing as an album."

Not exactly. In fact, Landau was thinking out loud, responding, he later recalled, to what he felt *Bruce* had already concluded. He and Bruce started talking in the empty studio at the end of the night's work. As they talked, Chuck and Steve wandered into the room. They all sat around a table while Bruce, ordinarily the quietest of them, expressed his frustration and a desire to finally nail the *Nebraska* songs down.

Landau had been mulling the problem over himself. He had come to no conclusions, but suddenly he found himself blurting out an idea he'd never intended to articulate. "Well . . ." he said. "We can just put the demo out the way it is." Bruce shot Landau a look, a mixture of uneasiness and relief. He'd already had similar thoughts himself but had been unsure how to go about saying so, especially since Jon seemed "a little bit resistant." Was Landau serious?

"I wasn't serious and I wasn't not serious," he said later. "I was thinking out loud, and basically I'm in a position of figuring out, Hey, we have this stuff. I know it's great, Bruce knows it's great, Chuck knows it's great, Steve knows it's great, and it needs to come out. We tried very hard with the band, who have always been able to successfully render anything that we wanted to get onto a record, and we haven't been missing by a little. If we were missing by a little, we could figure that out. But we're not in the ballpark. We're not even close."

Landau's folk background again came into play. "I had a lot of familiarity with music that doesn't have drums. Voice and guitar can be a completely satisfying record to me. I have many, many such records, and everybody knows a few—everybody's heard some Robert Johnson, and that's all that is. Not to make any extreme comparisons, but to me it's an utterly tenable idea that you can put a record out that's essentially voice and guitar."

They talked for a long while. All of the obvious questions came up. Musically, such material might be satisfying. But was it possible to release such music in the Eighties, at a time when the entire trend in pop was toward high-tech electronics—synthesizers, computer technology, video? People were writing articles wondering if the *guitar* was outmoded, and Bruce Springsteen was going to release an album of acoustic guitar and vocals recorded in a creaking chair in his bedroom on a portable tape deck?

Well, yeah, as a matter of fact he was. Columbia Records might not be pleased—although Landau maintained that they would readily release this album—and radio might have a hard time finding tracks to play. But as the conversation moved along, Landau became more and more convincing in his arguments. In the end, Steve Van Zandt's perception of the possibility of an album in the demo tapes became an unorthodox decision, put forward by the member of Bruce's production team—his manager—who was supposedly most concerned with Bruce's art as a commercial transaction. It was a perfect illustration of what made the relationship between Springsteen and all his collaborators, but especially Landau, so different from run-of-the-mill show business.

"One of the great things about the process the different groups of us working on Bruce's stuff have managed to evolve is just: You listen to the music. The music speaks to you. If you listen to it, it speaks to you. Whatever you think you're doing doesn't make any difference. It's what you are in *fact* doing. And if you listen hard enough, you can *hear* what you're doing; you can *hear* what you've done, which tells you what to include and what not to include—which take of a thing to use, which songs, which renditions. That's the whole thing. That's what you do: You put some music down and you listen to it.

"I think that it's one of the things that distinguishes Bruce from a lot of other artists. He, in fact, listens to his own stuff. He actually listens—in a way that's rather special, I think, for people who also write and play and sing. There is the feeling and ideas that go into creating the music, and then there is the process of stepping back and actually being able to hear what you've done as if you haven't just done it. Sort of separate yourself from the emotional rough and tumble of the creative process and listen. Listen hard.

"There's a fair amount of analysis that goes into it, but it's a very emotional process. There's a lot of flat notes on a lot of the records; there are things where the tempo isn't real solid. It's just, 'Does this thing make me feel my life in some deeper way that I otherwise would, in some new way than I otherwise have before?' And if it does, that's its job."

Bruce Springsteen may be a cautious, conservative man, but once the decision that the demo tape should become his next album was made, he never tried to hedge the bet. Someone proposed putting out the two sets of music together, as a double album. "Gee," Bruce said, "then most people would probably just listen to the other record. These songs will never get a fair hearing if we put them with the band stuff. This isn't the normal thing; it'll take more time. That's okay."

But, ran the argument, packaged together, more people would hear the *Nebraska* material.

Bruce was bemused. "I'm not worried about how many people get the record in their hands—I'm concerned with how many people *get it*. At least this way, I know if they're buying this album, they're buying it to get this album, not to get some other album."

So Bruce and Chuck Plotkin went to work turning the demo cassette into his next album.

Ordinarily, the hard part of finishing an album is mixing, placing the sounds so that they're heard in the proper proportions and perspective. Mastering, the final step, ordinarily is straightforward. Cutting a master disc from whose grooves LPs can be created is complicated and vital to the quality of the end product, but provided you're working with skilled technicians, the issues are mainly mechanical.

In the case of the tape that became *Nebraska*, nothing was nearly so simple. The tape deck on which Bruce had made his demo was a Tascam "home studio" that recorded at three and three-quarters inches per second (i.p.s. in studio parlance), double the speed of a nonprofessional machine. But in a recording studio, there are no such tape decks—the forty-eight-track master tapes there are two-inch reel-to-reel monsters rolling at thirty i.p.s., which are then mixed down to quarter-inch reel-to-reel "two-tracks" moving at the same speed. So the first job was to haul Bruce's Tascam deck into the studio and wire it up to the control board so its four tracks could be transferred to four tracks of a high quality studio tape rolling at thirty i.p.s. The idea was to mix the material from these tapes, using standard high-tech studio equipment, echo, equalization, and other processes.

But they quickly discovered that these "pro" mixes were, as Plotkin puts it, "also disruptive to the sensibility of the thing." What they were trying to do was not just reproduce the music accurately but retain its atmosphere, an intangible they couldn't even describe to each other very well, much less to anyone who hadn't experienced the failed sessions with the band.

At one point they even tried sending Bruce into the studio on his own with an acoustic guitar to rerecord the songs, but even then the songs didn't come out the same. Surrounded by the bright lights and huge machines controlled by studio professionals, they lost their feeling of isolation and became just stark and moody pieces, without the hair-raising quality of the originals. As Plotkin put it, "The better it sounded, the worse it sounded."

But that wasn't the worst of it. In order to play the three-and-three-quarters i.p.s. tape back on a conventional cassette player, Bruce had mixed it down by plugging his own conventional cassette machine into the back of the Tascam. Furthermore, it didn't have any alignment mechanism (by which the heads of one machine are matched up electronically to an industry standard), not that Bruce would necessarily have thought to align the heads if the facilities had been available. But then, that hadn't mattered, when all he was making was a demo. On Steve's machine, or Roy's or Clarence's, the stuff would sound good enough. It was only when you wanted to make several hundred thousand copies of those signals that you ran into trouble.

In January it didn't make any difference whatsoever that Bruce had mixed onto what Plotkin called "this completely screwed up, old battered blaster." But it mattered in late May, and sometime in the interim that machine died. "We never discovered the secrets of that machine," Plotkin sighed. They did know that it ran a little fast; they could tell because when they played the original Tascam master back through the studio board, the pitch was slightly elevated from the mixdown version, and that pitch shift could only have come from the machine that Bruce mixed with. So they were stuck.

"Once we discovered that these wonderful mixes that we were doing in the studio, where we brought in and remixed the stuff, were also depriving the stuff of some important element of its particularness, then we had no choice left but to take his original cassette mixes and try to master them," Plotkin explained. "So we got stuck with a very complicated set of technical problems."

Well, now at least they knew what they were going to try to master. So they took a thirty i.p.s. dub of the cassette to Sterling Sound and Bob Ludwig, the most experienced mastering engineer on the East Coast. And struck out.

"The cassette itself sounded fine," said Plotkin. "The problem is, cassette tape running across a head is one way of having the music transferred into a box that will give a signal and send it to a speaker. Another way is having a needle track a groove. A tape is soft; a needle's hard, vinyl's hard. And the mechanics of the contact between a needle and a groove are different than the mechanics of the contact of a smooth piece of tape passing over a smooth head.

"There was a kind of slap effect that Bruce got out of a little box— an Echoplex, the kind of little box that a guitar player ten years ago would have plugged his guitar into in order to get some slap on his guitar . . . When you take a noise like the beginning of 'oh' or 'uh,' and run it through a slap so it repeats . . . The needle would not reproduce that so that it sounded musical. It sounded like electronic distortion. It didn't sound like a throat. It was breaking up. It sounded like a piece of electronic gear crapping out."

They decided to try it in Los Angeles, so Bruce and Chuck flew to California and worked for a few days with Stephen Marcussen at Precision Lacquer. They learned a few things early on, and after several more days, they felt that they had it licked. They cut a reference disc. They played it all the way through, and the needle tracked and the voice didn't break up. They flew back to New York and played the disc for Landau. The problems returned. Bruce was reduced to the verge of tears; Landau and Plotkin weren't far behind him.

"Oh, it was just the most depressing thing," said Plotkin. "Here Bruce Springsteen, who takes years making records, has finally made an album in three days. And five weeks into the mastering process we haven't figured out how to get it on a disc. It was like God was looking down: 'Bruce, you cannot have anything fast. You have not suffered enough. You have not worked enough on this. You can't make a record in three days.'

"So we figured we just had to try something else." For a while, they discussed releasing the album only as a cassette. Cassettes were becoming the dominant musical medium anyway, outstripping sales of LPs by ever-lengthening margins. But putting the album out that way would make it look even more like an oddity, and Bruce wanted the music to be heard as open-mindedly as possible. And anyway, despite everything else, Plotkin knew they were getting closer. He wanted to try working more or less on his own at a less specialized mastering facility.

Plotkin called Atlantic Records studios, and engineer Jimmy Douglas agreed to work with him in their mastering room. Atlantic's mastering room was primarily a convenience for its patrons, and together with Douglas and Dennis King, Plotkin could pretty much do as he pleased there. He used what he had learned about how radically the record's peak sounds had to be limited, but he also took even more unorthodox steps. "And," he said, "I wanted to do it someplace where my high tech mastering cronies were not gonna think I was outta my mind. I wanted to experiment someplace."

Plotkin was no more an expert at mastering than he was at mixing. What he did know was that the normal standard level for cutting a master was zero—that is, a record's grooves were cut so that on the peaks, the v.u. meter on a tape machine would kick right to the edge of the red. It was even considered desirable to cut things a little "hotter" than that, to push the peaks up to +1 or +2. Records cut with a higher relative volume sound louder and more alive at the same playing level, and hotter sounds disguise a multitude of sins, burying hiss and other noise.

The tape that they were mastering from was two generations down from a cassette master, and cassettes are inherently much noisier than reel-to-reel tapes. The way Bruce had recorded was, compared to recording in a professional studio, also fairly noisy. No mastering engineer in his right mind would consider trying to cut a super-low-level master from such material, for fear that the pops, clicks, and hisses would make him a laughingstock. A completely reasonable attitude, but that's where Plotkin had an advantage—he was not a mastering engineer. For him, the only significant issue was to get a master that would track without the sounds cracking up. And so he pushed the level farther and farther down—they'd already tried cutting a −2 and a −3 disc at Precision—until finally he got something that worked.

The peaks were only pushing the needle up to −7 (take a look at the meter on any tape deck), meaning that most of the music was recorded even more softly than that, but he had a master.

They played it a few times to be sure, and then they played it for CBS Records President Walter Yetnikoff, who was very moved by its personal quality and wound up telling them tales of his own childhood. Then they went out to Bruce's favorite New York steak house and celebrated.

7 REASON TO BELIEVE

Take a good look at my face
You'll see my smile looks out of place

—*Smokey Robinson*

ebraska became an album for the best reason: When he'd switched on that Tascam tape deck in his bedroom, Bruce Springsteen had plugged into far more than he'd intended. As Quincy Jones noticed, every time Bruce played, he went as far as ability, instinct, and judgment could take him. At best, that meant discovering new territory every chance he got.

That doesn't mean *Nebraska* didn't rework a lot of familiar territory: The cars and highways, the guilt and quest for redemption—all the things his critics claimed were excessive in his writing—were abundantly present. In some respects, even the characters were extensions of those on the cycle of albums from *Born to Run* through *The River*. Joe Roberts and his brother, Franky, are adult relatives of the men in "Racing in the Street," "The River," and "Born to Run"; the narrator of "Atlantic City" relives a version of "Meeting Across the River"; the haunted wild men of "State Trooper" and "Open All Night" are virtually indistinguishable from the outmoded cruisers of "Ramrod" and "Stolen Car." You could even say that the dreamer of "My Father's House" is the same man whose nightmares are recounted in "Darkness on the Edge of Town" and "Wreck on the Highway." All these links and many more are firmly established. But even though they're connected, *Nebraska* didn't go where *The River* most logically would have flowed.

Nebraska gave Springsteen a new voice and his music a different feel; it also changed the population of his landscapes. Missing from the cast was the central character recognizable in "Badlands," "The Promised Land," "Hungry Heart," and "Thunder Road." Or maybe he wasn't missing—perhaps he'd just been warped beyond recognition. Springsteen and his characters had been rock and roll fundamentalists. Both *Born to Run and Darkness on the Edge of Town* opened with proclamations of faith and vitality: "This is a town full of losers, I'm pullin' outta here to win" ("Thunder Road") and "It ain't no sin to be glad you're alive" ("Badlands"). Now Springsteen stood those statements on their heads. In two of *Nebraska*'s first four songs, men virtually beg to be executed, and in the album's most heartbreaking moment, the protagonist of "Used Cars," a bright kid embittered by the humiliations of poverty, sings of a town full of losers from which he has no hope of pulling out: "My dad sweats the same job from mornin' to morn/Me, I walk home on the same dirty streets where I was born." This wasn't Bruce Springsteen's story; it wasn't the story of those whom he'd written about previously. It sounded different because, despite all the reference points, it was something new.

In part, the new album found its voice in the American folk and country music to which Bruce had listened so intently, especially Delta blues singers like Robert Johnson (whom Bruce first heard around this time) and bluegrass groups like the Stanley Brothers.

Folk music is palpably present in *Nebraska* as a wellspring of its energy and its stillness. Even "Open All Night," the closest thing to an all-out rocker on the disc, harks back to protorockabillies like Harmonica Frank Floyd and Hank Mizell rather than Chuck Berry and the R&B singers who inspired Bruce's usual songs. *Nebraska* is a species of folk music, but not since the first three Bob Dylan albums had any performer extended the folk tradition so effectively. Like Dylan, Bruce accomplished the feat by bursting through every rule and boundary folk cultists had established. But where Dylan was the product of a self-conscious community of urban folk singers, Springsteen was still not the folk-based singer-songwriter that John Hammond and Mike Appel thought they'd found in 1972. On *Nebraska* Bruce was responding to a more basic fact. He'd stripped his music until he laid bare the folk roots of rock and roll itself.

If folk tradition was the most significant musical influence on the *Nebraska* performances, it was hardly the most important force in shaping the album. Far more crucial was Bruce's recent personal experience. With *The River*, "Hungry Heart," and the ensuing tour—his graduation from a rapt cult to a truly mass audience—Bruce confronted the greatest challenge rock stardom presented. While out there working, he'd made the transition without dissolving or diluting the rapport between himself and his fans. Now he faced the moment of greatest dread.

Track the trajectory of all the rock and roll heroes who ever scaled the heights of fame Bruce now occupied and there comes a point, in every story from Presley's to Jagger's, where the line drops off the map. This moment arrives when the star's career is at a peak of commercial acceptance, acclaim, and often of artistry. It's as if each star looked his audience in the eye . . . and fled. For Elvis the moment came, perhaps, when he was seduced by Colonel Parker and Hollywood, or maybe when he returned from the Army—or for that matter, it might have been the day he quit his job at Crown Electric. With the Stones, you could locate it exactly—that grisly instant at Altamont when Mick Jagger emerged from his dressing room and found himself not revered but punched hard in the mouth.

In dozens of bad rock novels, the denouement is a Corn King ritual in which the audience slays the performer, usually because he has overexcited them erotically. It's interesting that this archetype has persevered through all the changes in popular culture since the 1950s, when the first such novels were written. After all, the fact is that every dead rock star but Lennon died a lonely, isolated death from drink, drugs, or a plane crash. But the facts have nothing to do with the legend. The myth expresses a basic relationship between the individual star and a truly massive audience. For all its thrilling potency, direct contact with such a crowd is also frightening, threatening every individual in its path with psychic, if not physical, extinction. For the performer who's the focus of all that attention, the threat is palpable—retreating from the spotlight glare means you're anonymous again, but holding your ground means risking being overrun by the crowd and its demands. Whatever would *really* happen, what feels most likely is death by catastrophe, and it feels that way not only to inept novelists, but to dozens of rock stars swaddled in bodyguard "security."

The enormous power of the mass audience can quickly become dictatorial, restricting performances to rote repetitions of outdated rituals. Mass audiences are less rapt, not so universally willing to put up with the more reflective aspects of the show, and they invariably pull the performance in the direction of the known. When it comes to sheer rocking out, a mass crowd is unmatchable, but simply meeting its demands is a trap. In the same way that not outgrowing cult status means withering and dying, giving in to the collective will of the mass audience—letting the crowd, in effect, determine creative decisions—can be devastating. Retreat in order to regroup is the only way for the artist to reassert control.

Once in retreat, most stars never make it back. Even if they stay famous and make hit records, the tendency is to avoid a repetition of the situation that caused them to retreat in the first place. The essential spirit of interaction with the audience disappears. Artists as influential and fascinating as Pete Townshend and Neil Young became lost in a maze of their own suspicion and dread. The Stones grew cynical, Lennon and McCartney just dropped out: one from playing music, one from trying very hard. Elvis mingled confusion, resentment, and terror of his own condition. Dylan blundered from pillar to post. By the early Eighties, the pattern seemed so irrevocably fixed that the new generation of rock stars became obsessed with keeping their careers within bounds so as to avoid any such moment of confrontation, willing to make music that promised nothing just so that the debt would never be called in. It was the heyday of the "semipopular."

On tour Bruce had been able to ignore or at least overwhelm these facts through an act of faith. He really did believe, to use Greil Marcus's words, "that rock and roll . . . has a coherent tradition which, when performed, will reveal possibilities of rock and roll the tradition did not previously contain." And he honestly felt that the source of all his fame and wealth was his talent for delving into just such questions while inviting damn near anybody who asked along for the trip. Yet, whether he was conscious of it or not, the crowds on the final leg of the American tour sent a message that disrupted this faith. They wanted to rock; they weren't especially interested in sitting through the somber songs that set up the explosive rock numbers, and they didn't try to hide their impatience. Springsteen was sufficiently willful to do what he needed to do anyway, and his moodier pieces were compelling enough to keep an unexpectedly high proportion of the audience involved. But audience rapport was an important part of the show, and although that never disintegrated, it was noticeably diminished. *Nebraska* didn't drive the mass audience away, but it certainly taxed its attention, and it served notice—to Bruce himself if no one else—that the dictates that ruled his life and music were still his own. This didn't solve the problem of how to regain contact with the mass audience, but it at least bought Bruce some space and time in which to figure out his next moves.

But even though *Nebraska* remains a rearguard action, it exhibited unmistakable growth, particularly in Springsteen's writing and singing. In their details and especially in their characterizations, songs such as "Used Cars" and "Highway Patrolman" were the most lifelike songs Bruce had yet written. Comparisons are difficult because the styles are so different, but on a purely lyrical level, for instance, these songs are more intriguing in their intricacy than those on *Born in the U.S.A.*.

Nebraska's songs are about the utter inability to communicate and the isolation that results. In that sense, it's a pure product of Bruce Springsteen's critical condition as a pop star. But it is also about family betrayals and failures, dreams that are wasted, hopes that are blasted, a longing for death as a release from the pitiful consequences of this life. The best of its songs—"Nebraska," "Highway Patrolman," "Used Cars," "Mansion on the Hill," "Reason to Believe"—are as horrifying as they are beautiful, not just because so many people die but because those deaths are so welcome to the singer, such a confirmation of his own despair. But the singer obviously didn't feel that disarrangement of all order simply because fans clapped and stomped through "Independence Day." Other, greater estrangements were at work.

◆

Anybody who traveled America in 1980 and 1981 would have been thrown out of kilter. Double-digit unemployment was only the most accessible measurement of the greatest economic disaster since the Great Depression. The United States was no longer the land of plenty, it was a land of limits; it was no longer the home of a dream of equality, but of a nightmare of inequity. If Americans expected nothing else, they expected a surfeit of personal possessions. Now hundreds of thousands had lost their homes, their jobs, and in the ensuing confusion and disruption, much of what they had thought was eternal. Families fractured, communities crumbled, tempers once sweet turned sour. An ugly spirit ascended, the most perverse rendering of "every man for himself." The greed behind it all wasn't anything new—in part, it was as old as the earliest European settlement on the continent—but it had rarely stood so naked and unapologetic. In this world, men saw each other not as brothers but as incomprehensible, threatening aliens.

In Europe, also in the throes of a new Depression, Bruce and the band experienced another kind of disparity, because the tremendous respect and devotion audiences there paid them wasn't based only in Bruce Springsteen's personality but also in his stature as a representative and disseminator of a version of the American dream, or at least a shared dream that was associated with America. The depth of their listening, which accepted all Bruce had to say and urged him on, said so decisively.

It's not entirely clear when Bruce Springsteen realized that he was writing about America, although since he was both ambitious and a native of the first country that was an idea before it was a nation, the topic was inevitable. Certainly, that must have been part of what drew him to John Ford, the greatest poet of the American cinema. But long before that, you could hear Bruce struggling to express something about it. When his storied Jersey Shore band, Steel Mill, played the Matrix in San Francisco in 1969, *San Francisco Examiner* reviewer Phil Elwood was struck by a tune called "American Song," composed of "political-military observations, ranging from Concord Bridge to the present." A similar number was prepared for Bruce's first Columbia album but dropped. Beginning with *Born to Run*, however, the idea of a specifically American dream began to loom larger and larger on his work. And beginning with *Darkness on the Edge of Town*, the frustrations of trying to realize that dream became Bruce's central subject.

That doesn't necessarily mean that Springsteen had grown especially political. In November 1976, playing a series of New York shows during the lawsuit period, Bruce treated the forthcoming presidential election as an occasion for jokes; his attitude seemed to be that politics was just something that could get in the way if you let it. But in November 1980 he took the stage at Arizona State University in Tempe on the night after the right-wing landslide and opened the show by commenting, "I don't know what you thought about what happened last night, but I thought it was terrifying." And by that time, he had released *Darkness on the Edge of Town*, an album suffused with class consciousness.

Even at that point, though, what made Springsteen so specifically American was less what he said than how he went about his business. On the surface he was almost childishly guileless, and the virtues of his show resided in straight-from-the-shoulder plain-spokenness, the restriction (which sometimes amounted to abolition) of irony, and the creation of drama without extravagant theatrical mechanisms. (Theatrical devices of a less tangible sort were everywhere, of course.) Furthermore, Springsteen developed a songwriting style that spoke in an unmistakably American fashion. The language of even his most artful songs—"The River" is the best example—is completely vernacular. And of course, his singing voice, with that odd combination of soul hoarseness, rockabilly twang, and Jersey nasality, was as unmistakably American as David Bowie's was British, and in the early Eighties that was uncommon in white rock.

But if America is a presence in Springsteen's songs before *Nebraska*, it's mostly through his remarkably specific sense of place. Looking back, it makes sense that he called his first album *Greetings from Asbury Park, New Jersey*. From the start, Springsteen's songs have been peppered with unforgettable places, although most are fictitious: Greasy Lake, Jungleland, "a rattlesnake speedway in the Utah desert," Stockton's Wing, the Trestles, Thunder Road, Bluebird Street, "that dusty road from Monroe to Angeline," "the fields out behind the dynamo." Often evoked just in the way Bruce sings their names, these places are vivid out of all proportion, compellingly rendered in the inflections of Springsteen's singing and recognizable archetypes for every American and everyone familiar with the landscape of American pop fiction, movies, and music. And because these songs are unified by their emotional portraits, even "Badlands" and "The Promised Land" are genuinely international beyond the bounds of their all-American titles.

Nebraska is different in many respects. Even its most specifically sited songs are primarily character studies. Several are directly grounded in the new depression of the early Eighties. In both "Johnny 99" and "Atlantic City" the protagonist complains of "debts no honest man could pay" and resorts to acts of desperate futility. Poverty is ever-present, and it's not the romantically bohemian poverty of the rock and roll singer in "Rosalita," soon to be dispelled by a grant from a large corporation, but poverty so crushing in its permanence that it saps all strength from the soul. There's not just a scarcity of jobs, as in "The River"; in "Johnny 99," when "they closed down the plant in Mahwah," it stayed shut. Bosses run wild over workers, and while one class hides behind "gates of hardened steel," the other works the night shift for penance and punishment.

In even the most glum of Springsteen's previous songs, people survive because they have roots, often connected to a love affair but always related to a dream. *Dream* was one of the biggest words in Springsteen's onstage vocabulary, and it was always linked with the redemptive power of rock and roll music and, through that music, to the entire purpose of playing and gathering. You could say that *Nebraska*'s story begins with "The River," when Springsteen finally imagines a character asking, "Is a dream a lie if it don't come true/Or is it something worse?" In Springsteen's universe, that is a very dangerous question because it dredges up an irreconcilable contradiction. And *Nebraska*'s characters have found the answer; it's about the only question to which they could respond in the affirmative. For these lost souls it's all over but the shrouding. In a vicious climate men go mad, turn crazy, and nothing is left to check their casual cruelty. Faith, hope, the possibility of redemption—all the concepts lurking behind Bruce's "dream"—are nothing less than absurd. In "Atlantic City," the singer toys with the idea of reincarnation as a signal that he's ready to test its truth. In "Reason to Believe" the idea of a life after death is seen as no more ridiculous than the idea that people will behave decently in this one.

It's not just that some of the characters are afflicted this way. They all are, even a stolid center of gravity like Joe Roberts, the highway patrolman. "Highway Patrolman" is *Nebraska*'s finest story; Roberts is Springsteen's most fully and lovingly drawn character and the performance is as beautiful as it is exhausted. Caught between family and responsibility, duty and love, Roberts obeys his most decent instincts and finds his life ruined by impossible choices. As he allows his brother's car to escape, he also watches himself cross the border into the forbidden. Springsteen's voice quakes as he sings the final verse, and when Joe finally watches his brother's "taillights disappear," the voice breaks and Bruce fumbles the guitar pick, which he has otherwise strummed steadily throughout the song. In the universe of Springsteen songs, making the right choice is always of the essence, but now he's telling a story in which right is not an available option and it feels absolutely shocking.

Nebraska's other great character sketch is "Used Cars," told in a child's voice (a voice not far from those O'Connor stories). It's a bitter tale, clearly drawn from life in a way that "Highway Patrolman" could not have been. "Highway Patrolman" has the atmosphere of a movie; "Used Cars" stinks of everyday reality and it's just as brutal in depicting lives so impoverished they feel counterfeit. Everybody is faking it, even the kid who makes another of Springsteen's breakout vows: "Now, mister, the day my number comes in/I ain't ever gonna ride in no used car again."

Springsteen spoke so often in his shows about his family's run of junkers that the personal context of "Used Cars" is inescapable. It's as if, having imagined his way out of the trap, he now returns to his despised neighborhood and "walks home on the same dirty streets where I was born," trying on the shoes of those who didn't escape . . . or, maybe, wondering how much of him made the break.

"Used Cars" isn't the only bit of elemental autobiography on *Nebraska*. "Mansion on the Hill" refers to an actual place Doug Springsteen and his son used to visit near Freehold, while "My Father's House," in which father and son achieve reconciliation in sleep that they cannot reach awake, is archetypal as only real dreams are.

And that's the final context in which *Nebraska* must be understood: as a deeply personal exploration of the private demons tormenting Bruce Springsteen. *Nebraska* is a study in crisis, and while a portion of that crisis was professional and a portion was political, another part was personal.

Born to Run proved that rock and roll dreams could come true. The albums that followed grappled with what happened when dreams were fouled. But all those records were predicated on the premise that the world is basically a decent place. *Nebraska* is not only bold enough to admit that it isn't, but that, in fact, living in it is an act of folly.

This might have been easy to ignore; it wasn't Bruce Springsteen's problem. But looking back over his life, he saw how thin the margin truly is. That is what accounts for the complete lack of distance with which he speaks through Charles Starkweather in "Nebraska," and for his almost eager acknowledgment of the other disasters and tragedies in these songs. When his career began, Bruce conceived himself as an explorer, and his searches had taken him not only all over the world but deeper into his own psyche than it was perhaps prudent to venture. Bruce describes himself as a basically psychological person, by which he means introspective and analytical. Since he always thought big, he found himself asking gigantic questions on that score, too. But when you get down to asking about life's meaning, you encounter questions that will not surrender to rational analysis. Now, pondering how it was that others got through life without his basic faith, the answer that came screaming back was *maybe he shouldn't be quite so sure*.

"Reason to Believe" stares down all of Bruce's rock and roll idealism and mocks its certainty. This happens in the specifics of the song, not on its surface, for this essay on the purposelessness of existence is ironically one of *Nebraska*'s jauntier numbers. The irony is that the title phrase could serve as an epitaph of his career. Its images are as bizarre as anything in *Wise Blood:* A man stands by the side of a highway, poking a dead dog as if he hopes to revive it. A woman stands at the end of her driveway every night, waiting for the return of a man who didn't care for her much when he was around, then left without notice. A child is baptized in the same instant that an old man is buried. A groom is left waiting at the altar and long after everyone else has gone, still stands there refusing to face the fact. And after each of these verses, Bruce puts the knife in:

> *Struck me kinda funny, seem kinda funny, sir,*
>
> *to me*
>
> *Still at the end of every hard-earned day people*
>
> *find some reason to believe*

As on so many of the songs here, the phrasing is flat not because the singer doesn't care but because his reserves are exhausted. But this time there's nothing ambiguous about the comments. If this stuff really strikes him funny, it's a cheerless joke. "Oh Lord won't you tell us, tell us what does it mean," he inquires after the baptism and funeral, but this time Bruce Springsteen, who has provided answers to such questions with every note of his best music, doesn't even pause long enough for God to get a word in. He just strums harder and keeps on singing. The stories and images rush out so fast that it's hard to take them all in. It takes a while for that verse to sink in, for example, to see that what passes in the instant between its second line and its third—between birth and death—is an entire lifetime, that the baby dunked in water and the old man flung back into the earth are the same person.

What Springsteen was saying contradicted almost everything implied in his other records, and it's impossible that he didn't know it. Maybe he could still stomp and shout, "It ain't no sin to be glad you're alive," each night during "Badlands," but now he also saw justice on the other side of the story.

Because in earlier songs Springsteen often found reason for optimism in the most terrible circumstances, many listeners (particularly reviewers) took the chorus of "Reason to Believe" to be an affirmation. But "Reason to Believe" said yes to nothing. It stared straight into the void about which Springsteen-as-Starkweather spoke and found there exactly what was expected: nothing at all.

If there's another song much like this in American music, it must be the Stanley Brothers' haunting bluegrass hymn "Rank Strangers," in which the singer returns after a long absence to his boyhood home in the Blue Ridge and finds there not one familiar soul:

> *Everybody I met seemed to be a rank stranger*
>
> *No mother or dad, not a friend could I see*
>
> *They knew not my name and I knew not their faces*
>
> *I found they were all rank strangers to me*

It's a song suffused with mysticism and terror, but in the end the singer is reassured by "the voice of a stranger," who assures him that he will rejoin his loved ones in heaven, "where no one will be a stranger to me." In Bruce's song, such hope of reconciliation was beyond consideration. His thoughts had now taken him closer to the Old Testament than the New, to the voice of that cranky old preacher Ecclesiastes, who despises life and all its activities and concludes, "Vanity of vanities . . . all is vanity."

If you were willing to hear what it was saying, it was frightening to listen to "Reason to Believe." But if it was scary to hear, it's hard to imagine what it must have been like to have to live it every day. And it would be a while before these badlands started treating their creator good.

8 BADLANDS

You broke my heart 'cause I couldn't dance
You didn't even want me around
And now I'm back to let you know
I can really shake 'em down

—The Contours

Finally having a master didn't mean that *Nebraska* was ready for release. Springsteen and art director Andrea Klein spent the better part of the summer working up an album cover. Bruce wanted something more evocative than a portrait of himself, something closer to the pictures he'd found in a rare copy of Robert Frank's 1958 photo essay, *The Americans*. Frank was known to rock and roll fans as the creator of the *Exile on Main Street* album cover. His long-out-of-print book explored, in the words of Jack Kerouac's introduction, "that crazy feeling in America when the sun is hot on the streets and music comes out of the jukebox or from a nearby funeral." Its portrayals were in a style of photography that directly connected to the *Nebraska* songs—staring without flinching at painfully mundane scenes and stirring the swarming life beneath.

Klein introduced Springsteen to the still-life and portrait photos of David Kennedy, and they arranged a marathon photo session at Kennedy's house in Brewster, New York. Three pictures emerged. Two are of Bruce. In one he's caught gazing apprehensively through a doorway; in the other he sits quietly at Kennedy's kitchen table. But the photograph that wound up on the cover was one that Kennedy had taken some time before, a shot of two-lane blacktop in the Midwestern flatlands that he'd grabbed through a windshield. Although the perspective is different, Kennedy's picture bears a startling resemblance to Frank's "U.S. 285, New Mexico," from *The Americans*. It also resembles pictures that Springsteen and photographer Eric Meola took in the Western desert in 1978. Its bleak tone succinctly sums up *Nebraska*'s mood.

Even with a cover, the album lacked a title. The record was slated to be released in early October, but Bruce debated about what to call it until nearly Labor Day. About half the song titles were considered; *State Trooper, Used Cars, and Reason to Believe* were among the finalists. But in the end, it was the first song, which was also the first one that Bruce had recorded, that set the mood and told the story. So the album became *Nebraska*. Columbia announced its release to a puzzled record world.

Nebraska wasn't a gimmick. Bruce didn't have a commercial need to get a record out. His core audience wouldn't drift away if it took him a long time to make his next album; most fans probably expected him to take two or three years in the studio. Even so, the new album had to be presented properly to whatever audience it could find. Oddment *Nebraska* might have been, but it still had to be marketed.

That wouldn't have been easy in any circumstances, and it was harder than ever in late 1982. The record business was in its greatest slump since before the advent of the Beatles; the mega-platinum boom years had been waning since 1979, and they'd ended with a thud in 1981. Even superstar sales expectations were typically cut in half. Increasingly, album oriented radio (AOR) stations were crowded out by singles-based competitors who simply moved Top Forty to the FM side of the dial, and the AOR stations that survived lasted by being programmed ever more rigidly. Because broadcasting dictated what music sold, records became equally conservative, and the result was a quagmire of stagnation: boring radio, boring music. Bored fans found other ways to spend their dough. In this climate, to release an album like *Nebraska*—an album without singles or prefabricated thrills—seemed next to suicidal. Experienced record businessmen guessed it would sell only 200,000 or 300,000 copies, less than a quarter of *The River*.

Yet Jon Landau, who as manager was responsible for such facets of Springsteen's career, was remarkably confident. "What I thought and knew was that we could put this tape out and it would be a sensational record," he said. "That's what I knew. I didn't know what would happen to it—how many people would hear it, what room there was for it on radio. All those things obviously required thought, but that wasn't the key decision. After all, even if we had gotten the band on all the *Nebraska* material, nobody thought that this was the most commercial stuff Bruce had ever written. That was not one of the reactions anybody ever had."

Springsteen and Landau adopted the attitude that the album would get enough airplay for people to know it existed and that it would sell enough to justify releasing it. "Clearly, it's something different; clearly it's not for everybody," Landau remembers thinking. "We're not going to try and pretend that this is the follow-up to *The River* in the normal sense. At the same time we're not gonna promote it in a fashion that makes it seem we're apologizing." So when someone proposed that the record be released in Columbia's budget-line series for a reduced price, Bruce simply laughed and asked whether it was now the policy to price albums based on how many musicians played on them. On the other hand, this was the sixth album he'd released but the first for which he did not plan an immediate concert tour; he also decided to shun the typical postrelease series of press and radio interviews. This time out, the music really would have to speak for itself.

Then again, if *Nebraska* was to find any audience at all, CBS needed some promotional tools. Dark as days were in the record business, there was a prosperous new phenomenon: MTV, the twenty-four-hour cable television channel broadcasting "music videos," short film clips designed to promote singles. Such clips had been a highly effective sales device in Europe for years. At a time when other forms of broadcast exposure for music were smothering innovation, MTV opened its programming to much that was new—it had to, because not that many videos existed. As a result, it had begun to capture a larger audience that bought impressive quantities of records. Record labels were eager to take advantage of its potential, although albums like *Nebraska* weren't what they—or MTV—had in mind.

That autumn Landau was visited by Arnold Levine, who headed up the in-house video department at CBS in the Seventies. Levine had filmed parts of a Springsteen concert in Tempe, Arizona, in August 1978, and the clip he made of "Rosalita" had been used in England and Europe, where it was an important factor in creating anticipation for the tour. (Although a snippet appeared in Malcolm Leo and Andrew Solt's 1981 ABC television special *Heroes of Rock and Roll*, the full "Rosalita" video didn't air in the States until 1984.)

Levine, now a free-lance video director, approached Landau to inquire about making a clip of "Atlantic City." He had been told that getting Springsteen to appear in the video was probably out of the question. But that was the case not because Bruce was hostile to the concept of video clips (in fact, he was intrigued, although plenty wary of the medium's ability to flatten imaginative content) so much as because he was heading for California to mix his rock and roll material. What Levine proposed was shooting street scenes in Atlantic City and putting together a video that would contrast the wealth of the casino strip along the boardwalk with the destitution of the rest of the town.

Springsteen agreed to let Levine try the idea, but everyone was extremely skeptical about winning Bruce's approval for something in which he'd have so little involvement. ("The only direction I gave was to say that it should be kind of gritty-looking, and it should have no images that matched up to the images in the songs.") In general, the watchword of the entire Springsteen camp was *control*, and letting Levine work on his own was, for them, a step as unusual and almost as daring as *Nebraska* itself. But what Levine created was simple, tasteful, and evocative, making its point without bludgeoning the viewer and working at an angle that didn't detract from the lyric narrative. Shot in black and white, it was one of the most impressive music videos anyone had come up with and, after Bruce gave his okay, universally well received. MTV played "Atlantic City" frequently, and the song's exposure there undoubtedly won the album many listeners it otherwise wouldn't have had.

The response to *Nebraska* was surprisingly intense. Before release, doubts ran rampant. When producer Jimmy Iovine, who had engineered *Born to Run* and *Darkness* and remained a close friend, heard the tape Landau sent him, he turned to Bob Seger, with whom he was working, and insisted, "This can't be it. It must be the roughs." Commented Bill Hard, editor of *The Friday Morning Quarterback Album Report*, an influential AOR tipsheet, "I think it's gonna do one of two things. Either it's gonna continue a trend toward softer, more personal music being accepted by radio, or it's gonna be a complete bomb."

In fact, neither happened. *Nebraska* was part of no trend—it flew in the face of the most important trend of 1982, which was synthesizer-oriented British pop. But as AOR radio programmer Lee Abrams, an extremely conservative practitioner, remarked, "With an artist of Springsteen's prominence, you owe it to the audience to expose it and let them make up their minds. I can't imagine a station's not playing it. You've gotta give it a shot." Most AOR stations did play it a bit, at least in the first couple of weeks after release. Audience reaction was divided—WMMS in Cleveland, a long-time bastion of Springsteen mania, reported that its call-in comments were split evenly between those who loved the album and those who hated it—but the response was there. And when *Nebraska* was played, it sold remarkably well for such a commercially off-the-wall venture, reaching Number Four on the *Billboard* album chart and selling about 800,000 copies in the United States alone.

Critical opinion was overwhelmingly in *Nebraska*'s favor. Even such long-time Springsteen naysayers as Robert Palmer of the *New York Times* had kind words for it. In the annual *Village Voice* critics poll, the album placed third (behind Elvis Costello's *Imperial Bedroom* and *Shoot Out the Lights* by Richard and Linda Thompson). *Rolling Stone* named *Nebraska* among its albums of the year and termed Springsteen artist of the year, top male vocalist, and best songwriter.

Reviews were exceptionally important to Springsteen. He was aware of the role critics had played in his early career, and he'd come to know several writers around the country and to count on their comments to help translate the more serious side of his work. If he was truly concerned not with how many people got the album but with how many *got* it, he must have felt as if he'd cashed the bet when he read the reviews.

Paul Nelson, who reviewed the album for *Musician*, was a folk music expert (he'd edited *Little Sandy Review* in the early Sixties and had the distinction of being one of the first people to play Woody Guthrie records for Bob Dylan). Nelson had known Springsteen since before the release of Bruce's first album. His review opened with an acknowledgment of how difficult the album could be to hear, because it "sounded so demoralized and demoralizing, so murderously monotonous, so deprived of spark and hope . . . Springsteen had the courage of his convictions, I decided, and had made an album as bleak and unyielding as next month's rent. Only one problem: I didn't want to hear it. So day after day, I circled *Nebraska*, attempting to listen, trying to escape."

Unlike most others who were initially so put off, Nelson finally found a way to get to the guts of it, tracing the record's roots to recent work by Neil Young and Bob Dylan, to Guthrie, and to those Library of Congress field recordings. Of course, few others had the background to place the album in such a broadly historical context.

But some critics found the record more accessible—after all, it did tap a mood astir in the nation. "A dark-toned, brooding and unsparing record, *Nebraska* is also the most successful attempt at making a sizable statement about American life that popular music has yet produced," wrote Mikal Gilmore of the *Los Angeles Herald Examiner*. Gilmore praised Springsteen's growth as a writer, particularly his use of vernacular language and the record's "submergence in point-of-view. . . . When Springsteen tells Charles Starkweather and Johnny 99's tales, he neither seeks their redemption nor asks for our judgment. He tells the stories about as simply and as well as they deserve to be told—or about as unsparingly as we deserve to hear them—and he lets us feel for them what we can, or find in them what we can of ourselves."

Others homed in on the album's politics. In a review presciently titled "Born in the U.S.A.," Greil Marcus wrote: "*Nebraska* . . . is the most complete and probably the most convincing statement of resistance and refusal that Ronald Reagan's U.S.A. has yet elicited from any artist or any politician. Because Springsteen is an artist and not a politician, his resistance is couched in terms of the bleakest acceptance, his refusal presented as a refusal that does not know itself. There isn't a trace of rhetoric, not a moment of polemic; politics are buried deep in stories of individuals who make up a nation only when their stories are heard together. But if we can hear their stories as a single, whole story, they cannot. The people we meet on *Nebraska* . . . cannot give their lives a public dimension, because they are alone; because in a world in which men and women are mere social and economic functions, every man and woman is separated from every other."

To Marcus this was a definition of what had taken place as a reactionary regime unraveled the accoutrements of liberal tradition, and the consequences were unmistakably totalitarian. "The only acts of rebellion presented on *Nebraska* have to do with murder," he concluded. "They are nihilistic acts committed by men in a world in which social and economic functions have become the measure of all things and have dissolved all other values. In that context, these acts make sense. And that is the burden of *Nebraska*."

Others, however, discerned that Bruce might be carrying extra weight. "Any artist who confronts the world around him in an attempt to define a set of values and a reason for living is running a risk," Robert Palmer concluded. "What if the world simply doesn't make sense? What if there is no reason for living? Several of the songs on *Nebraska* circle around these disquieting possibilities, and its final song, 'Reason to Believe,' attempts to come to terms with them. 'At the end of every hard-earned day,' it concludes, 'people find some reason to believe.'

"But 'people' and Bruce Springsteen are not necessarily the same thing, and the song fails to dispel the mood of profound unease engendered by the rest of the record. It's been a long time since a mainstream rock star made an album that asks such tough questions and refuses to settle for easy answers—let alone an album suggesting that perhaps there *are* no answers. Facing that possibility has driven more than one sensitive soul right up to the edge of the abyss, and over it. One can only hope that Mr. Springsteen will either find 'some reason to believe' or learn to live without one."

◆

The plan was for Bruce to come to California and spend several weeks mixing the rock and roll material with Plotkin. At the same time, Bruce arranged for Toby Scott to install a more elaborate twenty-four-track home studio in an outbuilding at his Los Angeles house. But it wasn't quite that easy to change gears from the gloomy and insulated world of *Nebraska* to the more open and friendly space of *Born in the U.S.A.*.

For one thing, Springsteen's tightly managed world was in turmoil. Bruce was able to retain such complete command of his work in part because the community within which he made music had for years been stable and protective. There had not been a major change in the band or management since the lawsuit, five years before. Now Steve was off working on his solo project, preparing to tour and planning his wedding for New Year's Eve, in the process completely absenting himself from the planned mixing sessions. Over Labor Day weekend, Landau was married to former *Rolling Stone* editor Barbara Downey, and he, too, stayed behind in New York. Plotkin had been separated from his wife and son in Los Angeles for months; he had some serious catching up to do. Bruce had broken up with Joyce Hyser, his girlfriend since 1978, soon after the tour ended, and he'd been mostly on his own since then. Aside from Steve, he socialized with the band infrequently, and he didn't have the circle of musician cronies common to most other rock stars. He was back to being a full-time loner.

Single-mindedness had made Bruce Springsteen rich and famous, an idol to millions, virtually King of Rock and Roll. But just as his music had matured, so had he, and now the loner was beginning to experience his condition in a different way—as nothing more than loneliness.

"That whole *Nebraska* album was just that isolation thing and what it does to you," Bruce said many months after the ordeal was over . "The record was basically about people being isolated from their jobs, from their friends, from their families, their fathers, their mothers— just not feeling connected to anything that's going on—your government. And when that happens, there's just a whole breakdown. When you lose that sense of community, there's some spiritual breakdown that occurs. And when that occurs, you just get shot off somewhere where nothing seems to matter."

It would have been difficult to deny that there was a more intimate connection. Bruce didn't even try, although he was never very forthcoming about how deep and immediate his own sense of emptiness ran and how difficult it proved to dispel. "The *Nebraska* record sounds a lot like me, in the sense of the feeling," he said. "I don't mean in the particular details of the stories, but the emotional feeling feels a lot like my childhood felt to me, a lot of the people I grew up with, the tone. . . . The whole thing is, when you tell a story, a story is only good if it's your story in some fashion. Even *Nebraska*, which is extreme emotionally, the thing that makes it real is knowing what that feels like. In a funny way, I feel it's my most personal album."

Wrapped up in his own thoughts, Springsteen thought to clear his head by doing what he always did: Get out and drive. Rather than flying to Los Angeles, he traveled by car, accompanied by his friend

Matty DiLea, proprietor of a North Jersey motorcycle shop. They took their time with the trip, lingering in the vast empty American landscape Bruce loved. "And when we got to my house in Los Angeles," Bruce remembered, "I wanted to get right back in the car and keep on going. I couldn't even sit down."

It seemed imperative to keep moving, to try to outrace whatever demons *Nebraska* had dredged up. But as Bruce traveled through the middle-American badlands, he felt cut off from real life, so lonesome he could cry.

Springsteen was certainly a person of black moods, but he had never encountered a cloud that rocking out couldn't disperse. Now he'd run into a darkness that floated in off the music itself. A complicated network of forces were at work—his own loner's life-style in conjunction with his remarkable antennae for touching the mood of his generation, coupled with the wrenching emotions of making the transition between *Nebraska*'s somber music and the ecstatic rock and roll represented by "Born in the U.S.A."

"I thought, 'This can't be happening to me. *I'm the guy with the guitar,*'" Bruce recalled, as if that should have rendered him immune to the consequences of dwelling upon cosmic questions.

As far as he could tell, music had always given him a kind of immunity from despair. The guitar had been an effective weapon in forging a better world for Springsteen, and he continually celebrated this. It was hard for him to imagine that it had also served as a protective shield. In truth, Bruce exercised such remarkable control over his work environment not only to enhance the quality of the music he created but also because he wasn't especially eager to be reminded of how many aspects of life—especially home and family, themes central to his work—he had closed off. As long as Bruce believed that he'd found a meaningful pattern to his existence, the trade-off was workable and beneficial. But the moment doubt crept in, the edifice crumbled and, with it, his remarkable assurance about how the world worked.

As a kid, he'd been smart enough to see that the order life had was generally imposed on it, and he'd been strong enough as an adult to work through his vision. But at the bottom of the questions he was asking—about what people believed and why and what happened to those who didn't believe at all—was a sense of the underlying fraud of all order, the undeniable fact that the universe contained as much randomness as structure.

The central tenet of everything Springsteen had ever done was hope. Bruce had always had his doubts that what worked for him would work for everyone else—he knew how extraordinary his own story was. But he believed in the validity of effort. Now, though, the rituals that made sense of his life had stopped working even for him. Things were spinning out of control.

"I guess for the *Born to Run* record I kind of established a certain type of optimism. After that I felt I had to test those things to see what they were worth. I guess in a funny way I began to do that test after *Born to Run* and through *Nebraska*. Those records were kind of my reaction, not necessarily to my success, but to what I was singing and writing about and what I was feeling—what I felt the role of the musician should be, what an artist should be. The one thing I did feel after *Born to Run* was a real sense of responsibility to what I was singing and to the audience. I didn't have an audience before that, not much of one. I was concerned with living up to that responsibility. So I just dove into it. I decided to look around. I decided to move into the darkness and look around and write about what I knew and what I saw and what I was feeling. I was trying to find something to hold on to that doesn't disappear out from under you. Eventually it led up to *Nebraska*, which was a record about the basic things that keep people functioning in society, in a community, or in their families or in their jobs. The idea is that they all break down.

"I was interested in finding out what happens then—what do my characters do, what do I do?" In the opening months of 1983, the question was not altogether rhetorical.

In a way, the problem wasn't even that grandiose. Maybe it was just the natural response of a guy in his thirties watching all his friends settle down into domestic routines and feeling himself odd man out. At some point, after all, life as a loner mutates into a life that's just lonely. At thirty-two, Bruce Springsteen seemed to have reached that point. He felt more than ever connected to the image of John Wayne at the end of *The Searchers*, turning away from the site of domesticity and returning to the bitter wilderness.

What he didn't do about it was follow his impulse to jump in the car and drive back East as soon as he'd hit L.A. Instead, he thought for hours about what had happened and began an even more basic questioning of his beliefs and motivations.

"It was very strange, because I felt that I'd done some of my best writing, and creatively I felt real vital. But maybe the thing that I was looking for from music, rock and roll . . . in some fashion it was either letting me down or it wasn't there, or I was demanding too much or . . . or . . . Something was wrong; something was dramatically wrong," he said a couple of years later.

"I think in the end, it was a real liberating experience. 'Cause I said, Whoa, I've made a big mistake here. I always had the idea that rock and roll will *save* you. It will do this, it will do that. Well, it won't. Not in and of itself it won't. It's not gonna. It's not gonna. That's all there is to it. It can't do it for me.

"It doesn't make anything less of it. It's just reality. I had a new sense of realness. And for the first time, I had maybe a sense of limitation, and it was a healthy sense of limitation. I know I walked on with a lot of different expectations after that moment. It did not in any way affect my devotion to my job or my work or what I wanted to do with it. But it may have been something that was as simple as, Gee, there's more to life than this. It's just a cliché, but that, in a funny sort of way, is it. Knowing that there are things I need that can only be provided by people. By contact. By . . . women. By . . . friends. You can't be the guy just blowin' the horn on the mountain."

But before Springsteen reached that realization, he needed more time alone, time in which he threw himself back in his work. But not the work of completing the rock and roll album that "Born in the U.S.A." had begun. He worked by himself in his Los Angeles home studio, creating a series of songs descended from *Nebraska*.

It wasn't that he necessarily wanted to linger in that gloomy world. It was more that he couldn't escape it until it was through with him. Meantime, the joy of rock and roll belonged to a separate universe, one in which Bruce Springsteen had temporarily lost interest.

"Whenever you start another record, you start from the point you stopped at," he said. "And when I stopped the *Nebraska* record, I just continued in my garage, in Los Angeles. I improved the recording facilities somewhat; I got an eight-track board. I drove across the country and I got to Los Angeles and I just set up shop in my garage and I just kept goin', you know. That's when I did 'Shut Out the Lights' and 'Bye Bye Johnny,' and I did a version of 'Follow That Dream' and

I did a whole bunch of other things. So I just continued because I was excited about the fact that I felt the *Nebraska* stuff was my most personal stuff."

For Bruce, *Nebraska* delivered the goods. "I enjoyed the record a lot, it was easy to make, for the most part; it was a real private kinda record, it was my most personal record, I didn't have to go to the studio to do it. I felt that the distance between me and the audience had been stripped, basically, to its minimum. That the distance between the actual creation of the music and the audience had been stripped down about as close as you could conceivably get it. There was no production values in the way; there was no band; all of these things became non-issues."

But of course, if the gulf you're trying to cross isn't just artistic but also personal—and in a broader way, social—things don't work out so neatly. "The other side of the coin was that the record seems accessible to me but it obviously wasn't as accessible as *Born in the U.S.A.* or *The River*, for that matter," said Springsteen, looking back. "Maybe just because of its subject matter, that alone. Or maybe it came out at a time when you didn't hear a lot of anything like that on the radio.

"I had a kid come up to me after the record came out and tell me it was too mellow. It was a young girl and I understood what she was saying; what she meant was that it didn't have a lotta loud noises on it. You know, it didn't have drums and all that thing, and hey, she was sayin', that's what she likes, you know?" He laughed.

"I'm always somebody who has a lot of ambiguous feelings about, not necessarily what I want to do but the style that I want to do it in. And the *Nebraska* album offered me a lot of privacy. I made the record, it came out, I got in the car, I drove across the country, I might have been recognized once someplace or somethin'. And I was really happy with the record, I really felt that it was my best record to that date as far as an entire album goes. I felt that it was my best writing, I felt that I was getting better as a writer. I was learning things. I was certainly taking a hard look at everything around me."

◆

Bruce briefly worked with Chuck Plotkin on rock and roll mixes, but his heart was elsewhere. The material everyone already thought of as the *Born in the U.S.A.* album just didn't seem urgent anymore. What held Bruce's attention was the new material he was writing, which sounded like a cross between *Nebraska*, sketchy rockabilly, and some of Neil Young's more melodic late-Seventies songs. As on *Nebraska*, Bruce built the songs around guitar and voice, but he fleshed them out with a Linn drum machine and comparatively extensive guitar and voice overdubbing.

The result was sketchy and moody. The songs included "Shut Out the Light"; "Sugarland," a song about disenfranchised farmers (with very different music from the stage rendition); and Bruce's rewritten version of Elvis Presley's "Follow That Dream."

As everyone soon realized, it was asking too much psychologically for Bruce to roll from one record right into another. As Jon Landau puts it, "Most artists who take their work very, very seriously are saying something to themselves, and they need to have time to just digest the experience. Having produced this record, whether it took two minutes or two years, Bruce basically seemed to be quite distracted right away. He was interested in working but not in any heavy goal-oriented fashion." Wisely, Landau and Plotkin pretty much left him alone.

After the holidays, Bruce called Landau and asked him to come and listen to what he'd been up to. In early January, Landau flew to California, listened, liked a lot of what he heard, and realized they were back to square one: Bruce had composed another group of songs that didn't blend naturally with the *Born in the U.S.A.* rockers. Once again, he'd come up with material that was for the most part ill-suited to the E Street Band. Together, they sat down to assess the situation.

Landau and Springsteen's relationship has little in common with such storied pairings as Brian Epstein and the Beatles or Tom Parker and Elvis Presley. As Bruce puts it, "There's basically nothing ordinary about our relationship. I don't know of any other situation even remotely like it."

Jon Landau has never been a typical manager—or even a record producer—any more than Bruce has been a typical rock star. In the beginning, Landau wasn't especially interested in a career as a manager. Even after he proved successful in the job, and other artists frequently came to him, Bruce remained his only client. As Bruce said, "The whole thing really evolved out of a unique type of friendship. Jon just happens to be my manager because nobody was my manager and I need a manager; there was nobody better for the job than him, but our relationship is not based around him being my manager. It's just one of the things that he does for me, and he does it real well. Before he met me, he had never managed anybody but it kinda grew out of the need of that situation."

Jon Landau is Springsteen's manager, then because he is the person best able to communicate with Bruce and because he can handle the even more difficult and important task of effectively communicating Bruce's ideas to others. Those are considerable qualifications, but there's an even more important one. Landau also has a gift for helping Bruce understand many of his own ideas.

Landau grew up in Brooklyn and the Boston suburbs. After attending Brandeis University, he played guitar and banjo in rock and bluegrass bands and worked in a Harvard Square record store, where he met Paul Williams, editor of *Crawdaddy!*, the first rock magazine, which his reviews of rock and soul albums immediately improved. In addition to attending shows and concerts everywhere from the folkies' Club 47 to the hippies' Boston Tea Party, Landau befriended many musicians, particularly such Boston stalwarts as Peter Wolf and Barry Tashian. In his early writing, however, he emphasized rhythm and blues taste above everything else, dwelling especially on the virtues of the records made by Stax/Volt in Memphis and by Motown. At a time when no other major critic paid anything close to sufficient attention to black rock, this made him stand out, particularly since his reviews were more likely to dwell on specifically musical—as opposed to social or lyrical—questions. Later, as editor of all *Rolling Stone* record reviews, a position of great authority in the pop world, Landau was also an early champion of the singer-songwriter movement. The catholicity of his taste was indicated by the first artists he produced. There was an unreleased session with Wolf's blues-based J. Geils Band, the proto-punk of the MC5, and the laid-back singer-songwriter stylizations of Livingston Taylor. Landau also served as *Rolling Stone*'s film critic for a time.

Landau was much more sympathetic than his critical peers about popular music as a business proposition. Coupled with his *Rolling Stone* tenure and his production experience, this gave him considerable clout within the rock industry. His friendship gave Springsteen's career its biggest boost since Bruce's discovery by John Hammond.

The intensity of their friendship stemmed from the very first time Landau saw Springsteen perform, in April 1974 in a tiny bar in Cambridge, Massachusetts. (Another show, about a month later, inspired the famous "rock and roll future" column.) Their friendship rapidly blossomed through a series of hours-long phone calls between Boston and New Jersey, in which Jon and Bruce talked about everything from the nature of the art to the details of record production to the mysteries of Gene Pitney's hit singles. Its first fruit was the production of *Born to Run*.

But all of that is only the relatively public aspect of their story. In the end, there were deeper and less tangible bonds. When he met Bruce Springsteen, Landau was thinking about leaving *Rolling Stone* to become a full-time record producer. He certainly hadn't planned to limit his work to one artist; that was just how the situation developed. And he was willing to let it, because he had absolute faith in Bruce Springsteen's capacities, not just as a rock star but as an artist. Landau gradually became manager because there seemed no one else—certainly no established manager—who met all of Bruce's needs and desires, the greatest of which was to have someone he could trust and confide in, someone with whom he could play a role more vulnerable than the loner.

Even though Jon was ordinarily imperious, he was continually patient with Bruce. He offered his guidance without insisting on a result or even a direction, even if he'd already made up his mind about what he hoped would happen. "A lot of times he won't say anything," Bruce said. "He lets the thing raise itself, rather than letting his opinion or his taste or his own prejudices get in the way. And that creates a tremendous amount of trust in his opinion."

Landau was able to operate this way because he and Springsteen shared a taste for restraint, an aversion to making public relations gestures for their own sake, and the desire to present Springsteen's music with as much dignity as they felt the best rock and roll deserved. The same thing applied in private discussions. Consequently, when either was moved to make a stand about something, he spoke with cumulative force.

"The essential part of me and Jon's interaction is that either of us can argue intensely about this issue or that issue, but in the end the music does the talking," Bruce said. "And we argue until what's right reveals itself, whatever that may be and wherever it may come from. We don't argue until he wins or I win.

"We both have a dedication to the idea, and we're just a couple of guys trying to get to it. That's the essence of our process. I don't have a dedication to my viewpoint on any particular issue, and I don't believe that he does, even though he has his arguing position that he feels is right and I have my arguing position. And we'll go at it until what *is* right or what feels right reveals itself. And I don't know of any time that we haven't agreed on what that was. No one has ever said, 'Well, I think you're wrong, but okay.' That has never happened. It's always come to, like, 'Well, all right. Yes,' or 'That seems like the right thing to do.' And I think that's because our dedication is to the idea.

"That's a real important thing about the way we work. And it keeps all the personal baloney that might normally come up in control. One of the things that keeps that under control is the trust we have in each other. From day one, when we first started to work together, I always felt Jon understood what I wanted to do and he was there to help me do that thing. It was as simple as that. He has always made me feel like he is there to help me do this thing that I wanted to do. Consequently, when we get into various different arguments over this song or that song or even if we get frustrated with each other, eventually we work our way through to the answer. And I think that's a real different thing and a real important thing."

Imperious as he, too, may have been, when the chips were down, Springsteen had a musician's necessary knack for collaboration. (Songs may be composed in solitude, but they're played—and recorded—by groups.) He was able to grapple with and use the ideas of a diverse group of people, which is the only way he could ever have made coherent albums working with a trio of producers who had quite a bit less in common than Holland-Dozier-Holland.

A manager's job is to rationalize art, translating abstractions into marketplace terms. A producer's task is similar. Often as not, Springsteen and Landau worked together in just that perspective: artist and translator. But when it came to specific pieces of music, they again violated the cliché. Often it was Jon who worked on instinct, fighting against Bruce's innate conservatism and caution, willing to let a piece that just rocked stand on its own. Bruce tended to be wary of what came too naturally. Landau struck everyone who met him as an extraordinarily controlled and rational person, but he loved wild music, from "Tutti Frutti" to "Kick Out the Jams." It was this one streak of recklessness that often proved most useful in making records and furthering Springsteen's career.

While making *Born in the U.S.A.*, this conflict centered around one song, "Cover Me." Landau says he knew the song belonged in the next (rock) album the moment he heard what was supposed to be nothing more than a tossed-off demo. Bruce was indifferent to the track from the start, often outright hostile to it. It struck him as too light, too pop, too obvious. These were among its virtues, Landau insisted, and anyway, none of that belied the intensity with which Bruce whipped home the crucial line: "Wrap your arms around and cover me!" Although the song was closer to pop than rock—and in its rhythms closer to postdisco dance music than either—it had a stinging guitar solo. Landau loved its modern sheen; Bruce knew its value—he'd created it, after all—but he wasn't sure what it said about him. The more anachronistic shape of his soul and rockabilly-based tunes was secure and comforting. In all their discussions about the album, Landau kept dredging up "Cover Me" and Bruce kept kicking it back under the rug, radical manager against conservative artist.

When they got together in Los Angeles that January, Bruce wasn't really in a mood to take any decisive actions and Landau was shrewd and sensitive enough not to push too hard. "At the time I felt that maybe this [solo recording] is where the whole thing is going in some fashion," Bruce said. "Maybe the idea is gonna be to just keep the thing real stripped down right now, almost like a *John Wesley Harding* type of thing."

Bruce did have one song that he wanted to try cutting with the band, and in February he flew back to New York briefly and in a short session recorded "My Hometown" at the Hit Factory, the studio at which the rest of the album would be made. "My Hometown" had something in common with the squalid, somber worlds of the *Nebraska* characters, but it was almost quiescent in its portrait of an American worker who witnesses the flower and the rot of post-World War II prosperity. The man teaching the rituals of a dead-end town to his son in this song lacked the rage of Johnny 99, and while that gave him the strength to think about pushing on, it also created a feeling of acceptance akin to the world of "Mansion on the Hill," with its horror-show class rituals. Taken on its own, "My Hometown" is a highly ambiguous statement, fraught with fear and reconciliation and detailing defeat. But it isn't nearly as desperate as "Used Cars," its opposite number from *Nebraska*, even though the circumstances are more mean and frustrated. "Foreman says those jobs are goin', boys, and they ain't coming back/To your hometown" are lines that lurk and linger in the heartland of America in the Eighties.

Successful as that session was, Bruce still headed straight back to his Hollywood solitude, once more leaving manager, band, and producers up in the air about his plans.

"I was living in L.A. and Jon was living in New York and I'm not a big person on the telephone so our communication wasn't as steady as it might be during the course of making a record," Bruce remembered. "Really, at the time we weren't consciously making a record. The *Nebraska* record had just come out and we had the bunch of cuts from the studio *Nebraska* sessions. It was just sittin' there, waiting to be mixed, because nothing else ever really happened on it again. We did that in two weeks, the same two weeks we spent tryin' to record some new *Nebraska* stuff."

In retrospect, it seemed to everybody that the problem was isolation, lack of contact and interaction. Bruce put it down to "my new method, which was initially begun for purely economic purposes. What do I spend all the money in the studio on? Writing the songs. I go in and record a hundred songs; some of 'em I finish, some of 'em I don't. It's a waste of time, it's a waste of everybody's time and money. Let's not do that anymore. I'll do that at the house.

"Now that I've begun to do that at the house, there's also something else happening. Nobody's seeing anybody else. The band's not seeing me, I'm not seeing the band, I'm not seeing Jon, Jon's not seeing the band or me. And it's been quite a while."

A few weeks after Landau went West, CBS Records president Walter Yetnikoff made a trip to Los Angeles and visited Bruce. Springsteen and the colorful record chief got along well and they met for dinner and had a great time. But Bruce didn't play anything for Yetnikoff, or even talk about his music.

When Yetnikoff returned to New York, he phoned Landau and expressed his concern. ("He never mentioned it to me," said Bruce, "but I do believe that he was concerned about me making another record in my garage or in my bedroom or wherever I was makin' it, you know.") Yetnikoff pointed out that although Springsteen was supposed to be working on his next album, that wasn't really possible, since his chief record producer and his band were a continent away.

Yetnikoff wasn't trying to pressure Springsteen, exactly. He didn't have much leverage, for one thing, since Bruce didn't need immediate transfusions of CBS cash. Anyway, it was inconceivable for him to make music under duress. What the record company president provided was an outside viewpoint that forced Landau and then Springsteen to face what was actually going on.

Jon phoned Bruce and they had a long talk about what they were trying to do. They agreed that the goal was still to make another album and that whatever else Bruce might have been accomplishing in California, that wasn't happening. "We realized that the studio is important because one of the things that happens is that everybody sees each other," Bruce said. "We get together and the band plays and sometimes we get something and sometimes we don't, but we do have a feeling that everybody's chipping in and working on a project. There's a little sense of something going on.

"We talked about this; we decided, that's right. Summer was coming up, I'd been in California quite awhile. It seemed like it's time to get back, get in the studio, do it the old way. Get the band in, spend a little time in there. And that's what we did."

In early May, Bruce came home—by plane—and went back into the studio with the band.

◆

Simply coming back home didn't end Bruce's turmoil. For one thing, his relationship with the band was still ambiguous. That was the chief reason Landau felt immediately making another *Nebraska*-style album could create serious problems. "To me, Bruce is the most unusual combination of talents that I know of, in terms of lyric-writing ability, music-writing ability, guitar-playing ability, arranging ability, band-leading ability, singing, everything," Landau said. "And when an artist has range, the most exciting thing is when you are doing all of the things that you know how to do, at the same time, at the peak of your ability. As I said to Bruce at the time, the problem with the *Nebraska* thing as a permanent approach or a main approach is that it is tremendous at what it is, but you have so many capabilities that are not utilized that it seems like it's less than you can be."

By making successive albums without the E Street Band, Bruce would seem to be signaling that he was no longer going to work with them. Furthermore, since he'd probably want to tour after the release of the next album, he would have the extremely difficult task of presenting twenty new songs into which the group didn't fit. Another round of enforced idleness might break up the group—players as skilled as Roy Bittan weren't going to sit on their hands forever. In any event, Bruce would be sending a very confusing signal to everyone concerned.

Landau wasn't absolutely opposed to making such changes, but he worried that Bruce hadn't thought everything through. "I just wanted to make sure that, if we were gonna go in this direction, all of these things were thought about. If Bruce had considered them all and said, 'Nope, this is really right; my thing with the band has changed; maybe I'm not gonna use them so much; maybe I'll do a tour without the band. . . . ' If he'd been prepared to make all those decisions, then fine. But I wanted to make sure that he understood that those were the decisions he was possibly making."

Bruce didn't want the group to break up, but he wasn't ready to get back into full-tilt rock and roll, either. As a method of music-making, *Nebraska* struck him right then as more than satisfactory. "There's nothing much more intimate than working with yourself," he said. "You're just working with your own thoughts and your own ideas. It is *not* something that you would want to do all the time, but at the time I wasn't exactly sure of that."

Bruce now needed to find music that reflected the ways in which he'd changed, and rock and roll still pulled him toward the same old mysteries, the same old ghosts. For the first time in his life, he felt wary of being in a band and rocking out.

"I think, and this goes to the general philosophy of the whole thing, the thing I liked about *Nebraska* was that it was kind of a private record. And in a way, I was able to maintain more privacy making that type of record. Basically, I'm a private person. So it appealed to me on a lot of different levels. And in a funny way, I'm somebody who has to be drawn out. That is one of the essential things Jon does for me, even in the face of my resistance.

"So I think that there was a point where I said, 'Gee, I could make a record like this, these types of records, and it's satisfying to me.' I was leading the type of life I was leading; it was totally suitable, it filled all my needs in a variety of different ways. I suppose I toyed with that idea because of the protection that it provides."

Furthermore, no matter what Bruce wanted, his relationship with the band *had* changed. The sessions called for in the spring and summer of 1983 were the first since 1975 without Steve Van Zandt on rhythm guitar. Even though Steve's presence was more often felt than heard, his catalytic personality had been an important component of Springsteen's relationship with the E Street Band, especially since Bruce often communicated with Steve even when he was basically noncommunicative toward everyone else. But that summer Steve was touring Europe in support of his first solo record and returning to New York to record his second album, *Voice of America*, in another part of the Hit Factory.

Steve Van Zandt had evolved his way in and out of Bruce's bands before, and this time he left without much discussion. "I felt that at that point I had something really significantly different to say," Van Zandt said. "Different enough that it would take full time, it would take leaving. And also, I felt that I had contributed everything I could possibly contribute: We'd recorded live, with no overdubs whatsoever, which is something that I had always worked for right from the beginning. . . . It was just a matter of getting the craftsmanship to the point where you can do that.

"Bruce and I talked off and on during this period. And it was just a real obvious point where I was anxious to get on with this new thing, because it was new, you know. I'd dedicated seven years of my life to making that thing happen, and we had accomplished everything that I hoped we could accomplish. It had never occurred to me until then to leave." However, Steve didn't talk much with the rest of the band about his plans—"not until it was comfortable," which was after they'd already done a few weeks work without him. And in keeping with the Springsteen organization's penchant for secrecy, his decision wasn't communicated to the outside world until many months later, on the eve of the release of *Voice of America* and Bruce's own record.

One result was rumors that Springsteen and Van Zandt were having a feud. One story even claimed that Steve's tracks had been erased from Bruce's masters, something that was impossible, given the way the music had been recorded. As Van Zandt said, "I did the mandolin solo on 'Glory Days' into my vocal mike. How you gonna wipe *that?*"

Van Zandt interpreted the rumors as a sign of public confusion. "I guess people had a tough time figuring out how I could leave at that point, not knowing how I felt, not knowing my own potential. 'Why would he leave?' Of course, it's because I had something to say that no one specifically had ever said before, and how could they relate to that if they've never heard it."

But if people were confused, it was also because the split—however amicable—disrupted the mythology of the E Street Band. Steve Van Zandt wasn't only Bruce's oldest friend in real life; onstage the role he played was the Sidekick. In many of Bruce's yarns, rock and roll functioned on the buddy system, and through them he and Steve and Clarence had achieved a kind of group identity. In real life, of course, being the sidekick of the King of Rock and Roll meant smothering your own talents or, at best, never getting a chance to discover what they were. As Chuck Plotkin put it in describing his own situation, "Anybody who works with Bruce can become overidentified with him. Your identity becomes subsumed in the identity of someone of Bruce's magnitude. It's difficult to get on with the next project, because the thing that people are interested in is how it was to work with Bruce."

Steve felt it necessary not just to leave Bruce's band and his production team but even to change his name from Miami Steve to Little Steven and eventually (with his second album) to abandon the soul music on which his earlier image was based. It was anything but the easy way out, but that was how he felt it had to be.

The absence of Steve Van Zandt didn't necessarily change Springsteen's rock and roll sound. The tracks without Steve's guitar include "No Surrender," "Bobby Jean," "My Hometown," and "Dancing in the Dark," which retain the same diversity of sound and feeling as the material Bruce recorded while Van Zandt was in the group. But Steve's absence still added to Bruce's uncertainty, and having just had a successful experience cutting solo, he was still inclined to think in terms of recording without the band. As Plotkin said, "It looked for a long time like we could end up with *Nebraska II.*"

With Bruce uncertain of his own direction, the music they made that summer lacked the confidence necessary for great rock and roll. They made some decent tracks in those long, hot weeks—"Stand on It" and a new version of "Pink Cadillac" (the one they ultimately released) among others—but nothing was up to the level of the material they'd recorded the previous May. Plotkin, the closest thing to a newcomer in the byzantine Springsteen recording process, felt almost estranged. He just couldn't hear the value in the songs they were cutting; he found them forced, the one thing good rock and roll can never be. Communication broke down.

Plotkin remembered the summer with a shudder. "Bruce would ask me what I thought about a guitar solo, and I'd say, 'I don't know. I don't know what the song's about. I don't know whether the guitar solo's the right guitar solo, because I'm not getting any hit off the song.' He'd say, 'Well, all right then, I'll just do this guitar solo.' After two or three of those responses, he just stopped asking me what I thought. I went through a period for about two months where we hardly talked.

"It sounded like Bruce was trying to recover from *Nebraska*. He was ready to rock again; he wanted to and he knew that was what he was gonna have to do or he couldn't finish, and he made a valiant effort to get a series of things to rock that were written from a place inside of himself that was just not rocking."

Landau, who had gone through less drastic versions of the same process on three other albums, was more sanguine. "Chuck's job is such that he has always gotta be grappling with the music as it is right at the moment," he said. "At those particular sessions, I was able to be less concerned about any particular song we were cutting (until we hit 'Bobby Jean') than I was about getting us back into an integrated working situation—the producers, the band, making this album together. Besides, the way we jump around is disorienting to anybody. Chuck was still getting used to songs that go into the black hole and you never hear from them again."

As the summer wound down, it became obvious that everyone needed a chance to get out and breathe, away from their nocturnal and pent-up studio existence. Bruce had spent the previous summer getting out almost every weekend to play with friends famous and obscure, joining bands like Beaver Brown and Cats at Jersey shore bars like the Stone Pony or sitting in with journeymen rockers like Nils Lofgren who were playing nearby clubs. He hardly took a day off all summer. Like everyone else, he'd clearly earned the chance to get some sun and to think about what they'd accomplished.

But workaholics don't make it so easy on themselves. As August approached, Springsteen proposed not that they needed a vacation but that they were finished with recording and ready to start final mixes. In retrospect, even Bruce doesn't quite understand his thinking. "When we started to mix the record, I don't really know what we thought we were doing. We must have thought we had an album."

The task of proving the point first fell to Chuck Plotkin, who began by asking Bruce to explain exactly which songs were on the record as he imagined it. "I said, 'Well, look, Bruce, you tell me what it is that we're gonna mix, what cards are on the table. I'll wade into the stuff and I'll take the best rough mixes that we have and let's string 'em together. I'd like to hear the record before we mix it.'" So Springsteen gave Plotkin a list of songs with a basic idea of their sequence.

Plotkin and Toby Scott went back into the Hit Factory by themselves and over five days assembled Bruce's version of the new album. What Plotkin heard confirmed his worst suspicions: They were a long way from finished. "And I was scared to death because our communication had just dwindled away to nothing," Plotkin recalled with a shudder. "That was one of the low points of my involvement with Bruce, because I was just scared to death. I was in a state. I strung the stuff together, and I said, 'I'm gonna master these rough mixes. Because I've got to figure out some way to get him to listen to this as if this is the record.'

"I'm talking to Jon every day about this. 'Jon, how can I tell him this?' 'You just have to tell him.' I said, 'My only hope is to get him to listen. I'm not gonna tell him anything. I'm gonna bring the disc down there, and I'm gonna say, "Bruce, look, let's just put this baby on and let's see how we're doin'."' Real nice and easy. And hope that he can hear it. He'll see the disc—he's taken a week off, he'll know. 'Cause I just can't say what I have to say. I know he won't take it from me right now.'

"So we set up a meeting in New Jersey and I walked in with the reference discs. I said, 'Let's put this baby on and hear it.' Bruce said, 'What do you mean?' I said, 'Well, I've got this all put together here. Let's just listen to it. We don't need to talk about it.' He says, 'I don't want to listen to it.' He says, 'Charley, you just spent five nights all by yourself in the studio, listening to this stuff. Tell me where we stand.' And I wanna go, 'But, Bruce, you haven't listened to a word I've said in the last eight weeks. We haven't talked. What difference does it make what I think?' I didn't say this, but that's what I was feeling. I said, 'Geez, I really think we oughta just listen to this stuff, you know. We'll just sit here together and we'll be able to hear what it is. You don't really want me to tell ya what I think.' He said, 'What the hell do ya think I hired ya for?'

"And I thought [*groaning*], 'He's not gonna listen to the thing. I'm gonna have to tell him.' So I said, 'Well, I can hear the album. I can hear the album we're making. This isn't it.' Because I couldn't be negative. 'This isn't it but I can hear it; I know what this record is about. And I know what of what we have is working, and I know what isn't working and I know what's missing. And we're real close. I can make one great side out of your song list, but I can't make two great sides out of it. I can make a great opening side or a great closing side. But I have a feeling that what we have is sort of like marking posts.' I said, 'If you listen to "Born in the U.S.A." into "My Hometown," that's the whole thing. That's the record.' "

It came down to Plotkin's vision of what it meant to produce a record with Springsteen. "It's simply caring enough about Bruce and his records to hang in until the record is right. That is, to hang in with him when his impulse is that it can be better and to force him to hang in with you when your impulse is that it can be better. It's the highest uncommon denominator. It's being able to hold your own in fairly strong company where the issue is, Is this thing as good as it needs to be yet? That's it. That's the job. Just somehow or another mustering the physical and emotional strength to stay at war until the thing is won. That's all. That's just . . . that's *it*."

"And he bought it—he bought the whole cloth."

As Plotkin and Landau saw it, the problem with the album was twofold. In the first place, there weren't quite enough songs that fit together in order to make a great album. In the second, a great deal of the best material they'd recorded was *not* on these reference discs. Springsteen's interest in "Downbound Train" had recently revived; "My Hometown" was part of the story from the time it was recorded, and Bruce had always regarded "Born in the U.S.A." and "Glory Days" as the core of the rock and roll LP. But "Cover Me," "I'm on Fire," "Working on the Highway," "Pink Cadillac," "I'm Goin' Down," and "Darlington County," all of them recorded more than a year before, had been abandoned. Those songs were among the best Bruce had ever recorded because they felt almost effortless—not casual or throwaway but sung as if Bruce were for once performing without burdens. In the months since, Bruce had felt just the opposite, and the new songs, no matter how hard the rhythm section kicked, showed the strain. He needed some more songs and everyone simply had to wait until he'd written the right ones.

Bruce's response to their conversation, Plotkin recalled, was almost immediate. "Two nights later, we went into the studio and he said, 'I have a song I want to cut.' We cut 'Bobby Jean' and it was like the fever had broken."

The song was a breakthrough for Bruce in several ways. Its accents were more modern than his usual rockabilly and soul-fixated rhythms. Tallent's bass chopped against Weinberg's drums, while Bruce's rhythm guitar and Bittan's perfectly placed piano notes roiled up out of a virtual dance groove. The song surged but also almost floated. This simple, spacious music was the essence of rock and roll: effortless, joyous, deeply grieved. It was the sound they'd spent the summer searching for.

Bruce wrote the lyric as a letter to a departed friend, and he sang it with the same mixture of mourning, wistfulness, affection, and anger. His voice was open, "young," showing no strain even as it hit a couple of awkward lines (e.g., "talking about the pain that from the world we hid"). The song is a one-way dialogue and, obviously, many of the details must have come from the circumstances of Steve Van Zandt's departure: "You hung with me when all the others turned away, turned up their nose/We liked the same music, we liked the same bands, we liked the same clothes." But it was more than just Miami Steve that Springsteen's singing sent away with this odd combination of reluctance and eagerness. In the end, as he sings lines that mingle love, grief, and rancor, Bruce might be singing to the old self burned up in the crucible and aftermath of *Nebraska*:

> *Maybe you'll be out there on that road somewhere, in some*
> *bus or train traveling along*
> *In some motel room there'll be a radio playing and you'll*
> *hear me sing this song*
> *Well, if you do, you'll know I'm thinking of you and all the*
> *miles in between and I'm just calling one last time*
> *Not to change your mind but just to say I miss you, baby,*
> *good luck, goodbye Bobby Jean*

But just making "Bobby Jean" didn't settle the question. Shortly afterward, Jon Landau drove down to Bruce's house, and that night they did play the acetate of the prospective LP.

"It just wasn't a record; it just didn't sound like one," Bruce said. "I've got a whole bunch of strange little songs that really, they're interesting but they don't seem to be mixing. It wasn't that all the stuff wasn't good on it. We had 'Shut Out the Lights' on it and 'Follow That Dream.' Individually the things were good but they just didn't add up—it didn't sound right, it didn't come together. And the difference in sound quality from the garage thing to the studio stuff was too haphazard. It left you flat."

The process had again become mystified and confusing. As Bruce admitted, "Of course, that's the inevitable question: We have a lot of material, why don't we have a record? It's mysterious—like why? And you know time is beginning to tick on and we had seen this before and we didn't want the same type of situation that we had on *The River* and *Darkness*."

The problem was that Bruce had cast aside most of the best material, which remained the songs from the band sessions done during the *Nebraska* period. As he said, when they failed to get mixes of them in California, "then I really dumped on them."

"All the stuff that got thrown out is pretty good," Landau said.

"Aw, no, that's no good," said Springsteen.

"No, that's good stuff," said Landau, and plunged a bit further: It had been thrown out while Bruce was in California; Jon hadn't really had a fair chance to work on it.

"Jon is good like this—he's patient, for one thing," Bruce said, laughing as he described it. "And he waits and he waits, and when he sees I'm down, then he makes his move. We reach a point of some confusion, then it's like, 'Hey, what about this stuff?'

"This was a central discussion that we got into one night. A lot of these songs had been thrown out without us really discussing the merits of them or whether they should be. And I had all my reasons why I didn't like it. I always have a million reasons. And they're arguable, you know; you can always make an argument.

"So that was when we sat down and we started discussing what type of record we were trying to make. The answer we came out with in the end was, we were making a rock and roll record. Before that we hadn't been trying to make exactly that particular type of record. A rock and roll band record. You know, with fast songs on it. Drums. Not too mellow. Something with loud noises on it.

"And this was a funny thing, because I had a lot of ambivalence about doing it. It's always a trade-off that you make. I guess part of it was I just wasn't sure that was where I wanted to go."

When it came to the actual composition of the *Born in the U.S.A.* album, Jon Landau had very specific ideas about where things ought to go. After their meeting in Rumson, Jon said, "I decided for myself that it was time to think about what my ideal album was, out of everything we'd so far recorded. It was something I'd never done before, but it seemed that it would be useful to have somebody's version of the record.

"So I made up a rough album sequence and sent it to Bruce with a letter, which was my own rave review of that sequence, giving all the ideas and arguments I could think of. In my own mind there was an element of provocation, because it was so unusual."

The letter ran five single-spaced pages of closely packed argument. Landau had arranged an eleven-song sequence. Side One consisted of "Born in the U.S.A.," "I'm Goin' Down," "Cover Me," "My Home-town," and "Bobby Jean." Flip it over and you got a still-unreleased ballad called "My Love," the revised "Follow That Dream," "Glory Days," Bruce's version of "Protection," the second song he'd written for Donna Summer, "Janey, Don't You Lose Heart," and "I'm on Fire." The idea, he wrote, was to make the album "a collage having to do with past, present, and future," with an eye toward expressing Bruce's current state of mind and opening doors for the future. "Born in the U.S.A.," Landau commented, "starts the album right in the middle—a man at the crossroads, by himself, disconnected from his past but not yet connected to any imaginable future beyond mere survival; a man at the beginning of a search."

Landau's letter also emphasized musical balance. He was encouraging Springsteen to step forward musically by using the dance rhythms and minor keys of "Protection" and "Cover Me." But most of all, he was concerned that the group of songs picked should reflect *adult* emotions.

Writing the letter was an eccentric approach to record production, but because Jon's positions were well stated and cogent, it helped break the bottleneck. "I think we all felt that we didn't have anything to lose at that point," Landau said. "I think one of the things that tape did was reintroduce the discussion of 'I'm on Fire,' 'I'm Goin' Down,' and 'Cover Me,' songs in which Bruce had seemed to lose interest."

Again Landau had stepped in at a key moment to help formulate a decision that felt like a step in the right direction. So they went off on their break, scattering from California to the Jersey shore, and returned refreshed for the next round in a battle that still had a long way to go.

◆

"When we went back to work in September, there was a looseness—there was an intensity but there was also a looseness," said Landau. "It opened up and everybody was shooting their mouth off. Everybody, including Bruce, sensed, 'Hey, we gotta figure a way to pull this all together and get it off our backs.' And we gradually just sifted through the material in the fall.

"We started gravitating very clearly back to a lot of the earlier stuff. Bruce was totally open-minded to it at this point: It's all on the table, anything's possible now, let's work until we're done. He took a lot of those songs and toyed with them and sort of tweaked them and, I think, brought them more up to date with his sensibility. He was more willing to look at some of that older material and say, 'Gee, maybe it's not the song or the track; maybe there's just something in the arrangement where if I can move it from here to here, it's gonna sit a little more comfortably for me.' And he wrote a couple of songs and he went and he did those."

In November Bruce took the band into the studio without Landau and Plotkin to record two songs, "No Surrender" and "Brothers Under the Bridges." Both songs are basically "Bobby Jean" turned inside out. Rather than dwelling on an old friendship at the moment of disintegration, Bruce's new songs surveyed the entire relationship and the values that can grow out of intense adolescent friendships and high school promises rashly made. Both songs obviously reflect the departure of Steve Van Zandt from the E Street Band, but "No Surrender" is by far the more effective.

"No Surrender" recapitulates not only an adolescent friendship but a whole style of recording. Working as his own producer, Bruce came up with his first "wall of sound" arrangement since *Born to Run*. "No Surrender" emerges as (barely) updated Sixties trash rock, far from the crisp electronics of the other *Born in the U.S.A.* tracks: Thunderous drums and surging washes of guitar support a vocal chorus straight off a 1965 Searchers' album.

The song's declaration of faith in the transformative power of rock and roll struck some as naïve, which was fair enough. The song was written as a character study but was clearly an intimate portrait of Springsteen's own values (an idea reinforced by his repeated dedications of the song to the absent Van Zandt during the 1984-85 tour). It's really a last gasping breath of innocence from a rocker who has embraced adulthood. But juxtaposed with the newer sounds and curdled optimism of "Bobby Jean," Springsteen's other recent song, "No Surrender," became a restless farewell, mingling a sure knowledge of the inadequacy of idealism with a stubborn refusal to renege on ideals.

In that way the song resembles not "Bobby Jean" but "Born in the U.S.A." "Born in the U.S.A." is the anthem of a man who has surrendered to adulthood; "No Surrender" outlines the convictions that sustained him long enough to make that decision. Once that connection is made, it seems not only sensible but inevitable that these characters "learned more from a three-minute record than we ever learned in school." And it's the very vividness of his teenage recollection that makes Springsteen believable in the final verse, where he sums up his rock and roll dream:

Now on the street tonight the light grows dim, the walls of my room are

  closing in

There's a war outside still raging

You say it ain't ours anymore to win

I want to sleep beneath peaceful skies in my lover's bed

With a wide open country in my eyes and these romantic dreams in my

  head

Brash as it is, "No Surrender" is perfectly confident as it lays out a purely "childish" set of values and acknowledges their continuing currency in adulthood. This is exactly the sensibility for which *Born to Run* was criticized, which means that "Bobby Jean" meets head-on the issues that had set Bruce to asking such hard questions of himself in the first place. Like the guy in "Born in the U.S.A.," he found himself running down the same road he'd always been on, albeit with a new look on his face.

Confident as he may have been, Springsteen was still unsure exactly which songs belonged on the record and what their sequence should be. The way that he makes records, those two steps—selection and sequencing—are the essence of the job. As Roy Bittan once said, "Bruce will throw a hit record off an album, as he did when we recorded 'Fire,' and everybody agreed 'Fire' was one of the best songs he wrote for that album. But he would not put it on because it's not what he wanted to say with *Darkness*. Ninety-nine percent of the other artists in the business wouldn't *think* of doing something like that. But to Bruce, what he says is more important than the commercial benefits he could gain from the commercial material. That's the story. That's how he does it. And that's why his albums stand up so well. That's why ten years from now people will be able to play those albums and those albums will say something."

But Springsteen got away with such tactics only because his gifts were so broad. "The guy's a great writer, he's a great singer, he's a great player, he's got great arrangement ideas," said Plotkin. "It's not like producing somebody else's records, where all of those things occupy most of your time and energy and you just cut whatever damn songs the artist can come up with. Most people write eight or nine acceptable songs and that's your album. But with Bruce, there is *no song* that isn't dispensable, in and of itself. And what you're always looking for is, What are we up to with this? What is he saying? What's the guy on about this year? What connects these things?

"With 'Born in the U.S.A.,' the night he cut it, we knew we had just started the album. On *Born in the U.S.A.*, he actually found what he was going to be going on about before he even recognized it as such."

"When people wonder about what goes on when you make a record for two years, this is what goes on," said Landau. "In other words, the main thing that does *not* go on is taking one song and overdubbing on it for three months to get it. Earlier in Bruce's career, we sometimes did that. But the process now is the creation of this huge mass of material and then the incredible complexity involved in sifting through it and ordering it and finally creating an album. Because that is what we are doing—we are making an album.

"In other words, are there songs that are not on the album that, if compared in pure isolation—song X to song Y—might it be possible that song Y, which is not on the record, might be in some sense a better song than song X, which is on the record? Yes! But that is not the discussion. The discussion is what plays best as an album—where's the unity, where's the balance of forces? That song that's not on there might have been one ballad too many or it might have been one rock song too many. And if we had that instead of the song we might take it off for, it might have tipped the overall emotional weight of the side away from where we really want it to be."

So crucial was this process of selection and organization that even once recording was essentially completed there was a fair amount of disagreement about what the record consisted of. Landau and Plotkin both felt that the best possible album would build around the core material recorded in May 1982. Bruce hoped to use more of the 1983 stuff. The difference was extremely significant, not because it meant much commercially—as Jimmy Iovine once remarked to Landau, in order to sell, all the album had to be was "Born in the U.S.A." and nine other songs—but because the material created with "Born in the U.S.A." had a cohesion of music and ideas that simply didn't exist among the songs from the other sessions. Certainly, nothing else fit so well with "Born in the U.S.A." and "Glory Days," which for Bruce were always the cornerstones.

Failing to persuade his coproducers, Bruce adopted an oblique stratagem. For the first time ever, he solicited a wide variety of opinions about song selection. The band was polled on its choices, which was the first time *that* had ever happened, but even more outlandish was Bruce's decision to solicit the opinions of assorted crew members and friends. Springsteen's penchant for secrecy made each of his projects something of a mystery even to insiders. Because some exciting songs didn't belong on any given album—though, as "Darlington County" from 1978 proved, they might linger long enough to find their place— it was risky to have anyone hear them out of context. Now Bruce had not only decided to play about twenty assorted songs for people outside the production process, he was also inviting his friends to list their choices, in sequence if possible.

One by one, he brought folks to his little house on the Navesink River. Seating them at a small table with the notebook in which he kept his lyrics spread out before them, he'd plug them—and sometimes himself—into a Sony Walkman Professional and play selections from half a dozen cassettes containing rough mixes. Then he might leave them alone with the songs for a time while he ran errands or simply got out and ran his daily six miles. When Bruce returned, a short discussion ensued and then the moment of truth, listing the picks. Turning to the back of the notebook, he would inscribe each person's selections.

Bruce took the process very seriously, although exactly what he got out of it is anybody's guess. Maybe it was just another part of shedding his isolation. However intently he listened as each of his friends and associates told him what should be on the record, surely no one had the impression that he was going to put out what *they* wanted. On the other hand, it was his willingness to hear everyone out that was the point. As Chuck Plotkin said, "Just because you're bright and independent and self-possessed and self-contained and ambitious, that doesn't necessitate your locking everyone else out of your processes." That was something Bruce had always believed, but it was only now that he seemed open enough to really try to make it work. Though the final choices had to be his, he paid attention and that by itself was rare for any artist. And who knows, maybe the popularity of "Cover Me" in the listening sessions helped put it on the record, although it's more likely that sheer quality and everyone's months of plugging got it over.

"When we went back in the studio that fall, the process was very focused," said Landau. "We put all this stuff on the table—a tremendous diversity of material—and we just kept playing all the different things, and over time there was a fairly natural consensus to go back [to the 1982 songs] because basically everybody involved came to feel it was the best stuff. It wasn't an ideological process at all. Hey, if there'd been more 'Bobby Jean's' from that late group, that's what would be on the record."

But Landau also felt that the early material asserted itself because of an intrinsic superiority. "The beauty of the *Born in the U.S.A.* group was that it had internal balance. I mean, we start with 'Born in the U.S.A.'—this is so intense—and then 'Cover Me'—although it's pop on the one hand, it's in a minor key and it's very dark; the lyrics are very serious. You say, 'Well, we need some relief.' Well, you get 'Darlington County.' It's already there; a great deal of it is there."

By Christmas they were ready to start final mixes of the fourteen or fifteen songs still in contention. The process of final mixing is so delicate that outside ears are always called for. As a result, specialist mixing engineers had emerged within the major recording studios. However, because of his technical unorthodoxy and the availability of Chuck Plotkin, Springsteen had never worked with one. But Plotkin had been involved with the recording on this album from the beginning and was far too intimate with the music to provide the necessary perspective. So they worked with Bob Clearmountain, the best-known mixer in Manhattan.

Clearmountain was a perfect choice. A former bassist and mathematics whiz, he is among the most musical engineers in pop music history. Originally based at the Power Station, which came to prominence in part because of his presence, Clearmountain earned his reputation working with Chic (Bernard Edwards and Nile Rodgers), who made some of the most high-tech recordings of the early Eighties, and with the Rolling Stones, who made some of the least polished. Clearmountain works fast but achieves remarkable results: extremely well-defined bass and electrifying drum sounds and vocals that are clearly intelligible and superbly integrated into the band sound. The latter was especially important in this instance because Bruce's records had often suffered from murky vocal mixes; not because Springsteen wasn't a good singer but because he was reluctant to fully expose his voice. Clearmountain knew just how to achieve the necessary balance between clarity and cover-up.

Yet as the mixing progressed, Landau remained uneasy. It struck him that even though they'd made an excellent record, it suffered from some of the same commercial flaws as Bruce's earlier albums. For instance, although there were plenty of hit possibilities, there was no sure-shot opening single. Equally important, the album lacked a clear picture of Bruce Springsteen at that moment. Clearly Bruce had undergone a great many transformative experiences since *The River*—or even *Nebraska*—but these weren't reflected in the songs they'd assembled for the new album. Even the newest material, "Bobby Jean" and "No Surrender," looked back rather than forward.

From the time they'd returned from the late summer break, Landau had adopted an unusually aggressive posture, something that only the manager/producer/best friend could do. "Part of Bruce's whole thing with Jon is that he has to bang into Jon," observes Plotkin. "Because

Bruce is Jon's exclusive client, Jon really does get to take the position, 'Look, Jack, this is my career, too. I've spent the last three years of my life on this. Chuck made a Bette Midler record; everybody else has other things. But this is my record, too.' He gets to say things . . . He doesn't have to say, 'Bruce, you don't want to do this. You don't want to put out a record without an obvious opening single after all this time.' He just says, '*I* don't.' " It's not quite that easy, but the point is well taken nevertheless.

"I felt like, 'Let's get on with it now.' So I started to behave somewhat differently than I have in the past. At this point, we'd been working together for so long that I just felt I could say things in a real direct fashion. Bruce knows that I know that he's always gonna make his own decisions; I'm gonna participate in them but he's gonna make them in the final analysis. And I'm gonna respect them, whatever they are."

In March, toward the end of the mixing sessions, Springsteen, Landau, and Plotkin spent a long Sunday reviewing everything they'd accomplished so far. It was an impressive body of work, and with the late substitution of "I'm Goin' Down" for "Pink Cadillac" (which was bumped to become the B side of the first single), they'd finally reached complete consensus on the song selection. Late in the afternoon, Plotkin left for the studio. Jon and Bruce would meet him there later that evening. Sitting with Bruce in Springsteen's room at the Lyden House, the East Fifty-third Street residential hotel where Bruce and Chuck had been periodically holed up since the previous summer, Landau blurted out what had been bothering him about the record.

Bruce recalled that Landau spoke "unusually forcefully," an understatement by Jon's own account. Landau wanted a first single, and by that he meant more than just a guaranteed hit. "When I used the word *single*, in my own mind I meant it in a much bigger sense. The type of single I was talking about was a single that would truly represent what was going on. And I was also searching for a way to express the idea that I wanted something that was more direct than any one thing that was on the record. As I said to Bruce, a song where a person who is a Bruce fan, who stayed with you on *Nebraska*, even if it was mysterious to him, a song where that guy's gonna say, 'Yeah, that's Bruce; that's what he's all about, right now, today.' "

"I don't have a song like that," Bruce said. Landau persisted, arguing his case strenuously and in great detail. "I don't know if I was doing it to be provocative or what. I was just doing it. I was saying things I hadn't planned to say," he remembered.

Springsteen balked, then exploded. "Look," he snarled, "I've written seventy songs. You want another one, *you* write it."

Landau took it on the chin but got in the final punch: The point wasn't just that he wanted such a song—although he frankly admitted that he wanted this as much as Bruce had wanted *Nebraska*—but that the album *needed* it, that it would be artistically incomplete until such a song existed.

By the time they left for the studio, Landau and Springsteen had calmed down, but both found the experience "weird," mostly because neither of them was given to such emotional roughhousing, at least not with each other. "It was a very explosive few moments, and it subsided very quickly and we went off and worked on the mix," said Jon. "It was as close as we get to almost the atmosphere of an argument, but it didn't hang in the air at all."

But later that night, alone in his hotel suite, Bruce found himself replaying the discussion. Sitting at the end of his bed in those hours before dawn that he still treasured most deeply, he picked up his acoustic guitar and began to strum a simple riff. He'd already thought up an opening line: "I get up in the morning," he sang and stopped. No, he thought, *I* don't wake up in the morning. What do *I* do? "I get up in the evening," he sang softly and thought, Well, how do I feel about that? ". . . and I ain't got nothin' to say/I come home in the morning, feeling the same way/Man, I ain't nothin' but tired, tired and bored with myself."

Telling the story even a couple of years later, Bruce still seemed a little bit in awe of what happened next. "It was just like my heart spoke straight through my mouth, without even having to pass through my brain," he said. "The chorus just poured out of me."

You can't start a fire, you can't start a fire without a spark

This gun's for hire, even if we're just dancin' in the dark

By sunup Landau had what he'd asked for: a song that summed up Bruce Springsteen's life in that moment. It was exactly what the album needed. But it was more—the most directly personal excavation Bruce had extracted from himself since "Born to Run," a song whose intimacies ran bitter and deep. Even the song's quotations from rock and roll classics were cuttingly ironic: Bruce Channel's mournful "Heeeey, baby!" and Elvis's "Have a laugh on me/I can help" each mutated into a statement of frustration.

In a way, the song was about everything Bruce had withstood since *Nebraska*. Through it all, Bruce's songs remained stoically philosophical. In "Dancing in the Dark" he finally let his bottled-up confusion explode. Through its verses, "Dancing in the Dark" sounds not so much bitter or angry as just plain *irked*, ticked off at events.

When he recorded the song, Bruce snapped off every line as if it were so brittle it might well shatter, and as if he didn't give a damn. Lonesome as some of those lines were, they were aggressively sardonic, too. "I wanna change my clothes! my hair! my face!" he cries, bemoaning "livin' in a dump like this," attacking his own loathing and fear of aging and responsibility and competition and the unending tug of each of these things. "Dancing in the Dark" becomes a jeremiad, as well as a replay of his rancorous discussion with Landau, this time with Bruce playing both roles. Juxtaposed against "You can't start a fire without a spark" is the rejoinder: "You can't start a fire, worrying about your little world fallin' apart."

This was a protest song worth keeping—a marching song against boredom , a battle cry against loneliness, and an accounting of the price the loner pays. And on top of that, it's also the moan of an extremely physical person who can't wait to hit the road again: "There's somethin' happenin' somewhere/Baby, I just know there is," he sings, and again, "I'm dyin' for some action." He was well on his way to finding as much as he—or anyone—could handle.

◆

Landau asked for a song about how Bruce was feeling. Bruce responded with a record that was about how he felt the second the song was proposed. In a way, "Dancing in the Dark" is about being caged in by one's own creation—its genesis is the desire to finish making *Born in the U.S.A.* Oddly, however, recording it proved difficult for Bruce. The session was one of the smoothest ever for the E Street Band—that day just Bittan, Weinberg, Tallent, and Springsteen, with Clemons's saxophone solo added later. But it came out as a record dominated by Roy Bittan's synthesizer and the supple drumming of Max Weinberg, while Bruce thought the song should be led by guitar. Over the next several days, he tried a variety of approaches to make it work that way. "In the end, it was just like any child," he said. "It was gonna be what it was gonna be, no matter what I wanted." Springsteen surrendered and the record was done.

The sequence quickly fell into place and changed little after mixing began. Side One included six songs, all recorded in 1982: "Born in the U.S.A.," "Cover Me," "Darlington County," "Working on the Highway," "Downbound Train," and "I'm on Fire."

Side Two mingled material from 1982 with the work done in 1983 and 1984: "Bobby Jean," "I'm Goin' Down," "Glory Days," "Dancing in the Dark," and "My Hometown." Clearmountain finished mixing these songs in about three weeks, along with enough extras for several B sides, and they began preparing to master. And then Bruce began to reconsider. If he could just record another song or two, he suggested, the record would be much stronger.

Landau reacted vehemently. He pointed out that they'd already cut about seventy tracks, which was a ratio of about six to one. To get two more worth keeping would likely require cutting about a dozen new songs. It was pointless to wait around to see if lightning would strike. Born in the U.S.A. spoke in the unified voice Bruce wanted for all his albums. It was time to let go of it.

The conversation ran deeper than that, though. In the course of it, Landau and Springsteen talked also about all the changes that had occurred since Born to Run. In a sense, the conversation was a way of reassuring each other about the new album's potential to create a massive, really disruptive success.

From the time they'd begun, Bruce had never been sure that he wanted to release such an album. "And then, of course, Jon tends to argue for the other idea, the louder noise. A lot of the things that I'm verbalizing now were implied at the time. And I'd bring up whatever— the ghost of '75—and say, 'Oh, that was a pain.' There were a lotta consequences that Jon was arguing for. And generally I guess I felt I'm the guy that has to face 'em," he said many months later. "And I was right." He laughed. "So on one hand, this always undercuts Jon's arguments in these areas, a little bit . . . but not that much," he added, sobering up again.

Bruce's arguing position was in favor of quiet, personal music—soft noises—that satisfied him and kept his profile low; it was all he needed to do. He stuck to it as he and Landau talked the matter through not one time or ten, but over and over again for weeks. He simply wasn't sure that he wanted to be that big, that exposed.

"We had made a record that was pretty off center for me, which I think is good. And I think those records should be made and I want to make other ones. But they're not the only records to make," Bruce said. "But that's where I was left—I was left out over there. And I spent a lotta time by myself, for a long time, where I did not have a lotta contact with everybody else. So I just kinda hung out there. That was part of the problem—it wasn't really that great a place to be left hung out at. But that's where it was and so then when we began to make a new album, the whole process was one of slowly kinda moving back, until bang! I locked in, I knew what we were gonna do, I knew what I really wanted to do. So Jon's place in this is he's just kinda there coachin' me. And we do this through arguing, and sometimes I just have to say a bunch of things and then once I say 'em, they're over. I'm arguing with myself is what I'm doin'.

"Part of myself is saying, 'Hey, don't do that, why do that? It's nice like this.' And then the other part of me is saying, 'Yeah, but if you could pull this off.' And then the other side: 'If you do that, you know, you're hangin' way out there and who needs it?' I'm sure it goes on inside of anybody who's a public figure and I suppose it goes on inside of everybody to one degree or another."

It went on with special relevance around the issue of what kind of record *Born in the U.S.A.* was going to be, however. The new trend in the record industry was for blockbuster albums keyed to a string of hit singles—Michael Jackson's *Thriller*, which produced seven Top Ten hits, is the archetype—resulting in mega-platinum sales: 5 to 15 million copies (*Thriller* sold 38 million). Coupled with the heightened visibility owing to video exposure (in the wake of MTV, music video programs had proliferated from the networks to local cable channels), the result was the most intensely saturated sort of fame. Just the kind of thing that Bruce had been dodging since *Born to Run.*

As finally released, *Born in the U.S.A.* had numerous potential singles—seven of its songs became Top Ten hits and there were at least two others ("Bobby Jean" and "No Surrender") which would have had a good shot if they'd been issued on 45. Clearly, if Bruce allowed this music to reach the public, his public profile would soar, and that was something that always—and justifiably—made him skittish. One way of looking at the whole arduous process of constructing *Born in the U.S.A.* was that it was a way of avoiding the specter of such celebrity.

"But at the same time, the big question came up. I had worked hard to get through a certain door and I had an opportunity that I had created for myself."

Consciously or unconsciously, Bruce's image of standing in a doorway, trying to decide whether to walk through, again threw him into the realm of John Ford's *The Searchers*.

In that film, John Wayne spends five years tracking his young niece, who has been kidnapped by Indian raiders who massacred the rest of her family. Wayne doesn't play an uncomplicated good guy; he is an unreconstructed Confederate soldier, he is a racist, and there are indications that he may be a highwayman. Although he initially intends to rescue his niece, he decides to kill her when he finds that she's been taken as a wife by the Indian chief. But when he finally does catch up to her, after a long ride across the desert, he sweeps her up in his arms and brings her home.

In the film's final scene, all the other characters enter a house, but Wayne is left standing outside, framed in the doorway (scenes viewed through the dark side of such portals are the film's recurring motif). He adopts a noble posture, holding his left arm with his right, but the film ends with the door swinging shut on him, forever barring him from what's inside the house.

"The John Wayne character can't join the community, and that movie always moved me tremendously," Bruce said. But if the experiences *Nebraska* and its aftermath had dragged him through had any value, it was to reinforce his desire to belong to just such a community, to cut him loose from the illusion of the romantic loner, to make him understand that in real (not mythic) life, making your stand all by yourself is a miserable impossibility.

"In the end," Bruce said, "it was a variety of things that kinda threw the argument in one direction, but my feeling was that I'd created an opportunity for myself and why cross the desert and not climb the mountain?" So, at the last moment when he could have turned back from superstardom and its threatened betrayal of self, class, and quality, he pushed forward precisely because it seemed the only way to preserve those things he most cherished.

"This was '84 when this was happening and I started in '64, so that had been twenty years. And where I was at that moment was the result of thousands of small decisions that I'd made daily since I was fifteen. The decision to stay inside and play guitar, the decision to watch the band all night long instead of chasin' girls around the CYO or whatever. The decision to watch the guy's hands on the guitar. The decision to quit school, to take my chances. There were just hundreds, thousands of 'em, throughout my whole life. And we had 'Born in the U.S.A.'—we had that cut, and that was kinda sayin', 'All right, come on.'

"I knew that that particular song was just a song that comes along once in a while, even if you write good songs. It had some power to it that seemed to speak to something that was so essential, similar to the way that 'Born to Run' did. It's not that you have better songs or worse songs, but that's a particular type of song.

"And I wrote that song with an intent. I had an intent. And I put a rock and roll band together with an intent. And the intent . . . was a loud noise intent." He had been speaking soberly, but now he found himself cracking up at the very idea.

"I guess that I felt that the rock band is there for use by the public. It is a public service situation. And I felt that essentially when it came down to it, that was my idea from the very beginning, because that was where my roots came from. The people that I admired the most were people who did that or tried to do that or made that attempt. They did not back down. Or turn away. They took it as far as they could take it. For better or for worse."

Jon Landau was not insensitive to what an enormous decision he was prodding his best friend to make. On the other hand, he continued to push in that direction for a simple reason: "I believed with all my heart that Bruce could do this." As they tumbled around the issue, Jon reminded Bruce that they had created structures that could withstand everything a massive hit would bring, a protective community that would help deflect some of the superstardom mania and might absorb and productively channel the rest. It was a huge task and a bigger risk. The question was whether Bruce was ready to take it.

"Me and Jon sort of get into these types of arguments," Bruce said. "And what is happening at the moment is, the answer is already there. We're not figuring something out, really. I'm in the process of centering myself and Jon is assisting me in doing this.

"At different times in my life, because obviously you can't stay there all the time, I'll go off to this side or that side. And particularly when I'm out of contact with Jon for a long time. Basically I'm a guy [who has] extreme emotions and extreme feelings but I act right down the center, most of the time. My behavior and my actions tend to be very focused and very centered. They always have been. So I would say, Jon's daily job is essentially that he centers me. And if I get way out on one side, we may have a series of discussions and eventually I'll feel myself coming back to the middle. So at this period this is kind of what was happening.

"It gets me in contact with what my real feelings are, what I really want to do. So essentially, it came down to a pretty simple thing. In the end, as much as I hate to say it, but in the end, what we did, that was what I wanted to do. You know, even if I had very strong feelings in the other direction—and I did. And what I wanted to do was what I'd set out to do. And if I had the opportunity to do it, I really wasn't going to be able to do anything else."

In the end, then, Bruce Springsteen accepted the mass mania—and all its consequences, imagined and beyond belief—because he really did believe what his songs said, including the part that didn't just welcome everyone's participation but openly and actively solicited it. So he chose the Loud Noise, and *Born in the U.S.A.* was up and running.

◆

Then Bruce played the assembled album for Steve Van Zandt, who was back in town from his European tour. Van Zandt loved what he heard. "Just that feeling of effortlessness, which is how you picture it when you first start playing—and you wonder why you can't do it. It's so frustrating. And there it was, man—the thing that you got into it for in the first place."

But Steve was also concerned. "I think he mentioned they were thinking about 'Dancing in the Dark' as the first single. And I said, 'This is a big mistake,'" he recalled, shaking with laughter. "And he played me 'No Surrender' as a song that wasn't even on the album. I said, 'Wait a minute, you got these songs reversed. If you're gonna throw something out, throw that one out and "No Surrender" should be the first single.' That's how much I know."

Though he was clearly incorrect about the song's suitability as a first single—it would not have signaled a modernization of Bruce's music and ideas but instead would have heavily reinforced links to Bruce's past—Steve was absolutely correct that the song belonged. CBS already had the eleven-song sequence for the record, but it was quickly pulled back and remastered with "No Surrender" slotted in at the top of Side Two. "There was enough time for it on that second side," said Landau. "We just put it first; we didn't worry about 'Where does it fit?' It makes the whole side rock a little more."

Well, rocking a little more seemed to be the order of the day. In early April they turned the master over to CBS and circled three dates on the calendar: May 9, when "Dancing in the Dark" would be released; June 4, when *Born in the U.S.A.* would enter the stores; and June 29, when the tour would start in St. Paul, Minnesota.

9 STILL DANCING

The show's first set ends in a rush of light and energy, the chords of "Thunder Road" bursting open the somber mood established by the preceding songs and making a promise of better times to come. At the end, Bruce skids thirty feet on his knees to wrap himself in the arms of Clarence Clemons for a soul kiss.

Backstage during the intermission, several rock stars, a few TV celebrities, the odd movie mogul, but mostly just family and friends mill about in a tent with refreshments: a couple of bottles of wine, some beer and soda, nuts and chips. The spread is limited in quality and quantity—one is invited to visit, not linger. Without a retinue of dope dealers, this backstage encourages less lurking about and less self-satisfied and attention-grabbing behavior than any other in rock. "Welcome to the Hardy Boys," someone remarked to *People*'s Chet Flippo near the start of the tour. But the atmosphere isn't squeaky clean; it's just businesslike. And not wasteful. The food and drink runs out just about the time the second set is ready to start.

Those with more productive reasons to be here wait out the half-hour break in the show's office, which is equipped with phones and computer terminals. Until tonight, this has been a place of light banter and rare bursts of activity. With the tickets sold out so soon after going on sale—a matter of minutes in most places—and an experienced and sober crew, there simply hasn't been much occasion for tension or dramatics. Good gossip has been hard enough to manufacture.

Tonight, though, plans are afoot. Equipment has to be shipped and warehoused; plane flights home have to be arranged and next jobs located. And after eighteen months of intense comradeship, there are farewells to be made. However, most of the crew have worked together before and most will be together again. For the past year and a half, these guys have done a superbly smooth and efficient job pulling off the longest, highest-grossing tour in rock and roll history without a single untoward incident. Part of the triumph of *Born in the U.S.A.* is theirs, but tonight they look back with ironic detachment. For the crew, bread and butter is hooking up with the next tour as soon as this one's over, and they'll move on with no regrets.

About ten o'clock, somebody goes to the Xerox machine and runs off a few copies of a single sheet of paper before the show shifts into gear again. It's a written set list, composed as a nightly ritual by Bruce in his dressing room while cooling down after the first half. The list is different every night; although there's a basic structure to every show, only the opening and the closing are fairly fixed.

In part, the intermission is there to give the band time to replenish its energy. But it also gives Bruce (who is so supercharged by the show itself that he is virtually inexhaustible) the time to calculate exactly how the rest of the night should run. The second-half set list, scrawled in Bruce's looping schoolboy handwriting, puts what the night is about into focus for anyone who reads it attentively. By choosing one song rather than another—the fairy tale of "Growing Up" rather than the agony of "Backstreets," say—Springsteen expresses his sense of the occasion, his reading of the crowd. Watching Bruce work, you can feel these things, but what's amazing is that by half-time he's worked out the gestalt of the evening well enough to write it down.

There's instinct involved, but equally there is intellect. It's the blend that makes this the greatest show on earth. The set is much more fixed than it once was, back in the club days, when Bruce was liable to call off just about any song he'd ever rehearsed and the only sure thing was "Rosalita" at the close. Now, when so much else is locked in, "Rosalita" is a variable element. Bruce is just as likely to end with something else, usually "Racing in the Street." In general Bruce has two shows—one for opening nights, which tends to concentrate on anthems, and one for the second night, which has a slightly larger proportion of oddities. (In cities where the band makes longer stands, all bets are off.) As it happens, a more predictable structure hasn't reduced the show's impact; the prominence of each night's variations is enhanced *because* the rest of the show is so tightly constructed.

Springsteen gives the set list to his major-domo, Jim McDuffie, who sees that it's copied and passed around. The band studies it as hard as the *Daily Racing Form*, mostly to make sure they're prepared for any unusual songs. A number can drift into regular rotation and then suddenly be replaced by something the group hasn't done for months or even years, and when that happens it means quick changes in synthesizer presets and guitar tunings have to be made. The crew also gives the list a hard look, in order to know where to be at crucial moments. For McDuffie and a couple of other crew members, there are cues to note: when to show up with the "Pink Cadillac" blackboard, when to don the bear costumes for "Growing Up."

Ready as they'll ever be, the band again sets out for the stage, Bruce's boots clicking on the concrete ever more decisively. Tonight the band seems caught between emotions. This is the end and yet it's a show they've done hundreds of times. They are friends destined for parting; they are also professionals.

Strobe lights hit Bruce in a tableau of sweat, muscle, and guitar as Patti Scialfa creates an echoed obbligato around the words *Cover me*. As her ghostly shrieks reverberate, the rhythm section kicks in and they're off and pounding again. The second set is designed to be light—"fun"; the first set is not. But "Cover Me" offers only a hint of this transition. The song has earned its place at the top of the last half of the night, it seems, because it suggests everything that has come before. It's a last bit of blues before diving into pure release. That release immediately presents itself through "Dancing in the Dark."

◆

A Springsteen concert is an event packed with rites, but as Boss-mania developed in the wake of *Born in the U.S.A.*'s ten-times platinum success, Springsteen no longer dove into the crowds. He'd stopped doing it regularly even when he was still playing in arenas rather than stadiums, not out of fear, it would seem, but because there wasn't much mystery left to the act. Rather than serving as a way of personalizing the event, physical immersion in the audience had simply become another star turn. Yet Bruce still wanted something that physically symbolized his interaction with his listeners.

The replacement rite that evolved actually had its origins in the 1980 tour. When the band played "Sherry Darling," a frat-rock trifle from *The River*, Bruce would sweep into the front rows to pick out a girl and bring her onstage to dance with him through the final bars. It meant something quite different from Bruce leaping into the crowd. Rather than reinforcing Springsteen's stature as mythic Everyman, it suggested that stardom was as much a matter of position and good fortune as skill. But "Sherry Darling" wasn't always a regular part of the show, much less central to it.

It was music video that codified the dancer-from-the-audience as an important and inevitable part of the show.

For their first 1984 video, Springsteen and Landau turned to their friend movie director Brian DePalma, whose films were mostly in the horror and thriller genres (*Carrie, Dressed to Kill, Scarface*). Although the stylistic disparity couldn't have been more complete—DePalma specialized in the overkill Springsteen disdained—it was outweighed by the virtues of working with a talented professional who could move quickly. "Dancing in the Dark" was already out and streaking up the charts, the album was ready to come out, the tour was set to begin.

DePalma, who'd seen many Springsteen shows, got together with Landau and cooked up a story line. Three girls arrive late at Springsteen's St. Paul concert (the first of the tour), forgetting their tickets in the rush. They talk their way in, buy tour shirts from the merchandise tables in the hallway, and find themselves seated in the first row. Springsteen comes out to sing "Dancing in the Dark" and, as the song nears its conclusion, he points down at one of them, then sweeps her up to dance with him.

DePalma worked with Springsteen and the band during their final week of rehearsals at Clare Brothers Audio in Lititz, Pennsylvania. On June 28, the day before the first show, DePalma worked with Springsteen, the band, a hundred extras picked off the Minneapolis/St. Paul streets, and his own crew, shooting close-ups and further rehearsing the interaction between Springsteen and actress Courtney Cox, who was playing the lucky concertgoer.

The stage in the cow pasture below Slane Castle, outside Dublin, where the 1985 tour of Europe began. Photo: Neal Preston

Clarence and Bruce, 1985. Photo: Neal Preston

On the backstreets of Amersterdam, 1981. Photo: Jim Marchese

In search of "Paradise by the 'C'," 1985. Photo: Neal Preston

Bobby Muller of the Vietnam Veterans of America introduces Brucc at the Los Angeles
Sports Arena benefit, 1981: "When you remember the divisions within our generation
about the war, it's a little bit ironic that it ultimately turns out to be the very symbol of
our generation–rock and roll–that brings us together." Photo: Neal Preston

Left to right: Clarence, Max, Bruce, Garry, Patti Scialfa, Roy, Danny, 1985.
Photo: Neal Preston

Standing around thinking about it during the filming of the "Glory Days" video, 1985. That's Dave Marsh with the pool cue at the far right. Photo: Bob Marshak

In Tokyo's Ginza district, 1985. Photo: Neal Preston

Boarding the train to Kyoto. Later, these fans crowded against Bruce's car while it stood on the platform, cameras flashing. Springsteen shot his own photos back through the windows. Photo: Neal Preston

The Aurora is rising behind him, 1979. Photo: Joel Bernstein

With Patti Scialfa, 1985. Photo: Neal Preston

Clarence, Bruce, Nils, Garry, Patti, 1985. Photo: Neal Preston

A close call for Nils, 1985. Photo: Neal Preston

A stadium-sized "Hungry Heart" sing-a-long, 1986. Photo: Neal Preston

Independence Day, 1986. Photo: Neal Preston

The big screen, 1985.

"Ten years burnin' down the road..." Photo: Neal Preston, 1985

Photo: Neal Preston, 1985

With sister, Pam, after dancing in the dark at the Los Angeles Sports Arena, 1984

Jan Landau in Dublin, 1985. Photo: Neal Preston

Photo: Neal Preston

Photo: Neal Preston, 1985

"...but it wouldn't shut up, so I tried to strangle it." Photo: Neal Preston, 1985

Photo: Neal Preston, 1985

In Japan, 1986. Photo: Neal Preston

The world's only saxophone-playing Santa discovers a long-lost guitar-crazy elf, 1985. Photo: Neal Preston

Photo: Neal Preston, 1985

The next night, in the midst of his first show in almost three years, Springsteen opened the second set with "Dancing in the Dark," singing it with the house lights up full for the cameras, and when he was done announced to the crowd that they were making a "movie" and that he was going to do the song again. Since the single was Top Ten already, this was hardly an unpopular move, but it still struck an odd note. Never before had Bruce Springsteen allowed an outside agenda to interfere with the spirit of his shows. When Levine filmed "Rosalita" in Phoenix in 1978, his cameras were severely restricted in their movements, to prevent them coming between Springsteen and the audience. At the M.U.S.E. No Nukes shows, the filmmakers were similarly constrained. Now Springsteen wasn't just giving the camera crew free rein, he was *lip-syncing*.

Although film critic J. Hoberman later praised DePalma's "sinister cool" and the video's "perversely radical realism" in presenting Springsteen as "a heroic model worker whose infinitely repeatable—and here artfully synthetic—rite climaxes with the dramatic selection of a partner out of the front row," from a rock and roll perspective that was just the problem. As Greil Marcus wrote, "On record, the song is about blind faith and struggle; here, as the comic Bob Goldthwait put it, Springsteen looks like a member of Up with People. . . . Moving across the stage in seemingly choreographed, marks-on-the-board jerks, he grins like a supper club singer doing 'Gloomy Sunday' while communicating boundless love for the crowd. One is made to see a wide-eyed girl pressing against the stage; Springsteen takes her hand, lifts her up, and dances with her as the video fades out. From show to show, he really does this—but this girl is too cute, and the routine makes something that actually happens into something that could never happen. The next time you pay your money, enter a hall, and see Springsteen sing his songs, it will make you think the woman whose hand he takes is a plant."

DePalma took most of the heat for the video, but that wasn't fair. The fact that Courtney Cox was completely unconvincing may be pinned on DePalma who cast her. But what was really unsettling about the "Dancing in the Dark" video was Springsteen's interpretation of the song itself.

Springsteen's self-conscious dancing and his enormous, fluorescent grin simply didn't jibe with the anguish in the vocal. And that wasn't DePalma's fault. Because the track was lip-synced, what the viewer heard was the dark urgency of the song. But when Bruce took the stage and sang about loneliness, the isolation the song portrayed disintegrated in the rush of the crowd's enthusiasm and the joyous look on his face denied the feeling in the record. The "Dancing in the Dark" video snagged on the most obvious pitfall of performance film—the simple fact that a song sung in the studio means something different from one sung under hot lights before a crowd.

However, video clips are advertisements, and what "Dancing in the Dark" was selling was a whole package: the song, the singer, the show. Picking a girl from the crowd and bringing her up to dance became a nightly drama in which the crowd took great delight, and not many thought that the dancers were "plants"—certainly not the women who paid ticket scalpers hundreds of dollars and jostled for space in those front rows, all for a chance to boogaloo with Bruce.

For them, at least, it seemed to be worth it, and looking on, it wasn't hard to figure out why. As the song ended, the stage went black and then the spotlights popped back on Bruce and the dancer, sometimes carried in his arms, sometimes swooning (one night in Tokyo, the girl fainted dead away), sometimes prancing too wildly to be held. Standing at the side of the stage one night at the Meadowlands arena, you could read the lips of the teenage girl he'd dragged aboard as she grabbed Bruce by the shoulders and pulled him close for a kiss. "I love you *so* much!" she gushed, then blushed and buried her face in her hands. But she'd only blurted out what all the others were feeling. Springsteen was supposed to sound downhearted in the face of *that*? Confronted with so much love, summoning just the memory of downheartedness was already an accomplishment.

◆

Tonight, "Dancing in the Dark" rides in straight off "Cover Me," one riff picking up from the other, a smooth yet abrupt transition from gloom to joy. Lately, Springsteen has been singing the song's blackest lines into the same echo used on "Cover Me." "You sit around gettin' older. . . . I wanna shake this world off my shoulders . . . there's a joke in here somewhere." Such morbid phrases rattle around the Coliseum for several seconds before the band kicks in, the echo drops out, and the real action starts. The song is now faster and looser than on record,

Bruce hanging onto lines that he spat out in the studio. The song becomes undulating where the record is staccato, and the result is less a confession than the shadow of a memory.

At the end Bruce's voice is doubled by Nils Lofgren's wavering tenor. Then, just when the sax is supposed to kick in, Bruce picks up the mike again and declares, "Sometimes I feel . . . I get feelin' so down-hearted . . . And I wanna reach out for some inspiration to somebody who . . . Heeeey, c'mon, baby!"

But tonight, rather than reaching into the front rows, he turns to the wing stage right and pulls out Julianne Phillips, his wife of six months. Swinging her around the stage as the Big Man resolves the song with his belated solo, Bruce looks as happy as a man can be. "Had to save the last dance for her!" he declares as Julie bustles back into the wings.

But that is hardly sufficient. Having had his personal fun, Springsteen gives the spotlight over to the whole crowd with "Hungry Heart." By now the crowd knows the ritual of singing the first verse without Bruce as well as the band does, but 80,000 voices in unison are startling and powerful even when you know what's coming. More than that, this crowd is burning with a sense of occasion.

The first set must have been just a warm-up for the audience. Although the response was strong by any standard, there's a frenzied edge now, like a football crowd invigorated throughout the game suddenly discovering new resources in its lungs during the waning moments of the fourth quarter. There are hundreds, maybe thousands out there who have been following this tour since the day it started, perusing accounts of it with the kind of attention ordinarily reserved for great sporting tournaments, and like those sports crowds, they rev themselves up and transmit their ecstasy to the players, whose exploits feed it back once more.

This crowd cheers Bruce Springsteen and the E Street Band, but in many ways it's equally celebrating its discovery of itself. As 80,000 throats grow hoarse, you can feel a great sense of satisfaction being released. However fragile and artificial it may be, right now this great spirit of community feels better than anything else in the world—especially in a world that spends so much time claiming that community is impossible to create. The rest of the show is turned over to celebrating the realization of the truth.

◆

Whatever else it may be, *Born in the U.S.A.* is Bruce Springsteen's friendliest record, welcoming everybody along for the ride. Of course, a lot of the journey is through scary and depressing territory, where friends fall along the wayside and lovers time and again turn cold shoulders, but that doesn't destroy the sheer thrill of making the trip.

This isn't necessarily Springsteen's best album. A strong case can be made for the stylistic unity and raw emotions of *Darkness on the Edge of Town* or for the excitement and innocent exploits of *Born to Run*. *Born in the U.S.A.* is more diverse than unified, and alongside the two finest tracks Springsteen has ever created—"Born in the U.S.A." and "Dancing in the Dark"—is the weakest song he's released since the second album, the incredibly sloppy "Downbound Train." (The protagonist's three jobs in five verses are only symptomatic of its problems.) From peak to peak, however, this is the boldest music Springsteen's ever made. "Born in the U.S.A.," "Cover Me," "I'm on Fire," and almost the entire second side update his sound, working in synthesizers and more contemporary rhythms so subtly that the transition goes all but unnoticed until the unmistakably modern "Dancing in the Dark," the album's eleventh track, kicks in.

Partly, this is just the result of what Chuck Plotkin called "the craft issue." "Bruce is a better record maker now than he was ten years ago. It's as simple as that. Recorded music is an art form; he's working in a medium, and I think he's grown enormously as a record maker," the producer told *Billboard*. From the standpoint of performance and production, that's certainly true. Roy Bittan's subtle use of synthesizers and his always magnificent piano playing, Max Weinberg's more fluid drumming, and Garry Tallent's supple bass work give these tracks a groove strong enough to match Springsteen's perpetual drive, and Clearmountain's mixes make what's going on brighter and more exciting. This lets Springsteen get away with even his slightest songs, far more than he'd been able to do on his previous three albums—compare "Darlington County" to "Cadillac Ranch," its sound-alike from *The River*. The result is an album that appealed to many who found his earlier, more elaborately anthemic records portentous. Springsteen had finally let loose his pop songs, with the attendant explosion of hit singles and celebrity trappings.

Although *Born in the U.S.A.*'s surface is hard rocking and joyous, the record begins and ends with songs about national tragedies, and in between there's not much solace. Muddled love affairs abound, from the bottled-up heat of "I'm on Fire," *The Postman Always Rings Twice* of rock and roll, to the frustrated horniness of "I'm Goin' Down." In both "Darlington County" and "Working on the Highway," everything seems swell until the very end, when the boom is decisively lowered. Despite its giddiness, "Glory Days" is as much about the fear of death as anything on *Nebraska*, while the rhythmic exuberance of "Dancing in the Dark" is just a frame for the depiction of an artist's nightmare. Throw in the shutdown friendships and closed-down dreams of "No Surrender" and "Bobby Jean," not to mention "My Hometown" and "Born in the U.S.A." itself, and you've got an album that's more painful than "fun."

Then again, Springsteen's willingness to leave the story wide open signified how much he'd changed. And that's the real story of *Born in the U.S.A.* From *Born to Run* through *The River*, Springsteen's records spoke through a series of characters whose vulnerability was somehow exactly what made them indomitable. Those folks maintained their integrity *no matter what*. The alternative (glimpsed only rarely and in passing through such songs as "Racing in the Street" and "Jackson Cage") was a spiritual death no less immediate than a wreck on the highway.

On *Nebraska*, the everyday characters Springsteen had worked so hard to bring to life with dignity were dragged down and distorted by forces so far outside their control that vulnerability was an obscenely inadequate description of their condition. Joe Roberts, the highway patrolman, and that little kid in "Used Cars" aren't just subject to pain, they're animate wounds. Now, on *Born in the U.S.A.*, the characters partake of all this experience. Even the best of them can be vanquished, and integrity is any thing but an unquestionable attribute—after all, the guy in "Darlington County" rides right on by his buddy Wayne's arrest. But these characters aren't the bizarre manifestations of good and evil found in *Nebraska*. They're just folks again. Even though you could halfway imagine the guy in "Born in the U.S.A." as Frankie, the bad brother of "Highway Patrolman," nobody here starts that low in the pit, much less as far down as the guys in "Atlantic City" and "State Trooper." And that's exactly why, when these people get kicked around, they stay down for the count.

"Foreman says those jobs are goin', boys, and they ain't comin' back," and that's final. The thirty-five-year-old father who sings this central message in "My Hometown" talks of moving on, but he imagines no way out, for none exists. It's not like there's some town out there unaffected by all the things that have happened in his hometown. And unlike the gas-guzzling dinosaur of "Ramrod," he's mature enough to know it.

In the face of such circumstances, the defiant slogans of "Badlands" and "Thunder Road" would seem worse than false; shouting them now would have been a betrayal of everything that sticking to those slogans had taught Bruce Springsteen. It wasn't that statements like "It ain't no sin to be glad you're alive" were suddenly untrue, but that the inadequacy of such incantations by themselves was now exposed.

There is a progression of understanding embodied in "Born in the U.S.A.," particularly in those haunted final lines: "I'm ten years burning down the road/Nowhere to run, ain't got nowhere to go." The speaker is a Vietnam veteran, but given his Motown allusion and the highway imagery, he's also unmistakably Bruce Springsteen.

That progression—call it growing up—is also embedded in the sequential structure of the album, which moves forward by oscillating between the desperate and the hysterical. "Cover Me" melts into "Darlington County," "No Surrender" becomes "Bobby Jean," "Glory Days" slides into "Dancing in the Dark," and that story erodes into "My Hometown," as if each speaker stopped the preceding one to say, "You think *you've* got problems."

It's tempting to see a basic contrast between the May 1982 material that comprises most of Side One and the later songs that make up the bulk of Side Two. But while there is a contrast, it goes back to the central 1982 songs, "Born in the U.S.A." and "Glory Days." At its heart, the difference is this: On Side One Springsteen sings through a variety of characters to whom he bears some relationship. On Side Two he most often sings as a version of himself. Side Two of *Born in the U.S.A.* is as personal as Springsteen's music has gotten. You can feel the transition edging in with "I'm on Fire," which closes Side One, and of course, Side Two opens with a restless farewell, "No Surrender," followed by a resigned one, "Bobby Jean."

The contrast is greater, though, the farther afield you gaze. Compare *Born in the U.S.A.* to earlier Bruce Springsteen albums, and you'll see as much difference as similarity. You can make a connection between the runaway kid on the bike in "Born to Run" and the middle-aged man in "My Hometown" or between the optimistic innocent of "Thunder Road" and the Vietnam veteran of "Born in the U.S.A.," but you can also see the discrepancy. Did the veterans of *Born to Run* fall so far? Did the expectations—much less the experiences—of the survivors of *Born in the U.S.A.* ever rise so high?

Move out a bit farther and try to fit these songs into the history of rock and roll. There is nothing about youth or juvenile experience in these songs. Almost every track on the album speaks of the experiences of young people but in the voice of someone much older and more experienced. The only teenage situation, in fact, is "I'm Going Down," and that song is written and sung with much more detachment and composure than any real teen could hope to bring to it.

The continuity lies elsewhere. *Born in the U.S.A.* is peppered with allusions to rock and roll history. Some of the links are obscure, as in the passing reference to Martha and the Vandellas' "Nowhere to Run" at the end of "Born in the U.S.A." and the pickup of a title from Chuck Berry's "Downbound Train," or the allusion to Bruce Channel's "Hey, Baby," which provides the most grievous motif of "Dancing in the Dark." But others are unmistakable; the titles "Born to Run" and "Born in the U.S.A." are similar by design, just as they're purposely similar to other titles: Chuck Berry's "Back in the U.S.A.," any juvenile delinquent's tattooed "Born to lose." In a way, that's exactly what *Born in the U.S.A.* is about: people who have lived out every note of rock and roll, who have believed in its promises and threats and have tried to live them out, and what happens when they grow up. That isn't the only difference between the parent and soldier of this album and the reckless youth of its 1975 predecessor, but it's the most important difference.

And yet the best way to understand the development of the central theme of *Born in the U.S.A.* isn't to explode the record outward but to focus inward at just "Born in the U.S.A." and "My Hometown." Chuck Plotkin was right: The whole story *is* in those two songs. The former is melodramatic and distanced from anything Bruce Spring-steen might ever have been (except in his worst nightmares). "My Hometown," just as much a fantasy of a life Springsteen never lived, is much more matter-of-fact, and despite its acceptance of a miserable reality, it's much more astute about the way things happen. In "My Hometown" broader, more material forces are at work, and even if the singer doesn't name them, he identifies them. Just as "Born in the U.S.A." contains the answer to the question implicit in "Reason to Believe" ("nowhere to run, nowhere to go," but you keep burnin' up the highway anyway), "My Hometown" extends "Born in the U.S.A.": When you take a good look around, you plant your feet—but that doesn't mean you can stop running.

This is a realm where the political and psychological come together in a grinding crunch. Too crazy to think straight, the poor fool in "Born in the U.S.A." finds himself dragged into a brutal and senseless war. Dwelling on what's been happening to his family and his town for generations, the discarded workingman of "My Hometown" feels every constant factor in his life wrenched apart. Both find themselves someplace they've never been before and without any choice but to accept it—for the time being. In the end, *Born in the U.S.A.* is about exactly the things that had plagued and preoccupied Bruce Springsteen for the past few years. If this isn't what made it popular, it's certainly what makes it fascinating.

◆

More than most albums, what *Born in the U.S.A.* meant depended upon how it was heard. Because its themes would later be misappropriated by politicians and their stooges, it's easy to forget that the record had a separate life in the hands of rock fans, who struggled to make sense of what it had to say or found their senses swept away by the pounding beat. Some waved flags, some just danced past them, a few fought their way deeper.

What Springsteen's massive audience, old fans and new, thought, we can only guess. There were soon far too many of them to hazard a survey, and even when they came together for the concerts, there was no way of knowing if those sufficiently fortunate and well-heeled to get tickets were representative—or if so, of what. But if we can trust those who wrote about the record—at least those who wrote about it early, before it became the thing to do and general-interest windbags from Leon Wieseltier to Jack Newfield chimed in—then *Born in the U.S.A.* managed to dissolve some feelings of isolation, and in the heyday of the hegemonic semipopular (Ronald Reagan's "landslide" was achieved with the votes of less than a quarter of the eligible electorate), that was also a welcome relief.

No song could have been more wildly misread than "Born in the U.S.A." Jingoists took its superficial salute to patriotism as an assertion of dumbskull pride and latter-day revisionism; too many on the left, domestically and internationally, grasped at the same straw. Yet to anyone who listened attentively the story was clear. As critic Greil Marcus wrote, "The song is about the refusal of the country to treat Vietnam veterans as something more than nonunion workers in an enterprise conducted off the books. It is about the debt the country owes to those who suffered the violation of the principles on which the country was founded, and by which it has justified itself ever since. In other words, the song links Vietnam veterans to the Vietnamese—or rather (because when he is on, Springsteen personalizes everything he touches), one veteran tries to make the link."

The key to "Born in the U.S.A." is its third verse—the incomplete, almost muttered verse in which the Viet Cong win the war: "They're still there, he's all gone." Springsteen isn't concerned that America lost; even Rambo knows that story. His concern is the lives that were lost and the facts that aren't being faced. It's hard to think of another postwar work of art in which the basic, irreducible fact of the war— that the Vietnamese won—is so plainly and forcefully stated.

In just the same way, after Ronald Reagan's attempt at expropriating Springsteen's image in a Hammonton, New Jersey, campaign speech, many leftists were confused about Bruce's nonconfrontational rejection of the President's kudos—he didn't make a speech, he just changed the way he expressed his ties to those the President despised. Yet at least one rock critic understood this perfectly. "I don't think the difference between the America of Ronald Reagan's landslide and the America of Laurie Anderson and Bruce Springsteen and Prince has anything to do with ideology or even values," wrote Steve Erickson in the *Village Voice.* "I think the difference is that Reagan's landslide was a colossal act of faith while these rock and roll records are, for the most part, acts of doubt—acts, I should say, of aggressive doubt. . . . Springsteen's record and tour find doubt and faith locked in protracted negotiations with no settlement in sight; the tour in particular seemed less a religious revival than a state of siege. Whether his fans get that same impression, I don't know. The media this year decided that Springsteen's importance as an American artist had to do with blue-collar economics; I think his importance has to do with the idea that doubt might be the antibody that saves a soul wracked by the toxics of blind faith."

This is true enough, as far as it goes, and prophetic, to boot, given what Springsteen had to say about "the toxics of blind faith" in the introduction to his 1986 hit single "War." But Steve Erickson and Greil Marcus are also a part of "the media," and they were far from alone. The great majority of press reviews of *Born in the U.S.A.* got most of the story right. You could almost draw a line between those who wrote about Bruce Springsteen because of his political agenda and those who wrote because they knew something about music. The music writers were the ones who got it right, and not because they ignored the politics. And this has nothing to do with whether they liked the record or not—aside from "Born in the U.S.A.," Marcus thought it "a piece of cheese." The best of what was written and discussed circled around the record itself and centered on what was happening in the environment in which *Born in the U.S.A.* existed, the environment that it helped create. This was true even of a review otherwise as single-mindedly zeroed in on musical artistry and songwriting craftsmanship as Stephen Holden's in the Sunday *New York Times.*

"If *Born in the U.S.A.* is an elegy to a vanishing breed of American, Bruce Springsteen represents a spirit that is also disappearing from our popular music," Holden wrote. "He is one of a very small number of rock performers who uses rock to express an ongoing epic vision of this country, individual social roots and the possibility of heroic self-creation. . . .

"Springsteen recognizes rock and roll as a product of the working-class culture he writes about . . . [T]his hard Saturday night party music for the common people wasn't invented to help examine the hard realities of life but to find a release [from] those realities. But on *Born in the U.S.A.*, Springsteen uses the music to do both. He has transfused rock and roll and social realism into one another, and the compassion and the surging brawn of his music make his very despairing vision of American life into a kind of celebration."

A dozen critics picked up the pieces of this story, seeing in *Born in the U.S.A.* the culmination of the long yarn that began with *Born to Run*, finding threads of continuity amid the rubble of the lives the songs described. But most of all, the music critics got it right because they were rejoicing that there was, even in the heyday of the semi-popular, a multi-platinum record that embodied more of rock and roll's virtues than its vices, a record whose mass appeal didn't cheapen either artistry or ideology. That is, critics were celebrating in Springsteen not their own good taste—many critics utterly uninterested in Springsteen or mainstream rock liked this album—but their audience's.

So more than anything, it was Springsteen's plain ability to communicate to a mass audience at all that people found inspiring. As Eric King put it in *Spin*, a magazine whose propensities unconsciously parodied the semipopular ethos, "If the '60s were supposed to be about the formation of a community that idealized rock music, Springsteen is the creator of a rock music that idealizes the idea of community."

When rock and roll criticism began—when people first began to admit, in public and in print, that they took this stuff seriously—one of its central precepts was that somehow the audience responded to the best stuff. But as time passed and some of what listeners sought out most avidly proved to be crap and some of what critics most favored was widely ignored, some critics came to revile the mass audience. But since, in the end, so much of rock's meaning derives from its use, that was a shaky position to occupy. In the end you were either a critic or fan of rock and roll, and to disdain the Loud Noise and its luxurious temptations meant surrendering the possibility that what you did would matter much.

Because almost everyone else had given up on getting through, it was impossible not to read enormous significance into Bruce Springsteen's proof that the ideal of balancing quality and success still held— if you were good enough to make it work and naïve enough to try. ("I was never much of a cynic, myself," Bruce said in one interview, almost apologetically.) People were invited to read as much into *Born in the U.S.A.* as they cared— or dared—*and so they did.* When that happened, they found out something about Bruce Springsteen and something about his audience. Those who most fully grappled with *Born in the U.S.A.* also found out something about themselves.

"I am a thirty-three-year-old man who has loved rock and pop music as foremost concerns for twenty years now, which is to say I have been fortunate to see great moments in American and English pop culture come, go, reignite and sometimes die off, in sad waste or injury," wrote Mikal Gilmore, who wrote a series of brilliant analyses of the record, the tour, and the Springsteen phenomenon for the *Los Angeles Herald Examiner.* "But when I see Bruce Springsteen reaching to his audience—to every corner of a large arena, to every mind in the hall—I find the kind of fulfillment and community that only the best friend-ships and kinships might bring one, which is to say, I see an oath of love and meaning played out with full heart."

In America, in those dark days of 1984 and 1985, when men had turned mean against one another and grubbing and greed were the order of the nation's business, such testimony was rare indeed. So Bruce Springsteen, who had himself walked cruel paths to get there, took his show back out on the road, where its spirit was needed.

PART 2

FOLLOW THAT DREAM

Here comes a banker, here comes a businessman
Here comes a kid with a guitar in his hand
Dreamin' of his record in the number one spot
Everybody wants to be the man at the top

—*"Man at the Top"*

10 NATIONWIDE

Nobody give me trouble 'cause they know I
  got it made.
Baby, I'm bad! Baby, I'm nationwide!

—ZZ Top

Bruce, photographer Annie Leibovitz, and art director Andrea Klein spent months working on a cover concept for the album. They were trying to find an illustration that conveyed the loving but critical picture of contemporary America *Born in the U.S.A.* created and yet remain distant from the rampant chauvinism frothing so heavily in the year of an American-based Olympics and the electoral coronation of Ronald Reagan. Jon Landau at one time thought of using a Jasper Johns flag painting because Johns's paintings had just the right combination of distance and respect to undercut the superficial patriotism of Bruce's title. Although that thought was never developed, it suggests what they had in mind.

Somewhere along the line, Springsteen had acquired a gigantic United States flag, and the best shots came from posing him in front of it, sometimes in action, sometimes stock-still. Springsteen and Leibovitz, formerly *Rolling Stone*'s principal photographer and a veteran of many such projects, did five or six sessions, but Bruce was uncomfortable with the result—the images were all too huge, excessively mythic. He must have understood the risk in linking his most commercial and accessible album to patriotic iconography; he needed something that worked against the mood of jingoism created in the

Carter and Reagan years but didn't push him into anything superficially "rebellious."

In the end, he and Klein settled on a picture Leibovitz disparaged as "a grab shot": Springsteen, wearing a white shirt and faded jeans with a hole in one back pocket and a red baseball cap hanging out of the other, stood with his back to the camera, his arms hanging loosely and his right leg set slightly forward, as if he were actually walking into the flag. Close cropping focused attention on Springsteen's back and, most of all, his jeans-clad ass, which had the Johns-like effect of reducing the flag to a design element. But it was still unmistakably the flag, especially with the album title spelled out in blue at the top of the frame. And somehow, even though you couldn't see his face, Springsteen was immediately recognizable, just from his posture.

That the picture effectively created the necessary distance from American chauvinism was proved by a rumor that circulated just after the album came out. Springsteen, it claimed, was pissing on the flag. "No, no," Springsteen told *Rolling Stone*'s Kurt Loder, who asked him about it. "We took a lot of different types of pictures, and in the end, the picture of my *ass* looked better than the picture of my *face*, so that's what went on the cover. I didn't have any secret message. I don't do that very much. We had the flag on the cover because the first song was called 'Born in the U.S.A.,' and the theme of the record kind of follows from the themes I've been writing about for at least the last six or seven years. But the flag is a powerful image, and when you set that stuff loose, you don't know what's gonna be done with it." Bruce was a long way from throwing caution to the wind, but his ability to live with the wide-open possibility of misinterpretation was another signal that he'd relaxed his need to rigidly control every nuance of his work and image.

Leibovitz's frustration was easier to understand when you saw the remarkable sleeve for the "Dancing in the Dark" single. It showed Springsteen in a leather jacket and black jeans, leaping in the air with his heels kicked up, a look of intense concentration on his face.

The shot happened on an April evening in an impromptu session in the basement of the house Springsteen had finally bought, a huge white-columned center hall colonial with a healthy six-figure price tag, which Springsteen referred to as "the mansion on the hill . . . the kind of place I told myself I'd never live in." It was located in Rumson, an extremely posh Monmouth County suburb, the kind of town Bruce always swore he'd never live in. He'd moved there for the obvious reason: The kind of house he wanted and needed and could afford wasn't readily available anywhere else in central New Jersey.

Leibovitz had just finished a photo session there that April evening with the E Street Band, including already-departed member Steve Van Zandt. At the end of the day; Springsteen brought out a tape of the just-completed "Dancing in the Dark."

"It was great," remembered Leibovitz. "It was the first time we heard it and it was *just great!* We had worked all day long with the band and everything, and everyone had left. We were the last people there and I said, 'Look, I just want to try one more thing. Come into the basement.' And he put on that song and he started dancing, and it was like *magic!* It was really like time stood still."

It was an ironic ending to the original version of the E Street Band, Springsteen dancing by himself to the tune of the loneliest song he'd ever written and looking locked into focus. He had to be, because there wasn't time for slacking off; the band had to be reconstituted before the concert tour could begin. Bruce could and did easily handle all the guitar parts in the studio—Van Zandt's most prominent solo on *any* Springsteen record is that brief mandolin bit on "Glory Days"—but onstage a second guitarist was essential, both to fill out the sound and because there were songs where Bruce needed complete mobility.

Springsteen had several guitarists in mind as potential replacements for Steve Van Zandt. Most of them were local people with whom he'd jammed in Asbury Park bars. He was also giving some thought to adding a woman to the group, to expand its emotional and imagistic range. But the name that kept rising to the top was more surprising: Nils Lofgren, the veteran guitarist and songwriter, who had made nine albums, first as leader of the band Grin and then under his own name.

Springsteen and Lofgren had known each other since 1969, when Bruce's band Steel Mill auditioned for Bill Graham at Fillmore West on the same night as Grin. After the *Born to Run* period, which also was the height of Lofgren's solo career, Bruce and Nils became more friendly, and for the past few years Springsteen had sat in with Lofgren whenever Nils played Jersey clubs, as he'd done several times in 1983 and 1984.

In the spring of '84, Lofgren didn't have a steady band and was without an American label, although he was on the verge of a record contract with the English label Towerbelle. Nils was a virtuoso guitarist and a more than able keyboardist, a skillful song-writer, and an effective if limited singer. But he'd never had a hit, and in the Eighties, without hits you were dead to the recording industry. (Typically, Gary Bonds was immediately dropped by EMI-America when his Springsteen-produced second album flopped.) All that notwithstanding, Lofgren and Springsteen grew more friendly as their circumstances diverged. As Bruce said, "I had spent some time with him, and I knew that he thought and felt about music and rock and roll the way that I did."

That spring Lofgren called Bruce, said he'd heard that Steve Van Zandt had left the E Street Band, and offered Bruce his services "if you ever need a guitar player." From Lofgren's own point of view, there was nothing shocking about the idea. He'd first come to prominence as a guitar and keyboard sideman with Neil Young soon after that Fillmore audition, and he'd played off and on with Young's groups ever since. But Bruce rarely formed any lasting bonds with musicians or celebrities outside his New Jersey network. Moreover, he and Nils had been perceived as rivals in the mid-Seventies because of the many similarities in the songs they wrote. It just didn't seem likely Springsteen would replace his long-time sidekick with somebody *famous*. But when you got right down to it, Nils Lofgren was the only sensible choice, because his musical skills were perfect for the job and because he had experience on superstar tours—whatever happened, he could keep it all in proportion.

In May Springsteen called Lofgren in Maryland, where Nils was staying with his parents. Bruce asked if he would come up to Big Man's West in Red Bank, where the E Street Band rehearsed, to jam with the group. Bruce wasn't proposing anything permanent but, Lofgren said, "I treated it like an audition."

"We jammed together for a couple days, and it felt good to Bruce and the guys in the band and they asked me to join," Lofgren recalled. "It was about four and a half weeks until the first show, so it was like a crash course. I basically put a ban on all music—I didn't listen to anything except Bruce's music day and night." During the weeks before the tour, he studied the band's huge repertoire with the aid of Bruce and bassist Garry Tallent, and because there were so many tunes to learn—more than forty floated in and out of the set—he kept up his studies during the first few weeks on the road.

But first he flew back to D.C. to settle his affairs. "The day that I was asked to join the band was a fantastic emotional day for me," he later recalled. "I was in New Jersey and I flew right home. And I had so much work to do, but just for that day I got my car and I just drove around town really feeling great, playing 'Dancing in the Dark' over and over again."

Lofgren was an ideal choice for many reasons, but the keys were his experience, professionalism, and virtuosity. Before inserting his own ideas, he devoted an incredible amount of time and concentration to simply mastering the parts Miami Steve had played. Even though Nils was an artist in his own right, his work with Neil Young meant he knew his role exactly. As far as he was concerned, he hadn't signed up to do a tour—he'd joined the band. "When Bruce needs me, I'm there. And when he's not working, I'll continue to do my own shows and records."

Lofgren proved to be much more than a guitar player. He even managed to fill Miami's shoes as onstage sidekick, becoming a "waifish little brother," as critic Joyce Millman put it. On "Cadillac Ranch" he took a careening solo while wearing a huge foam rubber cowboy hat with "HOBOKEN" felt-tipped on the side, indulging in leaps and flips learned during his years as a student gymnast. (For a time "Rosalita" featured Lofgren doing a trampoline flip while playing his guitar.)

Lofgren also helped steady the E Street Band's mix of personalities, partly just through his complete respect for them: "They needed all that time, ten or fifteen years, to all progress to this stage. To walk into the band at this moment is just fantastic."

Most of all, Lofgren fit in because of his empathy with Bruce's goals. "I was very surprised when he called me to come up and jam, but I definitely *wanted* the job," he said. "I've known Bruce, we're the same age, we grew up with the same music. I've always loved his music and, you know, saw his shows whenever I could, and it's just . . . it's osmosis . . . With Bruce you wind up treating those four hours [of the show] as if someone said, 'You've got four hours left on earth. What are you going to do with them?' "

For Bruce, seeing Nils fit in so skillfully must have been a relief and a joy. However much he missed Steve—and that was a lot, as all those dedications of "No Surrender" to his departed sidekick testify—Lofgren earned his highest praise: "He really brought an emotional thing to the band. At this point I think that the band is the only thing that counts. It's the emotional commitment you gotta have to get on that stage."

Nils Lofgren had it. Playing alongside the rest of the E Street Band, he helped increase it. Steve Van Zandt was never an especially eager guitarist; he was always most comfortable lying back in the shadows, playing rhythm. Nils Lofgren, a born guitar virtuoso, stepped forward to create high-profile parts, which proved particularly important on the sketchy mood pieces from *Nebraska*. That's not to make an invidious comparison. Lofgren simply brought different skills to the task than Van Zandt. But that difference was one of the determining musical factors in what the *Born in the U.S.A.* tour became.

Nils was also the band member who best expressed the reason for the abnormally disciplined backstage and offstage scene around the biggest tour of the Eighties. Some—even Pete Townshend, when he visited backstage in 1981—had criticized the Springsteen concert hall environment as too sterile, not sufficiently rowdy and sleazy for rock and roll. "Depends on what you consider is a rock 'n' roll atmosphere," said Lofgren. "The reason we tour is to do these shows. If you see it as a fairy tale rock and roll existence, you might get through two or three weeks, but you couldn't play a hundred and sixty shows over a year and a half. I won't beat around the bush. Offstage we're a boring band—normal, nice guys. If we weren't, it'd hurt the show."

As the tour progressed and Bossmania swept the land, out of all the band members it was Nils who best kept perspective, because he'd been there before, with Young in the early Seventies. Lofgren, whose parallel career gave him most reason for envying Bruce, assessed the situation without rancor, out of friendship and understanding. "Right now you've got seven or eight million people that are fanatic fans. Two years ago five or six million of them didn't know who Bruce was. There's electricity that won't ever quite be exactly like this," he said. "Nobody's happier about Bruce's success than me. I'm the guitar player in the band and we both know that and I'm happy with that. I'll just work my thing around whenever he needs me. The way it is now, it couldn't be much better."

There couldn't have been a better replacement for Miami Steve.

◆

As news leaked out that the Springsteen crew was finishing an album, the rumor mill began churning. Its best product was unquestionably columnist Herb Caen's February report in the *San Francisco Chronicle* that Bruce was the father of Nastassja Kinski's child. Springsteen and Kinski had never met.

Such outlandish tales were the result of public fascination with Springsteen's mystique, which was enhanced by his aloofness from conventional publicity machinery. CBS could never have engineered stories that preposterous, even with Landau and Springsteen's encouragement. But the label had known that a blockbuster album was on its way since January, when Landau had talked with CBS Records executive vice-president Al Teller. "Al called up to see how we were doing, just a checking-in type call," Landau recalled. "We were already mixing at that point. Generally, for peace of mind, our approach is to do things and tell people about them when we're done. Otherwise expectations get built up and then they get knocked down. It's just more civilized to wait until the end. So Al was taken by surprise because I started to tell him, 'This is how it's starting to shape up.'"

Springsteen had released commercially successful records before, but Landau already had the feeling that this album could be something much bigger. "I had a sense that certainly this was the most explosive record we would be putting out since *Born to Run*. I'm not talking about necessarily best or not best, but I just knew what its impact was likely to be. And I felt in particular that we were going to have some hit singles to a degree that we'd never had happen before. And I knew that the song "Born in the U.S.A." was something that was just . . . there was nothing like it. From the night that that song was cut, no matter what happened, sometimes at some fairly low moments where I just didn't know where the record was going, I knew that that was there."

Landau and Teller spoke again in March, the morning after the "Dancing in the Dark" session. Jon was so charged up he was practically floating.

"Well, we cut a hot one last night, buddy," Landau enthused.

"What's it called?" Teller asked.

"It's called the first single."

"Yeah, but what's its name?"

"Well, you're gonna tell me when you hear the album."

A couple of weeks later, when Springsteen and Landau played the album for Teller and Walter Yetnikoff for the first time, Teller grew excited at the first track, "Born in the U.S.A.," but reined himself in. Landau had said this one was a surefire hit. "Born in the U.S.A." was a strong possibility, but it wasn't what Teller was looking for. A couple of more times—with "Cover Me," "I'm on Fire," "Bobby Jean"—he leaned forward with a gleam in his eye.

"Dancing in the Dark" is buried, the eleventh song on a twelve-song album, which is not where you're supposed to hide the first single, but the instant Teller heard it, he knew not only that this was a strong album with a surefire first hit, but a record with the potential to become one of the biggest-selling ever released.

The multiple single possibilities on *Born in the U.S.A.* took advantage of new developments in Top Forty radio programming. Until the advent of the "contemporary hit radio" format in the early Eighties, there was almost no possibility of squeezing more than two or three hits out of even the most popular LP. Contemporary programmers, however, had decided that it was safer to program the fourth or fifth most popular track from a best-selling album than to take a risk on an altogether unknown quantity. In a time when most successful albums sold fewer copies than they would have in the Seventies, a few blockbuster LPs could break all previous sales barriers. It took at least one big single to take an album to the gold record threshold (sales of 500,000 copies) and two or three to take it to the platinum plateau (sales of a million or more copies). If you could get three or four (or more) singles, the possibilities were stratospheric: You could expect sales of more than 5 million copies, and by then, with all costs amortized, the profit percentage was extraordinarily high. The mid-Eighties saw a series of such blockbusters, spearheaded by Michael Jackson's *Thriller*, which had seven Top Ten singles and sold 38 million copies, and including Madonna's *Like a Virgin*, Cyndi Lauper's *She's So Unusual*, Prince's *Purple Rain* soundtrack, and *Born in the U.S.A.*, the second best-selling album, with eventual worldwide sales around 18 million units.

In addition to their abundance of Top Forty hits, these records and the performers who made them shared several features. Each skillfully used music video (and/or the movies) to build a broad but clearly defined image, each worked variations on older styles of rock and soul, each managed to make his or her sexuality simultaneously provocative and reassuring. On this last count, Springsteen might barely seem to fit, being commonly considered just another all-American. But scruffy outcasts have never been that welcome when you bring them home for dinner, and beyond that there was a running element of male bonding so powerful that its homoerotic undercurrent was undeniable. And, of course, there was that soul kiss with Clarence at the end of "Thunder Road." It wasn't the outrageousness of Prince or Madonna but it fit the bill.

Finally, all of them recorded for either CBS or Warner Communications, which each controlled about twenty-five percent of the American and worldwide record markets. Making the right kind of music was the irreducible base for blockbuster success, but after that you needed a marketing and merchandising and promotion army to get the records into the stores and on the radio. The result was both the greatest degree of hegemony in popular music history and also the most exciting Top Forty radio in more than a decade.

Bruce Springsteen didn't flog his records as hard as he could have, but he no longer stood in the way of his record company's marketing plans. Whereas Bruce had attempted to convince CBS that there should be no advertising at all for *Darkness on the Edge of Town*, he was willing to see the label roll out its big guns for *Born in the U.S.A.* The plan was to release "Dancing in the Dark" on May 9, a month in advance of *Born in the U.S.A.* That would not only build anticipation for the much more profitable album, it would focus radio station attention and prevent having the airplay split among other tracks even at the AOR level, ensuring that "Dancing in the Dark" would get the concentrated attention needed to fuel it up the charts. Columbia Records simultaneously began an "awareness" campaign aimed at retail stores.

On May 1 the label sent its sales and radio promotion men field kits containing a facsimile of the album cover and an announcement of the promotion campaign, emphasizing the company's heavy commitment to this project. T-shirts emblazoned *Born in the U.S.A. 6/84* were handed out to disc jockeys and record store clerks. Each CBS distribution branch got giant three-by-three-foot blowups of the LP cover for display in its record store accounts. Later in the month, as "Dancing in the Dark" swept up the charts, the distributors held advance listening parties for chain buyers and key radio programmers in eleven markets. The result was a boom in advance orders for the new album and a resurgence in sales of Bruce's back catalog.

According to Jack Rovner, Springsteen's Columbia product manager, the campaign was "designed to give rock radio stations and record stores an equal chance to climb on the Springsteen bandwagon." In fact, it was designed to make sure that nobody forgot there was a bandwagon to leap aboard.

In the late Sixties and early Seventies, when FM rock stations were considered "underground," it was commonplace for new albums by superstars—the Beatles, Dylan, the Stones—to leak unauthorized onto the radio several days, maybe even weeks before their official release. Except for the Beatles, Top Forty radio had almost never indulged in any such practice. In the Eighties, FM rock stations proliferated and became more competitive and cautious; album marketing strategies became more sophisticated and closely tied to the disc's availability in stores, so advance airplay all but ceased. Leaks were no longer arranged by zealous promotion men; radio stations were more likely to wait and see what happened than to offer sneak previews.

But in the case of "Dancing in the Dark," key radio stations all around the country jumped the gun. First on the air, on Saturday, May 7, was New York's Z100 (WHTZ), the highest-rated CHR station in the country. The city's top-rated AOR outlet, WNEW-FM, started playing its copy before Z100's had finished spinning. Both continued until Columbia's legal department sent them a "cease and desist" order by telegram. By then—it was Sunday—the record had leaked out to other stations around the country, more telegrams were sent, and the *Born in the U.S.A.* boom was off to a healthy prerelease start. Columbia wasn't heard complaining very loudly.

"All we had to do was make people aware that Bruce Springsteen was coming out with a new album," Rovner told the *Wall Street Journal*. But Columbia didn't just keep up the heat, it fanned the flames. Norman Hunter, buyer for the Carolina-based Record Bar chain, called it "the most expensive, best organized prerelease campaign I've ever seen." And Hunter was a doubter, certain that *Victory*, the album by the Jacksons (Michael and his brothers) that CBS was preparing for release later in the summer, was "going to be five times bigger and last ten times longer." (Despite a similar prediction by *New York Times* critic Robert Palmer, *Victory* sold only about 2.5 million copies and was a spent force by Labor Day. Nobody ever claimed much for it artistically.)

By May 18 record stores were loaded with posters, displays, reproductions of the record cover ("album flats"), and huge banners ("Gigant-O-Grams") announcing the album release date. On Memorial Day weekend, just five days before the album was to hit the stores, the three-by-three-foot slick of the album cover was plastered circus-poster style on walls and on hoardings in New York, Los Angeles, Chicago, Washington, Philadelphia, Cleveland, Detroit, Atlanta, Boston, Dallas, and San Francisco. The nine-and-a-half-minute "Rosalita" clip, which had never been seen in its entirety in the United States, was released to MTV, *Entertainment Tonight,* and other shows, while an MTV ad campaign also started. And on Monday, June 4, 1.25 million copies of the album were sent into the nation's record stores. Three days later, CBS had reorders for 300,000 more. *Born in the U.S.A.* entered the *Billboard* chart at Number Nine, the highest position reached by any new album upon release in two years. The next week it hit Number One. The album stayed in the Top Five for a year and in the Top Ten for several months more.

"Dancing in the Dark" faced much stiffer chart competition. It quickly climbed to Number Two but was blocked from the top spot by "When Doves Cry," the amazing first single from Prince's *Purple Rain,* a left-field movie hit. "When Doves Cry" and *Purple Rain* were the hegemonic blockbusters of the moment: newer, fresher, more revolutionary. Springsteen had reached the Top Ten with his last four albums; Prince had been there only once before. And while *Born in the U.S.A.* and "Dancing in the Dark" represented a striking evolution in Springsteen's personal style, Prince heralded a revolution (or at least a trend), leading a wave of Minneapolis-based black rockers that was still going strong three years later and paving the way for the resurgence of "black rock," like the heavy metal rap hits of Run-D.M.C.

Although it was easy to miss the resemblance, music's central heroes of 1984 also shared a lot. Among other things, both Prince and Springsteen were the product of regional isolation—practically and metaphorically, central New Jersey is as far from the media centers as Minneapolis—and both were especially interested in the collapse of domestic values.

As it happened, *Born in the U.S.A.* also became identified with a trend: the so-called American rock renaissance. In 1983 a "second British Invasion" had been ballyhooed. Now, with Springsteen, Prince, Jackson, Madonna, Lauper, Tina Turner, Huey Lewis, ZZ Top, and Van Halen crowding the top of the charts, the trend had turned the other way. It was probably inevitable that such a trend would develop that year, given the chauvinistic frenzy into which the country was whipped, first by the Los Angeles Olympics and then by the elections. Certainly, many performers—not only in music—exploited this mood, and *Born in the U.S.A.*, however critical its contents may have been, was helped along by the patriotic hysteria. The irony is that the so-called "heartland rockers" with whom Springsteen did share a great deal thematically and stylistically—Bob Seger, John Mellencamp, Tom Petty—were mostly absent from the '84 scene.

So maybe it was appropriate that the *Born in the U.S.A.* concert tour opened in St. Paul, just across the river from the town Prince called home.

◆

Bruce himself remained abstracted from the hoopla. As his record became an epicenter of pop, he simply went about his business. On May 19 he appeared at the Stone Pony in Asbury Park, where he sang "Fire," Wilson Pickett's "In the Midnight Hour," and Little Richard's "Lucille" with Clarence Clemons and the Red Bank Rockers. They topped the evening off with "Twist and Shout." That was the last show the Red Bank Rockers ever played. The next week Bruce and the E Streeters went into rehearsals at shuttered Big Man's West just up the coast in Red Bank.

A week later, on May 26, Bruce appeared with a group called Bystander at Club Xanadu in Asbury Park and sang "Dancing in the Dark" onstage for the first time. He played a lot in the shore clubs throughout the late spring weeks, as if to get his fill of the local night life he'd be missing through the months of touring ahead. On June 1 he sat in with John Eddie and the Front Street Runners (two years away from their own Columbia debut album), performing "Dancing in the Dark," ZZ Top's "I'm Bad, I'm Nationwide," Creedence's "Proud Mary," and Chuck Berry's "Oh Carol."

As the Big Man's West rehearsals progressed, so did some of the important auxiliary activities of the tour. Art director Andrea Klein and Winterland Promotions created a series of T-shirts, sweatshirts, and other "tour merchandise," including an elaborately illustrated and annotated program, all of which had to meet Bruce's approval before going into production. Bruce had accepted the need for selling his concertgoers some sort of merchandise, noting the demand of his audience for even the low-grade junk sold in the streets around his shows by "T-shirt bootleggers," unauthorized merchants preying upon rock-star images. Anyway, however superfluous such stuff might be, Bruce was at least avoiding the tug of an even more trivializing force, corporate sponsorship of rock tours, a system by which rock stars were paid to perform under the banner of consumer products (beer, cars, cologne, jeans).

Sponsorship was an issue Springsteen understood especially well, because friends like Bonds and Southside Johnny, all but ignored by radio and the record industry, had received their only recent paychecks from singing in beer commercials. Their acquiescence in Madison Avenue's post-*Big Chill* discovery of the power of rock and roll was understandable. But, as Springsteen must have known, a star who wanted to say something serious couldn't simultaneously present himself as a vehicle for flogging products or trumpeting the chimerical superiority of one brand over another.

"We get approached by corporations," Bruce later commented, beginning with a classic bit of understatement. Companies like Coca-Cola and Chrysler besieged Landau's office, proffering sums ranging from $5 to $10 million (as openers!) for the opportunity to snatch a piece of the all-American rock and roller. How much even Bruce knew about that was anybody's guess, because his instructions were that Landau's office convey a blanket "not available."

"It's just not something that struck me as the thing that I wanted to do. Independence is nice. That's why I started this—for the independence. I'm telling my story out there. I'm not telling somebody else's. I'm saying what I want to say. That's the only thing I'm selling. I had a few small jobs before I started playing, but when I picked up that guitar, that was when I could walk down my own path. That's just the way I like it. It's a lucky feeling, you know, because how many people get to set their own standards and kind of run their own circus?" He wasn't making even an implicit criticism of anybody else. Not collaborating with a tour sponsor was simply a reflection of Bruce's understanding of the luxury afforded by his own good fortune and of how that luxury ought to be used.

So the work continued as Bruce Springsteen's work, without much outside intrusion. Klein and photographer David Gahr appeared at one rehearsal for a photo session that included the shots of Bruce and the band grouped around the Sixties Chevy convertible "Dedication," a gift from Gary Bonds. Meanwhile, Nils Lofgren was living with Bruce at the Rumson house, and they studied the songs late into the night. Landau and Springsteen held frequent meetings, planning the De-Palma video, discussing various aspects of the tour, and coordinating the assembly of crew and management personnel with tour director George Travis. But Bruce also had time to relax, journeying into Manhattan one evening to have dinner with author Stephen King, for instance.

On Friday, June 8, the Stone Pony marquee again read "John Eddie and the Front Street Runners." Inside, the scheduled opening act, Eddie Testa and the Cruisers, became upset when told they were being replaced, although they'd still be paid. But Testa and his band were more forgiving when they learned why: John Eddie's show was to be followed by a full-scale set by Springsteen and the E Street Band, their first public appearance since 1981 and their first ever with Nils Lofgren.

The weeks after Memorial Day are the season in Asbury Park, so the Stone Pony probably would have been packed that Friday night to its full 1,000-customer capacity anyway. The club actually felt even more crowded. The temperature broke a hundred degrees, because one of the air-conditioning compressors malfunctioned. But as the night went on, nobody left. In fact, the lines at the telephone lengthened as one patron after another, spotting Clarence Clemons's bright brass tenor sax on the stage or catching a glimpse of Lofgren in the crowd, went to let a friend in on the open secret.

At 1:45 Bruce and the gang slammed into "Thunder Road," quickly following with "Out in the Street," "Prove It All Night," and "Glory Days," their first number from the just-issued new album. They paused to catch their breath and wipe the sweat from their eyes. "Man," Bruce gasped, "I hope I can remember the words to this song; it's been a while," then dedicated the next number, "The River," to Testa and the Cruisers.

They kicked back in with hard rockers: "Darlington County," "Dancing in the Dark," and "Promised Land." At quarter to three, the doors closed because of the liquor law curfew. "Who's here from North Jersey? Who's here from Central Jersey?" Bruce inquired. "Me, too . . . This song is a way of reminding me where I come from." They played "My Hometown" to thunderous approval and quickly followed it with "Born in the U.S.A." before closing with "Badlands." Inevitably called

back for an encore with chants of "Brooooce ... Broooooce," Springsteen responded with the inevitable "Born to Run."

That was it for the night, but on Sunday Bruce and Nils came back
to play with Cats, doing "Gloria," John Lee Hooker's "Boom Boom,"
the Animals' "We Gotta Get Out of This Place," the Stones' "The
Last Time," and "Rocking All Over the World."

A few days later they were in Lititz, Pennsylvania, doing full-dress
rehearsals with full sound and lights on the specially built stage with
which they'd tour. Later in the week they blocked out moves for the
"Dancing in the Dark" video under Brian DePalma's direction. On
June 21 the band took over the Village bar in nearby Lancaster for a
final warmup set, playing "Out in the Street," "Prove It All Night,"
"Glory Days," "Hungry Heart," "Dancing in the Dark," and concluding with "Rosalita."

Tickets had been going on sale in cities around the nation and selling out in record time. The measure of popularity for Bruce's shows
was no longer whether they would sell out or how many dates he could
play in a given town. The story was the pace at which the seats were
gobbled up. In most places the answer was a few hours. By the end of
May, tickets for twenty-nine shows had gone on sale; every available
seat was immediately snapped up at $15 to $16 apiece, and that included 201,000 seats for a remarkable ten-date stand scheduled for late
August at the Brendan Byrne Arena in New Jersey's Meadowlands
Sports Complex, the same arena Bruce had opened with five shows in
1981.

The Meadowlands tickets were gobbled up by a fanatic East Coast
audience in a bare twenty-eight hours on June 19 and 20. It took that
long only because Ticketron and Teletron couldn't spit them out any
faster. Meadowlands general manager Loris Smith estimated that demand was sufficient to have sold out thirty such shows. The $3.2 mil-
lion gross, the 16,000 seats sold in the first hour of sales, and the
29,000 seats sold by Teletron, the over-the-phone ticket agent, in the
first day were all records. (Teletron's first-day sale broke its record for
any previous *week*.) On June 19 New Jersey Bell registered 120,000
extra calls per hour through its central station in Hackensack, an over-
load foreshadowing things to come. On a slightly smaller scale, the
same story was repeated over and over in St. Paul, Cincinnati, Hartford, Philadelphia, and other cities.

The Springsteen tickets were sold with amazingly few glitches. Despite complaints by rabid fans about ticket scalping, such problems were far better controlled than in 1978 or 1981. This was in stark contrast to the other gigantic summer tour of 1984, the one starring Michael Jackson and his brothers. Promoted by figures from the sports world, sponsored by Pepsi-Cola, and playing the biggest football stadiums available with truckloads of special effects gimmickry and a huge stage that killed thousands of seats—and with a $30 ticket price—the so-called Victory tour was a public relations disaster and a financial debacle for principal promoter Chuck Sullivan, whose family wound up putting its New England-based National Football League franchise on the market to make up its multimillion-dollar losses. Part of what made Victory look so bad was the efficiency with which George Travis and the Springsteen crew ran their shows, but equally remarked on in the dozens of reviews comparing the two tours was the disparity between Michael Jackson's rote performance and Springsteen's searching one.

Bruce seemed impervious to comparison, whether it was to punks and New Wavers, to the so-called "heartland rockers," or most persistently during 1984, to Michael Jackson and Prince. Springsteen saw the Jacksons late in the summer at Philadelphia's Veterans Stadium and was impressed by what he heard. "I thought it was really a great show," he told *Rolling Stone*'s Kurt Loder. "Real different from what I do, but the night I saw 'em, I thought they were really, really good. Michael was unbelievable—I mean, *unbelievable*. He's a real gentleman, and he's real communicative . . . and he's *tall*, which I don't know if most people realize." As for Prince, Bruce was simply a stone fan, comparing the critically disparaged *Purple Rain* to "a real good early Elvis movie" and gushing over the live gigs he'd seen. "He is one of the best live performers I've ever seen in my whole life. His show was funny; it had a lot of humor in it. He had the bed that came up out of the stage—it was great, you know? I think him and Steve, right now, are my favorite performers."

Bruce was having second thoughts about the configuration of his own band. Not that there were any regrets about Nils Lofgren, but Bruce still hoped to expand the band's musical and emotional range. In the past he had occasionally performed (once done a whole tour) with a horn section, dubbed the Miami Horns as a result of Steve Van Zandt's tutelage, which later became La Bamba and the Hubcaps under the direction of trombonist Richie "La Bamba" Rosenberg. Bruce had become friendly with one of the group's singers, a redheaded Irish-Italian-American from Asbury Park named Patti Scialfa. Scialfa had auditioned for one of Bruce's Asbury groups while she was still in high school, but he'd turned her down then because she was still too young. Later Scialfa toured with Southside Johnny and the Jukes, who also used La Bamba's horn section. Earlier in the spring of 1984 she'd auditioned for Bruce again, but he'd never called back.

On the Sunday night before the band left for St. Paul, Bruce finally called Scialfa and asked if she'd like to join the tour as a background vocalist. "I wanted to tell him that I had to wash my hair, that I didn't have enough time to get ready," Patti told Steve Pond. It was virtually true—she had four days to pack and learn the show. But she said yes anyway. It wasn't the kind of opportunity a person could resist. "See," she later cracked, "you *can* meet a nice guy in a bar."

Bruce also seemed well satisfied, even though it would take some weeks to fully work Scialfa into the show musically. "It's real nice having her in the band," he told Don McLeese of the Chicago *Sun-Times* after the first St. Paul show. "It's kinda like, 'Yeah, everybody join in.' She's a local person, and it just feels like a bunch of people up there. It has a little of that community thing to it." Now his tableaus of male bonding would acquire a different dimension.

◆

At 8:37 P.M. on June 29, 1984, Bruce Springsteen and the new, expanded E Street Band raced onstage at the St. Paul Civic Center and launched into "Thunder Road." In only a few seconds, it felt just like old times as 17,500 voices joined Bruce's to complete the second verse:

> *Show a little faith, there's magic in the night*
> *You ain't a beauty but hey you're all right*
> *Oh and that's all right with me*

The song galloped to a close, and Bruce gasped, "Missed ya!" before snapping right into "Prove It All Night," which slid into "Out in the

Street," Patti Scialfa picking up Little Steven's duet lines and standing in for 10,000 female fantasies.

Bruce wore a blue shirt open to the neck and greasy jeans, the kind of uniform he'd always chosen. But the resemblance to tours past ended there. The most immediately noticeable change was in his arms—always muscular, they'd become huge, "biceps that would reduce Popeye to tears," as Joyce Millman wrote. His legs, neck, and chest had also grown to what seemed like NFL proportions.

In 1983 Bruce had begun attending a gym in Red Bank owned by physical therapist Phil Dunphy. Although Bruce claimed he'd "never exercised before in my whole life," he had always done a few things (notably, surfing) which kept him in decent physical condition. He'd never have made it through his own sweat-soaked concert marathons otherwise. On the other hand, the lingering effects of the leg injury from his high school motorcycle accident kept him limping and required frequent treatment, particularly after he was reinjured in a three-wheeler accident in 1979.

Springsteen had always been an extremely physical person; one of the things that "Dancing in the Dark" captures is how repressed he felt while sitting on his ass in a recording studio. So it made sense that he responded avidly to Dunphy's fitness regimen. Soon Bruce was doing strength and weight training and running six miles a day. He also radically altered his eating habits. ("All I knew was fast, fast food. That's all I had the dough for.") The result was a measurable increase in stamina as well as physique and a degree of dedication that included bringing Dunphy on the road as his personal trainer. As Bruce later told Chet Flippo. "It's really helped on the road. Before, I would come out the first night, and I'd almost die, wanna throw up, gaspin' for air." He was giddy and dizzy by the middle of that first night's set, but that was from the surge of adrenaline and the accelerated pace the band took in its initial excitement.

"Here we are!" Springsteen shouted after "Out in the Street." "It only took me three years. I should write, right?" Then he pulled the set back down with the first of the night's songs from *Nebraska*, "Johnny 99," performed with just drums, harp, guitar, and Clarence Clemons on pensive tambourine, following it with "Atlantic City" in a full band arrangement, with bagpipe effects reminiscent of the Celtic rock pioneered by U2 and Big Country, and a ghostly "Mansion on the Hill," introduced with words that emphasized its autobiographical nature: "This is a song about when I was a kid. My father was always transfixed by money. He used to drive out of town and look at this big white house. It became a kinda touchstone for me. Now, when I dream, sometimes I'm on the outside looking in—and sometimes I'm the man on the inside."

So the show oscillated, old songs ("The River"), new rockers ("No Surrender," "Glory Days"), and *Nebraska* numbers alternately presented as fictional ("Highway Patrolman") and as a species of autobiography ("Used Cars"). The show didn't really have a structure yet—or at least it was hard to follow the logic with which it was constructed, to fathom how each song was supposed to set up the next. (The sequencing had been the most original and unsettling quality of previous Springsteen shows.) But that wasn't surprising, because this tour presented an enormous amount of new material, far too much to digest immediately, even for someone as adept and instinctive as Bruce Springsteen. Between *Nebraska* and *Born in the U.S.A.*, there were twenty-two new songs to integrate. The band had two new players whose skills needed to be weighed and balanced with the others'. Beyond this, there were many technical differences. Everyone in the band except Tallent had the added mobility of playing with wireless amplification (and Garry would soon surrender his guitar cord, too), while Roy Bittan now played as much synthesizer as grand piano. There was a new lighting designer, Jeff Ravitz. The stage had a subtly different configuration from the one used on past tours. Bruce could hardly have known what his own new physique was really capable of. And of course, above all else, there was the altered content of all those new songs, which pushed the meaning of the show in unexpected directions—directions that often ran directly counter to the enthusiasms of the audience.

The day before, Brian DePalma had taken Bruce and the band through their paces, working with three cameras through eleven setups and several hours of repetitive shooting and posing, then polishing off the afternoon of lip-syncing with a live version of the "Detroit Medley," a sequence of Mitch Ryder and Little Richard hits. Bruce stayed cheerful and high-spirited through all that, but during the first night's show he seemed about as vulnerable and introspective as a pop star could be, struggling to find a structure for the show. The only time he projected a clear ebullience was for "Dancing in the Dark," which he ran through twice for DePalma's cameras. Although it surely had its exciting high points, moments of sheer fun, more than anything the first show of the *Born in the U.S.A.* tour was a struggle. Bruce did five songs from *Nebraska*, eight from *Born in the U.S.A.* For the most part, their purpose in the context of this performance was unfocused, cloudy, and uncertain.

Even so, there were galvanizing song sequences that came together in a radiant exemplification of what Bruce had been through and what he was pushing for. "Bobby Jean" was open, spacious, driving, *modern*, and it set up the wordless moans of "Backstreets" exquisitely. In introducing "My Hometown," Bruce put his finger on a lot of what he was fumbling to say elsewhere: "When I started playing guitar I had a couple of ideas in mind. One was to avoid all responsibility as much as I could for the rest of my life. We used to sit in bars and say, 'If I could just get this down.' The other idea was to get girls.

"Well, that idea didn't work out. Seems as you get older, you just can't get outta the way . . . I thought I was writing this song about the town I grew up in, but it turned out to be about responsibility. Whether it's done here or thousands of miles away, it's done in your name, and you share the shame and the glory." He followed that song with "Born in the U.S.A." and then, with his teeth gritted hard and staring straight into hot white spotlights, brought the first set to a brilliant, bitter close with "Badlands."

He brought the message back one more time, during the first encores, saying simply, "When I grew up, rock and roll was delivering a simple message: 'Let freedom ring!' But remember, you gotta fight for it!" then launching into a medley of "Born to Run" and "Street Fighting Man." Singing "What can a poor boy do/'Cept sing in a rock and roll band?" he emptied the question of Mick Jagger's cynical irony and brought it back home with bite.

Springsteen's reasons for choosing that song said a lot about what the show had to be and what he hoped to accomplish with it. "I just picked it out of the air a few days ago during rehearsal," he said. "It seems to fit in with the whole thing, for some reason. You come crashing down—it has that edge-of-the-cliff thing when you hit it. And it's funny; it's got humor to it.

"That's just me kinda being a fan. But that song did seem to fit in with the whole thing—with the whole feeling of the show and where it was kinda going. That one line, 'What can a poor boy do but sing in a rock and roll band?' is one of the greatest rock and roll lines of all time. It just seemed right for me to do it. In that spot of the night it just fits in there. It's just so driving, man. After 'Born to Run,' we got to go up. That's the trick. 'Cause it's hard to find songs for our encore. You gotta go up, and then you gotta go up again."

But then again, the other encores were some of the longest songs in his repertoire: the Detroit medley, "Rosalita," "Jungleland," great in themselves perhaps, but dissolving as much focus as they created. Did they take the show up? Yes, but in the end the encores became a parable of exhaustion, too damn much of a good thing.

However much instinct Bruce brought to the enterprise of each concert tour, he was clearly going to have to work hard to make this new set of circumstances reach the heights of his previous tours. To any random observer, the first show in St. Paul, so typical of the run of shows in the first few weeks of the tour, was nothing but excellent. But to the seasoned eye, it lacked the seamless, almost effortless quality of construction that earlier Springsteen concerts possessed.

You could almost imagine that Bruce wanted it that way. The show was no different than his current attitude about recordings and merchandising and publicity. All indicated that Springsteen wanted to *try things*. Control remained the central issue of his approach to his work, but now he was ready to try controlling less regimented situations; he wanted to take bolder risks.

The same day the tour began, Columbia issued a "dance mix" of "Dancing in the Dark" on a twelve-inch disc. "Dancing in the Dark" was already getting mixed reactions from the hard-core Springsteen aficionados, many of whom disdained its more limber and modern rhythms. The fact that "Dancing in the Dark" expanded Springsteen's appeal might have been just the problem from their point of view. But the dance mix, concocted by producer Arthur Baker, spun hard-core Springsteen buffs to a frenzy. As Bruce put it, "People kind of get a rigid view of certain things." Springsteen's Columbia A&R man, Joe McEwen, himself a former critic and deejay, was eager to have Baker rework the song, as he'd already done successfully with Cyndi Lauper's "Girls Just Want to Have Fun."

Baker and Springsteen were at once a perfect and a perfectly unlikely match. Baker grew up in Boston and went to school in one of that city's few integrated high schools. There he acquired an expertise in dance-floor beats totally belied by his beefy, long-haired appearance. Baker revolutionized dance music when he moved to New York and began producing records—"Looking for the Perfect Beat" and "Planet

Rock" by Afrika Bambaataa and the Soul Sonic Force and I.O.U.'s "Freez" and Planet Patrol's "Play at Your Own Risk"—ushering in an era of electronic beats and computer effects over hard-edged street raps.

Beginning with the Lauper record in 1984, Baker and his partner John Robie began remixing pop hits, radically restructuring each composition at the studio console, dismantling some sections of a song to its skeleton, doubling other parts, stretching and extending and bending the record into a danceable commentary upon itself. The result was almost a kind of computer-based rock criticism. It was also startling and a hell of a lot of fun.

Hearing what Baker was up to, Springsteen wanted in on it. "The entire thing is Arthur Baker. He's really an artist," he said. "It was fun to just give him a song and see what his interpretation of it would be. I was always so protective of my music that I was hesitant to do much with it at all. Now I feel my stuff isn't as fragile as I thought."

Springsteen wasn't dropping out of the process, though. He made sure that he was present for Baker's remix session. "Arthur's a character, a great guy. He had another fellow [Robie] with him, and they were really pretty wild. They'd get on that mixing board and just crank them knobs, you know. The meters were goin' wild. His overdubs were kind of connected to my songs. He would put in something that sounded like a glock or a twangy guitar. When I heard it, I just thought it was fun. This was kind of wild, man—this guy, he's got an unchained imagination. I thought it was real creative. You've gotta do different things and try stuff." Added Chuck Plotkin, "Some of the things that Arthur did on it we could very well have incorporated into the album version, and would have been glad to."

Baker was equally eager to work on the song. "First time I heard it, it freaked me out, because I could relate to the lyrics, and I just heard in my head all these parts that seemed to be missing." He took the master into the Power Station and rethought the song with Bruce looking on. Working with John Robie, engineer Chris Lord-Alge, and an electronic percussion team called the Latin Rascals (Albert Cabrera and Tony Moran), he overdubbed "tom-toms, dulcimer, glockenspiel, background vocals, sort of a bass synth part, a horn synthesizer part, and also some gunshots."

There was more than one purpose to creating such a mélange around *Born in the U.S.A.*'s most apposite, modern, and catchy track. As Baker pointed out, "The one last frontier Bruce has is obviously black people. I heard someone say that he had more black people on stage than in his audience." The exaggeration was very slight. Baker felt he not only knew the reason, he had the cure. "It's not like these people will come out in droves and flocks and be into Bruce, but he should realize that all these people are missing what he has to say because they can't relate to the music. Prince and all these other acts that are black but are doing rock and roll, they just know that they can relate to everybody. It isn't even a matter of selling more records, because once you're selling five million, what's the difference? It's just that it would be cool if black people knew Springsteen like white people know Prince."

As a good American populist, Springsteen was sensitive to the issue; it was disturbing, not ironic, to see exclusively white faces at a concert that was so concerned with injustice and inequity in America (a nation more than a third black and Hispanic). But populism by itself provided no solution, especially given the basic economic inequality that made even the Jacksons' tour—which presented itself as a triumph for black Americans, in that one of their own had become the world's single most popular entertainer—play to a crowd about ninety percent white.

But it wasn't just high ticket prices and low minority incomes that kept blacks away from Bruce Springsteen's shows and prevented that community from exhibiting much interest in his records. Nor was it skin color per se: Daryl Hall and John Oates, Boy George of Culture Club, and many other white singers were extremely popular with black audiences. The real dividing line was Springsteen's nervous aversion to syncopation, which he conscientiously avoided. It was hard to figure out why—whether Bruce feared some innate lack of ability in dealing with rhythmic nuance beyond a basic backbeat or whether years of trying to whip a band of white boys into shape to play with some semblance of soul had simply led him astray. If Springsteen had been more of a typical singer-songwriter, if the root of his music had been commercial folk music or even British rock, the lack of appeal would have been no surprise. But the basis of his music was soul, and in spirit, it was meant to be all-encompassing, so the lily-white composition of his crowd was a little frustrating and embarrassing.

Baker alleviated those problems with a radical restructuring of "Dancing in the Dark" that kept its darkness of mood while making the music lighter on its feet. The twelve-inch contained three versions of his work: a full-length (6:09) "Blaster Mix," a "radio" edit (4:50), and a "dub" with much of the vocal dropped out (which clocked in at five and a half minutes). The result, wrote *Newsweek*'s Jim Miller, "recasts the song as a rock and roll symphony in the spirit of 'Born to Run.'" Others compared it to the Phil Spector records on which "Born to Run" was based.

And no wonder. Springsteen now sang against an electronic background of voices and drums that exploded in the spacious mix like a bomb, with glockenspiel synthesizer effects shattering like glass against sharp guitar, his key lines—"You sit around getting older"; "Heeeey, baby!"; "This gun's for hire"—doubled, echoed, isolated, broken down to syllables, and reinforced by choral repetition. By the time he got to the last verse—"Stay on the streets of this town/And they'll be carvin' you up all right . . ."—Springsteen sounded even lonelier and more vulnerable than he did on the original track. Now when he cried, "There's somethin' happenin' somewhere . . ." there was no reassuring "baby, I just know there is" tagged on. If you listened closely enough, you found that Baker had stripped the smiling face from "Dancing in the Dark" and revealed a death's head lurking beneath, and did it in a way that pulled you from your seat to dance until breath ran out.

It was a monumental achievement, making a great record even greater. It even sold fairly well, although it won Bruce no visible long-term allegiance from the black pop audience, even after Baker did similar (and in some ways, even more striking) remixes of "Cover Me" and "Born in the U.S.A." Again, the primary reason was probably musical—in the strict sense, Springsteen's basic approach remained adamantly unswinging.

The sad part was that the Springsteen cult—by now beginning to resent its stature as a diminishing proportion of his audience anyway—liked it even less than the original. This left Arthur Baker annoyed, even angry. "I got really offended. What is so different? It has a fucking glockenspiel, which Bruce has used before, background vocals . . . it's no different. See, if any of those mixes had come out before, with no one knowing the other version, no one would have said a word. Even Bruce says it."

What Bruce actually said was predictably more measured and conciliatory. "I figured that a lot of people would like it and that the people that didn't like it would get over it. My audience is not that fragile, you know. They can take it," he said, then shifted gears to discuss what was really on his mind—his own altered approach. "I'm just into seeing some different things. I could easily go out and do just what I did before. But now we're playing outdoors on this tour, which I hadn't done before. And we did the blaster thing and the video thing. I want to learn it myself. I want to just step out and see what works. If something doesn't work, that's okay, and if something does, great. In ten years I've built up a relationship with my audience." Unfortunately, during this period of tremendous artistic and personal growth, Bruce was opposed almost every step of the way by the very cult that proposed to protect the integrity of his work.

Bruce ignored the claims of his retrograde older fans; that doesn't mean he was unaware of what they thought or insensitive to their attitudes. He told Chet Flippo that songs like "Born to Run" and "Thunder Road" were among "the most emotional moments of the night" because "I can see all those people, and that song to them is like—that's their song, man. A lot of times they mean so much to me now because they mean so much to the audience. They just take over. And that's where it becomes more powerful. They're like little touchstones for the people. And that's a great compliment. I like it when the lights are up, because you can see so much from people's faces. That's what it's about."

Right then, however, he was more concerned with fashioning new meaning from the old structure of his concerts, with exploring new recording possibilities, with speaking to the vast young video audience, fixed on getting over to ever larger groups of people without losing the essence of his message or, by the same token, leaving people stranded on the path that he had previously taken to the despairing outer darkness of *Nebraska*. That is, he wanted to communicate a remarkably idealistic sense of possibility balanced by a very worldly knowledge of restriction.

11 GROWIN' UP

"This is for all the *old* fans out there," says Bruce with a grin. He isn't thinking of age; he's referring to the hundreds or maybe thousands of fans out there who are attending their third or tenth or fortieth Springsteen show, the hard core who've followed him since *Greetings from Asbury Park*, or *Born to Run*, or at least *Darkness on the Edge of Town*.

There's no way to tell how many of the 100,000 spread out before him in the Coliseum are veteran concertgoers. Certainly it is proportionately far fewer than in the arena shows of 1984, when (especially in New Jersey and California) it sometimes seemed that the tiny turnover in the crowd from night to night gave Bruce an audience as predictable and homogeneous as the one that attends an urban parish's 6:00 A..M. mass. The arena shows of 1984 sold out so rapidly in part because the cult was now large enough to fill a substantial portion of an arena and wanted to come back night after night; the same number of cultists in a stadium soaked up a far smaller percentage of the tickets.

In one sense, Springsteen made the move to stadiums to keep from being strangled creatively by this cult (big as it is, there's no other term that accurately describes it in the mass context). He needed the artistic challenge the vast spaces of the football fields afforded, but he also had to open the gates to begin to preach beyond the converted. The move offended many cultists, who for years had misinterpreted Springsteen's resistance to larger-scale venues as an ideological commitment to remain "loyal" to them. When new conditions encouraged him to try an all-stadium tour, these fans felt some degree of betrayal, accusing him of abandoning the pledge of audience intimacy that had always been the key to his appeal.

Instead, the result has been a newer, fresher relationship between Bruce and his listeners, without altering the meaning of the show very much. You might even argue that the infusion of new and less attentive blood has enhanced the concerts, simply by forcing Springsteen to struggle to make sure he gets across with the darker parts of the program. The arena gigs could have been done on autopilot, and the cult's failure to notice this was telling.

But even among the new, expanded audience, the level of Boss recidivism is high, judging from the wave of applause and cheers that greets Bruce's dedication to the "old fans." Those who know only *Born in the U.S.A.* must be mystified by a great deal of this show (where have all these songs been hidden?), but even those who've traced the story back as far as *Born to Run* will be unfamiliar with the song the band now begins.

"Growin' Up" is a song from Bruce's first album, and like so much of *Greetings from Asbury Park,* you can't tell much about it from the halfhearted recording. It seems just a jumble of images more or less pertaining to the fantasies of youth, with a single gem that leaps out as a kind of Springsteenian signature: "I swear I found the key to the universe in the engine of an old parked car."

But live, in a full band arrangement that ranges from tinkling to thunderous, the song gains a life. It's only when the power of the music is enhanced, buttressed by big drums and crashing guitars, underpinned by glockenspiel and trebly grand piano, that the lyrics snap into focus and the fantasy suddenly seems pointed. This is Bruce Springsteen's story, announced in a whisper that quickly rises to a roar, and if you know a little about what he's been through, you can hear it as a kind of secret autobiography, written before he had a grip on the real thing. It may not have been his alone—"I combed my hair 'til it looked just right" is a sentiment not unfamiliar even to the likes of Rod Stewart—but it was certainly his in particular:

I hid in the clouded wrath of the crowd

When they said, "Come down," I threw up

"On my school shoes!" Springsteen interjects with a shout, spun away in the ecstasy of the moment. But when the first verse ends, he brings the music down. Now only the glock and piano continue behind him, repeating their little melodic riffs over and over again.

Veterans know what's coming as soon as the opening notes are heard. Over the years, Springsteen has opened the song up with a legendary series of shaggy-dog monologues ranging from episodic stories of parental conflict to an actual encounter with God (who explained that Moses forgot the Eleventh Commandment: "Let it rock"). But mostly these tales concern the myth of how Bruce the Loser discovered rock and roll magic—and his true identity. There have been various vehicles toward this realization, including wild bears, gypsy fortune-tellers, and drag-racing UFOs. (God was not such a vehicle; he just told Bruce that he was on the right track.) On this tour, "Growin' Up" has evolved into a skit, with assorted crew members in the cast.

In the age of high-tech rock extravaganzas, when it's hard to find an indoor show without lasers and computerized sets, Springsteen's skit is striking for its amateurishness. The couple of costumes used are rented or homemade; there are no sets; the visual effects come from the show's regular lighting rig; the few props are not even electric, much less electronic. It's just the same Boss and his buddies, hamming it up like any high school talent night. The comedy is broad: Bruce and Clarence now appear less as Huck and Jim than as Laurel and Hardy or, from time to time, Fred Flintstone and Barney Rubble, though there's some Ralph Kramden and Ed Norton and even some Yogi Bear and Booboo in there, too. The sketch works off joking asides to the audience and a "this'll get 'em" attitude. Springsteen is no more reluctant to go for the obvious here than in his rock and roll songs. And that's why it works.

With the piano and glockenspiel ticking away measure after measure, Springsteen begins to speak.

"Now *there I was*. I was still in high school, but I wasn't doin' too good. I was doin' bad in my studies, and they sent me down to see the guidance counselor. I walked in and he said [*in a threatening voice*], 'Mr. Springsteen, what seems to be your problem?' So I said, 'Well, sir, it's like, you see, I don't have any interest in anything. I don't know what I want to do with myself. I don't care what's going on around me. I ain't got any faith, I don't have any hope in anything; I don't have any *close interpersonal relationship with a member of the opposite SEX*. I don't have, uh . . . ' " He pauses, scratches his cheek, rubs his hair. "He said, 'No, that's too big a problem. You better go home and talk to your folks about it.'

"So I went home and I went in the kitchen, and my pop was in there and I said, 'Pop, man, I got sent home from school. I been in a lotta trouble lately. I really gotta talk to you about something. I don't know what's gonna happen with me. I don't have any interest in anything. I daydream in class alla time, and I don't have any faith in anything—in myself. I don't have any hope in anything.' And he said, 'Willya get me another beer outta the ice box?'

"So that was it," he says, picking up the microphone and walking off to his left a couple of paces. "I decided I was gonna do myself in. I was gonna *end it all*. I was gonna say, 'Goodbye, cruel world!' Yeah!

"So I got out and I hitchhiked down to Asbury Park. I was gonna drown myself. I was gonna jump in the ocean and drown myself." He sits at the edge of the stage. "I was sittin' there on the boardwalk, contemplatin' the water temperature, when all of a sudden, in the distance, this big, handsome dude came walkin' by." Into the spotlight strolls Clarence Clemons, derelict beefcake personified in white shirt and slacks with a white cap askew on his head. Bruce cracks up at the sight. Clarence sits down.

"He kinda sat down next to me; I started sayin' my prayers. But we kinda got talkin'. I was tellin' him all about my problems. Then he started tellin' me all about his problems. Then we cried on each other's shoulders for a while." They do that, mugging shamelessly. "But we decided we'd make a good team and we became partners."

"That's right, that's right, that's right," they tell one another, vigorously shaking hands.

"And Clarence, he said that he knew a gypsy lady that could help us out with our troubles. So over to the gypsy we went," Bruce continues. He rises and walks to his right, over past Danny Federici's keyboards, where sits a gypsy lady (Landau's managerial associate, Barbara Carr, togged in a gold turban and flowered print dress) seated at a table, waving her hands over an illuminated crystal ball.

"It was late at night; the boardwalk was deserted. We walked in, we paid our two-fifty each—I had to loan Clarence his two-fifty—and she looked into the crystal ball and she said, 'You guys are in a lotta trouble.' " The gypsy nods wisely. "Paid another two-fifty—I didn't get it back yet either—and she looked into the crystal ball, and then she said, 'You boys are gonna go on a real long trip. You're gonna seek out new forms of life. You're gonna explore new worlds. You're gonna go where no men have ever gone before . . . and stay twice as long. And have a lotta fun doin' it, too.' And she gave us a map to the secret of the world, and she said if we followed that map at midnight, we'd find the answer to all our troubles."

Clarence tucks the map into his shirt, and they return to center stage.

"So that night we got into Clarence's Oldsmobile and we started drivin' south down Route Nine. South through the rain. Down through *Free*hold, down through *Lake*wood, down through *Tom*'s River. And a hurricane hit! And then a tor-nah-do blew across the highway. And then a blizzard hit. And then a heat wave broke. And then the roof flew off the car; and then we got two flat tires; and then the fenders flew off; and then the engine block cracked; and then the carburetor went; and then the windows blew out. And then . . . and then . . . and then! THE RADIO BROKE!"

They shout this final disaster in unison and fall flat on their faces, pounding their heads. Spasm completed, they slowly rise to their knees. "You know what that's like," says Bruce.

"But there we were—on the side of this dark dirt road. And according to the map, what we were looking for was just on the other side of those woods." He points to his left, and he and Clarence reluctantly get back on their feet and move in the direction of a huge tree (Clarence's personal assistant, Terry Magovern).

"So into the forest we went. It was spooky in there," Bruce stage-whispers in mock-terrified tones that wouldn't frighten a three-year-old. "There were sounds comin' from all over the place." The audience picks up the cue and makes pseudospooky noises.

"Sounded like werewolves." From the audience, somewhat sinister snarls. "Sounded like homicidal cows." The crowd obliges with massive mooing. "Sounded like mad dogs barkin'." The fans approximate barking. "Sounded like the JERSEY DEVIL out there!" At the mention of this mythical creature from the South Jersey swamps, the crowd ditches pretense and simply hollers its lungs out.

Meanwhile, Clarence is cringing behind Bruce, who, with back bent in an exploratory posture, slowly creeps across the stage. He addresses Clarence as he stalks.

"Now, Big Man, I ain't never heard of no killer beasts like in New Jersey or nothin'. Did you? No? I hearda killer hamburgers but no killer beasts." He straightens up some, and they totter back toward stage right.

"I think we're safe out here, don't you?" Clarence denies this by vigorously shaking his head. From behind them, two bears appear (Bruce's aide, Jim McDuffie, and soundman Tom "Midget" Foelinger). The larger bear, a bit shorter than Bruce, wears a battered beige fishing hat. The smaller bear, diminutive next to Clarence, wears a blue LAPD baseball cap.

"I think I heard something behind us," says Bruce, and he and Clarence turn together to look over their left shoulders. The bears follow suit and therefore theoretically remain unseen. "I think I heard something behind us," Bruce says again, and again the quartet turns in unison.

"I think I heard something," Bruce whispers a third time, and now he and Clarence begin to whimper, Springsteen sounding just like Stan Laurel in his most fretful scenes. He grimaces piteously for the video screens. Suddenly Bruce and Clarence wheel about. The bears are caught by surprise, but it's the Boss and the Big Man who are startled. "Whoa!" they holler; the bears and Clarence scatter to the corners of the stage. Bruce barely holds his ground.

"And all of a sudden," he continues, "up behind us came these two big man-eatin' bears. But instead of jumpin' on us and making us their dinner, they were actin' kinda friendly." The bears make anthropomorphic gestures of affection, the larger one petting and stroking Bruce's arm and shoulder.

"And they said that they weren't mean but that they were just lonely, and that they'd been out in the woods for a long time by themselves, after they escaped from the circus, 'cause they got tired of livin' in them cages. And they said that if we'd be their friends, they'd help us find what we were lookin' for." Together the foursome begins to stalk the stage.

"And so back into the forest we went. And all of a sudden the clouds pulled away from the moon, and there in a clearing we saw the answer to our quest."

A pair of pinpoint white spots hit Bruce's guitar and Clarence's sax. The bears retrieve this equipment, the big bear bringing Bruce the horn and the little one carrying the guitar over to Clarence. Bruce puts the sax strap over his shoulder and tries to strum it. Clarence blows into the neck of the guitar. Nothing. They look at one another and exchange instruments.

Bruce walks back to center stage, strapping on his guitar. He looks lovingly at the instrument. For the first time since the story began, he replaces the microphone in its stand.

"And then we said goodbye to the bears, for the last time." He turns and hugs the big bear, then the smaller one. "And as we stood there in the moonlight, we knew that everything was gonna be all right. Because . . . because . . . when we touched"—he and Clarence stretch to tap their fingertips against one another, and lights and music explode and the song romps to its conclusion, Bruce concluding (as he always must) by interpolating a line from Chuck Berry and John Lennon: "And it was bye-bye New Jersey, we were *air*borne."

The song complete, he stands bathed once more in sweat. Then he looks out into the dark and a huge silly smile breaks across his face.

"And here we are tonight," he says, portentously as a five-year-old at the conclusion of a Christmas pageant, then twirls to count off the next number.

12 MONEY CHANGES EVERYTHING

"No substantial problem of art is soluble by art alone."

—Harold Rosenberg

The most significant change in performance Springsteen made during the early weeks of the *Born in the U.S.A.* tour was almost overlooked: He'd ended his long holdout against playing outdoors. But it was a tentative move at first. Bruce was fearful of a loss of control as well as about a lack of intimacy, doubtful about the havoc that those wide open spaces might wreak on his sound, and wary of the problems of communicating with audiences more than a hundred yards away.

Of course, he'd adopted exactly the same attitude about playing indoor sports arenas. But there were some precedents for succeeding in indoor arenas; *nobody* had ever created a satisfying outdoor rock and roll show. So the tour still ducked the massive football and baseball stadiums that other acts who'd reached Springsteen's level played exclusively. But an expanded audience and the threat of arena stagnation meant it was time to try something.

During the first month of the tour he played three open-air facilities—the "sheds," as they're known in the concert business—at Alpine Valley, Wisconsin, and Saratoga, New York, each of which drew an average of 25,000 for one-nighters, and Toronto's CNE Grandstand, a 22,000-seater across the street from the ball park housing the baseball

Blue Jays. (Springsteen did three shows in Toronto—and no wonder, since *Born in the U.S.A.* was, if anything, more popular in Canada than in the United States, eventually becoming the Northland sales equivalent of *Thriller*.)

It poured at Saratoga but the crowd refused to let Bruce cancel the show, as he told them he wanted to. Alpine Valley went fine, but Bruce found even good weather less than prepossessing in Toronto. The Grandstand seating was configured like a fairgrounds, so that the crowd was spread out before him broader than deep, which created weird sight angles and strange sound trajectories for both audience and performer. When the tour rolled into Detroit to play the Joe Louis Arena, Springsteen was relieved. "Man, it's great to be back inside again," he exulted backstage. And that feeling was confirmed by the shows, which were among the first in which the set really gelled, helped along a lot by the fact that "Born in the U.S.A." had finally asserted itself as the permanent set opener.

Those shows *had* to gel, because they were the prelude to the ten-night stand at the Byrne Meadowlands Arena in New Jersey. The incredible demand that created this unparalleled stand—Bruce would play to 210,000 customers over two weeks—symptomized the reasons that larger facilities (which only existed outdoors) had to be considered. The Meadowlands gigs were oversubscribed by a factor of ten, meaning that had they decided to fulfill the entire demand, the E Street Band would have been stuck in that one town—albeit their home turf—for several months. Something had to give.

Nevertheless, the Jersey stand was a love-in rivaled only by the M.U.S.E. concerts and the Meadowlands shows of 1981. Each night, ticket holders came out hours early to hang out in the parking lot, where they barbecued, sunbathed, threw Frisbees, squared off in touch football matches, and played Springsteen tapes through their car and portable stereo systems. By showtime the house seemed ready to implode.

"At first, watching Bruce Springsteen vault into the raging closing verse to 'The Promised Land' . . . I thought the band's supporting harmonies sounded uncommonly forcible—something like the roar of orchestrated thunder," wrote Mikal Gilmore. "Then, after a few moments, I realized that vocal blare wasn't issuing from on stage, but rather from above and below and beside and around me: from 20,000 young rock fans (many decked out in red, white, and blue, to honor the hard-bitten Americana that Bruce's new music espouses), gathered here in New Jersey's Meadowlands to celebrate the public return of a regional hero."

Springsteen gave these crucial shows a sense of event, helped along by special guests, including Gary Bonds, Southside Johnny, the Who's John Entwistle, and, on the final evening, Little Steven Van Zandt and the Miami Horns. Little Steven's return, even in a cameo role, was possible so soon after he'd quit the band only because Lofgren fit in so well that it was clear Steve's appearance didn't signal any change of heart. When Steve and Bruce rejoined their voices for duets on "Two Hearts" and a raw but moving rendition of Dobie Gray's "Drift Away" the full story of their comradeship was obvious to everyone one in ways that neither "Bobby Jean" nor "No Surrender" could ever tell. Dobie Gray's anthem spoke for both of them: "Thanks for the joy that you've given me/I want you to know I believe in your song."

Despite the emotional tenor of Bruce's homecoming, the lengthy run at the Meadowlands was in some senses as stultifying as it was rewarding; part of the idea of touring with a rock band is its hit-and-run quality, the constant moving from town to town, barnstorming round the planet, not settling in for Broadway-length stays. As Bruce put it, "To me, the idea is you get a band, write some songs, and go out to people's towns. It's my favorite thing; it's like a circus. You just kind of roll on, walk into somebody's town, and bang! It's heart to heart. Something can happen to you; something can happen to them." The fact that dispensing music this way in an age of instantaneous electronic access is a complete anachronism is beside the point. Moving on is what touring is about; staying in one place for so long violates the concept. Although maybe that meant a new concept was necessary—something that lingered longer.

Anyway, anyone who experienced the full complement of Meadowlands shows was as likely to be enervated as energized. The shows were epic in length and the crowds were ecstatic, but that only emphasized the way in which Bruce had to struggle to make them meaningful, to undercut the predictability of ritual and get *his* meaning across.

You could argue, as Mikal Gilmore did, that "the real glory of Springsteen's rise became increasingly apparent in the living drama of his 1984 nationwide tour, in which he . . . bound mass audiences together into an emboldened community that eventually took on a character and zeal all its own." But what made the process dramatic was that it was such a near thing. For Gilmore, seeing Springsteen perform "Born in the U.S.A." before those Jersey crowds meant witnessing "a segment of America coming face-to-face with the acerbic realities and undisguised goodness and hope that bind together the colors these fans waved." But that omitted several crucial facts. Many of those rock fans "decked out in red, white, and blue" weren't dressed up "to honor the hard-bitten Americana that Bruce's new music espouses," but to participate in the same jingoism Gilmore decried when it dominated that summer's other events: the Los Angeles Olympics, the Democrats' desperate Ellis Island histrionics, and the orgy of pseudopatriotism with which the Republicans moved to deify Ronald Reagan at the ballot box.

None of this was Bruce Springsteen's fault exactly. He was doing what he'd always done. But that didn't really address the new context his greater success created. Springsteen was pouring his heart out, at least the part of his heart that he dared to show and the audience deigned to notice, but it was hard to see these shows as creative activity in the way that his previous tours had been; instead, they were cele- brations of previous events or dramatizations of public assent in the star-making process.

Such problems are easier to spot retrospectively. During those months in 1984, Bruce Springsteen's across-the-board stardom was blossoming; for the first time his image blasted past the bounds of rock and roll into mainstream attention. It wasn't just New Jersey; across America "Bossmania" ruled the airwaves and print media, and as *Purple Rain* began to flag, dominated record store attention, too. Suddenly it wasn't just a mammoth cult of postadolescents and young adults who hummed Springsteen songs on their way to work. It was Mom and Pop and teens and grade school kids who found "Dancing in the Dark" and its Top Ten successor, "Cover Me," irresistible.

In a way, Bruce Springsteen was no different from Elvis Presley, Bing Crosby, Michael Jackson, or Paul McCartney. He made concessions for a run at the top. Except that Springsteen, so deeply imbued with a sense of tradition that he was in a sense the direct inheritor of each of those precursors, was more aware that what he was doing was com- promising.

The compromises didn't involve music so much as media. Spring- steen still did the show he'd always done, give or take the new material and a slight unbending in order to ride out the mania that couldn't control itself—he hadn't previously faced an audience composed purely of screaming teenagers, but that kind of adulation was now a nightly factor. Still, what remained remarkable about Bruce's performances was their constancy. He continued to eschew high-tech geegaws and he worked hard to undercut hero worship with dark mood pieces and pessimistic philosophizing. It was, in the main, a triumphant show, and one that cashed in on a promise that many thought no longer a possibility. As Christgau wrote, "It seems a simple thing—articulating the contradictions of freedom and powerlessness in America for both teenagers who still believe they're born to run and adults who know where they end up. But though many have set out to do it, nobody else has succeeded before cynicism and foolishness struck. And without doubt it's Bruce's passion for maintaining contact with his fans, his people, that has made the difference, to him and to them."

In media relations, however, Springsteen had begun to cut a few corners. "No, your eyes are not deceiving you," wrote Patrick Goldstein of the *Los Angeles Times* just after the Meadowlands run. "That *was* Bruce Springsteen on the cover of *People* magazine . . . and being interviewed on *Entertainment Tonight* . . . and yes, believe it or not, on MTV, promising that some lucky fan will get to win a week on tour as a roadie 'if you earn it!' "

But he was a rock and roll star, and anyway, it's not like anybody had an alternative. Since *The River*, the already wobbly rock press had further deteriorated. Yet Goldstein had a point. Bruce's stature as the most insightful rock interview subject since Pete Townshend was partly based on being interviewed by like-minded reporters and critics. Although he'd spoken briefly to a good one, Don McLeese of the *Chicago Sun-Times*, in St. Paul, there simply weren't that many of the old crowd still working the beat. Besides, Bruce simply didn't have that much energy for interviews. That being the case, both his management and CBS were steering him toward mass circulation enterprises: MTV, *USA Today, Entertainment Tonight, People.* Springsteen himself felt too preoccupied to handle a full-scale *Rolling Stone* interview, which remained the vehicle best suited for elaborating on his musical ideas.

The mass media interest in Springsteen coincided with his obvious interest in making music that reached beyond his hard-core rock audience, but that didn't mean that he had a very good idea of how to communicate what made him special to the newcomers—or that the mass media themselves had much idea what to do with such an odd fellow. His ambivalence about celebrity was legendary: "It's the old story of getting elected to a club you may not want to be a member of. But you are anyway. You're just another trivia question on *Jeopardy* or something." From time to time he seemed to view every aspect of fame as the nastiest trap of all. "Celebrity. That's a distraction. It's false. That's the false image," he told Kit Rachlis in 1981.

Bruce dwelt heavily on the topic that summer of 1984 during an interview with British disc jockey Roger Scott. "One of the problems is that the audience and the performer have got to leave some room for each other to be human, or else they don't really deserve each other in a funny kinda way," he said. "I think the position you get in is unrealistic to begin with,'cause you're just basically a guy. You know, you play the guitar and you do that good, and that's great, that's nice. If you do your job well, people like it and admire you for it or respect you for it or something; that's a plus. But . . . the idealizing of performers or politicians doesn't seem to make much sense. It's based on an image, and an image is always basically limiting and only a portion—and only the public portion—of that individual's personality. Which is not to say that it's necessarily false; it's just not complete.

"I guess I basically feel it's like Elvis. People say they got disillusioned or something. Well, I don't feel that Elvis let anybody down. Personally, I don't think he owed anything to anybody. I think that, as it was, he did more for most people than they'll ever have done for them in their lives. The trouble that he ran into, that's the trouble that you run into. It's hard to keep your head above the water, but sometimes it's not right for people to judge the way that they do."

On the other hand, he set a higher standard for himself. "I feel that the night you look into your audience and you don't see yourself, and the night the audience looks at you and they don't see themselves, that's when it's all over, you know?

"I don't feel that people 'sold out.' I don't think Elvis sold out when he lived in Graceland—people never sold out by *buying* something. It wasn't ever something they bought; it was something they *thought* that changed. . . .

"My audience, I always hoped, would be all sorts of people—rich and poor, middle-class people; I don't feel like I'm singing to any one group of people. I don't want to put up those sort of walls. That's not really what our band is about."

Bruce might get away with such complex and relatively long-winded expositions on album-oriented radio and in the rock press. In the mass circulation magazines and on television, however, his philosophical bent and skill as a raconteur undercut him. Bruce tended to warm up to interviews slowly and to express himself verbally only in roundabout ways, often through painstaking and indirect parables. He needed a great deal of time and space to express himself correctly, and he simply wasn't given that in the limited spaces provided by the mass media, who had to move on to the next celebrity.

Moreover, the people who were doing the interviews weren't especially interested in pursuing ideas or helping anybody—Springsteen or their audience—think things through. Barbara Howar of *Entertainment Tonight* knew nothing about rock and roll except the questions someone had written for her. While *USA Today* gave rock writer Bruce Pollock plenty of space, he presented only the most predictable quotes and commentary. *People* sent former *Rolling Stone* staff writer Chet Flippo, who did a fine interview (later printed in full in the rock magazine *Musician*), but the copy published in *People* was restricted to that magazine's personality gloss-over format. MTV's Mark Goodman was a professionally shallow boob who seemed most concerned that he look as hip as possible while also asking questions prepared by others; by the time Bruce's answers were cut up into the cable system's predigested bites, their substance was sucked dry. Worse, the "The Boss" contest, by trading on Springsteen's overused nickname, managed to trivialize the very idea of labor that Bruce's shows worked so hard to dignify.

But whatever the limitations of those entertainment business interviewers, the ultimate problem was Bruce's. It was exacerbated by his tremendous detachment from the ordinary processes and even desires of celebrities. As Landau said, "I don't think Bruce has ever identified with the conventional idea of success. And for that reason, he hasn't been overly affected by it." So he got over in arenas, when so few others had, by transferring his show almost unchanged from theaters and clubs; he made hit records by ignoring trends if not technology; he'd reached Europeans by speaking to them as straight-from-the-shoulder as he did to Americans.

Springsteen maintained an extraordinary detachment from the ordinary pop celebrity's goals and values. He wasn't especially interested in great wealth, although he was surely glad not to have to worry about the rent; he did not confuse size with quality (otherwise he'd never have released *Nebraska*). If anything, he was concerned with being *too big*, because that implied a loss of control and a restriction of mobility that was foreign to his nature. Had he been in less of a risk-taking mood, who knows if he'd ever have released an album like *Born in the U.S.A.*

Springsteen hadn't done things his way simply out of pop-star perversity. He'd moved at odd angles to stardom and skewed show-business procedure out of a deep need to secure and maintain the integrity of his life and work. If he couldn't do something similar now, his rise to superstardom would prove a net loss. But almost everyone who had ever risen to these precincts of fame was overwhelmed by them, forced into going along with the game. There were no road maps to show him how to avoid the pitfalls of celebrity rigamarole and still maintain access to a mass audience. If he was looking for new adventures, this was one that really counted.

That story was being played out as a private, almost secret drama, behind the scenes of Bruce's near-canonization as the All-American Rock and Roll Star. However much the mass media may have misapprehended what he was really about, they very much wanted a slice of his success because it was so palatable on their terms. Here was a performer who refuted the idea of the rock star as an outlaw, whose earnestness was beyond question, whose humility seemed complete, who was without visible vices—didn't smoke, drink, dope, or womanize to excess—whose dress was ragged but comfortably familiar, who spoke of America at a time when the country was enduring a festival of Americana. Any editor or news director with a pulse had to want in on this story. So they all checked in, from the lowliest dailies and weeklies on up to the network news. And if what Bruce Springsteen was about had been misinterpreted before, the story of his life and career was now butchered beyond all belief.

On September 12, 1984, the *CBS Evening News* ran a two-minute piece by correspondent Bernard Goldberg about the Springsteen phenomenon. "Bruce Springsteen sings about Americans—blue-collar Americans trapped and suffocating in old broken-down small towns," Goldberg declared. "His songs are about working-class people, desperate people hanging on to the American dream by a thread." So far, so good, and as the piece continued, playing fragments of "My Hometown" and "Dancing in the Dark," all was well . . . until his conclusion.

Trying to summarize what it all meant, Goldberg stumbled and in the process twisted Springsteen into just another free enterprise juggernaut: "He touches his fans and they touch him. His shows are like old-time revivals with the same old-time message: If they work hard enough and long enough, like Springsteen himself, they can also make it to the promised land."

Ironically, *Born to Run*, even *Darkness on the Edge of Town* and *The River*, might fairly have been interpreted in that way. But *Born in the U.S.A.* took pains to talk about the ways in which hard work was not enough, the ways in which the game was rigged to make honest effort and good intentions inadequate. In his shows, Springsteen did his best to make this clear. But if the ways in which his shows were being interpreted was any indication, it wasn't good enough.

Bernard Goldberg's piece was filed from Largo, Maryland, at the Capitol Center between Washington, D.C., and Baltimore, where four shows were scheduled for August 25, 26, 28, and 29, immediately after the Jersey run. Sadly, he wasn't the only political journalist to attend those shows and misunderstand them.

◆

When you start to get real popular, you have to be careful that there isn't a dilution into some very simplistic terms of what you're doing. There are times when you have to get up and say, "Wait a minute, this isn't right. This is it: This is the way I feel."

—*Springsteen to John Hammond, 1984*

Max Weinberg's wife, Becky, a high school history teacher, watched *This Week with David Brinkley* faithfully each Sunday morning. She was a fan especially of the prime antagonists on the program's round-table D.C. gabfest, liberal reporter Sam Donaldson and conservative pundit George Will. "So for the last three years we've been watching and saying, 'Gee, we should invite them when we come to Washington. Maybe they'd be interested in seeing rock and roll,' " Weinberg later told Craig Hankin and John Ebersberger in an interview for Baltimore's *City Paper*. As the Capitol Center dates approached, the

Weinbergs had a mutual friend call Will and ask if he'd like to attend. (Donaldson either never got invited or declined.)

"And he said, 'Yeah, great, I'd love to see it,' " Weinberg said. "He was really excited—he'd never been to a rock and roll—show. It was funny. He called me up and asked, 'What should I dress like?' So he came in his bow tie, of course, but he wore a sport jacket and slacks rather than a suit. That was casual. He really enjoyed the show. He got it. Unfortunately, he had just returned from the convention in Dallas and had to get up early to do *This Week*, so he left before the show was over."

But Will had some sort of vision that Saturday night: He saw a golden opportunity for Ronald Reagan to pick up more of the youth vote in the November election. After the concert, Will, who sometimes served as an unpaid Reagan campaign adviser, relayed the idea of Springsteen's endorsing Reagan to the White House, most likely through reelection staffer Morgan Mason (the young son of actor James Mason), who had originally come to prominence as the go-between in the Alfred Bloomingdale–Vicki Morgan sex scandal.

Mason played an important role in the reelection committee's attempt to create an image of broad-based unity around Ronald Reagan, attempting in particular to woo all sectors of show business for the actor-turned-President. He'd gone after rock star John Mellencamp in an attempt to recruit Mellencamp's "Pink Houses" as a campaign theme song. (A year after the election Mason married Belinda Carlisle, the former lead singer of the Go-Gos.) Similarly, the White House arranged an election year visit by Michael Jackson, who posed with Reagan as part of an anti-drunk-driving campaign; Billy Joel was also invited to dinner that year (a Democrat, he declined). Reagan attended a Grand Ole Opry salute to venerable country star (and sometime Republican candidate for Tennessee state office) Roy Acuff, at which Lee Greenwood agreed to sing "Proud to Be an American"—after Barbara Mandrell declined. The reelection committee's wildest move was attempting to associate ZZ Top guitarist Billy Gibbons (he of the Rip Van Winkle beard and hair) with the campaign because of the tangential fact that Gibbons's parents, prominent figures in the Houston classical music world, were close friends of Vice-President George Bush.

Eventually Will's plan for a Reagan–Springsteen linkage filtered through to presidential adviser and political fixer Michael Deaver's office. There it was duly noted that the President was scheduled to make a campaign stop in Hammonton, New Jersey, on September 19. Springsteen's popularity in his home state was enormous, and a Springsteen endorsement of Reagan would swing a lot of votes.

Deaver's staff knew no one in the Springsteen camp, but they did have an ally in the Virginia offices of Cellar Door Productions, the company that promoted the Capitol Center shows. Cellar Door contacted agent Barry Bell with a proposal that Bruce appear with Reagan in Hammonton. Bell politely declined, saying that Springsteen was unavailable for any outside appearances during the tour, which was true. Even so, he relayed the information to Springsteen and Landau, who took it as just another example of the weirdness associated with both Washington and the uproar over *Born in the U.S.A.* They'd deflected similar proposals in the past from politicians trying to glom a little pop-star glamor.

On September 13 Will's syndicated column was published under the headline "A Yankee Doodle Springsteen." Will's chosen label for his own political and cultural philosophy was "Tory," with all its implications of aristocratic conservatism and highbrow elitism, but from time to time, lest he register as a complete wimp, he liked to slum, usually abusing baseball in the process. In Springsteen Will found (or so he thought) an equally perfect icon, one that spoke explicitly to the antipopulism he wished to encourage.

"There is not a smidgen of androgyny in Springsteen, who, rocketing around the stage in a T-shirt and headband, resembles Robert DeNiro in the combat scenes of *The Deer Hunter*. This is rock for the United Steelworkers . . ." wrote Will. "Today, 'values' are all the rage. Springsteen's fans say his message affirms the right values. Certainly his manner does.

"Springsteen, a product of industrial New Jersey, is called the 'blue-collar troubadour.' But if this is the class struggle, its anthem—its 'Internationale'—is the song that provides the title for his 18-month world-wide tour. 'Born in the U.S.A.'

"I have not got a clue about Springsteen's politics, if any, but flags get waved at his concerts while he sings songs about hard times. . . ."

Will was not the first conservative to attend Springsteen's shows and become confused about the message. For instance, Barbara Carr's father, Harold Fitzgeorge, an oil executive, came away with the impression that Springsteen was implicitly proposing a national reorientation best realized through the "Reagan-Bush program." But George Will had quite a bit less excuse, for if he had listened more closely—or less selectively—that Saturday night, he would have heard Springsteen introduce "Nebraska" by saying, "It seems like one of the big problems we've got in the country today is people feeling isolated from their jobs, or from their friends, from their government. You get a sense of powerlessness sometimes and . . . uh . . . some people just explode." But this was not the optimistic, hard-working patriotism Will wanted to purvey, so the columnist simply ignored it (presuming he was still there to hear it).

"An evening with Springsteen tends to wash over into the A.M., the concerts lasting four hours," the column continued, though the author was hardly in a position to know. "Backstage there hovers the odor of Ben-Gay: Springsteen is an athlete draining himself for every audience.

"But, then, consider Max Weinberg's bandaged fingers. The rigors of drumming have led to five tendonitis operations. He soaks his hands in hot water before a concert, in ice afterward, and sleeps with tight gloves on. Yes, of course, the whole E Street Band is making enough money to ease the pain. But they are not charging as much as they could, and the customers are happy. How many American businesses can say that?

"If all Americans—in labor and management, who make steel or cars or shoes or textiles—made their products with as much energy and confidence as Springsteen and his merry band make music, there would be no need for Congress to be thinking about protectionism. No 'domestic content' legislation is needed in the music industry. The British and other invasions have been met and matched."

Since the politicians Will most avidly supported had done their best to deny adequate compensation and health care for workers who were not "making enough money to ease the pain," or simply denied the existence of such diseases as black lung and asbestosis, the column ended in even deeper smarm and hypocrisy than it began. George Will had never held a job in which his hands were more than metaphorically dirtied and was proud of it. The notion of his lecturing on the joys and rewards of labor to steel-workers who risked their lives in filthy, unsafe mills every day was such a perversion of what Springsteen was trying to communicate that it constituted an obscenity. Yet the column was well received.

Released as it was in a time of chauvinism masquerading as patriotism, it was inevitable that "Born in the U.S.A." would be misinterpreted, that the album would be heard as a celebration of "basic values," no matter how hard Springsteen pushed his side of the tale. (In 1986 Jackson Browne's much more explicit "For America" met the same fate, despite its being surrounded by a group of songs that attacked U.S. foreign policy in the most explicit terms.) Certainly, any popular song that honored the American Vietnam veteran in the age of Reagan and *Rambo* was going to be misconstrued as celebrating the war. Issued in the teeth of a presidential election being sold as a plebiscite on national virtue, such a song could expect to be misappropriated. Surrounding that song with others that presented equally mordant views of the country was no help.

Again, Springsteen just shrugged it off. Will's opportunism was as overripe and obvious as his prose; it wasn't likely to fool anyone who mattered. Bruce wasn't in the habit of making public statements to refute the mistaken ideas of newspaper columnists.

A week later Ronald Reagan made two campaign stops in the Northeast. At Waterbury, Connecticut, which John Kennedy had visited during the 1960 campaign, Reagan specifically identified himself with JFK. "Over there, on the balcony of the Elton [Hotel] one night in 1960, young John Kennedy stood in the darkness. He was exhausted, but the night was bright with lights and they lit the faces of the tens of thousands of people below . . . He smiled in the glow. And even though it was the fall, it seemed like springtime, those days," said Reagan, who had supported Nixon in the 1960 election.

"I see our country today and I think it is springtime for America once again. And I think John Kennedy would be proud of you and the things you believe in."

It was two weeks into the fall campaign, and Reagan had backed off from earlier comments exalting the interrelationship of politics and religion, which had proved controversial, in favor of optimistic themes "designed to identify himself with positive developments ranging from rising college entrance test scores to Olympic victory," as Francis X. Clines noted in the *New York Times*. "When America goes for the gold nothing can hold her back," Reagan enthused after noting a four-point rise in the national average SAT results. He was hunting Democratic crossover votes—and the youth vote, even though, if reelected, he would be the oldest chief executive in U.S. history.

Later the same day, the campaign plane moved on to Hammonton,

New Jersey, a town of 13,000 located in the rural southern part of the state. There Reagan appeared before a select audience. As at Waterbury, the event was a pure campaign stop, the audience brought out by the local campaign staff for the sole purpose of showering the President with affection, just part of the day's arrangements to ensure favorable attention on the evening news with its important national audience. Reagan spoke on essentially the same themes he'd touched on in Waterbury, but this time he added, "America's future rests in a thousand dreams inside your hearts; it rests in the message of hope in songs so many young Americans admire: New Jersey's own Bruce Springsteen. And helping you make those dreams come true is what this job of mine is all about."

As the *Christian Science Monitor* later commented, Springsteen thus became "the first popular singer to be recruited by a President of the United States as a character reference." It was hard to see the Reagan remarks as anything but the crudest sort of exploitation, especially since the campaign staff was unable to answer the obvious follow-up question: What was the President's favorite Springsteen song? (By the next day the answer was "Born to Run," but, as Johnny Carson remarked in his *Tonight Show* monologue, "If you believe that, I've got a couple of tickets to the Mondale-Ferraro inaugural ball I'd like to sell you.")

Well, Bruce Springsteen must have felt as John Mellencamp had: "I didn't know whether to be embarrassed for me or for the President." Still, it didn't seem necessary to do anything. "It just seemed like the same kind of thing the President did all the time, only this time he was doing it to me," Bruce said a couple of days later. His initial reaction was to treat the whole idea of a relationship between himself and the President—*any* president—as a preposterous joke. Springsteen may not have been an outlaw, but he'd grown up in the era of outlaw rock and roll, when the notion of any public official endorsing a rock star in the midst of an election campaign would have been a ludicrous impossibility.

In fact, there were certain similarities between Ronald Reagan and Bruce Springsteen, although these had little or nothing to do with a shared perspective on the problems facing America, as Reagan and Will and their ideological cohorts implied. What they shared was an unflappable attitude, a tremendous conviction of being the right person for the job at hand and a deep belief in their own authenticity.

This was easy to define. As early as 1975 Martin Nolan of the *Boston Globe* wrote, "Ronald Reagan may be the Bruce Springsteen of politics. And Bruce Springsteen may be the Ronald Reagan of rock," in an article that attempted to fathom how either man had ever wound up with simultaneous cover stories in *Time* and *Newsweek*. The common element has to do with what in Reagan's case has been called his "Teflon" quality but which in Springsteen has usually been appreciated as a survival instinct. Both men know almost automatically when to attack and when to back off; neither seems much troubled by existential doubt in the validity of his own enterprise. Examples pertaining to Reagan are an overfamiliar legion, although the quick shift in emphasis in his campaign, as reflected in the Hammonton and Waterbury speeches, is a particularly good example.

In Springsteen's case, the best example might be his reaction to Reagan's endorsement by imperial fiat. Bruce didn't respond quickly. Reagan made his speech on a day off for the tour, which had just finished a four-night run at the Philadelphia Spectrum. Bruce's initial reaction was a kind of shocked amusement, and since he wasn't the kind of performer who issued press releases, he simply said nothing, figuring the issue would blow over. Only the growing awareness that many in his audience—and in the press—who loathed Reagan and had faith in him expected some sort of reply forced him to react at all.

There are several obvious reasons why Bruce was slower to react than another performer might have been. In his own mind, he was utterly certain that Reagan had misinterpreted him. As Jon Landau pointed out, "Bruce has never thought the message or the lesson of his personal success was 'Hey, be like me, you can do it, too.'" To Bruce, this was obvious from all the songs he had ever written. He took it for granted that everyone interested knew all his work, not just *Born in the U.S.A.* Only when it was pointed out that this was an impossibility, since sales of *Born in the U.S.A.* were already over 5 million copies, more than twice as many as *The River* or *Born to Run* and about five times as many as his other albums, did he begin to feel differently.

But Springsteen was also extremely reluctant to speak in specifically political terms because he feared his own lack of expertise would prove embarrassing. He certainly had principles that he adhered to and tried to foster, and he also had a method of communicating those principles. Telling stories was a part of that method; making speeches wasn't.

Even when he played the M.U.S.E. shows, which involved taking a stand against the proliferation of nuclear power plants, he was the only artist who declined to make a statement on the issue in the tour program. His position was that his music spoke for him. But as he tackled more concrete issues and situations in his songs, that position began to prove inadequate. It risked making his work susceptible to all sorts of expropriation and dangerous misreadings, not only by opportunistic politicians but by his everyday listeners, too.

Like Reagan, Springsteen was also blessed with a larger than ordinary ration of good luck. As he was getting ready for a gig in Pittsburgh, perhaps the major city most devastated by Reaganomics, it became obvious that he would have to make some sort of disavowal of the President's endorsement. He had been asked to meet briefly that evening with Ron Weisen, president of United Steelworkers of America Local 1397, located in Homestead, Pennsylvania, legendary for decades as an outpost of union militancy—and under Weisen's recent leadership the most vocally dissident local within the USWA, consistently opposing "concessions" (givebacks of rights and wages) that both company management and the international union leadership insisted were necessary.

Springsteen was canny enough to know that a frontal attack on Ronald Reagan would never work. Reagan was the most popular President since Franklin Roosevelt and all direct assaults somehow redounded to his credit; denigrating the President would only make Springsteen seem an ungrateful hothead. Reagan's particular brand of Teflon was characterized by the ability to turn any awkward or unseemly situation into a positive advantage. Anyway, Bruce continued to abhor negativity. And talking with Weisen that evening must have helped him focus on what he needed to do, which was distance himself from the President and his policies by linking himself to their polar opposite, the disenfranchised workers exemplified by the men of Local 1397, who had, among other things, banded together to form the most thriving union food bank in the country, which aided hundreds of their laid-off brethren monthly. (This didn't stop the Pittsburgh area from having the highest suicide rate in the nation, but not much could have.)

In the midst of his first set on September 22, Springsteen made his statement. Finishing "Atlantic City," he said bitterly, "The President was mentioning my name the other day, and I kinda got to wondering what his favorite album musta been. I don't think it was the *Nebraska* album. I don't think he's been listening to this one." And he played a scorching "Johnny 99."

Before playing "My Hometown" at concerts, Bruce frequently told a story about growing up in Freehold and playing "out behind the Monument." He was in high school, he said, before he realized that the Monument was dedicated to the Battle of Monmouth in the American Revolution; the battle had been fought in Freehold. That night in Pittsburgh he described going to Washington, D.C., before the current tour began and making a "long walk" from the Lincoln Memorial to the Vietnam Veterans Memorial, and he concluded by saying, "It's a long walk from a government that's supposed to represent all of the people to where we are today. It seems like something's wrong out there when there's a lotta stuff being taken away from a lot of people that shouldn't have it taken away from [them]. And sometimes it's hard to remember that this place belongs to us—that this is our hometown."

It was a smart tactic, tackling exactly the issues that Reagan's "springtime" speeches evaded. Landau made sure that Springsteen's comments were relayed to interested journalists, and by Monday, three days later, several influential newspapers ran follow-up stories on the rock star's reaction to the President's rock criticism.

But if it was not Springsteen's style to make political speeches, it was even more unlike him to let such a traumatic incident pass by with a single gesture. He came back at his second Pittsburgh show, after the brief meeting with Weisen the night before, with much stronger and clearer remarks that amounted to a bill of particulars against the devastating winter that Ronald Reagan's administration had helped create in the real America.

"There's something really dangerous happening to us out there," he said. "We're slowly getting split up into two different Americas. Things are gettin' taken away from people that need them and given to people that don't need them, and there's a promise getting broken. In the beginning the idea was that we all live here a little bit like a family, where the strong can help the weak ones, the rich can help the poor ones. I don't think the American dream was that everybody was going to make it or that everybody was going to make a billion dollars, but it was that everybody was going to have an opportunity and the chance to live a life with some decency and some dignity and a chance for some self-respect. So I know you gotta be feelin' the pinch down here where the rivers meet." The sharp opening harmonica blasts of "The River" cut through the dead stillness his speech had created, and the crowd erupted. After the song was finished, he said simply, "That was for Local 1397, rank and file."

The next night the tour party moved on to Buffalo, another ravaged industrial city. There Bruce turned thirty-six, with a party at a local roller skating rink, and treated himself to a rare drunken night out. But he was fully recovered for the first of the two shows at the Buffalo War Memorial, where his raps showed he had turned a corner. Beyond reacting to Ronald Reagan, he was reasserting his own more positive vision.

"I dreamed something and I was lucky. A large part of it came true," he said just before singing "Born to Run." "But it's not just for one; it's gotta be for everyone, and you've gotta fight for it every day." It was the ghost of "Street Fighting Man" again, only this time Bruce was much more inextricably linked with that poor boy who had nothing to do but sing his heart out.

In all this Springsteen was careful not to hamstring himself by giving an endorsement to the Democratic ticket. The lack of a significant difference was brought home in the days after the Pittsburgh show when Democratic presidential nominee Walter Mondale told a press conference, "Bruce Springsteen may have been born to run but he wasn't born yesterday" and then claimed to have received a letter from Springsteen endorsing his candidacy. Landau's office denied that any such letter had been sent, and the next day Mondale was forced to the excuse that he had been "misinformed" by his staff.

Springsteen kept his distance from both the Democratic and the Republican parties. "I don't generally think along those lines," he told Kurt Loder. "I find it very difficult to relate to the whole electoral system as it stands." Election night would find him onstage in Los Angeles.

Bruce's political goal wasn't to elect candidates; it was much more basic. He meant to link his wealth and fame with the sort of people who were living in the circumstances in which he'd originated. By late 1984 there were millions of such people, thrown out of work permanently or reduced to menial, minimum-wage jobs without even such basic fringe benefits as health care, while industrial capital took flight from the United States and corporate profits were spent in a round of mergers and acquisitions that spiraled into outright scandal by the end of 1986. Springsteen operated from the understanding that his sympathies belonged with "my people." (The politicians' response to this was another matter. Mikal Gilmore guessed that Reagan probably dismissed this sort of concern "with his characteristic shrug of contempt," and after November 4 nobody cared what Mondale thought about anything.)

Bruce told *Rolling Stone*'s Loder, "I want to try and just work more directly with people, try to find some way that my band can tie into the communities that we come into. I guess that's a political action, a way to just bypass that whole electoral thing—human politics. I think that people on their own can do a lot. I guess that's what I'm tryin' to figure out now: Where do the aesthetic issues that you write about intersect with some sort of concrete action, some direct involvement in the communities that your audience comes from? It seems to be an inevitable progression of what our band has been doin', of the idea that we got into this for. We wanted to play because we wanted to meet girls, we wanted to make a ton of dough, and we wanted to change the world a little bit, you know?" He still hadn't fully learned his lesson, obviously, since the implications of *laissez-faire*—"people on their own can do a lot"—were exactly what misled Reagan and Will in the first place. Nevertheless, this was the dawning of something better than a candidate endorsement—it was the awakening of an actual political program independent of any candidate.

The Buffalo show ended the first leg of the *Born in the U.S.A.* tour. Everyone flew home for three weeks of rest and recuperation. Springsteen spent part of his time off planning a new course of action with Landau and Barbara Carr, who began researching groups around the country that worked with the hungry, the homeless, and the unemployed. Meanwhile, Bruce decided to make a $10,000 donation to the Local 1397 food bank. And he wanted to make similar contacts in every tour stop from then onward.

◆

The Reagan episode was a watershed. It unlocked Bruce Springsteen as a conscious political actor, by forcing him to see that he had to speak explicitly if he wanted to retain the right to choose his metaphors. Equally important, it demarcated the *Born in the U.S.A.* tour.

Now Bruce reasserted his previous style. No restrictions were placed on CBS's full-tilt record marketing, but Bruce regained his more personal and reserved focus. He canned plans for interviews in the mass circulation media and began preparing for a *Rolling Stone* interview with the excellent Kurt Loder. Although "Cover Me" had come and gone in the Top Ten with no video at all, Bruce was still attentive to the potential video presented. However, he wanted to pull back from the slickness of the "Dancing in the Dark" clip. Director John Sayles, who had made several significant films on funky budgets, was hired to direct a bare-bones live-performance clip of "Born in the U.S.A.," the album's third single, during upcoming shows at the Los Angeles Sports Arena.

The only public announcement of Springsteen's plans came when Columbia Records issued a late-autumn press release headlined: "Bruce Springsteen Announces New Tour Dates in Twelve Cities; Local Community Organizations Benefit from Tour Support; 'Born in the U.S.A.' Is Third Single, As LP Sales Top Four Million." Announcing a swing to begin on the West Coast and move through the South before winding up in the Northeast, the release also stated that Springsteen would henceforth be meeting local groups in each town he played, to express his "concern for depressed conditions in various communities."

The result was an active enhancement of Springsteen's prestige in many quarters. Meanwhile, growling back at the President had done nothing to slow down album sales. *Born in the U.S.A.* had now spent four months as the nation's Number Two best-selling album, and the title single entered the *Billboard* Hot 100 at Fifty-two, took a ten-point jump its second week, and eventually made the bottom rung of the Top Ten. By Christmas, sales had leaped to over 5 million copies in the United States, were nearly double that worldwide, and showed no sign of slacking.

"Born in the U.S.A." wasn't selected as the third single in order to capitalize upon the Reagan endorsement or to correct it. It wasn't even the top choice of the CBS promotion department, which would have preferred the softer, more surefire "I'm on Fire." But Al Teller, with Landau's concurrence, saw "Born in the U.S.A." as an ideal "image single," one that might not sell as well or receive quite as much airplay as a more obvious pop song but would lock in on exactly what Springsteen and his latest album were all about. It was a good call.

During the ten weeks that "Born in the U.S.A." spent on the singles charts, albums sold at a meteoric clip.

Bruce continued to work with Arthur Baker, whose controversial remix of "Dancing in the Dark" had been followed by a restructuring of "Cover Me" that even involved cutting a new bass line. (Because it was only meant as a demo, the song had been recorded in such haste that Garry Tallent had never had a chance to cut a proper track.) Baker also rescued an unused but outstanding background vocal sung by the well-known session singer Jocelyn Brown. His "undercover mix" drew the song's groove close to reggae and its density close to dub, a transformation so great that Bruce, who'd been reluctant to sing the song live at all, adopted several elements of the remix and began opening the second set with it, which also gave Patti Scialfa her only solo spot.

But Arthur Baker really outdid himself with his "freedom mix" of "Born in the U.S.A." If there was any lingering confusion about what the song said, the "freedom mix" dispelled it forever by enhancing every mournful accent Baker could find in the track. Baker also stripped the song, isolating synthesizer, drums, and voice in order to condense the E Street Band's brutally hard rock into electronic dance music played off against a martial snare. In a way, by featuring glockenspiel and synthesizer and deemphasizing guitar, Baker made the song prettier—as eerily beautiful as tracer fire. The effect is stark and scary. At the end of the second verse, Bruce's voice is simply overwhelmed, and for several minutes it jumps and skitters, fighting to be heard above the insistent rhythm. In the background, echoed and multiplied, one phrase rings time and again, like a Morse distress signal: "U.S.A.—U.S.—U.S.—U.S.A."

In the remix, parts all but hidden in the original are pulled into prominence: an acoustic guitar, a single zooming bass chord, Springsteen muttering "Oh my God, no." These things have been there all along, just waiting to be discovered, and Baker makes like Ali Baba. Finally, rather than the concert ending of the original, there's a violent finale, first the music and then Bruce's voice declaring "I'm a cool rockin' daddy in the U.S.A. now" sliced off. The last sound is the noise of a tape clipped to a halt, cruel as a last heartbeat.

The starkness of the "freedom mix" was matched by the 45's previously unreleased B side. "Shut Out the Light" is a song from Bruce's Los Angeles home studio; its musical atmosphere couldn't be farther from Baker's crashing electronics. It's just a guitar, a tambourine, a little synthesizer, and Eric Weissberg's fiddle. This time Springsteen sings a folkish melody as though telling a ghost story, his voice doubled an octave higher to sing harmony with itself on the chorus.

The lyrics are incredibly detailed and exceptionally brief. Vietnam is unmentioned but omnipresent, looming over each verse. The story is "Born in the U.S.A." set back ten years, to the evening of the protagonist's homecoming. His plane lands; he takes a taxi to a bar; he remeets his family and his wife, who love him utterly and think of the future. He cannot connect—or maybe he can't disconnect. It's more or less the Vietnam veteran's cliché but rendered with such passionate simplicity that it's as if you've never heard it before.

What's new is Springsteen's treatment of the presence of the war in these lives. It's like some mysterious disease in which part of the contagion is an inability to speak or think clearly. No one talks about it, because nobody understands it, least of all Johnson Linnier himself, who simply lies awake at night and cries a helpless prayer:

> *Mama, mama, mama, come quick*
>
> *I've got the shakes and I'm gonna be sick*
>
> *Throw your arms around me in the cold dark night*
>
> *Hey now, mama, don't you shut out the light*

. . . and then the harmonica and the fiddle, harmonizing as perfectly as bile and bitter tears. "Born in the U.S.A." is the Vietnam story as carried forward in one heroic life, but "Shut Out the Light" is something much more frightening: the dank aftertaste the war left in the mouth of the nations it poisoned.

◆

Springsteen's interest in working with community groups wasn't just a refutation of Ronald Reagan. He had spoken to Steve Van Zandt during *The River* tour about doing "something that would leave something behind" in the cities through which they barnstormed. He had mentioned similar ideas to Barbara Carr after the Vietnam Veterans benefit and during the album-making months. Landau also remembered talking with Bruce before the tour started about trying to "get into some kind of program on a sustained basis." There's plenty of reason to believe that Springsteen meant from the outset to do such things on the *Born in the U.S.A.* tour but then had simply become so wrapped up in his own phenomenon that he'd never started. The confrontation with the President was the catalyst, and it couldn't have come at a more opportune time.

Jon Landau pointed out that Springsteen's response was a typical example of his turning a negative into a positive. "He said, 'Okay, let's get our thoughts together on what we're doing and let's get a plan together. Now's the right time to start. Because rather than reacting to somebody else, this is the best way for me to get across my ideas about things in general.'"

"If I'm going around this country, I want to know what's going on where I'm playing, and I want to leave something positive behind," he told Landau. Perhaps there was a selfish motive, but it was not the crass need for a benevolent image—he already had that. Rather, Springsteen wanted to assuage his fear of becoming a star who lived cut off from "real life." But like any performer who had reached superstardom, Springsteen *was* now cut off from much information about the everyday world. Even in his ascetic backstage, the people who turned up were purely show-biz types, and if he met someone when he went for a walk, everything they said was most likely filtered through the knowledge of who he was. Anyway, trying to establish this kind of contact on a one-to-one basis was too haphazard.

"We talked and I said, 'How should we do this?'" remembered Landau. "'I mean, what type of thing are we interested in?'" If Bruce simply wanted to do charity work, there were dozens of worthy diseases and causes. But he was moved by the hungry and homeless of America, in no small part because he could easily imagine himself and his family among them. "For him this was the most personalized thing, and so this is where we channeled our efforts; this was our focus point. Things that you could say were having an effect on people that Bruce identified with, he feels close to, because they're the kind of people he grew up with.

"In other words, it is not merely about a quantity of money. It was not about that. It could be very helpful in that local area, but in terms of the needs of the situation, on a relative scale it was more symbolic than truly problem-solving." Instead, the contributions (which averaged $10,000 a night during the arena portion of the tour,

$25,000 nightly when the shows moved outdoors in the summer) would symbolize commitment and solidarity and perhaps serve as an inspiration to his fans. "Since his father was an unemployed blue-collar worker, he's naturally most concerned with groups like food banks for unemployed union members and groups that deal with environmental responsibility," Barbara Carr told the rock magazine *BAM*.

Carr did the advance work, identifying the one or two organizations in each city with ongoing programs that put them in direct contact with people in need. In the main, this meant food banks, some of them established by trade unions, some by churches, some by the food industry itself (the "Second Harvest" network). Occasionally Springsteen worked with citizens action groups that targeted specific issues—usually environmental—in their area. In Philadelphia, in the summer of 1985, they linked up with Chris Sprowal and the Committee for Fairness and Dignity for the Homeless, which spawned the National Union for the Homeless, the first organization to work for the empowerment of the homeless themselves.

Springsteen processed the information he received as an artist, not a politician. In all his meetings, he felt that he received at least as much from the community group as he gave to them. What was most remarkable wasn't his ability to remember names and figures and spiel them out to a crowd (that was just a basic show-biz skill at work) or even his plain courage and refusal to back off from supporting those shunned by society (that might even have been a good career move, since it preserved his image of unshakable integrity), but rather the way in which his community contact was integrated into the bedrock of his performances. Springsteen was integrating a new, unambiguous social vision into work still rich in metaphor. The result was an exceptionally powerful combination, especially since it meant he was able to champion radical causes and working-class dreams without ever losing his grip on a huge audience or the respect of the creative community.

And Springsteen's popularity continued to grow. By Christmas he'd have performed eighty shows before an audience of 1.3 million. In early October director Bob Giraldi chose "My Hometown" as the theme music to introduce the two-minute vignette he produced as a lead-in to the World Series telecasts—all seven games. Bruce probably didn't get to see it much, though, because it was during the Series, on October 15, that the next leg of the tour began with a show in Vancouver, British Columbia.

The show was as high-spirited as ever. During "Rosalita" Nils Lofgren brought out his mini-trampoline and essayed his nightly flip (complete with guitar). He missed on five straight attempts; Bruce finally just laughed, "Fuck it," and moved on to the climactic introduction of Clarence Clemons as "the king o' the world . . . the master of disaster . . ." "Rosalita" was the warhorse of warhorses; it had ended every Springsteen show since 1973, when Bruce wrote it. Sometimes it seemed that he did the entire show merely as an excuse to reach this epic, comic quarter-hour of rock-star bluster, cartoon poses, athletic leaps, and slapstick introductions—"Now you see him, now you don't . . . Phantom Dan Federici"; "The only member of the band with a high school diploma . . . Professor Roy Bittan." But "Rosalita" was also a ponderous pile, a somewhat bloated compendium of musical notions that had long since had its vital juices drained. Placed elsewhere in the set, that might not have mattered so much, but as the final pre-encore number, it had begun to drag somewhere around 1980. Yet it remained embedded in place, symptomizing Springsteen's root conservatism.

The tour moved on to Tacoma for two nights at the 25,000-seat indoor Tacoma Dome. Before each Tacoma show Bruce met in his dressing room with community representatives. The first night he saw people from Washington Fair Share, a two-year-old "nonpartisan coalition of church, labor, and community organizations" with a total membership of more than 15,000. Fair Share had helped pass a state "right to know" bill informing workers when they worked with hazardous substances (information companies ordinarily try to hide), worked to keep phone rates down after the AT&T bustup and to tighten toxic disposal laws, fought unsuccessfully together with steelworkers to keep area mills from closing, helped close dangerous toxic chemical plants in the Puget Sound area, and tried to stop cuts in Social Security benefits. The second night leaders of the Northwest Harvest Food Bank came along. Carr met briefly with the representatives, introduced them to Bruce (who had already read the literature about their work that they'd sent beforehand), then left them alone to talk. When they emerged ten minutes later, enthusiastic about Springsteen's intense interest, she requested that they meet her backstage again at the break.

The Tacoma shows opened the same way those on the first leg of the tour had, but toward the end of the first set Bruce paused and launched nervously into a new rap, one that seemed less prepared than his usual narratives. He spoke for a couple of minutes about Fair Share, about the danger of "blind faith—whether it's in your girlfriend or the government. This is 1984 and people seem to be searchin' for something." He praised Fair Share, saying, "They think that people should come before profit and the community before the corporation," and opened the encores by reminding his listeners, "Remember Fair Share—this is *your* hometown."

The next night was Northwest Harvest's turn. "This is a song, it's kinda about sharing some of the responsibility for the place that you live," he said, then hesitated. "Sometimes . . . I know when I was a kid I used to have a real love/hate relationship with the place I grew up. I felt like I didn't wanna . . . I didn't wanna belong. I guess I was afraid to belong to somethin'.

"But right here in your town there's an organization called Northwest Harvest. What they do is, they do somethin' real simple: They feed people—people that have been cut out by some of the injustices of our social system or by the economic policies of the current administration. There's people out there that are just hungry; they need something to eat. The name of the organization is Northwest Harvest, and they can use . . . ya got extra food, you got anything that you can give them, their number's gonna be out at the concession stands during the break. They're here in your town trying to make it a more decent place to live. If you get a chance, check 'em out and help 'em out—'cause this is your hometown."

Springsteen's very awkwardness helped him get over with a speech many might otherwise have found heavy-handed or inappropriate to "entertainment." Furthermore, his hesitancy and lack of polish worked toward establishing the kind of character who might tell a story like the one in "My Hometown." Over the next few months, various versions of this rap, elaborated and edited, became the prelude to the final section of the first set: "My Hometown" leading up to the explosion of "Thunder Road," with its last line, "It's a town full of losers/ I'm pullin' outta here to win." Inexorably, the kid who ran away from home was reining domesticity back into his orbit and doing it through the vehicle of joining the rock and roll circus.

Backstage during the break Barbara Carr again met with the community group representatives. Without any advance notice, she presented each of them with a check. The money wouldn't go far, given the scale of poverty, but Springsteen's onstage rap would be reported in all the reviews, and a press conference could be held the next day, announcing the donation and soliciting both more funds and greater community involvement.

But it was the end of the second night's show that really threw the old fans. As mordant organ and piano chords brought "Backstreets" to an end, veteran Springsteen concertgoers braced themselves for the "Rosalita" finale. But that night, for the first time in eleven years, the song that poured out next was not "Rosalita" but "Born to Run." And the old-guard Bossmaniacs were stunned.

Wrote Charles Cross, editor of the Seattle-based Springsteen fanzine *Backstreets*, "The crowd of twenty thousand was speechless, dazed, frozen in their places. Was the show over? Where was 'Rosalita'? As far as I can remember, ever since Springsteen wrote 'Rosalita,' he's ended every show with it—it was the great punctuation point to his body of work."

Even beyond the obvious fanzine hyperbole, it's hard to imagine that very many imaginations were as frozen as Cross suggests. But if all Springsteen had done was disrupt the ritual expectations of the fanatic fans Cross represented, he'd done himself a service, establishing through a burst of creativity just who *was* boss. He had also liberated the show from an albatross, a song that was too long and had long since stopped breathing. Refreshed, the band, as if working off excess energy, came back for an unusually lengthy and diverse group of encore numbers, including "I'm a Rocker," "Wooly Bully," the "Detroit Medley," the medley of "Twist and Shout" and "Do You Love Me," and finally—as Bruce shouted (probably telling the truth), "I can't go on. I'm *ill!*"—"Santa Claus Is Coming to Town."

After two shows at the Oakland Coliseum, marred only by promoter Bill Graham's inability to control ticket scalping, the tour moved on to a seven-night stand at Los Angeles Sports Arena. The show was evolving but it hadn't lost its high spirits. The final night of the Los Angeles run was Halloween, and Bruce entered like Screamin' Jay Hawkins, lying upon a black coffinlike box amidst billows of dry-ice smoke and spooky music. Flat on his back, Springsteen told the story of a Dr. Frankensteen who couldn't wake up. "They tried music," he intoned, as Clarence held a boom box playing "Louie Louie" to his ear. "They tried sex," he said, as Scialfà, outfitted in a nurse's uniform, bent close.

Then Jim McDuffie came out and presented him with a guitar, and Bruce leaped off the box and cranked into Jerry Lee Lewis's "High School Confidential."

In working with community groups, Springsteen wasn't looking for any publicity for himself—although working with them did help to take some of the media pressure off. Since he wasn't doing any interviews (the *Rolling Stone* story with Kurt Loder, who finally got Bruce to sit down in Los Angeles, was the last of the tour), his support for the food banks and other community groups gave the media something else to cover. The only restriction placed on what the groups did with Bruce's support was that they wait until after the first night's show to do it. Asked by the press why Springsteen didn't make a statement explaining his actions, Barbara Carr simply replied, "This *is* his statement," and that threw the reporters right back into the arms of the community groups, who wanted and needed the extra attention.

It worked, too. In Memphis, food bank director Virginia Dunaway found herself interviewed on the local rock station; the next month the station did a series on hunger issues. In Oakland Bruce worked with the Berkeley Emergency Food Project, whose manager, Becky Aiello, remarked, "No one knew we existed until the Boss said this is a good thing to contribute to. After that, even high school students came in to volunteer." A year later some were still helping out.

Even if Arthur Baker couldn't give Springsteen an audience among the dispossessed, who remain disproportionately black and Hispanic, Bruce's music already had a grip on many white community activists who worked with them. For instance, Dwight Pelz, executive director of Washington Fair Share, waited in line five hours for Tacoma Dome tickets; when a phone message came through from Jon Landau Management in New York, one of the Fair Share staffers recognized Landau's name from Springsteen liner notes. As a result, the dressing room meetings with activists didn't have the tone of politicos addressing a celebrity or of a media aristocrat deigning to notice representatives of the plebeians. They had the quality of a respected leader encountering peers. "I spent a night in jail in Wildwood [at the Jersey shore] when I was sixteen," said Pelz to break the ice. "Everybody did," Springsteen replied.

Additionally, the food bank directors were precisely the right people to help translate Springsteen's ideas to the media. Even their skepticism was useful. "We asked him quite candidly why he was doing this, and he said, 'Rock stars come into a community and leave,' " said Gene Hanlon of the Omaha Area Food Bank. "This was his way of coming into a community, thanking the community, and leaving something behind."

Many other performers made charitable gestures part of their shows by collecting canned goods or writing a check. Springsteen's approach was different. He plugged into ongoing processes. He carefully combed through the research Carr gave him; nearly every food bank director who met him was impressed with his command of the facts. He not only wrote a check, he made a speech placing local problems in a national context and prodded his listeners to do something themselves. Often, those things were worth more than the check.

As Bruce gained more experience, his confidence rose, and rather than worrying about the things he didn't know, he gave his audience as much as he could about what he did understand. Springsteen recited the appalling statistics of hunger in the richest, most agriculturally productive country in the world, noting the tons of food that rotted each year, the thousands of undernourished children. And at each stop he'd stick his neck out a little farther. "There are a lot of people out of work, seniors whose Social Security doesn't get them through the month, kids who don't have enough to eat," he'd say, adding, "and they ain't gettin' caught in no safety net." He talked about fighting for your community, about the importance of a hometown, about the ways in which joblessness robbed people not only of subsistence but of their human dignity. And he signed off with a slogan that was also a pledge: "Remember, nobody wins unless everybody wins." There were those on the left who'd argue that this was "just charity," but in fact, by asserting the reality of impoverishment for so many Americans (whose existence both political parties tried to downplay or deny), he was asking the well-off customers at his concerts to face serious questions about their own lives.

In Los Angeles, his second hometown, Springsteen worked with the Steelworkers–Old Timers Food Bank, based in Maywood, one of the string of working-class towns in the southeastern section of sprawling Los Angeles County. Following the Local 1397 example, this food bank had been established by out-of-work steelworkers from the defunct Bethlehem mill in Vernon, under the leadership of USWA Local 1845 president George Cole. By the end of 1984, it was feeding 5,000 families a month, almost 100,000 meals.

Like the Vietnam Veterans of America in 1981, the food bank was almost broke when Springsteen came to town. By the time he left, it had begun to thrive, building on his contribution, the first media attention it had ever received and new initiatives of its own. For instance, in Tacoma and Oakland the community groups had merely set out posters at the refreshment and merchandising stands. George Cole and his staff proposed setting up tables at which literature could be distributed and donations received, giving Bruce's audience an immediate opportunity to match his generosity and offering that much more opportunity to involve concertgoers in the groups' ongoing work.

Over the seven-night stand, and counting checks that poured in after the E Streeters left town, the audience contributed about $20,000, doubling Springsteen's contribution. Cole exulted that the donations would allow the Steelworkers–Old Timers group to buy "literally tons of food," but he also knew that it would be hard to keep up the pressure. Yet as he acknowledged, "Over the course of a week, [Bruce has] focused people's attention on organizations like ours. A lot more people are now aware that there's more to Los Angeles than Hollywood glamor and good times."

Following the Los Angeles shows, it was Cole and his staff who persuaded Springsteen to work with Dr. Jorge O'Leary's People's Clinic in the destitute mining town of Clifton, Arizona, where striking copper workers had been bankrupted by the strike-busting tactics of Phelps-Dodge and the lethargy of the United Steelworkers' international leadership. The clinic, located in a converted feed store, was only days from closing. The $10,000 Springsteen contributed, supplemented by more than $2,000 in audience donations, enabled O'Leary to move to better facilities in a mobile home and kept the clinic, which had become the center of resistance to Phelps-Dodge, alive for many additional months.

More importantly, there was an entire organization around the food bank in Los Angeles County. Even after the Bethlehem mill folded, Cole had managed to hold Local 1845 together, and he'd managed to get elected to the city council of Bell, another of the towns near the mill. (In 1985 Cole was elected mayor of Bell.) Included were dozens of different people, not just steelworkers but textile workers, machinists, and other unionists, many of them Hispanic or black, perhaps a majority over forty.

On one of his off-days in Los Angeles Springsteen drove down to the hall and met with a group of steelworkers. Springsteen donned a Local 1845 cap and joined the theater workshop organized by actress Susan Franklin Tanner. Tanner read some lyrics from "Downbound Train," and Springsteen participated in an exercise in which each participant imagined himself to be some sort of work tool. ("I'm a guitar," Bruce said without hesitation.) Many of the workers had seen the show; like other food banks, the steelworkers received six tickets for each evening's show and food bank volunteers could swap between seats and the donation tables in the course of the long night.

One who attended the shows and the workshop was Luis Rodriguez, a laid-off steelworker from the East Los Angeles barrio. Prompted by participation in Tanner's workshop, he wrote a brilliant poem, "Bethlehem No More," which recounted his experiences amid the ugly and dangerous conditions of life in the mill, evoking also the tremendous affection the workers developed for each other and for the steel with which they did nightly combat.

Like Rodriguez, the other laid-off steelworkers had little idea of their artistic abilities until they began meeting to swap stories and trade experiences. Out of such dialogue Tanner was helping the workers develop a play entitled *Lady Beth*, which had been their nickname for the mill. (In 1985 Springsteen went to see *Lady Beth* several times and participated in the final act, which was a discussion with the audience. He later sponsored and helped to fund a national tour by the Theater Workers Project.)

"Bruce is at a crossroads now," a "Springsteen associate" told Robert Hilburn in Oakland. "He's thinking about the connection between what he writes and the world. I think what you're seeing in these shows is him trying to find a way to make that connection in a way that's comfortable for him. . . . Rather than getting embroiled with personalities and endorsing candidates, the thing that seems to make the most sense to him is to keep it more personal."

The tour moved onward, through the heartland. Bruce played Ames, Iowa, and talked about the demise of the family farmers, then sang a revitalized "Sugarland," ending with a rare image of rebellion:

> *Well if land prices don't get no higher*
> *I'll fill this duster with gas and set these fields on fire*

Sit up on the ridge where the bluebirds fly

And watch the flames rise up against this Sugarland sky

The next night they moved on to Lincoln, Nebraska, where Bruce sang of Charles Starkweather. Then they crossed over to Kansas City, heading south into Texas and Louisiana, Alabama, Florida, Kentucky, Tennessee, and Georgia. In Memphis Little Steven turned up for the encores. In Atlanta they wound up the second leg of the tour with "Santa Claus Is Coming to Town." They'd played eighty shows in six months and only had about a hundred left to do.

◆

After a two-week Christmas break the tour reassembled in Columbia, South Carolina, swinging straight up the East Coast, from good weather into bad. By now the tour had its own momentum and, in a sense, its own life. While the outside world celebrated Springsteen as a superstar and hero of the underprivileged, the internal story was simpler—and maybe sweeter. With the changes he'd made in the ending of the show, Bruce had trimmed the event to a more livable pace and the result was some of the finest performances he'd ever given. Moving outside major media markets, the show became looser and freer.

In the outside world the legend simply grew. It was only marginally helped along by Bruce's second video. "Born in the U.S.A.," shot rough by John Sayles, had the kind of dark-tinged performance footage you'd expect from a grab-shot documentary or a low-budget heavy metal band. Bruce wore layers of sweatshirts and jackets, a headband, and several days' growth of stubble. (Because of the video shoot, the band had to wear the same stage clothes every night of the Sports Arena stand, and Bruce's beard had to be trimmed by hand each afternoon.) Sayles took a crew to various locations in New Jersey—most notably a Veterans of Foreign Wars hall—and came away with interesting cutaways that enhanced the message of the music. The problem was that the video had to be out before the single's run up the charts was finished. There wasn't time to do the painstaking mixing necessary to use the live soundtrack, and after "Dancing in the Dark" Bruce absolutely refused to lip-sync. The result was a hodgepodge: The documentary effect was undercut by the lack of live sound, and any inherent artfulness was dispelled because the sound didn't match Bruce's lip movements. (The effect was even odder because the live "Born in the U.S.A." Sayles filmed was played a little slower than the record.)

Nevertheless, the video increased recognition of Springsteen's face in the unlikeliest ways. While Christmas shopping with his mother in a San Francisco department store, Bruce felt his coattail tugged and turned to find a three-year-old looking up at him: "I know you. You're Bruce. I saw you on TV."

He'd become one of those one-name Eighties media stars—like Michael and Mick, Tina and Barbra, Ronnie and "heeere's Johnny"—but unlike the others, he didn't do regular press conferences or stage media stunts. The papers and television and radio worked twenty-four hours a day; their need for celebrity copy was insatiable, and stories about food banks and union halls could substitute only so far.

Springsteen's aloofness from the media was relaxed only twice in this period. In Greensboro he allowed a crew from the ABC show 20/20 to film the portions of the set in which he addressed the food bank issue for a story they were doing on the growing hunger pangs of American workers and the resurgence of activism among unemployed unionists. (Springsteen didn't do an interview for the show, but he did have a brief off-camera meeting with Hugh Downs, whose sons had made him a fan.) And the *Rolling Stone* interview with Kurt Loder appeared, in two parts—one in early December and the second (presented as a separate story but based on unused quotes and material from the first) in mid-February as part of the magazine's annual awards issue. (Bruce, the E Street Band, and the *Born in the U.S.A.* album and singles made a clean sweep of those.)

Loder's interviews were by far the most interesting and challenging Springsteen did in the entire *Born in the U.S.A.* period. Loder was particularly good at probing Springsteen's politics, probably because his questions were gently phrased and didn't scare Bruce by backing him into the limits of his knowledge of specifics. But Springsteen himself was also much clearer about his ideas. In 1981 he'd told his last *Rolling Stone* interviewer, Fred Schruers, "There's too much greed, too much carelessness. I don't believe that was ever the idea of capitalism. It's just gotta be voices heard from all places, that's my main concern," adding only that for him, the American dream "ain't about two cars in the garage. It's about people living and working together without steppin' on each other." With Loder he was much more concrete.

"I think what's happening now is people want to forget," he said about his reading of the country's mood. "There was Vietnam, there was Watergate, there was Iran—we were beaten, we were hustled, and then we were humiliated. And I think people have a need to feel good about the country they live in. But what's happening, I think, is that that need, which is a good thing, is gettin' manipulated and exploited. And you see the Reagan reelection ads on TV—you know, 'It's morning in America'—and you say, Well, it's not morning in Pittsburgh. It's not morning above 125th Street in New York. It's midnight and, like, there's a bad moon risin'. And that's why when Reagan mentioned my name in New Jersey, I felt it was another manipulation and I had to disassociate myself from the President's kind words."

In 1980, in an interview for *Musician* magazine, Springsteen had used the hustler image but had specifically resisted having the conclusions he'd drawn from that analysis applied as an answer to the reasons for his involvement in the antinuclear movement, reducing his perception to just another genre image: "It's just the whole thing; it's the *whole* thing. It's terrible, it's horrible. Somewhere along the way, the idea, which I think was initially to get some fair transaction between people, went out the window. And what came in was, the most you can get." He'd stopped and laughed, perhaps at his own audacity in presuming to tackle such an important idea. "The most you can get and the least you can give. That's why cars are the way they are today. It's just an erosion of all the things that were true and right about the original idea."

If one thing was clear from Springsteen's life and career, it was that he was far too cautious to put himself in a position of responsibility for things he didn't understand. Now, though, he seemed to have decided that he was ready to speak as if his ideas about the world counted in the most particular ways. He was by no means a politician; he wasn't even necessarily a "political" artist, if that meant that he had to stop singing and start campaigning. But if others were going to interpret his work in that way, then he'd make damn sure that his own interpretation was on the record—and that it was solidly grounded.

For the first and last time he specifically addressed his reaction to the President's endorsement-by-fiat. And he very typically did it by reducing the question to its most personal elements, disassociating himself from Reagan and Reaganism much more firmly than he could have done with political rhetoric or name-calling. "Well, I don't *know* him. But I think he presents a very mythic, very seductive image, and it's an image that people want to believe in. I think there's always been a nostalgia for a mythical America, for some period in the past when everything was just right. And I think the President is the embodiment of that for a lot of people. He has a very mythical presidency. I don't know if he's a bad man. But I think there's a large group of people in this country whose dreams don't mean that much to him, that just get indiscriminately swept aside.

"I guess my view of America is of a real big-hearted country, real compassionate. But the difficult thing out here right now is that the social consciousness that was a part of the Sixties has become, like, old-fashioned or something. You go out, you get your job, and you try to make as much money as you can and have a good time on the weekend. And that's considered okay."

◆

Swinging back into the frigid, winter-desolate Northeast, Springsteen was still having a good time, but he was also wrestling with a complex situation. Because he'd become so much more popular, the demand for his concert tickets had risen to ridiculous levels. The current tour ended with two shows at the 38,000-seat Carrier Dome in Syracuse, New York. After a few weeks break, he would spend the spring doing his first shows ever in Australia and Japan, then tour Europe in the summer months. Tickets in both Pacific basin countries had sold out in record-shattering time.

In Australia as well as in Europe there were logistical reasons obliging Springsteen to play outdoor stadiums. Neither continent contained the number and quality of indoor facilities to make it feasible to play arenas. If Bruce had insisted on not playing stadiums, he would have had to commit himself to spending months in just a few cities in order to fulfill the demand even fractionally. So he agreed to do both tours on the only practical terms.

Another decision needed to be reached as well. After Europe some sort of homecoming tour would be desirable. But the demand in most American markets now made the very idea of playing indoors out of the question—even ten more Meadowlands shows wouldn't begin to slake the thirst of "my people" to see the Springsteen show. And that demand might well grow. *Born in the U.S.A.* was still Number Two; it had cracked the 5 million sales barrier; and one of the album's most surefire hit singles, "I'm on Fire," was in the wings. If Bruce wanted to do another American tour in the summer of 1985, there wouldn't be any way to avoid playing stadiums.

Bruce wasn't sure he was willing to take that step. But for the first time since Philadelphia promoter Larry Magid had offered him a shot at 100,000-seat JFK Stadium in 1976, he wasn't sure that he didn't, either. Neither Jon Landau nor George Travis saw any creative or production problems with taking the show outside. Frank Barsalona and Barry Bell of Premier Talent, which had enormous experience with outdoor concerts, predating even Woodstock, were both certain that the shows would translate and that Bruce would satisfy far more of his audience than would be annoyed by the prospect of sitting farther away. Most significantly, Springsteen himself had sat in the crowd at the Who's final American shows in Los Angeles back in 1982, and he'd not only had a good time, he'd been inspired to think about how he'd perform in a similar situation.

The arena shows he was doing had about run their course. In the States, he'd been playing arena-size buildings for the most part since 1978, a total of four swings around the nation. He now knew almost exactly what would happen each night; so did the audience. Since he wasn't prepared to radically change the show, maybe the venue ought to be altered. That would open Bruce up to a new challenge, it would invite some new blood aboard (and give it a place to sit down), and it would make a strong statement about his inclusive artistic and political priorities. Presuming that the hard core would still want to go to every show, they would occupy a far smaller percentage of the total number of seats each night. Stadium gigs might even cut into the booming scalpers market, since that much more of the demand would be filled legitimately.

But it was the creative challenge that made Springsteen take the prospect of a stadium tour so seriously. He was always looking for a way to find out new things from his shows. He was at every one of those arena shows; he knew all their flaws as well as their glories. And he knew it was time to make a move.

"We build up so much horsepower that by the time we got out of the arenas, the band was tugging at the reins," he said. "From the beginning, my music fits a big place—it's big, it's a loud noise. And I sing at the top of my lungs. It works in a big place like that. I didn't think that the thing to do was to get overconcerned about it. Even with all those people out there, you're still in business that night to initiate some sort of one-on-one contact. So all you need is one person. And if there happen to be sixty thousand out there, they're all individuals. I'm basically trying to reach as many of them as I can, in as personal a fashion as I can. That's how I think in my head, anyway.

"That was the whole point from the very beginning, when there really were more people in the band than in the audience. And we had good nights, nights that were fine. We had a good time, the people that were there had a great time. I guess for me that was the important idea. It's not that big a deal, it's just something that just felt natural to me. It wasn't a plan or anything, it's just that that's the way we've always done it."

He'd resisted the move from club to arena, then, because it seemed possible that making that alteration would sacrifice that crucial idea. What he found out was that the opposite was true.

"Those places are great because, first of all, they have a roof, and the roof bottles in so much energy," he said. "And you get a band like ours and look out! It's like shakin' up a pop bottle. What we tend to do is, I wait until I have that feeling, that we *are* gonna blow the roof of this place, you know. And I wait until I feel that we have so much muscle behind us on that stage that like, hey, bring on what's next. We'd played every city twice, six nights or however we did it. When we were in clubs we did it—we'd play five or six nights in a club before we'd go into a theater. Played in a theater, we played five or six nights in a theater before we'd go into an arena. In the arena, we'd play five or six nights in the arena. Because I wanted to feel the tension, I wanted to feel before we went on, just for my own comfort or sense that it was time *to*; I wanted to feel that tenseness, like the place was just gonna explode. Like the band was carrying so much muscle, and it was so high-powered that it couldn't be contained here anymore."

The changes in Bruce's own personality made the transition easier. "I changed in a way that change became easier for me. It wasn't as difficult. I'm sure I agonized tremendously over it when we were moving from theaters; I can remember talking about it.

"So this time out, we planned from the beginning, before the tour started, that we'd end up in the stadiums. And at this point, it just seemed like that was the only thing to do."

The Australian and European shows made certain of that. The question was whether he and the band had the stamina and interest to come back and do the same thing in the States that summer. The answer, whatever it was, wouldn't be couched in theoretical resistance, just based on fact and feeling. As always, Bruce left the actual decision up to the last minute.

Outside the small world of the tour, the Syracuse Carrier Dome gigs looked like nothing less than a final cash-in—the gross for the two shows was more than $1.3 million—in a little-played part of Springsteen's prime Northeastern market. But in the final moments of the sound check before the first show there, on January 26, you could feel the added tension. The Carrier Dome shows were also a dry run in which the larger stage and runways, lights, and sound—even the digital delay lines and video screens that cut down the distance outdoors—would be put through their paces so that Bruce could get a feel for them. And Bruce appeared to have every intention to push these shows as far as he could, to find out if he really could communicate in such a vast space. At that sound check, as Springsteen played "Working on the Highway" in the emptiest space he'd ever faced, he was greeted in part by a huge burst of feedback, a voluminous warning signal.

For the first time on this tour (give or take Pittsburgh after the Reagan incident), there was *really* something at stake. The Meadowlands dates were a longer version of the inaugural run in that building three summers before; any performer's mettle is tested in a city like Los Angeles, but Bruce had safely passed that test long before; and although integrating the community groups into the rap preceding "My Hometown" was a delicate artistic maneuver, Springsteen had long found ways to shoehorn the unlikeliest of topics into his songs and shows.

If the stadium venture didn't work, however, he was going to be stuck. There was not much thrill left in the arenas, and no real challenge—in most places he'd gotten over the moment he took the stage. If he tried and failed in the stadiums, then Springsteen would have suffered the first blow to his image of integrity.

In St. Paul, at the very beginning of the tour, songs like "Atlantic City" and "Reason to Believe" had occupied too much of the show, and as a result, there he *was* blowing it in a way—but the band pulled the performance along so that it was hard to tell or to find the space where telling could be done. Now Bruce had cleared that space for himself.

As always, they came out smokin' in Syracuse, but Springsteen soon pulled the show back inward, spewing out songs in an unusual configuration. The sequence of "Johnny 99," "Atlantic City," "Reason to Believe," "Shut Out the Light," and "Bye Bye Johnny" was probably the longest set of somber songs he'd allowed himself since St. Paul. And given the mood that those established, even the anthemic songs that followed—"Glory Days," "Promised Land," "My Hometown," and "Trapped"—took on a darker cast, which was enhanced when he ended the first set without the ritualistic "Thunder Road." (It popped up in the encores.)

When Springsteen came out alone to sing "No Surrender" or to do the soft-spoken introduction to "Racing in the Street," there was a sense of intimacy as great as any in the smaller building. And as for the rockers . . . forget it. Like all party songs, they just sounded better when more people crammed the room. The essence of that show translated perfectly, and it became even clearer just what magic Bruce Springsteen could wring out of cheesy rock and roll chords and the trashy images of cars 'n' girls. As on any night when his show clicked, you could see the bones behind it all. Whether he was goofing on Clarence and himself getting old in "Glory Days," or honoring the arrival of Jon Landau's first child, Kate, with a rousing "Promised Land," Bruce brought his listeners into contact with their own mortality in the hardest and the kindest way. From such a show you emerged quickened to every breath you took.

To watch that show, especially the first set, was to be mesmerized. Here was Springsteen in a situation where he lacked his usual total confidence. You could feel that he didn't know. The moment when he had come down on Ronald Reagan in Pittsburgh was nothing next to this, for that night he'd been sure of having the crowd on his side. He'd learned since then the difference between making statements anyone can hear and saying things that were too unambiguous to be misunderstood. So he played a stadium; so he played the most acoustic/soft stuff he'd ever done. And in a sense, he confirmed his genius in the process, because he played the stadium with a show that had evolved in the arenas, and it translated perfectly.

The second show was the mirror image of the first. Not only did

Bruce know that he could make his more ponderous and difficult ideas work in such a venue, but this was the last night of the American tour. It was a night to pull out all the stops, to see how much fun you could have in a breakneck rock and roll show. He omitted nothing, including one of the hardest-hitting "My Hometown" intros he'd yet attempted. He even extended himself to ask if someone out there could donate a forklift truck to the new Food Bank of Central New York (and a week or so later, somebody did).

Bruce still hadn't told Landau or Barsalona or the band and crew whether they'd be working in America the next summer. He'd decided to end the show by crashing through John Fogerty's "Rockin' All Over the World," but that wasn't a clue, since they'd be playing Japan and Australia and Europe for the next few months no matter what. And who knows when he made his choice. Maybe it was the consonance between himself and one of the wildest crowds he'd ever played for that forced his hand. At any rate, as he slammed that last song to a halt, Bruce shook off his joyous sweat and shouted above the cheers, "That's it! Thanks for comin' down to the show. And we'll be seeing you next summer."

13 PINK CADILLAC

B ruce strides to center stage and stands, legs spread, behind the microphone and begins to deliver an oration in the fashion of his favorite television evangelist, the Reverend Jimmy Lee Swaggart of Ferriday, Louisiana, cousin of Jerry Lee Lewis and no mean player of honky-tonk gospel piano himself. Since Bruce's accents have always had a slightly Southern tang—the result of his youth in Freehold's "Texas," no doubt—the effect is extraordinarily convincing.

"Now *this* is a song about the *conflict* between worldly things and spiritual health," he declaims, his strange stresses and odd shifts in tempo perfectly evangelical, "between desires of the flesh and spiritual ecstasy.

"Now, where did this conflict begin? Well, it began in the beginning—in a place called the Garden of Eden." From the wings Jim McDuffie wheels out a blackboard-style map board.

"Now the Garden of Eden was originally believed to have been located in Mesopotamia," says Reverend Springsteen, using a long pointer to direct his congregation's attention to the proper area on the map. "But the latest theological studies have found out that its actual location was ten miles south of Jersey City, off the New Jersey Turnpike." McDuffie turns the map around, revealing a map of New Jersey with a small star at Trenton, the capital, and a larger star in the area Springsteen has just indicated. The pointer clacks down on the map. "That's why they call it *the Garden State*," Springsteen declares.

"Now, understand, in the Garden of Eden there were none of the accoutrements of modern living. I mean, there weren't any houses and there weren't, like, any Laundromats you could go down to and do your clothes. There wasn't no *toasters*—you couldn't pop no *Pop-Tarts* in that little toaster at night and go watch *Johnny Carson*. You couldn't go out on the highway and buy a *cheeseburger* if you wanted one.

"In the Garden of Eden, there was no sin, there was no sex," he says, in an urgently revelatory tone. "Man lived in a state of innocence." A Jack Benny pause, a brief glance downward, a quick running of fingers through tousled hair. "Now, when it comes to no sex, I prefer the state of guilt that I live in. But before the tour started, I decided to go on a spiritual journey to the location of the Garden of Eden to find out the answer to some of these mysteries—to what temptation is about, to why my body pulls to that spot, and I found out that it's now occupied by Happy Dan's Celebrity Used Car Lot.

"So I walked in. The man looked at me. He said, 'Son, you need a [*Bruce speaks rapidly*] yellow-convertible-four-door-DeVille with wire-chrome-wheels-air-conditioning-automatic-heat with a-fold-out-bed-in-your-back-seat, eight-track tape deck, TV, and a phone [*he slows so that each syllable is lasciviously distinct*] so you can speak to your baby when you're driving *alone*.'

"And I said, 'I'll take two.' " Bruce pauses, then draws out the sense of tormented mystery.

"But I said, 'Dan, now, that's not the reason I really came. What I want to know is, What's the answer to these mysteries? Why do I feel so . . . so torn apart by this conflict all the time?'

"And he said [*Bruce becomes Cal Worthington, a late-night television used-car evangelist*], 'Well, son, that's easy. Because right here at the beginning of time, on these ten beautiful, industrially zoned acres was the sweetest little paradise that man has ever seen. [*Now he speaks softly, swiftly, sensuously.*] And in the Garden of Eden there were many wondrous things. There was the Tree of Life. There was the Tree of Knowledge of Good and Evil. There was a man—Adam. There was a woman—Eve. And she looked fine. And when Adam kissed her, it was the first time that a man had ever kissed a woman. And she had legs that were long and pale. And when Adam touched her, it was the first time that a man had ever touched a woman. And then they lay down in the green grass, and when Adam . . . well, it was the first time."

The preacher returns: "But, son, somethin' else was in the Garden of Eden that day. *Satan* came slitherin' up on his belly! And somehow he turned their love into a betrayal and sent them running down into the darkness below."

Now it's Cal again, full tilt, making that last push to nail down the sale.

"But right here on this back lot—for ninety-nine ninety-five and no money down—I've got their getaway car. And if you've got *the nerve to ride!* son, I've got the keys . . . to the first . . . pink Cadillac!"

A rockabilly rhythm begins.

14 STRANGER IN TOWN

"Well, I'm no hero, that's understood . . ."

—"Thunder Road"

Bruce left Syracuse on a charter jet and arrived back in New Jersey around 3:00 A.M. He got up the next afternoon and drove to Newark Airport for a flight to Los Angeles, where he was scheduled to perform at the U.S.A. for Africa recording session that evening.

Even as Springsteen was creating his links with economically disenfranchised Americans, British rock star Bob Geldof began a move to involve pop musicians in feeding the starving in Africa. Spurred by a BBC news report on famine in Ethiopia, Geldof, leader of the Irish-originated band the Boomtown Rats, wrote a song he titled "Do They Know It's Christmas?" and recruited more than two dozen British pop stars to make a charity record. "Do They Know It's Christmas?" featured such noteworthy pop personalities as Boy George of Culture Club, U2's Bono, Phil Collins of Genesis, the Police's Sting, and parts of the black American group Kool and the Gang. Geldof dubbed the group Band Aid; proceeds from sale of the disc were assigned to the Band Aid Trust, whose mission was to spend the money quickly and wisely to allay the immediate effects of the famine that raged not only in Ethiopia but throughout the sub-Saharan region of Africa.

"Do They Know It's Christmas?" became the biggest-selling 45 in

British history, and it enjoyed similar success around the world. Geldof, who had planned on making a healthy donation to Save the Children, suddenly found himself with close to $20 million in the kitty and a full-time commitment on his hands. Over the next year he jetted into Africa and organized an even more profitable second event, the world-wide broadcast concert Live Aid, did thousands of interviews, and cajoled and hectored entertainers and governments into putting bread into the mouths of ravaged Africans. He was dubbed St. Bob by England's tabloid press, made a knight by Queen Elizabeth, and given serious consideration for the Nobel Peace Prize. Geldof resisted all attempts to make his work explicitly political (which left him free to make alliances with Western politicians) and in the process inspired dozens of other entertainers to make similar stands.

In America, after "Do They Know It's Christmas?" appeared, folk singer Harry Belafonte took notice and decided it was ridiculous that American performers weren't doing something similar. Several days before Christmas, Belafonte called talent manager Ken Kragen, a veteran from the folk music period who now handled such stars as Lionel Richie and Kenny Rogers. Kragen had managed the late singer-songwriter Harry Chapin, who had made ending world hunger a personal crusade, establishing in 1975 the World Hunger Year organization. Kragen explained that planning, financing, and running such a show was a long, cumbersome process; it would be logistically simpler to do a record.

Right after Christmas Kragen went to work. "Basically, I started at the top of the record charts and began making phone calls." He already held an ace: Lionel Richie was at the peak of his commercial and artistic influence, and Richie's commitment, given early, validated the record idea and helped persuade such other early participants as Michael Jackson and Quincy Jones, Ray Charles, Paul Simon, Willie Nelson, Bette Midler, and Smokey Robinson. Among the first to join was Bruce Springsteen.

"The turning point was Bruce Springsteen's commitment," said Kragen. "That legitimized the project in the eyes of the rock community." Most of the other acts that signed on early were black or middle-of-the-road stars. In order to have the greatest impact, though, some rock and roll stars were needed. Springsteen's credibility was now enormous and his credentials were unquestionable. By Christmas he'd already donated $225,000 to American groups working with the hungry. Once

Kragen could tell other artists that Bruce was in, offers to sing on the disc proliferated so much that the organizers wound up having to turn some down. (Bruce's importance was ironic, since, according to Jones, Springsteen's first reaction to the project was: "You sure you really want me to do this?")

The session was set for January 28 at the A&M Records studio, located on the old Charlie Chaplin studio right on Sunset Strip. Richie and Jackson wrote the song "We Are the World" about two weeks earlier, Lionel helping to polish the basic structure and lyrics that Michael provided. Richie, Jackson, Jones, and Stevie Wonder recorded the basic instrumental track and guide vocals over which the superstar choir would sing. The groundwork for a media extravaganza was already being laid: A video crew caught everything that went on throughout the session.

The first stars arrived by limousine, each attended by a small entourage, and all were quickly ushered inside, away from the crowd of star-spotters that had gathered outside. Jones had taped a handwritten sign on the studio entrance: "Please check your egos at the door."

Springsteen landed at Los Angeles International and picked up a rented Corvette, which he drove to a parking lot across the street that George Travis had told him would be a suitable place to leave the car. It wasn't exactly a Hollywood arrival. "I swear I walked out to the gate just as he was coming in," said an amazed Ken Kragen. "I was looking to see if there were any hangups out there, and in walked Bruce . . . by himself. He walked across the street away from the crowd and said, 'What do you want me to do?' "

It was still a night of hurry up and wait. Although vocal arranger Tom Bahler had come up with a brilliant and intricate scheme for recording both group and solo singing, the process couldn't begin until everyone turned up. In the control room Bruce found the Pointer Sisters, whom he knew slightly because they'd had a hit with his song "Fire," and more familiar acquaintances Bob Dylan and Billy Joel.

Control rooms are cramped quarters, and Bruce and the Pointers wound up sitting on each other's laps as they waited for the rest of the team to arrive. By ten thirty everyone was there, the cameras were rolling (they shot fifty hours of raw footage and boiled it down to a one-hour videocassette), and Jones was ready to begin. First they would record the chorus, then individual solos. The performers then heard from Bob Geldof, who talked about the horrifying things he'd seen in

Ethiopia (not failing to score a few points against the lavish buffet— "whole *bowls* of caviar"—laid out for the performers). Stevie Wonder then presented a pair of women from Ethiopia who tearfully expressed their thanks that people were helping.

The session had a dissonant beginning. At first the chorus was pitched far too high for most of the male singers. Springsteen, Dylan, and a couple of others just laid out, but so many others didn't that Jones had to bring the first take to a screeching halt and eventually lower the register. When they finally got rolling again, Jones noticed a strange jangling noise coming through the mikes. It was caused by Cyndi Lauper's jewelry. She removed it and they got on with the show.

Springsteen must have been beat, but he wasn't the only one. Paul Simon had just finished an all-night recording session, and Hall and Oates also arrived late from the East, where they'd been delayed by a snowstorm. But Bruce had a second problem. He never sang more than two nights running, because his concerts simply took too much out of him to do more. The two shows in Syracuse were more strenuous than average, and on this, the third night in a row, his voice was so raw it sounded as if someone had taken a rasp to his throat.

Nevertheless, Springsteen had been selected as a soloist, and it was clearly not going to be a short night.

The song opened with Richie, Wonder, Simon, Kenny Rogers, James Ingram, Tina Turner, and Joel singing the first verse, then Diana Ross and Michael Jackson completing the first chorus together. The second verse started with Dionne Warwick's perfect plum tones shading off into Willie Nelson's scratchy purple sage, the record's most unlikely transition (and because it sounded effortless, the finest tribute to vocal arranger Bahler's acuity). Al Jarreau was to complete the second verse, while Springsteen kicked off the second chorus. The third verse was sung by Kenny Loggins, Steve Perry, Daryl Hall, Jackson again, Huey Lewis, Lauper, and Kim Carnes. The record ended with legends shouting the full chorus: Bob Dylan, Ray Charles, then a final duet between Stevie Wonder and Springsteen. Charles and Ingram shouted out tag lines like preachers bringing the congregation to the altar.

By the time they got to Bruce's spot it was half past five in the morning. "You sounded fantastic, Dylan," he called to the man who'd just finished, then stepped to the mike. Dylan, Bette Midler, and a few others remained to watch him work.

Springsteen wanted direction. "It's like being a cheerleader of the chorus," Quincy Jones told him. "I'll give it a shot," replied Springsteen, sticking his sheet music in his back pocket. Bruce didn't have much voice but he pushed through the ache with a shattering bellow. He sang a mawkish line—"We are the world, we are the children"—but to the cliché he added rocks and gravel (the only material he had available) and blew everyone away. In effect, he stiffened the song for its final takeoff. Later, with Bruce's voice dubbed into a duet with Wonder's, the same line provided the single's climax.

Finishing that first take, Springsteen looked up shyly. "Something like that?" he asked.

Quincy Jones had to laugh. "*Exactly* like that," he said.

Springsteen left about dawn, drained by the events of the last few days but feeling good at all he'd achieved, too. As Bruce walked through the A&M gates toward his car, an A&M security guard asked if he wanted an escort. Springsteen just smiled. "No, thanks. I can make it on my own."

◆

In rock circles "We Are the World" was widely despised for what it was not: a rock record, a critique of the political policies that created the famine, a way of finding out how and why such famines occur, an all-inclusive representation of the entire worldwide spectrum of post-Presley popular music. Some of these criticisms were just; some were silly; none mattered much against what the record actually represented, which wasn't even the $40 to $50 million it raised for hunger relief. Sentimental as it might have been, "We Are the World" was a grand pop event with serious political overtones. While it was true that it barely challenged the political process by which food was produced and hunger created, it did a great deal to subvert the political process by which music and meaning are made. That is, "We Are the World" obliterated the often arbitrary stylistic boundaries set up in broadcast centers and by record companies and showed that musicians of diverse styles—and races—could work together creatively and productively. U.S.A. for Africa was an important element in the "crossover" boom of the mid-Eighties, which saw great numbers of black artists once again entering the pop music mainstream; by showing the interconnectedness of old and young artists, it helped create a sense of continuity amidst the endless newness of the Top Forty. Both had a value beyond charity.

It was just such undercurrents that made the record thrilling, despite the rather maudlin, sentimental song with its blissfully half-baked lyrics. The best elements of "We Are the World" were torn straight from gospel, and the best performances went to those who testified. With James Ingram and Ray Charles tearing it up to the very last note, "We Are the World" became the world's least likely choir hit, though its most salient highlights were the series of vocal solos. Half a dozen singers went straight over the top, reaching in a few notes pinnacles that were the equal of their own best records. Newcomers like Cyndi Lauper and Huey Lewis stood right alongside veterans like Dionne Warwick and Bob Dylan, and each served not only as a distilled essence of him- or her-self, but also as a link in a chain. So even though "We Are the World" was by no means a great song, it *was* a great record.

Everything came to a head in the final duet between Stevie Wonder and Bruce Springsteen. In the contrast and connections between Wonder's still-boyish purity and the leather-lunged shout that was all Bruce had to offer this night lay the whole story of rock and roll. Wonder was the only other performer present who'd gone out on a limb politically in recent years, single-handedly rescuing the Martin Luther King birthday holiday from Ronald Reagan's redbaiting dismissal, so teaming him with Springsteen offered a definition of the different ways in which hope might take shape.

Bruce Springsteen and Stevie Wonder are almost exactly the same age, but their experiences were radically different: one black, one white; one a child star in the greatest musical factory mankind has ever known, the other a product of Jersey isolation. Wonder is a composer with aspirations to the kind of quasiclassical stature Duke Ellington possessed; Springsteen is content to tread the paths worn by Chuck Berry and Elvis. Stevie is physically locked up by his blindness; Springsteen is the apotheosis of the artist-athlete. Yet it now became clear that what they shared was more important. Out of the poverty of their origins, each had created magnificent music; each had torn his songs from deep emotional well-springs and sung them in kind; both had refused to turn their backs upon their roots. Simply by bringing them together, "We Are the World" made an important statement.

The record was marketed with all the muscle CBS could put behind it, and with such low overhead that almost every penny went into the U.S.A. for Africa coffers. It was an easy Number One straight into the airplay charts, and sales didn't take long to catch up. Within the first month it had sold 4 million copies (sales of more than half a million singles represent a massive hit). It also spawned a hit videocassette documentary and a multi-platinum album (whose most widely aired track was Bruce's "Trapped," recorded live at the Meadowlands the previous summer). All told, U.S.A. for Africa raised about $200 million, a drop in the bucket but far more than any of the world's wealthiest governments provided in so short a span.

Why did it all happen? Bruce Springsteen best placed the artists' role in perspective. "Anytime someone asks you to take one night of your time to help people who are starving to death, it's pretty hard to say no. I think hunger all around the world—in the United States as well—is such an abstraction to most people that trying to bring it closer, to make it more real, is something that has to happen.

"It's unbelievable that with the amount of wealth we have here in this country, people are still hungry. Part of it, like I said, is that it's so abstract to people. It's very difficult if you're sitting in front of your TV in Iowa or New Jersey, seeing hungry people; nothing you see on TV is really real. Unless something touches people directly, they don't react to it. But when we get all of these [artists] together like this, in the same room, you don't turn away. I think that's what everybody was trying to say that night."

It was still true that his music spoke for itself; but the maker of the songs was learning to speak his piece pretty well, too.

◆

One reason Springsteen hadn't minded flying straight to California was that his new girlfriend, actress Julianne Phillips, was living there. Phillips, a twenty-five-year-old actress, grew up in the suburbs of Portland, Oregon, and modeled in Manhattan before moving to Los Angeles, where she'd appeared as the girl of .38 Special's dreams in a rock video, which led to starring roles in two television movies: *Summer Fantasy*, in which she played a lifeguard; *His Mistress*, in which she played the title role, with Robert Urich; and in Blake Edwards's 1985 film, *A Fine Mess*, a comedy with Ted Danson. She met Springsteen through his old friend and booking agent Barry Bell. Bell knew Phillips through acquaintances at the Elite Modeling Agency and because they both hung out at the same New York restaurant, Cafe Central.

Bell got them together for dinner after one of the Sports Arena shows (he characterizes it as "a good booking"), and they'd been seeing each other steadily ever since. Julie came to New Jersey for the holidays and flew to North Carolina to surprise Bruce, sticking around through the end of the tour in Syracuse. In February they'd even visited Julie's parents, Bill and Ann, when the latter were vacationing in Palm Springs. When Springsteen went to the Grammys (where *Born in the U.S.A.* had many nominations but won only an off-camera award for best male rock album), Phillips sat by his side in the front row.

It was extremely obvious during the American tour that Springsteen, without a serious girlfriend for the past couple of years, was dealing with some intense emotional conflicts. In fact, it was obvious even before that—back in the Asbury clubs when he was making *Born in the U.S.A.* and singing a new song called "On the Prowl":

> *Well, night after lonely night*
> *My head don't touch the bed*
> *I'm on a 2-lane blacktop*
> *cruisin' in my rocket sled. . . .*
> *They got a name for Dracula*
> *and Frankenstein's son*
> *They ain't got no name, now, mister*
> *For this monster I've become*
> *I'm on the prowl, I'm on the prowl*
> *I'm lookin' for a gal, gal, gal*
> *Hey, hey, hey, I'm on the prowl*

Similar thoughts could be heard in the introductions to "I'm on Fire," "Pink Cadillac," and "I'm Goin' Down"—and in the songs themselves—as well as in Bruce's frequent references to his youthful "lack of a close interpersonal relationship with a person of the *opposite sex!*"

Sexual frustration has always been a central theme in rock and roll, and Springsteen frequently dealt with it onstage, usually comically (as in his hilarious spoofs of "Fire"), but sometimes more poignantly, as he looked back on a life in which he had by no means always been a matinee idol. In a way, even the roiling conflicts of *Nebraska* weren't unrelated to this pent-up heat.

When he wasn't joking, Springsteen was ambiguous; when he sang about itching with a "bad desire" in "I'm on Fire," you had to wonder when he'd ever defined *any* carnal desire as good. (In that respect, it's emblematic that "I'm Goin' Down," a song of sexual frustration, made the album while "Pink Cadillac," which celebrated sexual expression, didn't.) But of course Springsteen wasn't just singing about getting laid but about having that "close interpersonal relationship." And here was a greater, weightier, far more troublesome problem, and one with even fewer ready-made solutions, because that all boiled down to the perpetual American artist's conflict between individual freedom and domesticity.

"I never wrote romantic songs," he said around the time of *The River*. "That was what everybody else did. . . . The romantic songs that I did write I tended to give away, like 'Because the Night' and 'Fire.' " Bruce felt he'd changed, and in some ways he had—that album contained a number of songs reconciled to at least the dream of domesticity (most obviously "I Wanna Marry You"). On the other hand, its biggest hit began: "I got a wife and kids in Baltimore, Jack/Went out for a ride and never came back." Introducing "Two Hearts," Bruce often talked a lot about hearing Marvin Gaye and Kim Weston's "It Takes Two" at the wedding of lighting designer Marc Brickman and how much the song meant to him. He also talked about what the rabbi performing the ceremony had said: "When you're alone, without anybody, your dreams and fantasies are all of what you got, and when you get married, when you get together with someone, that is the first step toward making those dreams and hopes a reality."

"Boy, that really got to me. I wrote a lot of songs after that," he said with a laugh when he told Kit Rachlis the same story in a 1980 interview. But Bruce quickly depersonalized the message, just as he did onstage. "It was like you can write a song up in your room by yourself, but it don't mean a damn thing unless people hear it." Similarly, the songs in which marriage features on *The River*—and on *Nebraska*—

mostly present it as a state of disaster: "The River," "Stolen Car," "Jackson Cage."

Springsteen's diffident attitude toward marriage and domesticity had deep roots. "I couldn't bring up kids," he told *Melody Maker*'s Ray Coleman in 1975. "I couldn't handle it. I mean, it's too heavy, it's too much. A kid—like you better be ready for them. I'm so far off that track. I'm so far out of line that it would be disastrous. I don't understand it. I just don't see why people get married. It's so strange. I guess it's a nice track, but not for me." Earlier he'd said he wasn't "ready to write married music yet."

By 1980 he'd modified his hard-line attitude somewhat, but he still talked about his work as if it were family. "To me, the type of things that people do that make their lives heroic are a lot of times very small, little things—little things that happen in a kitchen or something, or between a husband and a wife, or between them and their kids. It's a grand experience, but it's not always big. There's plenty of room for those kinds of victories, and I think the records have that."

More recently, however, Springsteen had begun to reassess. In North Carolina the previous December, doing an interview for a book Robert Hilburn of the *Los Angeles Times* was writing about him, Bruce showed himself clearly bending.

"I don't think I felt I was making any sacrifices until I was older— until probably relatively recently," he said, acknowledging that getting older and watching almost all his friends marry and settle into domestic routines and begin raising kids made a lot of difference. "I guess relationships have been [hard for me] just because I've traveled for my whole adult life, and it was difficult to settle into something and make those types of sacrifices," he said. ". . . I guess the most precious thing anybody has in the end is their time. That's what you can't bargain with quite a bit. It's not a question of wanting to do less. It's just more a question of wanting to round out your life." And that's when he also admitted, "To blame something on your job is an excuse, no matter what it is. It can make it difficult, no doubt about it. But in the end you do what you want to do. That's what I basically believe. All the rest is excuses."

This marked an alteration in attitude even from what he'd told Kurt Loder in the *Rolling Stone* interview. When Loder asked if Springsteen ever would marry, Bruce first tried to make it a joke: "I got an Italian *grand*mother, and that's all she asks me. She speaks half Italian and half English, and every time I go over it's 'Where's you girlfriend? When are you gonna get married?' "

Then he became a little defensive, before admitting that he harbored some desires along those lines. "I've had steady girlfriends in the past. I went out with a girl I met at Clarence's club. I'm just not really lookin' to get married at this point. I've made a commitment to doin' my job right now, and that's basically what I do. *Someday*, I'd like to have the whole nine yards—the wife, the kids."

It's romantic to believe that getting to know Julianne Phillips, which is what happened between those two interviews, had caused Springsteen to begin to speak of marriage in more concrete terms. But it's not necessarily unreasonable to see it just that way. After all, as Springsteen told USA *Today* the previous summer, "I don't rule out marriage. If it's the right moment, the right relationship, the right person, maybe you'll change the way you do the job. I love women. I love kids. I've been with my sister and her kids and see where certain feelings they have match the intensity that I get onstage. It's a different type of experience, and it's not something I want to miss out on."

So maybe he saw the moment not at hand but on the horizon.

And maybe he didn't. His other project while in Los Angeles during the break between the U.S. tour and leaving for the Orient was shooting a video for "I'm on Fire," John Sayles once more directing. The song was scheduled to be the fourth *Born in the U.S.A.* single, and this time Springsteen was determined to have a first-rate video to go with it, something that worked at an angle to what the song said, not just a performance piece.

So he and Sayles concocted a story line. Springsteen is an auto mechanic. A well-to-do woman (all we see of her are Cybill Shepherd legs and hem) brings her vintage Thunderbird into his garage for service, although it can't really need service, because he's only recently worked it over. She leaves him the keys . . . and innuendo. He tunes up the car and drives to her huge house, parking in front and walking slowly up the steps. Bruce reaches out his finger to push her doorbell, then thinks better of it. He smiles wistfully to himself, walks back down the steps and off toward the lights of the city below.

It was a terrific way to extend the meaning of "I'm on Fire" without rupturing its fragile allusiveness, but it didn't exactly strike anybody as the product of somebody getting ready to be hitched.

◆

The second week in March, Springsteen and the entire band flew to Honolulu for two days, a useful intermediate stop on their journey to Australia that also gave Bruce a chance to make a nonperforming stop at the CBS Records convention being held at the Kahala Hilton on the fifteenth. Just to get everybody back in shape, they rehearsed on the sixteenth and seventeenth, then flew to Sydney, Australia, where they arrived late Tuesday morning, March 18, two days before the first of five shows there. All 60,000 seats had sold out in just six hours when they went on sale the previous month, even though the ticket price ($27, Australian) was one of the highest Australia had ever seen.

Bossmania was the order of the day through the Antipodes. Bruce had agreed to play outdoor dates in Melbourne, at the 45,000 capacity Royal Agricultural Showground and in Brisbane at Queen Elizabeth Park, which held 37,000.

Dominated by the sleazy tabloids of Rupert Murdoch, the Australian press can whip itself into a frenzy over far less than a Springsteen tour. When Bruce left his plane at Sydney Airport, about 200 fans, attended by the press, were at the gates. Rather than attempt to negotiate a way straight through the mob, Springsteen's security chief, Bob Wein, naturally preferred to escort Bruce through a side exit to the waiting hotel van, but airport officials refused to allow that and the band had to push its way through. Murdoch's *Sun* managed to get a picture of Bob Wein and McDuffie escorting Bruce from the airport. BOSSY! screamed the tabloid's headline, as if Springsteen had breached his populist image.

Throughout the band's stay in Sydney, the papers fanned the flames. When the Springsteen tour management denied access to Jacobsen's so-called "ticket club," a device by which the promoter sold privileged clients good tickets at a premium, the New South Wales consumer affairs minister misinterpreted this as a ban on *credit cards*, and the press had a field day, running hysterical banner headlines:

PUBLIC TREATED LIKE A "BUNCH OF HILLBILLIES"

ROCK STAR CONCERT TICKET CHAOS

Meanwhile, reports of fictitious interviews proliferated. "During your concert, it's been reported that you give a long kiss to your black (male) drummer," one interviewer claimed to have inquired. "Is this a political symbol?"

The start of Bruce's first show at the Sydney Entertainment Center was delayed for half an hour due to electrical problems, but "Born in the U.S.A." was greeted with New Jersey-level pandemonium. (Australia, after all, was the country second most responsible for prosecuting the war in Vietnam, and it hadn't treated its vets much better than America treated hers.) Bruce pushed some of his grimmest material that night, and closed with "Racing in the Street." But in between it was a show typical of those he'd most recently done in the States. Springsteen was again determined to bring his show intact to foreign lands, making changes mostly for the sake of local color—"even Mad Max in that black Trans-Am," he sang in "Cadillac Ranch."

Bruce shared the wealth by making donations to three Australian charities: the Childrens Hospital/Youth Ward '85 fund in Sydney; the Prince Alexander Hospital Transplant Trust Fund in Brisbane; the Vietnam Veterans Association of Australia in Melbourne. He met with representatives of each of these groups as he'd done in the States, but the community connections weren't nearly as specific, largely because time was short and the terrain was so unfamiliar.

Naturally, it rained during his first ever stadium show, at Queen Elizabeth Park, a racetrack, but not long and not hard. In fact, the drizzle let up altogether after Springsteen played "Who'll Stop the Rain." The Melbourne and Brisbane dates also featured festival seating—nothing reserved anywhere in the stadium—which was regarded as risky since the death of eleven young people at a Cincinnati Who concert in late 1980. The reason for playing without reserved seats was that the Australian tour had to be brief and the demand was incredible. In the end, the audience response was so overwhelming that Springsteen found his dislike of the open-air format turning to enthusiasm.

◆

The Australian tour wasn't much different from the American one— the gap in cultures wasn't that marked. Despite enormous geographical distance and many distinctive local elements, the atmosphere was essentially Anglo-American. Sydney, where the band spent most of its time, was like an odd combination of London and Los Angeles.

Japan was strikingly different in every way. Even in cosmopolitan Tokyo, the contrasts were immediate and unmistakable. Although the promoter, Seijuro Udo, was the most impeccable and generous host imaginable, in Japan it simply wasn't possible to put on a typical Springsteen show.

To begin with, because of curfews the shows were scheduled to start at six P.M. Japan has strict regulations that insist on clearing most public events by nine P.M. This was extended to ten P.M., but that still meant the band had to be offstage by nine thirty. As a result, the Japanese shows were trimmed back to about two and a half hours plus intermission.

The Japanese venues were the smallest of the entire tour. The five Tokyo concerts were held at the 12,000-seat Yoyogi Olympic Pool (a covered swimming pool built for the 1964 Olympics) in the week between April 10 and 16. The facility was extremely modern and rarely used, but in advancing the tour, George Travis found it far preferable to the Budokan (where most such shows were held), with its odd sight lines. In Kyoto Springsteen played 5,000-seat Kyoto Gymnasium, the smallest place in which he'd done an official show since 1978. The tour finished up with two nights at 10,000-seat Osaka Castle Hall on April 22 and 23. Bruce might have been big enough to play stadiums on his first Japanese tour, but he wasn't eager to do so. The Japanese tour, with its frequent days off, was reminiscent of the 1981 European tour.

Because Springsteen was playing at closer quarters than usual, it was reasonable to expect he'd put on some of his most intimate shows. And beginning with the opening night, he certainly tried. When he burst onstage at Yoyogi to open his first show, he shouted, "*Konbanwa Tokyo!*" ("Hello, Tokyo") then ripped into "Born in the U.S.A." with the huge U.S. flag from the album cover displayed behind him. The roars were tremendous; the reviews the next day said what they said everywhere else—that there had never been a crowd response quite like this.

· But Springsteen's more venturesome moves simply fell flat. When he introduced "Atlantic City" by making reference to growing up in New Jersey, there was no response to indicate that the words—guaranteed to prompt a roar anywhere in the West—registered at all.

Bruce prefaced "My Hometown" with a long talk including several Japanese phrases. He bent and picked up the set list from the stage floor next to the microphone and explained what he had to say, haltingly reading the phonetic words he'd scribbled at the side of the page: "*Watashino foodoo sato cara meanasan no ko koro eh*" ("This song is from my hometown to your hometown"). With that the kids went crazy, but they quickly settled back politely for the song that followed.

The second set went much the same. The girl Bruce selected from the audience for "Dancing in the Dark" seemed startled and embarrassed, almost reluctant to have him put his arms around her. When Bruce tried his pent-up intro to "I'm on Fire," it never crossed the language barrier. And when he did his Jerry Falwell turn on "Pink Cadillac," it became obvious that the barrier was composed of more than just language. "There was temptation," said Bruce, giving the crowd the Japanese word, "there was sin (*sumi*), there was an apple"— here he said the word in Japanese and faked a bite—"and then there was a *pink Cadillac.*" Except for the odd American serviceman, nobody in the crowd had any idea what the hell he was talking about.

Springsteen intended to bring a lot more than a superlative rock and roll show, but in the Japanese context it just wasn't possible. In the first place, he spoke no Japanese and the audience understood only a smattering of English. More important, rock and roll existed in a different cultural dimension in Japan than it did in the United States. In America Springsteen was able to attach tremendous political significance to many of his gestures because of the specific context in which rock and roll had originated: among blacks, poor white Southerners, their transplanted brethren in Rust Belt factory towns, and to some extent, working-class ethnics in the Northeast.

All this gave American rock and roll a tradition not only of rebellion but of connection to the lives of its audience. In Japan this wasn't necessarily the case. There rock and roll was an import in every sense, and while it might signify a kind of rebellion, it doesn't seem likely that very many people used it to make sense of their lives. Japanese audiences responded avidly to rhythm, melody, and emotion, but the other cultural traditions Bruce evoked generally weren't accessible in this way. Such discrepancies could be felt even in Western Europe, but were much more total in Japan. There simply wasn't any tradition of Pentecostal preaching in the Swaggart style, so "Pink Cadillac" had no hope of having the same meaning. It could be fun, and an intellectual segment of the audience might apprehend some larger philosophical issues at stake, but there was little or no overall social impact at work.

In a sense, this was reflected most strongly in Springsteen's inability to find a community group to support. Given Japan's very different sense of social organization, nothing like a public food bank existed. After a long quest, Barbara Carr finally found an organization that did need help: The title didn't really translate, but the concept was to help the unmarriageable widows of men who had died in traffic accidents.

Springsteen remained unfazed; he just altered the shape of the show, talking much less and (after the first two shows) ending with the easier-to-grasp ecstasies of "Rosalita." On the other hand, he never abandoned his darker, more reflective material. For instance, there were two or three songs from *Nebraska* every night, and he talked a little bit in front of "My Hometown" in each show.

As a reward, he got the Kyoto show, which was like the old days of barnstorming clubs and theaters. Instead of fifty yards, the back of the room was perhaps fifty feet from the front of the stage, and the result was, among other things, breathtakingly loud, perfect for the kind of show Bruce was now doing. He opened with "Born in the U.S.A.," "Badlands," and "Out in the Street," slowed down just long enough so that Max Weinberg's hands could survive, and then pumped it up again, shooting off three-and four-song rock sequences like automatic weapons fire. Not only was the singing sweet on "Thunder Road," the kids also formed a ghostly echo to Bruce's acoustic "No Surrender" as if Bruce's memories were singing back to him, trying to soothe his cares.

"It felt like New Jersey," someone later told *Newsweek*, but it felt like Jersey in the Seventies, when everything was up for grabs and half the audience was discovering new horizons every night. When Bruce finished the show by hollering "Aishitematsu!" ("I love you!"), what came roaring back was simple affirmation. He'd gotten over in Tokyo, as he would get over in Osaka—he really was running the rock and roll tour all but guaranteed not to fail. But only in Kyoto did the audience finally crack through to the band, and that made it one of the most special events of the entire tour.

Julianne Phillips arrived in Tokyo on April 15. Phillips and Springsteen spent the rest of the Japanese tour together, seeing the sights in Kyoto and visiting the A-bomb memorials at Hiroshima during the stay in Osaka, then returning to Tokyo for a one-day shopping excursion and a party hosted by CBS/Sony Records in honor of the tour and *Born in the U.S.A.*'s double-platinum status in that territory. On April 25 Julie and Bruce flew to Maui for a brief Hawaiian vacation.

15 U.S. MALE

Where's everybody running?
Look at everybody go
Somebody please tell me, what's all the fuss
I'm gonna tell you: Babalu's getting married

— The Eternals, "Babalu's Wedding Day"

What the hell did Julianne Phillips and Bruce Springsteen have in common?

After all, not only was Julie ten years younger than Bruce, she'd lived what one high school friend called "a charmed life." Growing up as the youngest of an insurance broker's six kids (four boys, two girls) in the comfortable Portland suburb of Lake Oswego, her biggest trauma supposedly was having to wear braces. A representative of the Elite Modeling Agency in New York, which represented her in 1982, described her as "a perfect ten package" who could earn as much as $2,000 a day. Then she'd thrown that career over and moved to Los Angeles, where she had some success as an actress.

But they did have things in common. Julie Phillips only looked like a cheerleader; she was really an athlete who worked out intensely and race-walked several miles every day. Bruce Springsteen may have been a scruffy rock and roller, but he kept himself in physical trim. One of the first things they did together was visit Julianne's Los Angeles health club, Matrix One; when Phillips came east, Bruce took her to Phil Dunphy's New Jersey workout spot.

Bruce said he could remember "lying in bed and thinking about getting married and knowing that whoever's sittin' in that seat, it's not going to be the easiest place to sit in the whole world." Julianne seemed to fit the bill—in part, he thought, because "she was just tough; she had confidence and resilience and she wasn't afraid to confront facts or their implications." A second advantage was that Julie was "well versed musically," meaning that she was exceptionally familiar with "all the great older records," so that Bruce "never sensed or felt the age difference."

Besides, Springsteen was an eccentric rock star in part because he wasn't interested in being eccentric—all these years he'd been working hard to *fit in*. Conversely, even if Julie Phillips lived a "charmed life," she'd found reason enough to leave Oregon and attempt to build a different kind of life. So at least they shared a certain level of ambition.

Trying to account for the reasons anybody is attracted to anybody is risky business and thankless to boot. At any rate, it seems safe to say that if Springsteen was capable of using rock and roll individualism as a way of creating some kind of community, he was certainly capable of setting up shop with a beautiful actress-model who happened to have a completely different class and social background. And for that matter, who'd ever led a life more charmed than Bruce Springsteen's? What was its climax supposed to be—marrying Rosie the Riveter?

It was during their Hawaiian holiday that the prospect of getting hitched first arose, although they didn't say yes to each other until they'd been back in California a few days. Bruce told friends at the time that he'd decided to take the plunge because "it just didn't feel right" to introduce Julie Phillips as his girlfriend. As reasons go, that's not bad, but of course it's no more (or less) rational than any other he might have found.

They didn't tell anyone else until Sunday, May 5, when they went out to dinner with Bruce's parents and his sister Pam to celebrate both Mrs. Springsteen's birthday, which had been the day before, and Julie's, which was coming up on Monday. Bruce's family was surprised—and pleased. (The reaction of his Italian grandmother is not recorded, but it probably had something to do with grandchildren.)

When they got back home, they made a few phone calls—to Julie's folks in Oregon, to Bruce's sister Ginny in New Jersey, to Jon Landau and Barry Bell in New York. All the folks back east were contacted after midnight, but nobody complained.

Now that they were engaged, they wanted to be married quickly, before Bruce's European tour began on June 1. The quickest and simplest means of getting married would be a Los Angeles civil ceremony; a wedding reception could be held later wherever they chose. But they preferred to be married in church and feared that a church wedding in Los Angeles or New Jersey would too easily become a media circus. Billy Joel and Christie Brinkley hadn't had much privacy even though they had gone out into New York Harbor on a boat to say their vows; Keith Richard and Patti Hansen had been plagued by reporters even though they had wed at the tip of Baja California in Mexico. It seemed logical to go to the Phillipses' family parish church near Portland. The wedding was set for Wednesday, May 15, at Our Lady of the Lakes in Lake Oswego. Who'd be looking for a rock-star wedding there?

As public relations miscalculations go, this was a doozy. True, nobody was looking for Bruce Springsteen to turn up in the Portland suburbs. But in order to have a wedding you have to get a license, and that's a matter of public record. In order to plan a church wedding, you have to do business with florists and caterers, arrange for music, and rent a hall for the reception. With all those businesses in the know, it obviously didn't take long for word to leak out, and when it did Bruce and Julie were sitting ducks in her parents' living room. Portland hadn't seen a story this good since Mt. St. Helens had erupted. (*People* claimed it was the biggest news in Oregon since Lewis and Clark.) Paparazzi flooded in from all over the world, and there was nowhere to run, nowhere to hide.

Bruce's family understood his penchant for strict privacy as well as his business associates did. Throughout their son's twelve-year career, neither Doug nor Adele Springsteen, nor either of his sisters, had ever given a reporter so much as a one-line quote about him. It certainly was no accident that his closest advisers—starting with Jon Landau— also liked playing it close to the vest. In fact, Springsteen had been able to lead his personal life more privately than any other American celebrity of similar stature in the Eighties, largely because those around him worked overtime to shelter his life from prying eyes. It wasn't even something Bruce demanded, although he clearly preferred a modest approach to publicity, but you didn't have to know him long to understand that he needed a great degree of isolation.

Certainly, that secretive atmosphere added impact to his mystique. Anything he did publicly was an event: releasing an album, going on tour, making donations, participating in "We Are the World." But if

Springsteen had harbored any desire to expose his private life, the aura wouldn't have lasted. No one with enough ego to become a star could have maintained such a lock on exposure if keeping out of the lime-light hadn't fulfilled personal needs, too.

By now it was the conditioned response of everyone who worked with Bruce to stonewall all personal probing—not only because of Springsteen's personality but because of their own as well. Only people as concerned with control as Bruce himself could have worked with him successfully, and the first principle of control is to keep the spread of information within the tightest limits possible. Once information is widely shared, particularly once the public has access to information, control seeps away. And after the near-debacle with Reagan, Spring-steen, Landau, and their associates were more than ever devoted to complete control of his life, work, and image.

Julianne Phillips understood this very well. She was herself a minor celebrity and had the performer's natural instinct for self-preservation. But her family wasn't show-biz savvy, and they were eager to announce their daughter's engagement, as any proud parents would be. They knew reaction might be intense, but they never saw what was coming until it was too late.

The Phillipses didn't have any reason for such an understanding. As they began planning the wedding, rehearsal dinner, and reception, ru-mors naturally began circulating in the Portland area. And when a local radio station, working on a hot tip from a florist, called on Thursday, the ninth, to confirm them, Bill and Ann Phillips told the truth. Pan-dora's box flew open.

Naturally, Columbia Records and Jon Landau Management tried to put the lid back on. "We checked with his management, and they say it's not true," Columbia's Marilyn Laverty told reporters. "We haven't heard anything," Barbara Carr was heard to say from the offices of Jon Landau Management. "We haven't heard a thing about it. As far as we're concerned, there's no wedding," said Barry Bell for Premier Tal-ent.

It wasn't that Bruce Springsteen didn't want the world to know that he'd decided to marry; it was the attendant hoopla that he wished to avoid, the media circus that could trample and trivialize one of the most important days of his life.

From New York, Landau and Carr tried to explain the situation, and Bill and Ann Phillips listened and did their best to comply with what must have seemed the odd request that they make no further comments. But they didn't seem to grasp the idea that not talking about the wedding meant saying *absolutely* nothing—even one sentence could become a quote, and a quote could be inflated into a story, a story into a headline, and a headline into more disruption than any wedding could handle. Media professionals like Carr and Laverty could easily stonewall the story for as long as it took—at least long enough for the wedding to take place unburdened by paparazzi. But when the Phillipses looked out to their front lawn and saw reporters camped there, or when their listed phone rang with solicitous queries about the big event, they didn't see an enemy force besieging them. In fact, it struck them as absolutely rude not to answer the reporters' simple questions. One night Bill Phillips even brought out pizza and beer for them.

For the next week it was hilarious to watch the Springsteen camp try to hold on to the threads of the wedding story, only to have them unravel in their hands. Time and again over the next interminable week they'd think they had the situation in command, and then it would erupt all over again on the heels of some new minor tidbit blown out of scale by the supposed importance of this rock-star wedding.

And the stories were coming now, thick and fast. Robert Hilburn called it one of rock and roll's "hottest pieces of gossip since the 'Paul is dead' rumors in the Sixties." Bruce Springsteen's star was peaking: *Good Housekeeping* had just named Bruce one of its fifty most eligible bachelors, and Columbia Records had just announced that sales of *Born in the U.S.A.* had surpassed 6.5 million, making it the largest-selling album in the label's history.

Springsteen's media aloofness made any information about him newsworthy, and a wedding—a *church* wedding—for the Boss, Mr. All-American Rock and Roll Star, was the kind of thing that the tabloids and the TV shows, the gossip columnists and their electronic counterparts, could really sink their teeth into. They'd been trying to corner him for months, in some cases years, and when they did pin him down, all *he* wanted to talk about was rock music and spiritual values and the plight of the unemployed. At least now they had a story that made sense for kerchiefed housewives at the checkout stand, that played without comment—well, maybe a leer or two—on the six o'clock news.

Headlines about the Rock Star and the Beauty Queen immediately proliferated. In New Jersey the news was greeted with shock. "Reports of Springsteen Wedding Breaking Fans' Hearts," headlined the *Asbury Park Press,* adding, "You could almost hear the sound of hearts breaking all along the Jersey shore."

Bruce Springsteen had always done his best to live a normal life, which was abnormal only because he was a pop star. He avoided photographers, mostly by never going to paparazzi haunts, but when they snatched his picture he never made a fuss. He disdained gossip columns, but when they ran an item about him, no matter how outrageous, he never asked for a correction. Now the Associated Press was running an interview with the Reverend Richard Parr, the seventy-two-year-old Nebraska priest who'd been asked to officiate. (Parr said he had the flu and couldn't make it.)

If the situation looked fouled-up from New York, where Springsteen's damage control unit still sat, it was even hairier on the spot. Besides the media camped out in the Phillipses' driveway, there were excited fans, some of whom had driven long distances. Reporters claiming they represented *Rolling Stone* and *People* knocked on the door, were fobbed off with a couple of sentences, and went off to file stories in the sleazier tabloids. One local radio station set up a "Springsteen rumor hotline" and had no lack of callers.

All that was happening even before Bruce and Julie hit town; when the protagonists of the great event arrived, the proceedings just got sillier. A neighborhood teenager sneaked into the backyard next door and snapped blurry photographs from over the fence, which were later published in the tabloids. Reporters and fans continued to jam the driveway. It was soon arranged for Jim McDuffie to come and run interference, advising the Phillips family on media and security matters and assisting in getting the wedding license and other details in order. Springsteen had asked three of his closest friends to serve as best men: Jon Landau, Steve Van Zandt, and Clarence Clemons. Clarence came out early and brought with him his assistant, Terry Magovern, whose complete cool (and experience in barroom security) proved immediately useful.

Bruce and Julie weren't completely trapped. They were able to sneak out through a neighbor's backyard. On Friday Bruce and the Phillips men went to a local bar and grill, where they shot pool and ate pizza. Nobody recognized Springsteen even when "Dancing in the Dark" played on the jukebox.

Meanwhile Jon Landau and Bruce were spending hours on the

phone, plotting their way out of the mess. Finally, late Friday evening, they decided they might as well call Ringling Brothers as wait until Wednesday. Given five more days of this kind of coverage, such a horde of fans and reporters could be expected that it would create an enormous diversion outside the church and possibly even disrupt the ceremony itself. Nobody wanted that sort of wedding. Oregon has a forty-eight-hour waiting period before a marriage license becomes effective; that meant the wedding could take place any time after midnight Sunday—12:01 A.M. Monday.

Bruce had already notified the band and several of his East Coast friends of the Wednesday wedding ceremony; he notified as few as possible of the change in date. Those who got the word rushed to the airport; Landau himself didn't arrive until early Sunday evening. Ann Phillips contacted Father Paul Peri at Our Lady of the Lakes, who agreed to open the church at midnight and perform the ceremony as soon as all the guests had arrived.

Around eleven o'clock Sunday night, Bill Phillips took out the trash, rattling the cans loudly as he did so. He went back in the house and turned off the lights. The assembled reporters took that as a signal and went home for the night. "We were having fun," Bill Phillips later said. "It was like a cat-and-mouse game."

Most of Bruce's guests were staying at a downtown Portland hotel— except his parents, who were also staying at the Phillips home. At about eleven fifteen, Terry Magovern rounded them up and put them in two vans, which were driven to the parking lot of the Lake Oswego high school. It was a warm, starry night and when the vans pulled up to wait for several carloads of local guests, everyone got out to stretch their legs; they talked in low voices about the entire comical affair. By about ten minutes after twelve, all of the fifty-odd guests were present, and the caravan made its way to the church with a police escort.

All the lights in the church parking lot were off; a local police patrol car hovered outside, just in case word had leaked out and interlopers needed to be turned away. Inside, the church, a brick building with a low, modern altar arrangement, was lit only with candles. Guests stumbled into pews, barely recognizing friends in the dimness.

At about twelve thirty, the lights in the chapel came up full. After everyone's eyes had adjusted, organ music began to play and the procession down the aisle began. Bruce entered first, with his parents, one on each arm. He was wearing a blue silk suit but still proceeding casually—on his way to the altar he even said hello to a friend he hadn't expected to be present.

At the altar Bruce was joined by his best men. Julianne began her careful walk down the aisle, escorted by her parents. She wore an off-white antique lace dress, with ankle-high boots and a waist-length veil borrowed from her friend Ann Stucky Bickford, who had flown in from Alaska to serve as a maid of honor (along with Julie's sister Mary and Bruce's sister Pam) even though she was eight months pregnant.

There had been no time for a rehearsal, and there was a brief mixup during the ring ceremony, because the best men had lined up on the wrong side. Bruce made light of the error, but when he and Julie stepped forward alone to kneel at the altar to begin the ceremony, he was all seriousness. It was a typical Catholic ceremony, including Bible readings by two of Julianne's brothers and a brief sermon, but mass was not served.

By twenty minutes to one the wedding was complete. Bruce and Julianne grabbed a long kiss and then proceeded back down the aisle to the applause of their family and friends. Everyone milled around the chapel for another hour or so, taking pictures and relaxing; there was no champagne, but a couple of pints were passed around.

At about two A.M. Landau and Carr were talking back at their hotel, trying to decide when it would be appropriate to wake up Marilyn Laverty in New York so she could release a statement to the press. They finally decided that it could all wait until morning and went to bed, feeling relieved that at least the wedding itself had been pulled off without an untoward media crush. But although they didn't know it, the Portland radio stations had already been notified, and the next morning they were awakened by calls seeking to confirm the news. Bruce and Julie had already left for a couple of days in a cabin in the Oregon woods.

The press felt trumped, but there was little they could do. Most of the reporters packed their bags and headed for the next scene of celebrity non-news. Bill Phillips more or less apologized for being so sneaky, while the tabloids kept on sneaking, the *National Enquirer* even managing to snatch pictures from the Tuesday night country club reception that had originally been planned as a rehearsal dinner. The New York *Daily News* gossipmonger Suzy got a front-page headline for her report that the midnight wedding was just a tale, a swindle perpetrated by Jon Landau Management in order to clear the way for the originally planned Wednesday ceremony. The filing of the marriage certificate with the Portland civil records registrar shut her up.

A full-scale reception, at which the full E Street Band and a few dozen additional guests would be present, was scheduled for Wednesday afternoon at a house in rural Tualatin, from which Mt. Hood and the entire Willamette Valley were visible. Security was again tight, but word again leaked out and the occasion was badly marred by the presence of several news helicopters, which buzzed continually, drowning out conversation. A few paparazzi even managed to set up their gear in the yard next door; one snapped shots of Bruce and Julie as they walked and spooned in the fields, and these were later sold to the same Rupert Murdoch press organization that had plagued "the Boss's minders" in Australia. (Murdoch's *Chicago Sun-Times* deemed the wedding so important that it ran an editorial saluting it.)

The helicopters were the last straw, flying so low that the Federal Aviation Administration was eventually called and the pilots were ordered either to desist or maintain a much higher altitude. Late in the afternoon a beleaguered and exhausted Bruce Springsteen flopped on a couch and looked up at two of his friends. "I do not believe or comprehend the world that I live in," he said.

16 IT'S TOO LATE TO STOP NOW

I don't like the word "dream." I don't even want to specify it as American. What I'm beginning to understand is there's a human possibility. That's where all the excitement is. If you can be part of that, you're aware and alive. It's not a dream, it's possible. It's everyday stuff.

—*"Blue-collar housewife" to Studs Turkel,*
American Dreams: Lost and Found

Columbia Records scheduled the release of "Glory Days" as the fifth single from *Born in the U.S.A.* for May 31, the day before the European leg of the tour began. The single had the usual unreleased B side, a little rocker called "Stand on It," which would be featured as the final encore later in the summer.

Bruce also wanted this single to have a video. Most rock performers made their videos all at once, before their album was released and touring began. That way the record label could distribute the appropriate video as each single was issued; later all of them could be packaged—together with some not-too-probing interview footage—as an "MTV Special" or even as a commercial videotape. But Bruce only dealt with one thing at a time. That meant he was constantly playing video catch-up. Of the five *Born in the U.S.A.* singles, only the last, "My Hometown," had a simultaneously released video.

Rather than lack of forethought, this reflected Springsteen's wariness about form. "The main thing with my songs right now is that I write them to be complete things, and they're filled with a lot of geographical detail and a lot of detail about what people are wearing, where they live," he said. "The thing about a video is that you only really have a few choices about what you can do. Either you illustrate a song, which in my case I can't do—because it's like you're gonna paint a mustache on it or something. Or you create another story to go over the song, and that's kinda silly, because there's a story already there. That's the story I wanted to tell, so to create another story to go along with it, that doesn't make sense either.

"I've spent twenty years learning how to write so that when you hear a song you get the information you need—you get the experience and the emotion that you need. I write with a lot of detail, and I'm proud of doing it and I think that I do it well. And so I'm hesitant to mess with that. You've gotta respect the integrity of the song a little bit."

Springsteen was also wary of video, perhaps because the audience for it was so young—too young, in many cases, to have any hope of grasping the broader implications of his music. "The main audience video seems to be real important to is the little kids, from about six, seven—real young—up to like pre-concert-going age, where they can't go out yet. It's taken the place of cartoons, I think, actually, for kids," he told the BBC's David Hepworth. "Every house I go in, the kids are glued to it; they know all the bands. So there is a completely different audience out there."

Springsteen still hadn't written the medium off. "I don't know exactly what I'm gonna do," he told Hepworth. "I'd like to do something with it because it is a powerful tool. It is something that can reach a lot of people, and different types of people."

As an inveterate moviegoer, Bruce's most agreeable vision of video was seeing it as a way of exploring his cinematic ideas, but he was aware that its accessibility also concealed certain pitfalls.

"I always loved the movies. And, after all, music is evocative. That's the beauty of it. Which is also the danger of video. The tools can be great there, and obviously it can be used real well. But it can also be used badly because it's an inanimate thing in and of itself. The thing about a good song is its evocative power. What does it evoke in the listener?

"A song like 'Mansion on the Hill'—it's different to everybody. It's in people's lives, in that sense. That's what I always want my songs to do: to kind of just pan out and be very cinematic. The *Nebraska* record had that cinematic quality, where you get in there and you get the feel of life—just some of the grit and some of the beauty. I was thinking in a way of *To Kill a Mockingbird*, because in that movie there was a child's-eye view. And *Night of the Hunter* also had that—I'm not sure if *surrealistic* is the right word. But that was poetic when the little girl was running through the woods. I was thinking of scenes like that."

But after gaining some experience in video, he was less sanguine; the frustrations overwhelmed the potential. Most of all, video seemed an extraordinarily difficult thing to control. "It presents a set of unique problems which are very different from the way that I usually work," he told Hepworth. "One, it's very expensive most of the time, particularly since the production values of videos have gotten so high. And they're made very quickly, in a day or so; there's this enormous financial input and it's kind of a real roll of the dice.

"The way that I work is very different. I'll go in the studio and I'll spend a night, and if I don't like what I did, I throw it out. Basically, you can afford to do that. Plus, I work very slow; I don't work fast. I enjoy having the control over what I'm gonna say and what my work is. I work somewhat collaboratively but not near as much as, say, a video, with a director and all this other stuff. On my records I'm the director."

Film-making is such an elaborate art that control is far more diffused than it is even in a significantly collaborative medium like music. Though most successful films reflect a strong directorial personality, that's not always the case—great actors (particularly comedians) and writers and even cinematographers have sometimes had their say. Bruce didn't seem especially interested in becoming a director, but he had discernible talent as an actor—at least the camera loved him. (Film critic Andrew Sarris, who was not at all knowledgeable about rock and roll, had compared Bruce's turn in *No Nukes* to a John Garfield performance.) But in order to realize his ideas, Bruce needed to find compatible people to work with, just as he'd done in record-making.

In John Sayles he had found an ideal creative partner. John and Bruce were almost exactly the same age. Sayles grew up in a working-class neighborhood in Schenectady, New York, essentially a General Electric company town. Although he got a degree from Williams College (a "Little Ivy" institution), Sayles, like Springsteen, had never abandoned his ties to working-class culture. After writing three novels—the best of which, *Union Dues* (1977), Bruce read and liked—and a number of profoundly trashy screenplays (among them *Piranha, The Howling,* and *Alligator*), Sayles began making films on shoestring budgets. His first, *Return of the Secaucus Seven* (1980), was best known for its $60,000 budget (about one percent of what it would have cost in Hollywood), but what was really remarkable was its acute look at the lives of Sixties radicals nearing middle age. (Its plot was swiped and trivialized three years later for Lawrence Kasdan's odious *The Big Chill.*)

In 1983 Sayles made his only studio picture, *Baby, It's You*, for Paramount. The story of a mid-Sixties high school romance between a middle-class girl and a working-class boy, it featured an outstanding period rock and roll score. Sayles approached Landau about using Springsteen songs as more contemporary themes for the boy. Springsteen had never before allowed any of his songs to be used in movies—he just didn't want them exploited that way—but he approved *Baby, It's You* because he trusted Sayles. The film used four Springsteen songs, most memorably "It's Hard to Be a Saint in the City" in a high school lunchroom and "Adam Raised a Cain" as a travelogue that climaxed with an overhead shot of the Statue of Liberty.

However, Sayles and Springsteen did not meet until the spring of 1984. The night after they mastered *Born in the U.S.A.* Chuck Plotkin, Springsteen, and several other friends had dinner at the Hoboken home of Sayles and his producer, Maggie Renzi. (Among those present was Renzi's sister, Marta, a choreographer who'd created a dance piece based on Springsteen songs, "You Little Wild Heart," for PBS in 1982.) John and Bruce proved to be as personally compatible as the similarity of their work suggested they would be. But Bruce went on tour, and they didn't speak again until he called to ask if Sayles would direct the "Born in the U.S.A" video.

Sayles wasn't interested in music video formally or as a career move. He had already established his credentials as an independent filmmaker; he'd learned from *Baby, It's You* that studio productions weren't really his metier. While he hadn't struck it rich, his screenplays and a so-called "genius grant" from the MacArthur Foundation supported him well enough so that he could later donate his $10,000 fee from directing "I'm on Fire" to a fund that sent ambulances to Nicaragua. Like Springsteen, Sayles was more interested in doing good work and keeping control of it than in wealth and glory. He was interested in making a music video with Bruce because their work had such strong stylistic affinities and because Springsteen was one of America's great undeveloped moving-picture possibilities.

Bruce's proposal also came at a good time for Sayles. He'd finished his latest feature, *Brother from Another Planet*, and was in the midst of the arduous process of raising independent financing for *Matewan*, based on a segment of *Union Dues* that took place in the West Virginia coalfields during a strike in the early Twenties.

So Sayles agreed to make the "Born in the U.S.A." video, even though Bruce imposed severe restrictions on the shooting. Sayles was widely criticized for that clip's lack of lip-syncing, but the decision was entirely due to Bruce's dissatisfaction with the lip-syncing in "Dancing in the Dark." ("Lip-syncing is one of those things—it's easy to do, but you wonder about the *worth* of doing it," Bruce told Kurt Loder.)

"I'm on Fire" was much more a joint effort, but still it was shot and edited in haste, against the tight deadline of the single's chart life and Bruce's impending departure for Australia and Japan. Sayles was able to give Springsteen his first speaking lines, and Bruce pulled them off with aplomb; the look of mingled innocence and awareness that fills his face when his customer asks him to drop the T-bird off at her place is terrific.

"Glory Days" was also a collaborative venture, inasmuch as Springsteen and Sayles cooked up the story line together. This time they had the luxury of a three-day shoot (May 24, 27, and 28) spread over four North Jersey locations: a construction site and a decrepit baseball stadium in West New York; the Secaucus house of a bar owner Sayles knew; and Maxwell's, a Hoboken bar ordinarily the habitat of avant-garde rock and rollers but converted for this occasion into a sweaty working-class hangout. The video didn't exactly have a plot, but it was several minutes longer than the song; Bruce again spoke a few lines. It had a cast of four (Bruce's sons were played by Barbara Carr's nephews, eleven-year-old Jason Fisher and three-year-old James "Lucky" Dunning, and his wife by Julianne Phillips), plus about fifty extras for the barroom sequence.

In the "Glory Days" video Springsteen plays a construction worker with two kids who harbors big league baseball fantasies. He's seen at work, munching an apple while sitting atop a crane; at home watching Dwight Gooden on TV; contemplatively oiling his own glove; being awakened by his son, who smacks him with a plastic bat; and at the ball field, standing alone on the pitcher's mound throwing at a piece of board. (Sportswriter Shelby Strother of the *Detroit News*, a fan, commented that Bruce "throws a baseball like a man with a torn rotator cuff.")

In the barroom scene Springsteen leads the E Street Band, with Little Steven Van Zandt returned for the occasion to mug and play his mandolin solo. Although the story never spells it out, the singer/guitarist in the bar band and the baseball addict are probably meant to be separate but equivalent ider⁺ities—two guys who work day jobs and find fulfillment at night by sticking with things that they loved as children. (Baseball looks like hard work, while the shots of the bar band are radiant, a discrepancy surely not intentional.)

The energy and excitement of seeing the E Street Band live came across in a Springsteen video for the first time. The pained and scruffy poses of "Born in the U.S.A." had been almost as artificial as the exuberant and manicured stances of "Dancing in the Dark." (Bruce performed solo—and only a little—in "I'm on Fire.") But with "Glory Days" Sayles was given much more independence and Springsteen wasn't trying to alter his own pop-star image; they worked together to burnish that image, and in deepening its sheen they finally got it right. This isn't what a "real" Bruce Springsteen song looks like onstage, but it's exactly what it feels like.

The family scenes establish a Springsteen persona that steps outside rock and roll's myth of eternal youth. It's hard to think of another music video in which a star functions comfortably—and as an adult—in the interior of a nuclear family. The identity of most rock stars would explode in any version of this situation. But it enriched Springsteen's image and allowed the video to burrow much closer to the heart of the song, which is just as crucial to the *Born in the U.S.A.* album as "Dancing in the Dark," "My Hometown," and "Born in the U.S.A." but more easily missed because it doesn't sound as big.

"Glory Days" is about rock and roll's promise of eternal youth and the reality of aging. The music, which marries rinky-dink organ, honky-tonk piano, and garage-band guitar kicked along by an explosive tom-tom pattern, suggests a joke. Springsteen sings most of the song in a comic tone; when they get to the bridge he gleefully whoops and exhorts the group through its paces.

But "Glory Days" isn't really optimistic; behind its glee are some sad stories—the baseball pitcher who never topped his high school heroics, the good ol' girl whose marriage fell apart, the rock and roll singer who's embarrassed by his own fixation on the past. All are wasting away for the same reason, which isn't that they're living in the past but that they're missing the moment. The song's energy really comes from the contradictory atmosphere of the music, because it's the kind of trash—updated frat rock, archaic dance music—whose prime purpose is to propel you into the here and now.

Somehow its first verse defines "Glory Days" as a rock and roll song about baseball, an idea reinforced by the video and Bruce's comic on-stage raps about his preteen athletic ineptitude. In fact, the song says nothing much about the game; the singer just encounters the high school ballplayer who "could throw that speedball by ya/Make you look like a fool" but has now become a bar-hopping fool himself.

There's another reason baseball seems important to understanding "Glory Days," though. Rock and roll and baseball, despite the radical difference in the way they're paced—the former galloping, the latter ambling—share a common trait: In each of them, what seems so simple and easy when played by children becomes deeper and more complex when played by adults. There's nothing to that home-run swing when you're twelve; those songs are just three chords and a lot of attitude when you're sixteen. But as time goes by, both the sport and the music grow richer. Suddenly Chuck Berry isn't just outlining the ideal teenage life-style but illuminating the bitterness of a black man mocking everything he can't have; watching Ozzie Smith throw to first from deep in the hole, we realize the subtleties of positioning as a concomitant of grace. The blood squeezed from Pete Townshend's fingertips and the tears that fell from Wade Boggs's eyes at the end of the 1986 World Series have a lot in common.

In the last verse of "Glory Days" Springsteen prays to be released from his own obsession with the past and then laughs mockingly at the very idea, spitting in the eye of the idea that rock and roll is a toy for tots. "Well, but time slips away and leaves you with nothing, mister, but boring stories of . . ." he yelps, but the band won't let him stop. And when he whips the band onward in the final seconds—"All right, boys! We gonna go home now!"—he echoes Van Morrison, the most reluctant rock and roller of all: "It's too late to stop now."

Bruce had long been determined to find out what rock and roll became when it wasn't "youth culture" anymore. "Glory Days," in which he mocked his own nostalgia into proportion, is the first step in searching out a livable answer which is why it's the perfect lead-in to "Dancing in the Dark," where Springsteen finally stops "sittin' around thinkin' about it" and starts moving on. "Dancing in the Dark" boils "Glory Days" down to two lines—"You sit around gettin' older/

There's a joke here somewhere and it's on me"—and passes to a place where its author could face an interviewer in the fall of 1984 and say without sounding fatuous, "Maybe you can't dream the same dreams when you're thirty-four that you did when you were twenty-four, you know, but you can still dream something." And he told another, "After I wrote the *Nebraska* record, I said, 'Well, gee, I wonder what it'll be like when I sing "Born to Run." Do I still believe these songs?' And when I thought about it, I wasn't sure. But when I sang it, I knew that I did. It's just all different parts of life, you know. It's just all a different part of life."

In concert, "Glory Days" grew further. Wrote Joyce Millman of his Boston show, "Springsteen led off 'Glory Days' with a hilarious rant about the bad old times, skittering around like Richard Pryor, with his mouth scrunched up, his eyes bugging out, and his hands up in the air: 'I *hated* high school! I had a terrible time in high school! When fall comes around, I'm *still* glad I don't have to go *back* to high school!' Still, his ending shout of 'I can hear the clock ticking. It says, "Boss, you're 30–31–32–33–34 . . ." ' was ironic because, watching him hop around the stage in a loony kick-line . . . it seemed impossible that Springsteen will ever be too old for rock and roll. How can he ever look undignified or foolish when he's always been willing to risk looking undignified or foolish if the mood dictates? As he teetered on one clunky biker boot, then the other, swinging his guitar back and forth, with a gloriously spaced-out smile on his face, he made a convincing picture of both a tot and a dreamy old codger." Bruce put a finer point on it during his Ames, Iowa, show when, as critic Steve Perry reported, he halted the band and screamed, "I don't wanna die—ever!"

After that shout, Perry added, Springsteen looked startled, and that makes sense, for he'd just broken a mighty taboo or two. Humans are aware of their own death, but it's something they're supposed to contemplate alone. Rock stars have it worse; for them age is a constant, early arriving specter, but you're not supposed to admit that you crank up the amps in order to cheat the reaper—or at least to console yourself against his approach.

Rock and roll has been portrayed for so long as a child's game, and the facts that disprove the proposition are so rarely uttered that even most dedicated fans don't know that Chuck Berry was married and the father of two kids when he wrote all the hits that defined the first generation's glory days. "I was thirty-one years old, but I could *remem-*

ber," Berry told Bill Flanagan in *Written in My Soul*. But Berry didn't escape the fear that plagued everybody from Elvis to Pete Townshend to Elvis Costello. "I remember the first time I heard a kid say, 'Thirty-five years old! He's as old as my father!' I went, 'Oh, shit.'" And it wasn't just Chuck Berry: Fats Domino, Elvis Presley, Carl Perkins, Ray Charles , and John Lennon were all adults when they laid the ground Bruce Springsteen and his peers walk upon.

All of rock's other great performers felt they had to turn away from the essence of the music in order to be grown-ups. But there's more than one mythology of rock and roll. One of its more disabling specters is self-parody, in which the greatest, most experienced performers are paralyzed by the idea that what they're doing is a waste because they're no longer 'twixt twelve and twenty. (The audience also experiences this whenever some pompous ass asks a fan when he or she will "outgrow" such music or why he or she expects anything more than a hot time from it.) It seemed to happen to everybody: Chuck Berry and Mick Jagger got cynical; Little Richard and Carl Perkins got religion; Jerry Lee Lewis got drunk; Bob Dylan got lost; Elvis got confused; John Lennon got shot. For the Fifties rock stars, those who survived, there was the purgatory of the oldies circuit; for the Sixties stars, those who didn't overdose, there was the limbo of heartless craft. Seen in this light, "Glory Days" is a portrait of the rock star taking out the trash.

"I guess basically I always thought that I'd do it forever in some fashion," said Springsteen to an interviewer who asked how it felt to reach thirty-five. "I didn't think that you had to stop or that age was a factor. Age was just something to be dealt with—you grow into it. It just becomes a part of what you do. I mean, rock and roll anymore is not just somethin' for if you're seventeen. There'll always be fifteen-year-olds doin' it, but now there's gonna be forty-five-year-olds doin' it, too." He laughed; it's hard to say why.

Maybe even Bruce Springsteen felt the pressure not to "take it all too seriously." But most of his responses to such questions reflected how imperative answering them was. "You know, as you get older, the main thing that you gotta deal with is all the things you lose," he said, adding the even more heretical idea that aging could well be an advantage because it offers broader perspectives. "I guess basically as you get older your main battle is a battle to not give in to despair.

"Which is difficult." He laughed again. "It's difficult to do. And basically that's the fight most of my characters are fighting now in some fashion. Certainly the guy in 'Born in the U.S.A.,' his thing is just a survival thing. There's not the naiveness that there initially was in my earlier music. There's not a certain kind of youthful optimism— even though optimism may always be youthful in some sense. But it's not like you're gonna save the wo:'d. It's mainly people trying to find some place for themselves *in* the world—some place where they can live with some dignity and some decency, some sense of self-respect, to find some place in some community somewhere, to find some friends, to find a job, to be able to live with their wives or their kids, to make some sort of life for themselves."

And he not only knew that this was important, in the end he also knew why. "If you can deal with that, if you can deal with just that sense of leaving things behind . . . Or else you go crazy, you go crazy tryin' to hold on to the same dream you had when you were twenty-two."

The "Glory Days" video brought such ideas to life, in a far different way than a song could. Whether or not he ever made another great video, Bruce Springsteen had finally done one that lived up to the best parts of his music.

◆

Tickets for the European shows—eighteen dates, all outdoors—began going on sale the first week in May, only a month before the first show, on June 1 at Slane Castle in Dublin. As the cities were announced, one after another, many fell in the same fashion as the American towns that preceded them; even though capacities ranged between 50,000 and 100,000 (total attendance was just short of a million), most shows sold out in a matter of hours. In Gothenburg, Sweden, the only place Bruce was playing in Scandinavia, two 60,000-seat shows sold out in ten minutes. In Milan there were 250,000 applications for the only Italian date. In England, where a mail-order system was used, there were a million requests for only 300,000 seats.

As in Australia, the limited time available and the high demand required doing the largest outdoor facilities available; as in Japan, the shows started early—usually around four P.M., but at the beginning and end of the tour, at Slane and in Leeds, England, the concerts were set for one P.M. (There was no point waiting for full dark, which in the European summer comes only toward midnight.) In addition to

Slane, Gothenburg, Milan, and Leeds, Bruce would play two nights in Newcastle and three at London's 70,000-seat Wembley Stadium, two shows in Rotterdam, two in Paris, and single dates at Frankfurt and Munich, West Germany, and Montpelier and St. Etienne in the French provinces.

Born in the U.S.A. was a massive hit in Europe. When first released, "Dancing in the Dark" had stiffed, as had all Bruce's previous European singles, but it was revived after a remarkable one-hour Springsteen special on the British television program The Old Grey Whistle Test. The show, later rebroadcast in many countries on the Continent, featured a sensitive and intelligent interview conducted by David Hepworth, extensive footage of fans before the previous autumn's shows in Philadelphia, and an amazing amount of concert footage. Not only did OGWT have access to the "Rosalita" clip, "Thunder Road" and "The River" from No Nukes, and the "Dancing in the Dark" video, they were also able to film three complete numbers from the Spectrum: "Born in the U.S.A.," "Cover Me," and the "Detroit Medley" of Mitch Ryder hits.

The visceral excitement of this live footage spread the word about Springsteen as nothing else could have done. The interview also presold the show. Asked to define his ambitions for a concert, Springsteen gave a lengthy, seductive answer: "If it's a good night out, that's great—that's basically what it's meant to be. . . . I try to present a lotta different things so that it can be somethin'—I think you could come and maybe it'll change the way you think about something. Maybe about the way you think about your life or your job or your friends or . . . I think it can do that. We try to do it well enough so that it can do that. And at the same time, like I said, if it's a good date or somethin', that's good, too. Whatever people want—whatever they take from it—whatever they need at that moment is what I would hope that it would be." He hesitated, then plunged. "If you come and you need [a heavy sigh] some inspiration maybe, I would hope that you could find a little bit of it. But if you want to dance or if you wanna take your girl out—I'd hope it was a combination of all those things."

Springsteen explicitly offered an opportunity to have your life changed while you danced, yet his demeanor managed to make him seem modest while the concert footage more than backed up every word he said. But that didn't mean that "Born in the U.S.A." was any better understood in Europe than it had been in the States. Although the live version shown on OGWT sounded mordant and mournful, Springsteen still had something of a reputation as a mere flag-waver. Steve Van Zandt, who had built a small but significant audience in Europe with his leftist rock and r 'll, found himself having to explain the bitter criticisms contained in the song's lyrics to left-wing journalists who grasped its intricacies no better than conservative American pundits.

Springsteen got his ideas across better in a three-hour show, of course, than in a sixty-minute television special that steered away from social issues; taken alone, none of his songs summarized his perspective. That was the point. Throughout the European tour there was an arresting contrast between Springsteen's songs of dreams and disillusion and the stars and stripes that almost always waved here and there amongst the crowd. Still, Bruce was sure of himself. When they ran into each other after the first Paris show, Robert Hilburn asked him if he was surprised at the lack of an anti-American backlash. "Naw," Springsteen said. "Rock and roll has always been able to cut through all that. That's what's great about it; you don't have to intellectualize it. Everybody feels the same emotions. It's great out there when everyone sings 'Born in the U.S.A.' They put so much feeling into it that it's real for them, even if it's not technically true. They know what the song is about and they can relate to it. That's the real connection."

The biggest challenge of the European tour was the test of playing, for the first time, an entire tour outdoors in stadiums. The smallest crowds numbered more than 50,000, the largest about double that. In that sense, Syracuse and even Australia were nothing more than dry runs. Furthermore, Springsteen was used to playing at night, with extremely dramatic stage lighting. The European shows were played in such strong daylight that lighting director Jeff Ravitz didn't even bother with the majority of his effects, using just white-hot television lights.

Syracuse and the Australian outdoor dates had gone well, even in bad weather, and Bruce was ready to tackle the new challenge, eager to learn the secrets playing to such a crowd had to teach him and confident that he'd succeed. Hepworth asked how he'd made the transition from clubs and theaters to arenas. "It wasn't that different," Bruce replied. "It was really much more of a mental thing, once you got the physical things taken care of, like the sound and lights."

◆

On May 30, Liverpool, England's reigning soccer champions, faced Italy's leading club, Juventus, in a European Cup match in Brussels. The match was televised live across Europe and in the United Kingdom. As millions watched, the Liverpool fans, who already had a reputation for rowdiness to the point of riot, attacked the Italian supporters and in the process, hundreds were trampled. Thirty-eight died; hundreds were treated for injuries. In the wake of the riot, England's soccer teams were indefinitely banned from participation in international soccer, and people all over Europe became wary of stadium events for the next few months.

The Springsteen tour suffered some peripheral consequences. One result was a slump in ticket sales in those few places that weren't already sold out. In Paris authorities created so many new security restrictions for playing the Stade de Colombes, a soccer field, that the concerts had to be moved to Parc de La Courneuve, in the northern suburbs.

In Dublin preparations had been under way all week for the Saturday concert. Slane Castle is located about thirty miles outside the city, in County Meath, just beyond an ordinarily sleepy village. The castle is the property of Lord Henry Montcharles (who, like most Irish aristocrats, is British). Lord Hank, as Travis instructed his crew to call him, had converted a part of the castle to an inn; the previous winter, U2 had rented out several of the rooms and recorded *The Unforgettable Fire* there. For the past several summers, in order to help manage the expensive upkeep of the old monstrosity, Lord Hank had been staging rock concerts in the beautiful natural amphitheater (with a 65,000-person capacity) formed by the cow pasture just outside its walls.

Previous shows at Slane—by U2, David Bowie, and, in 1984, Bob Dylan—had proven so disruptive, with drunken kids littering the streets, pissing in doorways, and trashing store windows and private lawns, that the townspeople had vowed, "Never again." But Belfast promoter Jim Aiken and George Travis, by starting to negotiate the previous October, were able to swing a deal. They promised sufficient sanitary facilities, large, colorful litter barrels, and security personnel to protect the town, and eventually the local residents' association was convinced to allow the show, although it also insisted that it would be the last ever held there.

Bruce flew into Dublin at eight o'clock Friday morning, the day before the show. The Irish papers put his arrival on the front page, showing him arm in arm with Julie as they emerged from clearing customs. After resting up, Bruce and Julie left at six thirty for a seven thirty sound check and inspection of the site.

There was still plenty of light left as he walked through the tent city—with dressing rooms, hospitality tents, and eating facilities for the band and crew—like a general inspecting a battlefield. The tents were set up around a stream running perhaps twenty yards behind the stage—the River Boyne, trickling along about three miles from the spot where the Irish had lost the last vestiges of their independence to the British 300 years before in the Battle of the Boyne. (Kids without tickets would crowd the opposite banks the next day, as kayakers paddled past, getting a good listen.)

All around, assembly of the stage and sound system and barricades continued. The crew had even built a corduroy road leading to the stage from the dirt entrance road; it went off again to the security fence separating the crowd from the backstage. As Bruce traipsed into the field that spread out before the stage to listen from a fan's perspective, the ground was still muddy, although the heat of another day would firm it up.

Springsteen had hoped to see a demonstration of the Diamondvision screens, but they weren't ready to go yet and daylight was fading, however slowly. He took the stage and worked through a couple of numbers. "Born in the U.S.A." and "Dancing in the Dark" rang eerily through the beautiful and empty green hills, but not nearly as strangely as the final song Bruce pulled out of his hat, the Conway Twitty rockabilly arrangement of "Danny Boy." Roy Bittan made it seem as if those pipes acallin' had brought successive generations of Irish emigrants to America solely to learn to rock and roll.

At eight thirty there was still plenty of light, but it was becoming cold, so the band trooped into the castle's massive stone entranceway, which had been converted into a pub (closed for the evening). Equipment was set up in an anteroom for another hour's rehearsal. The band hadn't played together since Japan, and Bruce put them through almost a full hour's set before knocking off around nine thirty to head back to the Dublin hotel.

Saturday dawned bright and hot, by Irish standards, temperature peaking somewhere in the upper seventies. The *gardai* (Irish national police) set up roadblocks on the two-lane highways that were the only way into Slane, and travelers had to show their tickets to get by, precautions designed to prevent another outbreak like the one that had marred the Dylan show. But thousands of kids had camped out overnight in the village or in the fields near the castle. Hundreds of fans had wandered the streets long past midnight, often drunk, carrying sleeping bags or just as likely wearing black plastic trash bags in which they'd flop to the ground for a few hours snockered rest. Many were up early to visit the hundreds of vans stretched along the final mile of road leading to the castle and offering fast food and bootleg T-shirts. Beer and hard liquor were also easy to find.

Slane was barricaded against the onslaught. The bank and other shops on its main street boarded up their windows just in case of trouble; home owners removed the plants from their front gardens so they couldn't be torn up.

Sixty-five thousand tickets had been sold; counterfeits had made an appearance in northern England; some level of gate-crashing could be expected. Police estimated the real size of the crowd at 100,000. The only road to the castle was narrow and winding, and Travis had already worked out a plan to alleviate the traffic jam. Although the tickets stated firmly that no one would be admitted until three P.M., the gates would in fact be opened at noon. (There were plans to open them as early as ten if the hordes had already arrived by then.) Bruce took the stage promptly at five.

Unfortunately, Bruce Springsteen and the E Street Band were only the day's main attraction, not its only one. Slane was the place to be that Saturday, whether you were a big Springsteen fan or not. Most were, but the hundreds who jostled closest to the stage included dozens of drunks whose enthusiasm was expressed primarily by shoving forward; on the fringes, but within Bruce's view, some got into fistfights. Jostling and jockeying for position in the front rows was to be expected, but this was nastier, a restless pushing back and forth in waves that sent weaker and smaller people to their knees or crushed them against the barricade before the stage. Several dozen in the audience, mostly young girls, fainted and had to be passed up over the barricade and into the infirmary area backstage. No one was badly injured; an officer of the St. Johns Ambulance Brigade reported that only twenty to twenty-five had even minor injuries, and some of them were just suffering from sunburn.

Wearing jeans and a maroon-and-white-striped polo shirt, Bruce slammed through "Born in the U.S.A.," then "Badlands" and "Out in the Street" before pausing. Even on the video screen you could see distress and unease rush across his face. Maybe the danger wasn't real—"There is no built-in aggro, everybody there is a fan of one person," Jim Aiken told reporters who raised the specter of the Brussels riot; Pete Townshend smiled at Springsteen's distress and commented, "But it's always like this when you play outdoors." But this shoving and mauling and milling around wasn't at all what a Bruce Springsteen show was supposed to be about. How could you sing about self-respect before an audience that threatened to become a mob? How did you readjust their focus and get them to listen?

"What you gotta do is stop that swaying back and forth,'cause it's knocking people around, okay?" Bruce urged forcefully after "Out in the Street." "If anybody needs help to get out of there, raise your hand." He was probably a lot more freaked by the aggressive behavior than the crowd, but a look of fear could be seen in every band member's face, and on the ramp behind the stage, Jon Landau paced furiously, chewing his lip so powerfully it seemed he'd bite clear through.

Down in the pit between the barricade and the stage, crew members sprayed hoses on the crowd, to cool it off and perhaps help settle down some of the more drunken types. Julie Phillips worked backstage with the first-aid crews, soothing the brows of the kids who'd fainted in the crush.

Bruce swung into the *Nebraska* portion of the set, which today amounted to only "Johnny 99" and "Atlantic City," then dedicated "The River" to "all of you who ever needed a place to go when you couldn't go home." On the video screens, the song was paired with a view of the placid River Boyne, an ironic contrast to the turbulence of the song (and a shot kept on tape that was used for the entire rest of the tour).

The pace became a bit rushed, and when Bruce tried to speak again before "The Promised Land," the fans were so loud he couldn't manage the tone at all. Still concerned about what he was seeing before him, he again suggested cutting each other some slack. But when he spoke again, before "My Hometown," he never mentioned the Simon Community, the Dublin organization for the homeless to which he was making a contribution, perhaps because by then he'd accepted that he wasn't being listened to. (In fact, those who sat well back in the crowd experienced no problem; the problem only existed where Bruce would be most aware of it.) When he finished "Thunder Road" in Clarence's arms, the band left the stage looking almost thankful in its relief.

Eight hundred guests of Lord Hank, including Irish politicians, Townshend and his family, all of Spandau Ballet, most of U2, and Elvis Costello dressed like a rabbi, watched the show from the castle, where they ate smoked salmon and drank champagne. A hundred eighty came for breakfast; two hundred stayed for dinner. All day long, helicopters zoomed overhead, flying in wealthy and famous observers. During the break, many members of the "regular" audience clambered over the green wire fence into the "VIP enclosure" (less like a cage than it sounds) in front of the castle. Some, but by no means all, were stopped by gray T-shirted security men and sent back into the mass below.

The second set opened as usual with "Cover Me" and "Dancing in the Dark." Bruce had come to terms with the circumstances, reassured that no one had been seriously hurt. Besides, the worst of the swaying was over; maybe the rowdiest drunks had simply exhausted themselves or lost their places going for more booze at the break. Even so, the crush remained strong and during "Dancing" Bruce chose Patti Scialfa as his partner, although he did spot an old friend near the front during "Hungry Heart" and brought her up to dance along the front of the stage for a moment. On "Pink Cadillac" he delivered his Jimmy Swaggart spiel ferociously, as if trying to exorcise a bad mood; it didn't make much difference, because Catholic Ireland had no more experience of television evangelism than Buddhist Japan, and even attentive listeners were somewhat mystified.

The second set ended with "Rosalita," Bruce saying that the band would be "pissed off" if he didn't introduce them, a remarkable comment since he rarely swore even offstage. "You can call me lieutenant, honey," he snarled in the course of the song, "but don't ever call me Boss."

He came out for the first encore all alone, carrying an acoustic guitar, then sat down and played the Beach Boys' "When I Grow Up to Be a Man," his voice cracked and trembling. In that moment, he sounded as miserable as any misanthrope Elvis Costello had ever imagined.

When the band came back on, he turned to them with a look almost of supplication, and in the next few minutes you could see what they were really worth to one another. He shouted for "Ramrod," and they hit it viciously, playing their hearts out inside that dinosaur beat. In the midst of the song, you could practically feel the band pick Bruce up and try to turn his mood around. They finished with an exuberant "Born to Run" and the medley of "Twist and Shout" and "Do You Love Me?"

When it was over, the rest of the band and the part of the crew that didn't have to disassemble the show and get it to Newcastle dried off and repaired to the castle for a dinner the promoters had laid on. Bruce and Jon Landau, however, took the first chopper back to Dublin's Gresham Hotel, where they talked events over for the rest of the night.

Bruce had been making his adjustments all afternoon; he wasn't ready to make any radical alterations immediately. Landau was perhaps more worried than that. "I wouldn't say Bruce had a good time, but he was not feeling bad when the show was over," Landau said. "We had stuff to talk about, you know. . . . Let's put it this way, if that had been the third show instead of the first, it would have been a non-event. We got the wildest crowd in the first fifteen minutes of the tour. And the frightening thing was not what was happening here, but is it gonna be like this every night? Am I gonna have to go through six weeks of that, because that would have been a little difficult."

As it turned out, Slane was an anomaly in the course of the tour. George Travis had made one mistake, allowing the barricade in front of the stage to be laid out flat, rather than in a vee-shape (like a ship's prow), which would better disperse the crowding.

Landau took a single additional precaution. He gave interviews in each of the remaining cities to stress the idea that the show was a Bruce Springsteen concert, *not* a rock festival. He also made sure that the promotion for the upcoming U.S. dates took the same tone.

The rest of the European tour was almost completely devoid of negative events. This was so even in Milan, and it's a rock and roll industry cliché that all Italian shows are accompanied by riots and customers without tickets breaking in. George Travis, determined that this would not occur during one of his shows, successfully defused the situation by placing extra video screens in the plaza outside San Siro Stadium. At dusk, just as the crowd was gathering itself for a rush at the gates, he switched the screens on. Since the music could be adequately heard coming over the roof of the stadium, that left nothing to riot *about*.

In fact, you couldn't have asked for smoother shows than those in Newcastle, the tour's second stop. Newcastle is a town of coal-miners and industrial workers, the British equivalent of Wheeling or Youngstown. Bruce pushed the possibilities in both shows, concluding the first with the somber "Racing in the Street" and filling out the second with quieter numbers like "Shut Out the Light" and "Can't Help Falling in Love." The weather had cooled and, with everyone's adjustments in place, the shows went smooth as a dream.

Springsteen was continuing his policy of working with community groups in each city that he visited, and in Newcastle he chose to work with the Durham Miners' Wives Support Group, the wives of men left destitute after losing a bitter strike against the British government, which had decided to bust the union by closing most of the state-owned coal mines and importing scabs to run those that were left.

This earned him an attack by right-wing Member of Parliament Piers Merchant, who wrote a letter and raised questions in Parliament about the donation. "I think he was badly advised about the coal strike and the issues involved; it was an ill-judged decision," Merchant told Gavin Martin of *New Musical Express*. "I don't think he supports violence. The money will be going to miners who've been sacked, and they've been guilty of violence and vandalism. It's a great shame because it was great to have him in Newcastle." It turned out that this British version of George Will had in the past been supported by the fascist-style British National Movement and that Merchant had refused to disavow such support.

The reaction of Anne Fiddick, the Miners' Wives' representative with whom Springsteen met, was much more meaningful and symbolized the way in which Springsteen's "charity" work could have much broader political impact. Fiddick spoke of the group's amazement simply at being offered six tickets to the show. After all, once the Miners' Union declared the strike over, the majority of their media support had drifted away. (Gavin Martin and his colleague Cynthia Rose were significant exceptions.) "To me that was the *crème de la crème*," Fiddick said. "But when we were asked to bring information on the work we were doing now, I was taken totally by surprise.

"We met an incredible guy—he'd followed events on TV and in the press, and he wanted to know how we managed to live and organize the movement from within the communities so that it spread nationally. He told us about his own father, how being put out of work had drained his pride and spirit, and we explained how we were campaigning now to keep communities alive in places where pits are being closed down. His interest was obviously in the families and the communities.

"By doing this Bruce has become some sort of a symbol for the men up here. Since the strike ended they've become dejected and downcast. It seemed as if no one was interested and no one cared, with all the press campaigns dwindling. By proving he cares, Springsteen has reopened all the questions that have been left to die since the strike ended."

◆

Springsteen accepted a greater level of inattention at the stadium shows, as he'd had to accept an increase in distraction when he moved to arenas. "Hey, it's a rock and roll show," he said, shrugging off those who shouted and roamed during the slow songs. The nature of the event—outdoors, in a gathering more populous than Freehold, in the middle of the summer—didn't automatically grant the same ease of focus as indoor concerts. But that was part of the point; the adventure of these shows was figuring out how to center the crowd's attention and create a new kind of interaction.

In fact, Bruce changed the set very little. Basically, he stabilized the repertoire, making fewer changes each evening. This sort of thing had been a breaking point for every other rock act that reached stadium level; the vast audience came with its own expectations and the audience's sheer size gave its will enormous force. Mostly, a crowd of that size came to party more than listen, and to defy it risked not getting over at all.

Springsteen's show wasn't really an exception. It *was* measurably more difficult to pull off the slower, more thoughtful songs—the audience was restive through such quiet passages—but Bruce refused to back off. It was an extraordinary act of will. Apparently he simply decided that he was going to do *his* show and left it at that. And it worked.

As in 1981, the European tour peaked with the shows at Wembley, but this time Bruce was playing the 70,000 capacity soccer stadium rather than the arena, which was barely a fifth that size. Little international media attention was focused on the Continental dates, but the shows in London were intensely watched, not only in England but back home, where the rumors of a forthcoming stadium tour were circulating widely. Furthermore, the middle night of the three was the Fourth of July, which left Bruce to live up to the symbolism of playing the British capital on U.S. Independence Day.

The Wembley shows were packed with athletes and royalty, disc jockeys and movie and television stars, and such rock musicians as George Michael, Phil Collins, Sting, David Bowie, Pete Townshend and the other members of the disbanded Who, Mark Knopfler of Dire Straits (who were playing the Wembley Arena across the road), and Roger Taylor of Queen. Like all the other European shows, the seating was general admission, but the celebrities had access to the "royal box" and another section of preferred seating, where they could cluster with decent sight lines (about fifty yards from the stage) and be gaped at by the hoi polloi.

First-night (or rather, afternoon—the shows started just after six P.M. because of a local noise curfew) crowds in London hadn't changed in four years. They were still stiff, although this time there was no worry that industry guests would grab all the closest seats. Within a few songs Springsteen had knit the crowd together with their own mania. (When he'd first cracked Britain, he'd cracked it big, and between the stories of his previous U.K. shows and the success of "Dancing in the Dark," the crowd's anticipatory energy was just about palpable.)

Four songs into the first set, Bruce pulled his first surprise. Over a chunky boogie beat—like slowed-down ZZ Top—Bruce shouted a stentorian introduction. Because he'd just finished the hard opening push through "Born in the U.S.A.," "Badlands," and "Out in the Street," he was winded and almost panting. The reckless energy with which he paced and hollered despite that suggested anxiety, and his pauses appeared to be those of a man having trouble suppressing his anger. If he was just acting, it was the best job he'd ever done.

"When we were on the first part of our American tour, we were down in Texas," he said, and gulped for air. "Down there you saw a lotta folks that had come down from up north—outta Detroit, Pittsburgh. They'd gone down south lookin' for some work in the oil field and on oil rigs, and when they got down there the price of oil dropped. There wasn't no jobs.

"They'd end up sleepin' in tents out on the side of the highway . . . sleepin' in their cars at night, with their wives and their kids . . . with no work or no place to go [*pause*] and the cops just tellin' 'em to move along. This is called 'Seeds.' "

The music lumbered into gear, a great roar of synthesized brass and nasty guitar, as Springsteen spat out the lyrics in a leather-lunged voice:

> *Parked in the lumberyard freezin' our asses off*
>
> *My kids in the backseat got a graveyard cough*
>
> *Well, I'm sleepin' in front with my wife*
>
> *Billyclub tappin' on the windshield in the middle of the night*
>
> *Says "Move along, man,*
>
> *Move along."*

This was a song of a man hurt to the quick, not the "wounded not even dead" of "Jungleland," but the discarded, left for dead of real life, and not just life in Houston, Pittsburgh, and Detroit, but all over. It was a song that would have been well understood in Newcastle or, for that matter, in Dublin and Milan, industrial cities that had also suffered the ravages of Seventies "recession" and the false prosperity of the Eighties.

The music had a spare, surging power that Springsteen had rarely commanded before, based in the blues, not soul. And what could be heard of the lyrics was as completely vernacular as anything he'd ever written. In words and music, Springsteen had become that freezing migratory worker and his onstage demeanor captured the restless, furious passion of a man cheated not just of a dream but of the very staples of life. He ended with a curse and a warning, vowing that if he "could spare the spit," he'd gob at every limousine that passed him by, suggesting that anybody tempted to follow in his footsteps was "better off buyin' a shotgun straight off the rack." When Springsteen shouted the final line—"Movin' on, movin' on/It's gone, gone, it's all gone"—he wasn't idly echoing fifty years of highway blues; this was "Johnny 99" for real.

The rest of the show went as usual, until the encores. Bruce had saved "Bobby Jean" until then, and when it finished he turned to the wings and called out Little Steven, who came aboard decked out in a pink shirt, mauve bandanna, and tiger-print tights. They shot into the song that stated their case best of all, "Two Hearts," and then wound the evening down with the medleys of "Street Fighting Man"/"Born to Run," and "Twist and Shout"/"Do You Love Me?"

Bruce took the stage almost half an hour late on the Fourth of July, arriving alone with just his acoustic guitar. His face was gigantic on the huge video screen, overlaid upon an American flag snapping in the breeze as he sang "Independence Day," a ten-minute ballad, all by himself to this massive crowd. At the end he was joined by the full band for the final chorus. Opening the show all but naked took great nerve, but the song was the least arrogant Bruce could have chosen— its metaphors of reconciliation served almost as well for Britain and America as for father and son or loner and society. It even modified the meaning of "Born in the U.S.A." and "Badlands," which followed.

If there'd been any doubt that Springsteen could do stadium shows as poignant as those he'd created indoors, this performance dispelled it once and for all. Springsteen struck every emotional note he'd ever reached in smaller halls, and he did it without once violating the context of the stadium show. The energy, supercharged by the thrill of those first few minutes, surged even when he slipped into sequences of songs from *Nebraska*.

Introducing "Highway Patrolman," a song which in the abstract seems impossibly fragile for such huge spaces, he said, "This is a song about, I guess, the conflict between what your heart tells you to do and what you do with it." And with those simple words, which might have applied to his decision to tackle the biggest challenges as well, the song came home.

The final show of the European tour was something to savor from the very first notes, when Bruce, ready to kick off "Born in the U.S.A." shouted "One . . . two . . ." and the audience responded, "One, two, three, four!" in perfect cadence.

That show was held in Roundhay Park, which was (natives attest) the place to *park* in this Midlands city. Bruce was onstage by quarter past four, looking out at an audience that stretched beyond the open field spread out before the stage and spilled over into the trees nearly half a mile away. Eighty thousand tickets had been sold; there were at least another 10,000 counterfeits. When the temporary fencing was put up around the concert area, the joining bolts were left facing outward. They were easily unfastened by intermission, and then another 10,000 or so fans spilled through the gaps.

As with every other outdoor show Bruce had done in Europe, the weather was perfect—until the end of the day, when great black clouds began looming ominously overhead. As the band finished "Bobby Jean," Springsteen sat down and reached for a microphone. The air already felt damp as he began the story that led into "Racing in the Street," which would complete the second set in a somber mood.

It was another nervy move. Doing such a slow, sad narrative virtually invited any listener whose devotion was less than complete to rush for shelter or transport home. But as Bruce spoke and then sang, the crowd stayed almost completely still; there was no movement away from the stage. Bruce had transfixed them, held them in the palm of his hand, made them a part of the saga of his show as surely as if each had been able to look him in the eye.

17 SEEDS

As this show careens to its end, it's impossible not to be at least a little distracted by last-minute wishes and regrets. Springsteen takes so long between tours that the last night of every tour really seems to be *the* last. It's a feeling that grows stronger each time, not so much because he and the band are getting older but because the one constant in his work is change.

So even if your first thought on the first night of the whole tour was a cautionary reminder to wait, watch, and listen before judging, maybe you can't help anticipating the choices Bruce will make tonight. He's reached more than one pinnacle in the past eighteen months, and you figure the second set almost has to end giddy, with "Rosalita."

But if you're a fan, and not just someone who's along to take notes, then it's more than permissible to imagine another ending—another *kind* of ending, maybe another kind of triumph, less sweet but still worth savoring.

It's an ending Bruce has used recently and, in a way, it's the essence of the indefinable magic that he works in these dark evenings, because it explodes the bonds of genre—as song and as narrative. When they do it best, it goes something like this:

Roy Bittan begins to play an edgy, wistful synthesizer backdrop as Bruce walks to the edge of the stage, mike in hand, and sits down. It is so quiet onstage that you can hear every breath and holler in the crowd. Bruce puts the mike to his lips and begins speaking.

"It was around . . . it was around the end of summer, and I had this old convertible Camaro. I used to take it at night to this little place. There was this little strip off the river—I guess it was like a junkyard, where people from town would come down and they'd dump the things that they didn't want anymore and just leave 'em out there to rust.

"But there was this little spot where we'd all meet on Friday and Saturday, and that was the first place that I met her. And it was one of those . . . like, when you're first goin' out with somebody and everything's funny, it's easy—it's easy to be with somebody.

"But then time kinda passed, and I don't know what happened. It seemed like the things that made her happy once didn't make her happy anymore. And I was spendin' my time tryin' to figure out kinda what had happened, what I could do to make her happy again. And she got to where she didn't want to talk—she wanted to stay in at night. And she'd take my keys so I couldn't take the car out.

"And it was hard to get her to understand, and I *know* she knew because she remembered—she loved it once—that when I took the car out and when I won, that it was the only time that I really got to feelin' good about myself.

"And I don't know if people expect too much of each other sometimes—maybe they do. But to have just one thing—one thing in your whole life that you do, that you do good, that you feel proud of—that's not too much for anybody to ask."

The sound switches suddenly now, the synthesizer dying away as perfectly placed chords rise from the grand piano. It's the opening rhythm of "Racing in the Street," and the intro sustains through several repetitions before Springsteen rises and begins to sing:

> *I got a '69 Chevy with a 396*
>
> *Fuelie heads and a Hurst on the floor*
>
> *She's waitin' tonight down at the parking lot*
>
> *Of the 7–11 store*

This is the line of demarcation separating casual Springsteen fans from the fanatics. To those who keep their distance, it's an overblown metaphor, the Chuck Berry car song extended to the point of absurdity. For those who listen with their heart as much as their head, "Racing in the Street" is something else, maybe the best thing Bruce Springsteen has to give—it's the greatest imaginable subversion of the "Happy Days" illusions of rock and roll car songs; the genius bastard cousin of the ultimate automobile ballad, the Beach Boys' "Don't Worry Baby."

When Springsteen reaches the final lines, promising that tonight his baby and he will "ride to the sea and wash these sins off our hands," some shrug and walk away at this crazy guy's inflated notion of the importance of trash. Others stick around and hear something a lot better: a promise that if you let the little things add up, they count for more than all the monuments in the world.

By now, working off that opening story, Springsteen has added several layers of meaning to the song. He's made it a metaphor for his own life, an explanation of why he writes, sings, plays, tours. And in its junkyard images and allusions to the fact that we expect more from those we love than we do from life itself, he's created a description of why he has chosen the wretched and the despised as his allies.

Maybe—*maybe*—"Racing in the Street" was impossibly romantic in 1978, when it appeared on *Darkness on the Edge of Town*. But by now, in 1985, it has grown into the song that tells more about Bruce Springsteen and his accomplishments than any other, while still refusing to back off from its own romance. You can love it or hate it; you can love him or hate him. But the fact is that both the song and the singer speak the truth, in blind faith that someone will hear it. They reach and they connect, and sparks fly each time they do.

Bruce obviously can't let the story end with the simple absolution of guilt. At the end of the song Federici's organ and Bittan's piano and synthesizer rise together, not in combat but entwined in harmony, and the song bleeds through two or three more choruses as Bruce Springsteen sits back down and begins once more to speak, quietly and in a voice younger than you've heard all night.

"So that was the night that we left. Just packed up our bags. We still don't know where we're goin' yet, but I guess that'll come in time. As for this place, well, there's a lot here that we'll always remember. But sometimes it seems like time gets runnin' so short on ya that it's gonna run out. And so much gets lost and left behind that there's not much that you can do but to keep searchin' and to keep on goin', and to keep on goin', and to keep on goin', and to keep on goin', and to keep on goin', and to keep on goin' . . ."

Gently he lays the microphone on its stand and walks away, back toward the drums and the dark. As he does, the music rises once more, a solid wall of sound, the hearty wail of a dream being born out of one person's loneliness and pain. Born, rather than dying, because a single link is forged. And forged again, until it comes out right.

18 HOT FUN IN THE SUMMERTIME

Mama always told me not to look into the lights of
 the sun
Oh but mama that's where the fun is

—"Blinded by the Light"

After Leeds, the *Born in the U.S.A.* tour, about a year on the road, had played 128 shows with a total attendance of 2.9 million. The summer stadium tour of the United States would cover nine weeks, with twenty-eight dates in fourteen cities. Its total attendance would also be just over 2 million. The tour was already huge: 3 million people was more than Springsteen had played for in the previous decade. Now it became gargantuan: The 5 million total attendance represents the largest· live audience any rock act has ever reached in the course of a single tour. The tour grossed about $100 million from ticket sales alone, a sum greater than the annual gross national product of some countries, and that doesn't reflect revenue from records and concert merchandise, which might have come close to doubling tour income.

It was the summer of Bossmania. Columbia Records kept *Born in the U.S.A.* on the front burner; the album spent fifty-three weeks in the *Billboard* Top Five and remained in the Top Ten until the tour was over. Sales had passed 8 million copies in the United States; worldwide sales exceeded 12 million copies, and another Christmas shopping season was only a couple of months away. "Glory Days" was Bruce's biggest hit since "Dancing in the Dark," peaking at Number Five, and its humorous twists on nostalgia made it another important image single as well as perfect summertime blues. The video made Springsteen equally pervasive on rock and roll television. "Glory Days" was followed by "I'm Goin' Down," which became the sixth Top Ten hit taken from the album. (Only one LP in history—*Thriller*—had ever produced seven.)

Johnny Carson made Boss jokes—"Mick Jagger just had a baby boy; this kid has everything but he still can't get Bruce Springsteen tickets," he cracked one night. *Barron's* tried to divine the future of the stock market from the mood of *Born in the U.S.A.* Law firms around the country used Springsteen tickets as an enticement in recruiting desirable new law school graduates—according to *American Lawyer* magazine, one Cleveland firm had its staffers stand in line for six hours to buy seventy-two seats.

Magazines and newspapers ran lengthy articles by "serious" writers (meaning those who had no special knowledge of popular music) trying to assess what it all meant. Left (*In These Times*, the *Bay Guardian*), right (Leon Wieseltier in *The New Republic*, Norman Podhoretz in a column syndicated by Rupert Murdoch), and center (Jack Newfield in the *Village Voice*, Senator Bill Bradley in *USA Today*) all fumblingly tried to explain Springsteen's grip on the mass audience. None really succeeded because, of course, that grip derived its fundamental strength not from Springsteen's stand on the issues but from his perception of the importance of rock and roll music in the lives of his listeners and his ability to rock their butts off.

The previous summer's superstars—Michael Jackson and Prince— had faded from the front pages months before, each with his image sorely tarnished. In 1985 the only other pop stars the public found as fascinating as Springsteen were Sylvester Stallone, in his Rocky and Rambo incarnations, and Madonna.

Comparisons between Springsteen and Stallone were easy; they were bandied about everywhere, from casual conversations to the editorial page of the *Chicago Tribune*. The discrepancies were less instructive, given that Stallone's Rocky and Rambo were such obvious jingoistic stooges, with no depth, no humanity, and, in the end, a following that lasted only as long as the thrills were as fresh as the rivulets of stage blood that fueled them. If there was any purpose in comparing Springsteen to such brainless trash, it was primarily because *Rocky IV* and *Rambo* pointed up how completely the political and cultural right dominated all attempts to define "American" qualities, which suggests something of what Springsteen risked by daring to offer a separate vision.

Almost no one thought of comparing Bruce Springsteen to Madonna. In fact, their images formed a fascinating polarity. Madonna's presence was as divisive as Bruce's was unifying. While both were noted for being physically fit, her reputation for sexual expressiveness made her seem tawdry; his legendary wholesomeness was in part a by-product of libidinal restraint (a topic explored in songs as various as "Cover Me," "Pink Cadillac," "I'm Goin' Down," and "Dancing in the Dark"). Madonna's music was purely the creation of the recording studio; her concerts were the most suspect element in her musical arsenal. She was eager for movie success and began making her first top-billed feature (*Desperately Seeking Susan*) even before her musical star had fully risen. Springsteen was obsessed with society; Madonna's public image was a testimonial to narcissism.

Even so, they had things in common. The most important was that both were levelers in their way: Springsteen's denim and cotton were the contemporary equivalent of homespun; Madonna's flaunting of lingerie and foundation garments as outerwear infuriated arbiters of fashion at the same time that it spurred a gaggle of imitators ("Madonna wannabes"). Furthermore, neither seemed willing to slip into a one-dimensional image and stay there. Far from remaining a dumb sexpot, Madonna pursued both music and acting with serious purpose, and she exhibited genuine creative growth across her first three albums. Springsteen was set up to be the perfect all-American boy, not only the darling of presidential candidates but an absolute avatar of Horatio Alger rags-to-riches success; he didn't just decline the honors, he spurned the myth by bringing into focus the awful waste of human life in the community from which he sprang.

No one is immune to the consequences of being publicly held aloft for too long, particularly if disinclined to feed the media mill. In Madonna's case the potshots succeeded at least in driving her husband, Sean Penn, crazy. Springsteen seemed to shrug the whole process off, but it was hard to imagine how long he could keep it up. Later in the summer *Los Angeles Times* columnist Patrick Goldstein, for one, wondered aloud about how Springsteen might suffer, identifying a "backlash syndrome" that had recently affected everyone from Boy George to the BeeGees and inquiring of several industry figures what Bruce's eventual fate might be. Goldstein wrote of "familiar warning signs: Paparazzi have snapped pics of him smooching with his new wife . . . *Newsweek* put him on the cover even though he refused to give the magazine an interview . . . Politicians are quoting his lyrics, claiming be lifelong fans . . . Just the other day, *People* plugged him on its cover just so it could run three pages of photos from his stadium tour and speculate about what turn his career might take next . . . And *Time* ran 'the first-ever published portrait' of Mr. & Mrs. Boss. Columbia's release of a sixth single and plans to promote the album through Christmas increased the risk."

"Sooner or later, it's inevitable," a "veteran industry publicist" told Goldstein. "In a lot of ways, it's the media's fault, not his. The media has become expert at building someone up to epic proportions and then, just as quickly, tearing you down. It's hard to imagine Springsteen getting caught up in the same process, but he's being ballyhooed so much now that he may lose the mystique that has always made him appear different from every other pop star out there hawking themselves."

But Cliff Bernstein, manager of Def Leppard/Dokken, believed otherwise. "I think a sixth single is a little bit of overkill, but his audience hasn't really changed. When you went to see Prince or Michael Jackson after they got hot, it was a different audience—a fickle pop audience— who come to see artists on a one-time basis. But Bruce isn't attracting fans who've just read about him in *Newsweek*. He's kept the ones who were there from the beginning."

In fact, Springsteen remained a center of fan fanaticism. In November 1984 Bert Epstein, a twenty-year-old Beverly Hills Bossmaniac, started a "Bruce Party Line" in Los Angeles. It offered a thirty-minute tape-recorded phone message on which fans could relay rumors, enthusiasms, and critiques of shows, records, and ticket-selling practices. It received more than a hundred calls weekly for more than two years and eventually expanded to a second line in New York. Sustaining that level of cultish addiction was unprecedented and the best evidence that Springsteen had more than maintained the loyalty of the majority of his old fans; new ones were often absorbed in the same kind of devotion.

"I'm Goin' Down" was a legitimate hit, reaching Number Nine in *Billboard*. And although Springsteen was easy to caricature—you just dragged out the headband, the torn jeans, and sweaty shirts, strapped on a guitar, adopted a scratchy Jersey accent, and mumbled street philosophy—he subverted both the pop-star stereotype and the cartoon portrayal of the radical artist. He faced facts, but anger and frustration were never the core of his show, just the counterpoint to hard-rocking assent. He may have been the first left-wing star in show business history to make popular politics seem like a means of banishing drudgery. "Nobody wins unless everybody wins" is what he said, but "There ain't no party unless everybody's invited" is what he acted out. Since he also behaved as if he meant it, the only likely source of media burnout was the frustration of reporters, editors, and pundits trying to pigeonhole him.

◆

Plans for the U.S. stadium tour weren't finalized until the last night at Wembley, when Jon Landau and Premier Talent's Frank Barsalona and Barry Bell sat down to hash out requirements and possibilities. Bell made a series of telephone calls when he returned to New York. A tour like this wasn't really negotiated, since promoters, agents, and artists all understood the business parameters—and the artist had all the leverage. Premier then mailed out contracts; when the signed documents were returned, tickets could go on sale.

This left only about two weeks in which to sell the tickets for the shows on the first half of the tour, but that seemed no special problem, since demand for the arena shows had been at stadium level just about everywhere on the previous year's itinerary.

The tour was scheduled to start August 5 with a single show at RFK Stadium in Washington, which held about 54,000. Since Bruce had sold 60,000 tickets at the nearby Capitol Center the previous summer, this hardly did much to service the expanded demand (although it did help some, since there were many repeaters at the Cap Center shows). Tickets didn't go on sale until July 22.

This was either a great logistical error—owing to the decentralization of ticket sales through Ticketron and Telecharge, some people who'd camped out as long as four days in anticipation of the on-sale announcement were shut out—or accidentally a great piece of p.r. strategy. The show sold out in ninety minutes. Not only that, but between ten and eleven thirty on the morning of the twenty-second, the Bell system serving the District of Columbia, Virginia, and Maryland region registered more than 2 million calls—the previous Monday morning it had been used less than half as often. The difference was solely attributable to calls to Teletron for Springsteen tickets.

The flood of calls tied up the entire D.C. area phone system, affecting even the White House (but not the Oval Office) and systems as far north as New Jersey. This was worth national headlines, and it got 'em. And they repeated when phone systems also crashed in Pennsylvania, New York, and New Jersey as tickets went on sale for two Philadelphia shows, which sold out in six hours, and four shows at Giants Stadium in the Meadowlands. A couple of weeks later, when Chicago tickets went on sale, *Newsweek* reported, "Illinois Bell put on line a computer system that's usually used to control phone traffic on Mother's Day or to handle calls to towns hit by tornadoes."

In New York Ticketron sold 236,000 tickets for the shows at 70,000-seat Giants Stadium in one day, shattering their previous record. Ticketron officials estimated that the demand would have filled Giants Stadium more than twenty times. When dates in Boston fell through, two more Giants Stadium dates were added and the tickets for those were also gone in a day.

But it wasn't just New Jersey and the Northeast anymore; Springsteen was now an assured immediate sell-out throughout the country. Just as with the arena shows, the question became not whether he could sell out, but how many shows and how quickly. In Los Angeles he sold 340,000 tickets for four shows, "the biggest collective audience any single performer has drawn in this city's history," according to the *Los Angeles Herald Examiner*, and that wasn't untypical.

Once the tickets were sold, they were often avidly resold. In Toronto so many newspaper advertisements offered scalped Springsteen ducats that police began an investigation of promoter Michael Cohl and his staff (they were cleared). In Dallas scalpers paid homeless men and women up to $40 cash to stand in line and purchase tickets. In Philadelphia tickets went for $125 from scalpers; front row seats for as much as $400. Prices were similar elsewhere.

George Travis and his team had developed their own way of dealing with scalping. Besides doing their best to have any scalpers on the premises of a show arrested, they hoarded the extra seats made available by slight alterations in the production—moving the stage or sound and light mixing positions a few feet one way or another could open up a whole row. Those seats could amount to a couple of hundred additional tickets, which were put on sale just a few hours before show-time, either to fans already queuing outside the stadium or to fans notified by local radio stations, thus undercutting at least some of the scalpers. In Pittsburgh Travis's people were able to put 2,000 tickets on sale Saturday afternoon for a Sunday night show, which resulted in an attendance of 62,000 (the largest in Three Rivers Stadium history) and in tickets being scalped for as little as $5 two hours before show-time. "I'm getting stuck for sixty dollars, and I'm not the only one," moaned one scalper.

In Chicago, where the show was announced several days before tickets went on sale, the promoters instituted a lottery that scrambled the sequence of those waiting in line. One reason was that ticket brokers (legal scalpers) were "paying people to stand in line. They were already taking orders for this show," according to promoter Jerry Mickelson. That show was also the only one on the tour to be held as a general admission event, and it sparked fears recalling the Who tragedy at Cincinnati and the Brussels soccer riot. In fact, it wasn't until the Jacksons tour of 1984 that anyone had ever played stadium shows with reserved seating; until the Jacksons tried it, it was believed that a stadium audience would simply trample over any temporary alignment of chairs set down on the field. Nothing of the sort happened with the Jacksons, and their experience was what encouraged Springsteen to run a real concert tour, not just a series of wildcat outdoor dates in which the event overwhelmed the music.

Nevertheless, the reason for playing with reserved seating was artistic control more than crowd control, and everybody knew it. When the *Chicago Sun-Times* asked Chicago Park District Superintendent Edmund L. Kelly whether Springsteen fans or Chicago Bears fans were more likely to misbehave, he instantly responded, "Oh, the Bears," and criticizing the Bears in Chicago is sacrilege. As it happened, the day of the show did produce a tragedy, but one that had nothing to do with the seating arrangement: A speeding bus ran over a car trying to enter the stadium, killing all seven of the Springsteen fans in it and injuring sixty bus passengers.

A special area of reserved seating in the stands *was* provided for friends of the band and the promoters, which gave some well-connected Chicagoans a special vantage point. But in the end, its most fascinating by-product was a fistfight between former Bears quarter-back Bobby Douglass and George Cole of the Steelworkers—Old Timers Food Bank, who was in town for the founding convention of the National Rank and File Against Concessions (NRFAC). The Cole-Douglass bout was a draw, and Cole made a bigger point that day by bringing with him members of union locals from a variety of industries all over the country. One of the food banks Springsteen supported that night was run by Steelworkers Local 1014 of Gary, Indiana, representing what was left of U.S. Steel's once-massive Gary Works. The local, whose 3,500 still-employed workers were far outnumbered by the 5,500 who'd been laid off, was headed by Larry Regan, another key player in NRFAC, who was able to discuss with Bruce the problems faced by industrial workers in Gary and elsewhere and what the most progressive local union leaders were doing about them.

Indeed, it wasn't only politicians who found Springsteen's hardworking all-American image useful. Support of trade unions was so rare among celebrities that all of organized labor seemed eager to canonize him. But the support Bruce offered was not a blanket endorsement of American trade unionism; it would have been as contradictory to accord blanket approval to the AFL-CIO as to the Democratic and Republican parties. The AFL-CIO, with the encouragement of its major member unions, had avidly supported the war in Vietnam and, in the face of the Eighties Depression, also turned its back on the jobless and the homeless. The general principle of workers joining trade unions, which so many Americans failed to understand, was of course something that Springsteen endorsed. But he was careful to work with the kind of productive militants typified by Ron Weisen, whose USWA Local 1397 was (out of unfortunate necessity) almost as combative in its posture toward the Steelworkers International leadership as toward the steel companies.

Springsteen found Weisen and similarly minded local leaders such as Cole and Regan among his most natural allies because they were less concerned with abstract propositions about trade union solidarity than with protecting the lives of the workers the international unions often misrepresented. The best the AFL-CIO could offer was Walter Mondale and a package of "domestic content" legislation that was both rank protectionism and an assault on the living standards of workers outside the United States. Such trade unions no more believed in the principle that "nobody wins unless everybody wins" than Ronald Reagan did.

For better or worse, Springsteen was never called upon to make such fine distinctions explicit. The closest he came to such controversy was just before his Cleveland Municipal Stadium show that August. There Chicago concessionaire Andy Frain was attempting to push the 350 ticket takers, ushers, and security guards represented by Local 85 of the Service Employees International Union (SEIU) into accepting wage cuts. Unlike the militants of NRFAC, Local 85 wasn't opposed to such concessions in principle, but they felt that Springsteen's reputation as a union sympathizer gave them additional bargaining leverage and threatened a strike for the day of the show. It's hard to know whether Springsteen would have crossed a picket line if one had been set up. Ultimately, it was in part the power of his image and the reluctance of both the union and promoter Mike Belkin to damage it that won SEIU a one-night contract—but with Belkin, not Frain—which assured them regular wages for the concert.

◆

The stadium tour began at RFK Stadium for reasons that were practical rather than symbolic, but they couldn't have selected a better place to begin.

At most Washington shows the governmental elite are well provided with complimentary tickets or at least have special access to good seats. Springsteen's crew refused all requests, sending even the best-connected figures on Capitol Hill scurrying to the scalpers, which drove the prices way up.

The sole exception was New Jersey's Democratic senator Bill Bradley, who had been a fringe hanger-on in the Springsteen camp since visiting Bruce at the Power Station in 1980 during the making of The River. Bradley received tickets from Springsteen's crew and attended the show with Representative Thomas Downey, a Long Island Democrat (who headed the Congressional Arts Caucus, which provided for the special interests of so-called "serious" artists, writers, and musicians), and their wives.

Bill Bradley began running for President in 1963, when he was an All-American basketball star at Princeton. Upon graduation in 1965 he accepted a Rhodes Scholarship to Oxford University in England. There he organized pro-Lyndon Johnson demonstrations, despite Johnson's prosecution of the war in Vietnam. After returning to the United States, "Dollar Bill," as he became known, was for several seasons a star forward with the New York Knicks, NBA champions in 1970 and 1972. He first ran for office in 1978 and was elected by a substantial margin to the United States Senate from New Jersey.

Bradley's politics were definitively neo-liberal. The son of a banker, he was fiscally conservative and supported most military appropriations but tried to project himself as "young" and "hip," a pretty good feat for someone utterly lacking television presence. Even though his favorite record in college was "You'll Never Walk Alone," he tried to position himself as a rock and roll fan—in New Jersey, where Bruce Springsteen's "Born to Run" was named an anthem by the state legislature, liking rock music meant votes. In his office, reported the *New York Times*, Bradley kept a file on Springsteen between files labeled "South Africa" and "Strategic Petroleum Reserves." One could only wonder whether the senator made all of his file cabinets that easily available to the press.

On the day of the RFK Stadium show, *USA Today* ran a page 1 essay about Springsteen written by Bill Bradley. Had the prose been less wooden, one might have suspected it was composed by his staff. Bradley said that he wrote the article "because [Springsteen] burst on my imagination, when I was kind of reaching political maturity and trying to express the essence of New Jersey, and as I looked into the songs, I kind of felt in a funny way that we were trying to do the same thing."

If so, this was evident neither from Bradley's voting record nor from his article. After misidentifying Bruce as "a product of the New Jersey Shore," as though Freehold were a day at the beach, Bradley described a late-night episode in which he and his wife became fans after having their sleep disturbed by hearing "Born to Run" played from a nearby seaside home. Bradley wrote of Springsteen as if Bruce's subject were merely the landscape between the George Washington Bridge and Cape May and not America, or its working class, or the project of trying to become psychologically whole in a torn and bitter world. This parochialism was excusable, of course, since Bradley was for the most part writing as no more than a peculiarly elevated branch of the New Jersey Chamber of Commerce.

But Bradley then attempted to extend his vision of what Springsteen had to say, claiming that Springsteen's songs reflected Joseph Conrad's definition of work: "the sustaining illusion of an independent existence." Of itself this wasn't bad, but Bradley spent the rest of the article in barefaced contradiction of what Springsteen really had to say. "Bruce . . . doesn't delude himself with changing the world, or stopping war or creating a new consciousness. He simply isn't pretentious. He goes for the small, often sad, story, the insight into what makes us human. Above all, he goes for rock and roll." It was enough to make you wonder if Bradley had heard any of the songs Springsteen wrote *after* "Born to Run."

The senator concluded on an even more egregiously false note: "Forget that the factory closed or the marriage broke up. Forget—if just for a moment—and rock and roll. Remember the 'glory days.' Let the good times roll. The good and the bad, the highs and the lows—all part of a life, every life—and each life means as much as the next. Keep rocking, Bruce. Keep going. Let the good times roll." George Will and Ronald Reagan had practiced no greater distortion of what Bruce Springsteen's work was about. Yes, at the finest moments of a Bruce Springsteen show, listeners celebrated, but they never *ever* were left with the idea of fake "good times" that Bradley was trying to promulgate.

At the show that night Bruce Springsteen might have been directing himself straight at Bradley when he paused to introduce "My Hometown." Certainly what he chose to say was in part determined by an awareness of the many government employees in the crowd, as well as by the proximity of that scar in the earth that served as the unforgettable monument to Vietnam veterans.

Bruce never seemed very comfortable doing these introductions, partly because saying his piece this way was a little too close to actually making a speech, and partly, no doubt, because a little uncertainty was what the part called for. That night he was unusually awkward. Still wearing his guitar, his black shirt sopping wet, he looked absolutely distressed at what was about to issue from his lips. As he spoke, he nervously scratched at his temple, and from time to time he'd bring himself up short. In closeup on the video screens, he was visibly upset.

"When I was about, I guess, fifteen—I was fifteen years old," he began, stumbling nervously, "and there were these two brothers in town. And one was a singer and one was a guitar player. And I guess they had the first really adventurous band in my little town. One was named Ray and one was named Walter.

"I remember Walter was the first guy I'd ever seen tuck his pants inside his boots," he said with a nervous little giggle. "That was revolutionary at the time. You know," he added with a slight pant, pulling the mood back into line, "he was real good, a real good singer. And he got drafted and went to Vietnam—I guess it was in sixty-six." He scratched at his sideburns, disturbed, and continued in a hoarser voice. "I remember when his mother got . . got the word that he was missing in action. And Walter was the kind of guy, he didn't have the kind of talents that got ya . . . that kept you from gettin' killed in nineteen sixty-five and sixty-six. He just had a good voice and wasn't in college and . . ."

He looked down as the thought trailed off, as if summoning the strength for what came next.

"But, uh, I guess this next song is a song I wrote and after, quite a while after I wrote it, I guess I realized that what it was about was responsibility.

"And a lot of you young guys out there—and girls, too—the next time there's a little war, whether it's in Central America or wherever it might be, you're gonna be the ones that"—his voice sagged, hitting a sad note—"that they're gonna wanna go. And you're gonna need a lot more information than you get in the six o'clock news to know what to do."

Cheers stopped him. He reflected a second, then plunged on.

"And I guess, whether . . . whether we like it or not, it's our money that gets spent, either for makin' bombs, or it gets spent for feedin' people or it gets spent for wagin' little covert wars or for educatin' people. And we all get sucked into it, one way or another. There's no way around it." He said this as though describing a mountain he'd once explored, with a sense of painful assurance, in a tone that suggested how hard he'd looked to find such a path. And having no option, he continued.

"I guess a couple of years ago, I read a history book, *History of the United States*. I remember, when I was in school, I always hated history. But I read this book and I felt like I learned a lot about where we were comin' from, where we are today, and where we're goin'. And where we're goin' is pretty scary." He paused again and looked away. "Uhhhh . . ." he began, and broke again, as if unsure how to conclude or whether any conclusion at all was wise. He looked a little scared.

"So I guess all you really gotta do is take a walk from that Lincoln Memorial over to the Vietnam Veterans Memorial." Again cheers forced a pause, but this time he pushed through them to complete his thought. "Read. Read the names of the dead, and you get an idea of the stakes you're playing for in 1985"—he hesitated before making one last plunge—"when you were born in the U.S.A."

The cheers renewed, but Springsteen kept speaking, now as much to himself and the band as to the larger audience. "So this is your hometown, but you gotta put your stake in for it; you gotta make a claim for it." The cheers swelled again, but he still had a little left that he needed to get out. "Gotta find out what's going on around you," he muttered into the roar, and turned to sing his song.

It was a beautiful moment, a revelation of Springsteen's gift as a storyteller as well as of his ability to recapitulate the most intimate occurrences in epic terms. It was, as well, a summary of the past five years of struggling to make sense of what he'd read in his history book, seen in his travels around the world, written in his songs, heard as an echo from the crowd, felt—and feared—in the depth of his soul. In a sense, you could say that story retraced the path from the ingenuous optimism of *Born to Run* to the unraveled pessimism of *Nebraska*, and, with that statement about what it means "when you were born in the U.S.A.," wound up in exactly the same place.

There were many national reviewers in attendance that night. Almost all of them made some reference to his powerful introduction, but none picked up on the crucial sentence in which Bruce Springsteen made his most ardent and loving assertion of his right to dictate the meaning of his own song.

That was too bad. The deliberate distortion practiced the next day by Senator Bradley on national television was something worse. In the course of a bumbling interview on the *CBS Morning News*, in which both interviewer and interviewee revealed their complete ignorance of American popular music (Bradley referred to Bruce as an heir to "Buddy Holiday"), Phyllis George asked what Bradley thought of the antiwar sentiments Springsteen had expressed the night before.

"Well, I don't think he gave a lecture," Bradley claimed, backpedaling furiously. "I think he was simply saying that people should be aware of the world around them and inform themselves because there's a lot at stake. I think that's particularly true for all Americans. That's a positive message. That's a message of participation and involvement, and it's done with enthusiasm. I mean, Bruce Springsteen is an incredible talent, and there he is engaging you to be involved in the democratic process."

Did George Will practice any greater distortion? Had Ronald Reagan committed a greater perversion of Springsteen's words and actions? Well, if perhaps they had—and the point is arguable—certainly they didn't do so by speaking on network television in the assumed voice of a crony. Bruce Springsteen was talking about choice, all right, but he was also talking about situations in which there was only one correct selection to be made.

As it developed, Springsteen found an even clearer and louder way in which to voice his loathing of American foreign policy and what it had done to his bandmates. Bill Bradley also found a clearer way of saying what he really thought. In 1986 he voted twice to send military aid to the counterrevolutionary Nicaraguan *contras*.

In 1985 liberals moved to appropriate Bruce Springsteen's image and work just as conservatives had tried to do the previous year. Despite the myth, most leftists are uncomfortable around rock and roll; they prefer folk music—in particular the pseudofolk produced by white, urban acoustic writer-performers of topical songs, the preferred musicians of the New Left as well as of the old. Liberal pundit Jack Newfield, for instance, who wrote articles for the *Village Voice*, *Playboy*, and even *ASCAP in Action*, had an extremely difficult time coping with Springsteen's aesthetic. In a *Voice* article he described Elvis Presley as "a negative role model" and claimed that Springsteen's "canon of socially important songs numbers only twelve or fifteen at this point," as if the explicitly polemical utility of his works was their only salient characteristic (which is not true politically, much less artistically). It was feeling himself roped in by such agit-prop demagoguery that had driven Bob Dylan away from leftists in 1965.

Springsteen's activities also left left-wing pundits politically confused. Newfield could find no one better to compare Springsteen with than Robert Kennedy, a rather lame selection, given that Bruce is identified in the same passage as "neither a liberal nor a Democrat." David Corn, of the prominent socialist newspaper *In These Times*, referred to him as "the Mario Cuomo of pop music," which is *really* praising with faint damns.

Springsteen, it seemed, needed to exercise as much caution when dealing with leftists and liberals as with the right. Once absorbed into the cultural mainstream, most performers willingly surrender their "radicalism," since it is, after all, not much more than a gimmick.

Springsteen's was more organic; he could no more give it up than turn in his fingers and stop playing guitar. As it was, leftists and liberals were as isolated from the homeless and the hungry as the right. It was in his alliances with the dispossessed, not with the politicos of whatever stripe, that Springsteen found a clear space in which his ideas could fight their way free.

So he carried on, doing the best he could, which was a hell of a lot better than anybody could have expected or would have dared to imagine.

◆

Springsteen debuted a "new" song at the Washington show—"Man at the Top," another *Born in the U.S.A.* leftover. Although Bruce had sung it once or twice on the 1984 U.S. tour, at RFK Stadium it was a lot more site-specific. It had a light Ricky Nelson pulse, and Bruce sang it a little bit as Nelson might have, as a kind of quiet rockabilly. The lyrics inverted Randy Newman's mocking "Lonely at the Top":

> *Man at the top says it's lonely up there*
>
> *If it is, man, I don't care*
>
> *From the big white house to the parking lot*
>
> *Everybody wants to be the man at the top*

If Bruce was feeling the strain of being America's favorite son, that was as close as he came to showing it. Otherwise he treated the stadium shows as he would have treated performances in clubs or theaters or arenas, as occasions for hard work and dancing, spiritual probing and near-orgasmic release.

The national reviewers who attended the D.C. concert arrived skeptical that even Bruce Springsteen could pull off a meaningful show in such vast spaces. For the most part, they left convinced that he had managed to do exactly that.

"The size of the crowd seemed to intensify the music's impact rather than diminish it," wrote Don McLeese of the *Chicago Sun-Times*. "A Springsteen concert generally creates a sense of community; here the community was larger than ever.

"Even so, part of Springsteen's instinctive brilliance as a performer has been his ability to make his darker, more brooding and painful material as powerful in concert as his full-throttle rockers. At RFK, he was far less successful at running the gamut of emotion within his performance than previously. Later in the evening, some of Springsteen's extended introductions w…re impossible to hear from certain sections of the stadium. The crowd was filled with younger fans who know Springsteen primarily from his recent string of hits; many of them became restless and impatient during the quieter, less familiar material."

As he became more experienced in outdoor touring, Springsteen picked up some tricks. From time to time, particularly during the skits accompanying songs like "Pink Cadillac" and "Growin' Up," he played to the cameras, a useful change, since the majority of the audience could see him clearly only on the video screens. And he was careful to rein in the energy as he prepared to speak. Mainly, though, Springsteen seemed looser, more exploratory. He never seemed regretful about what had been left behind in smaller venues, only eager to find out what could be learned in the new ones. And it was his very directness and enthusiasm that transformed the stadiums from spaces of mass isolation to the temporary but thrilling condition of community. When Springsteen reared back during each night's encores and asked, "Do You Love Me?" the assent that came roaring back was enough to make you feel goofy and dizzy. The exhilarated eruption seemed to be the crowd's way of saying, "Yes, that's just what's on our minds." Whatever risks success of such scale posed, Bruce seemed unfazed by them, just eager to keep on pushin'.

He was able to continue performing such a straight-ahead show in part because his set lacked the lasers and other gimmicks on which other outdoor acts relied. This hardly made the stadium tour a small production—the stage, sound, and light gear traveled in a total of fifteen thirty-foot tractor trailer trucks, and there were a few more for the video equipment. It took a hundred stagehands to rig the 18,000 pounds of lights, mount the sixty-foot stage; and assemble the 400 speakers over three layers of scaffolding. Load-in lasted close to two days, and it took another day to pack all the stuff up and put it back on the highway again.

The only person who remained undeterred by the stifling 100-degree-plus temperatures at Bruce's Philadelphia show was Chris Sprowal, head of the Committee for Dignity and Fairness to the Homeless, who was there to meet with Bruce and receive a donation. "I spent eighteen months living on the street," Sprowal remarked, "and after that it took me another six months to get warm. It'll *never* get too hot for me again." Sprowal was (and is) unique among leaders of the homeless because he had been homeless himself. He started the Committee and later the National Union of the Homeless (NUH) with other homeless people as a way of fighting for basic rights; the central premise of both groups was to provide homeless people a means of battling for themselves instead of relying on more affluent surrogates. The Committee had won homeless Philadelphians the right to vote and to welfare. (They had previously been disenfranchised and disqualified from governmental aid because they lacked addresses.)

With the $10,000 Springsteen gave it, the Coalition was able to expand its activities from Philadelphia to Camden, across the river in New Jersey, renovating a house there, and to train organizers for the NUH in five additional cities.

Sprowal, a black man in his mid-forties, came to the show (with Bob Brown of the United Electrical Workers, another NRFAC partisan, who'd made the contact) expecting nothing more than a useful handout. By intermission he was raving, especially about "Seeds," which the NUH adopted as its unofficial theme song, and about what Springsteen had said before "My Hometown": "The Committee was started by homeless people who try to let other homeless people be productive members of society. Right now they need all the help they can get. The things I'm singing about in my songs are things happening in your everyday life. In a country as rich as ours, it's a shame that fifteen percent of the population lives below the poverty level. There's absolutely no reason for it, but it affects all of us."

Sprowal was also impressed by his conversation with Springsteen. "He talked to us about how he hopes his music will bring to the attention of Americans the poverty and misery in this country," Sprowal said. In the end, the homeless leader felt, "the money is not that important. But Springsteen, by singling our group out, has raised the issue of homelessness before the whole country."

Springsteen's reputation as an ally of the poor was growing not only in the media but among the destitute themselves. "When we played the Cotton Bowl, I got a call in the hotel from a woman with a Spanish accent," remembered Barbara Carr. "She started to tell me all these terrible problems, and I was thinking, 'Oh no, she'll want Bruce to give her money; that's what this is leading up to.' But then she just asked me to thank him—for bringing the food bank to her attention. She had already phoned them up and received help." As well as being a pathetic comment on the inability of the American poor to receive even the most minimal information about where to receive assistance, that story also suggests the real potential for increased activity among the disenfranchised themselves when given even a minimum of information.

As it was, a call from the Springsteen organization had become the community organizer's version of a visit from television's mythical Michael Anthony of *The Millionaire*. And the shrewder organizations continued to line up many new donors and volunteers via the resulting publicity. Unfortunately, taking donations at the shows had to be discontinued when in several cities members of the Hare Krishna sect were discovered to be soliciting donations fraudulently in the name of the legitimate food banks and homeless organizations. Bruce actually had to warn people from the stage that anybody taking money in the halls at intermission was a crook. Even so, and despite skeptics left and right, every food bank or homeless union organizer the tour worked with in 1984 testified that the attention Springsteen had focused on the shameful problems they were working to address had carried over into the next year, and the effect of his work during the stadium shows was equally long-lasting.

The point, of course, is not that Springsteen was doing something saintly but that he was once more forming a substantial set of ties with the people to and for whom he most wanted to speak. Since it was unlikely that many of them could afford concert tickets, this was the only way of reaching out he had. For Bruce it was a two-way street; he felt he left each city a little more aware of what was really going on, which had always been part of his purpose in touring. When Springsteen's show came to town the hungry and homeless made headlines, and that was a step in the right direction. In the best cases—in cities like Pittsburgh, Gary, Los Angeles, and Philadelphia—the battle waged by the unemployed and discarded on their own behalf ceased being invisible and received a blast of fresh energy. As the flyer handed out by the Steelworkers–Old Timers group at the Los Angeles Coliseum shows put it, "Bruce Has Set the Tone."

◆

In New Jersey people just went nuts. Cops were accused of ticket scalping in more than one community; New Jersey Bell suspended five employees for illicitly commandeering access to the Ticketron lines; the governor, the attorney general, the state's police superintendent, and the state consumer affairs director announced a crackdown on scalping, alleging that tickets with a face value of $18.50 were going as high as $300 for the front rows. Officials at the Meadowlands pledged to double security and set up patrols by undercover state police in order to quell scalping.

Governor Tom Kean, a conservative Republican, issued a flatulent proclamation of Springsteen's virtues in *Rolling Stone* (he was running for President, too). "During his latest concert tour, Bruce's support for regional food banks and other organizations to help the unemployed made a lot of people think about those problems for the first time," Kean wrote in unctuous agreement, but driving through Newark or Red Bank or Camden, you had to wonder how much thought the governor himself was giving to those problems.

In Freehold Mayor Mike Wilson and four other members of the town council boasted to the *New York Times* of attending high school with Bruce (nobody in Jersey knew he had a last name). Wilson, who'd been in a band, The Legends, which shared manager Tex Vinyard with Springsteen's Castiles, wanted to place a plaque on the Springsteen "homestead" or rename South Street Springsteen Boulevard. (The move was headed off by its subject's noticeable lack of enthusiasm and a realization that the signs were certain to be stolen as collector's items the moment they were put up, as the town councils of Liverpool and Memphis had already learned.)

Every reporter on the East Coast wanted a Springsteen story as the Giants Stadium dates approached, but neither Bruce nor the E Street Band were giving interviews. So camera crews and reporters flooded into Asbury Park and Freehold, digging for background and local color. Former sidemen, acquaintances from school, Asbury bartenders and club regulars spent most of August with notepads, cameras, and microphones shoved in their faces. The fact that none of them had much to say didn't matter. For the moment they were good copy because they were the only copy available.

Following the first Giants Stadium dates, the tour went up to Toronto for a few days, then came straight back to play Giants Stadium again on August 30 and 31—these were the extra shows that replaced the Boston dates. On the afternoon of the thirtieth the weather was growing bad, but so far the tour hadn't been rained upon once since Australia; the near-perfect conditions were an inside joke among the crew, a sign of the luck that blessed the whole tour. But that Friday night's forecast was for severe thundershowers, and that meant lightning, a hazard among all that equipment and scaffolding. At six o'clock, an hour and a half before showtime, George Travis made one last call to the weather bureau at nearby Teterboro Airport. Then he grabbed Jon Landau, and they went into Bruce's dressing room, where they decided to postpone the show until Sunday, September first.

Many of the nearly 70,000 ticket holders were already in the stadium parking lot; almost all the rest were on their way. Traffic snarled in the lots and on the highways as thousands of cars turned around and headed home. To top it off, it barely rained a drop, and aside from an occasional flash of heat lightning, there was no electricity in the air.

In less charmed circumstances this might have been an omen. As it happened, it was just somebody else's turn to be fortunate.

For several months Little Steven Van Zandt had been working on a song he'd written after returning the previous fall from a "fact-finding" trip to South Africa. Steven was appalled by everything he saw there, especially the so-called "homelands," a variation on the United States government's reservation system, which had all but destroyed unity and community among American Indians. Van Zandt understood the parallel quite well. He was particularly horrified at the way one such homeland, the so-called independent state of Bophuthatswana, had been transformed into an African Las Vegas, complete with pop music concerts that were used to legitimize both apartheid and its homelands system.

The song he wrote as a reaction, "Sun City," was an infuriated mixture of American black dance music, a few African inflections, and kick-ass rock and soul. Its lyrics denounced the homelands fraud and lambasted the apartheid regime, the American government's hypocritical policy of "constructive engagement," and the spectacle of international performers playing a resort surrounded by such total oppression and misery. This rock and roller was not for sale, Van Zandt declared. In a classic rock and roll stammer, he took a solemn oath: "I . . . I . . . I . . . ain't gonna play Sun City."

Little Steven made a demo of the song early that summer. When Arthur Baker heard it, he was so excited that he proposed they produce the record together at his Shakedown Sound studio. Journalist Danny Schechter, who heard a second demo featuring vocalist Will Downing, pushed them toward making "Sun City" into a more political "We Are the World" type of production, using a broader cross-section of pop musicians, including many who wouldn't have been deemed big enough for the U.S.A. for Africa supersessions.

So they began to assemble a series of sessions, spending their own time and money. (Steve was between record deals.) First they called upon New York musicians and old friends: rappers Afrika Bambaataa, Melle Mel, Duke Bootee, and Run-D.M.C.; Darlene Love, the veteran great of Phil Spector sessions; *salsa's* Rubén Blades and Ray Barretto; Peter Wolf, late of the J. Geils Band; reggae singers Big Youth and Jimmy Cliff; punk godfather Joey Ramone; demimonde giant Lou Reed. But as more artists found out about "Sun City," they clamored to be a part of the project. Soon Jackson Browne had a separate set of master tapes in Los Angeles, where he recorded himself, Daryl Hannah, and Bob Dylan. Meanwhile such impressive names as Miles Davis, Herbie Hancock, Bono of U2, and Peter Gabriel were among those who visited Shakedown Sound in New York to add their voices to the "Sun City" tracks. In July Van Zandt flew to London, where he recorded Pete Townshend, Ringo Starr, Bob Geldof, dub poet Linton Kwesi Johnson, and several others.

At this point Bruce Springsteen was just about the only pop star with progressive sympathies who *wasn't* involved in "Sun City." Steve Van Zandt was one of his best friends, but that meant, among other things, that Steve was sensitive to exploiting Bruce. Additionally, Steve undoubtedly felt some need to achieve a hit on his own. Also, Bruce was busy on the road; he didn't really have time to make a record date. So Van Zandt didn't say a word to Springsteen about it; Bruce heard the demo and received further word of the sessions through mutual friends (including Clarence Clemons, who also appeared on it).

Once aware of the project, Bruce was naturally enthusiastic. "Sun City" represented not only a significant political gesture but a huge musical leap for his friend. Still, it didn't seem likely that he would have time to appear on the record—and then the Giants Stadium gig was postponed. After the traffic cleared on the evening of the thirtieth, Bruce drove into New York City and met Steve at Shakedown Sound to review the tracks.

"I knew of Steve's involvement during the past couple of years, and that he'd been down [to South Africa] and back a couple of times," Bruce told the "Sun City" video crew. "I don't think I could just sit back and watch what was going on without feeling that I had to say something about it. The funny thing about it is that [racism] is so out in the open down there, but I was hoping that by helping bring attention to what's going on in South Africa it'd also make us look in our own backyards, at the terrible problems we have with racism right here in this country right now. So when Steve said, 'Come on,' I said, 'Sure.' "

Bruce quickly added in his part. The approach taken on this recording was completely opposite to that Quincy Jones had taken with "We Are the World." Because the sessions were catch-as-catch-can, Steve had each singer separately perform the entire song (five verses); then he selected key lines to mix together into a composite version. On the finished record, Bruce completes the second line, bouncing off Eddie Kendricks of the Temptations to sing, "We're stabbin' our brothers and sisters in the back." In the award-winning "Sun City" video, made later, Springsteen appears paired with Kendricks and fellow Temptation David Ruffin.

"Sun City" was not the international multi-platinum smash that the Band Aid and U.S.A. for Africa records were, but that's not surprising, for it was musically and politically much more adventuresome. The record was a substantial hit in England and Holland, got significant attention in many other European nations, and, of course, had the honor of being immediately banned in South Africa. In the United States it cracked the Top Forty and sold several hundred thousand copies, and the video opened MTV to integrated music almost for the first time, testimony to the way its message came back home, just as Bruce—and Steven, who had expressed similar sentiments—hoped it would.

On Sunday evening, in closing out the postponed Giants Stadium show, Bruce brought Little Steven onstage to sing "Two Hearts." "Two hearts are better than one," they sang, shouting with one voice into the mike. "Two hearts get the job done."

◆

And I said, 'Hey, gunner man, that's quicksand;

that's quicksand, that ain't mud

Have you thrown your senses to the war or did you

lose them in the flood'

—"Lost in the Flood" (1972)

In Los Angeles, on one of the last days off before the Coliseum show that would end the tour, Jon Landau and Bruce Springsteen went for a drive through the canyons above Hollywood. In the course of their conversation they discussed how to approach the Coliseum dates. "It seemed like, Los Angeles is the last show; this is a unique event and we need to personalize it in some fashion," said Bruce. Landau mentioned the idea of doing Edwin Starr's "War," and Bruce said he'd thought about the same thing.

"It was funny," Bruce said, "because it was a song that Jon suggested maybe a year before. And we just couldn't get it down—it seemed too hard to play or we didn't have the patience at the time. Or at the moment it didn't make enough sense. And then we just tried 'War' one afternoon and we just got it fine. So I taped the words to my arm and we did it."

"War" was an extremely bold choice, though. Starr's original made Number One in 1970, and in retrospect it served as a signal. The song began with an unforgettable gravel-voiced shout: "WAR! What is it good for?/Absolutely nothin'! Huh!" It made Number One legitimately—by never backing off from its opening premise and backing its ideas up with equally tough and funky music. If ultraconservative Motown was willing to go that far, then Vietnam had to be coming to a conclusion (though it took four more terrible years to do so).

It was quite a different thing to sing "War" in 1985, when America was not at war but was behaving so belligerently around the world that war seemed imminent in various places from the Middle East to Central America. It meant taking a stride beyond what Bruce had written in "Born in the U.S.A.," or even what he'd said at RFK Stadium.

"War" was the one song that could make every implication of U.S. policy unmistakably explicit.

Obviously, as a devotee of complexity, Bruce Springsteen couldn't just leave it at that. Constructing the previous shows on the stadium tour had been a fairly simple matter of juggling the well-established set pieces of the arena show; the alterations were so minimal they were almost invisible. Simply adding "War" without other adjustments would disrupt the show's balance. It had to be surrounded with just the right blend of prefatory explanations and opportunity for release.

On earlier tours Springsteen had rehearsed the band rigorously through hours of daily sound checks. For a variety of reasons, those rituals had been trimmed down until, by the end of the 1985 dates, they were sometimes skipping the sound check altogether. Bruce had begun doing such rigorous sound checks because he placed an extremely high value on consistency. The ritual persisted as long as it did because it had another value. "In the end, what I was really doing was just familiarizing myself with where we were going to be working that night. Going out there, seeing the place, talking with a few people—personalizing it."

That part of the ritual was a valuable and healthy sign of commitment, and adding "War" to the set caused it to be revived for the Los Angeles stand. When it was, everyone from band to crew responded heartily, as if at the end of this cycle of shows as well as at the beginning, all concerned welcomed the opportunity to reaffirm their devotion.

The Los Angeles shows opened just before dark; the stage was framed within the Coliseum's beautiful synthesis of Californian and Grecian architecture so that the day's last rays glinted off it as off a devotional object. The concert opened with a triad of rockers—"Born in the U.S.A.," "Badlands," and then either "Darlington County" or "Out in the Street"—slammed out hard and fast, one after the other, without pause for breath or comment. The tone darkened with "Johnny 99," just as it had in all the other shows on the tour. But then out rumbled the bluesy grunge of "Seeds," a clatter of guitar and synthesizer introduced with almost exactly the same words Bruce had used in London, only with a few more American specifics.

As "Seeds" ended, the Dylanesque chords of "Darkness on the Edge of Town" arose, a perfect segue from rampant rage to suppressed fury. After that the stage went black, then a single spot illuminated Nils

Lofgren as he strummed a folkish melody; Roy Bittan swirled reedy synthesizer over it. After a few bars Bruce strode forward, wearing a black leather jacket over a couple of sweaty shirts. As he stood up to the mike, he gazed into the darkness, as if contemplating the wistful music.

"How ya doin' out there tonight?" he asked with a shy smile, his voice surprisingly loud against the softness of the playing. Anyone who'd ever attended a concert had heard the question asked, but even. if you'd been to a thousand, this might be the first time the answer seemed to matter.

The answer swept back over him in a wave.

"That's good," Bruce said. "That's good." As he began to speak again, the music rose a bit, creating a backdrop for the story he would tell.

"When I was growin' up, me and my dad we used to go at it all the time. It seemed like it was over anything. But, uh, I used to have really long hair, like way down to my shoulders." He gestured broadly, holding his hands six inches away from his head and well below his shoulders. "When I was seventeen or eighteen, oh, man, he used to hate it. He used to hate it so much that he used to wait for me at night in the house.

"It got to where we were fightin' so much that I'd stay outta the house a lot. In the summertime it wasn't so bad, but when the winter came . . ." He paused to button his jacket and cross his arms, left over right, a posture he held. He shivered a little, or maybe it was just a tremble—it's colder in L.A. after the sun's gone down, but not that much.

"I remember bein' downtown and it would get so cold. And when the wind would blow I used to have this phone booth that I used to stand in. I used to stand there and call my girl and get her to call me back," he said with a short, nervous laugh, "and then talk to her for hours at a time, all night." He hesitated a beat, to let the squeals die down.

"Finally, when I'd get my nerve up to go home, I'd stand in the driveway and he'd be waitin' there in the kitchen. I'd tuck my hair down so he couldn't tell how long it was, and I'd get up on the porch and I'd get into the kitchen and he'd always want me to sit down and talk to him. And he'd sit there with all the lights out and I could never see him. And he'd always ask me the same question—what I thought

I was *doin'* with myself. And the worst part about it was that I could never explain it to him.

"I can remember one time I had an accident—motorcycle accident. I was laid up in bed and he had a barber come in and cut my hair when I couldn't walk. I can remember tellin' him that I hated him. I told him that I hated him and that I would never, ever forget."

Another beat; he shifted his arm. The left still held the right, which was now aimed straight ahead, rigid yet shaking.

"He used to tell me, 'Man, I can't wait 'til the Army gets you. Man, when the Army gets you, they're gonna make a man outta ya. They're gonna cut all that hair off, and they'll finally make a man outta ya.'

"I remember the day I got my draft notice in the mail, I hid it from my folks. Then, three days before I was supposed to go up for my physical, me and my buddies went out and we stayed up all night.

"I remember when we got in the bus that mornin', we were so scared. 'Cause it was in sixty . . . sixty-eight, and the Vietnam War was goin' on. There was a lot of guys leavin' town that didn't never come back, and there were guys that came back that just weren't the same no more. And we were so scared goin' up on that bus. And we went up and we took the physical and I failed." He laughed, a couple of nervous barks, then quickly admonished, "It's nothin' to applaud about.

"But I can remember comin' home—comin' home, walkin' in the kitchen . . . and my mom and pop sittin' there. And they asked me, "Where you been for three days.' And I said, "I had to take my physical.' And my dad said, 'What happened?' And I said, 'I failed.' And he said, 'That's good.' " The cheers rose almost to a scream, but Bruce said nothing, just uncradled the microphone and blasted into it with a harmonica wail so sharp it felt like a knife.

"The River" poured out of him, and old fans caught their breath as he sang. In a single tale Bruce had combined and resolved themes he'd been exercising for years. That short story, built on the framework of the raps Bruce had used to introduce "It's My Life" and "Independence Day," not only brought them up to date but uncovered their secret heart. And this song rocked harder than ever; it felt unhinged, cut free.

As it finished Bruce stepped out of the spotlight and the stage went black again. A diffused red spot caught Nils Lofgren, who picked up a new riff, threatening and bluesy. After a moment Bruce stepped back to the mike, his jacket off, his shirtsleeves rolled above his massive biceps. He closed in tight, head turned slightly to the right. He moved little more than his lips as he spoke. His right hand held the mike hard, like a tool or a weapon. His voice was steely, even though he was slightly breathless from the exertions of "The River."

"I want to do this next song for all the young people out there tonight," he said sternly. "When you grew up in the Sixties, you grew up with war that your country was involved in every night on television. And, uh, I remember . . . I remember a friend of mine, the drummer in my first band, comin' over to my house with his Marine uniform on, sayin' that he was goin' to Vietnam and that he didn't know where it was. And kinda laughin' about it.

"I'd like to do this song for you, 'cause if you're seventeen or you're eighteen out there, the next time, the next time they're gonna be lookin' at you. And you're gonna need a lot more information before you're gonna be able to make a decision about what's right for you to do. Because in 1985, blind faith in *anything*—your leaders—will get you killed."

He picked up the mike, took a couple of steps to his left, then turned. "Because what I'm talkin' about here is"—suddenly he was screaming as the lights exploded to full brightness—"WAR!!!"

The song erupted into action; the lights flashed bright as Bruce sang, referring from time to time to the handwritten lyrics that he'd taped to his left wrist. He mostly matched Edwin Starr lick for lick, "Good God, y'all" for "Good God, y'all." But Max Weinberg was delivering a sledgehammer beat, not funk, and as Bruce cracked down hard on each line, the words were as sundered from their original musical context as they were from Motown's political meaning. When Bruce sang, "They say we must fight to keep our freedom/But Lord there's got to be a better way," he found irony—and discarded it.

The song came to a halt on another blast of "WAR!" this time swamped in reverb and echo. The band shifted into "Working on the Highway" so suddenly that it was as if Bruce were deliberately deflecting the audience response (which was extremely intense), turning it aside as he'd finally reached the point in that long dialogue where he wanted to say, "I don't know what you think; it doesn't really matter right now. But this is what I think."

Bruce Springsteen sang those songs that way for four nights running, and in the process he recast his show. Packaging the new version of

"The River" so tightly with "Seeds" and "War" and "Born in the U.S.A." did what Bruce's shows had always aimed for and promised: It knit together the threads of many years, so that each song knew its own heart and read new meanings into the hearts of the others, opening itself to all who were willing to listen. It was tempting to construe this suite of songs as "political," but that was too narrow an interpretation. The point wasn't that Springsteen had finally found a way to speak his mind in a fashion that couldn't be co-opted. It was that he was finally sure enough to speak with all the talent and power he commanded. What made "War" so ferocious was not just its appropriateness to the occasion—after all, anyone could have sung the song—but the utterly personal way in which Bruce put it across, so that its rage took on a dimension that went far beyond melodrama.

Toward the end of each of those four nights, Bruce sang "Twist and Shout," the lights flooding the entire stadium as he threw back his head and looked up, circling the building with his finger to acknowledge each section. And he crooned, "Do you love me?" It was another lost Motown classic, a silly song by the Contours. But those nights it never seemed silly. And the answer was right at hand.

The last two nights Bruce invited Jon Landau onstage to play guitar on "Travelin' Band," a resurrected Creedence Clearwater song. On the last night, just before he collapsed to one knee, he turned back to his manager and friend and shouted gleefully, "Hey, Jonny, it's too late to stop now!"

19 FORTUNATE SON

fter "Rosalita" the band goes backstage and towels down, but everybody knows they're not going anywhere. This is a rock and roll encore—a necessary part of the show, an especially important moment in the Springsteen liturgy because it's traditionally the part where all debts have been paid and you're free to bop 'til you drop.

Tonight Bruce retakes the stage by himself, harp rack 'round his neck, an acoustic guitar in his hand. He does this sometimes as a kind of final "balance due" notice—there are some dues no one ever stops paying.

The nervousness Bruce occasionally shows when he's about to talk, rather than play or sing, is completely absent. He speaks confidently but with an air of fatigue, staring into the middle distance, thinking through the topics he needs to cover.

"I guess I'd like to take a minute and thank people who don't get thanked very much. I guess first and foremost is my crew and all the people who work behind the scenes at my show." The crowd cheers; a smile blossoms on his face. "Yeah!" he says, pumping his fist in the air. "Right! Let 'em hear it!" Then, more soberly, "We've traveled all year; they've put this show up in the cold, they've put it up in the rain, they've put it up when it's ninety-nine degrees and ninety percent humidity. And they've just done the best job that's ever been done.

"Now I'd like to thank . . . uh, I'd like to thank all you guys for comin' down to the show tonight. And I guess I'd especially like to take the chance to thank all my fans for all the years of support that they've given me and the band. This has been the greatest year of my life"—he pauses to blink—"and I wanna thank yas for makin' me feel like the luckiest man in the world.

"And, uh, I'd like to do this song for yas," he says, and now the fatigue really shows. But it's not the weariness of having performed for so long; it's the kind of tired a man feels when he's butted his head against a wall. "This is, I guess, the greatest song that's ever been written about America. It's by Woody Guthrie and it gets right to the heart of the promise of what our country was supposed to be about. And, as we sit here tonight, that's a promise that is eroding for many of our fellow citizens every day, with thirty-three million livin' at or below the poverty line.

"I guess I'd just like to do this for ya tonight, askin' you to be vigilant, because with countries, just like with people, it's easy to let the best of yourself slip away."

Bruce begins "This Land Is Your Land," not the melodic rendition he first uncovered in 1981 or the cheerleading version used at gatherings of patriots and protesters. He sings the song as a stark and somber confession of beauties and indignities seen and unseen; the equation of individual lives with whole societies that he's made in the introduction is carried through into the music. Tonight Bruce Springsteen sings the song that ideologues of any stripe will never get—the part that's alive and still changing fifty years after the writing, the part that's so fragile any reasonable person never stops marveling that it survives, but so strong that it requickens each time someone comes along who's strong enough to pick it up. You might call it blues. Whatever it is, it's about the saddest damn thing you've ever heard.

As he sings it, someone sitting alone in the dark may be remembering what Bruce said earlier that evening as he introduced "My Hometown." That was so long ago; the show has pushed its way through so much that it's a little hard to believe it's all one thing. But it is, and in thinking back the connections are tangible.

"I remember when I was a kid, I walked to school in the morning, it used to seem like the loneliest walk in the world," Bruce says, standing alone in the spotlight, holding his guitar, without even the harp rack for armor. "And I remember the first thing we'd do when we'd get into class is, we'd . . . you know, they get you all standin' there and you'd say the Pledge of Allegiance. You know how it goes." He executes an extremely rapid mumble of the Pledge. "The one thing I always remembered from when I was young, that if somebody asked me what the flag meant . . . I guess even when I was a kid, I used to think, well, it meant fairness—that this was a place where the fair thing was supposed to happen. And we've been all over this year—we've been just about all throughout the States—and I've gotta say I've learned some things that have given me a lotta hope, and I've learned some things that have made me sad. I guess the fair America was not the one that I found there often enough for most people.

"I guess I'm bringin' it up tonight because I guess I think we all got—have—a chance and a responsibility to do something about it. And tonight in the audience there's some folks from the Community Food Resource Center of Los Angeles. That's a food bank, and they're connected to food banks in Long Beach, in Orange County and Riverside and San Diego. And there's some folks from the Steelworkers–Old Timers Food Bank in East Los Angeles, who we worked with the last time we were out here—"

He breaks off, then resumes speaking suddenly, as if something important has just occurred to him.

"And one thing I *have* found out over this year is that *every* place you go, no matter where it is, when you mention the name of that place people go *nuts*. Like, we'll give it a try here for a minute. Los Angeles [*monotone—eight-second cheer*]. That happens every place you go. And I finally figured it out that that happens because people are proud of where they come from. And if you're proud of where you come from, [think about] the folks from these food banks that are out there every day takin' some of these ideas that I'm singin' about up here tonight and tryin' to make 'em a reality in people's lives. They're tryin' to make Los Angeles and the whole surroundin' area a better and fairer place to live for all of its citizens. Without them, what I'm doin' up here tonight don't amount to much more than words."

If you're looking for answers, there are some here. He sang these songs, it seems, in order to fit one life into many, in order to feel that he's accomplished something—when he looks back over his shoulder the world has to be a different place because of it. Tonight is a night for such glances, some hasty, some lingering. And if the task for an attentive listener when this tour started way back in Minnesota was to hold back judgment, things have now come full circle: Now's the time to weigh events and find out if they balance.

"From the redwood forest to the Gulf Stream waters," Bruce Springsteen sings. "Yeah, this land was made for you and me." He sounds so lonesome he could cry, and the song trails off.

Then in the next moment all is transformed with a simple shout of "ONE...TWO..." The band kicks in, and Springsteen, no longer alone, can shout out the story's other side. It begins in a rush:

> In the day we sweat it out on the streets of a runaway
>
> American dream
>
> At night, we ride through mansions of glory in suicide
>
> machines

Where it ends, nobody yet knows. But the stadium lights have turned night into day, and all around, 85,000 fists punch the air and 85,000 voices chant the words, the multitude ready to come along.

20 NO SURRENDER

I can recall a time when I wasn't afraid to reach out
to a friend
Now I think I've got a lot more than my toys to
lend . . .
A little bit of courage is all we lack
So catch me if you can, I'm goin' back

—The Byrds, "Goin' Back"

The *Born in the U.S.A.* tour ended just after midnight on October third. Still toweling themselves dry, Bruce and the E Street Band immediately dove into vans and were driven to their West Hollywood hotel, the Sunset Marquis. Rather than staying at his house, Bruce had rented a large suite there for the evening, the better to accommodate the end-of-tour party.

The ritual festivities at the end of a tour are usually mildly uproarious, featuring hard dancing to tapes of British Invasion and soul hits and large quantities of a Kahuna punch concocted by Clarence Clemons. At the end of *The River* tour, in Cincinnati, Springsteen danced fifty people into the ground and everybody stumbled aboard the next morning's plane looking happily ravaged.

But the *Born in the U.S.A.* tour party was subdued. Music played but there was little dancing; Clarence made up his mixture, but most contented themselves with sipping beer or wine. Band, crew, and a scattering of friends talked quietly in small knots. The evening still bore a glow, but it stemmed from simple satisfaction at a massive job well done.

The air was also melancholy. Off the road many of these people didn't see each other, and after so many months together their partings were reluctant and regretful. For that matter, it wasn't only a question of the tour coming to an end. What about everything else that *Born in the U.S.A.* had stirred up? Did that just stop, too? No one knew and Bruce wasn't offering any clues.

But Springsteen knew what they'd just accomplished. It was no mystery at all.

"This particular tour, everything seemed pretty clear to me. And not only did it seem clear to me, but it seemed clear to other people. I remember there was a year-end *People* magazine where they had one page on the tour, and it was about things that we did—it was about the work we were doing. And I said, Gee, if that weird light of celebrity or whatever you want to call it [can be focused in that way], I felt that we'd done a good thing. On that particular page, that was what it was about. It was about what we were doing, what we'd done over that year. I said, Well, if it was gonna get lost, what we were trying to do would get lost here. But I felt that we'd kept the focus on the important stuff, and the superfluous stuff that attracts a lot of attention was minimized for the most part—and that I was pretty comfortable in the shoes I was in."

Bruce stayed in his Los Angeles house for a while after the tour's close, getting reacclimated to life without a next show in front of him, sorting out a domestic routine with Julie. The couple weren't doing anything in particular, so the following Tuesday, when Bruce was invited to see a production of *Lady Beth*, the play written by the theater project at the Steelworkers–Old Timers Food Bank, they went.

In the year since Bruce had visited with the former steelworkers, they'd developed a two-act presentation. The first act of *Lady Beth* presented the workers reciting reminiscences of lives surrounded and engulfed by the steel mill and relating what happened to those lives when the mill ceased to exist. (The Vernon Bethlehem steel mill lay idle for four years and then was dismantled and its machinery sent to Japan, where it was melted down and sold as scrap.)

The second act was an audience participation discussion, in which the steelworkers and their audiences confronted the myths and attitudes on both sides of the stage. At its best, that act could be as revealing and legitimately theatrical as the first. Springsteen, whose own approach to involving an audience was equally direct, loved what happened.

That night's audience was especially good. In addition to Bruce and

Julianne, George Cole and the staff of both the union local and the food bank, those in attendance included the legendary Alabama civil rights activist Albert Turner. Turner, the father of the Selma march, the man on whose living-room floor the 1965 Voting Rights Act was first drafted, and Martin Luther King's chief Alabama organizer, was in Los Angeles on a fund-raising mission. He and twenty other west Alabama civil rights veterans had been indicted by federal authorities for so-called "vote fraud," which really meant so efficiently organizing their heavily black counties that it threatened white power all the way to Washington.

Turner and his wife, the first to be indicted and tried, had already been found innocent, but their house was fire-bombed the night they were acquitted. In the end, the government was able to secure only one minor conviction out of more than two hundred charges brought, and the federal prosecutor in these cases, Jefferson Sessions, became the first nominee for a federal judgeship to be rejected by the Senate in decades. But for Bruce, who had just sung on "Sun City" for the purpose of bringing the fight against racism back home, the connection couldn't have been clearer.

Turner's comments following *Lady Beth* reflected the decade he'd spent at Martin Luther King's side, and the rest of the discussion was almost as stirring. Afterward, everyone repaired to a nearby restaurant, the Guadalajara Inn, where they ate and drank and hung around for several hours more. "We had a great time," said Cole, when the *Los Angeles Herald Examiner* asked him about it. "We had a little trouble getting the dancing going, even after we moved the tables to one side. But then we got 'Glory Days' on the jukebox and turned it up real loud and everyone was up on their feet."

There were those who found it perplexing that a wealthy celebrity who had married an actress-model and drove a Corvette felt so easy with such a crowd, but what made Bruce Springsteen's relationship with organizations like the Steelworkers–Old Timers Food Bank a matter of equality rather than charity was that they also had something *he* needed. In addition to pink Cadillacs and the adulation of millions, what rock and roll had promised Bruce Springsteen was that he would find a community where his loner heart fit in.

◆

"I'm Goin' Down" was completing its chart run, and with Christmas again on the horizon, it was time for one last single (the album's seventh). The choice was "My Hometown," a song with heavy resonance during the holidays. Putting out another single didn't require much from Bruce besides assent. Put by now it was expected that each of his singles would have a flip-side not taken from the album—there was hardly anything left on the album that hadn't been released as a single or given saturation AOR radio play—and there was also the question of video.

The first idea was to make the B side a live take of "War" from the Coliseum shows. But when Jon Landau went back and listened to the Coliseum shows, something bigger leaped out. Rather than sending Bruce "War" in isolation, he sent a tape that included four songs in sequence: "Born in the U.S.A.," "Seeds," "The River," and "War." Strung together like that, with their spoken introductions intact, the songs owned a startling unity.

Landau was thinking about a live album. Bruce was a lot less certain. In fact, when they'd discussed the possibility just after the tour ended, he'd simply said no.

"I was against it," he said. "I never listened to any live tapes, really, and it just seemed like you were rehashing things. Maybe I was superstitious about it. But he sent me down that tape, and that was when I started to think that maybe there was something to it."

In any event, "War" was clearly too powerful to toss off as a B side. Instead, they used "Santa Claus Is Coming to Town," a live recording made in 1975 at C. W. Post College on Long Island.

As for the A side, Arthur Rosato, the video director of the live shows, was already sequestered in an editing room at the Cherry Hill studios of NFL Films, cataloguing all the footage from the tour for future reference. He quickly put together a video of "My Hometown" based on Bruce's live performance; it was released to MTV on November 19, 1985, two days before the single came out. It was Bruce's most modest video; the song spoke in the quiet, simple voice it had found onstage.

"My Hometown" took off commercially, becoming *Born in the U.S.A.*'s seventh Top Ten hit, matching the record set by *Thriller*. *Born in the U.S.A.* sold like a blockbuster for a second Christmas season. Its sales topped 18 million worldwide and 10 million in America, making it, according to *Billboard*, the fourth best-selling LP of the past decade (after *Thriller*, Fleetwood Mac's *Rumours*, and the *Saturday Night Fever* sound track). By Christmas *Born in the U.S.A.* had also surpassed *Thriller*'s seventy-eight weeks in the Top Ten of the LP charts. It didn't drop out until the chart of February 1, in its eighty-fifth week—the longest Top Ten chart run of any album since *The Sound of Music*. With "Sun City" also riding the charts, Bruce Springsteen still seemed almost as ubiquitous as he had while touring.

◆

Bruce had hardly been back home for a week when events in his real hometown caught up with him. On October 17, 1985, Stanley Fischer, president of Oil, Chemical and Atomic Workers (OCAW) Local 8-760, wrote Bruce a letter outlining the plight of his 450 members, who operated a Minnesota Mining and Manufacturing (3M) professional audio and video tape plant in Freehold—3M had just notified OCAW that it would be shutting down the Freehold plant in 1986 because the facility wasn't worth modernizing.

"You wrote a song about your hometown and about a factory that was shut down and what it meant to the town. When we hear that song, it strikes a very painful chord," Fischer wrote. "It's painful because it's happening all over again . . ."

It was literally true; a number of the 3M workers had been employed at the A and M Karagheushian rug mill, "the textile plant across the railroad track" of the song, before that plant moved south in the Sixties.

But that wasn't the only similarity. The rug mill moved to an area with cheaper wages and lower taxes. 3M, a company with almost $8 billion in annual sales and profits of more than $700 million, claimed it was closing the Freehold plant "as part of a program to reduce costs and improve product efficiency." The company maintained it would cost $20 million to make the Freehold plant "competitive" with Japanese plants. It was cheaper, the company insisted, to use its more modern plants in Hutchinson, Minnesota, and Wahpeton, North Dakota, and cheaper was all that mattered. The company had an obligation to make money for its shareholders and none at all to the workers whose livelihoods it controlled six and seven days a week through compulsory overtime.

"This shutdown will really hurt us," Fischer wrote. "Fifteen to twenty percent of us are single parents. This is by far the best job we will ever find around here. Twenty-five percent of us are minorities. Our average wages are $20,000 per year. . . . We must be honest with you. Many of us feel like there is nothing we can really do. This is a big company and there are no laws to stop this kind of thing.

"But . . . we believe the company might respond to a positive public campaign that would encourage them to keep the plant open ('3M and Freehold . . . We Need Each Other'). . . . Because of your special connection to Freehold and the entertainment industry, we believe that an open letter to the 3M Company signed by the Freehold workers and by you would have a tremendous impact on this situation. . . . We are not looking for your financial support. What we need is to make a positive public statement that will cause the International Board of Directors of 3M to take notice of our hometown. . . ."

Since Springsteen's interest in working with the needy and disenfranchised had become apparent, the Jon Landau Management office was daily besieged with propositions from charities, union groups, and individuals who were broke or sick or both. It's a familiar accompaniment to celebrity, in Bruce's case intensified by the specific content of his songs and by the fact that he actually took corresponding initiatives through the tour and on records like "We Are the World" and "Sun City." All Landau's office could do was screen the requests; there were far too many for all to be answered.

When Bruce saw Fischer's letter, sent to Landau's office through Lee Ballinger, associate editor of the *Rock & Roll Confidential* newsletter, his interest was immediate. Not only was the tie-in with "My Hometown" obvious, but Bruce's father and grandfather had been among the laborers in that rug mill. His response was personal as well as political. A meeting with Fischer was soon arranged; Bruce and Julie drove to Freehold for a lasagna dinner with Stanley and his family, and the drive to keep the plant open began.

Country singer Willie Nelson had already agreed to sign a public appeal if Bruce would. So Fischer and Les Leopold of the Labor Institute in New York drafted an open letter to 3M. After some tinkering it became a two-part ad—the first part a letter to the company from the Local 8-760 workers, the second a shorter message to 3M from Springsteen and Nelson.

The ad appeared on December 4, 1985, in the *New York Times*, *Variety*, the *St. Paul Pioneer Press*, and the *Asbury Park Press* (Freehold doesn't have its own daily newspaper). "3M: Don't Abandon Our Hometown!" read the headline.

The workers' letter followed a quote from the "textile mill" verse of "My Hometown," using much the same language in Fischer's appeal to Bruce: "For 25 years we have produced professional quality video and audio tapes for the broadcast and entertainment industries. Our work allows performers to share their images, words and sounds with the world.

"But now you are shutting us down. For many of us, this is not our first plant shutdown. Some of us actually came to 3M from the textile plant shutdown that Bruce Springsteen refers to in his song 'My Hometown.' We can't just let this happen again and again."

The ad told of the local's efforts "to meet with management to find a way to keep the plant open" and reported 3M's rebuff: "This wasn't a labor issue. . . . it would be more cost efficient for 3M to move the work elsewhere." "But what about the costs to human dignity?" the letter asked.

The workers' letter praised 3M's donation of the tape on which "We Are the World" was recorded, but pointed out, "Here is suffering that you and only you can alleviate. We are not asking for charity. All we want is the chance to work."

Appearing slightly below the OCAW plea, the second letter read: "On behalf of the working people, their families and the community of Freehold, New Jersey, we urge you to reconsider your decision to shut down the 3M video and audio tape facility.

"We know that these decisions are always difficult to make, but we believe that people of good will should be able to sit down and come up with a humane program that will keep those jobs and those workers in Freehold."

Springsteen and Nelson's signatures followed, along with an informal P.S.: "We ask that other entertainers voice their support and concern. . . ." More than a few did. A week later a similar ad appeared in *Variety*, signed by virtually the entire cast of *Hill Street Blues*. On January 28, 1986, a third ad appeared, bearing the signatures of Springsteen, Nelson, the Hill Streeters, and a large group of entertainers ranging from actors Ed Asner and Robert Foxworth to musicians like John Mellencamp, Joan Jett, and the Blasters. It was headlined "3M: VIOLATING THE HUMAN RIGHTS OF OUR HOMETOWN" and proposed a "national bill of rights" for communities faced with plant shutdowns, including the right to rebuild careers through higher education, the right to full medical protection and income security, and the right to child care. Stanley Fischer undertook a national informational tour to present the workers' case.

To all this 3M responded with a stone wall of meaningless corporate clichés. "It was a difficult decision, but our analysis makes it clear that no alternative to consolidation is possible, and production must be moved now for 3M to remain competitive in this advanced technology market," said plant manager Kenneth R. Dishno. This boiled down to saying that the company was entitled to do whatever it wanted, employees be damned, an especially ironic position given that only a few weeks after the Freehold plant closed, 3M's professional tape production capacity was so diminished that it had to put its labels on tapes made by Sony.

The company wouldn't budge, but the workers kept fighting. A benefit concert for the beleagured local was arranged for Sunday, January 19, at the Stone Pony in Asbury Park. Ten bands, mostly little-known local acts, were scheduled to play from two P.M. to two A.M.

Naturally, the event was jammed all day, as rumors circulated that Springsteen and the E Street Band would make their first post-tour appearance. Several E Streeters were visible early in the evening, but that didn't mean much since Garry Tallent had been involved with Jersey Artists for Mankind, the group putting on the show, and one of the acts on the bill was J. T. Bowen, formerly lead vocalist with the Red Bank Rockers. But just after eleven, Bruce himself turned up, and the club's phone lines were soon flooded as friends went to spread the word.

Bruce took the stage just after midnight, supported by Tallent, Clarence Clemons, Danny Federici, Max Weinberg, and Patti Scialfa. (Roy Bittan and Nils Lofgren were out of town.) Before beginning to play, Bruce calmed the crowd and spoke in a cold, angry voice.

"The marriage between a community and a company is a special thing that involves a special trust," he said. "What do you do after ten years or twenty years, you wake up in the morning and you see your livelihood sailing away from you, leaving you standing on the dock? What happens when the jobs go away and the people remain?

"What goes unmeasured is the price that unemployment inflicts on people's families, on their marriages, on the single mothers out there trying to raise their kids on their own."

Now he spoke with ice in his words. "The 3M company: It's their money, it's their plant. But it's the 3M workers' jobs. I'm here to say that I think that after twenty-five years of service from a community, there is a debt owed to the 3M workers and to my hometown."

Bruce said nothing more, just broke into the tautest "My Hometown" he'd ever played. Though his voice soon started to unravel, the band slugged through a set of anthems: "Promised Land," "Badlands," and "Darkness on the Edge of Town," the last dedicated to Fischer and the Local 8-760 membership. Springsteen was hoarse when he paused after that song. But instead of stopping he reversed the mood with a series of rockers—"Stand on It," "Ramrod," "Twist and Shout"—before calling it a night just before one A.M.

That was it. Over the next few months, 3M closed the Freehold plant in stages. By January 1987 only about a quarter of the workforce still held on to its jobs. (At least one of the dislocated workers got a job at a chemical plant further north in Sayreville, Stanley Fischer reported, but in less than six months, that plant, too, folded.) Stanley Fischer and the OCAW local fought for state legislation on plant closings and filed lawsuits against 3M, but to little avail. For the most part the dismissed 3M workers were consigned to the growing heap of discarded Americans. Corporate reputation might be affected by rock stars—3M was near the top of the *Fortune* magazine list of most admired corporations in 1985; in 1986 it didn't make the list—but not the process of dismantling the American worker's standard of living. That was inexorable.

◆

Late in the year Bruce briefly visited California. During that trip he was surprised by an invitation from his father. Doug proposed spending a week fishing in Mexico. They didn't catch much, but the weather was fine and the pair enjoyed their time together immensely.

When Bruce returned to the East Coast, he and Jon began seriously talking about a live album for the first time since *Born to Run*. For just that long, fans and businessmen had campaigned for such an album, the former because they wanted a souvenir to take home, the latter because Springsteen's live-performance reputation would make it a guaranteed gold mine. Both points were underscored by the proliferation of "bootleg" live albums; according to record collectors, by

1985 Springsteen was the most bootlegged artist in history. Bootlegs—the term refers to music recorded and manufactured without the artist's permission—were difficult to find, extremely expensive (averaging about $20 per disc), usually poorly recorded, and haphazardly packaged. Yet hundreds, perhaps thousands of Springsteen buffs cherished bootlegs and clandestinely recorded tapes of his shows.

Springsteen made his disapproval clear by allowing CBS and the Recording Industry Association of America (RIAA), an industry trade group, to pursue bootleggers aggressively in his name. (A couple of them even went to jail.) Even prosecution didn't end the practice. It only slowed from a flood to a trickle.

Bruce's personal animus seemed to be simply artistic, not mercantile. "I guess nobody likes the feeling that they wrote a song and in some way the song is bein' stolen from them, or presented in a fashion they don't feel they'd want to present it in—the quality isn't good, and they're so expensive," he said to *Rolling Stone*'s Kurt Loder. "I always tell myself that some day I'm gonna put an album out with all this stuff on it that didn't fit in. I think there's some good material there that should come out. Maybe at some point, I'll do that." So when Springsteen spoke of bootlegs, he was thinking of surreptitiously taped live shows as much as of tapes containing unused or unfinished songs that had leaked out over the years from recording studios.

His reasons for not releasing a concert album were significantly different. "I never wanted to do just a live record," he told Robert Hilburn. "It wasn't ever interesting enough for me. What I was interested in was finding out what kind of songs I could write and finding my way around the studio to get some of the feeling that the band gets on stage. . . . I get interested in what I can do next; I get curious and anxious about writing more songs." In a way, then, Bruce's reluctance to satisfy the demand for live material was akin to his avoidance of hit singles, embedded in his general suspicion of things that came too easily.

David Hepworth confronted Bruce with the same question during the *Old Grey Whistle Test* interview in 1984 and got a different kind of answer.

"A lot of what we do at this point is about *being there*, which is why we haven't done much television or too much of the video thing," Bruce said. "A lot of the problem is that it allows too much distance. What our band is about is about breaking down distance, and I think it's important that people come out, they come down, they go someplace where there's a bunch of other people.

"And then the other thing was, [on] a live record, a lotta times you're doing things that you've done already. I think it'd probably be a little boring to work on, maybe."

In this sense, then, Springsteen's avoidance of a live album stemmed from a feeling that concerts were a distinct medium, quite separate from the process of songwriting and album-making, that what was special and spontaneous onstage probably wouldn't translate into the careful and considered world of the recording studio. He was interested in going out and performing his songs night after night, but if he was going to spend all the time and energy it took to fix a song on tape, it seemed right to do it with new material.

However, he was starting to bend now, perhaps because some of his recorded songs—often the best ones—acquired a different and larger life onstage. "There are songs that I want to re-record, that I was unhappy with the original studio recordings of," he told Hepworth. "Mainly the *Darkness* album, which was a record that I thought had some of my best songs, but I always felt was a little dry recordingwise. I felt we kinda underplayed and oversang a little bit, you know. That stuff sounds quite a bit different in performance, and I'd be interested in getting different versions of some of those songs."

To those aware of previous Springsteen pronouncements on the subject, this was a fascinating change—not just another sign of his relaxation about the uses to which he could put his work but evidence that he was thinking seriously about something he'd previously dismissed. Still, it seemed likely that when it actually came time to make a new record, Bruce would want to cut new songs.

The tape Jon Landau sent Bruce changed that because it included both new songs ("Seeds," obviously; "War," too) and new ways of looking at old ones. "Born in the U.S.A.," taken slightly more slowly than in the studio, was much more emphatic in the verses, and that made the ironies of the chorus unmistakable. The stories Bruce told before "The River" and "War" were not only worthy of repeated listening (always the central problem with spoken material) but cast the music itself in a different light. As a piece of music, "War" had a brittle intensity that the band had never captured in a recording; as a public statement, it affirmed Bruce's beliefs more pungently than anything else he'd ever sung.

Bruce later acknowledged that he'd been wary of a live album in part because he just didn't know what had gone onto the live tapes they'd been making for the past decade, usually when near the so-phisticated remote recording facilities of New York and Los Angeles. "I didn't understand that the band had played really well over the years," he said. "I mean, I knew we'd been doing something right, but I didn't know exactly what. And I wasn't so sure I wanted to find out. It seemed things were going well, and I was kinda superstitious about it."

Landau *had* listened to those tapes, and he knew that the band was playing well (if not always impeccably) straight through. And once Bruce listened, he agreed: "I'd never really heard the band until I heard the tapes," he said, sounding a little like someone who'd just heard his first E Street Band concert. "When I heard the band on the tapes, it gave me a whole new insight as to what it sounded like and what we had been doing over a ten-year period. And mainly, they were just doing their job really well. Like Danny—on the record, he's incredible.

"I was never completely satisfied with any of the recorded versions of things that we did—certainly not before *The River*. I never felt the band learned to play in the studio before *The River*. On 'Badlands' or 'Darkness,' the live versions are the way that stuff was supposed to sound. And we couldn't have ever got that in the studio, even if we had been playing well—because the audience allows you to attack something with a lot more intensity, and if you did it the same in the studio, it would sound overdone or oversung.

"So the surprise when we listened to all the tapes was that we could just mix 'em and put 'em out. Even when the playing wasn't at what you'd call a technically high level, the enthusiasm was so crazy that it kinda lifted the whole thing. Like, listen to 'Rosalita.' 'Rosalita' is so funny, there's so many strange parts, but people were playing so hard and so intensely and so happily, that the whole thing just kinda takes off."

Making the decision for a live album proved quick and easy; deciding what shape that record would take was a bit more complicated.

"Once I heard the sequence tape, the question became, Are we going to make one record or two records? One record wouldn't be enough; two records felt limiting," Bruce said. But from the beginning, Landau's concept was that the live album was worth doing precisely because it didn't have to be a condensation of Bruce's show, it didn't have to be drawn entirely from the *Born in the U.S.A.* tour or from any single tour.

Columbia Records was eager for a live Springsteen album; they'd happily issue an expansive (and expensive) multidisc set. The advent of compact discs, which could accommodate more than seventy minutes of music per disc, made multi-hour recordings more practical and even more desirable. And the CD technology could be tested—even given a public boost—by the most recent live tapes (from 1984 and 1985), which were digitally recorded.

Most important, once Bruce and Jon came upon the idea of doing a record that wouldn't be a live album or a greatest hits album so much as it would be the *next Bruce Springsteen album*, the issue resolved itself: This album would be as long as necessary to tell the story, and since the story was an epic, that might be real long.

Still, Bruce Springsteen was cautious, and he moved slowly. At first, he and Landau spent some hours together just listening to tapes. A key moment came when Jon dredged up the tape of "Thunder Road" from Bruce's show at the Roxy (a Los Angeles club) during the *Born to Run* tour in 1975.

"Bruce and I were sitting one day that December [1985] and just playing cassettes and starting to get into the process of making that record," Landau said. "We put it on and one of us said, 'Well, if we ever did do a live album and it was a retrospective, *that's* what should open it.' And from that point on that's always been the song that opened the album. Looking back, that was probably the first thing we knew about this album. If it existed, it was gonna start with this version of this song. And I think that that was almost a handle for Bruce to get into the album, because that already established the idea that we could make a live album that would just be a creative endeavor. Because that was a creative decision."

For Bruce, "Thunder Road" was the key to understanding the record's historical reach. "That kinda opened the thing up to take in the time span, 'cause we knew we wanted to use that version. And if we're gonna use that and 'War,' what's the matter with all the stuff in between?"

That Roxy version of "Thunder Road" was remarkable at the time by virtue of Bruce's simple audacity in opening the show with such a radical revision of one of his best-known numbers. As the opening track of *Born to Run*, "Thunder Road" was presented in full-band grandeur, a sweeping statement of romantic questing on a broadly mythic American landscape, from the opening reference to Roy Orbison to the final declamatory "This is a town fulla losers/And I'm pullin' outta here to win." But when the *Born to Run* tour began, Bruce wasn't playing the song with the full band. Instead, he came out and did it as the first number of the night, standing stock-still at the microphone, guitar slung behind his back, accompanied only by Roy Bittan on piano and Danny Federici playing electric glockenspiel. The result was a tender and vulnerable recasting that transformed a promise into a plea. By situating this revision at the very beginning of his shows, at a time when his image was just being locked in, Bruce suggested a more open, less monolithic vision of both self and show. You felt that between the time he'd recorded the song and began performing it, Springsteen had outgrown its conceits without letting go of its hopes.

In preparing the live album's sequence, it wasn't memories that Bruce Springsteen was seeking—and finding. It was a decade of "Growin' Up," to give it the name of the song in which he first spoke clearly about the relationship between early days and adulthood.

Springsteen and Landau had access to about thirty professionally recorded shows, far fewer than the number that had been bootlegged. But those shows were more than sufficient to their purpose, and anyway, they couldn't have used any less technically sophisticated material and maintained the necessary sound quality. In the end, the digital tapes from the *Born in the U.S.A.* concerts set an extraordinary standard for everything else. This meant that some memorable moments simply weren't available. For instance, the concert rendition of "Racing in the Streets," preceded by and concluded with Bruce's narration, didn't make the record because it had never been professionally recorded.

And while they didn't stint themselves in terms of quantity of songs or time, it wasn't just the warhorse concert staples they sought, either. As Bruce put it, they were looking for the songs "before they were institutionalized," while their meanings were still fermenting.

Around Christmas 1985 Jon Landau sent Chuck Plotkin a rough assemblage of what became the live album's first side: the piano-and-glockenspiel "Thunder Road," a frothing "Adam Raised a Cain" that began with shouts and feedback akin to the MC5, and a pair of songs from Bruce's first two albums, "Spirit in the Night" and "4th of July Asbury Park (Sandy)," in sleek late Seventies/early Eighties arrangements. Landau put the tape together from low-fi cassettes on his home dubbing deck, and Plotkin described what arrived in Los Angeles as "a third-generation cassette copy of lousy rough mixes. There was as much noise as there was music."

Landau sent more tapes, and eventually Plotkin finally began listening with an open ear. The first thing he reviewed was the 1978 tape from the Roxy, recorded in the same club as "Thunder Road" but three years later. Plotkin had been among the 500 patrons at the original '78 show. "And when I got done with it, I just said, 'Oh yeah. Jon's right.' "

By the time Springsteen himself arrived in Los Angeles, a couple of days after the benefit for the Freehold 3M workers, Plotkin had done his homework. "I've done a lot of work with him, and I can jump in quickly and catch up very fast. And hey, listen, I love that 'Thunder Road.' "

They spent the next two months sitting together, assessing a stockpile of shows that, with a bit of research by engineer Toby Scott, grew to fifty or sixty, a total of about 200 hours of music. They had reached an apotheosis of the process Plotkin described as the essence of Bruce Springsteen's record-making: "You listen to the music. The music speaks to you. If you listen to it, it speaks to you. Whatever you *think* you're doing doesn't make any difference—it's what you *are* in fact doing. And if you listen hard enough, you can hear what you're doing; you can hear what you've done."

Except in this case it wasn't just the essence of the process—it *was* the process. The songs were written; the performances were done. The job was picking which songs and which takes and deciding the order in which they'd best be heard.

"We just tried to pick the best takes," Bruce recalled. "Charley's real good at knowing when you have the best take of something. He's the kind of guy who hears something and sees a diagram of everything that's going on. I don't hear that at all. For the most part, I listen to it the way a kid would listen to it. I never listen to the bottom or this or that; I just listen to it, from the very beginning.

"Charley sees through the whole thing really quickly, and he can tell you pretty quickly. He can just tell when something feels right, is moving right, and also has the heart and soul, which is ultimately what we based the choices on. Like 'Born in the U.S.A.,' which is the rawest one we had that held together, the wildest one we had."

Picking the takes took only two or three weeks. Given such a huge body of material, it could have been a fearsome task for a pair of perfectionists, but Plotkin makes it sound like a cruise.

"It was the easiest thing in the world. Once we got into it and you could see what was shaping up, Bruce and I spent about six hours a day, five days a week, essentially trying to come up with the right songs to use, come up with little segments of sequences, and to come up with the right takes of the songs.

"It was an enormous amount of work and it was easy as hell. First of all, we didn't do it in a studio. We just went to Bruce's house. We just listened to music. And if you're listening to music, even when it's his music, it's fun.

When they'd picked takes of between forty and fifty songs, Jon Landau flew to Los Angeles, and they set to work on sequencing, a much more delicate process. Gradually the live album revealed itself by a process of elimination, as a sculpture will sometimes reveal itself to an artist who knows just how to view a chunk of stone. Chip by chip, bit by bit, they fit it together.

"Sequencing was real important, because that was how we were setting up the story to be told," said Bruce. They chose the right takes of as many songs as seemed fitting. But sequencing this album was also a matter of narrowing it down, putting the right songs in the right order to reflect the personal and musical evolution of an entire decade. They didn't want to make a record of curios, so the rarity of a song counted for nothing and, when the chips were down, neither did any individual song's everyday power. For instance, "Badlands," Bruce's original post-"Born to Run" anthem, was the last song added to the sequence, and then not until the following summer.

Everyone endured some frustrations, including Bruce. "In the end, there's no 'Glory Days,' which is one of my favorite songs. Like, hey, I got my complaint, too," he said, referring to the moans of fans disgruntled by the lack of this or that selection. "I would've liked to put that on, and I tried to the bitter end, and I just couldn't fit it on."

They'd decided to shoot for a five-record set, which would be the equivalent of five vinyl discs or three cassettes or compact discs, similar to Bob Dylan's retrospective *Biograph*, issued in early 1986. "There could have been twelve sides as easily as ten," Plotkin said. "At fourteen sides, you're into a different thing. But there were some close calls. There was at least one side of close calls—I think probably two sides of close calls.

"For instance, there's a solo version of 'No Surrender.' Bruce said, 'I don't think we have room for it.' I said, 'Bruce, this solo version of "No Surrender" has literally saved me from depression and self-contempt on more days than I choose to tell you about—just from putting it on and listening to it.' It's a beautiful, highly particular, and stirring version of a song that basically just gets lost in the shuffle on [Born in the U.S.A.]. That's what the album had to have; it has to have things that you only got to find out about because of the show." ("No Surrender" made the record.)

They weren't trying to recreate a concert but, as Plotkin pointed out, what they came up with is about the same length as a concert, and the sides actually take a shape resembling segments of shows and they're paced accordingly. As the central criterion of selection, they wanted versions that were alive—"either the most alive or alive in a very particular way," as Plotkin said. "That is, nothing got on the record because the song needed to be on the record. We came close to not putting 'Born to Run' on the album. We were cruising into the end of the sequencing without an acceptable take of 'Born to Run.' "

The reason was simple: They had comparatively few workable takes of any given song; and there was no way to get more. "Born to Run" was a special problem. "That was a song that for a long time we didn't know how to play," Bruce admitted. "It was hard to sing and hard to play." In the end they used a rendition from the Giants Stadium shows of August 1985, more than eleven years after they'd begun performing it. "I was so happy when I put that version of it on, because I never thought we were gonna have a good live version of that song on tape."

"Badlands" was another such problem. In fact, that song might not have made the lineup at all if the version recorded November 4, 1980—the night after Ronald Reagan's first election as President—hadn't turned up late in the game.

In general, they followed the chronology in which the songs were composed, though not always the sequence in which they were performed. For instance, "Sandy," which crops up on Side One and has a "club" feel, is actually from the arena tour of 1980.

To increase the sense of continuity, they relied heavily on certain shows in each period: the 1978 Roxy date for the club and theater years, the 1980 New Year's concerts at Nassau Coliseum for the arena material, the second night of the Los Angeles Coliseum shows for the stadium tour. Other shows also cropped up, notably those from the inaugural Meadowlands stand in 1981 and the Jersey shows of 1984 and 1985. The continuity was further enhanced because the original playing was for keeps. "There were no vocal overdubs, no resinging anything, no replaying anything, unless something was actually broken or a channel wasn't on or something like that," Bruce said.

The record's key transitions came at the beginning of Side Four, as the show entered its arena phase, and at the top of Side Seven, when the fullscale stadium show kicked in. (Although the six-sided cassette and CD versions probably outsold the LP, everyone refers to the record in terms of its breakdown into ten album sides, a convenience born from tradition.)

But they weren't sticklers about chronology for its own sake. The transition to arenas comes with "Hungry Heart," even though none of the material from *Darkness on the Edge of Town* has yet been heard. But the choice is correct—"Hungry Heart" is thrilling before you hear a note of music, because the crowd sounds impossibly big and wild. The lead-in to the stadium shows is both more subtle (because the rock material is prefaced by a trilogy of *Nebraska* songs, themselves prefaced by "This Land Is Your Land" from 1980) and more stunning (because "Born in the U.S.A." emerges in such a mighty roar). At the end, arena and stadium performances are again mingled in order to fit the larger plan.

Bruce's raps presented another sort of problem. However fascinating they might have been in the heat of a moment, spoken passages can be deadening on record, because generally they survive repetition less well than music. On the other hand, Bruce's storytelling at its best was exquisite and integral. For example, in the sequence running from "Born in the U.S.A." to "War," what Bruce says determines the meaning of the music he plays. Again, the task was to sculpt the mass of material, carving the structures they wanted to show. So Bruce's spoken interlude in "Growin' Up" made the record because it foreshadowed future developments, while a moving introduction to "Independence Day" wound up on the cutting room floor because it wasn't as necessary to the overall tale. In other places they managed to edit with remarkable effectiveness pieces that were originally heavily visual: "Fire," with its extended mugging with Clarence Clemons, was snipped to the bone and yet retained its sense of humor.

In general, the idea was that this was a *record,* and that meant it had to reward the casual listener as well as the one who paid close attention—you had to be able to simply sit back and listen. When it was finally released, the live album was criticized for wandering away from the point after "War," but, as Bruce pointed out, that was part of the concept, too.

"It's just a break in the action. The whole point is, there's times when you have to take the record as a whole. And at that point, you're not gonna put 'Jungleland' in there. You need songs for what they're *not* saying right then. You gotta bring it back down to everyday life. Life goes on, man, life rolls on," he said. "The whole idea of the record was that you could put on any side at any time, that it would be a record that would contain a certain group of ideas but that those ideas were not necessary—it was just a rock record, it was just like a rock and roll record. Dance to it, listen to it, do whatever you wanna do with it. That was the point of the thing, you know.

"From the very beginning that was how we wanted to present the thing, you know. And this came up in the sequencing a lot. When we began to sequence the thing, if we began to construct it too intellectually or too conceptually—too superficially conceptually—it started to sound like, 'What are you trying to do?' The whole point was, it had to roll. And in the end, that's what made it what it was. So after 'War,' we're rolling a little bit, you know. It's gotta keep going, and it's gotta scale back down.

"We wanted the record to rock, and one of the most important things we were trying to do with the record, we were tellin' a story. There's a story bein' told here. And the record had to have its internal logic. It wasn't a greatest hits album; there were certain songs we knew we would like on. But nothing was sacred; anything could've been left out if it really and truly wasn't gonna work."

If anything made assembling the live set truly difficult, it was this dual purpose: trying to capture accurately the spirit of the moment on which the concerts were built, while building a retrospective that would document the periods of Bruce's career and his growth as man and artist—his transition from aspiring young singer-songwriter fumbling in the dark to adult confidence in the full spotlight of rock and roll stardom. The result was an unusual set of choices, a hybrid of expectations and necessities, neither a catalog of obscurities to replace the bootlegs nor a simple concert documentary.

"The thing is that you don't actually know what's coming, even if you know what's coming," said Plotkin, referring to both the actual Springsteen concert experience and what he helped shape from it. "You may have heard the songs; you may know what it's like to sit there and have that experience. But it's a slightly different experience each night. The stuff isn't canned. He tells stories; the stories are a little different each time. I've heard stories for the seventh time that I thought I knew, and you'll see this funny expression on his face and you realize that he's remembering some detail of that story that he didn't remember before *that moment*. And you realize that there is a live thing taking place. That it's not simply some guy getting up and repeating a series of songs—that it is a live celebration, in that moment, in real time. And that's what you have to try to get this album to catch."

They caught more than their share of moments. But what was just as startling was the sense of continuity that the live album demonstrated. In introducing "Growin' Up" in 1978, Springsteen relied upon almost the same experience that he later developed for the introduction to "The River" at the Los Angeles Coliseum. (Just as, for instance, his 1981 raps about his history book became the RFK Stadium introduction to "My Hometown," which evolved into the "War" intro.) The same kind of development was expressed in his songwriting, as the characters of "Thunder Road" and "Backstreets" became those of "Darkness on the Edge of Town," and those in turn became the forebears of the folks in "Born in the U.S.A.," "Bobby Jean," and "My Hometown."

Certainly his themes hadn't changed much, although, of course, his way of looking at them had altered drastically. But from "Backstreets" to "Racing in the Street" to "Bobby Jean," and from "Sandy" to "Two Hearts" to "Reason to Believe" and "I'm on Fire," the quest and the pain and the triumph all evolved from the same stem.

◆

Throughout 1986 Bruce Springsteen's legend continued to expand, even without any public activity. In 1985 year-end media polls ranging from trade magazines to television shows, he scooped up dozens of awards (although he won no Grammies). He was named *Rolling Stone* Artist of the Year for the second straight year, outpolling runner-up

Phil Collins three to one, and won best male singer, songwriter, and live performer as well.

In the end, though, Springsteen's omnipresence had little to do with that sort of thing. He'd become a reference point in American popular culture, even though he remained intensely private, as uninterested as ever in the conventional mechanisms of creating and sustaining celebrity. He made no talk show appearances or cable television specials, ignored every one of the dozens of movie offers that flooded Landau's office, went out to dinner in out-of-the-way places that never hit the gossip columns, never did interviews—didn't even have a press agent—and was rarely if ever troubled by paparazzi. Somehow, this homespun life-style only stirred the juices of exploitation in others to a froth.

Perhaps the first indication of this was the song parody written by Cheech and Chong: "Born in East L.A.," a good single and an even better video about the consequences of being born brown in America. In the Cheech and Chong version, the Immigration and Naturalization Service deports the singer, born in the Chicano ghetto of East Los Angeles, "back" to Mexico because he "doesn't look American" and confuses Ronald Reagan with John Wayne. He then has to fight his way home from Tijuana ("Now I know what it means to be born to run," he sings against a mariachi version of Roy Bittan's synth riff), a home he recognizes by the glow of the golden arches. The video, which wreaks havoc both with the imagery of the original song and with the blue-jeaned iconography of Springsteen the pop idol, is a fabulous act of guerrilla rock criticism.

Ironically, in satirizing and vulgarizing Springsteen's original song Cheech and Chong tapped into its darkest heart. The song hit the *Billboard* chart just as the *Born in the U.S.A.* tour was ending, and though it missed the Top Forty, it prefigured the coming commercial exploitation of Springsteen's imagery. As Bill Lane of the J. Walter Thompson advertising agency predicted during the summer of 1985, the coming trend in advertising would be "the Springsteen heartland of America approach."

"Just wait until you hear how many Bruce Springsteen sound-alike songs are on commercials this fall," Lane predicted. "I can feel in my bones that we're on our way to Boss Land." And he was right. The Safeway grocery chain, AM-PM convenience stores, Stroh's and Miller beer, and dozens of local ads all picked up on the superficial details of Springsteen, *Born in the U.S.A.*, or both.

Of course, not every "made in America" commercial was a Spring-steen exploitation. Ronald Reagan's virtual deification, the new cold war spirit, and the impending celebration of the Statue of Liberty restoration all helped turn the concept into a trend. Nevertheless, Springsteen was still at the center of the phenomenon. As Joan Neary, the New York jingle producer who made Chrysler's "The Pride Is Back" commercials, pointed out, "Now 'all-American' commercials are all over the place. But if you think about it, about the only 'American' commercials I recall *before* 'Born in the U.S.A.' were those union com-mercials—you know: all those people standing around singing 'Look for the union label'—which were really kind of corny."

Neary had good reason to know, for as she told Jimmy Magahern of the Phoenix (Arizona) *New Times*, she and partner Marc Blatte (com-poser of the Four Tops hit "When She Was My Girl") wrote "The Pride Is Back" as a deliberate knock-off of "Born in the U.S.A." Indeed, they were hired only after Chrysler had found Springsteen himself to be unapproachable.

Chrysler had been so eager to obtain Springsteen's endorsement that they made an initial offer estimated to be worth $12 million for his services—to sing and show his face in a sixty-second commercial. Ac-cording to one advertising industry source, Chrysler was so certain that this enormous offer would land Springsteen that they actually had written and begun production on a "Born in the U.S.A." ad campaign. The auto manufacturer and its ad reps were confident not so much because the money was so lucrative as because *Rolling Stone* had iden-tified Chrysler chairman Lee Iacocca as "the Bruce Springsteen of busi-ness," while Iacocca had projected himself—through his autobiographical best-seller, *Iacocca*—as a kind of folk hero of capital-ism. The mass media had cheerfully contributed to sustaining that bit of hype.

"Actually, the reason they thought he *might* do the commercial in the first place was because Chrysler was such a real American success story," Neary told Magahern. "A story of a company coming back from the grave—from practically going down the tubes, with all those people in danger of losing their jobs—that just came up incredibly under Lee Iacocca's leadership. And we all know that Springsteen's *all for* the working man—he's all for people working and having jobs. And there are a lot of people working now making Chrysler cars who were very nearly in the unemployment lines. So in that respect, we did kinda think that Springsteen might be interested in working specifically for Chrysler, as opposed to, say, a cola company or something. But as it turned out, he wasn't even into doing that."

Apparently Springsteen, along with the rest of America, was supposed to ignore the fact that Lee Iacocca's "leadership" consisted of several billion dollars of government loans; that Iacocca tried to welsh when it came time to pay off those loans; and that Chrysler's success was built on the backs of concessions by the members of the United Automobile Workers union, who continued to work for the lowest wages in the American automobile industry for more than a year after Lee Iacocca's salary had risen from a dollar a year to several million.

But chances are, Bruce Springsteen never had to confront such ugly facts. His distaste for doing commercials or endorsements remained total. If Landau ever brought up the offer with him, it could only have been as a joke: "Guess how much money we turned down today?" (Of course, other companies had weighed in with similarly hefty bids.)

For those who had to endure the "Pride Is Back" jingle through the next six months of prime time TV, the laughs were less enduring. Sung by Kenny Rogers and Sandy Farina (management clients of U.S.A. for Africa's Ken Kragen), the song was abrasively memorable. (Ironically, the Plymouth minivans being pushed via the ads weren't "born in America" in the jingoist sense the song intended anyway; they were assembled in Canada.)

"We knew from the start that Chrysler really wanted 'Born in the U.S.A.', " Neary said. "So obviously we didn't want to go way in the opposite direction.

But it doesn't specifically *sound* like 'Born in the U.S.A.,' either. There's a certain bell sound in there that's definitely Springsteen. And, of course, the hook line—'The pride is back, born in America'—is pretty similar. But the commercial didn't really copy his song. It's just got the *spirit* of his music."

Actually, as Neary knew, the jingle violated that spirit. "Even though what came across most in 'Born in the U.S.A.' was the chorus, we do realize that the lyrics of that song were more critical of America—all that Vietnam veteran stuff and all," she told Magahern. "The lyrics weren't as positive as 'The pride is back, born in America.' So from that angle, I don't know. But I think 'Pride' just makes a statement the way that 'Born in the U.S.A.' did. It's like, the pride in our country was gone for a long time, and now it's back, you know?"

The reaction of the advertising industry and the record industry was nearly as blithe. "The Pride Is Back" won an *Advertising Age* award for best "original" music; the jingle was publicly credited by Chrysler as one of the big reasons for its boost in '86 sales. And RCA released Kenny Rogers's secularized version of the song as a single. (It wasn't a hit.)

As part of a trend of increased usage of rock music in commercials, often songs that played on sentimental themes without mentioning products, "The Pride Is Back" was nothing special. But it was an indication of how deeply Springsteen's image had penetrated into contemporary American mythology that he could be exploited in the same way that the telephone company abused children's guilt about being out of touch with their parents.

It wasn't only corporations and ad agencies who wanted a piece of the Springsteen myth and were willing to settle for mimicry. Ads for *American Ninja*, a summer '85 exploitation flick, knocked off the *Born in the U.S.A.* album cover; a drive-in-level loser called *No Surrender* and several others featured huge flag backdrops or behinds encased in faded Levis.

One movie did benefit from Bruce's actual contribution, although it wasn't released until 1987. While in Los Angeles for the final shows of the tour, Bruce took director Paul Schrader out to dinner, apologized for swiping the title of his *Born in the U.S.A.* script, and offered to provide a title song if Schrader still wanted to go ahead with the story. Schrader did, and Bruce sent along "Just Around the Corner to the Light of Day," a song from the band sessions the summer after *Nebraska*. Schrader made the film, *Light of Day* (Bruce's title was marquee-proof), in late 1986, starring Michael J. Fox and Joan Jett.

So whether he wanted to or not, Bruce Springsteen stayed in the spotlight. But no one guessed what he was really doing until he'd been at work on the live album for many months. One measure of the mass success of *Born in the U.S.A.*, after the crisis surrounding *Nebraska*, was the extraordinary degree to which Bruce had managed to maintain his privacy. And in the case of the live album, for which so many had various expectations, it was a good thing he did. Even without additional weeks of anticipatory speculation, it proved hard enough to get people to hear the album for what it was, rather than for what it could or should or might have been.

◆

In the end, making the live album went more smoothly than any other Springsteen album project. By March Springsteen, Landau, and Plotkin had arrived at a sequence that was altered only slightly in the final release.

Beginning in June and continuing through October, Bob Clearmountain mixed close to fifty songs at Right Track studio in New York. Forty of these wound up on the album, with a few—"Merry Christmas, Baby," "Incident on 57th Street," "For You"—reserved as B sides for anticipated singles off the album.

The digital recordings of the stadium material gave Clearmountain a very tough standard to live up to when mixing the analog recordings from the earlier years, but he was up to the task. As Bruce remarked, Clearmountain managed to circumvent the artist's mercurial sense of production values by "taking that and putting it on automatic pilot."

Clearmountain's confident expertise with the technical details freed the production team to work on the big picture. It must have been clear soon after they began that the live album would be more than just the next step in the sequence of albums that began with *Born to Run*. It would be a culmination—not only a recapitulation but the closing of the door on one story as the next began to unfold.

What made the live set a distinctive part of the album series to date was its continuity and its narrative quality. "I guess what I was always interested in was doing a *body* of work—albums that would relate to and play off of each other," Bruce had told Kurt Loder in his *Rolling Stone* interview. "And I was always concerned with doin' *albums* instead of, like, collections of songs . . . I was very concerned about gettin' a group of characters and followin' them through their lives a little bit."

The live material took the measure of how well he'd done. Like its brethren, the album told a tale—not a simple or necessarily obvious one, but a story nevertheless. The album had no title until very late, and the name eventually selected was the most neutral possible: *Bruce Springsteen and the E Street Band Live/1975-1985*. But that was just a feint. At heart this album was the latest in a series through which a rock star and his cast of characters struggled from innocence to maturity.

The exact nature of the underlying story is best revealed via this question: How do you get from the innocent glory of "Thunder Road," as performed at the Roxy in 1975 before an audience of perhaps 500, to the harrowing rampage that runs from "Born in the U.S.A." to "War," sung in the same city ten years later before an audience of 100,000? Posing that question, with all its internal and external implications, unlocks *Bruce Springsteen and the E Street Band Live*, adding dimensions that few rock albums—let alone live albums or retrospectives—have ever possessed.

Because the live album was a five-record boxed set, it was frequently compared to Dylan's *Biograph*, whose five discs spanned the length of a twenty-five-year career. That album had sold relatively well—more than 200,000 copies—and it probably did help inspire Springsteen and Landau. But the album that *Live* really resembles most is Neil Young's *Decade*, a three-record set from 1976 programmed and annotated by Young himself with an eye toward making a case for his artistic development and achievements. (*Biograph* was put together without Dylan, and it includes many minor rarities at the expense of some of his core material and greatest performances.)

As Bruce looked over the music he'd made in the previous decade, he found himself, like Young, recapitulating the entire journey of his passage from childhood dreams of rock and roll glory to grappling with the real thing as an adult. It was an intensely personal story but, at its broadest, it was also the rock and roll archetype come to life and brought up to date. The album did *not* conform to rock and roll mythology; these descendants of Johnny B. Goode grew up, and the ending of their story was collected, not chaotic, open rather than closed, nurturing rather than wasteful.

By the time he released each of his preceding albums, Bruce had invariably come to understand the implications of what he'd done, but rarely much before then. This time the music's secrets revealed themselves to him more rapidly; that was one reason the assembly could proceed so swiftly. That only made sense: He was gathering up old friends, not creating new ones. But as these familiar faces shifted themselves into position, Bruce found them telling a new version of their stories.

"The record opens with 'Thunder Road,' and as I've said before, when the *Born to Run* album came out, the record was so tied in with who I was, I felt like, hey, I felt like I was born," Springsteen said in early 1987. "I felt like it was a birthday. I know that's why those words are in the title. *Born*—why is that word there? That's there because it's real. And"—he began to laugh at his own presumption—"that's probably why the word *run* is there—that's real, too.

"And that 'Thunder Road' is the birth song; it's the panorama, the scene and the characters, setting the situation. So that was why, from the very beginning, we knew that that was gonna start the live album.

"Then you get 'Adam Raised a Cain'; we wanted a gut punch right after that, just so you'd be ready for what was gonna happen. And then you get to 'Spirit in the Night,' which is kinda the cast of characters— friends. It's a real localized situation. Then you get 'Sandy.' That's the guy and he's on the boardwalk, and I guess that was me then, when I was still around Asbury. And there's the girl.

"That first side, that's the whole idea: Here it is. This is the beginning of the whole trip that's about to take place. All those people. Some of 'em are gonna go, some of 'em are gonna stay, some of 'em are gonna make that trip, some of 'em aren't gonna make it. And let's see what happens.

"And then you flip the thing over. 'Paradise by the "C" '—the Clarence instrumental—that's bar-band music, that's who we are. And that's real important. That sets the tone. That's what we were doing in those clubs—we were blowin' the roof off with that kinda stuff. People were dancin' and goin' crazy and havin' a great time.

"And then you get that 'Growin' Up.' That's sort of a little bit of a statement of purpose. Sort of. And then there's the rest of that—'Saint in the City,' 'Backstreets,' 'Rosalita,' and 'Raise Your Hand.' 'Rosalita' was funny because, even though it came before 'Born to Run,' the guy gets the girl—or he's trying to get the girl. And he's got the record deal, and he's trying to get away. And if he gets all these things, he thinks everything's gonna be *great*. And I guess that was kind of . . . *That happened*, I guess.

"Then the 'Hungry Heart' side with all those songs from *The River*, which is funny, because that side felt right there even if it was a little out of chronological order . . . and I think felt right because the next thing you hear, you hear that big crowd. Right after 'Rosalita,' you get 'Raise Your Hand,' and that's the idea: You want it and then, Bang! You got it.

"And the rest of that side is kind of 'Two Hearts' and 'Cadillac Ranch' and 'You Can Look but You Better Not Touch.' And now the underside starts to kinda sneak in there; you start to pick up a little undercurrent there."

That undercurrent motivated B⁻uce's best songs from *Darkness on the Edge of Town* to *Born in the U.S.A.*, from "Badlands" to "Reason to Believe" to "Dancing in the Dark"—that is, from the confidence of youth to a crisis of faith to the realization that you overcome only when you keep moving. Like all journeys to experience, it began with questions that seemed simple: Why me? What about everybody else? What next?

"At some point I said to myself—and I know this is one of the things that caused me a lot of distress—I said, Well, okay, what if I am the guy in 'Born to Run,' with the bike and the girl, shooting down the road," Bruce said. "But when you get out there a little ways, there's not that much traffic. And you can't see the people in the cars next to you; all the windows are tinted. And all of a sudden you're out there, but where is everybody? So I guess I kinda thought, Well, all right, you know; so maybe I get to do these things, but what about everybody else?

"And that didn't come from a real selfless motivation or some idea to do good. Because I understood that it was a self-preservation question. I realized that you will *die* out there, simple as that. I understood that underneath this illusion of freedom was an oppressiveness that would kill me. And that where maybe I was different was that I knew it.

"So when I got in that situation, I felt tremendously threatened, and I did not know why. It was totally instinctive. Matter of fact, I don't think I really knew why until not that long ago. But initially, when I was twenty-five, it was just instinctive—I felt threatened, I felt in danger. And it was funny because those were the exact opposite responses that people generally have. But I didn't know why I was havin' 'em; I was just havin' 'em.

"So initially, I wanted to just reject the whole thing—'This is bad; all this is bad'—as people have done before. I think you look at some of the older rock and rollers, they've chosen to reject it and their opposite choice was to move to religious fundamentalism. But I got so alienated from religion when I was younger that there was no way that

that was ever gonna be an alternative, in that sense, for me. I just could never see it.

"I think when I got in that spot, I really did feel—and not in a paranoid fashion—attacked on the essence of who I felt that I was. So at that point I realized that, unattached from community, it was impossible to find any meaning. And if you can't find any meaning, you will go insane and you will either kill yourself or somebody will do the job for you, either by doping you or one thing or another.

"I began to question from that moment on the values and the ideas that I set out and believed in on that *Born to Run* record: friendship, hope, belief in a better day. I questioned all of these things. And so *Darkness on the Edge of Town* was basically saying, You get out there and you turn around and you come back because that's just the beginning. That's the real beginning.

"I got out there—hey, the wind's whipping through your hair, you feel real good, you're the guy with the gold guitar or whatever, and all of a sudden you feel that sense of *dread* that is overwhelming everything you do. It's like that great scene in *The Last Picture Show* where the guy hits the brakes and turns around. The *Darkness* record was a confrontation record: 'Badlands,' 'Adam Raised a Cain,' 'Racing in the Street'—all those people, all those faces, you gotta look at 'em all. Right through to 'Darkness on the Edge of Town'—that was a whole other beginning.

"Now, you strip a whole bunch of things away from the thing, and you lose a lot of your illusions and a lot of, I suppose, your romantic dreams. And you decide . . . you make a particular decision. And that is a decision, I believe, that saves your life—your real life, your internal life, your emotional life, your essential life. Because you can live on, and a lotta people do; there's all sorts of people livin' on out there, you know. But I knew—and this ties right in with the discussion I had with Jon about *Born in the U.S.A.*—that the reason I began to do what I did was for connection. I desperately needed connection. I couldn't get it; I wanted it.

"And that's why the guitar was my lifeline. That was my connection with other people, more than anything else. Because other things will not sustain you. Maybe for a while you'll be distracted and have some fun, but in the end, your real life, you'll die, you will really die. And then once that happens, I believe there's only a certain amount of time before the physical thing catches up to you.

"So you've got that situation, where I turn around—on the live record, that's where 'Badlands' fits. Then you're there—from 'Badlands' through to 'War' really. But from 'Badlands' through to 'Reason to Believe,' that's kind of an investigation of that place."

Springsteen began to question not only the values he'd found in rock and roll but whether rock and roll itself, which offered the most romantic illusion of heroic Yankee individualism imaginable, was worth the effort. It all came back to the questions he'd asked himself as he put together *Born in the U.S.A.*

"Is making the Loud Noise worth it?" is how he put it in the winter of '87. "That's a question that I feel like I'm constantly asking myself, and the only answer I come up with is, Well, you don't know unless you try.

"I think that when I did the *Nebraska* record, obviously I was in a deepening process of questioning those values that were set out on *Born to Run*. I did the *Darkness on the Edge of Town* thing, and with *The River* thing I allowed some light to come in, part of the time. I had to—had to. In a funny way, I felt that I didn't have the center, so what I had to do was I had to get left and right, in hope that it would create some sort of center—or some sense of center. That probably wasn't embodied in any one given song or something, and that was the juggling that I had to do on that record."

So the same Bruce Springsteen who had sung "I'm pullin' outta here to win" at the beginning of *Born to Run* found himself opening *Nebraska* by imagining someone being hurled into a "great void." But that wasn't all.

"Here's where this thing breaks down all the social-type barriers that we put up in society. That void that you feel in that situation is the same one you can feel breathin' down your neck when you got that sun behind you, drivin' down the road; you got the girl, got that guitar. It's the same, for some reason. Because of that isolation. There are guys who come home from the factory, sit in front of that TV with a sixpack of beer, that are as isolated as the *Nebraska* record, if not more so."

It's the specter of that void that sends men down to the river when their dreams fall through or their marriages crumble or the plant closes and leaves them not just without a paycheck but empty of purpose. And rich men or poor, when they've stared long enough into that void, they make a leap. They may jump into the abyss of doubt or across a chasm of faith, but they leap.

Having reached that desperate place himself, Bruce Springsteen pushed forward, not because he rejected the hopelessness he found, but because he accepted it. "That was the subject of the *Nebraska* record," he said. "And it's the central thing at this moment in our band; we're kinda locked in with this thing. That was just the idea of the band, from the very beginning, from the minute when I touched the guitar for the first time. That was what moved me, what motivated me. And that's why as you follow the way the whole thing has developed, the moment after *Nebraska* and before *Born in the U.S.A.* is where I'm having this exact conversation with Jon . . . about these things. These are what the records are about.

"When you're in the live record, you run up to 'Reason to Believe' and at that point—well, that was the bottom. I would hope not to be in that particular place ever again. It was a thing where all my ideas might have been working musically but they were failing me personally.

"I always feel like I was lucky. I got to a point where all my answers— rock and roll answers—were running out. All the old things stopped working—as they should've and as they have to, and as time and the world and the way it is demands and dictates, in order for you to go on. They run dry, not as a joyous thing in and of itself, but as some sort of shelter for your inability to take your place in the world, whatever that may be. That's when either you recognize that that's happening or you don't and you continue with your trappings and your ceremony, whatever *that* may be, and slowly you just get strangled to death and you die. You just die."

It was at this point that Bruce Springsteen did a remarkable thing. Rather than surrendering to the "trappings and ceremony" of showbiz rite or retreating into a cocoon of protective "artistic independence" (as Young and Dylan had done), he reached out, opening himself in a way that very few public figures have ever done. He found a response as powerful as any public figure has ever known and learned to live with it. Was he another Elvis? Of course not. He didn't start something; he helped put it on the road to completion. But Bruce Springsteen had finally become like Elvis in another way. He used popular music to change himself and the slice of history he could affect. And rather than dying, he lived more whole than before.

Bruce Springsteen had finally circumvented—or rather, defused—
the trap depicted by the Band's Robbie Robertson:

See the man with the stage fright

Just standin' up there, givin' all his might

And he got caught in the spotlight

But when we get to the end, you wanna start all over again

Springsteen escaped this Sisyphean fate by ignoring the advice given
in "Stage Fright": "You can make it in your disguise/Just never show the
fear that's in your eyes." On the contrary, he'd taken the risk of turning
the glare of his personal terrors full upon his audience and, what was
most startling, found that many recognized them as their own.

When they did, Bruce Springsteen crossed the line between idol and
hero as defined by the art critic John Berger: "The function of the hero
in art is to inspire the reader or spectator to continue in the same
spirit from where he, the hero, leaves off. He must release the spectator's potentiality, for potentiality is the historical force behind no-
bility. And to do this the hero must be typical of the characters and
class who at that time only need to be made aware of their heroic
potentiality in order to be able to make their society juster and nobler.
. . . The function of the idol is the exact opposite to that of the hero.
The idol is self-sufficient; the hero never is. The idol is so superficially
desirable, spectacular, witty, happy, that he or she merely supplies a
context for fantasy and therefore, instead of inspiring, lulls. The idol
is based on the *appearance* of perfection, but never on the striving
towards it."

But what Springsteen achieved also confounded Berger, because he'd
done it through the mechanism of popular culture, mediated by one
of the country's largest industrial corporations. Like most good leftists,
Berger believes that culture to be bankrupt; like any pragmatic member
of the working class, Bruce Springsteen worked with the tools that
came to hand.

If Springsteen proved able to restore a sense of center to rock and
roll without entirely dulling that idiom's status as the cutting edge of
popular culture, it was not only because he'd dared expose to a mass
audience what seemed to be his least conventional thoughts and feelings but also because he'd done that while risking the inconveniences

and dangers of genuine mass popularity. It would have profited him not at all to gain the pink Cadillac and lose his own soul, but it would have served him equally poorly to have hardened his heart against the public from which he sprang. In that regard, his success was genuinely antibohemian, because it sprang not from a refusal to participate in social conventions, but from a refusal to be excluded from them.

For its first five sides, then, *Bruce Springsteen and the E Street Band Live/1975-1985* defines a dream and chronicles its dissolution and the ways that dawning realizations transform the dreamer. Its final four are concerned with how you live with what's left. The transition is expressed on Side Six, which runs from "This Land Is Your Land" to "Reason to Believe," a leap every bit as long as it looks. Introducing Woody Guthrie's greatest hit, Springsteen acknowledges that Guthrie wrote in anger, but when Bruce sings the song it's about dreams and visions. What's emphasized isn't the grandeur of the landscapes or the mockery society makes of them, it's the voices that call out at the end of each verse, promising something better.

"Nebraska" and "Johnny 99" are songs about people who cannot hear those voices, the consequence of which is a death sentence. But "Reason to Believe" is something worse: a requiem for those who have heard the voices, pursued them to the end, and then discovered that they were lying. It's about the greatest menace that lurks in the darkness on the edge of town, about the compulsion to leap into the river and be swept downstream, about the temptation to run and keep on running, not toward freedom but away from the facts. Springsteen defines the song precisely: "That was the bottom."

"But at the end of *Nebraska*—it's kind of ironic—I wrote another song with the word *born* in it, which is really weird," Springsteen observed. "And from that point on, the answer to 'Reason to Believe' was 'Born in the U.S.A.'—I guess either record, but particularly the live version. That's the answer to it. That's the only answer that I can perceive. And that connects back to 'Badlands,' you know. And that was the moment that I felt I'd gotten things in a little healthier perspective, and that I stopped—I didn't stop using my job; I stopped abusing my job, which I felt part of me had been doing. In the end, I just understood a lot more about what it takes to get by.

"No, it ain't gonna save you; you gotta save yourself. And you're gonna need a lotta help."

The rest of the record—and, it is not entirely unreasonable to imagine, the rest of Bruce Springsteen's work—is about giving that help and, just as important, receiving it. It begins with "Born in the U.S.A.," with that singer "born down in a dead man's town," but at the end, standing in the shadows of a prison, the singer has made a choice: He will run, and keep on running, but he will never *fail* to look back. He will always remember what's been done to him—and his friend at Khe Sanh, that woman he loved in Saigon, and the Viet Cong—and those memories will shape his future, no matter where it leads. In order to be "a cool rockin' daddy in the U.S.A.," you have to go beyond hearing the voices Woody Guthrie wrote about; you have to try to answer them back—you have to join them. And that is exactly what "Seeds," "The River," and "War" do.

"The 'Born in the U.S.A.' side, that's everything I know—at the moment, or at that time," Springsteen said with a short laugh. "And I know Jon felt that the opening section of 'The River' was the real center of the record. It moves out in all directions. The band on that night, the thirtieth of September 1985, they were great that night. They just played better than other nights. And it was a thing where just intensity and the forward thrust of the music was the best it's ever been."

Springsteen knew exactly what he was doing in the live show when he didn't stop for a reaction after "War." He compared his sense of what to do with Alfred Hitchcock's *Vertigo*—the entire film leads up to James Stewart stepping out onto a ledge, a shot that lasts less than ten seconds and is almost immediately followed by the picture's end. Springsteen calls what he learned from watching this "the integrity of the moment," which, he adds, "is a lesson I can use, because I'll be excessive. I've got the energy and I'll crank on forever. But you get to a point, you gotta have the confidence not to do that. You need confidence to do less and let it be more."

At the end of the album version of "War," the cheers are quickly faded out, and the record moves with barely a pause into "Darlington County" and "Working on the Highway," the most modest of the *Born in the U.S.A.* songs and the most embedded in the workaday world. But as life goes on, what might be missed is that it doesn't end with the "Born in the U.S.A." to "War" sequence. It carries the story onward, forward, and since that means eschewing melodrama, what's left is a finish that's as oddly muted as the start.

Yet it would be a mistake to think the story's over. It couldn't be, not as long as Bruce Springsteen's juices still flow. Even when anthems like "The Promised Land" and "No Surrender" crop up in the aftermath of "War," they are cooled down, taken in stride, without a hint of finality.

Ending the album proved one of the most difficult aspects of making it. Bruce knew that he didn't want to finish with the rock and roll medleys that always concluded his shows. But knowing what he didn't want only emphasized the magnitude of the question: So how do you end the record?

"The first time we played it through the way it was, I wasn't sure. And then we played it again and it started to really sync in—'cause 'Born to Run' tops the tenth side and you go all the way back to 'Thunder Road.' And it restates the central question.

"And the central question of 'Born to Run' is really 'I wanna know if love is real.' That's the question of that song. We go from there; we go to 'No Surrender,' a modern-day reaffirmation and restatement of all those things in the present tense. Then we get to 'Tenth Avenue'; believe it or not, that kinda connects back up to 'Spirit in the Night.' That's the cast of characters and friends; it's the band. And hey, that's what we did, you know."

At one point the plan was to end the album right there. The song told the band's story and it was modest. "We didn't want to end it with something big," Bruce said. It was Jon Landau—arguing for the softer noise for once—who suggested that a love song would be more appropriate. And although "Jersey Girl" had already been issued (as the B side of the "Cover Me" single in 1984), although it was one of only three songs in the set that Bruce didn't write, although it was obscure and quiet and ended the record somewhat mysteriously, it still felt like the right ending.

"That's the same guy that's on the boardwalk in 'Sandy,' back in the same place," Bruce said. "The same guy in 'Rosalita'—you know, he got that Jersey girl. I guess I wanted the record to feel like the middle of summer—real soft moonlight, you're takin' a real slow ride in that convertible, and you're back in that place where you began. You got somebody beside you and you feel good, and you've been through all those things.

"When I listened to that song, I'd always see myself ridin' through Asbury. There'd be people I know a little bit on the corner, and we'd just drive by. I guess that you feel in some way you're changed forever.

But you also have all those connections, so you feel really at home.

"The most important thing, though, is that the question gets thrown back at 'Born to Run.' 'I wanna know if love is real.' And the answer is yes."

◆

The live album project remained almost perfectly secret. Not even the band was in on it until there was already a preliminary sequence; CBS Records executives didn't find out until midsummer. They were given just enough notice to arrange pressing plant time, gather the huge stockpile of materials—vinyl, paper, cardboard for the boxes—and work out the logistics of distributing a five-record set that they projected would sell well over a million copies.

Columbia Records chiefs Walter Yetnikoff and Al Teller were not only willing but eager to release a massive Springsteen live set. Manufacturing the sets on such short notice would prove enormously disruptive to the company's day-to-day business, but the profit potential from a live Springsteen album was so great that the temporary chaos was worthwhile. Besides, *Live* sounded so good and was so much easier to play on compact disc that it had the potential to inaugurate a CD boom equivalent to the boom in stereo sales prompted by the Beatles' *Sgt. Pepper's Lonely Hearts Club Band*.

Manufacturing, particularly of the CD, was problematic because it threatened to outstrip the capacity of the industry to produce so many albums, cassettes, and discs that fast. No other five-record set in record industry history had sold more than a quarter of a million copies (*Biograph* and RCA's eight-disc *Elvis Aron Presley* both sold in that neighborhood). But CBS planned to manufacture more than 2 million copies of *Bruce Springsteen and the E Street Band Live/1975-1985* and stockpiled materials for several hundred thousand more.

As it turned out, that was barely enough, since the company got initial orders for more than 1.5 million sets, 500,000 more than advance orders for *Born in the U.S.A.*, which was, after all, much cheaper for stores to buy. (Wholesale price for each cassette or LP box was about $18; for the CD, around $28. Estimates were that *Live* grossed $50 million out of the gate.) For three weeks in October CBS reserved its only American CD pressing plant exclusively for pressing the Springsteen box; the 300,000 CD sets they pressed virtually sold out by the end of the set's first week of release, and no new CD pressings could be produced until January 1987. CBS had to order a million pounds of paper and hire extra trucks because only 16,000 Springsteen sets could be loaded on one tractor trailer, compared to 100,000 units of a single album. At the Carrollton, Georgia, LP pressing plant, the boxes alone filled a space equal to five football fields.

Security around the project remained tight. Even when the album was officially announced on September 11, 1986, Columbia's release kept information to an absolute minimum: the album's title and that it would contain forty tracks on five LPs or three cassettes or CDs and be accompanied by a thirty-six-page booklet. Because the mixes weren't yet complete and Bruce and art director Sandra Choron were still putting together the cover and the booklet, not even a specific release date could be stated, although dealers were told that the label was shooting for November 10, just in the nick of time to cash in on holiday gift buying.

The Springsteen/Landau style was to maintain as much secrecy about their doings as possible, but this time the motivation was much more than a desire to maintain control. As Chuck Plotkin told *Rolling Stone*'s Michael Goldberg, "Someone hears Bruce is doing a live record. Is there any way for it not to be disappointing, really, given the level of expectation that one has to have? Yet the only thing I can tell you for sure: The damn thing is *not* disappointing."

Record retailers almost drooled at the prospect of a live Springsteen set. Russ Solomon, owner of the Tower Records chain, called it "this year's Beatles album," referring to the Beatles' practice of releasing their albums just before Christmas. Jim Thompson of the Record Bar chain (the same company that had predicted that *Born in the U.S.A.* would be outsold by the Jacksons' *Victory*) went even further: "It'll definitely be *the* hit of the Eighties," he told *USA Today*. *Billboard* reported that the Springsteen live anthology was "on its way to generating the biggest dollar-volume preorders of any album in history."

◆

Bruce didn't have his nose continually to the grindstone of the record-making machinery. He spent part of September in Paris, where Julianne was costarring with Treat Williams in *Sweet Lies*, a film directed by Natalie Delon. He was home by the end of the month, though, in time for a performance of *Lady Beth* at the Stone Pony on September 28. The Los Angeles-based troupe was on a six-city national tour that Springsteen had partially funded. Bruce spoke for about five minutes during the second set discussion period, talking about the idea that "a plant owes a responsibility to a community," a particularly appropriate sentiment, since Stanley Fischer had helped organize the Asbury Park performance and many of the Freehold 3M workers were in the audience.

Springsteen had to get back to New York both to finish work on the album and in order to prepare an acoustic set for an October 8 benefit he'd agreed to do in California. Neil Young and his wife, Pegi, were staging the benefit at the Shoreline Amphitheatre in Mountain View, near their home, to raise funds for The Bridge, a San Francisco-based program that would make available vocal computers for severely handicapped children who otherwise had no way of speaking. (The Youngs have two children with that problem.) Bruce finished the album mixing on October 5 and the next morning flew to San Francisco, where he spent the weekend with his parents, who lived not far from Mountain View themselves.

Shoreline Amphitheatre holds 17,000, which would have been ludicrously inadequate for a show with the E Street Band. But on his own—even with support acts including Young, Don Henley, Tom Petty, Robin Williams, and Nils Lofgren—the facility was manageable, although the tickets sold out instantly, of course.

There was a certain irony to the benefit. It was Young's night, but it was unquestionably Springsteen who sold the tickets. The alliance between Springsteen and Young proved that music was thicker than politics: Neil Young was an ardent supporter of Ronald Reagan. Moreover, Young was raising funds for a program that couldn't get federal education funds because his President's "free market" policies had all but eliminated them.

That was barely relevant at this point. The night opened with Pegi Young introducing ten-year-old Alan Forderer, who typed a message into the computer on his lap, which then rang out over the p.a. system: "Talking computers are neat . . . It makes you feel like one of the gang. I'll be glad when other kids like me have talking computers, too."

Neil Young opened the show, but for his second song, "Helpless," he brought out "my friend Bruce" to sing harmonies, which Bruce did even though they were far out of his range. Springsteen, dressed in black jeans and sweatshirt, came and went to thunderous applause, matched only by the rousing ovation for Young's erstwhile sidekicks David Crosby (just out of jail), Stephen Stills, and Graham Nash. CSNY sang Young's "Only Love Can Break Your Heart" and an amazingly powerful "Ohio" (with Crosby dominating) to close his set and put hefty musical chips on the table.

The rules of the benefit were that each performer could bring as many sidemen as he wished but that all the instrumentation had to be acoustic. So Nils Lofgren performed by himself (including a great solo on "Keith Don't Go" and a rendition of Bruce's "Man at the Top"), while Don Henley, a harmony expert from his years with the Eagles, sang with J. D. Souther, ex-Eagle Timothy B. Schmit, and southern California all-'rounder Danny Kootch. Tom Petty also came on solo, which, he confessed, he'd never done before, and acquitted himself well. He was followed by a hilarious verbal blitzkreig from Williams, which left the crowd roaring and raring for Bruce. Bruce stepped to the mike with no band behind him and without so much as a harmonica in his hand. He took a deep breath and began to rap out the lyrics to "You Can Look but You Better Not Touch," which turned into an arm-waving a cappella boogaloo somehow reminiscent of North Beach poetry readings of the Fifties. It was a deliberately eccentric performance, reminiscent of the kind of willfully odd music that defined recent Neil Young albums, and it set up a performance that oscillated between the brilliant and the weird.

From this near-naked beginning, Springsteen built up his music sequentially. For his second number, he pulled up a chair and strummed a red-trimmed acoustic guitar. "This is a song about a snake that comes around to eat its own tail," he said, and began a version of "Born in the U.S.A." unlike anything heard before. He sang it slow and with an odd meter, banging out the downbeats by stomping his feet on a tambourine, which gave the song the accents of classic country blues—it was "Born in the U.S.A." as Skip James or Son House might have done it. The result was ravishing and as integral to the song as "You Can Look" had seemed artificial.

Bruce seemed to feel edgy or maybe just strange. "Big Man, where are ya when I need ya?" he rasped after "Born in the U.S.A." Then he brought out his sidemen, Lofgren on acoustic guitar and Danny Federici on his original instrument, accordion. Bruce sang "Seeds," with the same introduction he'd used during the tour but pared down to something like a talking blues, and then, adding a harp rack, he lurched into the story that usually introduced "Open All Night," but which now became "Darlington County."

Confronted with momentary technical confusion, he pointed to Federici: "Danny, 'Lady of Spain.'" Federici began the song in an instant; after a chorus or eighty, Bruce cut him off with a curt "Thanks" and sat back down. He told a story about his father and began "Mansion on the Hill," his tone and rhythms again closer to speech than song. More technical glitches, then Danny's accordion solo on "Satin Doll" led into "Fire."

Bruce had now built the show into something all his own. However purposeful it may have been, he'd built from the most basic element of music—the human voice—to a point where you could feel the need for a band: "Ummm . . . rock and roll, huh?" he said. "I dunno. I can't get too excited."

Bruce sang the first half of "Fire" sitting down, then paused at the spot where he usually faced off with Clarence Clemons. "No," he said, as if to himself, "I gotta stay calm—this is acoustic." From the wings Jim McDuffie appeared and took his chair away, leaving him no choice but to stay on his feet and do his best to rock the house—which he did pretty well. By the time "Fire" was finished, the entire crowd was on its feet and hollering. Bruce let the music flow right into a beautiful arrangement of "Dancing in the Dark," which somehow managed to retain the size and dynamics of the original.

"Glory Days" followed, but that didn't work as well. By now it felt like Springsteen was having too much fun at the expense of the acoustic idea. He'd been onstage the better part of an hour, and he'd avoided the bulk of the songs most likely to benefit from acoustic treatment—material like "The River," "Highway Patrolman," and "Used Cars." As long as he was offering something different and just as good, if not better, his mockery made sense. But with "Glory Days" Bruce seemed simply to be longing for a band to work with, and that seemed to play into this audience's simplest expectations of him: He was playing the hard rockin' fool.

But that impression was partly dispelled by "Follow That Dream," the first song he did that seemed to have a direct connection to The Bridge. When that was done, he called out, "Where's those old-timers?" and Crosby, Stills, Nash, and Young joined him for a ragged but gorgeous "Hungry Heart." After that everybody got into the act and the show closed, inevitably, with Nash's "Teach Your Children."

It was hard to discern just what Bruce's Bridge benefit performance meant. Was it just an oddity, a chance for him to be as weird for one night as Young, one of the contemporary artists he most admired? Or was it an omen, an exploration of a musical approach he'd pursue in the future? Chances are, Springsteen himself couldn't have told you for sure.

◆

A few days after the Bridge benefit, Bruce flew back to Paris to stay with Julianne in a Left Bank apartment while she continued work on *Sweet Lies*. Matty DiLea, the same friend who'd driven with him to California in 1982, also came along. Bruce wasn't nearly as recognizable in Paris as he was in New York or Los Angeles, and it was a good chance to get out and stretch.

The first week in November, Huey Lewis and the News played Paris, and Bruce went along to the show. Backstage, Lewis and another visitor, Bob Geldof, razzed Springsteen about the frenzied anticipation over the live set. Both had new albums out, but everything was being swallowed in Bruce's wake. At the end of the show Bruce and Geldof joined Lewis to sing the Robert Parker soul hit "Barefootin'."

On Monday, November 10, Bruce got up early and went to DeGaulle Airport with DiLea. They boarded the Air France Concorde for JFK, where they landed around nine A.M., then got into a car and drove into the city.

They couldn't have imagined what they were walking into. It was the live album's release date and record stores all over the United States were madhouses. Columbia had released an eight-song sampler, led by "War," to radio stations the previous Friday, and those tracks dominated national airplay throughout the weekend, which further piqued anticipation for the live set. As *Boston Phoenix* music editor Milo Miles wrote, to lead in to what was easily the most perceptive review the live set received, "Many visions of stardom fueled Bruce Springsteen in his adolescence, but he surely never imagined that someday local and network crews would flock to record stores to film lines of fans waiting to buy his latest album. *Born in the U.S.A.* became news as it was scooting toward the 10-million sales mark and Springsteen was bringing down stadiums across the country. *Live/1975-85* (Columbia) was born news on November 10."

Record stores were poised to do land-office business. There had been some concern at CBS about the album's selling price, but competition was so avid that many stores sold it for only a few cents more than it cost them: Tower Records offered the LP and cassette for $19.95; Record World's $24.88 price was more typical. Both were cheap.

When the stores opened that morning, many already faced lines. "We're selling them as fast as we can get them out of the box," Don Bergentry, manager of Sam Goody's Rockefeller Center store, told the *New York Times.* "This is the biggest thing I have ever seen in records." In Times Square, Disc-o-mat sold 500 of its 1,000 sets between ten A.M. and two thirty P.M. By one P.M. the Sam Goody's in the Monmouth Mall was completely sold out of the live set.

But this was no regional success story. "Nobody has seen anything like this since the madness when Elvis died," said Hays Carlock, purchasing manager of Music City Record Distributors in Nashville. "It's the craziest I've seen it since then. I wish I had a pressing plant." Record Bar owner Barrie Bergman called the entire week "the wildest I've seen in twenty-five years in the business. There wasn't this kind of money involved with the Beatles' albums," and Bergman's chain operated in the Southeast, one of Bruce's weakest markets.

Billboard reported the next Monday that most retail outlets sold out their entire initial shipments the first day. California's Music Plus chain ordered 22,000 sets; by close of business on the tenth, they'd reordered another 15,000. There were shots on the television news of customers walking out with stacks of boxes; some reportedly bought the CDs even though they didn't yet own compact disc players. By the end of the first day, Columbia had 300,000 reorders for all three configurations.

Nor was Bossmania confined to the United States. The album was expected to be the biggest-selling international record of 1986 in Japan, with an initial pressing of 150,000 and the anticipation that CBS/Sony could double that figure before the end of 1986. The goal seemed easily attainable when, only a week after release, twenty front office employees had to be transferred to a factory to box albums by hand. In England, *Live* became "the biggest CBS money grosser ever in terms of prerelease orders," according to Paul Burger of CBS International. Sweden surpassed England in advance orders, and out-of-the-chute sales were also strong in Norway, France, and West Germany. A consignment of 10,000 box sets on its way from Holland to Italy was hijacked.

Burger estimated that *Live* would be the biggest CD package ever issued in Europe. "Our prediction is that 250,000 CD box sets will be sold in Europe alone," he said. By the end of the year the box set was Number One in the United States and Canada; Top Ten in England, West Germany, Australia, and Italy, and on the "Pan-European" chart.

But if America wasn't the only site of triumph for *Bruce Springsteen and the E Street Band Live/1975-1985*, it was the principal one. Saturation airplay ensured that. "It's Here: All-Bruce Radio," headlined *Billboard* the next week, and the facts backed up the hype. Some stations were airing all forty of the album's tracks; the *Album Network* tipsheet reported that of 1184 new playlist additions at its reporting stations, fully *half* were from the Springsteen album. Boston's leading music station, WBCN, said it was playing at least two cuts an hour; in Los Angeles KLOS program director Tom Kelly said, "We'll probably hold off to about ten cuts pretty soon." As Kid Leo, the veteran Bossmaniac who programmed Cleveland's WMMS, put it, "To call this a big deal is kind of badmouthing the event."

All this held up for several weeks. Over Thanksgiving weekend, Dallas stores reported that *Live* outsold the Number Two album (Bruce Hornsby's debut) by three to one. Radio stations tapered off their airplay, but when "War" was issued as the first single it was immediately added to almost eighty percent of the Top Forty (CHR) playlists in the country. Supported by an agonizingly powerful video directed by Arthur Rosato, which added a fictionalized intro and epilogue and interwove Bruce's rap with footage from Vietnam and Central America before letting the music speak for itself, "War" soon became Springsteen's eighth straight Top Ten hit.

Bruce Springsteen and the E Street Band Live/1975-1985 would become only the third album in the past three years to debut in *Billboard*'s Top Ten. (The others also featured Springsteen: *Born in the U.S.A.* and *We Are the World.*) But something even more stunning happened: The album debuted on the chart at Number One, something that had happened with only three previous albums in history: Stevie Wonder's 1976 *Songs in the Key of Life* and two 1975 Elton John albums, *Captain Fantastic and the Brown Dirt Cowboy* and *Rock of the Westies.*

In the face of all this, the rich got richer. By the end of 1986 *Bruce Springsteen and the E Street Band Live/1975-1985* had sold about 3.5 million sets. *Time* estimated gross revenues at more than $450 million and guessed that Bruce's royalties were over $7.5 million for the first *week* of live set sales. Wild figures were tossed around, with people guessing that *Live* might sell as many units as *Born in the U.S.A.* Given the price barrier, that seemed pretty unlikely—not that the guaranteed reality of 4 to 5 million units sold was just your everyday hit record.

Bruce wasn't going to tour in support of the live box. He posed for the cover of *Rolling Stone*, where the readers voted him Artist of the Year for the third consecutive time, but he did no accompanying interview, although he did do a television interview with the BBC's Hepworth for Europe. *Live* would spawn more singles—"Fire," the second, was even accompanied by a strange and funny video from the Bridge benefit—but it was out there on its own now.

Bruce Springsteen was not. When MTV ran a Thanksgiving weekend contest in which fifty CD boxes were given away (along with the players to go with them), entrants had to call an AT&T 900 number. Knowing how Bruce might feel about that, MTV proposed donating its end of the fifty cents per call to an organization specified by Springsteen. He chose Chris Sprowal's Committee for Dignity and Fairness for the Homeless, which subsequently received more than $25,000, enabling the National Union for the Homeless to organize in several additional cities during a cruelly cold winter. Tour or no tour, Bruce Springsteen still meant what he'd said to his Philadelphia fans: "The ideas that I sing about in my songs these people put into action in real life. Fifteen percent of the population in this country lives below the poverty line, and for no good reason. It's gotten so we just accept this as a fact of life—that some people are poor and will stay poor— and that's not right."

Yet in some ways Bruce remained the loner. On his day of maximum celebrity, with *Bruce Springsteen and the E Street Band Live/1975-1985* as ubiquitous a presence as any record since *Abbey Road*, Springsteen stepped off the most famous plane on the planet, at the most famous airport in the world, and not one paparazzo snapped his picture.

When Bruce reached Manhattan, he went up to Jon Landau's office, expecting to pick up his copies of the album. They hadn't arrived yet. So he went out for his first cheeseburger in a couple of weeks, then took in a movie. In the midst of the mania, he was able to walk public streets undisturbed.

Was it too much to think that he'd really beaten the system? Not at all. Just as long as you understood that he hadn't done it alone.

21 GLORY DAYS

Springsteen's idea of what a rock concert should be is fairly simple—it should be Christmas, something anticipated, slow-coming, cherished and festive.

—Joyce Millman

You can feel the show beginning to complete itself. Most nights that means careening through a veritable history of rock and roll—some basic Springsteen originals, a little Creedence, and a lot of rhythm and blues.

All the numbers are present in their proper order tonight: "Bobby Jean" and "Ramrod," "Travellin' Band" and the inevitable medley of "Twist and Shout" and "Do You Love Me." But the feeling is different. There's no rush; it's as if the band and crowd are conspiring to set a pace that will keep this show on the brink of becoming a complete madhouse without ever letting it end.

The entire stadium is bathed in light now, enough light to televise a football game, and if you had binoculars and the inclination, you could count the smiles and the tears as parting looms inexorably closer. Warding off any unwanted sobriety is that perfect fool up on the stage. He's dancing in the light, wearing a blue cap backwards and a little-boy grin, chasing his own tail now that he's brought this massive crowd as close together as it could possibly be. The step and the smile express many things, but not the thought that this night is the end of something. At most, Bruce Springsteen's bright face seems to promise, what's coming is only a pause in the action.

So it makes sense that, as the rhythm and blues medley dies down, he turns round and shouts to the band, "Hey, guys, I think we forgot one." The entire E Street Band and Jon Landau look at Bruce blankly; he's winging it now. But when he grinds out the opening chord of "Glory Days," they burst into grins and a moment later, when they pick up the signature sound of the song, so does the entire crowd.

They take the song at an almost ambling pace, as if they've just started playing and have all the time and energy in the world. Reaching the final chorus, Bruce begins to toy with the terrors of aging, as he always does. "I can hear that clock tickin' away," he shouts. "It says, 'Boss, you're thirty—thirty-one—thirty-two—thirty-three—thirty-four—thirty-five—thirty-six!" Reaching his actual age, he groans and flails even harder at his Fender.

But then his face brightens again and he looks to Clarence Clemons, standing at his right. "Big Man," he hollers, shaking his fist. "We're adults, man!"

"Right on," says the Big Man.

"We're *adults*!"

"Right on."

"Right on," says Bruce, quite happily. "Let's dance."

22 SPARE PARTS AND BROKEN HEARTS

No need to prolong it
Too much needless pain
And it just don't make any sense
To go through it all again
—Van Morrison, "Domino" (live)

lory Days is a book with a bunch of endings. In my favorite, Bruce Springsteen, who has just returned from France for the release of his five-record *Live 1975–1985* album, appears in the guise of the protagonist of Joni Mitchell's "A Free Man in Paris": "You know I'd go back there tomorrow/But for the work I've taken on/Stoking the star maker machinery/Behind the popular song."

Mitchell's song, a portrait of a career-obsessed mogul very similar to her then-manager, David Geffen, offers heightened irony: The "free man" would clearly be lost without his work, but he'd rather be caught in a barefaced lie than be so uncool as to admit it. Bruce Springsteen, an actively antiironic artist, would also be lost without his labors, but rather than denying or poor-mouthing the fact, he celebrates it.

"A Free Man in Paris" may be fiction, but it's easier to believe than what was really happening to Bruce Springsteen. Public figures who embrace their stature as wholeheartedly as he does are rare indeed. At the time, though, Springsteen seemed to have beaten the star making machinery Mitchell views with such contempt, through intelligence, perseverance, and most importantly, by finding active collaborators who enabled him to pursue his work and vision without sacrificing his humanity. In the process, he'd found the courage to speak to a mass audience with clarity and without reservation in a voice that struck nearly everyone who heard him as emotionally authentic. Obviously, this is quite a bit different from the stories of such pop stars as Madonna and Michael Jackson, who don't beat the system because they don't challenge it, instead settling in with varying degrees of comfort at its crest. And so, the two most important endings of the book are the final direct quotation from Bruce, in which he explains the entire past decade of creative pursuit and achievement as an attempt to answer the question of "Born to Run" ("I wanna know if love is real") and says that the answer is yes; and the final scene onstage in which he not only acknowledges but revels in his ability to both assume the mantle of adulthood and keep on dancing, in total contradiction to the pop idol's dream of eternal youth.

Like a lot of great yarns, this one played out easier on the page. *Glory Days* needs its endings, because books aren't published in the open-ended way that lives are lived. No matter how many endings they might have, books are only born when they reach their conclusion. But the life of a complicated man in his mid-thirties, though it might provide material enough for many books, has barely reached midpoint. After the events recounted in *Glory Days*, Bruce Springsteen's life not only went onward, but proceeded at angles that sometimes confounded the ideas in the book. This was right and natural.

Glory Days is genuinely nonfiction, which doesn't mean that it's unerringly "factual." Facts in that simplistic sense barely exist in human lives, and anyway, you can't make a biography out of birth date, graduation announcement, wedding invitation, album release date, tombstone inscription. At least, not a readable one. Like any biography, this one presents a selection of events from an angle chosen by the biographer. Nobody else saw these stories this way.

So all *Glory Days* does is present the Bruce Springsteen of 1980-1986 as true as I could make him. And though it's been damned as hagiography, my Springsteen is anything but an invulnerable rock star—unless you think that the near-suicidal depression that infests the central chapters here is the mark of invincibility, or that the indecisiveness and psychological isolationism that precede and trigger that depression are meant as guideposts for living. What "hagiography" really means, in a cynical age, is that I wrote it the way I found it: as a true story with a happy ending.

Truth to tell, *Glory Days* ends when it does at least as much because I was done with that part of my life as because Bruce Springsteen had completed a phase of his life and career (which he had). Whatever answers Bruce had found in the previous decade, I felt happy, even privileged, to report, but my greatest joy came in understanding that I'd finally finished the story I'd been trying to tell since *Born to Run*, and through the books I'd written about Elvis Presley, the Who, and Michael Jackson. I didn't want to know if love was real. I wanted to know that somebody could make a life in the spotlight work without being mentally and morally shattered; that within the pursuit of fame, fortune, and mass communication there was a possibility of retaining personal freedom. *Glory Days* helped me get a grip on what that question meant and why it was important, and for that reason alone I'll always love this book in a different way than anything else I've ever written.

Meantime, Springsteen's life went on, in ways that noticeably impinged upon the terms of his triumph. You may think that all this upsets my conclusions. But I believe that it confirms them. Personal freedom is many things, but mainly it's an opportunity. I have never believed that heroes don't fuck up.

◆

When something goes wrong, I'm the first to admit it

The first to admit it, and the last one to know.

—Paul Simon, "Something So Right"

Glory Days was published in the spring of 1987, straight into the teeth of the so-called "Boss backlash." Since *Born in the U.S.A.* Springsteen had seemed all but impervious to criticism. But even though the *Live 1975-1985* box set spent three weeks at Number One and eleven in the Top Ten, selling four and a half million copies, a negative mood began to swell for the first time since *Born to Run*. "Fire," the second live single, flopped, and with program directors talking about "Bruce burnout," there were no further attempts to generate a hit from the set. With no airplay, sales died out.

The concert box didn't just sell (the next-biggest-selling box set, Bob Dylan's *Biograph*, had sold only about 250,000 copies), it played a major role in establishing the compact disc market and set an industry-wide trend toward multivolume box sets that continues to this day. But neither CBS nor any other record company could have sold so many records so quickly without generating a large overstock; after two centuries, overproduction remains a bugbear of capitalism. *Live 1975–1985* returns were in pretty normal proportions: Between ten and twenty percent of total sales. But the size and price of the box meant that several hundred thousand unsold records represented many millions of dollars in potential returns. CBS wouldn't have been eager to assume such a debit at any time, but especially wanted to avoid booking it at a time when its record division was in the process of being sold.

So CBS worked out a scheme that gave stores an incentive to delay returns. Since the details were as dull as they were intricate, the consumer press confused the issue, assuming that the return rate should have been zero and implying that the concert box was some kind of hype, rather than one of the most profitable recording projects in history. (Four and a half million sets sold represented a gross revenue of more than $100 million.)

Backlash, burnout, or bust, Springsteen remained a tabloid favorite. "Bruce Springsteen: I Want to Be the Next Governor of New Jersey," the *National Enquirer* trumpeted on its March 31, 1987 cover, and reporters around the nation phoned Landau, CBS, and beleaguered biographers to know if it was true. Yet nobody divined the real story, which was that Springsteen had begun making a new album in the studio he'd installed in the small carriage house at his Rumson, New Jersey, home. Springsteen had always worked so slowly that nobody imagined he would quickly turn out another album, his fourth in five years.

Springsteen not only recorded his new songs rapidly, he'd come up with one of his best records, a far more consistent and mature set of songs than *Born in the U.S.A.* and one which, rather than gazing over his shoulder as all his previous records had done, broke into new territory (though not without a few glances).

Tunnel of Love wasn't a rock and roll record. Bruce made much of the music solo, using a drum machine and playing guitar, piano, synthesizer, bass, adding the various E Street Band members for minimal overdubs. With the exception of the title track, *Tunnel*'s music resembled a fleshed out *Nebraska*, modest, country and folkish in mood, though with touches from the Del Shannon /Lou Christie/Gene Pitney grab bag that had been among Springsteen's building blocks since *Born to Run*.

That wasn't such a surprising mixture; you could get there by merging the musical styles Springsteen had used previously. The break came in the record's subject matter, and most of all in its point of view. *Tunnel of Love* eschews the broad social vision of previous albums; rather than trying to provide Big Answers to Big Questions, it concerns itself with love relationships. The perspective is miniaturized and demystified: in one song, a character actually eyed an open highway "and he didn't see nothin' but road," rather than a metaphor of freedom and release. In most of the rest, the solitary pursuits of driving and dreaming are replaced by images of dancing, a totally collective activity. It's also the only Springsteen record that smacks of direct autobiography.

It opens with a musical knockoff and lyrical rewrite of Billy Boy Arnold's classic Chicago jump blues, "I Ain't Got You" (as filtered through the Animals and the Yardbirds). But rather than taking the song uptown and polishing it, as he usually did with blues themes, Springsteen stripped it down to harp, guitar, voice, and hand percussion. Rather than Arnold's El Dorado, tavern, liquor store, closet full of clothes, and "women to the left of me, women to the right of me, chicks all around me," Springsteen declares himself possessed of fortunes in diamonds and gold, houses from coast to coast, priceless art, and "a hundred pretty women knockin' down my door."

It's a mockery of the tabloid vision of Springsteen's circumstances (not that he couldn't have had many of those things, if he'd wanted them; not that he didn't actually have some of the art and real estate). But in its final few lines, Springsteen's "I Ain't Got You" summarized the excesses of his existence through eyes that could have been no one's but his own:

> *I been around the world and all across the seven seas*
>
> *Been paid a king's ransom for doin' what comes naturally*
>
> *But I'm still the biggest fool, honey, this world ever knew*
>
> *'Cause the only thing I ain't got, baby, I ain't got you*

The rest of *Tunnel of Love* presents Springsteen's search to replace his lack of love. "Tougher Than the Rest" and "All That Heaven Will Allow" detail infatuations; "Spare Parts" and "Cautious Man" are about the consequences of evading commitment, the impossibility of surviving without it; "Walk Like a Man" finishes out the first side by showing him actually taking the plunge, an emotionally charged portrait of his thoughts as he walked down the aisle.

Those first half-dozen pieces from *Tunnel of Love* are different from any other songs Bruce Springsteen had ever written. Only two are character pieces (and "Cautious Man" is so thinly veiled, it's as if only the names have been changed). "Walk Like a Man" is the first of Springsteen's many father songs that speaks directly to his experience of Doug Springsteen, the first in which his mother's strong role in his childhood is addressed, the first, after all the years of describing such relationships purely in terms of conflict, in which he acknowledges spending his life trying to follow in his father's footsteps. It's certainly the only song in which Springsteen ever confessed so directly the strangeness of his own life. And finally, there is a reconciliation of all the anger and bitterness and sense of betrayal into the lonely last line: "I'll walk like a man . . . and I'll keep on walkin'."

Tunnel of Love may have been made in the age of CD, but it's divided in the old vinyl sense into side one and side two, separate but interacting sides of the same story. "Tunnel of Love" doesn't pick up from "Walk Like a Man" so much as explode past it in a surge of carnival percussion and guitar/synthesizer warfare. The music is the one really ensemble piece on the album, Nils Lofgren's guitar surging out of the mix like the louder voice in a bickering couple's terminal argument. The singing is all portent and turbulence; the lyrics fill in the shadows without illumining any of the details:

> Oughta be easy, oughta be simple enough
>
> Man meets a woman and they fall in love
>
> But the house is haunted and the ride gets rough
>
> And you've got to learn to live with what you can't rise
>
> above

It was as if Springsteen's conception of what happened after you got married came from his first draft of the 1980 song "Stolen Car," in which the bride and groom's relationship sours at the instant of the nuptial kiss. Butt-ended with "Walk Like a Man," "Tunnel of Love" dashes the whole idea of romantic love—the kind of love Springsteen's been seeking throughout the first side of the album. It isn't an abrupt transition; there *is* no transition, just an immediate leap from the wedding to the shattered crockery. And the tension doesn't really let up for the whole side, as Springsteen rips through a series of songs that quietly but firmly tear the mask off true love and good intentions. "Now look at me, baby! Strugglin' to do everything right/And then it all falls part/Oh, when out go the lights," he cries and then, "I wanna know if it's you I don't trust/'Cause I damn sure don't trust myself."

Bruce put those words, from "Brilliant Disguise," in the Top Ten but he put their resonances into all of the final songs on *Tunnel of Love*. All but the last one. In "Valentine's Day," Springsteen's vision of wedded bliss becomes so gorgeously seductive that at the end, he dies and comes back to life renewed and made whole to the synthesized sound of chiming wedding bells. "Valentine's Day" might have borne a banner: MARRIAGE! THE WAY IT OUGHTA BE!

I don't mean that "Valentine's Day" is dishonest. If *Tunnel of Love* is a fable of marriage, wedded bliss needs to be included prominently alongside marital woes. But the sequence, at least, is improbable. It makes more sense to run the songs backward, from "Valentine's Day" to "Tunnel of Love," which happens to correspond with their chronology of creation. Certainly, that sequence would more closely conform to what we now know Bruce Springsteen's experience to have been. Either way, what's at the center of this cycle of songs are songs of doubt and remorse and deep confusion—and smack dab in the middle, "One Step Up, Two Steps Back," as miserable a cheating song as even Nashville ever knew.

And either way, what you'll feel, listening straight through, is the ebb and flow of these affairs, the waxing and waning of desire itself, and the urgency of making a commitment to carry on. Earlier, Springsteen had committed himself to finding Purpose, something large and outside himself. Now, he's either decided or realized that the purpose is in the doing; meaning isn't found in life, it's inserted there, as the result of what we do day by day. This is the true tunnel of love, in which marriage takes place among sweaty sheets, dirty kitchens, at the top of our lungs, and in the shakiest sectors of our quivering guts. But never alone—someone you love is always there too. With "When You're Alone," Springsteen sweeps away his earlier romantic conception of a loner's existence, and he does so because his experiences leave him no choice:

> *With just the shirt on my back I left and swore I'd*
> *   never look back*
> *And man I was gone, gone, gone*
> *But there's things that'll knock you down you don't*
> *   even see coming*
> *And send you crawling like a baby back home*
> *You're gonna find out that day, sugar*
> *When you're alone, you're alone*

So from beginning to end *Tunnel of Love* comes to terms with the fact that, even if you achieve what passes in these parts for "freedom," you're still stuck with what to do for an encore.

Tunnel of Love hit the stores in late 1987; it sold five million copies or so. Those weren't blockbuster numbers, but in spirit, this album was closer to *Nebraska*. Springsteen had now established a creative oscillation of sorts, between mass-appeal projects and more personal, "artier" ones, a balance unlike any other superstar's. This was important for reasons of image and sanity, but it counted for nothing at record stores, which cared only for tonnage. As singles, "Brilliant Disguise" and "Tunnel of Love" both hit the Top Ten, but without igniting public attention as "Dancing in the Dark" and "Lover Me" had done. Artistically, Springsteen had hit another peak, but the star-making machinery of which he was now so firmly a part has other standards, and by those terms, *Tunnel of Love* was perceived as another dubious achievement.

In early 1988, Springsteen began a concert tour. Rather than returning to outdoor stadiums, he went back to the indoor arenas that had sustained him for the decade before. But at least initially, the tour departed in startling ways from previous E Street Band extravaganzas:

it was somewhat shorter (a little under three hours) and many of the seemingly irreplaceable warhorse concert pieces, even (or perhaps especially) such landmarks as "Badlands," "Thunder Road," and "The Promised Land," were discarded. The first ninety minutes featured only two pre-*Born in the U.S.A.* songs, and those were "Adam Raised a Cain," the most raucous song from *Darkness on the Edge of Town*, and the 1981 B-side, "Be True." The rousing climax wasn't a celebration of possibility but the hard facts: "War" straight into "Born in the U.S.A."

The second set superficially lightened up, but the two new songs, "Part Man/Part Monkey," a reggae tune prefaced by a diatribe that both parodied Jimmy Swaggart-style confessionals and acted as a refutation of "creation science," and "I'm a Coward (When It Comes to Love)," a rewrite of Motor City soulster Gino Washington's "Gino Is a Coward," each were edgy and agitated—which fed into the best of the old tunes, "She's the One" and "Dancing in the Dark." The ending was "Just Around the Corner to the Light of Day," the song Springsteen had given Joan Jett to sing in Paul Schrader's rewritten movie, *Light of Day* (the one originally called *Born in the U.S.A.*), a powerfully positive signal. But Bruce encored with an acoustic "Born to Run" that was sobering and somber. As on the *Tunnel* album, the emphasis was on limits, not possibilities; the theme for this tour was all that heaven would allow, not everything that man could imagine.

This was a great show, because it challenged the perceptions and expectations of Springsteen fans—not just the mass audience that had first been reached by *Born in the U.S.A.*, but also longtime fans nurtured to expect Bruce to deliver anthemic optimism. All that marred it was the finale, a long series of predictable encores—the Detroit medley, "Rosalita," "Sweet Soul Music"—that seemed to say that his listeners *didn't* have to come to grips with the intensity and maturity of his new work. Or else, that Springsteen once again felt himself on such shaky ground that he needed to exhaust himself before leaving the stage, drain every ounce of energy until he'd burned out not the crowd but himself. Soon enough, the shows were back up to four hours.

As it worked out, the greatest tension in the show came from the intensity with which Springsteen worked with singer Patti Scialfa. The lithe redhead replaced Clarence Clemons as Bruce's principal foil. They put their heads together intimately at the mike, gazed passionately at each other across the narrowest distances, as they teased, flirted with, and tormented one another. Bruce ordinarily epitomized the cautious man when it came to public expressions of sexuality. Nobody'd ever seen him like this before. And as the tour went on, the interplay with Scialfa intensified until it became the centerpiece of the show.

They weren't just acting. They'd fallen in love in real life. Neither of them has ever publicly discussed how or why it happened, not that it's anybody's business. You could listen to the second group of songs on *Tunnel of Love* and make your own guesses. You could figure the statistics: forty percent of American marriages end in divorce, the figure is higher for first marriages, and the rate of marital success between rock stars and actress/models who've known each other less than a year must be infinitesimal.

By early May, when the tour reached California, Springsteen had told Julianne Phillips the bad news. They separated. At least within the community of the tour, he and Patti were now openly a couple. Yet so far as the world knew, Springsteen remained the contented husband of "Valentine's Day." Rumors had the couple wrangling over when and whether to have children. But apparently nobody imagined Bruce Springsteen, the all-American rock star, having his marriage crash and burn in only three years.

Springsteen's wholesome image, which for some contradicted the whole idea of rock stardom, had just been boosted by making an album about the travails of monogamy. But his wariness of making public statements outside the context of his shows led to a major media miscalculation: he decided that the end of his marriage was a private matter that did not require a press release.

In the end it was Julianne's divorce lawyer who made the public announcement of the split. But Bruce and Patti didn't keep their affections private. In Italy, paparazzi caught Springsteen and Scialfa in their underclothes, necking on a hotel-room balcony. The pictures flashed to tabloids worldwide, and Springsteen looked like a heartless man cheating on a unsuspecting wife a continent away. For Julianne, who had respected her own sense of privacy by making no public statement about their breakup, the photos were humiliating. Patti's image now descended to the housewrecker, the classic "other woman," though in fact, her friendship with Bruce predated her residency in the E Street Band.

Bruce finally issued a press statement, apologizing to Julianne, though without making it clear that the paparazzi hadn't broken the news to her. To many fans, even those who'd never really warmed to the idea of the workingman's rocker marrying an ex-cheerleader, the incident seemed a significant breach of faith. The Tunnel of Love tour ended in Europe in a jumble of mixed emotions.

At one of the last shows, broadcast worldwide live from Stockholm on July Fourth, Springsteen announced from the stage that he would be headlining a worldwide tour for Amnesty International, the human-rights group. Numerous other acts had been mooted for the venture, but the lineup eventually became Springsteen, Sting, Peter Gabriel, Tracy Chapman, and Youssou N'Dour.

Ostensibly, the tour was to celebrate the twenty-fifth anniversary of the International Declaration of Human Rights, a document ratified by most of the world's nations, but enforced in its entirety by none. It was a true world tour, leaping from Europe to North America to Asia, back to Europe, then to Africa, Central America, and South America. But its time frame was telescoped, running at a killing, energy-depleting pace from the September-second night at Wembley Stadium, London, to the conclusion, at the huge football stadium in Buenos Aires on October fifteenth. Before long, many roadies and technicians sported T-shirts on which the Declaration's Article 24 was spelled out:

> *Everyone has the right to rest and leisure, including*
>
> *reasonable limitation of working hours and periodic holidays*
>
> *with pay.*

Springsteen ordinarily isolated himself from other pop stars so much that the Amnesty tour almost amounted to a coming-out party for him. The tour's necessities shoved him into a somewhat awkward role: closing the show with the night's only up-tempo rock and roll set, which led him to the kind of abbreviated, hit-after-hit performance of familiar favorites the band hadn't done since the M.U.S.E. concerts in 1980, a stark contrast to the antistar turn of the *Tunnel of Love* tour, and one that set Springsteen up as a sort of *capo di tutti capi*, Boss of all Bosses.

But each night's performances at least began and ended in togetherness: a collective sing-along on the Wailer's anthem, "Get Up, Stand Up," and a roundrobin set of choruses on Bob Dylan's "Chimes of Freedom." (Columbia released a Springsteen EP featuring the latter song, with proceeds donated to Amnesty International.) The overall show developed other rituals: Sting's set grew to include a duet with Bruce on "Every Breath You Take," while Bruce invariably brought out Sting to sing along on "The River."

Sting proved the greatest foil Bruce had ever come across. One night, he appeared during Bruce's solemn introduction of "The River," pushing a vacuum cleaner, an unmistakably pointed jab at Springsteen's self-seriousness. At the press conference held before the first show in each nation, Sting and Springsteen began referring to each other as long-lost friends, key spiritual and career advisers and in other mock-heroic ways designed to keep two of the pop world's larger egos in something approaching proportion.

On the final night of the tour, during the worldwide radio broadcast, Sting and the quietly off-his-rocker Peter Gabriel appeared onstage dressed as Bruce Springsteen clones, right down to the black jeans and red bandana. It evoked a small, hearty chuckle, appropriately for an event whose purpose was not fund-raising or any direct political goal, but simply the raising of awareness about Amnesty International.

Within those modest terms, the Amnesty Tour succeeded. As a pop event, it worked out less well. The package show drew less well than any of the individual acts—certainly Springsteen—might have done alone, particularly in America, where ticket sales were meant to subsidize the unprofitable Third World performances. With each show cut to about an hour, none of the performers was really able to play at their peak, and five hours of music a night wore on the attention span of even the most avid audiences. The HBO special about the tour, though well directed by Larry Jordan and featuring excellent performances and sometimes moving offstage footage, was a ratings bomb.

This tour came down to faith and conviction more than numbers. In that respect, perhaps it put Bruce Springsteen back in a more comfortable groove—and once again, not alone.

23 THE PRICE OF THE TICKET

The irreducible price of learning is realizing
that you do not know.

> —James Baldwin

Baby once I thought I knew
Everything I needed to know about you
… But I didn't really know that much
The joke's on me but it's gonna be okay
If I can just get through this lonesome day.

> —Bruce Springsteen

Bruce Springsteen takes advantage of memory onstage all the time. Unlike any other rock singer, he knows how to fit together the parts of his work into a series of contiguous statements that overarch seemingly unrelated facets and time periods. He does things like drop "Lost in the Flood," a song from his first album, into his set list between "Darkness on the Edge of Town," which came twelve years later, and "Empty Sky," or "Worlds Apart," from his 2002 album, *The Rising*. He sings a slide guitar version of "Born in the U.S.A." as if he he'd recorded it either yesterday or in 1938. He sings a brand new song, "Land of Hopes and Dreams," which takes most of its structure and imagery from "People Get Ready," and makes you realize how much Curtis Mayfield and Woody Guthrie had in common.

This requires effortlessness *as an illusion*. People who attended his Asbury Park rehearsals in 2002, which he opened to the public in a departure from his legendary cloistered work process, emerged startled that Springsteen worked as hard on perfecting the specific stage activity as on the band and vocal arrangements. In the days when he talked more onstage, you could hear him practicing a yarn at soundcheck.

Springsteen remains immune to the incongruous because of a work method so internalized that predicting its next turn remains all but impossible for even those who have watched him longest. Sometimes, he does just what you know he's going to do and still makes it a surprise. Sometimes, he does just what you wish he'd do—up to a point. Sometimes, he comforts his listeners and unsettles them in the same moment. Always, he makes of himself an open book and an ongoing mystery.

The lackluster response received by his two 1992 albums and the 1992–1993 tour with the non–E Street Band in the United States suggested an artist whose heyday had come and gone. A year later, he turned up with "Philadelphia," one of the biggest hits of his career, and won an Oscar and a Grammy for record of the year. He parlayed the awards into a brief return to #1 on the album chart with *Greatest Hits*, a concise summation of what he'd done since *Born to Run*. Most notably, the album reunited the E Streeters for two new songs, "Secret Garden" and "Blood Brothers." "Secret Garden" became a minor hit when some enterprising disc jockey did a mix interweaving it with some of the corniest dialogue from the film *Jerry Maguire*, and Bruce, apparently feeling immensely less controlling than he usually does, failed to smother it in its crib. More important, "Blood Brothers" provided a statement of purpose, commitment, and brotherhood that evoked a history that reached back to before he'd ever made any records.

He seemed on the verge of a public revival, so the next thing he turned up with was a solo (but not acoustic) album, *The Ghost of Tom Joad*. A friend of mine who teaches high school in Los Angeles defined it: "This is what it's like to live in Pete Wilson's California." As such, it should feel dated eight years later. I started to play it yesterday, and the first words that registered were "Welcome to the new world order," which in the wake of the invasion of Iraq seemed nothing so much as contemporary.

Tom Joad has some great lyrics and a static musical atmosphere that builds a sense of desperate tension. It's not quite a great album, though. It relies too much on words, and that musical stasis demands a relief it doesn't get. The tenor is journalistic except on songs like "Straight Time," "Dry Lightning," and the direct quotations from *The Grapes of Wrath* in the title song, where it becomes literary. Springsteen's interest in music seemed to have become secondary.

Springsteen turned *The Ghost of Tom Joad* into a solo show that was great because he *was* still interested in what things sounded like. He came up with an unsettling vocal wail that could chill your bones; I remember the first night he did it, at the end of "Promised Land" in

Detroit. The weird starkness of this noise, coming in the midst of all those endless words, suggested our closest glimpse ever of the tightrope as a noose knotted around one man's neck.

As I point out in *Glory Days*, *Nebraska*, *Joad*'s obvious precedent, is an album about personal turmoil in the guise of social commentary. *The Ghost of Tom Joad* contains virtually no immediate personal subtext. It shows nothing of the life he was living—in a beautiful house in a Beverly Hills cañon, with a wife he loved and three very young kids whom he treated as the miracles they are. Maybe *Joad* is the product of reading the newspapers while even more isolated than usual—he hadn't toured in a couple of years. More likely, it's a way of projecting himself and his family into the lives they had evaded but which Springsteen, from his childhood, knew as a tangible possibility: destitute, desolate, hopeless, frustrated, furious, a life of wasted possibility, a life that ridiculed dreams. What *Joad* said was that this was not only wasteful but wrong, not only unnecessary but criminal. Not a political statement, though. A moral one.

The album's finest song, "Across the Border," pays homage in its title, mood, and imagery to "Across the Borderline," a song popularized by one of its writers, Ry Cooder, and originally written for the 1982 Jack Nicholson movie, *The Border*, a film about an INS agent trapped in a relationship remarkably similar to the INS agent in another *Joad* song, "The Line." Bruce had played "Across the Borderline" live several times. But his own song took the same scene and played it from the other perspective.

Springsteen plays the melody of "Across the Border" on an acoustic guitar, the band coming in quietly as a fog around a campfire, as he tells the tale of a Mexican man, his wife and child about to cross the Rio Bravo (the Mexican name of the Rio Grande) into the U.S. His voice is full of the hopeless hope it takes to leave your home and enter America illegally. "Across the Border," then, returns Springsteen to his greatest subject: dreams and the strivings of ordinary people to realize them. But it appears after nine previous songs have outlined the virtual impossibility of a happy outcome. As the immigrant speaks in the fullness of possibility—"For what are we / without hope in our hearts / That someday we'll drink from God's blessed waters?"—you realize two things: The border he's going to cross lies between life and death, and he damn sure knows it. There, and only there, "pain and memory have been stilled."

Death has been Springsteen's other great topic. In his most anthemic early songs—"Born to Run," "Thunder Road," "Badlands," "Darkness on the Edge of Town"—the central character finds a way to assert that death is preferable to living without fulfillment. The forty-five-year-old Springsteen sang well aware that for every success story like his own there are millions for whom death is neither a metaphor nor a welcome juvenile fantasy. It's what most often comes from reaching for things as simple as "Pastures of gold and green / Roll down into cool clear waters."

The youthful Springsteen saw death in its relationship to life's boundless potential for freedom. The adult Springsteen sees it in its relationship to life's endless potential to crush that spirit. For the first time, his writing recognizes that for a lot of people, the prospect of realizing hope is an obvious fiction. In the end, "Across the Border" answers the question of "The River" (the similarity in setting cannot be accidental): A dream's not just a lie if it doesn't come true, and it is not something worse—it is something *much* worse. A dream that has no chance of coming true is a kind of death. And dead is what we are without hope in our hearts.

Bruce couldn't end with a message that savage. It may have been true as to the facts, or at least most of them, but it wasn't right for Bruce Springsteen—not because he's a person for whom life did provide abundance and love, but because he hadn't lost the conviction of the main message of his art, which is simply that, given the chance, people want to be decent. So he wrote "Galveston Bay," a song about Le Bin Son, a Vietnamese immigrant who comes to Texas and fishes for shrimp in the Gulf of Mexico, and a Vietnam vet, Billy Sutter, who joins the Klan and tries to oust the Vietnamese. The attempt fails, and Sutter decides to seek private revenge. But when the moment comes to stick a knife in Le Bin Son's ribs, he puts his knife in his pocket, goes home, kisses his wife, and goes out on his own shrimp boat.

This is as much hope as Bruce Springsteen, the world's champion hope finder, could locate in Pete Wilson's California, George W. Bush's Texas, and Bill Clinton's America. Even he couldn't end there—so "My Best Was Never Good Enough" finished things off.

The Ghost of Tom Joad came out in November 1995. Bruce toured behind it until the end of May 1997—a tour as long as the one he did behind *Born in the U.S.A.* This one did little to expand his audience, although it did something to solidify the remainder of his following, particularly in Europe.

For the next several months, he fell silent. He worked in the studio, on his own, and with various musicians and producers Chuck Plotkin and engineer Toby Scott. (Jon Landau had withdrawn to become man- ager-only after *Human Touch/Lucky Town*.) If Bruce came up with much, it's not apparent from *Tracks*, his four-CD box set of outtakes, rarities, and leftovers released at the end of 1998. Only two of these tracks were written after 1992. One of them, "Back in Your Arms," appeared in Blood Brothers, the 1995 sessions for new *Greatest Hits* material. The other, "Brothers under the Bridge," a rewrite of a title he'd used during the *Born in the U.S.A.* sessions, featured E Streeters Garry Tallent and Danny Federici. *Songs*, a collection of his lyrics published as a book that fall, featured nothing newer.

In January 1999 Bruce faced induction to the Rock and Roll Hall of Fame. The excellence of his last record and concert tour made the case that he was that rare artist who remained creative twenty-five into his career. But in the rock world, the three-and-a-half years between albums constituted a meaningful lapse. When the Hall announced Springsteen's election the previous autumn, he'd come up with noth- ing new to follow *Joad*.

Despite Lone Genius mythology, most successful music making results from a collaborative process. Springsteen's best music resulted from collaborations with long-term associates. Now, they'd scattered: Steve Van Zandt became a TV star with the HBO series *The Sopranos*; Max Weinberg led the band on Conan O'Brien's late night NBC show; Garry Tallent produced records in Nashville; Roy Bittan played sessions and worked as a producer, mainly in Los Angeles. Nils Lofgren and Clarence Clemons made records and toured with their bands; Danny Federici had never seemed more the "phantom." Since Bruce announced the breakup of the E Street Band he'd never attached himself to another group. He now seemed as isolated musi- cally as he had been psychologically when he made *Nebraska*.

The music, it turned out, resumed flowing when he rejoined his old band. I can't remember anymore whether he announced it before or after the Hall of Fame ceremony, but by that night everyone knew that he'd gathered the old gang back together. He didn't say what they were going to do, except make some music.

When they announced a tour, it wasn't called a reunion, much less a comeback, but it was. In theory, there was plenty of new material — of the sixty-five songs on *Tracks*, more than a dozen, enough for at least one album, could be performed well onstage. After all, a song is just as new if the audience has never heard it before as it is when it's just been written.

On the tour, though, Springsteen did just the opposite of what you'd have thought. He played very little of the new material in most sets—"Don't Look Back" and "My Love Will Not Let You Down" became regular features, sometimes opening the show. He also played a few that he'd been doing occasionally for years anyway—"Roulette," "Rendezvous," "Janey Don't You Lose Heart." "This Hard Land" showed up, but he'd been doing that one off-and-on since the 1992 tour, one reason he included it as the final song on *Greatest Hits*. The tour focused on Springsteen's warhorses: "Prove It All Night," "Badlands," "The River," "The Promised Land," "Atlantic City," "Out in the Street," "Tenth Avenue Freezeout," "Backstreets," an acoustic "Born in the U.S.A." developed during the *Joad* tour.

But Springsteen held aces. First, the quality of the E Street Band's playing took a leap. Everyone just got better. Max Weinberg acquired more finesse, Garry Tallent bore deeper into the grooves, and the return of Steve Van Zandt gave the group a thunderous three-guitar attack (although virtuosic Nils Lofgren often played other instruments—including steel guitar, which he learned by rehearsing between shows). The transcendent versions of "Youngstown," from *The Ghost of Tom Joad*, hinted at what some of that album's songs might have become if the E Streeters had gotten a crack at them in the studio. Of the warhorses, "Darkness on the Edge of Town," in particular, reached new heights of power (and depths of emotion)—many nights, it was the best number in the show—and "Tenth Avenue Freezeout" grew into a twenty-minute gospel-soul rave-up.

Another ace was the growth in Springsteen's singing. A new arrangement made "The River" swing, and that started with the singing—you'd almost think he'd learned a few tricks hanging around with Frank Sinatra just before the great saloon singer died. But for the most part, Springsteen relied on resources taken from soul music and, more often than before, gospel. "Tenth Avenue Freezeout" became an extravaganza because Bruce used it as a platform to sermonize on "the power, the glory, the *majesty* of rock 'n' roll!" (An unbeliever could be forgiven for feeling thankful that the boy had been born a Catholic and infected early with the rock 'n' roll virus.) A lot of nights, it went on for a full twenty minutes, incorporating into its basic Stax-Volt structure not only Bruce's exhortations and proclamations but audience chants, band introductions, and bits of the Curtis Mayfield's Impressions' hit, "It's All Right," Bobby Moore and the Rhythm Aces' "Searchin' for My Baby," Sam and Dave's "Soothe Me," and Al Green's "Take Me to the River."

The sermon stayed on the same topic Springsteen always preached: "I want to go to that river of resurrection, where everybody gets a second chance ... but you gotta work at it!" he proclaimed. "You just don't stumble onto those things, you don't find those places by accident. You've got to seek them out and search after them. And that's why we're here night after night after night after night. Because you can't get to those things by yourself. You've got to have *help.*"

At one level, the message just set up Springsteen's introductions of the band members; at another, it spoke to what he had gained by returning to work with the very people he publicly dismissed, the builder reconsidering the foundation stone he'd rejected. At a third level, it represented the entire saga of Bruce Springsteen's life and career, a journey from loneliness to community.

It also spoke to a nation and a world where the individual in his or her supposedly realistic, allegedly splendid isolation had reached the outer limit of estrangement. To a land and a time when the inability to reach out to one another had become the cross under which each and all had stumbled and fallen into the dust. To the fact that you could get killed just for living in your American skin—or any other kind—and everyone looked the other way because those were just the breaks.

For God's sake, did Bruce Springsteen still think that rock 'n' roll could save the world?

Not without a lot of hard work. Not by itself.

This was the message of the Bruce Springsteen and the E Street Band's Rock 'n' Roll Revival (to give it its most appropriate name). The spirit of that tour came in two less bombastic songs.

"If I Should Fall Behind," the hidden jewel of *Lucky Town,* started out as a kind of wedding song, a pledge between two lovers. It grew into something else after Bruce sang it with Dion at the *Joad* tour's Miami stop. The band worked up fine solo vocal parts. ("He writes great doo-wop songs," was all Dion said.) It took off when Springsteen incorporated his dramatic sense. He placed it near the end of the show. The band's singers stood in a group at the back of a blacked-out stage. Each in turn came forward to sing a single line, Patti and Nils harmonizing on the chorus—"I'll wait for you / If I should fall behind wait for me." Then a solemn Clarence Clemons sax solo, which yielded to Clemons singing the next two lines in a doowop bass, which gave into Bruce's first turn. Then each member in turn—Clarence, Patti Scialfa, Little Steven, Nils, Bruce—sang the chorus. And finally, in one chord searching for a subway echo, all together in harmony the more glorious for its imperfections.

"10th Avenue Freezeout" told you what you could do. "If I Should Fall Behind" showed a way to do it.

On the last night of the tour, July 1, 2000, Bruce stepped to the mic as soon as "If I Should Fall Behind" was over. "The first night we played, I came out and we did this song, and I said I was hopin' that our tour would be the rebirth and the renewal of our band and our commitment to serve you," he said. "I hope we've done that well this year, and we'll continue to try and do so."

Then he said what he said every night just before the last song. "This is 'Land of Hope and Dreams.'" The only new song in the set, going in, it proved beyond dispute that Bruce Springsteen still had it in him to write a great rock song. It even included his specialty, a bridge that contained as much emotional energy as the rest of the song but of a whole different order:

> *This train carries saints and sinners*
> *This train carries losers and winners*
> *This train carries whores and gamblers*
> *This train carries lost souls!*
> *This train, dreams will not be thwarted*
> *This train, faith will be rewarded*
> *This train, hear the steel wheels singin'*
> *This train, bells of freedom ringing!*

There were many others aboard this train—kings and fools, brokenhearted, and souls departed. What came through clearest was that if you drew the usual lines—"This train don't carry no ramblers, no lost souls, no midnight gamblers"—it wasn't only the people left at the station who lost. "Nobody wins unless everybody wins," Springsteen used to tell his audiences. He hadn't changed his mind. Here he was, with the family he'd longed for and all the riches he'd never let himself dream about, and the price of today's ticket must have seemed more, not less. In any event, he seemed, as ever, not only willing but glad to pay it.

Springsteen closed his tour that night with the most emotionally focused performance I've ever witnessed from anyone. When he played his old '70s ballad "The Promise," sitting alone at Roy Bittan's white grand piano, I remember staring at his back, because everywhere else I looked, a sob awaited.

When he finished that song, the band stood before him on the stage and applauded. From band to leader, who could imagine a greater tribute?

They played some more songs—he was not about to let *that* crowd loose without having drained himself—and then he called the group to the front of the stage. Against a droning chord, he began to sing "Blood Brothers," the song he wrote when the band first reunited at the *Greatest Hits* sessions.

When he finished the last verse, he motioned for the band to stay close by him and keep playing. He started to sing a new verse, and he sang it with tears in his eyes:

> Now I'm out here on this road
> Alone on this road tonight
> I close my eyes and feel so many friends around me
> In the early evening light
> And the miles we have come and the battles won and lost
> Are just so many roads traveled, so many rivers crossed
> And I ask God for the strength, and the faith in one another
> 'Cause it's a good night for a ride, 'cross the river to the other side
> My blood brothers

"We'll be seein' ya!" he shouted and then they were done with their new beginning.

◆

One can speak, then, of the fall of an empire at that moment when, though all of the paraphernalia of power remain intact and visible and seem to function, neither the citizen-subject within the gates nor the indescribable hordes outside it believe in the morality or the reality of the kingdom anymore—when no one, any longer, anywhere, aspires to the empire's standards.

That is the charged, the dangerous moment, when everything must be reexamined, must be made new; when nothing at all can be taken for granted.

—James Baldwin

There ain't no storybook story
There's no never-ending song
Our happily ever after Darlin'
Forever come and gone

—Bruce Springsteen

If you traveled due north from Rumson, New Jersey, where Bruce Springsteen has lived for the past couple of decades, you'd wind up on the southern tip of Manhattan. There are spots in the Jersey Highlands where, on a very clear day, you could see the Twin Towers of the World Trade Center.

So Rumson made a convenient home to many of the investment banking and stockbroker types who worked there. When suicide pilots flew jets into the towers on September 11, 2001, the shockwave rolled into Rumson early and with particular force, and it has taken—will take—a very, very long time to stop reverberating.

Bruce and Patti were home that morning. His kids were at school across the street.

On the North Jersey coast, Bruce isn't such an unfamiliar sight. He lives in privacy, but he lives as a member of a community, doing his best to shrug off his status as a big celebrity in a small town.

Everyone in a community has a role to play. Sometimes that role isn't noticed until there's a crisis. Sometimes, the crisis changes the role. Both happened to Bruce in the days after September 11. The way he tells the story, one day soon afterward, a man drove by him, slowed, and yelled, "Hey Bruce! We need ya!" and drove on.

That happened. But it wasn't an isolated shout-out. Many bereaved families reached for Bruce. He didn't spend all day every day reaching back, but he did his share or more. For one family, he made a tape of himself singing "Thunder Road" to be played at the funeral of a husband lost in the attacks. He made the tape because his presence at the funeral would have knocked the funeral ceremony off center. Anyway, it wasn't like he knew the man or his family. Just another thread among the millions woven into his life.

There were several examples like that, involving families all through the area. As a result of what Bruce gleaned from such experiences, they have been portrayed as "research," but that's a distortion. He didn't seek them out—he didn't need to, because there were already so many bereaved wives, husbands, and children as he could accommodate. What he saw and heard, over and over again in one form or another, would have broken the heart of a Tin Man. It wasn't carnage, blood, and dust—the things that workers at Ground Zero went through every day. It was another kind of tragedy, a tragedy of absence, the psychic devastation of lives that once had seemed altogether orderly, secure, and prosperous. It wasn't just that the breadwinner in these families was gone without a second's preparation. So were the order, the security, and, often as not, the prosperity.

Bruce had been thinking of ways to move forward again with the E Street Band, and the first step had to be making an album of new material. He had a few songs, including "41 Shots" and "Land of Hopes and Dreams." But he lacked a theme, and throughout his career, it's finding a thread linking songs that's motivated the making of Springsteen albums. He recognized, not so much in the 9–11 catastrophe but in its reverberations through his community, a topic for songs. But that topic had yet to resolve itself into a theme.

Jon Landau thought he ought to try a new producer. He had in mind Brendan O'Brien, a former guitarist and engineer best known for producing Pearl Jam, Rage Against the Machine, Stone Temple Pilots, and Train (the last a new Jon Landau Management client). O'Brien eagerly anticipated working with Bruce—some of his friends called it his dream gig.

Bruce met O'Brien and agreed to try doing a session in Atlanta, where O'Brien works. Bruce brought five songs to the studio expecting to cut two or three. Before the weekend was over, all five had been cut, and they were making an album.

The material didn't yet have what would later be called its "9–11 theme" (more accurately, its "9–12 and forever after" theme). It did include "Into the Fire," which related to the World Trade Center attacks, but the 9–11 undercurrent in songs like "You're Missing," "The Fuse," and "Mary's Place" seemed just one layer among many—which may yet prove to be the most accurate way to look at them. Only when "The Rising" emerged did the album's theme come into focus.

The sessions at O'Brien's Southern Tracks Recording excited Bruce not because he'd found his theme but because he'd found his music. O'Brien produces records—he doesn't just try to realize the artist's ideas, he comes in with plenty of his own. Part of his idea for working with Springsteen involved recentering the E Street Band sound from keyboards to guitars, which upped the energy level and brought the sound closer to the band onstage. Where the song called for keyboards, synthesizers replaced piano and organ, giving the soundscape a fresher, more modern feel.

O'Brien also works quickly. They did the first session in January 2002 and were done by April. Springsteen hadn't made a band record that rapidly since his debut album.

Springsteen worked fast because he became inspired. He hadn't made a record with the E Street Band since *Born in the U.S.A.*, fifteen years earlier (*Tunnel of Love* features the entire band but the band members were overdubbed onto Bruce's solo tracks). He hadn't truly made a *rock* record in all that time. Brendan O'Brien makes rock records.

Take "Mary's Place," whose structure most resembles primordial E Street Band material: roadhouse rhythm, multiple sections, blaring sax solo, improbable giddy lyric narrative—it's a regular "Rosalita." The differences become apparent as soon as the song starts. A see-sawing violin riff, a rock steady bass drum and what sounds like wood blocks, a plucked guitar, a brief synth riff that sounds like a ringing phone—all recorded very dry, and with no dynamic shift as Springsteen's voice enters. The electric bass is a two-step heartbeat until the explosive chorus, which is brief, relative to previous E Street-vaganzas, and filled with female—not male—voices, with surging ensemble playing underneath the vocal verses. The sax steps forth for an instrumental verse and chorus. "Turn it up!" cry the girls, leading into familiar Van Morrison territory, but this exploration of white soul is much more disciplined than usual. The whole thing sounds leaner, denser, tidier—more a producer's arrangement than one that developed from the band tinkering with the song as they learned it.

In recent years, Springsteen developed the habit of using melodies that feel, and sometimes are, unresolved; he did this even on a big hit like "Philadelphia." O'Brien's arrangements tended to make those melodies feel much more complete, even when, as with "You're Missing," they really aren't.

Like any thematic album, *The Rising* has its share of program numbers—"Worlds Apart" and "Paradise"—and there are plenty of loose ends: If, given sufficient scrutiny, "Let's Be Friends" and "Nothing Man" fit the general theme of healing after catastrophe, if "Further on Up the Road" makes sense as a song about resurrection, the connection to "The Fuse" remains opaque.

For me, it was the music that provided the tug. I heard *The Rising* about twenty-five times before I ever read the lyric sheet. (This cost me my favorite line, "musta been your science degree," which turned out to be the much more comprehensible "musta been you sighin' so deep.") My favorite tracks, "Sunny Day," "Mary's Place," "Worlds Apart," "You're Missing," and "My City of Ruins," registered first as sound then as stories. They aren't even best heard as statements about 9–11 and what came next, since Springsteen did his best to strip them of political specifics.

The lyrics of "You're Missing," "The Rising," and "Paradise" rank with Springsteen's best. There are no false steps, no attempts to cram too many syllables into a line. They flow as words meant to be sung, and Bruce sings beautifully throughout, which can be demonstrated by comparing songs like "Mary's Place," "Sunny Day," and "Countin' on a Miracle" with their obvious antecedents—"Rosalita," "Hungry Heart," and "Leap of Faith."

The vocal command of "You're Missing" has no antecedent in Springsteen's work. Set here, above a ceaseless synthesizer cello, the way he labors through the verses (and the way the tambourine hiss symbolizes a deep breath between phrases), Springsteen's singing conveys relentless sadness through little more than the texture of his voice. The lyrics speak vernacular American as well as any he's written since "The River"—and here, he's portraying almost exactly the opposite social situation: Not a guy who can't connect, but a person—it doesn't have to be a woman, although most assume it is—who has made a true heart connection, the kind Bruce Springsteen preaches about onstage, and had it snatched away in one missed beat of that heart. Thus, the cryptic conclusion—"God's drifting in heaven, devil's in the mailbox / Got dust on my shoes, nothin' but teardrops." Nothing is right, nothing will be right, nothing can be right.

"Can't see nothin' in front of me / Can't see nothin' comin' up behind," begins the very next song. This is Springsteen in flat-out rock 'n' roll mode, with an organ riff honing the tension's edge. "The Rising" is no vengeful call to arms. It's a song about those things that do survive sudden tragedy: ghosts, memories, faith, "a dream of life / Like a catfish dancin' on the end of my line."

Or it is the things that Madison, WI writer Mary Kay Feingold wrote about it the day that the record officially hit the Internet:

> The words of this song can be heard as a firefighter talking to God, or heard as God talking to Father Judge [the priest who died with the firefighters who were his congregation], or as a firefighter talking to his wife ... with all conversations taking place in the context of resurrection and what that implies. First, there's the simple lifting of a soul—God telling the dying to "come on up for the rising." Then there's the reminder inherent in the story of the Resurrection: that the most meaningful thing that can be done about suffering you can't stop is to share it—"may you feel your arms around me" (or "may I feel your arms around me"; it's apparently written "I," but seems to be sung "you.")
>
> No matter whose voice, though, the message is the same: may you not have to get there by yourself. May someone hold you and acknowledge your suffering; may someone share it. And may there be angels, human or heavenly, to sing you on your way.

No catfish dance in the waters of "Paradise." Instead, a suicide bomber—perhaps in Israel, perhaps in the U.S.—prepares to die, while a mourner in the Virginia hills finds life stopped by a loss caused by just such action. In the second verse, Springsteen even more unequivocally equates the bomber with the mourner who can't let go. The third verse could be a story told by either of these characters, it could be told by both, it could be told by anyone who dives into the treacherous waters and finds them empty of promise, mere oblivion.

What matters is that the swimmer in that verse lets himself see, through the eyes of his most beloved, that such a paradise is empty; so he fights back into the sunlight of the everyday.

The next thing you know, "My City of Ruins" has begun. Now the singer's back on the night-lit streets of Asbury Park, another place praying for resurrection, and in its guise as seaside wonderland, another symbol of false paradise. Here young men rot away without anyone's second glance. If their strength gave you strength, their hope gave you hope, their love gave you love, you'd be hollowed out.

Does Springsteen understand what it *really* means to encourage such people to "rise up" as he and a gospel choir chant at the end of the song? I think he does. It means that, having suffered great tragedy, the human's responsibility is to the here and now. We can do nothing constructive for the dead except honor their lives by working to set things straight. In the part of his "Tenth Avenue Freezeout" sermon where Bruce swears he can't offer eternal life he adds that he can offer the spirit of rock 'n' roll: "Right here! Right now!" At this altar, rock 'n' roll is the bread of life.

Choosing life over death provides no security, no freedom from care. It incurs the greatest obligations. "I was instructed to feed the hungry, clothe the naked, and visit those in prison," wrote James Baldwin. "I am far indeed from my youth, and from my father's house, but I have not forgotten these instructions, and I pray upon my soul that I never will."

Like every important album that Bruce Springsteen has made, *The Rising* organizes itself around a thematic progression. You could term the progression this time as theological—Springsteen speaks continually of the resurrection of the spirit, and he frankly addresses himself to God in more than one song. But ultimately the progression from "Lonesome Day" to "My City of Ruins" is ideological. "A little revenge and this too shall pass," he sings in "Lonesome Day." The thirst for revenge can't be denied—what you have to do is recognize that it won't work. "Better ask questions before you shoot / Deceit and betrayal is bitter fruit," he sings before the song ends. But if revenge won't do the job, what will?

"Nothing Man," the album's fourth song, portrays the disintegration of a former hero—he might be a firefighter who survived the towers' collapse, he might be a Vietnam vet, he might be one of Timothy McVeigh's comrades from the Gulf War. He has been into the fire, and "Around here, everybody acts like nothing's changed.... The sky's still, the same unbelievable blue." So he makes a decision: "You want courage," he says, no more hopelessly than he speaks in every other syllable of the song, "I'll show you courage you can understand / The pearl and silver / Restin' on my night table. / It's just me Lord, pray I'm able."

No Bruce Springsteen character except Charles Starkweather in "Nebraska" so actively chooses death. All the rest see some way out: running away from home, driving all night, teaching your guitar to talk. Even sliding down to the river might revive you, as the character in "Across the Border" prays. But the Nothing Man is dead at heart. Though Bruce slotted "Nothing Man" between the album's too most brightly lit songs—"Waitin' on a Sunny Day" and "Countin' on a Miracle"—even he couldn't deny that such people now had permanent roles in his community. He'd spent too much time in Asbury Park, where he worked to help with the city's economic revival and played benefit shows at Christmas the last few years.

When *The Rising* came out, a media frenzy akin to those around *Born to Run* and *Born in the U.S.A.* ensued. It constituted a resurrection, and no surprise: Springsteen created the first significant artwork to emerge from 9–11, and the major players all wanted to participate. The *Today* show moved its site to Asbury Park for the day of release, July 2, 2002. Springsteen did a pair of long, intense interviews with Ted Koppel for *Nightline*. *Time* once more put his face on its cover. The album went straight into the charts at Number 1 and stayed there for a second week.

But it wasn't a huge hit. Outside the Northeast, radio played it little after the initial week or two. None of the singles broke into the Top Ten. In part, radio remained too closely wed to satisfying teenage tastes to accommodate such adult rock—no matter how much Brendan O'Brien modernized the sound, it still came unmistakably from grown men, not kids.

More important, *The Rising* and Bruce Springsteen could not entirely be digested in 2002 America. In 1984 Bruce stood out as the symbol of humanist culture, an anti-Reagan. After four more years of Reagan, eight years of Clinton, and six of one Bush or another, that culture had no popular context. It had been swept away as surely as the prosperous promise of '60s America had been pulled out from under the characters in "Independence Day." For all its innumerable references to life after death, for all its moral courage, *The Rising* could not synch up with the spirit of the day. That's one of the best things about it.

The very best thing is that millions of people heard *The Rising* as a tool for healing. But millions more probably heard it as potential license for America to strike back against the terrorists. Millions more heard it not at all. There was no overlap. A sad-but-true summation of how things stand.

Bruce and the band saddled up and hit the road again. They played great shows—they played better than they had on the reunion tour, which astonished me—and they played places they hadn't played in decades.

This time, Bruce would not let the jingoes take away his songs or define his Americanism. He played an electric "Born in the U.S.A." for the first time in more than a decade, but when the war drums began beating harder, he shifted back to the fierce acoustic slide guitar version he'd developed on the *Joad* tour. He said nothing about the invasion of Iraq, except that he started opening some of his shows with one of his old hits: "War! What is it good for? Absolutely nothin'! Say it again!"

One of the stranger qualities of being a concert performer is that you *do* say it again—and again and again and again. All artists who last reiterate their themes for decades. The best of them, like Bob Dylan, weave endless variations, but even the Rolling Stones keep finding new nuances of joyous cynicism to add to their shows.

Bruce Springsteen's greatest virtue may turn out to be that he never felt trapped by his theme, perhaps because, more than most, he has always been answering questions for himself. He says at the end of *Glory Days* that the central question comes from "Born to Run": "I wanna know if love is real."

Years later, he asked another question that probably better defines this middle part of his journey. During the *Born in the U.S.A.* tour, some friends of mine got into a fight with a little Nebraska town that tried to ban their bar band from playing there. When Ben Eicher, the group's bassist, started telling Bruce the story, he got just to where they'd been banned before Bruce interrupted. "What'd you do about it?" he demanded to know. Ben, one of America's great attorneys, told him in detail. They won, too. As Ben tells it, though, one reason they knew that they had to do something about it was because they were Bruce Springsteen fans.

Springsteen asks of those of us who love his work nothing more and nothing less than he asks of himself. "What are you going to do about it?" An end to his story is not in sight because he's out there writing the story as it continues to rise up.

"I don't know what happens next, but I do want to add my voice." In the land of hope and dreams, it will always ring out.

INDEX